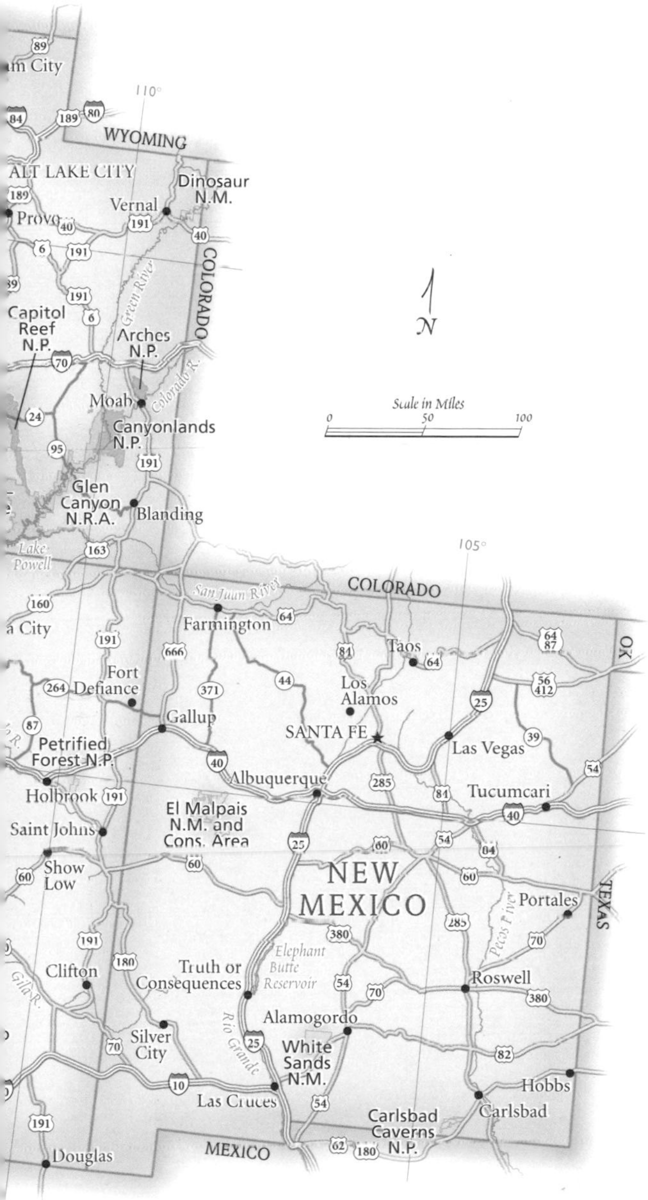
WYOMING
SALT LAKE CITY
Dinosaur N.M.
Vernal
Provo
COLORADO
Green River
Capitol Reef N.P.
Arches N.P.
Moab
Colorado R.
Canyonlands N.P.
Glen Canyon N.R.A.
Blanding
Lake Powell
San Juan River
COLORADO
Farmington
Taos
Los Alamos
SANTA FE
Fort Defiance
Gallup
Petrified Forest N.P.
Holbrook
Albuquerque
Las Vegas
Tucumcari
El Malpais N.M. and Cons. Area
Saint Johns
Show Low
NEW MEXICO
Portales
TEXAS
OK
Pecos River
Elephant Butte Reservoir
Truth or Consequences
Clifton
Gila R.
Roswell
Alamogordo
Rio Grande
Silver City
White Sands N.M.
Hobbs
Las Cruces
Carlsbad
Carlsbad Caverns N.P.
Douglas
MEXICO
110°
105°
Scale in Miles
0
50
100
N

NATIONAL AUDUBON SOCIETY®

FIELD GUIDE TO THE Southwestern STATES

A Chanticleer Press Edition

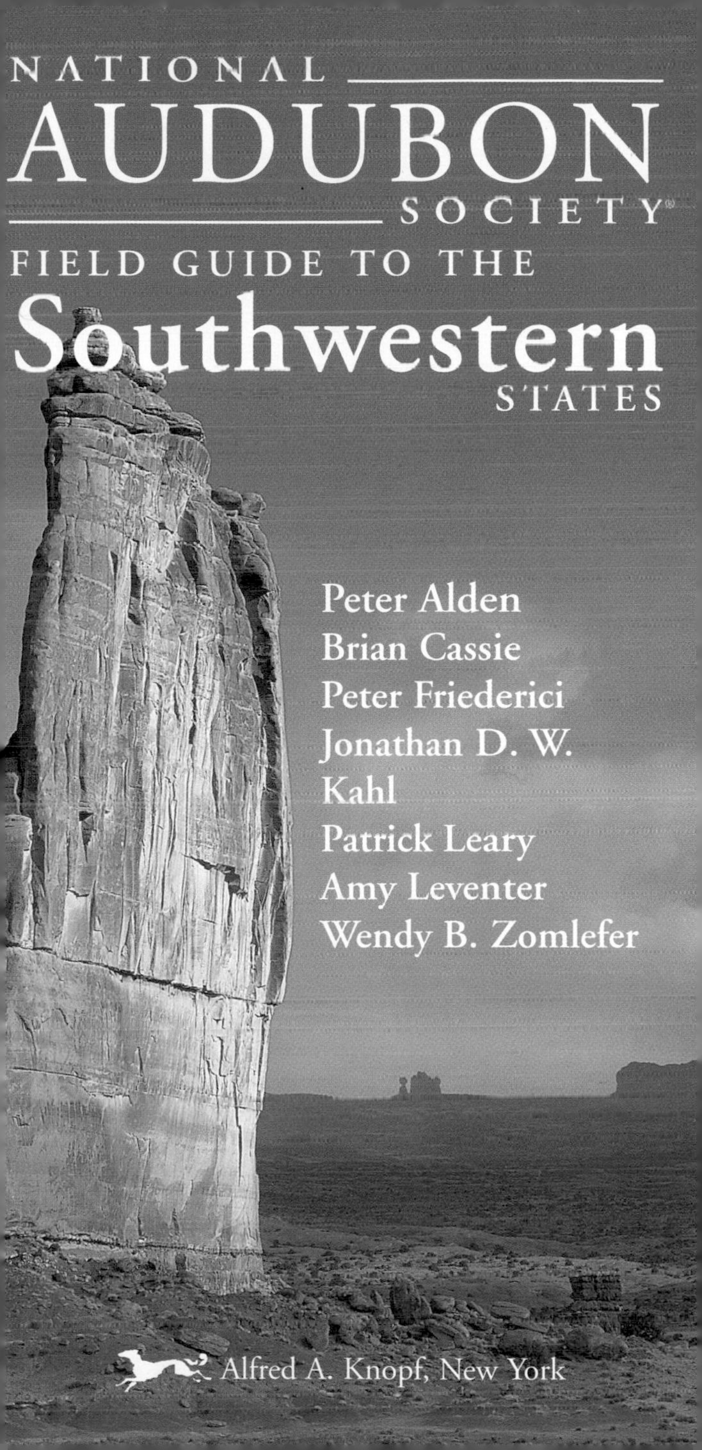

NATIONAL

AUDUBON

SOCIETY®

FIELD GUIDE TO THE

Southwestern
STATES

Peter Alden
Brian Cassie
Peter Friederici
Jonathan D. W. Kahl
Patrick Leary
Amy Leventer
Wendy B. Zomlefer

Alfred A. Knopf, New York

This is a Borzoi Book.
Published by Alfred A. Knopf, Inc.

www.randomhouse.com

Prepared and produced by
Chanticleer Press, Inc., New York.

Printed and bound by
Dai Nippon Printing Co., Ltd., Korea.

First Edition
Published September 1999
Fourth Printing, November 2003

Library of Congress Cataloging-in-Publication Data

National Audubon Society field guide to the southwestern states /
Peter Alden ... [et al.]. — 1st ed.
p. cm.
Includes index.
ISBN 0-679-44680-X
1. Natural history—Southwest, New Guidebooks. 2. Natural areas—Southwest, New Guidebooks. 3. Parks—Southwest, New Guidebooks. 4. Southwest, New Guidebooks. I. Alden, Peter. II. National Audubon Society. III. Title: Field guide to the southwestern states.
QH104.5.S6N38 1999
508.79—dc21 99-27920

National Audubon Society

The mission of NATIONAL AUDUBON SOCIETY *is to conserve and restore natural ecosystems, focusing on birds, other wildlife, and their habitats, for the benefit of humanity and the earth's biological diversity.*

One of the largest, most effective environmental organizations, Audubon has 550,000 members, 100 sanctuaries, state offices, and nature centers, and over 500 chapters in the Americas, plus a professional staff of scientists, educators, and policy analysts.

Our award-winning *Audubon* magazine, published six times a year and sent to all members, carries outstanding articles and color photography on wildlife and nature, presenting in-depth reports on critical environmental issues, as well as conservation news and commentary. Audubon also publishes *Audubon Adventures,* a children's newsletter reaching 450,000 students in grades four through six. Through Audubon ecology camps and workshops in Maine, Connecticut, and Wyoming, Audubon offers nature education for teachers, families, and children; through Audubon Expedition Institute in Belfast, Maine, the Society offers unique, traveling undergraduate and graduate degree programs in Environmental Education.

National Audubon Society also sponsors books, field guides, and on-line nature activities, plus travel programs to exotic places like Antarctica, Africa, Baja California, and the Galápagos Islands.

For information about how you can become an Audubon member, subscribe to *Audubon Adventures,* or to learn more about our camps and workshops, please write or call:

NATIONAL AUDUBON SOCIETY
Membership Dept.
700 Broadway
New York, New York 10003
212-979-3000 or 800-274-4201
http://www.audubon.org/

Contents

Part One: Overview

Part Two: Flora and Fauna

Part Three: Parks and Preserves

Appendices

Overview

Natural Highlights

Defined by clear skies and long horizons, and molded by aridity, the Southwest is among the most distinctive of North American landscapes. Its rugged mountains, mesas, and canyons are often ungentled by vegetation, resulting in striking landforms. An outdoor enthusiast's paradise, the region is rich with public lands. Its extreme heat, cold, floods, and droughts make it an ideal biological laboratory in which naturalists can explore how plants and animals have adapted to environments that may seem unimaginably harsh to humans.

Wasatch National Forest, Utah

Mountains

Whether products of volcanism or of geologic uplift, the region's mountains rise above surrounding lowlands, many reaching high enough to create their own storms. Thanks to reduced temperatures and increased precipitation, these mountain "islands" are often cloaked with spacious pine forests. Canyons and high slopes support dense stands of fir and spruce; alpine tundra tops some peaks. Animals more often associated with high-latitude forests, such as Red Squirrels, Blue Grouse, and Three-toed Woodpeckers, live in isolated populations almost as far south as the Mexican border.

Canyon along Blue River, Arizona

Canyons

Bearing abrasive sediments washed from areas with little vegetation, the Southwest's creeks, rivers, and washes carve steep-walled canyons that form some of the region's most distinctive scenery and that multiply its biological diversity. From slots no wider than a backpacker to the mile-deep Grand Canyon, canyons often hide small microclimates in which heat, cold, and moisture conspire to support plants and animals unable to survive in the surrounding landscape. Replete with natural surprises and striking views, they are an irresistible temptation to explorers.

Mojave Desert, Lake Mead National Recreation Area, Nevada

Deserts

Deserts cover much of the Southwest, but a single term scarcely does justice to their diversity. Biologists recognize four distinct deserts here—the Sonoran, Chihuahuan, Mojave, and Great Basin—and each of these contains numerous habitats that vary according to rainfall, temperature, topography, and soil type. These deserts include areas that rarely freeze and places that are snow-covered each winter, sparse sagebrush flats in northern Nevada and lush foothill gardens, rich in cacti and ephemeral spring wildflowers, in southern Arizona.

Buenos Aires National Wildlife Refuge, Arizona

Grasslands

Grasslands in the Southwest include both the western fringes of the Great Plains and transition zones between the low, hot deserts and the higher, moister woodlands and forests. Perennial bunchgrasses once ruled these open spaces, but livestock grazing, fire suppression, and the spread of nonnative species have substantially changed their composition. American Bisons, Pronghorns, and a host of other grassland wildlife can still be seen at many sites.

Bosque del Apache National Wildlife Refuge, NM

Wetlands

The importance of water is magnified in an arid land. The Southwest's marshes, lakes, and riparian areas are vital to a multitude of creatures. Unfortunately, the area's river corridors have been degraded by human activities, endangering many fishes, amphibians, plants, and other species. A handful of healthy rivers persists in preserves. Some native species, and many introduced ones, have benefited from the construction of reservoirs and from other alterations to the region's hydrology.

Topography

The Southwest is a land of topographic contrasts. Deeply incised rivers of the Colorado Plateau, like the Colorado River and its tributaries, run their course as deep as 6,000 feet below the rim of the plateau. Many mountain peaks of the Basin and Range Province, which covers almost all of Nevada and parts of Utah, Arizona, and New Mexico, rise to more than 10,000 feet, towering above valley floors that range from 4,500 to 6,200 feet in average elevation. The Rocky Mountains pass through Utah and New Mexico, and the Great Plains sweep across the eastern third of New Mexico. Kings Peak, in the Uinta Mountains of Utah, is the region's highest point, at 13,528 feet; the lowest point, at 70 feet, is along the Colorado River, near Yuma, Arizona.

Canyonlands National Park, Utah

Colorado Plateau

The Colorado Plateau is a 130,000-square-mile, high-elevation tableland, deeply engraved by steep canyons, that covers southeastern Utah, northern Arizona, northwestern New Mexico, and southwestern Colorado. The Colorado River and its tributaries—the Green, Little Colorado, and San Juan Rivers—cut through the plateau's "layer cake" of sedimentary rocks, forming a maze of cliffs, escarpments, mesas, and canyons, including the celebrated Grand Canyon in Arizona.

Wasatch Line

The Wasatch Line divides Utah roughly in half from north to south, separating the Basin and Range Province to the west from the Colorado Plateau to the east. Composed of high mountains, often covered with volcanic rock, in the north, and plateaus in the south, it includes the Uinta Mountains, the Bear River and Wasatch Ranges, and the Wasatch, Sevier, Aquarius, Markagunt, and Paunsaugunt Plateaus.

Wasatch Range, Uinta National Forest

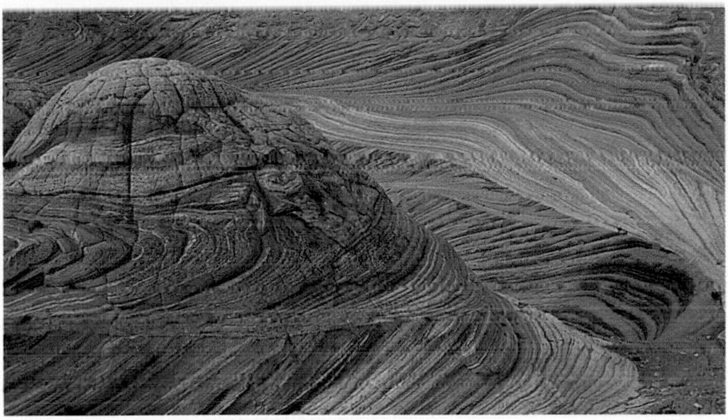

Vermilion Cliffs, Arizona

Grand Staircase

A succession of cliffs that straddles the border between Arizona and Utah has come to be known as the Grand Staircase. The colorful Vermilion, White, Gray, and Pink Cliffs are composed of sandstone and other hard sedimentary rocks that have resisted erosion by wind and water over eons of time. At 3,000 feet, Vermilion Cliffs is the lowest (and oldest) step. Pink Cliffs is the highest (and youngest), at 10,000 feet.

Central Highlands of Arizona

The diagonal band of the Central Highlands of Arizona is a transition zone between the Basin and Range deserts to the southwest and the Colorado Plateau to the north. Unlike much of the rest of the state, this region of rugged mountains is relatively wet and is forested with pinyon, juniper, Ponderosa Pine, and Douglas Fir. The highlands divide the state in two, running northwestward from the New Mexico border to Lake Mead. The Mogollon Rim, an escarpment (steep slope) that runs for hundreds of miles, forms the border between the highlands and the Colorado Plateau.

Great Basin, Nevada

Great Basin

Covering 75 percent of Nevada, much of Utah, and parts of northern Arizona, the Great Basin is the largest desert in the Southwest. It is a desert characterized by interior drainage—no water flowing into the Great Basin flows back out. Instead it empties into lakes, disappears into sinks, or simply evaporates. From above, the Great Basin looks like corrugated cardboard. Its narrow north–south trending mountain ranges average 50 to 100 miles long and 10 miles wide, and are separated by broad, flat valleys, called basins.

Tectonic Origins

Between 200 and 250 million years ago, all the earth's landmasses existed as one huge continent. Utah, Arizona, and western New Mexico lay on the shallow, western shelf of this supercontinent. The formation of California's Sierra Nevada cut off much of Utah and Arizona from any source of moisture, creating a vast desert. About 200 million years ago, the supercontinent began to splinter into plates. Collision of the North American and Pacific plates led to the birth of the Rocky Mountains and later the formation of the mountain ranges of Nevada, California, and Idaho. The Colorado Plateau began to rise about 6 million years ago, but for the most part remained intact.

Plate Tectonics

According to the theory of plate tectonics, the earth's surface is broken into a dozen major plates that constantly move as a result of convection currents generated by the planet's internal heat. Three types of motion occur along plate boundaries. At **divergent** boundaries, plates move away from one another, or rift apart; magma (molten rock) rises from within the earth and fills the void that was created, solidifying under the ocean as new seafloor or on land as a rift valley. At **convergent** boundaries, two plates collide, causing a buckling of the crust and/or forcing one plate beneath the other in a process called subduction, which can result in earthquakes and volcanoes; all major mountain chains and most volcanoes are located along convergent boundaries. **Transform** boundaries, or fault lines, where plates slide past one another, are the sites of earthquakes.

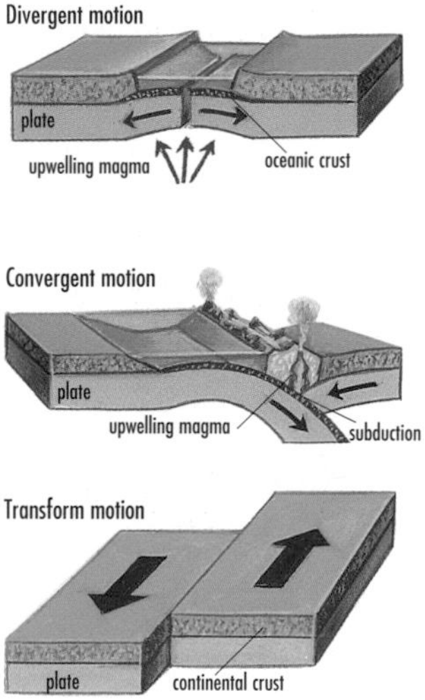

Basin and Range Tectonics

Bulging of the earth's crust around 17 million years ago stretched and cracked the North American crust between the Sierra Nevada and eastern Utah, leading to the formation of the Basin and Range Province. This region covers about 300,000 square miles—nearly a tenth of the continental United States—and comprises all the North American deserts. Basin and Range topography is characterized by extremely flat-floored valleys, or basins, separated by narrow, straight mountain ranges that rise as high as 13,000 feet above the valleys.

Rio Grande Rift Valley

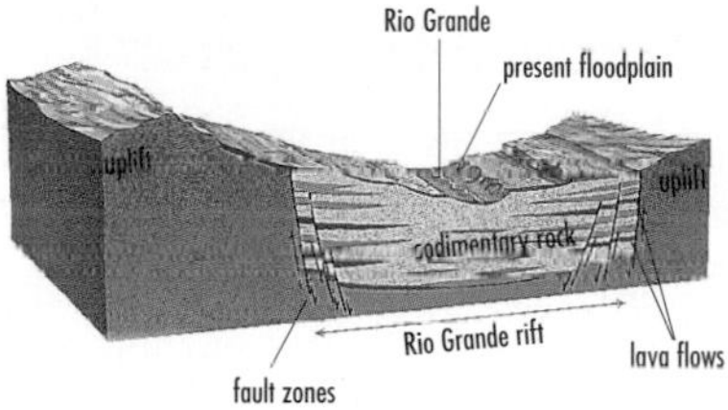

The Rio Grande rift valley originated about 30 million years ago, the result of divergent forces breaking apart the North American plate. Fault zones, punctuated by basaltic volcanoes, lie on either side of the rift, which has dropped down as much as 25,000 feet relative to either side. Running from Mexico into Colorado, the valley measures about 30 miles wide near Albuquerque, New Mexico, and narrows to the north as it bisects the state. The Rio Grande runs through much of the length of the valley. The rift is filled in with clay, gravel, sand, lava, and volcanic ash.

Waterpocket Fold, Capitol Reef National Park

Waterpocket Fold

The Waterpocket Fold in Utah is a classic example of a monocline—a bending of rock with one very steep side in an area of otherwise nearly horizontal layers. It was formed 50 to 70 million years ago during the Laramide Orogeny (a stage in the building of the Rocky Mountains); that event reactivated an ancient buried fault that warped the earth's crust. Rock layers on the western side of the monocline were lifted more than 7,000 feet higher than those on the east. Over time, many of the uppermost layers of rock have eroded. The 100-mile-long escarpment is visible at Capitol Reef National Park.

Turtlebacks

Many of the mountain ranges in western Utah, eastern Nevada, and western Arizona are metamorphic core complexes—ancient domes of igneous or metamorphic rock with outer shells of very deformed (stretched and sheared) metamorphic rock. These "turtlebacks" are associated with detachment faults—nearly horizontal faults that separate the earth's brittle upper crust from its lower crust. Geologists speculate that overlying blankets of sediment slid westward during faulting; with the overlying pressure reduced, the core complexes popped up, bringing the detachment fault to the surface.

Turtlebacks, Ruby Mountains, Nevada

Volcanic Features

Many fascinating geologic formations found in the Southwest are volcanic in origin. Volcanoes form at the earth's surface when magma (molten rock) is extruded through a vent in the earth's crust. The type of volcanic structure built depends on the chemistry of the lava. In the Southwest, volcanism between 20 and 40 million years ago was characterized by silicic lavas. These thick, sticky lavas contain large amounts of silica and have a tendency to clog up volcanic vents and then violently explode, sending ash and other volcanic materials great distances. The spires and columns of Chiricahua National Monument in Arizona are composed of "welded tuff"—fine ash particles that exploded as an incandescent avalanche and fused

Shiprock

together under intense heat 25 million years ago. More recent volcanism in the region has been characterized by basalt-rich lavas, which flow easily and quietly and tend to erupt less explosively. Lava flows and cinder cones, common types of basaltic volcanoes, can be seen near Grant, Carrizoza, and Capulin, New Mexico; in the San Francisco Volcanic Field and at the Grand Canyon in Arizona; and in the Black Rock Desert of Utah. New Mexico has the largest number and the greatest diversity of volcanoes in North America.

Shiprock

Located in New Mexico near the four corners (where Utah, Colorado, New Mexico, and Arizona meet), Shiprock is an ancient volcanic pipe that rises 1,100 feet above the desert floor. A violent volcanic explosion 12 million years ago left an existing volcanic conduit filled with large fragments of solidified magma. Erosion has since stripped away the surrounding rock, exposing the skyscraper. Cracks emanating from the central vent also filled with magma are now visible as three black dikes in the surrounding area.

Sunset Crater

Sunset Crater

Cinder cones form when basaltic lava eruptions are accompanied by escaping gases and steam. Steep conical hills build up around volcanic vents from coarse rock fragments, ash, and cinders pushed out by the escaping gases. Only 900 years old, Sunset Crater is the most recent addition to a field of about 400 cinder cones in the San Francisco Volcanic Field near Flagstaff, Arizona. This 1,000-foot-tall volcanic structure was built up over a 200-year period, beginning in A.D. 1064 or 1065 (studies of trees burned by the eruption make it possible to fix the date so precisely). Sunset Crater is named for its red and yellow tints, which result from the oxidation of minerals containing iron and sulfur.

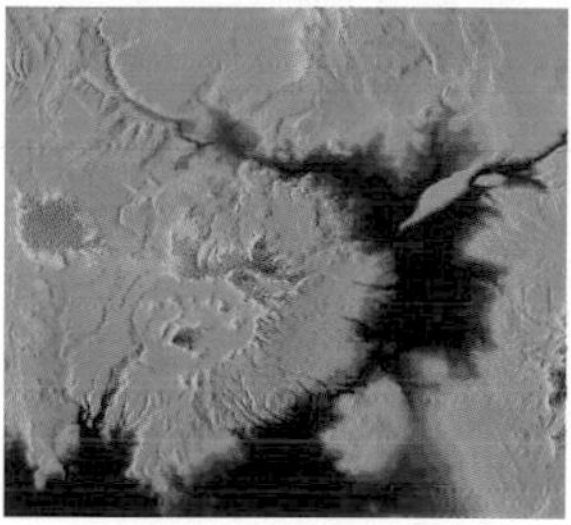
Valles Caldera ringed by Jemez Mountains (left), and Rio Grande rift valley (right).

Valles Caldera

Valles Caldera, located in the Jemez Volcanic Field of New Mexico, is an example of a resurgent caldera. This enormous depression, more than 10 miles in diameter, formed 1 million years ago, when an exceptionally powerful volcanic eruption evacuated a magma chamber, forcing the collapse of the overlying volcanic material. It is called "resurgent" because it lies on top of the older Toledo Caldera, which formed 1.4 million years ago, during a previous volcanic cycle. In the center of Valles Caldera is Redondo Peak, the highest point (11,254 feet) in the Jemez Mountains. Redondo Peak is a volcanic dome, a bulge of lava formed shortly after the caldera collapsed.

Grand Canyon Volcanoes

Vulcans Throne

Rocks of the Grand Canyon record a fascinating history of volcanism; there have been more than 150 lava flows into the canyon over the past 1.5 million years. Among other remnants of eruptive activity are lava dams and frozen lava falls, as well as Vulcans Anvil, the neck of an ancient volcano, and Vulcans Throne, an extinct cinder cone perched on the rim of the inner gorge.

Glacial Features

The great sheets of ice that covered much of northern North America until about 10,000 years ago never reached the Southwest. However, during the last ice age, smaller alpine glaciers increased in extent as a result of colder temperatures (less evaporation occurs at colder temperatures) and a change in atmospheric circulation (southward displacement of the jet stream by the elevated Laurentide Ice Sheet to the north). The expansion of alpine glaciers brought increased moisture to the region, especially present-day Nevada and Utah. Today, at higher elevations (above about 9,000 feet), the land both reflects erosion by the glaciers and contains forms the glaciers deposited.

Glacier below Wheeler Peak, Nevada

Alpine Glaciers

The Snake Range in Nevada and the high peaks of Utah, including the Uinta Mountains and the Wasatch and Bear River Ranges, were once covered by alpine glaciers that reached their maximum size between 15,000 and 20,000 years ago, during the last ice age. A small glacier that originally formed during that period persists below the summit of Wheeler Peak in eastern Nevada. Cirques, such as those that mark the crest of the Wasatch Range in Utah, are amphitheater-like hollows sculpted out of the rock by alpine glaciers. These depressions are commonly found at the head of a glaciated valley.

Pluvial Lakes

During the last ice age, much of the Southwest received considerably more rainfall than it does today; the result was the formation of pluvial lakes—lakes filled by rainwater and increased flow from streams. Great Salt Lake, for example, is a remnant of glacial Lake Bonneville, which covered an area of about 20,000 square miles and was nearly 1,000 feet deep. Ancient shorelines of Lake Bonneville, formed between 16,000 and 45,000 years ago, can be traced throughout western Utah. Glacial Lake Lahontan in Nevada covered nearly one-third of Nevada 50,000 years ago. Pyramid and Walker Lakes are vestiges of that immense body of water.

Caverns

Underground caverns form when acidic groundwater percolates through underlying limestone and gradually dissolves the stone. The water eventually drains away, revealing passageways and hollow rooms. In the later stages of cavern formation, lime-rich water drips down into the caverns and evaporates, leaving behind tiny crystals of calcium carbonate that grow into stalactites (icicle-like deposits hanging from the ceiling), stalagmites (columns rising up from the cave floor), and other cave formations, collectively called speleothems. Some of the most spectacular cavern formations in North America are found in the Southwest.

Shields and other speleothems, Lehman Caves

Lehman Caves

Lehman Caves is a single cavern that extends a quarter-mile into the limestone and marble at the base of Nevada's Snake Range, in Great Basin National Park. The cavern's rare and unusual formations include helictites (twisting and turning twig-like projections), snow-white clusters of carbonate needles, and knobby lumps of "cave popcorn." Lehman Caves is best known for its shields—circular plates that extend out from the walls, with stalactites and other string-like formations often hanging below, making them resemble parachutes.

Giant stalagmites, Carlsbad Caverns

Carlsbad Caverns

The 83 separate caves that make up New Mexico's Carlsbad Caverns reach as deep as 1,597 feet below the ground. The limestone of the caverns was formed in an inland sea about 250 million years ago as part of a 400-mile-long reef-like structure, similar to the modern Australian Great Barrier Reef. The fossil remains of marine organisms, such as corals, shells, and algae, are visible in the rocks today. After the sea evaporated, the area was uplifted and fractured; caverns formed where groundwater seeped through the cracks. Two of the most striking formations in the caverns are the Giant Dome, Carlsbad's largest stalagmite, and the Chinese Wall, a beautiful "rimstone dam" (a wall of calcium carbonate that once rimmed a pool of water).

Erosion and Weathering

Mechanical weathering—physical processes that force rocks to break apart without causing a chemical change—has dramatically shaped the landscape of the Southwest. The erosive power of running water is evident in the countless canyons incised into layer upon layer of rock. As erosion progresses and steep walls are undercut, bridges, mesas, buttes, columns, and spires are formed. The effects of erosion depend on the type of rock involved. Cliffs generally form from rocks resistant to erosion, such as limestones and sandstones, while softer shales commonly weather to form slopes.

Landscape Arch, Arches National Park, Utah

Fins and Arches

Fins and arches are common in the Colorado Plateau region. The story of their formation starts 300 million years ago when the region was covered by a shallow sea. When the sea evaporated, thick beds of salt formed over the plateau. Subsequently covered by layers of rock—formed from marine sediments and sand dunes—the salt was forced by the overlying pressure to flow laterally to areas where the pressure was less. The movement of the salt led to buckling and doming of the overlying rock and the formation of deep vertical cracks in the rock. Over the millennia, erosion has worn away at the cracks, forming fins, narrow walls or blades of sandstone, and arches, where sections of the fins have eroded away. Landscape Arch, in Arches National Park, is the world's largest natural arch, measuring 306 feet from base to base. One day this fragile arch will collapse, leaving only two pillars standing.

FORMATION OF FINS AND ARCHES

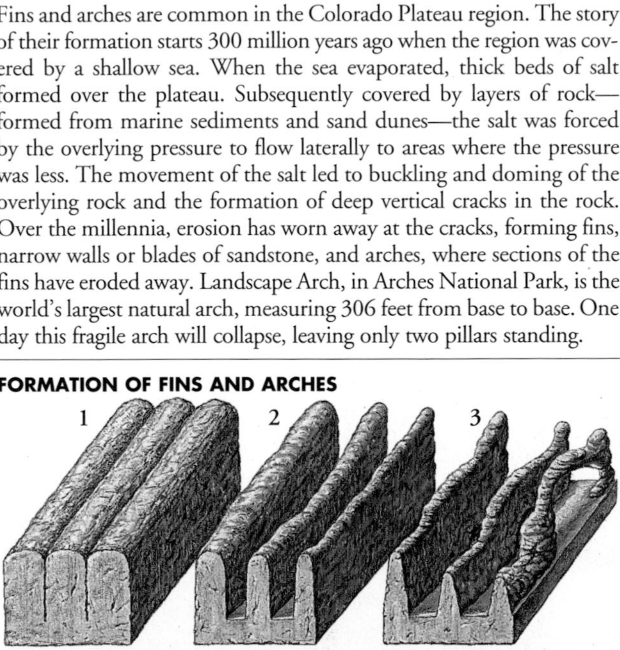

1. Vertical cracks penetrate rock layers. 2. Erosion widens the cracks, creating fins. 3. Arches form where fins are broken through.

Monument Valley Navajo Tribal Park, Arizona

Mesas

Mesas—flat-topped elevations bounded by steep cliffs—represent one of the more advanced erosional stages of the Colorado River. As streams and rivers cut narrow canyons, the cliffs became undercut, and large masses of rock crashed down to the valley floor. This progressive "scarp retreat" formed mesas and then buttes, as the mesas further eroded. Monument Valley in Arizona and Utah showcases these spectacular formations.

Canyon de Chelly National Monument

Canyons

Deep, vertically walled cliffs and canyons carved by powerful rivers, including Rio de Chelly and the Green, Little Colorado, Virgin, and Colorado Rivers, are characteristic of the Colorado Plateau. The Grand Canyon may be the most famous one, but equally spectacular canyons can be seen at Canyon de Chelly National Monument in Arizona and Canyonlands National Park in Utah, where the sandstone cliffs rise as high as 1,000 feet above the valley floor.

Badland Weathering

Badland weathering occurs in soft, easily eroded sedimentary rock, such as shale, that is still cohesive enough to maintain steep faces. Rain splash and surface runoff over slopes devoid of vegetation carve myriad steep and narrow features, including columns, spires, and accordion-like folds. Multi-colored badland topography exists in the Painted Desert of Petrified Forest National Park in Arizona, Capitol Reef National Monument in Utah, and Fantasy Canyon, near Bonanza, Utah.

Painted Desert

Hoodoos

The fantastically shaped rock pillars and narrow spires of Bryce Canyon in Utah formed from erosion by a myriad of tiny streams along the rim of a plateau. Water moving along the steep slopes carved out gullies, which widened over time, leaving thin blades of rock. Continued erosion of sections of the rock walls left behind tens of thousands of vertical columns, or hoodoos. The red, orange, yellow, and white colors of the rocks are the result of minor concentrations of iron-containing minerals.

Hoodoos, Bryce Canyon National Park

Goosenecks, Goosenecks of the San Juan State Park

Goosenecks

Over flat terrain, rivers often meander, winding back upon themselves like ribbon candy. In the Colorado Plateau region, many streams established their courses before uplifting created the plateau. As the land rose, the meandering paths cut trenches down into the rock. Extremely tight meander loops, termed goosenecks, can be seen in Utah at Canyonlands National Park, Natural Bridges National Monument, and Goosenecks of the San Juan State Park.

Owachomo Natural Bridge, Natural Bridges National Monument, Utah

Natural Bridges

Although similar in appearance to arches, most natural bridges in the Southwest form by stream erosion through thick-bedded, strong sandstone. As meandering streams incise into the bedrock, the rock on either side of a tight loop in the stream's path erodes. Eventually the stream breaks through the rock wall, forming a natural bridge above. The loop is abandoned and stream flow is rerouted under the bridge, enlarging the hole until the bridge weakens and collapses.

FORMATION OF GOOSENECKS AND NATURAL BRIDGES

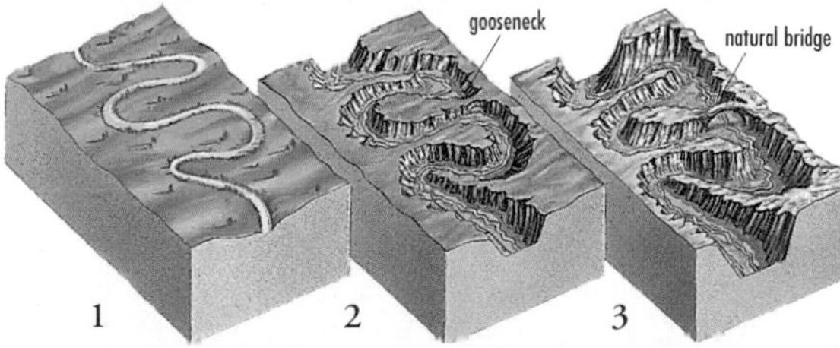

1. Streams meander across flat terrain. 2. Streams cut deep into rock as plateau rises. 3. Tight loops form goosenecks. Water cuts through walls where impact is greatest, forming natural bridges.

Desert Geology

Both wind and water play significant roles in shaping the desert landscape of the Southwest. With only sparse vegetation to anchor the surface, strong winds pick up loose grains, forming fields of sand dunes wherever the wind speed drops enough to release the grains. Removal of the finer-grained sand leaves behind a pebbly ground cover, known as desert pavement. Although water is limited in the region, intermittent streams fed by episodic rainfall are an equal if not greater agent of erosion than wind. Alluvial fans—cone-shaped formations of sediment—are formed when torrential rains carry weathered material down from mountains and deposit it at the base of their slopes. In the Basin and Range Province of Nevada and in southern Arizona, these structures are so extensive that they coalesce to form alluvial sheets, or bajadas. In much of the Basin and Range Province, eroded mountains flank enclosed flat basins, which have only interior drainage; though flooded from time to time, the basins are more commonly dry and covered by playas or salt flats.

Cross-bedding in Navajo sandstone, Zion National Park

Ancient Sand Dunes

Navajo sandstone, which forms the massive walls and towers of Zion National Park and many of the cliffs in Canyonlands National Park in Utah, is characterized by broad, sweeping cross-beds that originally formed in desert sand dunes that covered the Southwest from 135 to 190 million years ago. At that time, the area was a vast, arid, sandy desert, probably similar in size to the modern 3½-million-square-mile Sahara in Africa. The immense thickness of this stone—up to 2,220 feet in some places—attests to the longevity of the desert.

Gypsum dunes, White Sands National Monument

Modern Sand Dunes

White Sands in New Mexico is the world's largest gypsum dune field, covering an area of 275 square miles of the Tularosa Valley in the northern end of the Chihuahuan Desert. The gypsum, which has its ultimate source in rocks of the nearby San Andres and Sacramento Mountains, is dissolved and carried through groundwater flow to an ancient lakebed, Lake Lucero. Capillary action draws up the dissolved gypsum (like a sponge absorbs water), where it is precipitated as solid crystals on the ancient lake floor. These crystals are picked up and carried northeastward by seasonally strong winds and deposited as brilliant white grains, forming dunes.

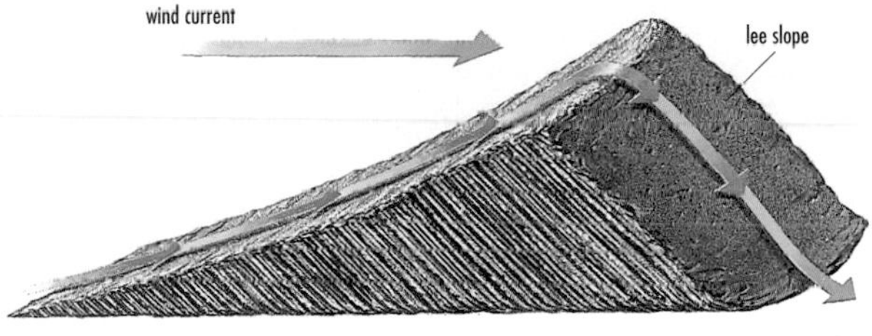

CROSS-BEDDING

Many of the sandstones in the Southwest exhibit spectacular cross-bedding. Cross-beds—layers of sedimentary rock inclined at angles of up to 35 degrees from horizontal—form from deposits of sand on the steep, down-current side (lee slope) of a sand dune. The slope of the cross-beds tells geologists the direction of prevailing winds at the time of dune formation; different directions of cross-bedding indicate changes in wind direction.

Playas

Salt ridges left by receding water, Bonneville Salt Flats

Playas, dry lakes that are intermittently filled with shallow water, can be found in the arid, closed basins of many mountain valleys in western Utah and Nevada. As the water in the lake evaporates, calcium carbonate and salt that were dissolved in the water are left behind, forming brilliant white surfaces. Bonneville Salt Flats, stretching 40 miles east–west and 100 miles north–south, is the largest playa in Utah. Some playas are covered with clay or other sediments, instead of salt. Black Rock Desert in Nevada is the site of a playa made of fine-grained sediment, or silt.

Desert Varnish

Petroglyphs etched into desert varnish, Newspaper Rock

Many rock surfaces in deserts are covered by a dark brown, shiny coating called desert varnish, which is composed of a combination of clays and manganese and iron oxides. Desert varnish is the result of chemical oxidation, although its mode of formation is not well understood. Black streaks of desert varnish, which look like spilled paint, are seen on many cliff walls of the Colorado Plateau region. The petroglyphs at Newspaper Rock, at Canyonlands National Park, in Utah, are scratched into desert-varnished sandstone.

Grand Canyon Geology

Arizona's Grand Canyon, by far the best known of the many canyons that cut through the Colorado Plateau, was carved by the erosional power of the Colorado River over the past 5 to 6 million years. The distinctive shape of the 277-mile-long canyon is the result of differential erosion. Easily eroded shales form the slopes, and more resistant limestones form the cliffs. The steep inner gorge is composed of rocks very resistant to erosion—ancient schists and granites.

Rock Layers of the Grand Canyon

Rock exposures of the Grand Canyon record almost half of the earth's 4.6-billion-year history. The oldest rocks—Vishnu schist—are found in the inner gorge of the canyon. These dark gray to black rocks are between 1.7 and 2 billion years old and are the roots of an ancient mountain range. Above this layer is a suite of sedimentary rocks that were deposited between 825 million and 1.2 billion years ago. Overlying these Precambrian rocks is an unparalleled sequence of layers that reveal the changing marine, freshwater, and desert environments of the Southwest through the Paleozoic Era, between 250 and 550 million years ago. The lowest of these units is 545-million-year-old Tapeats sandstone, a dark brown sandstone that contains marine fossils and ripples formed by ocean waves. The uppermost unit is whitish-gray Kaibab limestone, which is about 250 million years old and marine in origin. Between these two units lie fossilized sand dunes, marine and freshwater limestones, shales that contain terrestrial fossils, and shales that contain marine fossils.

THE GREAT UNCONFORMITY

No rocks between 545 and 825 million years old are found at the Grand Canyon. This gap, the Great Unconformity, lies between the Precambrian and Paleozoic rocks. Unconformities occur when sediment deposition stops, erosion removes some layers of sediment and rock, and then deposition resumes. The Great Unconformity in the Grand Canyon marks a period when advancing oceans eroded away the rocks that are now missing. The Precambrian layers show another unconformity from 1.2 to 1.7 billion years ago.

Fossils

A fossil is any indication of prehistoric life, including petrified wood, dinosaur bones, ancient seashells, footprints, or even casts in the shape of an animal left in rock after the organism itself disintegrated. Almost all fossils are discovered in sedimentary rocks, usually in areas that were once underwater, which explains why most fossils are of aquatic species. For many millions of years the Southwest was a shallow sea, and the rocks here are consequently full of marine fossils from that time. As sea level fluctuated, tropical terrestrial environments also formed, providing a rich habitat for hundreds of plant species, as well as dinosaurs and other vertebrates that all became part of the area's fossil record.

DINOSAUR FOOTPRINTS
At Clayton Lake State Park in northeastern New Mexico, more than 500 dinosaur footprints have been preserved and identified along the lake's spillway. Most were made by iguanodons, three-toed plant-eaters that lived here about 100 million years ago. The tracks are easily recognized by their square heels and lack of claw marks. Other tracks from carnivorous dinosaurs are distinguished by their pointed heels and clawed toes.

ICHTHYOSAURS
The largest specimens of the predatory "sea lizard" *Shoshonisaurus* have been found near Berlin, Nevada. These ichthyosaurs were not dinosaurs, but a separate group of marine vertebrates that breathed air, as modern whales do. They swam in a shallow arm of the Pacific Ocean that covered the area 225 million years ago. *Shoshonisaurus* reached 50 to 60 feet in length and probably weighed between 50 and 60 tons.

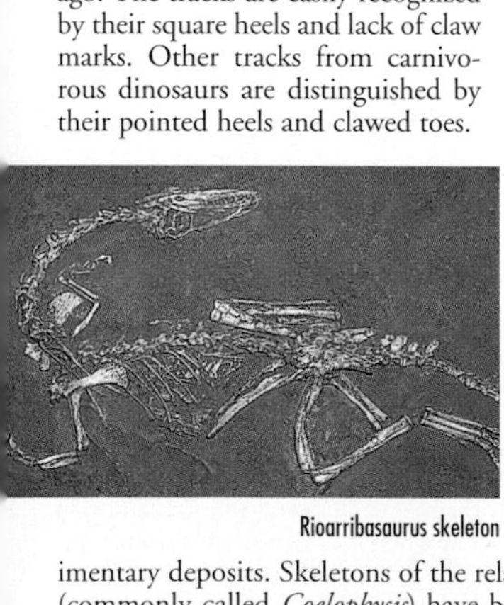

Rioarribasaurus skeleton

DINOSAURS
Fossils of *Apatosaurus* (better known as *Brontosaurus*), a 70-foot-long plant-eater, are common at Dinosaur National Monument in Utah and Colorado. Discovered there in a ridge of sandstone, the bones were probably originally deposited on a river sandbar by floodwaters, mineralized by percolating groundwaters rich in dissolved silica, and preserved by overlying sedimentary deposits. Skeletons of the relatively small dinosaur *Rioarribasaurus* (commonly called *Coelophysis*) have been recovered from Ghost Ranch, in Abiquiu, New Mexico. This meat-eater, which lived 215 million years ago, weighed between 50 and 100 pounds, and walked on its hindlegs.

The Best Places to See Fossils in the Southwest

ANTELOPE SPRINGS TRILOBITE QUARRY Delta, Utah. Trilobites from 500 mya.
BERLIN-ICHTHYOSAUR STATE PARK Austin, Nevada. Ichthyosaurs from 225 mya.
CARLSBAD CAVERNS NATIONAL PARK Carlsbad, New Mexico. Ancient reef environment from 200 mya and bird bones from 60 mya.
CLAYTON LAKE STATE PARK Clayton, New Mexico. Dinosaur footprint trackways from 100 mya.
CLEVELAND-LLOYD DINOSAUR QUARRY Price, Utah. Dinosaurs (*Allosaurus, Stegasaurus, Camarasaurus,* and others) from 147 mya.
DINOSAUR NATIONAL MONUMENT Colorado and Utah. Dinosaurs from 145 mya (million years ago).
GHOST RANCH Abiquiu (near Taos), New Mexico. *Coelophysis* from 215 mya.
GRAND CANYON Arizona. Marine invertebrates from 600 mya.
PETRIFIED FOREST NATIONAL PARK Holbrook, Arizona. Petrified wood from 225 mya.

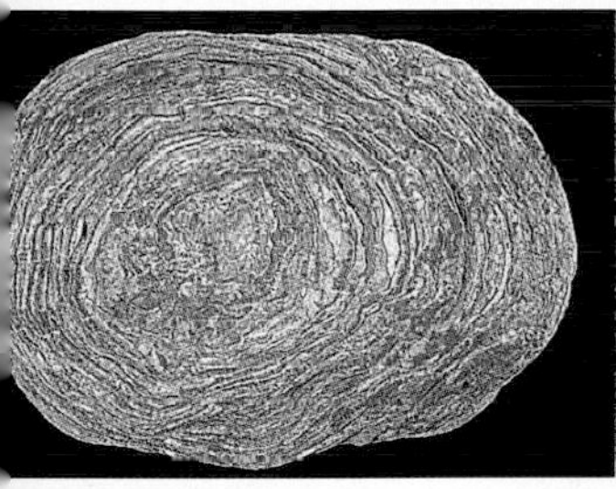

STROMATOLITES

Stromatolites are reefs built out of colonies of blue-green algae that look like heads of cabbage. These ancient organisms are estimated to have lived more than 1 billion years ago, probably in shallow water. Stromatolites are found in rocks of the inner gorge of the Grand Canyon, in Arizona, and at Bald Mountain Pass, in Utah.

TRILOBITES

These ancient marine arthropods, the dominant life-form between 500 and 570 million years ago, were one of the first organisms with a hard exoskeleton. At Antelope Springs Trilobite Quarry, in western Utah, about 45 species of trilobite can be found, including *Elrathia kingi.* The trilobite *Paradoxides harlani* can be seen in the Bright Angel shale in the Grand Canyon, Arizona.

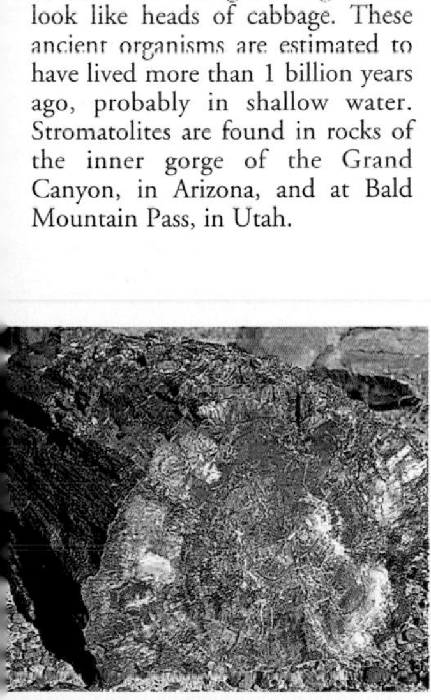

PETRIFIED WOOD

Most of the fossilized trees of Petrified Forest National Park, in Arizona, are of the ancient tree called *Araucarioxylon,* which is similar to modern-day conifers. These trees grew to be 200 feet tall, with straight trunks and few limbs. The logs were preserved when volcanic eruptions quickly killed, burned, and buried the trees. Fossilization occurred as silica replaced the wood fragments. The striking colors of the fossil logs, formed 225 million years ago, are the result of impurities—iron, manganese, copper, and lithium—present in the wood during fossilization.

Minerals

Minerals, the building blocks of rocks, are naturally occurring substances with characteristic chemical compositions and crystal structures that determine their external appearance. A mineral may be a single native element, such as copper or gold, or a compound of elements. Minerals are recognized by such physical properties as hardness, cleavage or fracture (the way they break), luster (the way the surface reflects light), and crystal structure. Minerals are ductile if they can be shaped into strings; they are malleable if they can be hammered into various shapes. Color may be an unreliable identifying feature, since it is often the result of impurities. The brief accounts below describe visible physical properties of common minerals in the Southwest, the rocks in which they occur, and areas where they are likely to be found.

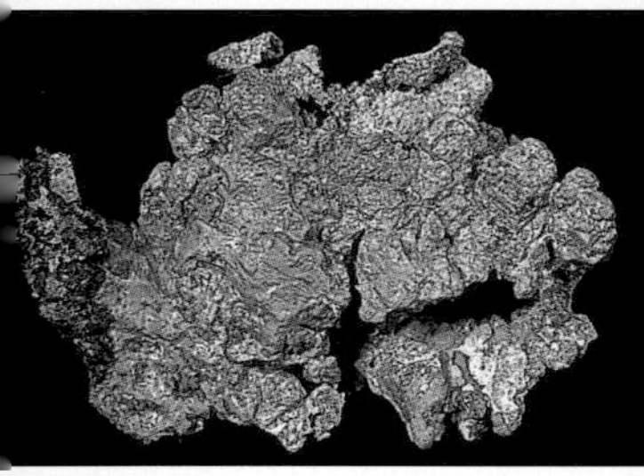

COPPER
Cubic and 12-sided crystals; also scales, lumps, and branching forms. Reddish brown, turning black, blue, or green with tarnish; metallic luster. Can be scratched by a knife; ductile; malleable; lacks cleavage. Bingham Mine outside Salt Lake City, Utah, is one of the world's largest open pit mines; old copper mines dot the San Francisco Mountains in Utah; open pit mining occurs in the Pima Mining District south of Tucson, Arizona. Arizona produces more than half of the copper in the United States.

FELDSPARS
Large group of aluminum silicates; earth's most common minerals. Flat crystals, square to rectangular in cross section. Color varies depending on relative amounts of sodium, calcium, and potassium; most commonly white, pink, or gray. Many forms, including orthoclase (a potassium-rich form; pictured) and andesine (a sodium and calcium form). Very common in both igneous and metamorphic rocks; a main constituent of granite.

SILVER
Scales, wires, or in massive form. Silvery white, with exposed surfaces tarnished; metallic luster. Ductile; malleable; lacks cleavage. Comstock Lode near Virginia City, Nevada, is largest silver strike in world. Other silver strikes near Tonopah, Eureka, and Hamilton, Nevada, and near Magdalena and Georgetown, New Mexico.

QUARTZ
Crystals commonly six-sided, with pyramidal ends. Many colors: white, gray, red, purple, pink, yellow, green, brown, or black; transparent or milky; glassy luster. Cannot be scratched by a knife; lacks cleavage. Most common mineral in sandstone.

CALCITE
Occurs in more forms than any other mineral. Commonly white or light gray. Can be scratched by a knife; fizzes with vinegar or hydrochloric acid. Key component in limestones; found in deserts as a whitish crusty deposit called caliche.

GYPSUM
Evaporite mineral formed when seawater or salt lakes dry up, leaving behind minerals that had been dissolved previously. White or light gray; translucent. Soft; easily scratched by a fingernail. Often found in reddish sedimentary rocks as gray-white layers or thin white veins. Common on surfaces of playas, such as Bonneville Salt Flats in Utah. Also found in dunes of White Sands, New Mexico. Gypsum mines operate today near Sigurd, Utah.

MICA
Thin sheets or flakes. Dark brown to black (biotite) or colorless to white (muscovite); transparent to translucent; glassy luster. Easily scratched with a knife or fingernail; fractures in sheets. Common constituent of many rocks, including granite, sandstone, and gneiss; mostly found in igneous and metamorphic rocks.

GOLD
Grains, flakes, or nuggets. Rich, bright yellow; metallic luster. Ductile; malleable; lacks cleavage. Found in Utah (near Cedar City, Silver City, Dividend, Eureka, and Tintic) and Nevada (Pyramid, Ortiz, Sangre de Cristo Mountains, and Rio Grande valley). Nevada is world's fourth-largest producer of gold.

Rocks

A given rock may be composed of only one mineral or may be an aggregation of different kinds. A tangible record of the geologic processes that made them, rocks provide information about many such processes that are impossible to observe directly—for example, the melting of rocks in the earth's interior. Rock identification can be difficult, but clues are provided by a specimen's constituent minerals, color, grain size, and overall texture.

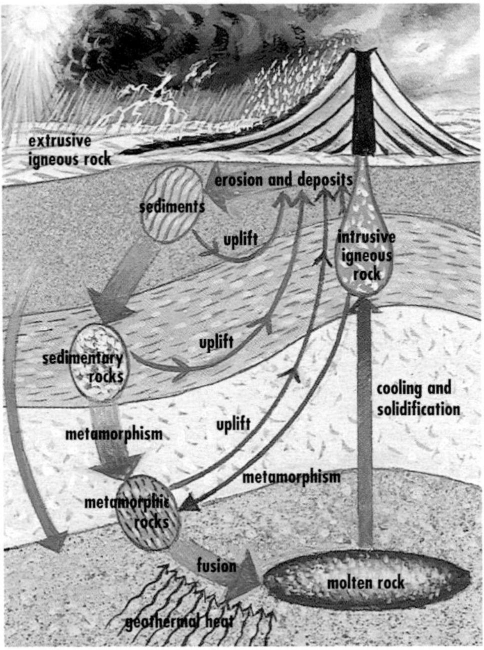

The Rock Cycle

The three basic classes of rocks undergo processes that convert them from one form to another. *Igneous* rocks form through solidification of molten material from the earth's interior. Extrusive igneous rock forms on the earth's surface from solidified molten material; intrusive igneous rock solidifies below the surface. *Sedimentary* rocks form from fragments of older, weathered rock ranging in size from submicroscopic particles to boulders, and from organic or chemical matter deposited at the earth's surface. *Metamorphic* rocks form when other, pre-existing rocks are transformed, through heating and/or pressure. As the small arrows on the drawing indicate, the complete cycle can be interrupted at any point. Though all rock types are found in the Southwest, many of the most spectacular features are made of sandstone.

GRANITE

Intrusive igneous rock formed as magma cools beneath the surface of the earth. *Constituent minerals:* quartz (clear to white), feldspar (pink or white), and mica. *Appearance:* speckled pink, white, and gray-black; large, coarse grained crystals. Found in Zuni, Organ, Sandia, Tusas, and Capitan Mountains, New Mexico; McCartys Basalt Flow near Grants, New Mexico; Ruby Mountains and East Humboldt Range, Nevada; inner gorge of Grand Canyon, Arizona (Zoroaster granite).

SANDSTONE

Sedimentary rock. *Constituent minerals:* predominantly quartz, with feldspar, mica, and other minerals. *Appearance:* white, orange, pink, or reddish; fine- to medium-grained; often cross-bedded (with inclined layering due to grain movement by wind or water); often contains fossils. Common throughout Southwest: Grand Canyon, Arizona (Tapeats, Coconino, and Wingate sandstones); Arches National Park, Utah (Entrada and Navajo sandstones); cliffs of Capitol Reef and Zion National Parks, Utah (Navajo sandstone).

SHALE

Sedimentary rock formed as mud or clay turns to stone. *Constituent minerals:* predominantly quartz and clay minerals. *Appearance:* multi-colored, including gray, black, green, red, and purple; very fine-grained; often breaks in relatively flat sheets and weathers to form sloped surfaces. Common throughout Southwest; dominant rock type in badlands.

LIMESTONE

Sedimentary rock. *Constituent minerals:* calcium carbonate. *Appearance:* fine- to medium-grained; often contains fossils of varying size. Common throughout Southwest, including Muav, Temple Butte, and Redwall limestones in Grand Canyon, Arizona.

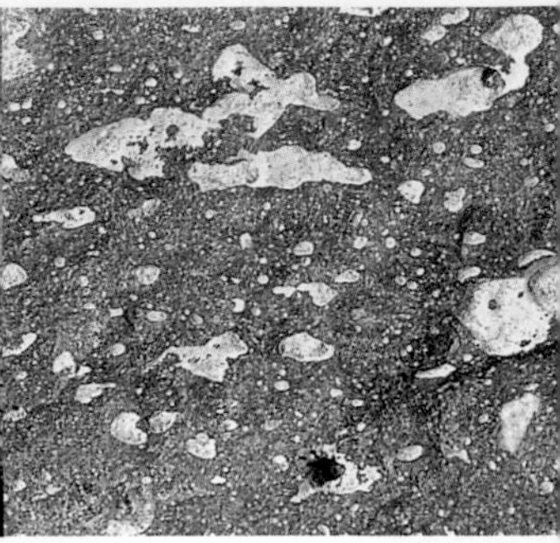

RHYOLITE
Extrusive igneous rock formed as lava erupts explosively at or near the earth's surface. *Constituent minerals:* quartz, feldspar, and biotite mica. *Appearance:* light-colored; pink, white, or gray; very fine-grained; may contain small cavities. Found in San Francisco Mountains, Arizona, and in Valles Caldera, New Mexico.

BASALT
Extrusive igneous rock formed as lava erupts at or near the earth's surface. *Constituent minerals:* feldspar and pyroxene. *Appearance:* dark green to black; very fine-grained; ropy or blocky textures, depending on where rock came to surface. Common in western Nevada from Pyramid Lake area south to Walker Lake; Capulin Mountain and Raton-Clayton Volcanic Field, in northeastern New Mexico; region of Zuni Mountains, New Mexico.

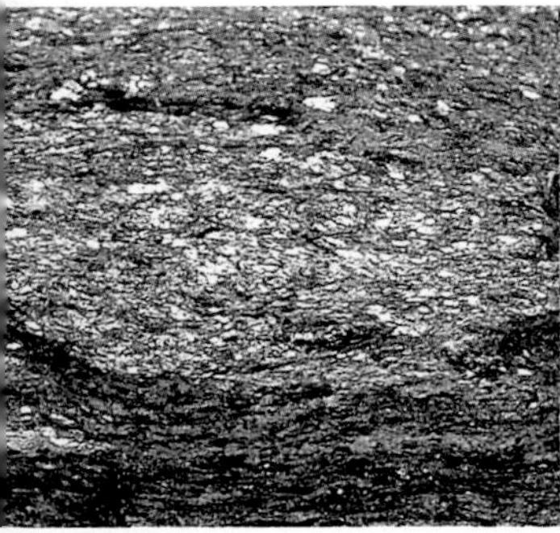

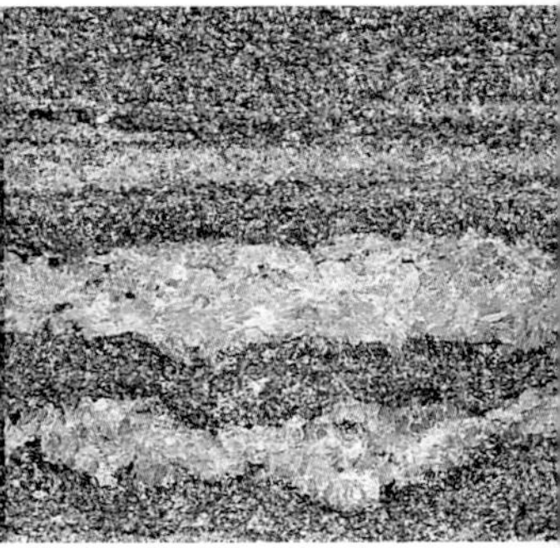

SCHIST
Metamorphic rock formed under conditions of medium temperatures and pressures. *Constituent minerals:* quartz, feldspar, and mica; often segregated into layers with foliated or wavy banding. *Appearance:* gray or greenish gray, depending on relative amounts of constituent minerals; medium-grained. Found in Ruby Mountains and East Humboldt Range, Nevada; inner gorge of Grand Canyon, Arizona (Vishnu schist).

GNEISS
Metamorphic rock formed under conditions of high temperature and high pressure. *Constituent minerals:* quartz (clear to white), feldspar (pink to white), and mica (dark- and light-colored). *Appearance:* varying shades of white, black, gray, and pink; discontinuous, alternating light and dark bands; medium-grained. Found in Sangre de Cristo Mountains, New Mexico, and Santa Catalina Mountains, Arizona.

Habitats

At first glance, the habitats of the Southwest may seem an astonishing patchwork. Cold-loving Douglas Firs grow within a stone's throw of cactus and agave plants; sedges and willows thrive around springs surrounded by drought-tolerant Creosote Bushes. Deserts, grasslands, and woodlands intermingle. But in the Southwest, as elsewhere, the lives of plants and of the animals that rely on them are governed by largely predictable conditions.

In general, the climate grows cooler and moister as one travels from south to north, as well as from low to high elevations. For each rise of 1,000 feet, the temperature drops about 3 degrees Fahrenheit, while annual precipitation increases an average of 2 inches. In the Santa Catalina Mountains near Tucson, a motorist can ascend in 30 miles from Giant Saguaro–studded Sonoran desert at 2,400 feet to cool fir stands at over 9,000 feet, passing through desert grasslands, oak woodlands, and Ponderosa Pine forests. This rise in elevation is the ecological equivalent of a 2,000-mile trip from southern Arizona to Canada.

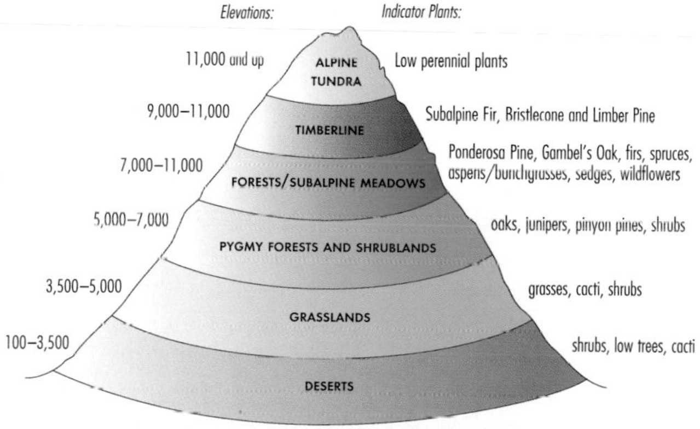

This diagram shows the elevations (in feet) at which the major habitat types of the Southwest occur, along with the indicator plants that dominate at each elevation.

The details of habitat are not dictated by elevation alone. Cacti and other heat-loving plants grow high on south-facing slopes, while firs descend into cool, north-facing canyons. Drainages capture cold air, while rock outcrops retain heat. Precipitation patterns—in some places more falls in winter, in others more in summer—often have a greater influence on which plants grow than does the total annual amount. Rock and soil types, too, have a profound effect.

Most habitats in the Southwest have evolved to deal with severe disturbances, such as fires and floods. In recent centuries, the pace of change has accelerated as humans have introduced domestic livestock and large-scale agriculture, logged forests, and altered drainage patterns. The challenge now is to ensure that future changes do not further reduce the area's rich diversity of plants, animals, and ecosystems.

Deserts

The Southwest lies in the rain shadow of the Sierra Nevada and Coast Ranges to the west. Winter storm systems moving off the Pacific Ocean shed much of their moisture in those mountains; by the time they reach Arizona and Nevada, most produce little precipitation. As a result, rain and snow are infrequent and irregular across much of the region. This dearth, coupled with ample sunshine and frequent high temperatures, ensures that most of the land remains arid. Some areas along the Colorado River receive, on average, as little as 2 inches of rain per year.

Deserts of the Southwest

Climate, topography, soil type, and other factors interact with this predominant aridity in such diverse ways that experts identify not one but four deserts in the Southwest. All are interrupted by isolated mountain ranges that allow islands of moister or cooler habitats to persist.

Sagebrush and grasses, Great Basin, Nevada

Great Basin

The Great Basin, the northernmost American desert, covers most of Nevada, much of Utah, and parts of northern Arizona. This desert is high and often cold; large sections receive most annual precipitation in the form of winter snow. The Great Basin is dominated by a few shrubs that often form vast monotypic stands: several species of sagebrush, Shadscale, Blackbrush, and others. These plants are unappetizing to most herbivores, and they offer relatively little shelter, so animal diversity is fairly low here. But some species have come to make a living on sagebrush; indeed, some depend on it almost entirely. Both the Sage Grouse and the Pygmy Rabbit rely on sage buds and leaves for much of their diet.

Mojave Desert with Joshua Trees, cacti, and grasses, Utah

Mojave Desert

Centered in southern California, the Mojave Desert stretches into Nevada, Arizona, and barely into southern Utah, and Mojave vegetation extends upstream in the depths of the Grand Canyon. This desert includes some of the hottest and driest places on the continent. Some of its expanses are sparse indeed, dotted with widely spaced and extremely drought-tolerant Creosote Bushes. Large yuccas, especially the imposing Joshua Tree, are important to wildlife in many areas, such as around Lake Mead in northern Arizona and southern Nevada. After fall and winter rains, poppies, phacelias, globe mallows, and many other spring-blooming wildflowers form carpets of color on the desert floor.

DESERT ANIMALS

Desert animals commonly avoid heat and drought by remaining hidden underground during daylight hours, dry spells, and cold winters. Many species obtain all their needed water from their food; some, such as kangaroo rats, can gain all the water they need from a diet of dry seeds.

Banner-tailed Kangaroo Rat

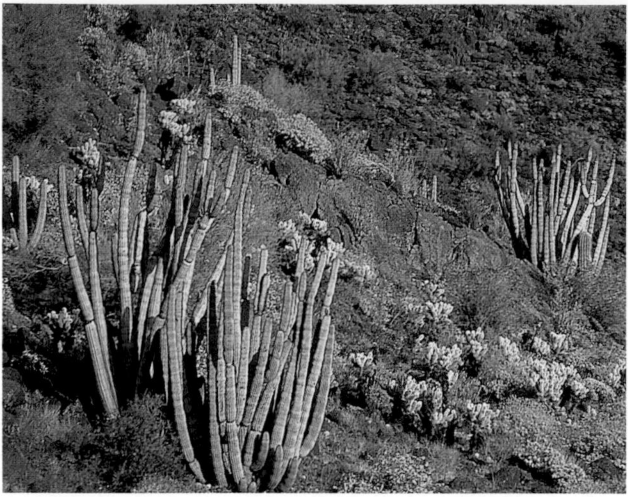

Organ Pipe Cacti, Organ Pipe Cactus National Monument, Arizona

Sonoran Desert

The most species-rich of North American deserts, the Sonoran stretches across southern Arizona and California and deep into western Mexico. In the United States its lushest portions can be found in Arizona, where violent summer thunderstorms produce spectacular lightning displays and nourish a wide array of subtropical vegetation. Tall Giant Saguaros, Organ Pipe Cacti, and a variety of other cactus species, along with Desert Ironwood, Velvet Mesquite, and Foothill Paloverde trees, give this desert a great structural diversity. Animals take advantage of that diversity in many ways. Cavities hammered into Giant Saguaros by Gila Woodpeckers and Gilded Flickers, for example, shelter the nests of about a dozen bird species, while paloverde and mesquite seeds are a nutritious food source for animals from bruchid beetles to Coyotes.

Gila Woodpecker, Saguaro National Park, Arizona

DESERT PLANTS

Perennial desert plants minimize water usage and exposure to drying sun and wind by producing small, ephemeral leaves, as Ocotillos do, or none at all, as in the cactus family. Leaves and stems are often coated with layers of waxes or oils that reduce water loss. Some succulent species, such as Giant Saguaros, can store sufficient water during storms to weather long dry spells. The ephemeral wildflowers that infrequently produce spectacular spring displays in the Mojave and Sonoran Deserts use another tactic: They freely use water during their short lifespan, but their dormant seeds can wait in the soil for years or decades until sufficient moisture triggers germination.

Ocotillo in bloom

White Sands, New Mexico

Chihuahuan Desert

A high midcontinental plateau, the Chihuahuan Desert extends from southeastern Arizona and southern New Mexico through west Texas and into Mexico; at its fringes it often merges with desert grassland. It receives most of its moisture in the form of summer storms that move inland from the Gulf of Mexico. They nourish low-growing shrubs, such as Creosote Bush and Tarbush, that often fill wide basins; slopes sprout gardens of Ocotillos, agaves, yuccas, and a wide variety of small and often inconspicuous cacti. At White Sands National Monument in southern New Mexico, a wide, slowly moving sea of gypsum dunes has resulted in the evolution of specialized plants and animals, including perennials that can survive burial by sand and Lesser Earless Lizards, whose exceptionally pale scales allow them to move about camouflaged on the dunes.

Grasslands

Most grasslands in the Southwest occur at elevations above the true deserts and below moister woodlands. The perennial grasses that thrive here can withstand fires, drought, and some grazing pressure, thanks to their deep root systems. As a result, they are able to dominate places too dry, windy, and exposed for trees. But this toughness has not prevented grasslands from becoming among the most severely altered of the region's habitats. Most have been heavily grazed by domestic livestock since the coming of the Spaniards in the 1500s, to the detriment of native plants and animals alike. Grasslands that retain most of their original biological diversity are scattered in remnant pockets today.

Semidesert grassland, Arizona

Semidesert Grassland

In southern New Mexico and southeastern Arizona, grasslands often have a large complement of shrubby species, including Velvet Mesquite, Catclaw Acacia, Ocotillo, and several varieties of yuccas and agaves. Grasses exhibit a great diversity here, with more than a half dozen species often found growing in close proximity. Summer thunderstorms also promote the growth and blooming of many wildflowers. Some desert animals, such as Desert Bighorn Sheep, Greater Roadrunners, and Western Diamondback Rattlesnakes, extend their range up into these areas. Black Bears and other species more often associated with montane forests wander down in search of seasonal food bounties, such as the succulent fruits of pricklypear cacti.

ARTHROPODS

Tiny but mighty, arthropods dominate grassland ecosystems. In the Southwest, a single acre of grassland may harbor some 250 pounds of termites that gather and digest plant material from dead grass stalks, woody stems, and the droppings of herbivores. Their excavations significantly aerate the soil, promoting plant growth. Following summer rainstorms that help perennial bunchgrasses grow, large grasshoppers, predatory tarantulas, and tiny chiggers are among the other arthropods that make their presence known, not always amicably, to human visitors.

Great Basin grassland, Wupatki National Monument, Arizona

Great Basin Grassland

Sharing many species with the true shortgrass prairie, these grasslands exist in scattered valleys, canyons, and plateaus throughout the Great Basin as far south as northern Arizona. The vast majority of these areas have been heavily altered by livestock grazing, resulting in a shift from the dominance of grasses to dominance by Big Sagebrush, Broom Snakeweed, Green Ephedra, and other shrub species unpalatable to most herbivores. The best places to view this habitat are areas off-limits to grazing, such as Wupatki National Monument in Arizona and Canyonlands National Park in Utah. Pronghorns, Coyotes, and Spotted Ground Squirrels are among the animals often seen or heard here.

Black-tailed Prairie Dogs

Great Plains Grassland

The Great Plains abut the Rocky Mountains in eastern New Mexico, where shortgrass prairie meets pinyon-juniper and oak woodland; island pockets of similar grassland lie scattered as far west as central Arizona. Though these extensive, generally flat habitats may seem monotonous, a close inspection reveals fine gradations. Short perennial grasses, such as Blue Grama and Buffalo Grass, dominate dry areas, while Big and Little Bluestem and other taller species grow in swales and other moist places. Some desert shrubs, such as saltbushes and prickly-pear cacti, may also be common. In late spring the aerial songs of Mountain Plovers and Horned Larks fill the air. Many once-common animals, including American Bison, Black-tailed Prairie Dogs, Burrowing Owls, Lesser Prairie-Chickens, and Massasaugas, occur in much-reduced numbers today, because of livestock grazing and the conversion of grasslands to agricultural fields.

Pygmy Forests and Shrublands

Pinyon Jay

Above the open lowland basins and below the tall pines lies an in-between realm that is neither desert nor grassland nor true forest, a place where widely spaced, seemingly stunted trees grow to majestic stature in their own right. The oaks, junipers, and pinyon pines of these pygmy forests seldom grow taller than 35 feet, but they are often thick-trunked, gnarled, and long-lived. Their seeds form an important food source for many animals, from Black Bears to Wild Turkeys to several species of jays. These woodlands tend to receive an average of 10 to 20 inches of rain per year. Because wet periods may be separated by long dry spells, fires are not uncommon. Fires were probably more frequent before extensive livestock grazing lowered the abundance of the perennial bunchgrasses that often formed much of the understory in earlier times.

Madrean evergreen woodland, Canelo Hills, Arizona

Madrean Evergreen Woodland

Mexico's Sierra Madre Occidental boasts an exceptional diversity of oak species, some of which—such as Emory, Silverleaf, and Mexican Blue Oak—extend north into the foothills and mountains of southern New Mexico and southeastern Arizona. Most of these oaks are evergreens, though they may drop their leaves in times of extended drought. They grow intermingled with Alligator Juniper, Mexican Pinyon, and a few other trees. Naturalists flock to these woodlands to see animals more characteristic of the Mexican highlands, such as the White-nosed Coati, Apache Fox Squirrel, Montezuma Quail, Hepatic Tanager, and Rock Rattlesnake. As a transition zone between grassland and forest, this habitat supports many species characteristic of both; in some cases, oak woodlands form important travel corridors that allow Black Bears, Mountain Lions, and other animals to move between the higher forests of otherwise isolated mountain ranges.

Chaparral, Prescott National Forest, Arizona

Chaparral and Shrublands

Mid-elevation hills and mountainsides in central and southeastern Arizona and western New Mexico are often covered with tangled thickets of drought-tolerant shrubs that grow to five or six feet high. This chaparral, often kept free of trees by periodic fires, includes such species as Shrub Live Oak, Desert Ceanothus, and several types of manzanita. Farther north, the slopes of Great Basin mountain ranges often support patches of high-elevation brush made up of Gambel's Oak, New Mexico Locust, and various types of manzanita and mountain mahogany. Both types of shrubland grow so dense that wildlife-watching is often difficult, but the distinctive calls of Spotted Towhees, Western Scrub-Jays, Bushtits, Virginia's Warblers, and a number of other birds are often heard.

Pinyon-Juniper Woodlands

Covering mid-elevation slopes and plateaus throughout southern and central Utah and Nevada and northern Arizona and New Mexico are extensive woodlands made up primarily of several species of junipers and pinyon pines. Thriving mostly between about 4,800 and 7,500 feet in elevation, these often scrubby trees rise above perennial grasses and sometimes a shrub layer characterized by Big Sagebrush and the gangly branches of Cliffrose. Whether growing densely, as on some flat-topped mesas and plateaus, or widely dispersed, as on the sandstone swells of the Colorado Plateau, these stands can appear monotonous. But they support a wide web of life. Large, nutritious, and tasty, pinyon seeds are a particularly important food source, attracting Pinyon Jays, Clark's Nutcrackers, many species of rodents, and other animals; they have also been relished by human beings for millennia.

Pinyon-juniper woodland, Colorado Plateau, Arizona

Forests

Forests grow at high elevations throughout the Southwest, forming a continuum from open, dry growths of pine at lower elevations to densely shaded spruce-fir stands higher up. Along with climate and topography, fire plays an extensive role in the composition of these forests. Ponderosa and Lodgepole Pines and Quaking Aspens are among the species that generally benefit from periodic fires, while spruces and firs take over on cooler, wetter sites that rarely burn.

Coronado National Forest, Arizona

Mixed Conifer Forests

Just above the belt of monotypic pines, and in sheltered drainages, conditions become cool and moist enough for Douglas Firs, White Firs, and other conifers. They mingle with pines and such deciduous trees as Gambel's Oak and Quaking Aspen. Some of these conifers can grow to well over 100 feet, particularly in protected canyons; such old-growth stands are the preferred home of such threatened animals as the Mexican Spotted-Owl and Northern Goshawk.

Spruce-Fir Forests

At high elevations, from about 8,000 to over 11,000 feet, mountains in the Southwest often support dense forests of Engelmann and Blue Spruce and Subalpine Fir. Snow lingers late in these cool, moist places; frosty nights are possible even in summer. Precipitation—occurring at any time of year, but most often in the form of heavy winter snows and frequent summer thunderstorms—can exceed 40 inches a year. This habitat's affinity with boreal forests is revealed by the presence in Utah and Nevada of such northern species as Snowshoe Hare, American Marten, and Lynx. Boreal birds extend even farther: Gray Jays, Pine Grosbeaks, and Three-toed Woodpeckers nest as far south as the White Mountain massif of east-central Arizona.

Boulder Mountain, Dixie National Forest, Utah

Quaking Aspens, Manti–La Sal National Forest, Utah

Aspen Groves

When conifer forests are disturbed by fire, wind, or logging, Quaking Aspens are often among the first trees to take advantage of newly available space and sunlight. Often resprouting from roots, they can quickly form large stands of even-aged trees. Their succulent leaves provide forage for Elk and other herbivores, while their appearance is a feast for the eyes, especially when golden-yellow leaves ripple against white bark in autumn. Birds encountered here include incessantly singing Warbling Vireos and cavity-nesting Violet-green and Tree Swallows. Though fast-growing, aspen groves do not last long. They are typically replaced after a few decades by the young conifers that sprout in their shade.

Pine Forests

Apache National Forest, Arizona

Ponderosa Pine dominates throughout the Mogollon Rim country of central Arizona and New Mexico; it also grows on isolated highlands and in canyons throughout the region. Ponderosas often form pure stands, though clumps of Gambel's Oak also occur. Snags and woodpecker holes provide homes for American Kestrels, Western Bluebirds, roosting bats, and other species. Abert's Squirrels and Common Porcupines are among the most commonly seen mammals. On Utah's northern mountains, especially the Wasatch Range and the Uinta Mountains, are darker, denser Rocky Mountain forests of Lodgepole Pine—a species that requires hot fires to open its seed cones and establish new generations.

High Mountain Habitats

In the Southwest, high montane habitats exist as small islands surrounded by forest; the High Uintas of northern Utah, with 60 miles of continuous tundra, are a notable exception. Conditions for life are harsh in these exposed places. Dessicating wind is almost incessant; soil is sparse or nonexistent. Temperatures remain low throughout the year, though heat from the sun can be intense in summer. Many of the species that can survive these conditions are found in alpine and subpolar habitats throughout much of the Northern Hemisphere.

Subalpine daisies, Manti–La Sal National Forest, Utah

Subalpine Meadows

Often intermingled with spruce-fir forests, subalpine meadows can range in size from small glades to extensive grasslands of thousands of acres. They can occur anywhere from about 8,000 to above 11,000 feet. Subject to heavy snow in winter, they often remain moist or even saturated throughout the year, resulting in the growth of bunchgrasses, sedges, and many wildflowers. Grizzly Bears, now extirpated in the Southwest, once foraged for roots in these areas. Elk, Pronghorns, and Mule Deer are still frequently seen in some meadows, and nesting Broad-tailed and migrant Rufous Hummingbirds forage among the flowers on their edges. A few reptiles and amphibians, including Wandering Garter Snakes, Short-horned Lizards, and Western Chorus Frogs, live in these cool, moist places.

Wheeler Peak, Snake Range, Nevada

Timberline

Timberline marks the place where conditions become too windy, dry, and cold for trees; in the Southwest it varies in elevation from about 9,000 to over 11,000 feet, depending on latitude and local conditions. Its trees—most often Subalpine Firs and

Bristlecone, Whitebark, and Limber Pines—grow in distinctive shapes. Some are "flagged" with all their branches pointing in the same direction, away from the prevailing wind; others are known as krummholz, a German term for fantastically gnarled, crooked trees. Some woody species grow in extensive low mats, shielded from winter winds by protective snow cover. Though often noted more for scenery than for wildlife, timberline habitats are a good place to observe a few species, such as Clark's Nutcrackers, White-crowned Sparrows, Yellow-bellied Marmots, and American Pikas.

Montane Pine Woodlands

Bristlecone Pine

Some of the earth's oldest living things live atop high peaks in the Great Basin. Whitebark and Limber Pines, growing in open stands on exposed ridges above about 8,500 feet, can live for centuries, but their longevity is dwarfed by that of Bristlecone Pines. Tree-ring studies have shown that some Bristlecones in Nevada's White Mountains and Snake Range have been alive more than 4,000 years. They accomplish this remarkable feat by growing extremely slowly, by possessing dense wood that resists decay, and by thriving in a difficult environment, thereby minimizing competition with other plants.

Alpine Tundra

The icing on the altitudinal layer cake of habitats, most tundras in the Southwest are, practically speaking, as much desert as the wide basins far below. Tundras begin at about 11,500 feet in Arizona and New Mexico, a little lower farther north. They may receive much snow and rain, yet there tends to be little soil to hold moisture, and much wind to evaporate it. The plants that grow here are low, tough, and perennial—a short summer growing season makes long lifespans a necessity. Because of the isolation of many ranges in the Southwest, some tundra areas support a number of endemic plant species.

Alpine tundra, Uinta Mountains, Utah

Riparian Areas

In a region defined by aridity, water means life. The richest habitats in the Southwest are the riparian oases where water occurs on the surface. Islands of cool shade amid the baking desert, these areas support unique aquatic ecosytems, sprout lush vegetation, and attract large numbers of animals of all sorts. Many waterways in the Southwest have perennial upper reaches separated by intermittent, often sandy lower reaches. This isolation has resulted in the evolution of numerous endemic fish species and subspecies. Unfortunately, human alteration of the area's hydrology has resulted in the endangerment and extinction even of widespread species (see Lost Fish of the Colorado River, page 242).

Elegant Trogon

Canyon Woodlands

Chiseled into rugged mountains, canyon woodlands support an array of plants and animals, nowhere more so than in southern Arizona and New Mexico. Arizona Sycamores, Arizona Madrones, and evergreen oaks sometimes form considerable canopies along perennial or intermittent streams here; a few canyons are lush enough to support the growth of subtropical epiphytes. This vegetation lures primarily Mexican birds such as Elegant and Eared Trogons, Sulphur-bellied Flycatchers, and many hummingbirds. Border canyons are among the best places to spot White-nosed Coatis, sometimes in bands of more than a dozen, and a few Jaguars and Ocelots have been documented. Subtropical reptiles, amphibians, and arthropods are equally well represented.

Wasatch-Cache National Forest, Utah

Mountain Streams

Mountains in the region wring moisture from the air. Some nourishes montane forests, but much of it tumbles downstream toward desert and grassland. Along the way, it sustains a riparian ecosystem that at high elevations is characterized by such water-loving deciduous plants as alders and willows, often interspersed with spruces, Douglas Firs, and other conifers. American Beavers build dams along these waterways. Moose occur along them as far south as the mountains of central Utah. Some streams are large enough to foster the presence of waterbirds, such as American Dippers and Belted Kingfishers. The few amphibians that thrive in these cool conditions include Northern Leopard Frogs and Tiger Salamanders.

Cliffs

The impressive erosive power of creeks and rivers in the Southwest creates habitats defined not by vegetation but by topography. Many species can be found only where cliffs or talus slopes (areas of broken rock worn from higher slopes) create nesting, roosting, or feeding sites. The sweet, descending trill of the Canyon Wren is one of the most characteristic sounds of riparian cliffs. Rock Squirrels are common on talus piles. Peregrine Falcons and White-throated Swifts nest, respectively, on ledges and in crevices. Desert Bighorn Sheep perform amazing feats of agility on near-vertical terrain.

Arches National Park, Utah

Riparian Woodlands

Ribbons of life, the area's few perennial lowland streams are of great value to wildlife. Fremont Cottonwoods and Goodding's Willows grow quickly after periodic floods, forming thickets vital to such species as Gilbert Skinks, Yellow-breasted Chats, and the endangered Southwestern Willow Flycatcher. Numerous migrant songbirds, too, use these linear oases as travel corridors. Though streamside woodlands have been much diminished by urban and agricultural development, the altering of river flows, and the growth of nonnative species, their resilience is displayed at such preserves as the San Pedro Riparian National Conservation Area in Arizona.

Fall cottonwoods along the San Pedro River, Arizona

Wetlands

Though the Southwest is governed by aridity, wetlands do occur. Lakes and playas, whether perennial or intermittent, are formed where surface runoff collects. Seeps and springs appear when the ground level intersects the water table, or where groundwater rises to the surface through geological faults. Though most springs are small, a few are noteworthy for their size. Blue Springs feeds some 200 cubic feet of water per second into the Little Colorado River just above its junction with the Colorado River in the Grand Canyon.

American Avocet, Bear River Migratory Bird Refuge, Utah

Marshes

Marshes are rare in the Southwest, and where they exist they are almost invariably magnets for resident and migrant birds. Many, such as the cattail marshes in New Mexico's Bosque del Apache National Wildlife Refuge, are human-constructed with the aid of dikes and irrigation ditches, and heavily managed for the benefit of waterfowl and shorebirds that feed in nearby fields. Small marshy areas also occur in backwaters along some rivers. The endangered Yuma Clapper Rail is largely restricted to cattail stands along the lower Colorado River.

Seeps and Springs

Water can spring up unexpectedly even in the driest areas. The Colorado Plateau, where water percolates through porous limestone and sandstone, is particularly rich in seeps and springs, many of them found at the head of small canyons in such areas as Utah's Glen Canyon National Recreation Area and Canyonlands National Park. Even the smallest water sources may be sufficient to irrigate tiny patches of maidenhair ferns, columbines, and other plants. Larger ones can sometimes be spotted from a distance, thanks to the shimmer of the pale green leaves of Fremont Cottonwood or Western Redbud trees.

Holemen Spring, Canyonlands National Park

Ruby Mountains reflected in Ruby Lake, Nevada

Montane Lakes

Though lakes are nonexistent in many of the Southwest's steep, arid mountain ranges, they do occur in some numbers, generally in the northern reaches of the region; the Wasatch and Uinta Mountains in Utah, and the Ruby Mountains in Nevada, are noted for their lakes. Montane lakes run the gamut from small snowmelt patches that freeze solid during the winter to much larger lakes that support such indigenous fishes as Cutthroat Trout, and often introduced species of trout as well. Northern River Otters and American Beavers are among the larger animals sometimes seen cruising the waters.

Marshy shoreline, Great Salt Lake

Lakes and Playas

The Great Basin, which covers much of Nevada and Utah, is a huge area with no outlet to the sea. Snowmelt and rainfall course from its mountains into extensive valley basins, where water collects at the lowest point. Some of the resulting lakes, such as Utah's Great Salt Lake and Nevada's Pyramid Lake, are large enough to be perennial, though their levels fluctuate considerably. Many others in the Great Basin and elsewhere are ephemeral playas (dry lakes) where water may linger for weeks or months after heavy runoff. Playas are generally too short-lived, or too alkaline, to support much plant life. But many are rife with algae and small arthropods, especially Brine Shrimp, that attract huge concentrations of shorebirds.

Human Environments

Though urban sprawl, grazing, and water diversions have had devastating impacts on many landscapes in the Southwest, they have also created new ecological niches. Many native animals, including Inca Doves, Great-tailed Grackles, Anna's Hummingbirds, and some butterflies, have expanded their ranges in response. Some introduced species, too, from House Sparrows and European Starlings to Mediterranean Geckos, thrive in cities, suburbs, and agricultural areas.

Truckee River flowing through downtown Reno, Nevada

Cities

By means of groundwater pumping and the diversion of rivers, city dwellers in the Southwest have surrounded themselves with lush growths of native and introduced trees, shrubs, and other plants. Many wild animals tolerant of the presence of humans have found homes in sprawling cities that are essentially artificial riparian areas—rich in food and shelter, and with no hunting. Tree Lizards forage in gardens. Hummingbirds and Southern Long-nosed Bats gather at bird feeders. Cooper's Hawks, Great Horned Owls, Greater Roadrunners, and other avian predators nest in trees and shrubs. Coyotes, Collared Peccaries, and several species of skunks find abundant food in the form of garbage, handouts, and garden plants.

Urban Parks

Most cities in the Southwest have grown in the midst of relatively undeveloped and often rugged land; in some places, subdivisions abut wilderness areas. Foresighted citizens have campaigned for the preservation of parts of these unique natural settings. As a result, some cities have developed extensive parks that preserve large wild areas close to their borders. They offer outstanding recreational opportunities and valuable wildlife habitat, even for such usually retiring animals as Mountain Lions and Bobcats.

Tucson Mountain Park, Arizona

Sandhill Cranes in field

Farms and Ranches

The advent of domestic livestock and large-scale agriculture created new environments throughout the Southwest. Brown-headed Cowbirds, other blackbirds, and Cattle Egrets feed on pasture lands in close proximity to cattle. Sandhill Cranes, Snow Geese, and Long-billed Curlews forage on stubble fields after harvests. Large rodent populations on open agricultural lands also support large populations of predators, from Gray Foxes and Coyotes to Northern Harriers and Red-tailed Hawks.

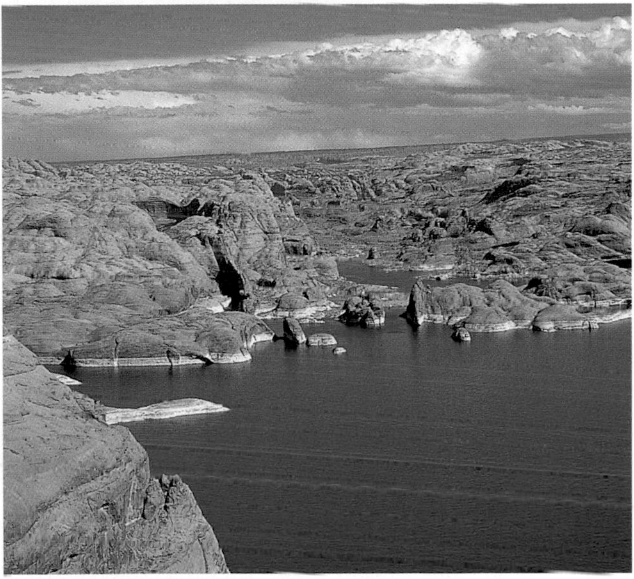

Lake Powell, Utah

Reservoirs and Canals

Manipulation of the Southwest's scarce water resources has allowed a large human population to live here. The reservoirs that store water on river systems and the canals that transport the water to farms and cities comprise stable aquatic habitats that were scarce or nonexistent before the modern era. Among the beneficiaries of that change are numerous nonnative fish species, from Striped Bass to Channel Catfish, that live in reservoirs and rivers. Changed aquatic populations have benefited predatory species, such as Bald Eagles, which now concentrate in winter in such fish-rich places as the Colorado River below Glen Canyon Dam.

The Effects of Human Habitation

Since the arrival of humans thousands of years ago, the hand they have laid on the ecosystems of the Southwest has been sometimes light, sometimes heavy. Some forms of human activity, such as the setting of fires and the ancient gardening practices of some native tribes, have contributed to the area's biodiversity. Other practices, such as over-hunting and the diversion of surface waters, have been less benign.

Ancient cliff dwellings, Navajo National Monument, Arizona

Native Peoples

No one knows how long people have lived in the Southwest. Stone spear points indicate that hunters roamed eastern New Mexico 11,500 years ago, while some archaeologists claim to have found evidence that humans inhabited the region as early as 40,000 years ago. Some believe that human hunting was responsible for the extinction of many Paleolithic animals, such as the Woolly Mammoth. More certain is that some later cultures substantially altered their environment. The Hohokam of the Sonoran Desert, for example, practiced large-scale agriculture, which they were forced to abandon, possibly because an over-reliance on irrigation resulted in soil salinization. Still, most peoples who have lived in the Southwest have existed in relative harmony with their surroundings. Native peoples continue to live here today, both on and off reservations, and many continue traditional occupations, such as farming and livestock grazing.

Hunting and Trapping

American Beaver

Some of the first Americans in the Southwest were trappers in pursuit of American Beaver pelts. Animals such as Bighorn Sheep and Elk were much reduced by big-game hunting, and predators such as Grizzly Bears and Mexican Wolves were wiped out in the region with the aid of federal programs in support of the livestock industry. Hunting and trapping continue, although habitat alterations are a greater threat to species survival.

Grazing

Domestic livestock have roamed the Southwest since the coming of the Spanish conquistadores in the 16th century. To this day cattle—and, to a lesser extent, sheep—graze throughout most of the Southwest, including huge tracts of public lands. Heavy feeding on grasses has promoted the growth of Broom Snakeweed, Green Ephedra, and many other unpalatable, shrubby species, and has converted great expanses of grassland into scrubland. It has also contributed to the spread of nonnative weedy plants, such as Cheatgrass, that have little value for wildlife or livestock.

Roads and Urban Development

Air-conditioning and cheap gasoline have been primary forces in building towns and cities in the Southwest, where sprawling suburbs have become the norm. The rampant pace of development threatens the regional survival of some species, such as the Ferruginous Pygmy-Owl and Flat-tail Horned Lizard of southern Arizona. Because housing tracts, shopping malls, and roads also sever travel corridors between wild areas, they cast doubt on the long-term survival of Black Bears, Mountain Lions, and other wide-ranging animals that are still fairly common. Even two-lane roads can be fatal. Desert Tortoises, snakes, amphibians, and countless arthropods are among those often killed by fast-moving traffic.

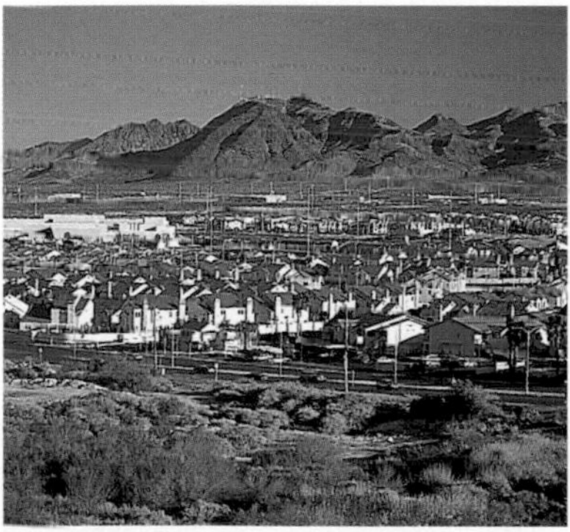

Urban sprawl, Las Vegas, Nevada

Tamarisk trees

Introduced Species

Whether brought here deliberately, or by accident, some introduced species have become plagues. Tamarisk and Russian Olive trees choke native plants out of riparian areas. Cheatgrass and other nonnative grasses dominate rangelands. Aquatic ecosystems have been particularly hard-hit. Bullfrogs from eastern North America feast on endangered native frogs, and the fish fauna of most lakes and rivers is dominated by introduced species such as Striped Bass.

Logging and Fire Suppression

Many habitat types in the Southwest evolved in the presence of periodic fires that swept along too quickly to kill large trees. But the Americans who arrived in the 19th century saw fire as a hazard to lumber and ranching interests. Fire suppression, along with the logging of large old trees, has turned many open forests into dense thickets of young, highly flammable trees. On ranchland, it has combined with heavy grazing to promote the growth of shrubby species and the decline of fire-loving perennial grasses.

Clearcut logging, Arizona

Dams and Water Diversions

The Southwest has the highest per-capita water use in the country, and most people live where there is insufficient water to support large populations. Such sprawling cities as Phoenix and Las Vegas have been able to swell to their current size only through large-scale diversion of the Southwest's scarce surface water. The Colorado River is so heavily used that most of the time no fresh water reaches its delta. By turning free-flowing rivers into reservoirs that lack sediment-rich currents and irregular floods, and by sometimes drying them up entirely, dams have massively degraded riparian and wetland habitats.

Central Arizona Project Canal, near Aguila

Conservation in the Southwest

Aldo Leopold Wilderness, Gila National Forest, New Mexico

The Beginnings of Conservation in the Southwest

Strong conservation sentiments were voiced virtually from the beginnings of American settlement in the Southwest. Early in this century, Aldo Leopold worked as a forest ranger in Arizona and New Mexico. He codified many of his conservationist beliefs here, from an understanding of the ecological role of predators to the concept of land ethics. The work of other writers and artists of the region—Mary Austin, Edward Abbey, Eliot Porter—has had an impact on the modern environmental movement far beyond the region's boundaries.

Glen Canyon Dam, Arizona

Dam Battles

In the middle of this century, with development of the American West proceeding at a rampant pace, doubts began to be voiced about the changes caused by humans. Nowhere were debates more heated than in battles about the damming of the Colorado River. Though conservationists defeated proposals to build high dams in the Grand Canyon, they failed to stop construction of Glen Canyon Dam, which drowned a lovely, isolated canyon system. Proposals to drain Lake Powell, the reservoir behind the dam, still arouse strong emotions.

Efforts at Reconciliation

Arguments between resource users and conservationists have often reached fever pitch in the Southwest. Recently, though, proponents on both sides have begun efforts to work cooperatively. Ranchers, loggers, environmentalists, and land managers are increasingly looking at regional issues together, attempting to preserve the area's rich natural diversity while maintaining a role for humans in the landscape.

Threatened and Recovering Species

The controversial federal Endangered Species Act (1973) has helped protect and restore the populations of many threatened plants and animals in the Southwest. It has also helped restore an ecological balance that in many areas had been severely altered by human-induced changes in the landscape. Elimination of predators, for example, has allowed populations of herbivores such as Elk to swell in some areas, resulting in overbrowsing and the degradation of riparian areas.

Twin-spotted Rattlesnake

Endangered Reptiles

The Southwest is rich in reptiles, many of which are prized by unethical collectors who sell captive specimens to hobbyists. Gila Monsters, Rosy Boas, and Twin-spotted and Ridgenose Rattlesnakes are among the species whose populations have been diminished in some areas by illegal collecting.

Riparian Species

Most riparian areas in the Southwest have been severely altered or destroyed by grazing, agricultural and urban development, and water diversions, and the species dependent upon them are among the most threatened in the Southwest. The endangered Southwestern Willow Flycatcher and Yuma Clapper Rail both breed only at widely scattered sites now. Some amphibians, such as the Chiricahua Leopard Frog, have also lost a great deal of their habitat.

Desert Bighorn Sheep

Desert Bighorn Sheep

Exceptionally well adapted to arid conditions, the desert subspecies of the Bighorn Sheep were common when European settlers arrived; as many as 2 million of these herbivores may have ranged mountains and canyons in the past. By 1975 their population had shrunk to about 10,000, the result of a combination of hunting, diseases transferred from domestic sheep, and habitat fragmentation. Reintroduction programs and habitat protection have since increased their numbers, but some herds are still in danger of dying off as urban and suburban sprawl separates them from other sheep populations.

Mexican Wolves

The Mexican Wolf and Other Predators

Until recently, ranching interests, supported by federal aid, promoted the outright extermination of predators. Though Coyotes and Mountain Lions survived the onslaught of shooting, trapping, and poisoning, the Grizzly Bear and the Mexican Wolf (a subspecies of the Gray Wolf) did not; both were extirpated from the Southwest. In 1998 captive-bred Mexican Wolves were reintroduced in eastern Arizona's Blue Primitive Area, in hopes that a wild population will assure the subspecies' survival and restore the area's ecological balance.

Endangered Plants

One result of the Southwest's topographic diversity is that many plant species are endemic—restricted to small hospitable patches surrounded by large expanses of unsuitable habitat. The natural scarcity of many species has been exacerbated by habitat changes caused by humans. The Dwarf Bearclaw-poppy, as well as a species of solitary bee *(Perdita meconis)* that specializes in pollinating it, were both naturally restricted to a handful of sites in southwestern Utah; both have become quite rare due to habitat destruction.

Other Reintroduction Programs

Reintroduction plans have brought a number of species, including California Condors, Wild Turkeys, and Black-footed Ferrets, back to their former haunts in the Southwest. But not all reintroduction programs work. In the late 1980s, a plan to restore a breeding population of Thick-billed Parrots to the mountains of southeastern Arizona failed. The released parrots, many of them captive-bred birds with little experience in the wild, became easy targets for Northern Goshawks, Ringtails, and other predators.

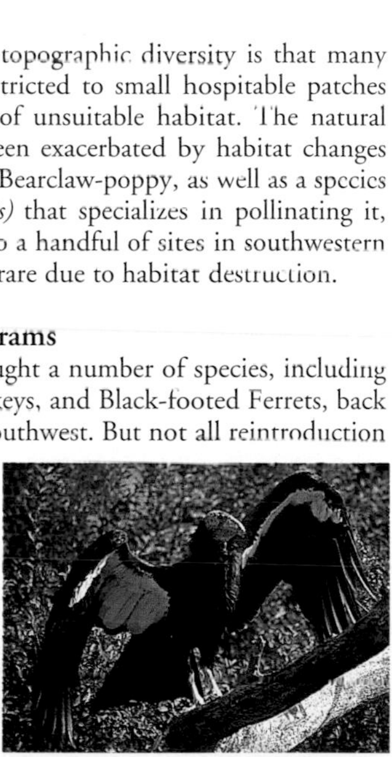

California Condor

Weather

The Southwest encompasses vastly different geographical features that combine with large-scale atmospheric flow patterns to produce greatly varying climate conditions. From 100-inch annual snowfalls in the mountains of Arizona and Utah to searing 120-degree-Fahrenheit heat in the Arizona and Nevada deserts, the weather of the Southwest can be fascinating. The Rocky Mountains pass through Utah and central New Mexico, whereas high plateaus and canyonlands are the rule in northern Arizona, northwestern New Mexico, and southeastern Utah. The Sonoran Desert of southern Arizona and the Great Basin in Nevada, Utah, and northern Arizona add to this incredible diversity. In addition to the influence of local geographical features, weather in the region is also controlled by the contrasting effects of large-scale airflows from the Pacific Ocean, the Canadian Arctic, and Mexico.

Major Influences on Southwest Weather

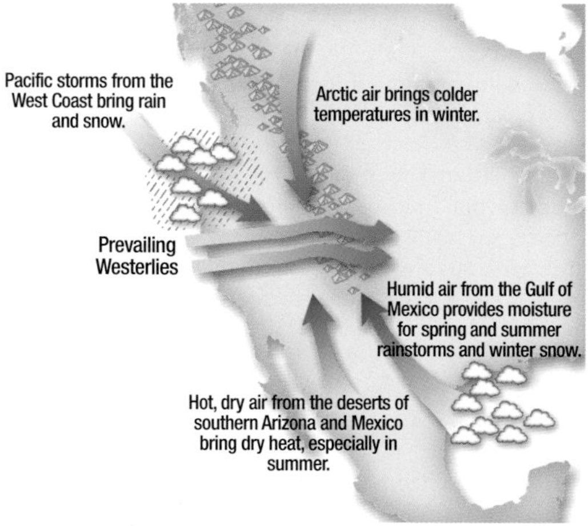
Pacific storms from the West Coast bring rain and snow.
Arctic air brings colder temperatures in winter.
Prevailing Westerlies
Humid air from the Gulf of Mexico provides moisture for spring and summer rainstorms and winter snow.
Hot, dry air from the deserts of southern Arizona and Mexico bring dry heat, especially in summer.

Wind Patterns

The earth's atmosphere is driven into motion as hot tropical air rises and spreads toward the poles and cold polar air sinks and flows toward the equator. The earth's rotation warps this north–south exchange of warm and cold air into vast wind patterns, including the prevailing westerlies, a broad west–east current of air that flows over most of the United States and southern Canada. Because of these westerlies, as well as the westerly subtropical jet stream, most of the weather patterns in the Southwest approach from the west. Large frontal storms also form off the Pacific Coast and sweep through the region, bringing clouds, precipitation, and significant changes in weather conditions.

Highs and Lows

Embedded in the prevailing westerlies are a succession of whirls and eddies: systems of high pressure (fair weather) and low pressure (high humidity, cloudiness, storms) that form and dissipate along fronts, which are the boundaries between warm and cold air masses. Winds blow in a circular pattern around the center of weather systems; in the Northern Hemisphere they blow counterclockwise (as seen from above) in a low-pressure system and clockwise in a high-pressure system. Weather in the Southwest is dominated by alternating influences of high and low pressure; each type of system lasts for 3 to 5 days before being replaced by a new pattern. The Pacific High, a large, semi-permanent system located off the Pacific Coast, controls many of the weather patterns experienced in the region.

Rain

Annual rainfall in the Southwest ranges from 2 inches in the deserts to 50 inches in the mountains. Rainfall is greatest in summer, and often occurs as a thunderstorm. The southwest monsoon, a wind circulation that brings moist, southerly winds into the region during July and August, produces regularly occurring afternoon showers and thundershowers. Because humidity is often low, rain frequently evaporates before reaching the ground; these evaporating streaks of precipitation are called virga. During winter in the high country, temperatures slightly below freezing cause rain to freeze on contact and to cover trees, roads, and power lines with a glaze of heavy ice that can restrict transportation and cause widespread damage.

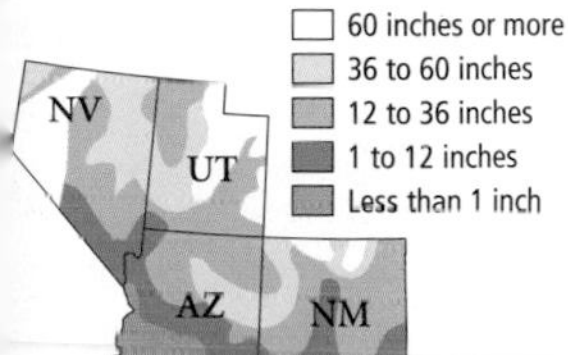

Average annual snowfall

Snow

Annual snowfall throughout the Southwest varies from more than 60 inches in the mountains of Nevada, Utah, and New Mexico to less than one inch in southwestern Arizona. Locally heavy snows can occur throughout all mountainous areas within the region. The heavy snows that fall in the alpine areas of Utah and Nevada create desirable conditions for skiing. Frequent lake-effect snows occur downwind of Utah's Great Salt Lake.

Thunder and Lightning

Lightning is an electrical discharge between one part of a cloud and another, between two clouds, or between a cloud and the earth. In a typical year, lightning strikes in the Southwest several hundred thousand times, and perhaps ten times as many flashes arc across the sky without reaching the ground. Lightning is a deadly weather hazard that kills dozens of people each year. Thunder, the sound of air expanding explosively away from the intense heat of lightning bolts, is a common sound from late spring to early fall.

Flash flood in Canyonlands National Park, Utah

Flash Floods

Flash floods can occur throughout the Southwest. Mountainous areas are particularly susceptible to flooding, as narrow valleys channel water that originates over large tracts of upstream areas. Slow-moving thunderstorms can dump enormous amounts of rain over narrow mountain valleys, causing a raging torrent of water that may destroy everything in its path. Desert areas are also susceptible to flash floods, since hard, dry soil does not allow heavy rains to soak in before rolling across dry creek beds. The springtime melting of heavy winter snowpacks can also create flooding.

Extreme Heat

The deserts of the Southwest are known for their searing heat. Throughout Arizona and portions of Nevada and New Mexico, the sun shines during more than 80 percent of all daylight hours. The hot temperatures help to produce thermals, rising pockets of warm air that frequently produce a cumulus cloud at their top. The combination of hot and dry air produces low relative humidities, causing water to evaporate readily from skin and other moist surfaces. Hikers and other outdoor enthusiasts are advised to wear hats and to carry water with them at all times.

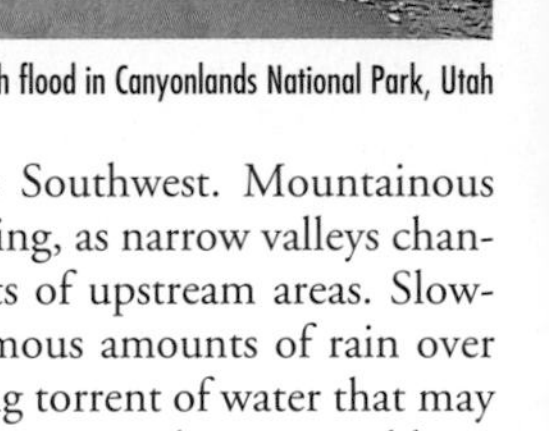

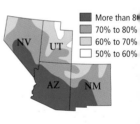

Average daily sunshine

Record-setting Southwest Weather

COLDEST EVER –69° F at Peter's Sink (30 miles east of Logan), Utah, February 1, 1985.

HOTTEST EVER 128° F at Lake Havasu, Arizona. June 29, 1994.

WETTEST PLACE Silver Lake (35 miles southeast of Salt Lake City), Utah. Average 43.81 inches of annual precipitation.

MOST RAIN IN 24 HOURS 11.4 inches fell at Workman Creek (near Roosevelt, 50 miles east of Phoenix), Arizona, September 4 and 5, 1970.

Dust Devils

Small whirlwinds of dust, called dust devils, frequently occur in the deserts of the Southwest. Dust devils form on clear, hot days as warm air rises above the heated ground. Typically several feet across and a few hundred feet high, dust devils are short-lived and generally do not cause much damage. Occasionally a large dust devil may produce winds exceeding 75 miles per hour and cause damage to roofs and small buildings. Unlike tornadoes, dust devils are not associated with thunderstorms.

Double rainbow

Sunsets, Sunrises, and Rainbows

The frequently clear skies over the desert portions of the Southwest create excellent visibility, allowing opportunities to view many optical phenomena in the sky. Some of the most spectacular and most common displays are sunrises, sunsets, and rainbows. Sunrises and sunsets frequently exhibit vivid colors as the low-altitude light travels through clear, dry air. Rainbows are observable when you stand between the low-altitude sun and a raining cloud; in deserts, they regularly occur in the late afternoon and early evening. Rainbows are particularly intense after heavy rains, when they often exhibit both primary and secondary arcs, a phenomenon called a double rainbow.

GREATEST SNOWSTORM 67 inches fell at Heber Springs (40 miles south of Winslow), Arizona, December 13–16, 1967.

HOTTEST PLACE Yuma, Arizona. Average annual temperature 73.9° F. Fourth hottest city in the United States.

SUNNIEST PLACE Yuma, Arizona. The sun shines during 90 percent of all daylight hours.

LEAST HUMID CITY Las Vegas, Nevada. 31 percent average relative humidity.

LEAST PRECIPITATION IN A YEAR Less than 0.01 inch of precipitation fell in 1898 at Hot Springs, Nevada.

Seasons

The Southwest undergoes significant seasonal weather changes throughout the region. Its location nearly halfway between the equator and the North Pole makes the region particularly sensitive to the changing angles of sunlight striking the ground over the course of a year, which is what causes the change of seasons. In the mountains, the average annual temperatures span a 50-degree-Fahrenheit range between summer and winter; in the deserts the range is closer to 35 degrees.

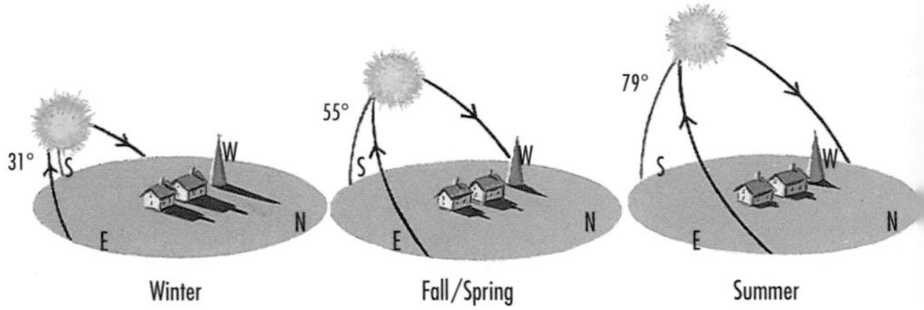

At 35° N (the latitude of Albuquerque, New Mexico), the noontime sun at the winter solstice has an altitude above the horizon of 31°; at the spring and fall equinoxes, its altitude is 55°; and at the summer solstice, the noontime sun rises 79° above the horizon.

As the earth moves around its orbit, its 23½-degree tilt on its axis means that for half the year the Northern Hemisphere is inclined toward the sun and the sun's rays shine on it more directly; for half the year it is tilted away from the sun and the sun's rays are more oblique. The latitude that receives the greatest heat from the sun is farther north during the summer months (though the earth's surface—land and sea—takes a while to warm up, so that early August is actually hotter than late June). Large-scale wind patterns, like the prevailing westerlies, shift toward the north in summer. Higher sun angles and longer days in the Arctic during summer warm up the polar air masses, and the northern position of the westerlies keeps the coldest air north of the Southwest.

Spring

Organ Pipe Cactus National Monument, Arizona

Spring officially begins on March 21 or 22, called the spring (or vernal) equinox, when the sun appears directly overhead at noon at the equator. Cold fronts still sweep across the Southwest in spring, triggering showers and thunderstorms (a few of which may spawn tornadoes), but the high-pressure systems that follow in their wake are much milder than those of winter. March can be snowy and cold, but sunshine begins to increase in April and May.

Summer

Mountain Lion

The sun reaches its peak over the Northern Hemisphere on June 21 or 22, the longest day (that is, daylight period) of the year, known as the summer solstice. As the sun's more direct rays heat the high Arctic, tempering the Southwest's source of cold air, and the Pacific High moves northward, the region experiences prolonged periods of heat and low humidity. A thermal low-pressure system develops over the deserts, causing pockets of warm air to rise and form scattered cumulus clouds and virga. Desert temperatures above 110 degrees are common. Frequent showers and thunderstorms, particularly in July and August, bring temporary relief to the blistering heat of the Southwest deserts.

Zion National Park, Utah

Fall

As it does at the spring equinox, the sun "crosses" the equator again at the fall (or autumnal) equinox, on September 21 or 22. Temperatures begin to decrease across the Southwest, with the first frost typically occurring in November in the deserts, and in August in the high country. Frequent afternoon showers and thunderstorms occur during fall, followed by spectacular rainbows. Cold polar air masses dropping down from the north clash with warm tropical and desert air, creating the cold season's first snowstorms.

Winter

Winter arrives on December 21 or 22, the winter solstice. As long winter nights settle in over the Arctic, cold fronts increase, bringing cold air and more frequent frosts to the Southwest. In the mountains most precipitation falls as snow, while in the deserts rain or a mixture of sleet and snow is quite common. Late January often brings the season's coldest outbreak, and winter conditions generally persist into March.

Snow-covered prickly-pear cacti

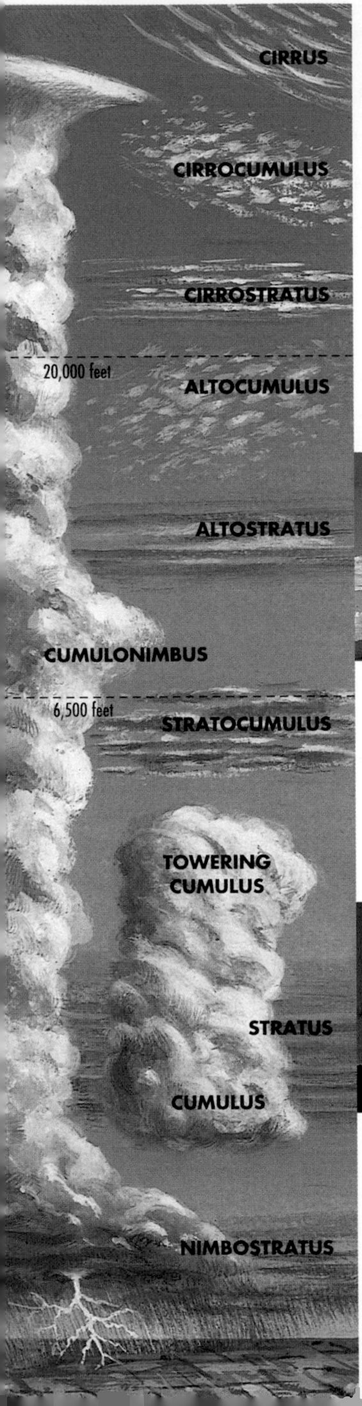

Typical Clouds

Clouds form when moist air is cooled, causing water molecules to condense into water droplets or ice crystals. While most types of clouds can be spotted over the Southwest, the ones described here are among the most common and can be seen year-round throughout the region. The illustration at left shows the relative common altitudes of the different cloud types; distances are not shown to scale.

CUMULONIMBUS
Tallest of all cloud types; commonly called thunderheads. Lower part composed of water droplets; fuzzy, fibrous top—the "anvil"—made of ice crystals. Produce lightning, thunder, heavy rain, and sometimes hail, high winds, or tornadoes. Most common in summer.

LENTICULAR CLOUDS
Stationary, smooth-edged clouds that form at crests of air currents over mountainous terrain. Indicate high winds at mountaintop level and turbulence above. Also common are more ragged cap clouds, formed directly on summits of higher mountains.

CUMULUS
Water-droplet clouds formed at tops of rising air currents set in motion by uneven heating of ground by sun. Domed tops, like bright white heads of cauliflower. Typical clouds of fine summer days. Very common over hilly or mountainous terrain.

TOWERING CUMULUS
Cumulus clouds grow into towering (or swelling) cumulus (also called cumulus congestus) if atmospheric moisture is sufficient, and if it is much warmer at ground level than in air aloft. Can grow taller and develop into thunderstorms—watch for rapid billowing in tops. Most common in summer.

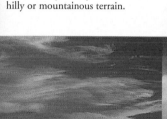

CIRRUS
High (5 miles or higher), thin, wispy clouds made of ice crystals. Cirrus thickening from west or south may signal approaching rain or snow; however, cirrus often come and go without bringing any lower clouds or rain.

ALTOSTRATUS
Middle-level clouds, mainly made of water droplets; usually appear as a featureless gray sheet covering the sky. The sun is dimly visible through altostratus clouds as a weak yellow disc. Thickening, low altostratus often bring steady widespread snow or rain within hours.

VIRGA
Streamers of evaporating rain hanging below a cloud. Commonly occur over deserts and other areas with low humidity. Streaks of evaporating snow are called fall streaks.

MAMMATUS
Series of pouch-shaped, gray to pale-blue cloud elements that form when air pushes downward out of a cumulonimbus cloud. Look like cow's udders hanging down from cloud. Can indicate severe weather because they form in well-developed thunderstorms. Most common in summer.

Our Solar System

The sun, the nine planets that revolve around it, and their moons make up our solar system. Venus, Mars, Jupiter, and Saturn are easily visible to the naked eye. Mercury, Uranus, Neptune, and Pluto are more difficult to see. Other objects in our solar system are transient: The large orbits of comets make them rare visitors near earth, and meteors flash brightly for only seconds before disappearing.

Observing the Sky in the Southwest

The Southwest is the best region in the continental United States for astronomical viewing. The challenges that impede outdoor sky observing—clouds and precipitation, temperature, urban light pollution—are all lessened in this region. The climate is dry and relatively warm and population is low. The air flow is relatively free of turbulence in southern Arizona, resulting in generally good viewing and making it one of the major professional astronomical centers of the world.

FULL MOON

The full moon rises at sunset and sets at dawn. It is highest in the sky in December, up to 87 degrees above the horizon in northern Arizona and New Mexico (in summer, it rises only about 30 degrees). Some features show up best when the moon is full—the dark "seas" (hardened lava flows) and the "rays" of bright material splattered from craters. Craters and mountain ranges are best seen before and after full moon, when the angle of sunlight throws them into relief; look especially near the terminator, the dividing line between the moon's day and night sides. Because the moon is locked in the earth's gravitational grip, the same side of the moon always faces us.

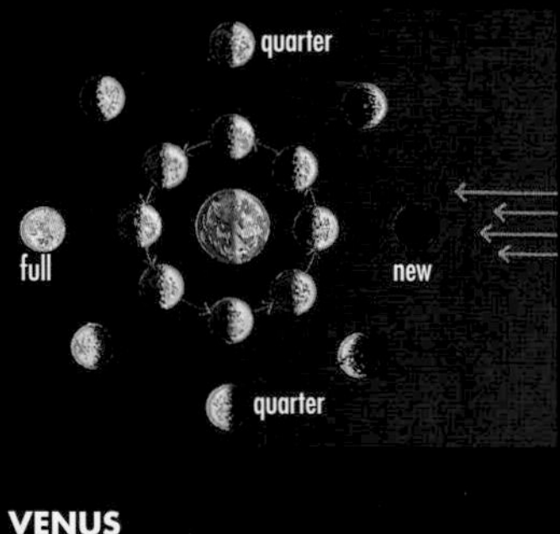

PHASES OF THE MOON

As the moon makes its monthly orbit around the earth, the illuminated lunar surface area appears to grow (wax), shrink (wane), and even disappear (at new moon). The center of the illustration shows the phases, with sunlight coming from the right. The outer drawings show how the moon looks from our perspective on earth.

VENUS

Cloud-shrouded Venus alternates between being our "morning star" and "evening star," depending on where it is in its orbit. This brilliant planet usually outshines everything in the sky except for the sun and moon. As it circles the sun, Venus displays phases, which can be viewed through a small telescope or high-power binoculars.

MARS

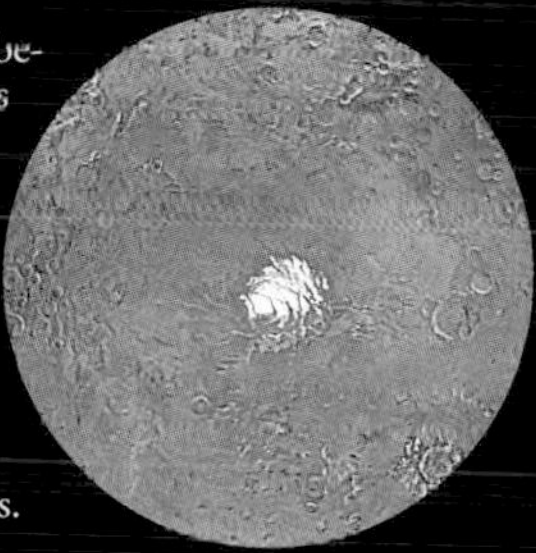

Every 25½ months, when the earth is aligned between Mars and the sun, Mars is closest to us and at its brightest and most colorful, appearing orange-red to the naked eye. At this time, called opposition (opposite in the sky from the sun), Mars rises at sunset and remains in the sky all night. Bright, white polar caps and dusky surface markings may be glimpsed through a small telescope at opposition. Mars rivals Jupiter in brightness at opposition, but fades somewhat at other times.

Jupiter (top) and moons

JUPITER

Visible in our morning sky for about five months at a stretch and in our evening sky for five months, Jupiter appears brighter than any star in the night sky at all times. The largest planet in our solar system, it has a diameter of 88,850 miles, 11.2 times that of the earth. Jupiter's four largest moons—Ganymede, Io, Europa, and Callisto—can often be spotted with binoculars.

SATURN

Visible most of the year, Saturn appears to the naked eye as a slightly yellowish, moderately bright star. A small telescope reveals its rings, composed mainly of rocky chunks of ice, and the two largest (Titan and Rhea) of its more than 20 known moons.

METEORS

These "shooting stars" are typically chips ranging from sand-grain to marble size that are knocked off asteroids (tiny planets) or blown off comets and burn up as they strike our atmosphere. The strongest annual meteor showers are the Perseids, which peak around August 12, and the Geminids, which peak around December 13.

MAN-MADE SATELLITES

During the first hour after dark and the hour before dawn, even a casual observer is likely to see several man-made satellites crossing the sky—a tiny fraction of the 8,000 or so catalogued objects in orbit. Many of the brightest are about the size of cars or buses. As with our natural moon, satellites are visible due to reflected sunlight. When observing satellites, look for the blinking of tumbling objects, brilliant flashes of sunlight reflecting off solar panels, and sudden fading as they pass into the earth's shadow.

COMETS

Comets are irregular lumps of ice and rock left over from the formation of the solar system. Occasionally a notable comet approaches the sun as it travels in its far-ranging elliptical orbit. The sun's energy vaporizes the comet's surface, generating a tail of gas and dust that may be millions of miles long.

Comet Hale-Bopp, 1997

Stars and Deep-sky Objects

As the earth orbits the sun in its annual cycle, our planet's night side faces in steadily changing directions, revealing different stars, constellat[redacted] views of our own Milky Way. People in anc[redacted]mes na[redacted]tellations after mythological figures and familiar creatures whose shapes they saw outlined by the stars. The best k[redacted]f these constellations lie along the ecliptic, the imaginary line t[redacted]es the apparent annual path of the sun through the sky. T[redacted]our moon, and other planets orbit in nearly the same plane, [redacted] tra[redacted]ing along a band roughly 16 degrees wide centered on the ecliptic and called the zodiac. The zodiac is traditionally divided into 12 segments, but 13 constellations actually intersect it.

Modern constellations are simply designated regions of the celestial sphere, like countries on a map. Most constellations bear little resemblance to their namesakes. Beyond the approximatel[redacted]000 stars visible to the naked eye lie other fascinating deep-sky ob[redacted]ts—star clusters, galaxies, nebulas (gas clouds)—that can be seen[redacted]ome with the naked eye and others with binoculars or a small telescope.

The Zodiac

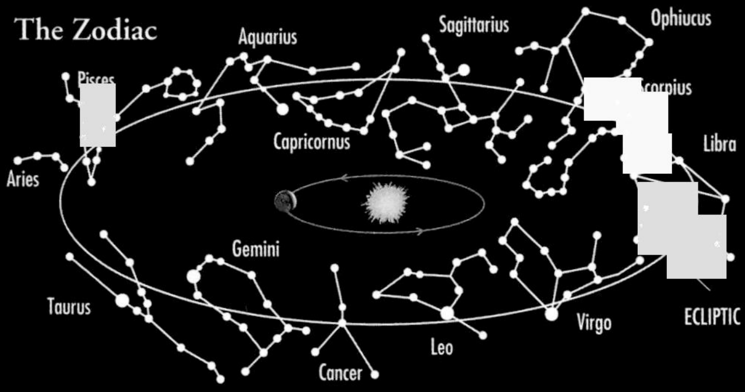

Seasonal Sky Maps

The following pages show star maps for each of the four seasons, drawn at a latitude of 40 degrees north for the specific tim[redacted]nd dates given. (If you wish to observe at a different time or dat[redacted]note that the same stars appear two hours earlier each month[redacted]ne hour earlier every two weeks.) The map for each season is divided into four quadrants: northeast, northwest, southeast, and southwest. Start by facing the direction in which you have the clearest view[redacted]our b[redacted]v is southeastward, use the southeast map. The maps plot the constellations and major stars. The wavy, pale blue areas represent the band of the Milky Way; the zenith, the point directly overhead, is indicated. The key to finding your way around the sky is to locate distinctive constellations or star groups (a few[redacted]re described at right) and then use them to find others. The maps do not chart the planets of our solar system, whose positions change continually; their locations are often listed in the weather section of newspapers.

WINTER: ORION

On winter nights, we look outward through a spiral arm of our disk-shaped galaxy. Many hot, young blue or white stars (such as Sirius, Rigel, and Procyon), along with some older, cooler yellow and reddish stars (Betelgeuse, Capella, and Aldebaran), dominate the sky. New stars are being born in the Orion Nebula, a mixture of young stars, gases, and dust visible to the naked eye or with binoculars as a fuzzy area in Orion's sword, which hangs from his belt.

SPRING: THE DIPPERS

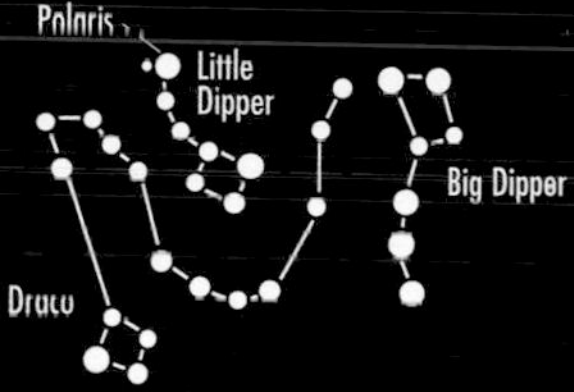

The spring sky features the well-known Big Dipper, part of the constellation Ursa Major, the Great Bear. The two stars at the end of the Big Dipper's bowl point almost directly at Polaris, the North Star, a moderately bright star (part of the Little Dipper, or Ursa Minor) that lies slightly less than 1 degree from the true north celestial pole. Polaris sits above the horizon at an altitude equal to the observer's latitude (32 to 42 degrees in the Southwest).

SUMMER: MILKY WAY

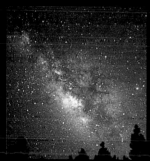

During the summer months, the earth's dark side faces toward the bright center of the Milky Way, making that hazy band of light a dominant feature in the sky. A scan with binoculars through the Milky Way from Cygnus to Sagittarius and Scorpius reveals a dozen or more star clusters and nebulas. High to the northeast, the hot, white stars of the Summer Triangle—Vega, Deneb, and Altair—are usually the first stars visible in the evening.

FALL: ANDROMEDA GALAXY

On autumn evenings, the earth's night side faces away from the plane of our galaxy, allowing us to see other, more distant ones. The Andromeda Galaxy can be found northeast of the Great Square of Pegasus, just above the central star on the dimmer northern "leg" of Andromeda. (On the Fall Sky: Southeast map, the galaxy is near the first D in Andromeda.) Appearing as a fuzzy elongated patch of light, it is 2.5 million light years away.

The Winter Sky

The chart is drawn for these times and dates, but can be used at other times during the season.

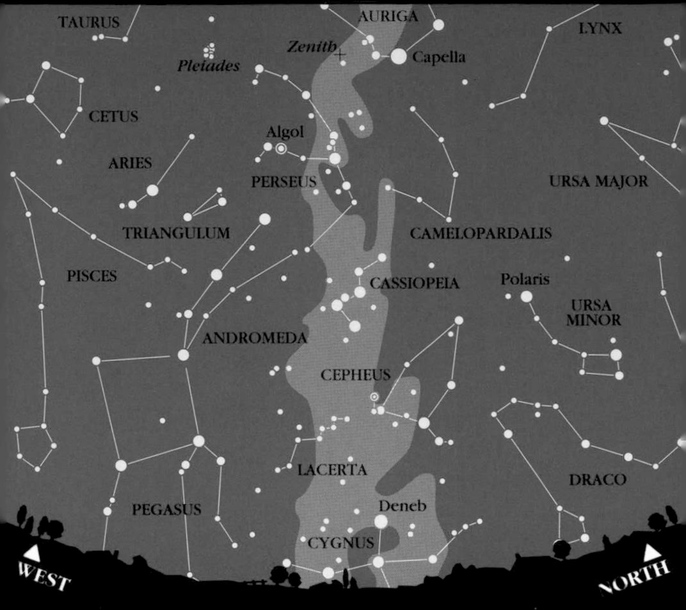

NORTHWEST

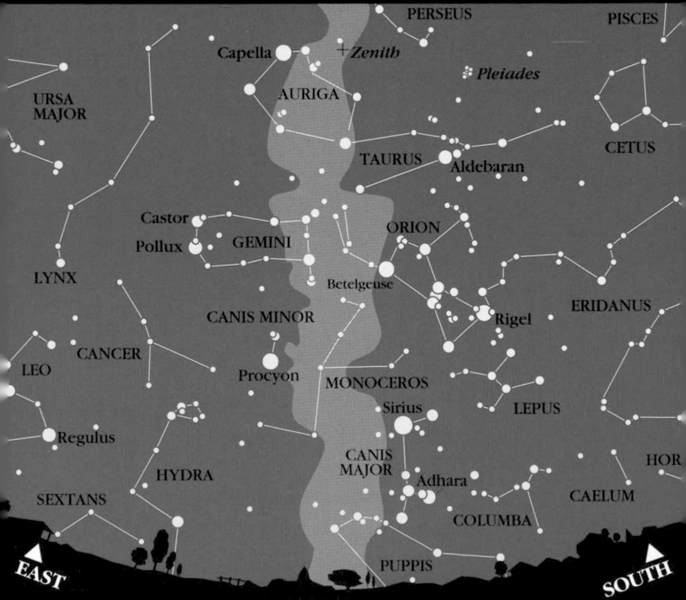

SOUTHEAST

December 1, midnight; January 1, 10 P.M.; February 1, 8 P.M.; March 1, 6 P.M.

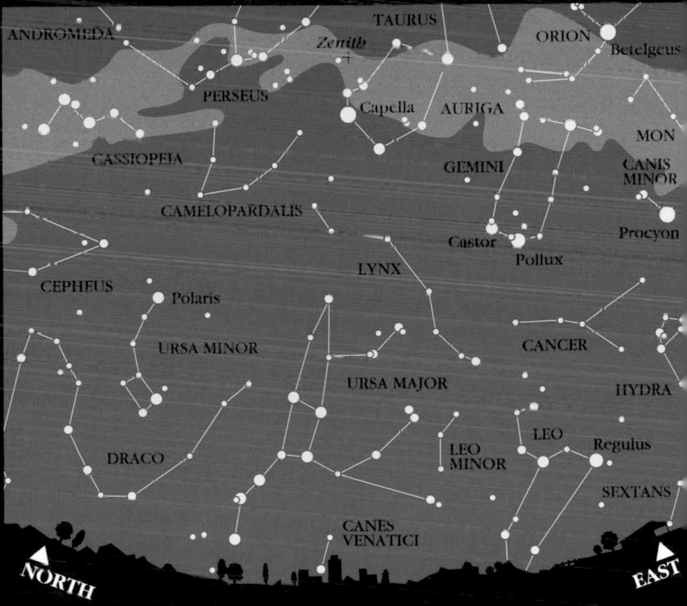

NORTHEAST

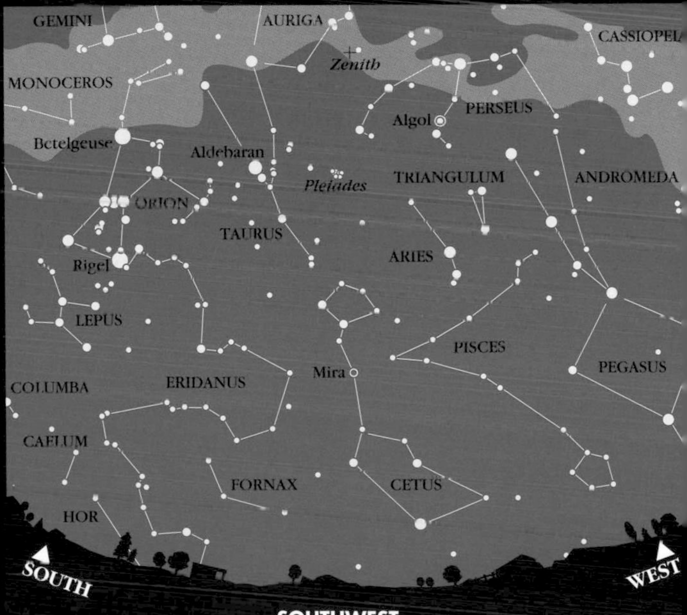

SOUTHWEST

The Spring Sky

The chart is drawn for these times and dates, but can be used at other times during the season.

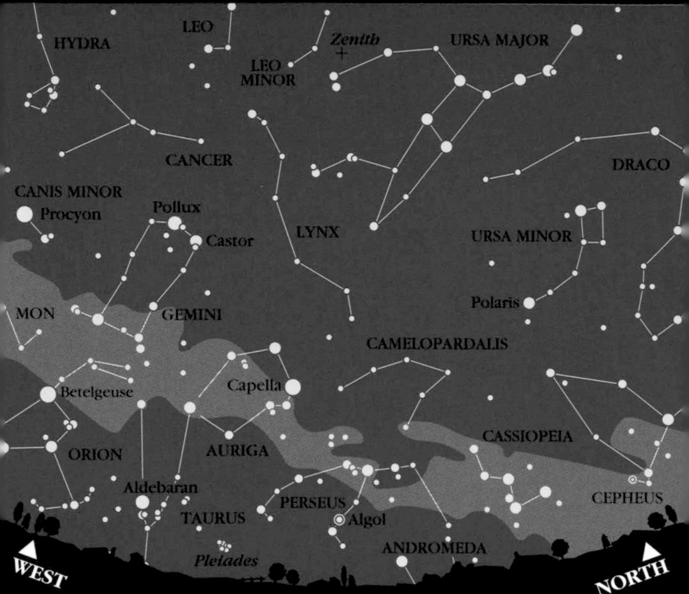

NORTHWEST

SOUTHEAST

March 1, midnight; April 1, 10 P.M. (11 P.M. DST); May 1, 8 P.M. (9 P.M. DST)

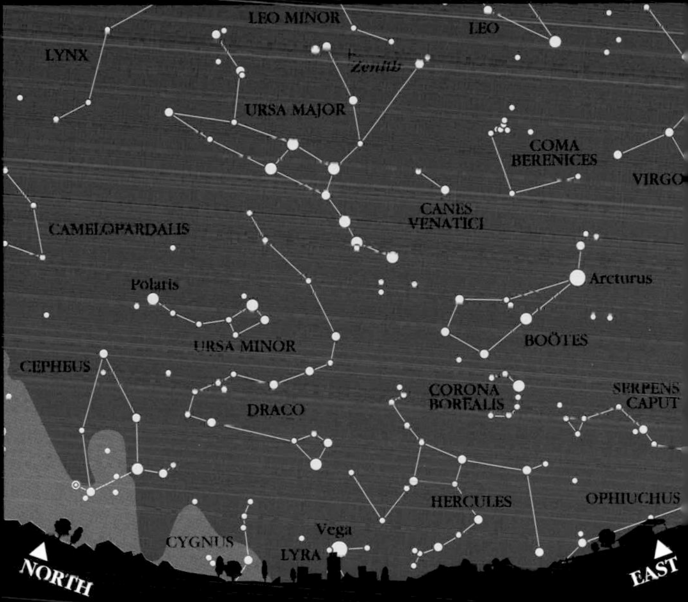

NORTHEAST

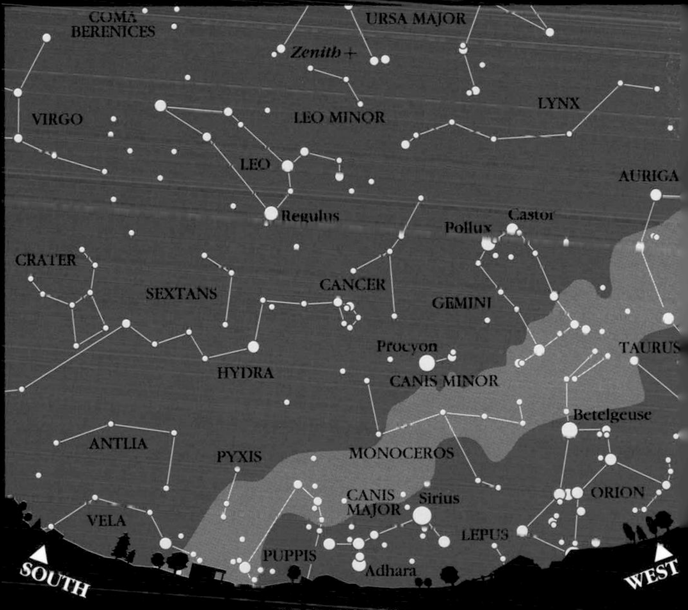

SOUTHWEST

The Summer Sky

The chart is drawn for these times and dates, but can be used at other times during the season.

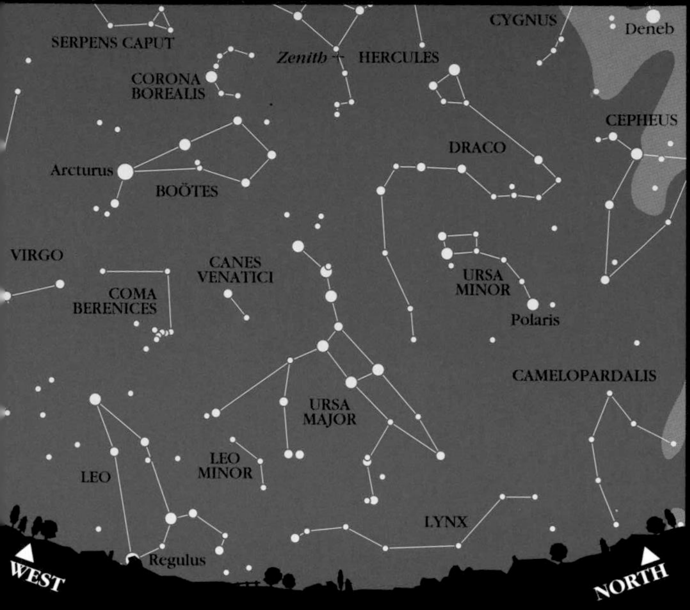

NORTHWEST

SOUTHEAST

June 1, midnight (1 A.M. DST); July 1, 10 P.M. (11 P.M. DST); August 1, 8 P.M. (9 P.M. DST).

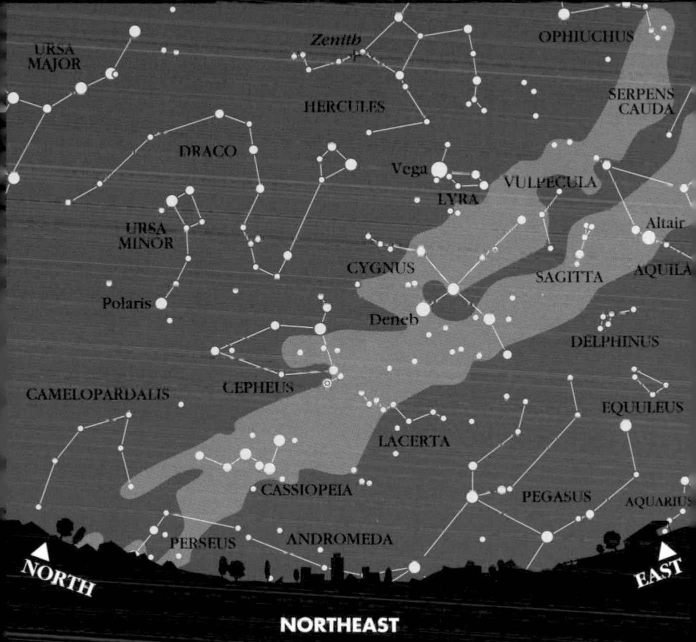

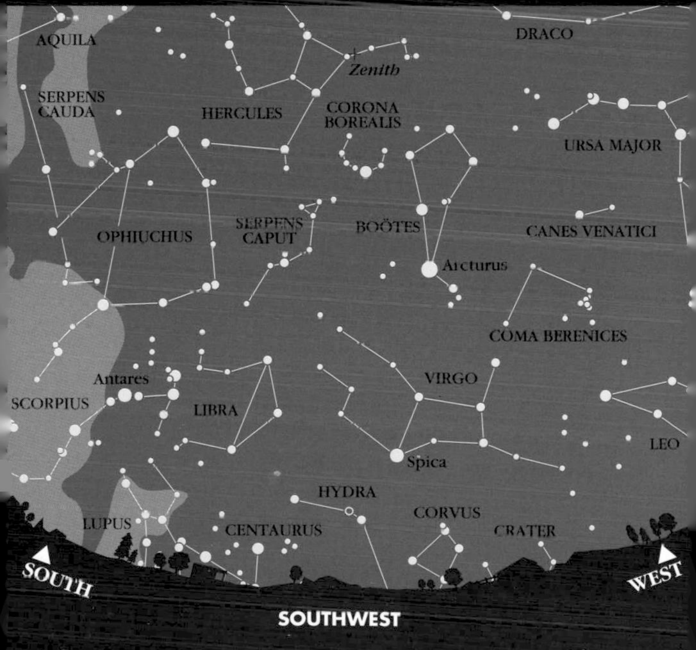

The Fall Sky

The chart is drawn for these times and dates, but can be used at other times during the season.

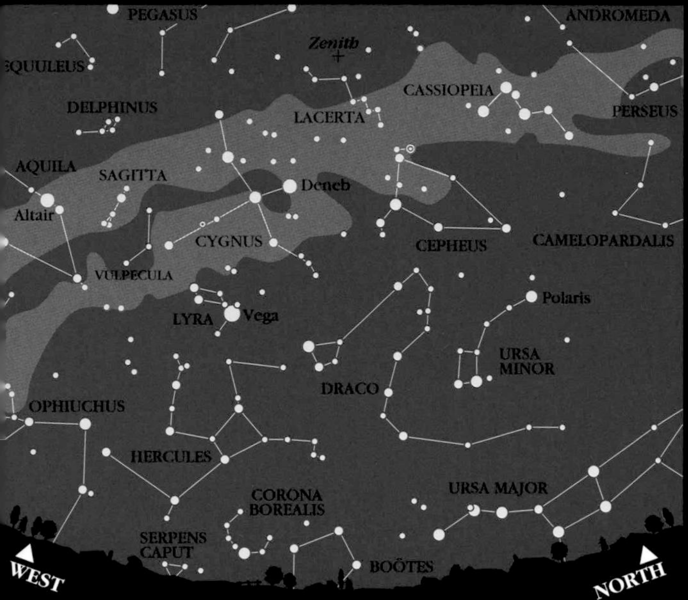

NORTHWEST

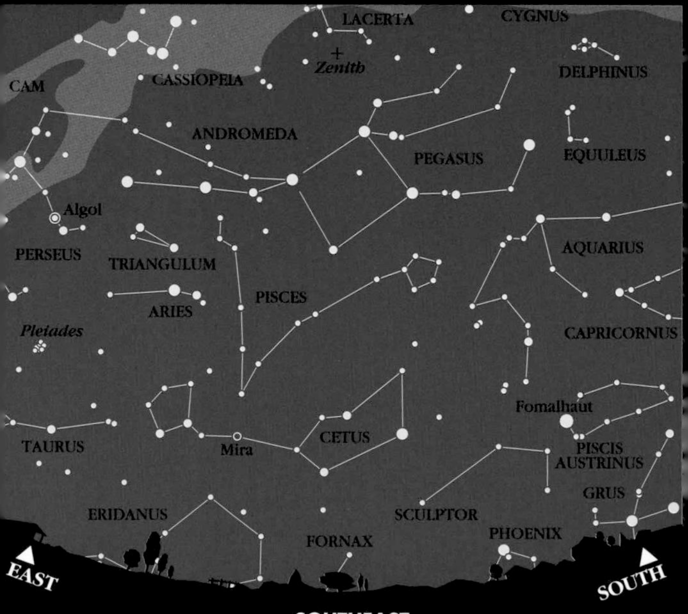

SOUTHEAST

September 1, midnight (1 A.M. DST); October 1, 10 P.M. (11 P.M. DST); November 1, 8 P.M.; December 1, 6 P.M.

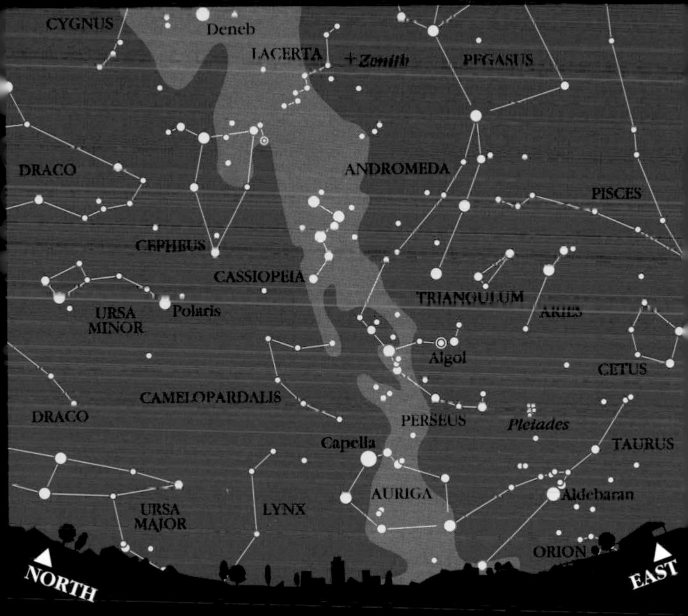

NORTHEAST

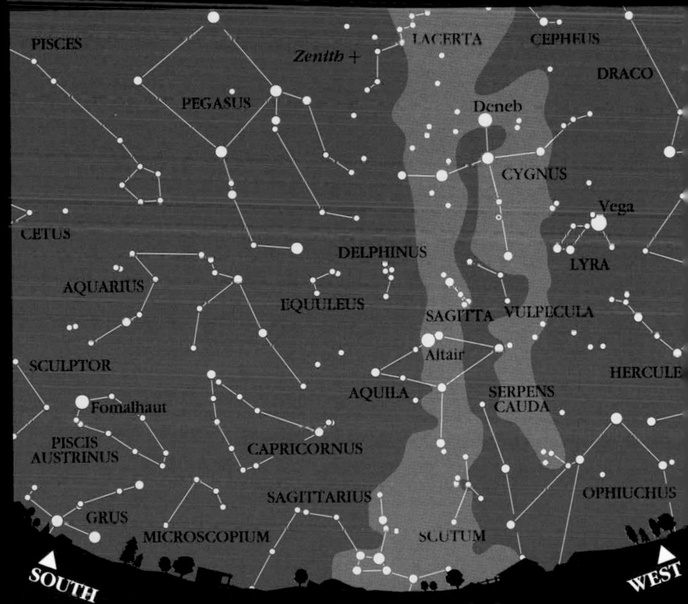

SOUTHWEST

Flora and Fauna

How to Use the Flora and Fauna Section

Part Two of this book presents nearly 1,000 of the most common species found in the southwestern states, beginning with mushrooms, algae, lichens, ferns, and other spore plants, and continuing with trees and shrubs, wildflowers, invertebrates (mostly spiders and insects), fishes, amphibians, reptiles, birds, and mammals. Flora species are presented alphabetically by family name. Fauna species are sequenced according to their taxonomy, or scientific classification. The classification and the names of species in this guide are based on authoritative sources when these exist for a given group.

Introductions and Other Essays

Most major sections of Part Two—for example, trees, wildflowers, marine invertebrates, birds—have an introduction, and some groups within the larger sections are also described in brief essays. The introductions should be read along with the species accounts that follow, as they present information that is fundamental for understanding the plants or animals in question. For groups without introductory essays, shared features are sometimes given in the opening sentence of the first species in the sequence.

Names

Each account begins with the common name of the species. Common names can change and may differ in other sources; if a species has a widely used alternate name, that is given within quotation marks, directly below the common name. The scientific species name, shown below the common name, is italicized (alternate scientific names are also sometimes listed). In a few cases (some flowers and invertebrates), organisms are best known on the genus level and are presented as such here. For example, the deer flies are presented as a group: the *Chrysops* species. Below the scientific name is the name of the group (class, order, family) with which the species is most commonly associated.

Description

The species accounts are designed to permit identification of species in the field. An account begins with the organism's typical mature or adult size: length (L), height (H), width (W), diameter (D), tail length (T), and/or wingspan (WS). The size is followed by physical characteristics, including color and distinctive markings. We use the abbreviations "imm." (immature) and "juv." (juvenile). The term "morph" describes a distinctive coloration that occurs in some individuals.

Other Information

For every species, the typical habitat is described. Other information may also be given, such as seasonality (bloom times of flowers or periods of activity for mammals) or the need for caution (species that

Names — **AMERICAN ROBIN**
Turdus migratorius
THRUSH FAMILY

Description — 10″. Breast orange; gray-brown above; head blackish; white eye ring; yellow bill. Juv. has blackish spots below.

Other Information — VOICE Song: *cheery-up cheery-me.* Calls: *tut tut tut; tseep.* HABITAT Woodlands, fields, gardens, towns. RANGE Resident in SW; to high elev. in summer, low in winter.

can cause irritation, illness, or injury). Similar species are sometimes described at the end of an account. The range (the area in which the species lives) is not stated if the species occurs throughout the Southwest region; the one exception to this rule is the birds, for which the range is always given. The term "local" means that a species occurs in spotty fashion over a large area, but not throughout the entire area. In describing the geographic range of species, we use the abbreviations e (east), w (west), n (north), s (south), c (central), and combinations of these (sc for south-central). For state names, we use the two-letter postal codes.

Readers should note that color, shape, and size may vary within plant and animal species, depending on environmental conditions and other factors. Bloom, migration, and other events can vary with the weather, latitude, and geography.

Classification of Living Things

Biologists divide living organisms into major groups called kingdoms, the largest of which are the plant and animal kingdoms. Kingdoms are divided into phyla (or divisions, in plants), phyla are divided into classes, classes into orders, orders into families, families into genera (singular: genus), and genera into species. The species, the basic unit of classification, is generally what we have in mind when we talk about a "kind" of plant or animal. The scientific name of a species consists of two words. The first is the genus name; the second is the species name. The scientific name of the Common Muskrat is *Ondatra zibethicus. Ondatra* is the genus name, and *zibethicus* is the species name.

Species are populations or groups of populations that are able to interbreed and produce fertile offspring themselves; they usually are not able to breed successfully or produce fertile offspring with members of other species. Many widespread species have numerous races (subspecies)—populations that are separated from one another geographically; races within a species may differ in appearance and behavior from other populations of that species.

Flora

The flora section of this guide includes flowering and nonflowering plants as well as algae and mushrooms, which are no longer considered part of the plant kingdom. Botanists have developed classification systems that place most algae outside of the green plants group. Mushrooms, members of the fungus kingdom, are covered here because they are somewhat plant-like in appearance and are often found on plants or plant matter.

The first part of the flora section begins with mushrooms and lichens. The next group is the nonflowering spore plants, such as mosses, horsetails, and ferns. Trees follow, beginning with conifers, then broadleaf trees and shrubs, and finally agaves and cacti. Wildflowers, including grasses, water plants, and terrestrial herbaceous plants, end the flora section.

In most of the flora subsections, species are grouped by family. The families are sequenced alphabetically by the English family name. Within each family, the species are sequenced alphabetically by Latin name. The measurements given in the species accounts are approximate, typical mature sizes in the Southwest. Colors, shapes, and sizes may vary within a species depending on environmental conditions. Bloom times vary widely throughout the region—later northward and at higher elevations—and can also be affected by the weather conditions in a given year. The geographic range is specified only when the species is not found throughout the region.

Users of this guide are warned against eating or otherwise consuming any plants or parts of a plant (including mushrooms, fiddleheads, or fruits) based on the information supplied in this guide.

Mushrooms

The organisms known as fungi—including molds, yeasts, mildews, and mushrooms—range from microscopic forms to mammoth puffballs. Unlike plants, they do not carry out photosynthesis and thus must obtain food from organic matter, living or dead. The fungi in this book are of the type commonly known as mushrooms.

Most mushrooms that grow on the ground have a *stalk* and a *cap*. The stalks of different species vary in shape, thickness, and density. There is often a skirt-like or bracelet-like *ring* midway up or near the top of the stalk, and the stalk *base* is often bulbous or sometimes enclosed by a cup at or just below the surface of the ground. Bracket (or shelf) mushrooms, which grow on trunks or logs, are often unstalked or short-stalked. A mushroom's cap may be smooth, scaly, warty, or shaggy, and its shape may be round, flat, convex (bell- or umbrella-shaped), or concave (cup- or trumpet-shaped). The caps of many species change as they mature, from closed and egg-shaped to open and umbrella-like; the cap color may also change with age.

Fungi reproduce through the release of single-celled bodies called spores. Many mushrooms bear their microscopic, spore-producing structures on the underside of the cap, either on radiating, blade-like *gills* or within tiny tubes that terminate in pores. In others, the spore producing structures line the inside of a cup-shaped cap or are located in broad wrinkles or open pits on the sides or top of the cap. Mushroom seasons are generally shorter in dry areas than in moist areas. In the accounts that follow, sizes given are typical heights (for stalked species) and cap widths of mature specimens.

CAUTION
Some of the Southwest's mushroom species are deadly poisonous to eat, even in small amounts, and others cause mild to severe reactions. The brief descriptions and few illustrations in this guide do not provide adequate information for determining the edibility of mushroom species. Inexperienced mushroom hunters should not eat any species they find in the wild.

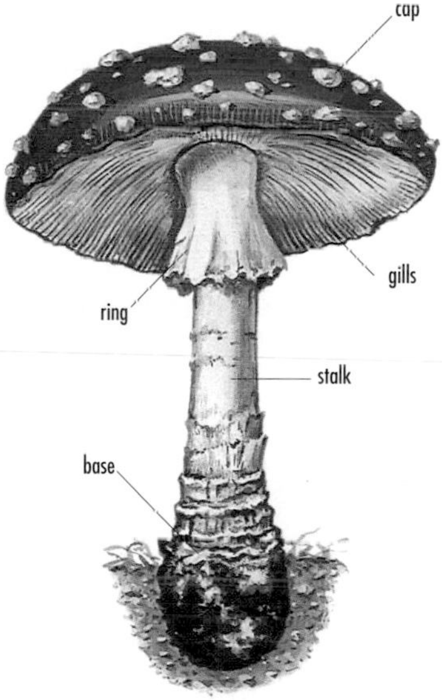

Parts of a Mushroom

PANTHER AMANITA
Amanita pantherina
AMANITA FAMILY

H 5″; W 5″. Cap umbrella-shaped; tan to brown, with paler warts; edge has fine radial lines. Stalk white, cylindrical or tapered upward, with skirt-like ring; base bulbous. Gills white, thin. **CAUTION** Deadly poisonous. **SEASON** Aug.–Apr. **HABITAT** Under conifers.

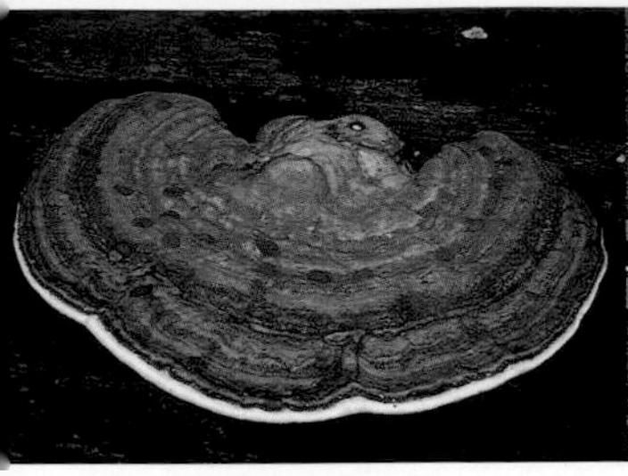

ARTIST'S FUNGUS
"Artist's Conk"
Ganoderma applanatum
BRACKET FAMILY

W 16″. Cap flat to convex, semicircular; shiny dark brown or gray, lighter at edge; wrinkled, hard; attached directly to wood. Underside white, bruises brown; with pores. **SEASON** Year-round. **HABITAT** Low on trunks of dead or dying trees.

MEASURING EARTHSTAR
Astraeus hygrometricus
EARTHSTAR FAMILY

H ¾″; W 3″. Puffball-like when young. Fruting body 2-layered: inner layer 1″, thin, spherical, splits open to release spores; outer layer tough, with 6 or more pointed, leathery, tan (black at maturity), 1½″ rays. Stalkless. **SEASON** Sept.–Nov. **HABITAT** Sandy areas, beneath pines and oaks.

HORSE MUSHROOM
Agaricus arvensis
FIELD MUSHROOM FAMILY

H 5″; W 5″. Cap umbrella-shaped, white, bruises yellowish; smooth or slightly fibrous; sweet anise or almond fragrance. Stalk usu. cylindrical, with felty white skirt. Gills fine, crowded; white when young, maturing pinkish gray to blackish brown. Often fruits in fairy rings. **SEASON** June–Oct. **HABITAT** Among grasses.

GREEN-GILL
Chlorophyllum molybdites
FIELD MUSHROOM FAMILY

H 7″; W 7″. Cap umbrella-shaped or broadly conical; white, with coarse cinnamon scales. Stalk slender, tapering upward, with broad often movable skirt. Gills white when young, maturing gray-green. Often fruits in fairy rings. **CAUTION** Poisonous. **SEASON** Aug.–Sept. **HABITAT** Lawns, pastures, disturbed ground.

SHAGGY MANE
Coprinus comatus
INKY CAP FAMILY

H 8″; W 2½″. Cap bell-shaped, white with brown tip, shaggy-scaly; edge turns black, dissolves upward. Stalk white, usu. hollow, with ring. Gills white to pink, then black and liquefying. **SEASON** Dec.–June, Sept.–Oct. **HABITAT** Grassy areas, disturbed ground, gardens.

LAWN MUSHROOM

"Haymaker Mushroom"

Psathyrella (Panaeolus) foenisecii

INKY CAP FAMILY

H 3¾"; W 1¼". Cap conical, maturing to flat or convex; tan to dark brown; cracks and fades if dry, thin, fragile. Stalk hollow, spindly. Gills dark to purple-brown, black when spores mature. **SEASON** May–July. **HABITAT** Lawns, parks, pastures.

INDIGO MILKY

Lactarius indigo

RUSSULA FAMILY

H 3¼"; W 4". Cap dark blue fading to gray-blue, green-stained, sticky silvery sheen; if cut, white flesh and milky juice turns blue then green. Stalk hollow, blue-spotted. Gills dark blue, yellowish when spores mature. **SEASON** July–Oct. **HABITAT** Oak and pinewoods, floodplains, leaf litter.

COMMON LACCARIA

Laccaria laccata

TRICHOLOMA FAMILY

H 4"; W 2". Cap flat to convex, with central depression, wavy upturned margins; pinkish to brown, fading whitish; smooth then breaks up into rough scales. Stalk fibrous, slender, firm. Gills thick, widely spaced, pink to flesh-colored; spores pale lilac. **SEASON** June–Nov. **HABITAT** Moist, sandy soils, streamsides, pinewoods.

FAIRY RING MUSHROOM

Marasmius oreades

TRICHOLOMA FAMILY

H 3"; W 2". Cap tan, umbrella-shaped, with central bump. Stalk slender, yellowish brown, finely velvety. Gills white. Grows in radiating rings or arcs. **SEASON** May–Oct., after rain. **HABITAT** Pastures, lawns.

OYSTER MUSHROOM

Pleurotus ostreatus

TRICHOLOMA FAMILY

H 4"; W 8". Bracket. Cap fan-shaped, white to yellowish. Stalk absent or very short, attached to one side of cap. Forms overlapping clusters. **SEASON** Sept.–May. **HABITAT** Limbs and trunks of dead trees.

Lichens

A lichen is a remarkable dual organism made up of a fungus and a colony of microscopic green algae or cyanobacteria ("blue-green algae"). Such a relationship—dissimilar organisms living in intimate association—is known as *symbiosis* and may be detrimental to one of the participants (parasitism) or beneficial to both (mutualism). In a lichen, the fungus surrounds the algae and takes up water and minerals that come its way from rainwater, fog, and dust; the algae supply carbohydrates produced by photosynthesis. It is not definitely known whether symbiosis in lichens is mutually beneficial or mildly to wholly parasitic. The balance is most likely different in each lichen species.

Lichens occur in a wide range of habitats, including some of the harshest environments on earth. They can also be found in woods, along roadsides, on man-made structures, and on mountaintops. During droughts they dry up and become dormant; they rapidly absorb water when it becomes available and spring back to life. Lichens range widely in color, occurring in white, black, gray, and various shades of green, orange, brown, yellow, or red. Their color often varies dramatically with moisture content.

Most lichens grow very slowly, about 1/25 inch to ½ inch per year, and they can have extremely long lifetimes; specimens estimated to be at least 4,000 years old have been found. Many lichens have special structures for vegetative reproduction—tiny fragments that break off easily or powdery spots that release tiny balls of algae wrapped in microscopic fungal threads. In others, the fungal component produces spores on conspicuous fruiting bodies, which may be disk-like, cup-like, or globular.

Lichens are an important source of food and nesting material for many mammals and birds. Since lichens are sensitive indicators of air quality and ecosystem continuity, they serve as natural tools for monitoring the environment. In the accounts that follow, sizes given are typical widths of mature specimens.

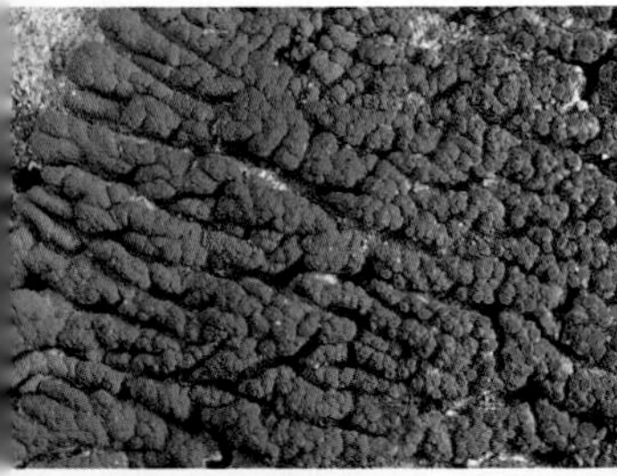

DESERT FIREDOT
Caloplaca trachyphylla
1″. Yellow-orange patches of narrow lobes radiating outward with numerous round fruiting bodies in center. Fruiting bodies darker orange in center, with rims same color as lobes. **HABITAT** Rocks.

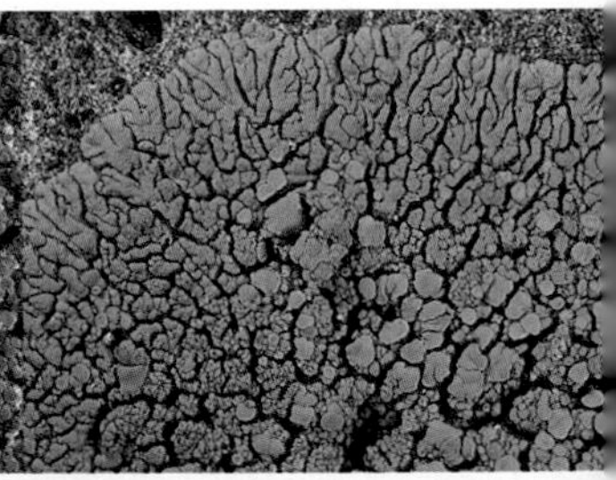

MEXICAN YOLK LICHEN
Candelina submexicana
1″. Circular-like patches of bright yellow to yellow-orange lobes radiating outward from lumpy center. Fruiting bodies same color, round, rimmed, numerous. **HABITAT** Rocks.

EARTH-SCALE LICHEN
Catapyrenium lacinulatum

1″. Clusters of tiny, dark brown scales, sometimes overlapping. Edges of each scale dark; may become white where eroded. Fruiting bodies minute, black spots. **HABITAT** Desert soils, esp. around small bushes; not on steep slopes.

LEATHER LICHEN
Dermatocarpon miniatum

1″. Irreg. patches of white, pale gray, or tan lobes, crowded and usu. overlapping. Each lobe attached at central point. Numerous black dots on upper surface; lower surface pale tan. **HABITAT** Sandstone and limestone rocks, occ. in watercourses.

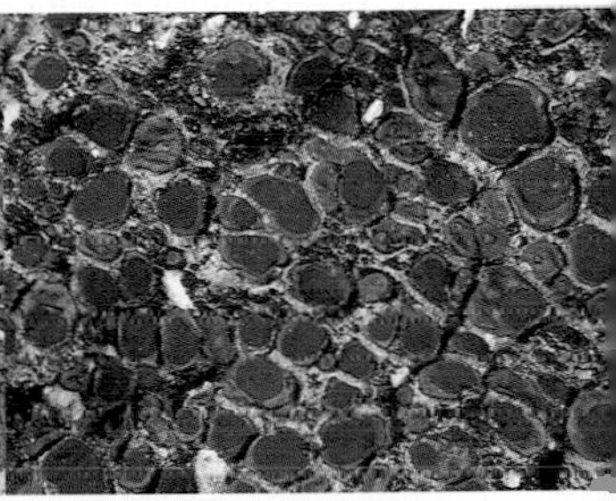

SOUTHWESTERN GREENSHIELD
Flavopunctelia praesignis

4″. Broad patches of yellow-green lobes with tiny white pores on upper surface. Numerous fruiting bodies form raised cups; dark brown inside, green with white spots outside. Undersurface black with sparse hairs. **HABITAT** Tree trunks in mid-elev. woods. **RANGE** se AZ, s NM.

OLIVE EARTH LICHEN
Peltula richardsii

1″. Scattered tiny red scales with olive-green rims on soil; resemble miniature stuffed olives. Each segment slightly separated by small area of soil. **HABITAT** Low-elev. desert soils.

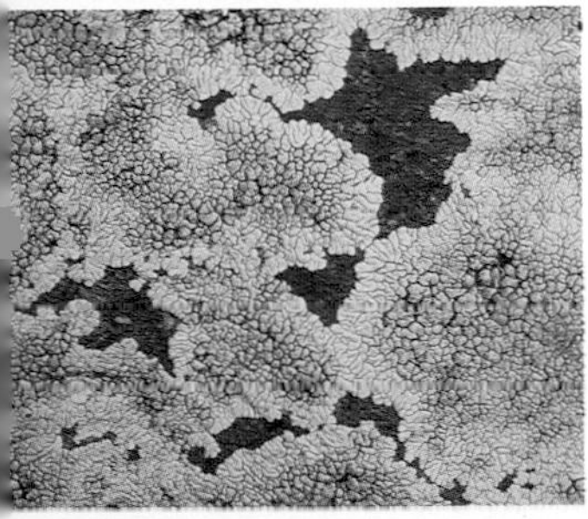

YELLOW PAINT LICHEN
Pleopsidium oxytonum

1″. Very bright yellow or greenish-yellow patches on rocks; divided into tiny segments by network of cracks, sometimes following joints in rock. Fruiting bodies tan, forming groups of slight depressions in individual segments. Several species in this genus and in genus *Acarospora* look similar. **HABITAT** Exposed rock.

ANTLER LICHEN
Pseudevernia intensa

2″. Irreg. bunches of very pale gray straps, creating bushy, antler-like appearance; side branches smaller; older straps become wrinkled. Fruiting bodies shiny dark brown, cup-like, with white underside when mature. **HABITAT** Dead branches of conifers in mid- to high-elev. woods. **RANGE** se AZ, NM.

DESERT BRAIN LICHEN
Psora cerebriformis

1″. Small lumpy clusters of irreg. white or very pale gray (occ. dull yellowish-brown) lobes with dark fissures. Fruiting bodies usu. dark gray; round, scattered throughout. **HABITAT** Soil in semiarid areas, esp. soil derived from limestone.

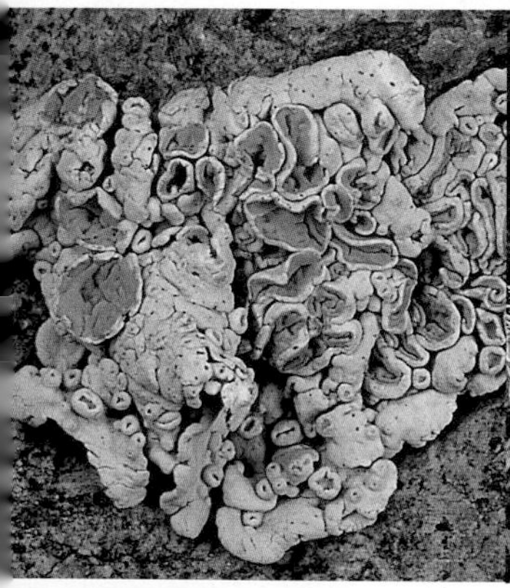

ROCK-POSY LICHEN
Rhizoplaca chrysoleuca

1″. Whitish to pale yellow-green, in lumpy rosettes attached to rock at central point. Fruiting bodies pale orange to salmon or tan, with pale rims; flat to folded disks. Underside tan to brown. **HABITAT** Exposed granite rock. **Green Rock-posy** *(R. melanophthalma)* is yellowish green, with dark greenish fruiting bodies.

ARIZONA BEARD LICHEN
Usnea arizonica

3″. Yellowish, bushy to hanging, stringy branching tufts with perpendicular bristles. Fruiting bodies large, disk-like, edged with bristles; at branch ends; white central cord revealed when branch stretched. **HABITAT** Trunks, branches, twigs of trees, esp. oaks. **RANGE** s AZ, s NM.

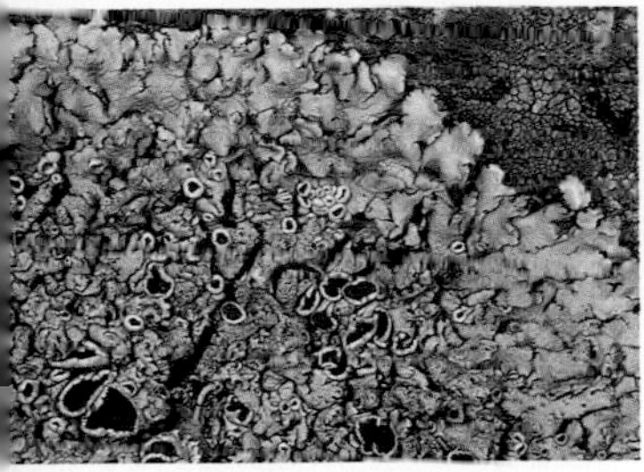

CUMBERLAND ROCKSHIELD
Xanthoparmelia cumberlandia
4″. Round, yellowish to greenish patches of crowded lobes, with scattered, tiny black dots. Center often has large, brown, cupped to nearly flat fruiting bodies. Underside tan to brown. **HABITAT** Rocks.

Spore Plants

Spore plants are green land plants—such as mosses, horsetails, and ferns (introduced separately on page 92)—that reproduce from spores rather than seeds. Among the earliest evolved land plants still present on earth, these plants do not produce flowers or fruits. The most conspicuous part of their reproduction is the *spore*, a cell that divides and develops the structures producing the sperm and egg, which fuse to form a new adult plant. Mosses are mat-forming plants usually found in shady, moist habitats; they typically absorb water and nutrients directly from the environment because they lack a sophisticated vascular system for conducting water and nutrients internally. When "fruiting," their spores are released from a lidded capsule often elevated on a *fertile stalk*. Horsetails have well-developed vascular systems. They have conspicuously jointed stems with whorls of tiny, scale-like leaves and branches at most joints. Spores are produced in tiny sacs called *sporangia*, found along the edges of umbrella-like structures grouped in a cone-like cluster atop a brownish, whitish, or green stem. The following accounts give heights of mature specimens; sizes are not given for very low, mat-forming species.

SMOOTH SCOURING RUSH
Equisetum laevigatum
HORSETAIL FAMILY
3′. Green, hollow, unbranched, jointed aerial stems, produced each year from an underground stem. Each joint topped by sheathing ring of 10–25 tiny, scale-like leaves appearing to form a dark band. Cone produced on 1″ terminal spore. **HABITAT** Streamsides, moist meadows, marshes, ditches.

HAIRCAP MOSS
Polytrichum juniperinum
MOSS CLASS
Green carpet of bottlebrush-like, erect, wiry stems with narrow, hair-pointed leaves. Fertile stalks reddish; each topped by golden-brown, cylindrical capsule. **HABITAT** On soil in mid- to high-elev. woods or open areas. **RANGE** UT, AZ, NM.

TWISTED MOSS
"Star Moss"
Tortula ruralis
MOSS CLASS

Loose mats of erect stems, with tongue-shaped, hair-tipped leaves; reddish green when wet, very dark and erect-spiraling when dry. Fertile stalks rarely encountered. **HABITAT** Dry to moist soil, deserts to high-elev. mtns.

ROCKY MOUNTAIN SPIKEMOSS
Selaginella densa
SPIKEMOSS FAMILY

Erect, 4-sided, spore-bearing spikes rise from small mats of prostrate branches covered with closely pressed, tiny, needle-like leaves, each tipped with 1 white hair. Spikes and leaves grayish when dry, greener when moist. **HABITAT** Rocky ledges, outcrops, talus slopes, pinyon-juniper and coniferous woods, above tree line. **RANGE** UT, AZ, NM.

Ferns

Ferns, the largest group of seedless vascular plants still found on earth, are diverse in habitat and form. In the Southwest they occur mainly in shady woods and near fresh water, but several fern species thrive in open sunny areas. Some ferns grow in soil, often in clumps or clusters. In the Southwest, most ferns grow at seeps, on cliff faces in fissures, and beneath rocks.

Frond types

Ferns have a stem called a *rhizome* that is typically thin and long and grows along the surface or below the ground. The rhizome bears the roots and leaves and lives for many years. Fern leaves, called *fronds*, are commonly compound and may be *pinnate* (divided into *leaflets*), *bipinnate* (subdivided into *subleaflets*), or even *tripinnate* (divided again into segments). They are often lacy or feathery in appearance.

Ferns reproduce through the release of *spores* from tiny sacs called *sporangia*, which commonly occur in clusters *(sori)* on the underside of the frond. The sori may cover the entire frond underside, form dots or lines, occur only beneath the frond's curled-under edges, or be covered by specialized outgrowths of the frond. Fronds that bear sporangia are called *fertile fronds*; those that do not are called *sterile fronds*. In some species, the sterile and fertile fronds differ in size and shape.

The foliage of most of the region's ferns dies back each year with the autumn frosts. Each spring the rhizome gives rise to coiled tender young fronds called *fiddleheads*. Fiddleheads of some ferns are popular delicacies, but identification is difficult. The shoots of some deadly poisonous flowering plants (including various poison hemlocks) can be mistaken for fern fiddleheads, and many fiddleheads are edible at certain stages and poisonous at others. Only local experts should collect fiddleheads for consumption.

In the accounts that follow, sizes given are typical mature heights. For illustrations of leaf shapes, see page 144.

Parts of a Fern

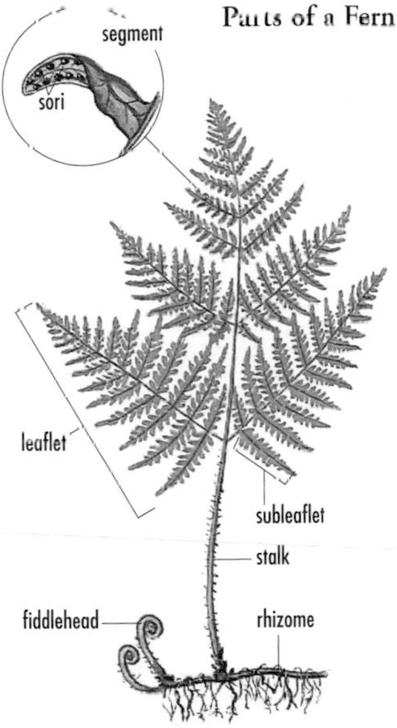

BRACKEN
Pteridium aquilinum
BRACKEN FAMILY

4′. Stalks longer than blades. Blades divided into 3 broadly triangular, stalked, bi- or tripinnate leaflets, each with many pinnate subleaflets. Sori dot curled-under leaflet edges. **HABITAT** Moist to dry mtn. areas, streamsides, seeps, shaded woods, clearings, slopes.

GIANT CHAIN FERN
Woodwardia fimbriata
CHAIN FERN FAMILY

9′. Stalks stout, smooth. Fronds huge, blades pinnate, with lobed leaflets; grows in vase-like clusters of 5–12. Sori oblong, arranged end to end, near veins. Rarely encountered, found only in small, isolated populations. **HABITAT** Moist areas, streamsides, springs. **RANGE** e NV.

SOUTHERN MAIDENHAIR
Adiantum capillus-veneris
MAIDENHAIR FERN FAMILY

20″. Stalks reddish brown to black. Blades twice pinnately compound, approx. same length as stalk; smallest divisions of leaflets lobed; lobe margins may be reflexed, bearing sori. **HABITAT** Seeps, springs, streamsides, moist cliffs.

PARRY'S LIP FERN
Cheilanthes (Notholaena) parryi
MAIDENHAIR FERN FAMILY

8″. Stalks brown to black. Blades wide, hairy, twice pinnately compound; gray-green above, rusty-brown below. **HABITAT** Cliff fissures, beneath large boulders, among limestone and granite rocks. **RANGE** NV, UT, AZ.

LADY FERN
Athyrium filix-femina
WOOD FERN FAMILY

3′. Stalks blackish, scaly. Fronds arch outward, taper at both ends; blades pinnate or bipinnate, with lobed, fine-toothed leaflets. Sori under J-shaped flaps. **HABITAT** Mtn. streamsides, meadows, moist woods.

FRAGILE FERN
"Brittle Fern"
Cystopteris fragilis
WOOD FERN FAMILY

10″. Stalks straw-colored, smooth, fragile. Blades usu. bipinnate, both ends tapering; leaflets fine-toothed. Translucent pouch partly covers sori, soon withers. **HABITAT** Moist to dry, shaded mtn. areas, streamsides, meadows, cliff fissures, among rocks.

ROCKY MOUNTAIN WOODSIA
"Cliff Fern"
Woodsia scopulina
WOOD FERN FAMILY

12″. Stalks reddish brown. Blades bipinnate, both ends tapering; leaflets white-hairy underneath. Sori surrounded by star-shaped membranes. **HABITAT** Cliff fissures, talus slopes, among rocks.

Trees and Shrubs

Trees and shrubs are woody perennial plants. Trees typically have a single trunk and a well-developed crown of foliage and grow to at least 16 feet tall; some attain heights of more than 300 feet. Shrubs are usually less than 20 feet tall and often have several woody stems rather than a single trunk. This guide covers two major categories of trees and shrubs: gymnosperms (including conifers) begin on page 96; broadleaf trees and shrubs (including the Southwest's only palm) begin on page 102. Agaves and cacti begin on page 133.

Individual tree size varies according to age and environmental factors. The heights given in the following sections are for average mature individual trees on favorable sites in the Southwest. Younger trees and those exposed to harsh conditions are smaller; older specimens may attain greater heights in optimal conditions. Trunk diameter, which also varies greatly within a species, is cited only for very large species.

Identifying a Tree

Trees can be identified by three key visual characteristics: crown shape, bark color and texture, and leaf shape and arrangement (illustrated on page 144). Below are common crown shapes for mature gymnosperms and broadleaf trees. These shapes are idealized and simplified for illustrative purposes.

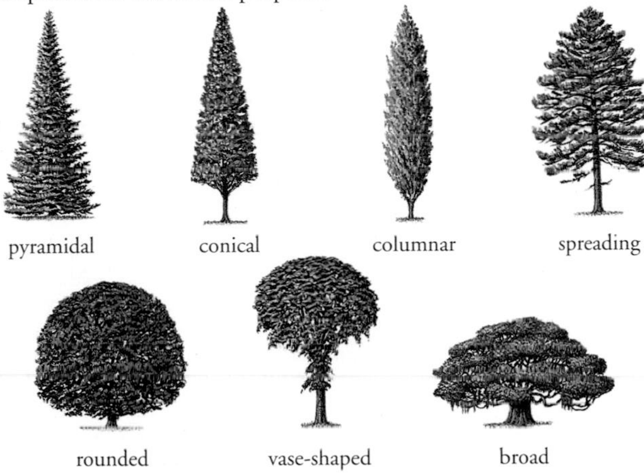

The roots, trunk, and branches of most trees and shrubs are covered in bark, a protective layer consisting mainly of dead cells. The bark of young trees often differs in color and texture from mature bark. As a tree grows, the bark splits, cracks, and peels. In junipers the bark shreds in vertical strips; the bark of birches peels horizontally. In many trees the bark may develop furrows, ridges, or fissures, break up into plates, or flake off. Unless otherwise noted, the species accounts describe mature bark.

Beneath the bark is the wood, most of which is dense, dark, dead tissue (heartwood) that provides structural support for the plant.

Between the heartwood and the bark are many pale, thin layers of living tissue (including sapwood) that transport water and minerals and produce new wood and bark. Concentric rings, each representing a period (often a year) of growth, are visible in cut trunks and branches.

Gymnosperms

Gymnosperms ("naked seeds") are trees and shrubs that produce exposed seeds, usually in cones, rather than seeds enclosed in an ovary, as in the angiosperms (flowering plants). Members of the pine and cypress families are commonly called "evergreens" and are known as conifers or "softwoods." The gymnosperms covered in this guide are conifers, with one exception: Green Ephedra. Conifers have leaves that are needle-like (long and slender) or scale-like (small and overlapping), typically evergreen, and, due to a thick waxy coating and other protective features, are well adapted for drought and freezing temperatures.

The distinctive cone is a reproductive structure composed of a central axis with spirally arranged scales bearing pollen or seeds. A single tree usually has both pollen-bearing (male) and seed-bearing (female) cones; males are usually produced on lower branches than female cones or are lower down on the same branch. Male cones appear in spring, shed pollen, and soon fall from the tree. Female cones are larger, more woody, and have scales that protect the seeds until the cones expand to release them. Unless otherwise noted, cones described in this guide are female.

Most conifer species in the Southwest belong to the pine family (Pinaceae). Those commonly known as pines (genus *Pinus*) bear long needles in bundles of two to five. Other pine family members have much shorter needles. Spruces (genus *Picea*) have rough twigs, hanging cones, and flat needles borne on tiny, raised, woody pegs. Douglas Firs (genus *Pseudotsuga*) also have hanging cones and flat needles, but they grow directly from the branches. True firs (genus *Abies*) have upright cones that shed their scales and seeds while still on the tree and needles arising from tiny depressions on the branches. Other conifers in the Southwest are in the cypress family (Cupressaceae). Cypresses and junipers have narrow, scale-like leaves covering their branches; the small cones of the cypress are woody and globe-shaped and those of the juniper are fleshy and berry-like.

In some areas of the Southwest, conifers are often part of a continuous woodland canopy in which the shapes of individual trees cannot be discerned. Most conifers are pyramidal in shape when young, especially if they grow in an open area; they mature to a ragged columnar shape with a conical (commonly broken) top and a limbless lower half. The following species accounts specify shape only if it differs from this description. Typical crown shapes are illustrated on page 95, and leaf shapes, including the needles and scale-like leaves of conifers, are shown on page 144. Unless otherwise noted in the individual species description, needle or scale color is green, fading to yellowish or brown when shedding, and cone color is brown.

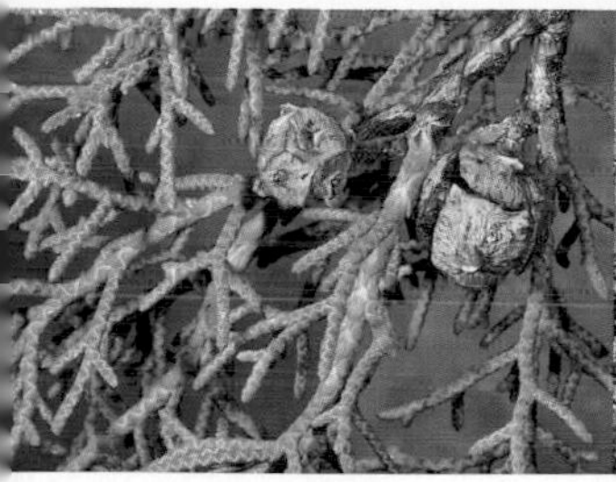

ARIZONA CYPRESS
Cupressus arizonica
CYPRESS FAMILY

90′. Crown rounded to conical. Leaves scale-like, opposite, overlapping. Male cones tiny; female cones 1½″, globose, with 3–4 pairs of woody scales bearing numerous winged seeds. Frequently cultivated; found only in small, isolated populations. HABITAT Canyon bottoms, pinyon-juniper woods. RANGE c and se AZ, sw NM.

COMMON JUNIPER
Juniperus communis
CYPRESS FAMILY

30″. Usu. sprawling, mat-forming shrub. Needles ½″, whitish above, sharp; crowded. Cones ¼″, berry-like, green to blue-black, resinous. Bark reddish, shredding. HABITAT Mtns., high-elev. woods, rocky areas.

UTAH JUNIPER
Juniperus osteosperma
CYPRESS FAMILY

20′. Shrub to rounded, sometimes many-stemmed tree. Scales mostly tiny, gray-green, in pairs; stems 4-sided; some leaves (esp. on young plants) ¼″, needle-like. Cones ¼″, berry-like, tan to red-brown, resinous, 1-seeded. Bark gray-brown, aging whitish, shredding. Sometimes forms pure stands. HABITAT Arid, rocky areas on flats, slopes, low-elev. drainages, dry pinyon-juniper woods.

ROCKY MOUNTAIN JUNIPER

Juniperus scopulorum

CYPRESS FAMILY

30′. Shrub to tree with dense, rounded to conical crown. Scales mostly tiny, gray-green, in pairs; stems 4-sided; some leaves (esp. on young plants) ¼″, needle-like. Cones ¼″, berry-like, blue-black, resinous, 2-seeded. Bark red-brown, shredding. May live more than 2,000 years, become massive. **HABITAT** Mtns., canyons, slopes.

GREEN EPHEDRA

"Green Indian Tea" "Mormon Tea"

Ephedra viridis

EPHEDRA FAMILY

3′. Erect shrub. Stems upright and parallel, bright green. Leaves tiny, scale-like, opposite; bases at maturity forming black ring. Cones paired or numerous at nodes; sexes separate: male cones with stamen-like structures, female with 2 tiny brown seeds. **HABITAT** Arid rocky areas, flats, slopes, cliffs.

WHITE FIR

Abies concolor

PINE FAMILY

H 130′; D 4′. Branches short, horizontal. Needles 2″, silvery blue-green with white lines; flat, up-curved in broad U. Cones 4″, cylindrical, greenish or purple; upright, on highest branches. Bark gray, furrowed. Forms pure stands. **HABITAT** Woods, dry, rocky mtn. slopes.

SUBALPINE FIR
Abies lasiocarpa
PINE FAMILY

H 80′; D 18″. Tree with spire-shaped crown; matted shrub above tree line. Needles 1″, white-striped, flat, usu. up-curved; camphor-like aroma when crushed. Cones 4″, cylindrical, purplish; upright. Bark gray, smooth to fissured. **HABITAT** Subalpine coniferous woods.

ENGELMANN SPRUCE
Picea engelmannii
PINE FAMILY

H 150′; D 3′. Tree with drooping branchlets; dense low shrub above tree line. Needles 1¼″, blue-green, white-striped, sharp, 4-sided. Cones 2¼″, cylindrical, with paper-thin scales; hang down. Bark grayish, thin, scaly; young twigs minutely fuzzy. **HABITAT** Subalpine coniferous woods.

BLUE SPRUCE
Picea pungens
PINE FAMILY

H 150′; D 24″. Crown pyramidal; stiff branched. Needles 1¼″, bluish or green, white-striped, sharp, stiff, 4-sided. Cones 3″, cylindrical; hang down. Bark gray or brown, thick, furrowed. UT state tree. **HABITAT** Subalpine coniferous woods, dry, rocky slopes. **RANGE** UT, AZ, NM.

COLORADO PINYON PINE
Pinus edulis
PINE FAMILY

45′. Crown conical to rounded; trunk contorted. Needles 1¼″; usu. in bundles of 2; fragrant. Cones 1½″, egg-shaped; seeds edible, in hard ½″ shells. Bark yellowish to reddish brown, scaly. Source of American pine nuts; choice firewood; dominant member of pinyon-juniper woods. **HABITAT** Arid, rocky flats, slopes. **RANGE** UT, AZ, NM.

LIMBER PINE
Pinus flexilis
PINE FAMILY

60′. Crown rounded; shrub-like at tree line. Needles 3″, white-lined, sharp; in bundles of 5. Cones 5″, egg-shaped, yellowish. Bark gray to dark brown, furrowed, scaly. Forms pure stands. **HABITAT** High-elev. woods, often at tree line.

CHIHUAHUA PINE
Pinus leiophylla
PINE FAMILY

50′. Crown conic to narrowly pyramidal, more rounded at maturity; slender-trunked. Needles 5″; in bundles of 3. Cones 3″, persistent. **HABITAT** Arid, rocky slopes, plains. **RANGE** AZ, NM.

BRISTLECONE PINE
Pinus longaeva
PINE FAMILY

45′. Crown open, irreg.; branches hanging, twisted. Needles 1¼″, stout, stiff, blunt; crowded, in bundles of 5. Cones 3″, cylindrical, reddish; scales have bristles. Bark gray or red-brown, furrowed, scaly. Forms pure stands; considered to be longest living tree. **HABITAT** Windswept alpine and subalpine limestone slopes, ridges. **RANGE** UT, NV.

SINGLELEAF PINYON
Pinus monophylla
PINE FAMILY

30′. Crown spreading, rounded, with many low horizontal branches; often shrubby. Needles 1½″, gray-green, stiff, sharp, often curved. Cones 2½″, nearly round. Bark gray, furrowed, scaly. Forms pure stands; dominant member of pinyon-juniper woods. **HABITAT** Arid, rocky flats, slopes. **RANGE** UT, NV, AZ.

PONDEROSA PINE
Pinus ponderosa
PINE FAMILY

H 150′; D 4′. Needles 8″, yellowish; in bundles of 3, in tufts at branch tips. Cones 5″, egg-shaped, reddish; scales have out-curved prickle. Bark yellow-brown, thick, scaly plates. Often dominant species. **HABITAT** Open woods on flats, slopes, canyons.

DOUGLAS FIR
Pseudotsuga menziesii
PINE FAMILY
H 150′; D 4′. Needles 1¼″, flat. Cones 3½″, egg-shaped; scales have protruding, paper-thin, 3-pointed bracts. Bark reddish brown, deeply furrowed. **HABITAT** Wooded areas in mtns., sheltered canyons, on north-facing slopes.

Broadleaf Trees and Shrubs

Trees belonging to the angiosperm (flowering plant) group are called broadleaf trees because their leaves are generally broad—obvious exceptions are the Southwest's cacti and agaves—in contrast to the needle-like leaves of most gymnosperms. The seeds of gymnosperms are exposed, while those of angiosperms are enclosed in an ovary that ripens into a fruit. This section also includes shrubs: trees typically have a single woody trunk and a well-developed crown; shrubs are comprised of woody stems growing in a clump.

In much of North America, many broadleaf trees (known as "hardwoods") are deciduous, shedding their leaves for the winter because the leaves cannot survive long periods of freezing weather. Most of the Southwest's flowering trees are also deciduous. Some species that grow in dry areas shed their leaves in summer to conserve moisture. Many are found only alongside water or in well-shaded canyons; such areas are moist throughout the summer and average colder temperatures in winter, resembling climates where trees are commonly deciduous. Evergreen species are noted as such.

The species descriptions in this guide note leaf color only if it is not green. The term "turn" indicates fall leaf color. Leaf arrangements and shapes are illustrated on page 144. As most broadleaf trees and shrubs bear their leaves in an alternate arrangement, only exceptions are noted in the accounts. Measurements indicate length, unless otherwise stated; leaflet measurements are given for compound leaves.

Illustrations of flower types and parts, and a discussion of the structure and function of flowers, appear on pages 145–148. Only conspicuous flowers are noted in the species accounts. Many of the Southwest's broadleaf trees and shrubs have beautiful spring flowers and/or colorful summer fruits. They typically flower from late winter to late spring; fruits mature mainly in late spring to summer.

DESERT HONEYSUCKLE
Aniscanthus thurberi
ACANTHUS FAMILY

8′. Shrub. Leaves lanceolate, opposite, entire. Bark white. Flowers solitary, axillary; corollas 1½″, tubular, red to orange, irreg.; bloom Apr.–Oct. Fruit stalked, flattened, 4-seeded capsules. **HABITAT** Dry hills, mesas, canyons, washes, watercourses. **RANGE** NM, AZ.

WHITE BURSAGE
Ambrosia dumosa
ASTER FAMILY

24″. Low shrub with rigid, brittle branches. Leaves ¾″, silvery, with several narrow, toothed lobes. Bark pale gray to white, hairy. Flowers tiny, pale yellow, in spikes; bloom Apr.–Oct. Fruit tiny spiny burs that attach to clothing, fur. A dominant plant with Creosote Bush. **HABITAT** Desert slopes, plains in Creosote Bush scrub. **RANGE** UT, NV, AZ.

TARRAGON
Artemisia dracunculus
ASTER FAMILY

5′. Hairless, shrub-like; from short rhizome. Leaves 3″, bright green, linear, entire or rarely cleft. Flowers tiny, in 18″ clusters; bloom July–Nov. Widely distributed. **HABITAT** Desert shrub communities to subalpine woods.

WORMWOOD
"Louisiana Wormwood"
Artemisia ludoviciana
ASTER FAMILY

3′. Shrub-like, white, densely matted with hairs, from rhizome. Leaves 4″, lanceolate to linear, entire to deeply lobed or cleft; lobes or cleft segments sometimes further cleft or toothed. Flowers tiny, yellow to tannish, in 12″ clusters; bloom July–Oct. **HABITAT** Rocky, sandy areas, shrub communities to woods.

BLACK SAGEBRUSH

Artemisia nova

ASTER FAMILY

12″. Low shrub, somewhat dark in appearance. Leaves 1″, entire or three-lobed at apex, hairy, covered with minute glandular swellings. Flowers tiny, yellow to tannish, in 12″ clusters; bloom July–Oct. **HABITAT** Shallow flats, hillsides where Big Sagebrush does not grow.

BUDSAGE

Artemisia spinescens

ASTER FAMILY

12″. Low shrub; old branches thorny. Leaves 1″, palmately 3–5 cleft; segments again cleft, hairy. Flowers tiny, yellow to tannish; bloom Apr.–June. The only spring-flowering *Artemisia*; drought resistant. **HABITAT** Dry silty, clay, or gravelly flats, slopes in mixed desert shrub communities.

BIG SAGEBRUSH

Artemisia tridentata

ASTER FAMILY

6′. Rounded, gnarled shrub. Leaves 1½″, gray-green, narrowly oblanceolate, with 3-lobed tip, fuzzy; spicy-aromatic. Stems brown, shredding. Flowers tiny, drab yellow, in loose spikes; bloom July–Oct. Indicator plant of the Great Basin Desert. **HABITAT** Arid flats, slopes in variety of communities from mixed desert shrub to coniferous woods.

SEEP-WILLOW

Baccharis salicifolia

ASTER FAMILY

10′. Leaves 3″, bright green, elliptical to linear, mostly hairless, resin-coated; margins smooth or toothed to lobed. Twigs angled, ribbed. Flowers ¼″, yellow to tannish, numerous; sexes separate; in clusters; bloom Mar.–Dec. **HABITAT** Streamsides, moist meadows.

SWEETBUSH
"Chuckwalla's Delight"
Bebbia juncea
ASTER FAMILY

4'. Rounded, intricately branched shrub, often rough-hairy. Stems slender, photosynthetic. Leaves 3", linear or linear-lobed, opposite, sparse. Flowers ½", disk florets yellow, lacking ray florets; bloom year-round. **HABITAT** Low-elev. rocky hillsides, gravels along washes, canyons.

MOJAVE BRICKELLIA
Brickellia oblongifolia
ASTER FAMILY

18". Glandular, hairy shrub, somewhat woody at base. Leaves 1½", lanceolate to linear, stalkless. Flowers 1", solitary, at branch ends; bracts striated; disk florets whitish, lacking ray florets; bloom May–Sept. **HABITAT** Dry rocky areas, from Blackbrush communities to pinyon-juniper woods.

Plants That Cause Allergies

An allergy is a sensitivity in certain individuals to ordinarily harmless substances. "Allergy plants" typically have inconspicuous flowers that produce copious airborne pollen, which causes hay fever in susceptible individuals (reportedly at least 10–20 percent of the population). The cold-like symptoms include respiratory irritation, sneezing, and eye inflammation and may lead to more serious conditions, such as ear infections and asthma.

The amount of pollen in the air generally peaks three times during the year in the Southwest, depending on the plant species in bloom: mainly early-flowering trees, such as White Bursage, in the early spring; grasses, especially Bermuda Grass, in midsummer; and Big Sagebrush in the fall.

Some plants are unfairly blamed for allergies. In the Southwest region, for example, the conspicuous, insect-pollinated Canada Goldenrod and Sparse-flowered Goldenrod are not responsible for late-summer–autumn allergies; Big Sagebrush is probably the culprit.

RUBBER RABBITBUSH
"Gray Rabbitbush"
Chrysothamnus nauseosus
ASTER FAMILY

8′. Dense, broom-like shrub. Leaves 3″, gray-hairy, linear, soft. Stems shredding; twigs fuzzy. Flowers tiny, bright yellow, profuse, in rounded clusters; bloom July–Oct. Increases with overgrazing; widely distributed. **HABITAT** Mostly dry areas from woods to desert shrub communities, dry wash margins, cliff fissures.

BRITTLEBUSH
Encelia farinosa
ASTER FAMILY

3′. Rounded, many-branched, leafy shrub with flowers protruding on long stalks. Leaves silvery-gray, ovate. Flowers 5″; ray florets yellow; disk florets yellow-orange or brown-purple; bloom Nov.–May. Dominant species in some areas. **HABITAT** Rocky to gravel-covered slopes, hillsides. **RANGE** UT, NV, AZ.

TURPENTINE BRUSH
Ericameria laricifolia
ASTER FAMILY

30″. Leaves ¾″, linear, shiny, numerous, resinous; smell like turpentine when crushed. Flowers ¼″, with 3–10 golden ray ray florets, 9–15 disk florets; bloom Aug.–Nov. **HABITAT** Rocky to gravel-covered slopes and hillsides, in and along margins of dry washes, seeps.

ROSE-HEATH
"Baby Aster" "Heath Aster"
Chaetopappa ericoides
ASTER FAMILY

7″. Diminutive; from woody base, spreading underground stem; stems, leaves somewhat glandular, hairy. Leaves ½″, entire, linear to oblong; upper stem leaves reduced. Flowers ½″; ray florets white to pink; disk florets yellow; pappus of capillary bristles; bloom Mar.–Sept. **HABITAT** Rocky areas, Blackbrush to pinyon-juniper woods, southern deserts.

MOJAVE GOLDENBUSH
Ericameria linearifolia
ASTER FAMILY

4′. Rounded shrub; twigs and leaves resinous. Leaves 2″, linear. Flowers ¾″, solitary on stalks, with 10–20 yellow ray florets, numerous disk florets; pappus of many fine white bristles; bloom Mar.–June. **HABITAT** Among rocks, coarse sandy to gravelly areas, low-elev. shrub communities to pinyon-juniper woods. **RANGE** UT, NV, AZ.

BROOM SNAKEWEED
Gutierrezia sarothrae
ASTER FAMILY

24″. Many-branched subshrub or shrub; old growth often persistent. Leaves 3″, linear. Flowers ¼″, yellow to tannish; in flat-topped, crowded clusters, with 3–7 tiny ray florets, 3–6 disk florets; bloom May–Nov. **HABITAT** Slopes, flats, rocky areas, low-elev. desert mixed shrub communities to wooded mtns.

ARROW WEED
Pluchea sericea
ASTER FAMILY

10′. Dense, willow-like shrub; straight-branched, many-twigged. Leaves 2″, lanceolate, white-hairy. Stems gray-brown, grooved. Flowers tiny, purplish, at branch tips; bloom Apr.–Oct. **HABITAT** Low-elev. sandy or gravelly areas, streamsides, springs, marshes.

SPINELESS HORSEBRUSH
"Gray Horsebrush"
Tetradymia canescens
ASTER FAMILY

30″. Rounded shrub. Leaves 1″, linear to oblanceolate, white-wooly. Stems finely wooly. Flowers ½″, vase-shaped, with several cream to yellow petal lobes sticking out at odd angles; in clusters at branch tips; bloom June–Oct. **HABITAT** Arid, open areas in various mixed shrub communities, chaparral, pinyon-juniper woods.

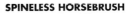

WHITE-STEM PAPERFLOWER
Psilostrophe cooperi
ASTER FAMILY

3′. Rounded shrub with white felt-like hairs on stems. Leaves 2″, simple, linear; felty-hairy when young, nearly hairless at maturity. Flowers 1¼″, yellow, with 4–8 papery, 3-lobed ray florets, 4–12 disk florets; pappus of 4–6 scales; bloom year-round. **HABITAT** Alluvial fans, rocky areas, Creosote Bush, low-elev. mixed shrub communities.

MOJAVE ASTER
Xylorhiza tortifolia
ASTER FAMILY

18″. Subshrub; lower woody, gnarled, old growth; upper current season's growth. Leaves 4″, lanceolate to elliptical, with marginal spine-like teeth; covered by wooly hairs and glands; nearly hairless at maturity. Flowers 2½″, ray florets white or lavender, disk florets yellow; solitary; bloom Mar.–June. **HABITAT** Arid, open, sandy or gravelly areas in mixed shrub communities, chaparral, pinyon-juniper woods. **RANGE** UT, NV, AZ.

CREEPING OREGON GRAPE
"Creeping Barberry"
Berberis aquifolium (repens)
BARBERRY FAMILY

24″. Prostrate shrub. Leaves 9″, pinnately compound; leaflets 3″, 3–9, ovate, spiny-edged; evergreen. Flowers ½″, yellow, with 15 petal-like parts in concentric whorls; bloom Mar.–June. Fruit ½″, blue berries; edible (tart), ripe Aug. Spreads by runners. **HABITAT** Mainly coniferous woods.

DESERT BARBERRY
Berberis fremontii
BARBERRY FAMILY

10′. Stout, multi-stemmed shrub. Leaves pinnate; leaflets 1″, 3–7, each with 5–7 spiny teeth; evergreen. Flowers ¼″, yellow, with 6-parted perianth (calyx and corolla); in clusters of 3–8; bloom Apr.–July. Fruit ½″, blue-black berries. **HABITAT** Open areas on slopes, canyons, Blackbrush communities to pinyon-juniper woods.

ARIZONA WHITE OAK
Quercus arizonica
BEECH FAMILY

40′. Round-topped tree with spreading branches at low elevs.; shrub at high elev.; evergreen, or deciduous just prior to formation of new spring growth. Leaves 3″, blue-green, leathery; elliptical to obovate with heart-shaped base, turned-under margins, entire to spiny-toothed. Flowers minute, yellowish, petals lacking, with 6 sepals and 4–10 stamens; unisexual; in elongated catkins; bloom May–June. Acorns 1″, narrow. **HABITAT** Dry areas, among rocks, canyons, margins of washes, oak and pinyon woods, chaparral. **RANGE** AZ, NM.

SHRUB LIVE OAK
Quercus turbinella
BEECH FAMILY

15′. Shrub to tree; often thicket-forming. Leaves 1½″, stiff, thick, elliptical, with 2–6 pairs marginal spiny teeth; evergreen. Male flowers in 1″ catkins; female flowers mature into 1″ acorns; bloom Apr.–May. **HABITAT** Canyons, slopes, chaparral, pinyon-juniper woods.

GAMBEL'S OAK

Quercus gambelii

BEECH FAMILY

10′. Thicket-forming shrub; tree occ. to 40′ or more. Leaves 4″, elliptical, bluntly 6- to 10-lobed; turn brown, stay on tree. Bark light gray or brown, scaly. Flowers minute, yellowish, petals lacking, with 6 sepals and 4–10 stamens; unisexual; in elongated catkins; bloom Apr.–May. Acorns ¾″, solitary or paired. **HABITAT** Mixed shrub, sagebrush, pinyon-juniper communities, slopes, washes, Ponderosa Pine woods.

DESERT WILLOW

Chilopsis linearis

BIGNONIA FAMILY

20′. Large shrub to small tree; crown rounded, spreading. Leaves 5″, linear, occ. sticky-hairy. Bark dark brown, scaly. Flowers 1¼″, bell-shaped, light pink to lavender, with yellow ridges and purple lines inside; bloom Apr.–Aug.; attract hummingbirds. Fruit 8″, brown, linear seedpods. Not a true willow. **HABITAT** Low-elev. desert washes.

YELLOW TRUMPETBUSH

Tecoma stans

BIGNONIA FAMILY

24′. Irregularly branched shrub to small tree. Leaves 5″, odd-pinnate; leaflets usu. 7–9, lanceolate to linear, serrate margins. Flowers 1½″, yellow, tubular with irreg. symmetry; bloom May–Oct. Fruit 6″, narrow capsules; seeds flat, winged. **HABITAT** Arid, exposed, well-drained rocky or gravelly slopes. **RANGE** AZ, NM.

MOUNTAIN ALDER

Alnus incana var. *tenuifolia*

BIRCH FAMILY

15′. Thicket-forming, low to almost tree-like shrub. Leaves 4″, ovate, doubly toothed, wavy-edged; finely white-wooly below. Bark smooth, brown to gray. Male flowers in 3″, green catkins; female flowers ½″, brown cones; bloom Apr.–June. **HABITAT** Streamsides, springs, seeps, lake-shores, moist meadow margins.

WATER BIRCH
Betula occidentalis
BIRCH FAMILY

30′. Tall shrub to tree with rounded crown. Leaves 2″, ovate, doubly toothed; shiny above, pale and dotted below; turn yellow-brown. Bark shiny red-brown, smooth with horizontal slits. Flowers in 1½″ catkins; male flowers yellowish, drooping; female flowers greenish, upright; bloom Apr.–May. **HABITAT** Streamsides, springs.

MOJAVE CEANOTHUS
"Desert Ceanothus"
"Desert Mountain-lilac"
Ceanothus greggii var. *vestitus*
BUCKTHORN FAMILY

6′. Rounded shrub with stout branches. Leaves ¾″, narrow, thick, leathery, mostly entire, opposite. Flowers tiny, white or purple; bloom Apr.–June. Fruit ¼″, globose or with wart-like projections. **HABITAT** Gravelly slopes in mixed shrub communities, pinyon-juniper woods.

BIRCH-LEAF BUCKTHORN
Rhamnus betulifolia
BUCKTHORN FAMILY

8′. Shrub; branches red to green when young, gray at maturity. Leaves elliptical, on ¾″ stalks; blades 6″. Flowers with tiny, greenish-white petals; bloom May–June. Fruit ½″, green to red or black. **HABITAT** Among boulders, canyons, cliff bases.

CALIFORNIA BUCKWHEAT
Eriogonum fasciculatum
BUCKWHEAT FAMILY

H 4′; W 10′. Low, spreading shrub. Leaves ¾″, dark green above, white-hairy below, linear to oblong, rolled under; densely bundled along stem. Flowers tiny, white to pinkish, in 1″ branched clusters above 3″ of bare stem; dead flowers persistent, rust-colored; bloom Mar.–Sept. Favorite of bees, butterflies. **HABITAT** Dry, sandy to gravelly, rocky slopes, canyons, washes, Creosote Bush and Blackbrush communities. **RANGE** UT, NV, AZ.

WESTERN WHITE VIRGIN'S BOWER
Clematis ligusticifolia
BUTTERCUP FAMILY

L variable. Prolific climbing, woody vine. Leaves 6″, pinnately compound; leaflets 2″, 5–7, coarse-toothed. Flowers ¾″, creamy, with usu. 4 petal-like sepals; in open, 2″ clusters; bloom May–Sept. Fruit seeds have 1″ white plumes, in abundant fluffballs. **HABITAT** Moist canyons, streamsides, bottomlands.

CREOSOTE BUSH
Larrea tridentata
CALTROP FAMILY

9′. Rounded, multi-stemmed shrub. Leaves ½″, opposite, compound, with 2 oblong leaflets, waxy; evergreen; pungent after rain. Stems gray and black. Flowers ½″, bright yellow, 5-petaled; bloom Mar.–Nov. Fruit tiny, white, hairy capsules. Dominant on arid plains, slopes, hillsides. **HABITAT** Widespread at low elev.

SQUAWBUSH SUMAC
Rhus trilobata
CASHEW FAMILY

5′. Rounded shrub. Leaves 2″, usu. compound, with 3 round-lobed , 1″ leaflets; turn orange-red. Flowers tiny, yellow, in clusters at branch tips; bloom Mar.–June, prior to appearance of leaves. Fruit ¼″, red-orange, flattish, sticky-hairy berries; used for ersatz lemonade. **HABITAT** Streamsides, canyons, among rocks, cliff bases, rimrock.

DESERT RUE
"Turpentine Broom"
Thamnosma montana
CITRUS FAMILY

24″. Broom-like, spiny shrub; aromatic. Leaves ½″, linear, simple; short-lived. Stems yellow-green, photosynthetic, densely gland-dotted. Flowers ½″, with 4 dark purple petals, erect; doubly lobed ovary on stalk; bloom Mar.–June. **HABITAT** Arid, gravelly, or stony slopes in Creosote Bush, Joshua Tree, Blackbrush communities. **RANGE** UT, NV, AZ.

NET-LEAF HACKBERRY
Celtis reticulata
ELM FAMILY

20′. Shrub to small tree. Leaves 3″, lanceolate to ovate, entire or 4-toothed margins, with conspicuous network of veins; usu. with insect galls; base oblique, asymmetrical. Flowers minute, greenish, petals lacking; bloom Apr.–May. Fruit ½″, reddish, spherical drupes, on ½″ stalk; persistent. **HABITAT** Canyons, washes, streamsides, springs.

FOUR-WINGED SALTBUSH
Atriplex canescens
GOOSEFOOT FAMILY

6′. Rounded shrub. Leaves 1¼″, gray-green, oblanceolate, scaly. Young bark whitish, scaly; later peeling. Flowers minute, greenish; males often reddish; bloom Apr.–June. Fruit ½″, 4-winged. **HABITAT** Sandy or gravelly flats, slopes in Creosote Bush, Joshua Tree, sagebrush, Blackbrush communities, pinyon-juniper woods.

PICKLEWEED
"Iodine Bush"
Allenrolfea occidentalis
GOOSEFOOT FAMILY

5′. Succulent, hairless, highly branched shrub; woody below. Leaves tiny, scale-like, triangular. Stems constricted into rings at nodes; internodes fleshy. Flowers minute, greenish, petals lacking; in clusters on 1″ erect, cylindrical spikes; bloom Apr.–Nov. Tolerates salty soils by taking up salt into plant tissues. **HABITAT** Salt flats, saline areas, playa margins.

DESERT HOLLY
Atriplex hymenelytra
GOOSEFOOT FAMILY

3′. Rounded, silvery shrub. Leaves stalked; blades 2″, round, irreg. dentate. Male flower clusters erect, yellow turning purple, 1½″; female flowers surrounded by round, leaf-like ½″ bracts; sexes on separate plants; bloom Mar.–Dec. Foliage gathered for Christmas decoration. **HABITAT** Low-elev. gravelly flats, slopes. **RANGE** UT, NV, AZ.

SPINY HOPSAGE
Grayia (Atriplex) spinosa
GOOSEFOOT FAMILY

3′. Rounded shrub with spiny twigs. Leaves 1½″, entire, oblanceolate, slightly fleshy. Flowers in spike-like clusters; male ¾″, female 7″; sexes on separate plants; bloom Mar.–Aug. Fruit surrounded by fused pair of orbicular, spongy, bractlets that enlarge in fruit, becoming reddish. **HABITAT** Dry, rocky plains, foothill slopes, in Blackbrush, sagebrush, pinyon-juniper, mixed shrub communities. **RANGE** UT, NV, AZ.

GREASEWOOD
Sarcobatus vermiculatus
GOOSEFOOT FAMILY

5′. Dense shrub, with white thorny branchlets. Leaves 1½″, bright green, linear, fleshy. Bark pale gray, smooth. Flowers tiny, greenish, in 1¼″, catkin-like spikes; bloom June–Sept. Marvelously adapted to an extreme environment. **HABITAT** Arid, saline, or alkaline plains, playa margins.

WINTER FAT
Krascheninnikovia lanata
GOOSEFOOT FAMILY

3′. Shrub; woody at base. Leaves 1½″, lanceolate, edges rolled under. Wool on stems and leaves whitish; turns reddish brown. Female flowers minute, buried in willow-like ¼″ tufts; male flowers in smaller tufts in uppermost axils; bloom May–Dec. Valued in winter as sheep browse; sometimes forms pure stands. **HABITAT** Arid, somewhat alkaline rocky plains, hill and mtn. slopes, Creosote Bush, sagebrush, pinyon-juniper, mixed desert shrub communities.

CANYON GRAPE
Vitis arizonica
GRAPE FAMILY

L 20′. Branched, woody vine, with shredding, peeling bark; clambers over rocks, shrubs, trees. Leaves roughly heart-shaped, hairless to quite hairy, simple, lobed or not, with toothed margins, stalked; blades 5″. Tendrils formed opposite leaves, provide attachment or support. Flowers tiny, with white petals; in 1½″, dense clusters; bloom Apr.–July. Fruit ¼″, deep purple to black, waxy; relished by birds, small mammals, and humans in spite of large seeds. **HABITAT** Streamsides, springs, seeps, canyon bottoms.

ARIZONA MADRONE
Arbutus arizonica
HEATH FAMILY

50′. Red-branched, with peeling bark. Leaves thick, broadly lanceolate; evergreen. Flowers ¼″, pink or white, urn-shaped; in 3″ clusters; bloom Apr.–May, Sept. Fruit dark orange to red, warty, berry-like. **HABITAT** Well-drained areas in open mixed woods, oak mtn. woods, slopes, washes. **RANGE** AZ, NM.

MYRTLE BLUEBERRY

Vaccinium myrtillus

HEATH FAMILY

10″. Small, open shrub. Leaves 1″, elliptical, fine-toothed. Stems sharply angled. Flowers ¼″, pink, globose, minutely 5-lobed; bloom May–Aug. Fruit ¼″, blue-black berries; edible, ripe July–Sept. **HABITAT** Open woods, hillsides in coniferous woods.

MEXICAN MANZANITA

"Point-leaf Manzanita"

Arctostaphylos pungens

HEATH FAMILY

6′. Rounded shrub, often forming dense thickets. Branches with smooth red-brown bark. Leaves 1″, ovate to lanceolate; evergreen. Flowers ¼″ with pink corollas; bloom Feb.–June. **HABITAT** Mixed shrub and sagebrush communities, pinyon-juniper woods, drained sandy to gravelly areas, canyons, lower mtn. slopes. **RANGE** UT, NV, AZ.

ARIZONA HONEYSUCKLE

Lonicera arizonica

HONEYSUCKLE FAMILY

L variable. Trailing or climbing vine. Leaves 3″, oval to elliptical, simple, opposite, finely glandular-hairy; lower leaves on short stalks, upper pairs stalkless, united at base. Flowers tubular, with 1½″, red to purplish corollas; in terminal clusters of 2–4; bloom June–July. Fruit red berries. **HABITAT** Mtn. areas, open coniferous woods. **RANGE** AZ, NM.

BLACK TWINBERRY

"Bearberry Honeysuckle" "Bush Honeysuckle"

Lonicera involucrata

HONEYSUCKLE FAMILY

8′. Erect shrub; often thicket-forming. Leaves 5″, opposite, elliptical. Bark light brown, shredding. Flowers ¾″, pale yellow, tubular, 5-lobed, in pairs, with 4 green bracts that turn magenta; bloom June–July. Fruit tiny, black, paired berries. HABITAT Coniferous woods, meadow margins, moist streamsides.

BLUE ELDERBERRY

Sambucus cerulea (mexicana)

HONEYSUCKLE FAMILY

12′. Tall shrub. Leaves 12″, opposite, pinnately compound; leaflets 5″, 5–9, lanceolate, fine-toothed. Bark gray, furrowed. Flowers tiny, white, in flattish, branched, 8″ clusters; bloom May–Sept. Fruit tiny, blue or white berries; in rounded clusters; edible, ripe Aug.–Sept. HABITAT Streamsides, woodland openings, moist slopes, valleys.

ROCKY MOUNTAIN ELDERBERRY

Sambucus racemosa

HONEYSUCKLE FAMILY

20′. Tall, weak-stemmed shrub to tree. Leaves 10″, opposite, pinnately compound; leaflets 5″, 5–7, lanceolate, toothed. Flowers tiny, white; bloom May–July. Fruit tiny, red berries; black in mtns. CAUTION Raw berries poisonous. HABITAT Streamsides, wooded or open areas, low-elev. hills to upper mtn. slopes.

RED TWINBERRY
"Utah Honeysuckle"
Lonicera utahensis
HONEYSUCKLE FAMILY

6′. Shrub. Leaves 2½″, lanceolate to oblong, entire, opposite. Flowers in pairs, enclosed by lower, narrow, papery bracts; corollas ¾″, yellowish, tubular; bloom June–July. Fruit ½″, red berries. **HABITAT** High-elev. shrub communities, wooded slopes, coniferous woods. **RANGE** UT, AZ, NM.

MOUNTAIN SNOWBERRY
Symphoriocarpos oreophilus
HONEYSUCKLE FAMILY

5′. Branched shrub. Leaves 2″, elliptical to ovate, entire. Flowers borne singly or in pairs in leaf axil; petals pink or white, fused to form tubular, ½″ corollas; bloom May–Aug. Fruit ¼″, white berries. **HABITAT** Open slopes, coniferous woods, foothills to high elev.

LONG-FLOWER SNOWBERRY
Symphoriocarpos longiflorus
HONEYSUCKLE FAMILY

4′. Highly branched shrub; branches often arching. Leaves ½″, elliptical to oblanceolate, entire. Flowers borne singly or in pairs in leaf axil; petals pink, fused to form tubular, ½″ corollas; bloom Apr.–Aug. Fruit ¼″, white berries. **HABITAT** Rocky mtn. slopes, sagebrush, pinyon-juniper communities.

CLIFFBUSH
"Waxflower"
Jamesia americana
HYDRANGEA FAMILY

3′. Rounded to straggly shrub. Leaves 2″, opposite, ovate, toothed, gray-wooly below; turn bright red. Bark reddish, peeling. Flowers ¾″, waxy-white to pink, with 5 narrow lobes, in clusters; bloom May–July. **HABITAT** Rocky slopes, cliff faces, canyon walls, mixed shrub communities, coniferous woods.

LITTLE-LEAF MOCK ORANGE

"Desert Mock Orange"

Philadelphus microphyllus

HYDRANGEA FAMILY

6′. Shrub. Leaves 1″, opposite, 3-veined, entire, ovate to lanceolate, hairy, margins slightly turned under. Flowers showy; 4 sepals; 4 white, 6″ petals; bloom June–July. Fruit ¼″, woody capsules. **HABITAT** Arid rocky slopes, cliffs, pinyon juniper to coniferous woods.

CLIFF FENDLERBUSH

Fendlera rupicola

HYDRANGEA FAMILY

30″. Branched shrub. Leaves 1″, opposite, 1-veined, some seemingly whorled, elliptical, usu. hairy, edges usu. rolled under. Twigs tan to red, aging gray. Flowers 1¼″, white, pink in bud, with 4 spoon-shaped petals; single to clusters of 3; profuse; bloom Apr.–Oct., sometimes repeating later. **HABITAT** Dry, rocky, gravelly slopes in Blackbrush and sagebrush communities, pinyon-juniper woods. **RANGE** UT, AZ, NM.

RANGE RATANY

Krameria erecta (parvifolia)

KRAMERIA FAMILY

24″. Low, branched, dark grayish shrub. Leaves ½″, entire, linear. Flowers bilaterally symmetrical, borne singly on silky stalks; sepals pinkish; 5 petals, ¾″, purplish, the 2 smaller ones reduced to glandular tissue that attracts pollinators; bloom Apr.–Oct. Fruit ¼″, with minute, downward-pointing barbs cloaking prickles. **HABITAT** Arid, gravelly, rocky areas, low-elev. slopes, plains in Creosote Bush and Blackbrush communities.

ROCKY MOUNTAIN MAPLE
Acer glabrum
MAPLE FAMILY

18′. Shrub to small tree. Leaves 4″, opposite, palmately 3- or 5-lobed; turn red-orange. Bark gray to reddish, smooth. Flowers tiny, greenish, saucer-shaped, in branched clusters; bloom Apr.–June. Fruit 1″ reddish, dry, hard, 1-seeded, with right-angled wings. **HABITAT** Arid, well-drained areas, mid-elev. mtn. slopes and canyons in pinyon-juniper, coniferous woods.

BOX ELDER
"Ash-leaved Maple"
Acer negundo
MAPLE FAMILY

50′. Crown broad, rounded; trunk short. Leaves 8″, opposite, pinnately compound; leaflets 3″, 3–7, ovate, toothed; turn yellow or bronze. Bark gray-brown, furrowed. Flowers minute, greenish, petals lacking, with 4–5 sepals; sexes in separate clusters on same plant; bloom Apr.–May. Fruit 1¼″, pale yellow keys, with 45-degree-angled wings. The only maple with compound leaves; planted as an ornamental. **HABITAT** Washes, streamsides.

DESERT LAVENDER
Hyptis emoryi
MINT FAMILY

10′. Erect shrub. Leaves 2½″, whitish, ovate, toothed, with wooly hairs; semievergreen; lavender-scented. Bark gray. Flowers tiny, blue-violet, 2-lipped, in clusters at leaf axils; bloom year-round; attract bees and hummingbirds. **HABITAT** Arid, low-elev. rocky slopes, washes, canyons. **RANGE** NV, AZ.

BLADDER SAGE
Salazaria mexicana
MINT FAMILY

4′. Rounded, highly branched shrub. Leaves ½″, ovate to elliptical, opposite, entire. Stems green, photosynthetic, arching, somewhat thorny. Flowers with calyx enlarging to 1″ while fruit develops, becoming bladdery; corollas with irreg. symmetry: upper lip white, lower lip purple; bloom Mar.–Oct. **HABITAT** Dry, low-elev. rocky slopes, washes, canyons. **RANGE** NV, UT, AZ.

PURPLE SAGE
Salvia dorrii
MINT FAMILY

30″. Low, rounded, aromatic shrub; glandular, finely silvery-hairy; occ. mat-forming. Leaves 1¼″, opposite, spatula-shaped to oval. Flowers ½″, in 2–5 separate clusters along elongated axil; corollas blue, tubular, 2-lipped; stamens thrust out; bloom Apr.–July. **HABITAT** Dry, open gravelly slopes, outcrops, washes, plains, Blackbrush communities to high-elev. coniferous woodland openings. **RANGE** NV, UT, AZ.

TREE TOBACCO
Nicotiana glauca
NIGHTSHADE FAMILY

15′. Thicket-forming shrub to small, sparsely branched tree. Leaves 6″, blue-green to grayish, ovate, long-stalked. Flowers 2″, yellow, tubular; hang in loose clusters from branch tips; bloom year-round, attract hummingbirds. Introduced from South America. **HABITAT** Disturbed, moist areas, lakesides, streamsides, ditches. **RANGE** NV, AZ, NM.

ANDERSON'S WOLFBERRY
"Waterjacket"
Lycium andersonii
NIGHTSHADE FAMILY

8′. Intricately branched, thorny shrub. Leaves 1″, thick and fleshy; shape and size variable, depending upon seasonal moisture. Flowers borne singly or in pairs in leaf axils; calyx tiny, green; corollas ½″, white to yellow, bluish above and on lobes, tubular; bloom Feb.–May. Fruit ¼″, red, juicy berries. **HABITAT** Fine gravelly plains, washes, rocky slopes in Creosote Bush, Joshua Tree, Blackbrush communities.

OCOTILLO
Fouquieria splendens
OCOTILLO FAMILY

15′. Shrub with cane-like stems; resembles bundle of spiny sticks. Leafless stems carry out photosynthesis; quickly form 2″, ovate, fleshy leaves and stalks; become stiff-spined after heavy rains. Flowers 1″, red, tubular, in terminal clusters; bloom Mar.–June. Occ. produces leaves and flowers more than twice a year. **HABITAT** Hilltops, mesas, dry plains, rocky slopes. **RANGE** NV, AZ, NM.

RUSSIAN-OLIVE
Eleagnus angustifolia
OLEASTER FAMILY

20′. Thorny-branched. Leaves 3″, lanceolate, covered with stellate scale-like hairs, fewer on green upper surface, silvery below. Flowers ½″, lacking petals; emit heavy fragrance; bloom Apr.–June. Fruit ¾″, olive-like, silvery-scaled, yellow to brown at maturity. Introduced as an ornamental from Eurasia; naturalized around rural communities. **HABITAT** Irrigation ditches, springs, streamsides.

SINGLELEAF ASH
Fraxinus anomala
OLIVE FAMILY

20′. Shrub to small tree; twigs 4-angled. Leaves 4″, opposite, usu. entire, smooth or serrate margins; occ. with 3–5 leaflets. Flowers tiny, greenish to creamy, lacking petals; bloom Apr.–May. Fruit dry, hard, 1-seeded. **HABITAT** Rimrock, rocky drainages, slopes, pinyon-juniper woods.

VELVET ASH

"Arizona Ash"

Fraxinus velutina

OLIVE FAMILY

30′. Crown rounded, open; branches spreading. Leaves 5″, opposite, pinnately compound; leaflets 3″, 5–9, lanceolate, toothed; turn yellow. Bark gray-brown, furrowed. Flowers minute, greenish, petals lacking, with 4-lobed calyx; sexes separate, male flowers with only 2 stamens; bloom Mar.–May. Fruit 1¼″, light brown, 1-winged keys; in clusters. Extensively planted as an ornamental. **HABITAT** Canyons, washes, streamsides.

CALIFORNIA FAN PALM

Washingtonia filifera

PALM FAMILY

50′. Crown rounded; trunk gray, scarred, partly to completely covered with dead leaves (thatch). Leaves 5′, fan-shaped; cut into many narrow thready segments on spiny-edged stalks; evergreen. Flowers ½″, whitish, funnel-shaped, in 9″ clusters; bloom May–June. Fruit ½″, black, berry-like; in loose clusters. Most plant biologists consider this to be the only palm native to Southwest; widely cultivated as an ornamental. **HABITAT** Permanently moist areas, springs, streamsides, canyons. **RANGE** sw AZ.

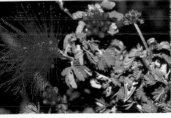

FAIRY DUSTER

Calliandra eriophylla

PEA FAMILY

12″. Intricately branched. Leaves 1½″, twice pinnately compound. Flowers reddish purple; sepals and petals small; stamens 1″, numerous, thrust out; in sparse clusters in leaf axils; bloom Feb.–May. Fruit 2″, thick pods. **HABITAT** Sandy, gravelly slopes, flats, low-elev. washes. **RANGE** AZ, NM.

CATCLAW ACACIA

Acacia greggii

PEA FAMILY

15′. Spiny, thicket-forming shrub to small tree with rounded crown. Leaves 3″, bipinnately compound; each main leafstalk has 2–3 pairs of side stalks with 3–7 pairs of tiny leaflets. Bark gray, furrowed. Flowers tiny, yellow, in cylindrical clusters; fragrant; bloom Apr.–Oct. **HABITAT** Dry streambeds, alluvial benches along washes, canyon bottoms.

FOOTHILL PALOVERDE

"Yellow Paloverde"

Cercidium microphyllum

PEA FAMILY

25′. Large shrub to tree, with scattered thorns. Leaves bipinnately compound; leaflets 3″, 1–3. Bark green, smooth; photosynthetic on young stems, branches. Flowers ¾″, yellow, in clusters; bloom Apr.–May. Fruit 4½″, green drying brown pods, constricted between seeds. **HABITAT** Low-elev. plains, rocky slopes in foothills, mtns. **RANGE** AZ.

WESTERN REDBUD

Cercis occidentalis

PEA FAMILY

12′. Shrub to small tree. Leaves 4″, heart-shaped, simple. Bark gray, hairless. Flowers ¾″, petals pink, bilaterally symmetrical; in clusters on spur shoots; produced before leaves; bloom Mar.–June. Fruit 3″, chestnut-brown at maturity, flat, oblong; persistent. Grown as an ornamental. **HABITAT** Sandstone areas, canyons, washes, streamsides. **RANGE** UT, NV, AZ.

WESTERN CORAL BEAN

Erythrina flabelliformis

PEA FAMILY

15′. Shrub to small tree; stems and leaves with scattered, hooked prickles. Leaves pinnately trifoliate; leaflets 2½″, triangular to ovate. Flowers 2″, corollas red; produced before leaves; bloom Apr.–May, Sept.–Oct. Fruit 10″, linear, thick-walled pods, constricted between several red, ½″ seeds. **CAUTION** Seeds poisonous. **HABITAT** Arid, rocky mtn. hillsides, canyon slopes. **RANGE** NV, AZ, NM.

DESERT IRONWOOD

Olneya tesota

PEA FAMILY

25′. Crown rounded, dense, broad; trunk short; twigs spiny. Leaves 2¼″, blue-green, pinnately compound, with up to 10 pairs oblong leaflets. Bark gray, shredding. Pea-flowers ½″, purple, in short clusters; bloom May–June. Fruit 2½″, brown pods. **HABITAT** Low-elev. sandy to gravelly washes, low hills, plains. **RANGE** AZ.

HONEY MESQUITE

Prosopis glandulosa

PEA FAMILY

15′. Spiny, thicket-forming shrub to small tree with short trunk, crooked branches. Leaves 8″, bipinnately compound, each axis with 7–17 pairs of tiny, oblong leaflets. Flowers minute; in 4″ spikes; bloom Apr.–Sept. Fruit 8″ pods, constricted between seeds. Found in areas where water table is high. **HABITAT** Low-elev. alkaline flats, playa margins, washes, sand dunes, springs.

SCREWBEAN MESQUITE

Prosopis pubescens

PEA FAMILY

20′. Spiny, thicket-forming shrub to small tree with long, twisted branches. Leaves 3″, grayish, bipinnately compound; each axis with 5–8 pairs of tiny, oblong leaflets. Flowers tiny, yellow; bloom May–June. Fruit 2″, brown or yellow, coiled pods. **HABITAT** Low-elev. saline springs, meadows, with salt-grass, sandy and gravelly washes, associated benches.

SMOKE TREE

Psorothamnus spinosus

PEA FAMILY

15′. Shrub to small tree with irreg. crown, short crooked trunk, many spiny branches. Leaves 1″, gray, spatula-shaped, hairy; shed in a few weeks, before flowers bloom. Bark pale gray, scaly. Pea-flowers ½″, purple, in 1¼″ clusters; fragrant; bloom Apr.–July. Fruit ½″, brown, acorn-shaped pods. **HABITAT** Low-elev. broad, sandy, gravelly, rocky washes, floodplains. **RANGE** NV, AZ.

FREMONT INDIGO-BUSH

Psorothamnus fremontii

PEA FAMILY

5′. Open, branching shrub; gland-dotted, silver-gray. Leaves 2½″, pinnately compound; leaflets ½″, 3–9. Bark white. Flowers ½″, indigo, in 5″ clusters; bloom Apr.–June. **HABITAT** Sandy to gravelly washes, slopes, benches, flats, dunes, in Creosote Bush, Blackbrush, Joshua Tree communities. **RANGE** UT, NV, AZ.

NEW MEXICO LOCUST

Robinia neomexicana

PEA FAMILY

25′. Shrub to small tree; thicket-forming; stout, slightly recurved, paired 1″ spines at nodes. Leaves 10″, odd-pinnate; leaflets 1½″, 9–19, oblong. Flowers 1″, purplish pink, in crowded clusters; bloom May–July. Fruit 3½″, glandular, hairy pods. **HABITAT** Moist streamsides, talus slopes, pinyon-juniper to Ponderosa Pine woods, chaparral.

GRANITE GILIA

Leptodactylon pungens

PHLOX FAMILY

24″. Open-branched shrub; stems woody at base. Leaves alternate above, opposite below; palmately parted or divided, minutely spine-tipped; rigid, flat against stems; in clusters. Flowers 1″, corollas white or suffused with purple on outside, tubular, radially symmetrical; solitary or in small terminal clusters; bloom May–Aug. **HABITAT** Dry, rocky areas to tree line, plains, slopes, cliffs, mixed shrub communities, pinyon-juniper to Ponderosa Pine woods.

UTAH SERVICEBERRY
Amelanchier utahensis
ROSE FAMILY

10′. Low shrub to small tree. Leaves simple, stalked; blades 1″, ovate to round, serrate margins above middle half. Flowers with white, ½″ petals, showy, in clusters of 3–6; bloom Apr.–May. Fruit ½″, purplish, globose; juicy but usu. dry and brownish at maturity; persistent. **HABITAT** Streamsides, arid mtn. slopes and canyons, sagebrush, mixed shrub, pinyon-juniper, Ponderosa Pine communities.

CURL-LEAF MOUNTAIN MAHOGANY
Cercocarpus ledifolius
ROSE FAMILY

20′. Crown rounded; branches twisted. Leaves 1¼″, lanceolate, with rolled edges; aromatic; evergreen. Bark reddish to gray, furrowed. Flowers ½″, yellowish, funnel-shaped; bloom Apr.–June. Fruit seed-like, with long, white, hairy tail. Often forms pure stands. **HABITAT** Dry, rocky mtn. slopes, sagebrush, pinyon-juniper, open coniferous woods. **RANGE** UT, NV, AZ.

BIRCH-LEAF MOUNTAIN MAHOGANY
Cercocarpus montanus (betuloides)
ROSE FAMILY

15′. Large shrub to small tree. Leaves 1¼″, elliptical, with tapered base, grayish below; evergreen. Bark brown, scaly. Flowers ½″, yellowish, funnel-shaped; bloom May–July. Fruit seed-like, with long, white, hairy tail. **HABITAT** Mtn. slopes in pinyon-juniper woods, sagebrush, open coniferous woods. **RANGE** AZ.

FERNBUSH
Chamaebatiaria millefolium
ROSE FAMILY

6′. Aromatic shrub; glandular, stellate, hairy. Leaves 3″, finely twice pinnately compound, fern-like. Flowers ¾″, petals white, stamens yellow, showy; in 4″ clusters; bloom Apr.–Nov. **HABITAT** Dry, rocky slopes, mtn. canyons, limestone areas, pinyon-juniper, coniferous woods, mixed shrub, sagebrush communities. **RANGE** UT, NV, AZ.

BLACKBRUSH
Coleogyne ramosissima
ROSE FAMILY

5′. Intricately branched, thorny shrub. Leaves ½″; in opposite clusters on short, lateral branches. Flowers ½″, yellow, 4-sepaled, lacking petals; numerous stamens borne on membranous, hairy structure enveloping ovary; bloom Mar.–June. Forms pure stands. **HABITAT** Bajadas, lower mtn. slopes, shallow bedrock. **RANGE** UT, NV, AZ.

BLACK HAWTHORN
Crataegus douglasii
ROSE FAMILY

15′. Thicket-forming shrub or tree with rounded crown. Leaves 2½″, ovate, toothed, lobed. Bark gray-brown; twigs red, spiny. Flowers ½″, with 5 white petals, pink stamens; in rounded clusters; bloom May–June. Fruit ½″, reddish-black berries. **HABITAT** Moist areas, streamsides, floodplains, canyons.

SHRUBBY CINQUEFOIL
Pentaphylloides fruticosa
ROSE FAMILY

24″. Rounded to mat-forming shrub. Leaves 1½″, pinnately compound; leaflets ¾″, usu. 5, linear, hairy. Stems red, smooth to shredding. Flowers 1″, yellow, 5-petaled; bloom June–Sept. Fruit tiny, white-hairy seedpods. **HABITAT** Rocky areas, floodplains, alpine meadows, sagebrush, coniferous, aspen woods.

APACHE PLUME
Fallugia paradoxa
ROSE FAMILY

6′. Slender, many-branched shrub. Leaves ¾″, pinnately 3–5 lobed, turned under margins, rusty-hairy below; in clusters on short, lateral branches; occ. evergreen. Bark white. Flowers 1″, petals white, long-stalked, numerous stamens and pistils; unisexual, one or the other sterile; bloom Apr.–Oct. Fruit pink to purplish, feathery plumes, formed by styles, above seed-like base. Cultivated for flowers and fruit. **HABITAT** Dry, rocky slopes, alluvial washes, canyon bottoms, mixed shrub, Blackbrush, pinyon-juniper communities.

MOUNTAIN NINEBARK
Physocarpus monogynus
ROSE FAMILY

5′. Stellate-hairy shrub. Leaf blades 1″, rounded, palmately lobed. Bark brownish, matures gray; peels off in strips. Flowers ½″, petals white; in flat-topped clusters of 9–25; bloom May–July. **HABITAT** Well-drained canyon bottoms, mtn. slopes, mixed shrub communities, coniferous woods. **RANGE** NV, AZ, NM.

DESERT ALMOND
Prunus fasciculata
ROSE FAMILY

6′. Intricately branched, thorny. Leaves 1″, spatula-shaped; in clusters on short, lateral branches. Flowers with tiny, white petals; solitary or in clusters of 2–5; bloom Mar.–May. Fruit hairy, resemble tiny almonds. **HABITAT** Dry, rocky areas, mixed shrub, Joshua Tree, pinyon-juniper communities. **RANGE** UT, NV, AZ.

CHOKECHERRY
Prunus virginiana
ROSE FAMILY

15′. Thicket-forming shrub or rounded to straggly tree. Leaves 4″, elliptical, toothed; turn yellow. Bark gray-brown, smooth. Flowers ½″, white, 5-petaled; bloom Apr.–July. Fruit ½″, red to blackish cherries; flesh edible, bitter, used for jam, ripe June Aug. **HABITAT** Hillsides, canyon bottoms, springs, streamsides, ditches, sagebrush, pinyon-juniper, coniferous woods.

WOODS'S ROSE
Rosa woodsii
ROSE FAMILY

6′. Thicket-forming, weak-stemmed shrub. Leaves 4″, pinnately compound; leaflets 1½″, 5–9, ovate, toothed. Stems sparsely prickly or with prickles only near base. Flowers 2″, pink, 5-petaled, in clusters; fragrant; bloom May–Aug. Fruit ½″, red rose hips. **HABITAT** Moist hillsides, canyon bottoms, springs, streamsides, ditches, often with willows, sagebrush, pinyon-juniper, coniferous woods.

CLIFFROSE
Purshia (Cowania) mexicana
ROSE FAMILY

9′. Straggly shrub; occ. tree with open crown, crooked trunk. Leaves ½″, with 5–7 narrow lobes, leathery; crowded at branch tips. Bark reddish; shredding as ages. Flowers ¾″, with 5 white to cream to pale yellow petals, 5 smaller sepals; bloom Apr.–Sept. Fruit ¼″ seeds, with 2″ curling plumes; in clusters of 5–10. **HABITAT** Dry, rocky mid-elev. hills, wash margins, mtn. slopes, canyons, Blackbrush, mixed shrub, pinyon-juniper, Ponderosa Pine communities.

BITTERBRUSH
"Antelope Brush"
Purshia tridentata
ROSE FAMILY

6′. Stiff, branched shrub. Leaves ¾″, oblanceolate, with 3-lobed tip, edges rolled under; white-hairy below. Flowers ¾″, yellow, funnel-shaped, with 5 flat petals; bloom Apr.–July. Fruit ¾″, dry, hard, 1-seeded. **HABITAT** Sandy, gravelly, rocky areas, canyons, open slopes, flats, sagebrush, pinyon-juniper, coniferous woods.

WILD RED RASPBERRY
Rubus idaeus
ROSE FAMILY

6′. Many-caned shrub. Leaves compound; leaflets 3″, 3–5, ovate, toothed. Stems cinnamon-brown, peeling; usu. prickly; live 2 years, flowering the 2nd year. Flowers ½″, white, 5-petaled; usu. in clusters; bloom June–Aug. Fruit ½″, red berries; edible, delicious, ripe July–Sept. **HABITAT** Streamsides, moist talus slopes, aspen stands, coniferous woods.

THIMBLEBERRY
Rubus parviflorus
ROSE FAMILY

5′. Shrub. Leaves 6″, 5-lobed, toothed, hairy. Stems green to light brown. Flowers 2″, white, with 5 rounded crinkly petals; bloom May–Sept. Fruit ¾″, crimson, cup shaped berries; edible, ripe June–Aug. **HABITAT** Humid, moist areas, rich streamsides, canyons, open aspen and coniferous woods.

ARIZONA SYCAMORE
Platanus wrightii (racemosa)
SYCAMORE FAMILY

H 80′; D 3′. Crown spreading. Leaves 10″, palmately 5-lobed. Bark peeling, smooth; white at maturity. Flowers tiny, greenish, mature tan to brownish; in series of ball-like clusters along pendant stalks; bloom May–Sept. **HABITAT** Canyons, washes, streamsides. **RANGE** AZ, NM

ELEPHANT TREE
Bursera microphylla
TORCHWOOD FAMILY

20′. Young branches reddish; mature trunk white. Leaves 3″, hairless, odd-pinnately compound; leaflets ½″, 7–33. Flowers with tiny, white petals; bloom July. Fruit drupe-like. **HABITAT** Arid, rocky slopes. **RANGE** AZ.

ARIZONA WALNUT
Juglans major
WALNUT FAMILY

H 50′; D 3′. Crown broad; branches spreading. Leaves 12″, pinnately compound; leaflets 9–15, serrate. Male flowers minute, greenish, in 3″ catkins; female flowers separate, solitary or few, mature into fruit with fibrous, fleshy outer layer, bony inner layer (the nut, containing 2-lobed seed); bloom Apr.–May. Other members of family produce hickory nuts and pecans. **HABITAT** Canyons, streamsides. **RANGE** AZ, NM.

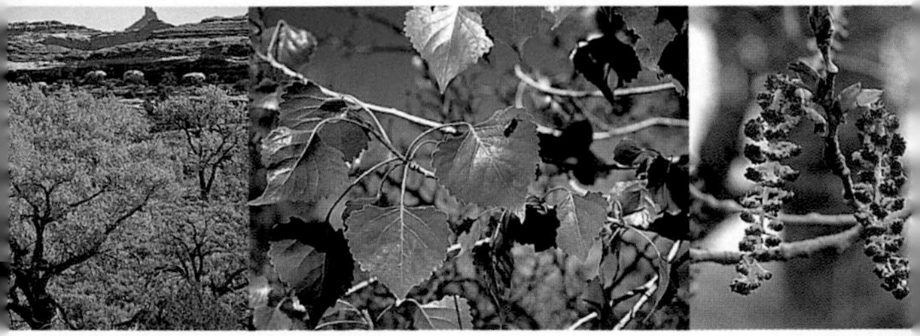

FREMONT COTTONWOOD
Populus fremontii
WILLOW FAMILY

H 65′; D 3′. Crown broad, open, flat; branches wide-spreading. Leaves 2½″, shiny yellow-green, triangular, usu. broader than long, round-toothed; turn yellow. Bark gray, thick, deeply furrowed. Flowers in 2″, reddish catkins; bloom Mar.–Apr. Fruit ½″, brown, egg-shaped capsules; contain cottony seeds. Occ. cultivated. **HABITAT** Canyons, streamsides, ditches.

QUAKING ASPEN
Populus tremuloides
WILLOW FAMILY

50′. Crown narrow, rounded. Leaves 2½″, heart-shaped to rounded, fine-toothed, on flat leafstalks; "quake" in slightest breeze; turn yellow. Bark greenish white, smooth. Flowers in 2″, brownish catkins; bloom Apr.–June. Fruit tiny, green capsules; in 4″ catkins. Occ. cultivated. **HABITAT** Canyons, mtn. streamsides, slopes.

COYOTE WILLOW
"Sandbar Willow"
Salix exigua
WILLOW FAMILY

20′. Thicket-forming shrub to small tree. Leaves 3″, usu. gray-wooly, linear; turn yellow. Twigs reddish or yellowish. Flowers tiny; in 2″, yellowish catkins; bloom Apr.–May, some with leaves, some later. **HABITAT** Streamsides, springs, marshes, ditches.

ARROYO WILLOW
Salix lasiolepis
WILLOW FAMILY

25′. Small tree, mostly shrubby. Leaves 5″, broadly lace-shaped, elliptical, pointed at tip, margins entire to finely toothed. Flowers yellow to yellow-green; in 3″ catkins; bloom Feb.–May. **HABITAT** Springs, marshes, streamsides, ditches.

Agaves and Cacti

Agaves (including yuccas) and cacti are xerophytes (plants adapted to arid conditions). Water conservation has probably been the greatest selective pressure to shape the unique architecture of these plants. Cacti are all placed in the Cactaceae family, a group native to the New World. Yuccas and agaves have been variously placed in different families; for the purposes of this guide, agaves and yuccas have been classified in the Agavaceae family.

Cacti are easily separated from yuccas and agaves. The long, fibrous leaves of yuccas and agaves form the most conspicuous portion of the plant. Cacti have sharp leaves and usually rigid spines, formed to diminish the surface area from which water could potentially be lost. Spines are found within definite, circumscribed areas

Claret Cup Cactus blossoms

known as *areoles*. Each areole is above a leaf or the potential position of a leaf. A spine cluster is actually a modified, condensed lateral branch that never elongates, its leaves converting to spines. Most cacti also have ribs or knobs of tissue that allow the stem to swell or contract as water is stored or lost. Prickly-pears and chollas also possess numerous *glochids*, barbed hairs located at the base of spine clusters. These small glochids may often be more dangerous than spines to desert vistors because they are easily overlooked.

Members of these families typically produce shallow root systems in order to enable absorption of large quantities of water during brief rains in which only superficial soil layers are moistened. These plants have a "skin" that is coated with a waxy layer to form an effective barrier that prevents water loss from the stem surface.

In order for photosynthesis to occur in these plants, carbon dioxide enters through microscopic pores covering the stem. Precious stored water also exits through these pores; in order to reduce water loss, the pores open at night when the carbon dioxide taken up is chemically stored as an organic acid. Throughout the following day, the carbon dioxide is chemically released from the acid and made available to the plant. This unique method of conducting photosynthesis is called Crassulacean Acid Metabolism.

Flowers in the agave and cactus families are generally quite large and striking. The flowers possess regular symmetry and the normal flower parts are all present. (Illustrations of flower types and parts, and a discussion of the structure and function of flowers, are on pages 144–148.) Cactus flowers have many greenish sepals that surround and intergrade with numerous colored petals. Next to the petals are numerous stamens, the pollen-bearing portion of the flower. At the very center of the flower are four to eight stigmas placed atop a stalk-like style. Yuccas have six cream to white perianth (the floral structure composed of the calyx and corolla) segments, and agaves produce yellow flowers on very tall stalks; both have six stamens and a three-lobed stigma. The ovule-producing ovary of cacti and agaves is found at the base of the petals and sepals and is therefore classified as inferior; yuccas have a superior ovary. The cactus fruit that develops is considered to be a berry, but it varies from juicy to dry and leathery; areoles, glochids, and spines generally cloak the fruit. A capsule fruit typifies both agaves and yuccas.

PARRY'S AGAVE

Agave parryi

AGAVE FAMILY

18″. Leaf blades 16″, blue-green, narrow, concave on upper surface; with terminal spine, lateral prickles; form rosettes. Flowers yellow, on 12′ stalk; bloom June–Aug. Cultivated as an ornamental; utilized for food and fiber by Native Americans. **HABITAT** Arid, rocky slopes in mixed shrub to pinyon-juniper communities. **RANGE** AZ, NM.

UTAH AGAVE

Agave utahensis

AGAVE FAMILY

12″. Leaf blades 14″, narrow; with terminal spine, lateral prickles; form rosettes. Flowers yellow, on 12′ stalk; bloom May–Aug.; plant dies after flowering. Utilized for food and as source of the beverage mescal by Native Americans. **HABITAT** Canyons, rocky slopes (generally limestone) in mixed shrub to pinyon-juniper communities. **RANGE** UT, NV, AZ.

DESERT SPOON

"Sotol"

Dasylirion wheeleri

AGAVE FAMILY

3′. Leaf blades 3′, narrow; with lateral, forward-curving teeth; form rosettes. Flowers yellow, on 14′ stalk; bloom May–Aug. Utilized for food, beverage, and to construct baskets by Native Americans. **HABITAT** Canyons, rocky, gravelly slopes in mixed shrub to pinyon-juniper communities, generally limestone. **RANGE** AZ, NM.

BEARGRASS NOLINA
Nolina microcarpa
AGAVE FAMILY

4′. Lacks conspicuous stem. Leaf blades 4′, narrow; tips split into fibers. Flowers tiny, yellow, on 3′ stalk; bloom May–June. Not a true grass; utilized to construct baskets by Native Americans. **HABITAT** Arid, open rocky slopes, dry plains. **RANGE** AZ, NM.

BANANA YUCCA
Yucca baccata
AGAVE FAMILY

3′. Stemless. Leaves 30″, blue-green, narrow; concave on upper surface; with coarse marginal filaments; form large rosettes. Flowers marked with brownish red on outside, cream on inside; on 24″ stalk; bloom Apr.–July. Pollination accomplished by small, nocturnal moths. **HABITAT** Arid, open rocky slopes, Joshua Tree, Blackbrush, pinyon-juniper woods.

JOSHUA TREE
Yucca brevifolia
AGAVE FAMILY

40′. Crown broad, open; usu. branched, forking; trunk short, stout. Leaves 12″, serrate margins, spine-tipped; in rosettes at stem tips; evergreen; gray, dead leaves cloak branches. Flowers 3″, creamy, in 18″ cluster; bloom Mar.–May (in favorable years). Fruit 4″, oval-shaped, green turning brown; numerous flat, black seeds at maturity. A dominant and conspicuous plant; indicator of Mojave Desert. **HABITAT** Arid, open sandy flats, rocky slopes. **RANGE** UT, NV, AZ.

SOAPTREE YUCCA

Yucca elata

AGAVE FAMILY

15′. Unbranched or occ. few-branched, palm-like. Leaves 24″, narrow, flexible, linear, with fibers along margins. Flowers 2″, white; in clusters on 6′ stalk; bloom May–July. Utilized for food, fiber, and soap by Native Americans. **HABITAT** Arid, open sandy plains, rocky slopes, tablelands. **RANGE** UT, AZ, NM.

GIANT SAGUARO

Carnegiea gigantea

CACTUS FAMILY

40′. Trunk columnar, massive, simple- or few-branched; trunk and stems with 12–25 lengthwise ribs. Spines 2″, in clusters of 10–25 on ribs. Flowers 6″, white, near ends of stems; open at night; bloom May–June. Fruit plump; outside green, inside red. Fruit was important source of food for Native Americans. AZ state flower; indicator of Sonoran Desert; cultivated in warm regions. **HABITAT** Hills, plains, slopes in well-drained areas. **RANGE** AZ.

ORGAN PIPE CACTUS

Cereus thurberi

CACTUS FAMILY

20′. Trunk columnar, branched from base; stems with 12–18 lengthwise ribs. Spines 1½″. Flowers 3″, white, outer petals reddish, near stem apex; open at night; bloom May–July. Fruit 3″, globular, with red pulp. **HABITAT** Rocky hills, plains, slopes in well-drained areas. **RANGE** AZ.

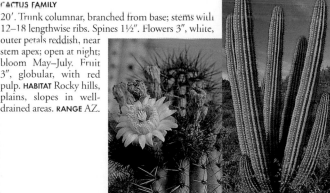

SENITA CACTUS
Cereus schottii
CACTUS FAMILY

16′. Trunk columnar, branched from base; stems with 4–7 lengthwise ribs. Spines 2″, dense, on upper flower-bearing portions of stems, giving the plant its distinctive shaggy appearance. Flowers 1½″, white to pink, near ends of stems; open at night; bloom Apr.–Aug. Fruit 1½″, red, plump, egg-shaped; mature in late summer. Found in U.S. only at Organ Pipe Cactus N.M. **HABITAT** Hills, plains, slopes in well-drained areas. **RANGE** s AZ.

ENGELMANN'S HEDGEHOG
Echinocereus engelmannii
CACTUS FAMILY

H 24″; W 3′. Stems spiny, cylindrical, clustered in mounds. Main spines 2″. Flowers 3″, magenta to purple, funnel-shaped; bloom Feb.–May. **CAUTION** Spines are extremely sharp. **HABITAT** Rocky slopes, drained areas in Creosote Bush, Blackbrush, pinyon-juniper communities. **RANGE** UT, NV, AZ.

CLARET-CUP CACTUS
Echinocereus triglochidiatus
CACTUS FAMILY

10″. Ribbed; forms large, dense mounds. Spines 1″, usu. gray; in clusters on ribs. Flowers 3″, red to orange, funnel-shaped; bloom Apr.–July. Fruit 1″, pink to red, egg-shaped, initially spiny. **HABITAT** Rocky slopes, canyons, drained areas in mixed shrub communities, pinyon-juniper woods.

BEEHIVE CACTUS
Escobaria (Coryphantha) vivipara
CACTUS FAMILY

6″. Stems usu. solitary, cylindrical. Spines 1″, densely cover stem; central spines white, radial spines white with dark tip. Flowers 1¼″, pink, magenta, or purple to straw-yellow; bloom May–July. **HABITAT** Limestone, rocky, sandy, drained areas in Creosote Bush or Blackbrush communities, pinyon-juniper woods.

CALIFORNIA BARREL CACTUS
Ferocactus cylindraceus (acanthodes)
CACTUS FAMILY

5′; occ. to 10′. Young stems globose, more cylindrical at maturity, with 18–30 thick, prominent ribs. Spines dense; 1–4 central spines, 3″, yellowish or reddish, flattened, curved but not hooked, ringed; 6–12 radial spines 1½″, white. Flowers 2½″, yellow; bloom Apr.–July. Fruit 1½″, yellow, scaly. **HABITAT** Rocky slopes, canyons, cliffs, flats in drained areas, mixed shrub communities, pinyon-juniper woods. **RANGE** UT, NV, AZ..

FISHHOOK CACTUS
"Pincushion Cactus"
Mammillaria milleri (microcarpa)
CACTUS FAMILY

6″. Young stem globose, more cylindrical at maturity; single or clumped. Central spines ½″, 1–3, reddish to black, straight, longest hooked; radial spines ¼″, 15–30, tan to red. Flowers 1″, pink; bloom June–July. Fruit 1″, bright red, smooth; persistent. **HABITAT** Rock and cliff crevices, rocky hills, slopes. **RANGE** AZ, NM. The very similar *M. tetrancistra*, which is also commonly called Fishhook Cactus, has a corky appendage on the seeds and is found in UT, NV.

BUCKHORN CHOLLA
Opuntia acanthocarpa
CACTUS FAMILY

5′; occ. to 10′. Open, branching shrub. Stem joints 18″, thick. Spines 1½″, 6–20 per areole. Flowers 2½″, yellow-orange to copper; bloom Apr.–May. Fruit 1″, dry, spiny. **HABITAT** Well-drained rocky to sandy areas, plains, slopes, hillsides in Creosote Bush communities to pinyon-juniper woods. **RANGE** UT, NV, AZ.

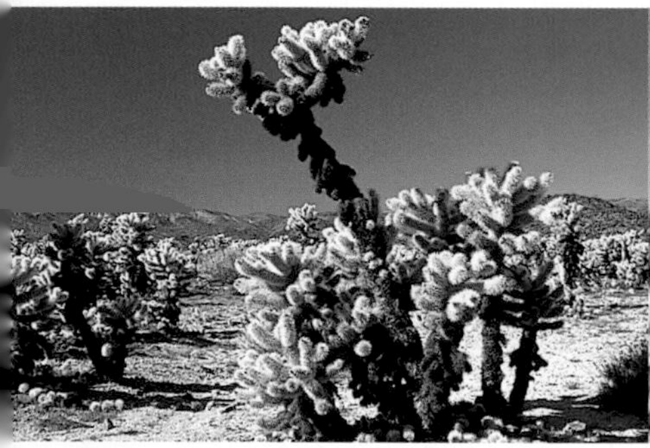

TEDDYBEAR CHOLLA
Opuntia bigelovii
CACTUS FAMILY

5′. Tree-like, with single trunk-like stem and short, fuzzy-looking branches. Stem joints 2″, cylindrical; densely covered with straw-colored, 1″ spines; lower branches on stem turn black. Flowers 1½″, with pale yellow petals, green stamens; rarely encountered; bloom Feb.–May. Propagates mainly via easily detached, spiny joints. **CAUTION** Spiny joints readily attach to passersby. **HABITAT** Well-drained rocky to sandy areas, alluvial plains, slopes, hillsides in low-elev. desert shrub communities. **RANGE** NV, AZ.

BEAVERTAIL PRICKLY-PEAR
Opuntia basilaris
CACTUS FAMILY

15″. Stems form sprawling clumps of flat, pad-like, gray to lavender joints. Lacking large spines; glochids tiny. Flowers 3″, pink-magenta, numerous petals, showy; bloom Mar.–June. **CAUTION** Glochids difficult to remove from skin. **HABITAT** Sandy to gravelly areas, alluvial plains, bajadas, rocky slopes, Creosote Bush communities to pinyon-juniper woods. **RANGE** UT, NV, AZ.

PANCAKE PRICKLY-PEAR
Opuntia chlorotica
CACTUS FAMILY

6′. Often with a trunk. Stem joints 8″, flattened; covered with golden, ¼″ glochids. Spines 2″, yellow, reflexed, 3–8 per areole. Flowers 2½″, yellow; bloom Apr.–June. Fruit 2½″, red, juicy. **HABITAT** Cliff crevices, among boulders, rocky hillsides, low-elev. mixed shrub communities to pinyon-juniper woods.

PORCUPINE PRICKLY-PEAR
Opuntia erinacea
CACTUS FAMILY

H 15″; W 3′. Clump-forming. Stem joints 8″, flattened. Spines 5″, turn downward (curve and twist in some varieties), 1–10 per areole. Flowers 2½″, rose to yellow; bloom Mar.–June. Fruit 1½″, green with reddish tint, drying tan; dry and spiny at maturity. **HABITAT** Rocky hillsides, low-elev. mixed shrub communities to pinyon-juniper, Ponderosa Pine woods.

DESERT CHRISTMAS CACTUS
Opuntia leptocaulis
CACTUS FAMILY

6′. Many slender, cylindrical branches. Stem joints vary from 5″ to 16″. Spines 1½″, sparse to nearly spineless. Flowers 1″, green-yellow; bloom May–June. Fruit ¾″, red, fleshy; spineless but with some glochids. **HABITAT** Sandy to gravelly areas, alluvial plains, bajadas. **RANGE** AZ, NM.

DESERT PRICKLY-PEAR
Opuntia phaeacantha
CACTUS FAMILY

H 3′; W 5′. Colony-forming. Stem joints 18″, bluish green, yellow in dry areas, flattened. Spines 24″, 1–6 per areole. Flowers 3″, yellow to red; bloom Apr.–June. Fruit 1½″, red-purple, fleshy at maturity; spineless but covered with glochids. **HABITAT** Among boulders, rocky hillsides, sandy areas, low-elev. mixed shrub communities to pinyon-juniper and Ponderosa Pine woods.

DEVIL CHOLLA
Opuntia parishii (stanleyi)
CACTUS FAMILY

8″. Clump-forming. Stem joints 3″, club-shaped. Spines 1½″, dagger-like, flattened. Flowers 2½″, yellow; bloom Mar.–June. Fruit 2″, yellow, fleshy; spineless but with numerous glochids. **HABITAT** Sandy flats in Joshua Tree woods, grasslands, desert shrub communities. **RANGE** NV, AZ, NM.

PLAINS PRICKLY-PEAR
Opuntia polyacantha
CACTUS FAMILY

H 3′; W 5′. Colony-forming. Stem joints 7″, bluish green, flattened. Spines 1½″, 6–10 per areole. Flowers 2½″, yellow, bronze, pink, or violet; bloom May–July. Fruit 1½″, dry at maturity. Hybridizes with many other species of the subgenus *Opuntia*. **HABITAT** Among boulders, rocky hillsides, low elev. mixed shrub communities to pinyon-juniper, Ponderosa Pine woods.

WHIPPLE CHOLLA
Opuntia whipplei
CACTUS FAMILY

24″. Low-growing shrub; occ. mat-forming. Stem joints 6″, thick. Spines 1″, 4–10 per areole. Flowers 1½″, yellow to yellow-green; bloom Mar–Oct. Fruit 1″, yellow, fleshy; covered with glochids. **HABITAT** Mixed shrub, grasslands, pinyon-juniper communities.

DESERT NIGHT-BLOOMING CEREUS
"Reina de la Noche"
Peniocereus greggii
CACTUS FAMILY

4′. Stems 4′, slender, 4–6 ribbed; arising from underground fleshy, turnip-like tuber (reported to weigh 80–85 lb). Radial spines ¼″, 6–11; central spines ½″, solitary. Flowers 7″, white; open at night; bloom June–July. Fruit 2½″, orange-red, fleshy. Tubers were used as food by some Native American groups. **HABITAT** Rocky hillsides and plains in Creosote Bush, mesquite, paloverde communities. **RANGE** AZ, NM.

Leaf Shapes

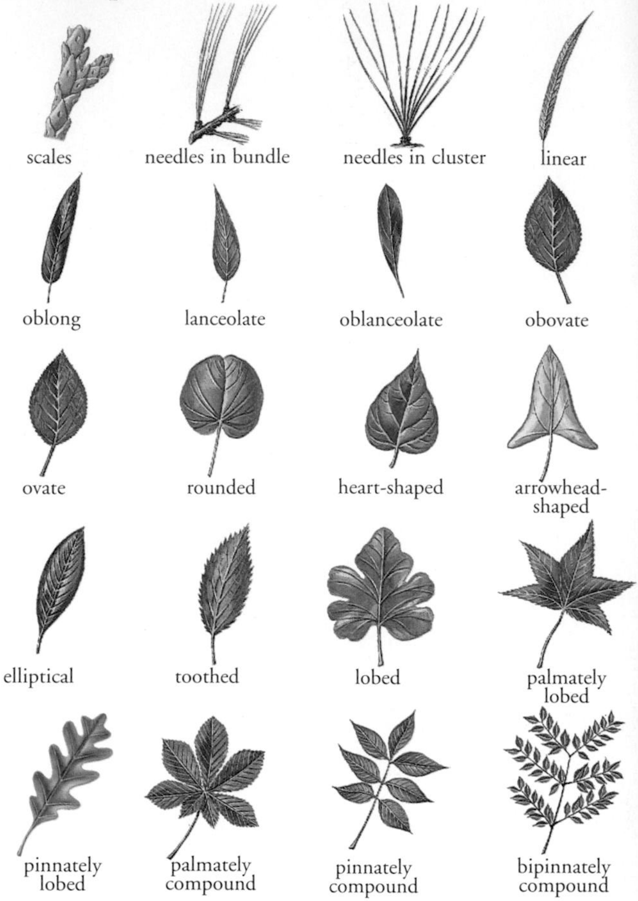
scales
needles in bundle
needles in cluster
linear
oblong
lanceolate
oblanceolate
obovate
ovate
rounded
heart-shaped
arrowhead-shaped
elliptical
toothed
lobed
palmately lobed
pinnately lobed
palmately compound
pinnately compound
bipinnately compound

Leaf Arrangements

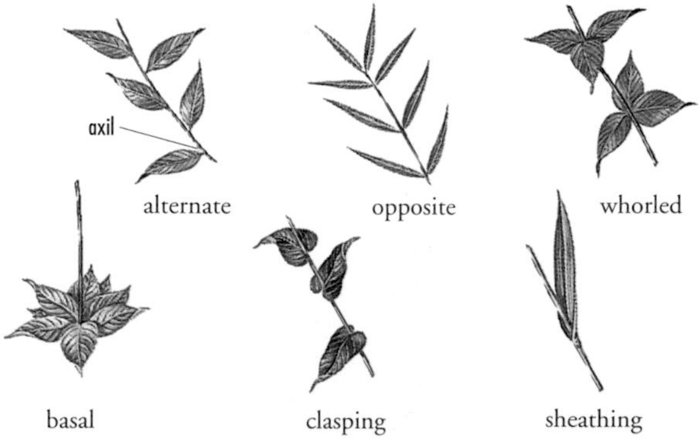
axil
alternate
opposite
whorled
basal
clasping
sheathing

Flower Types

regular

irregular

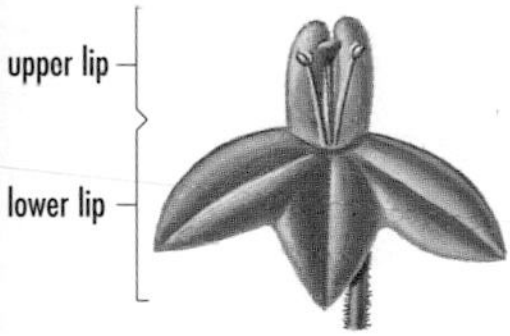

two-lipped

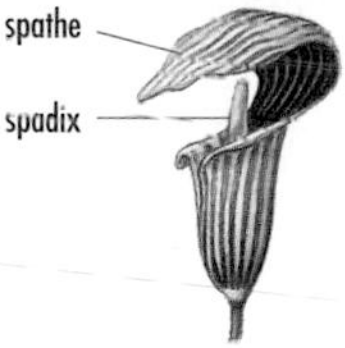

arum

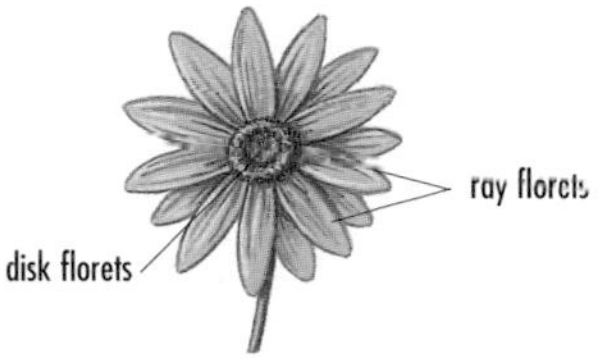

composite

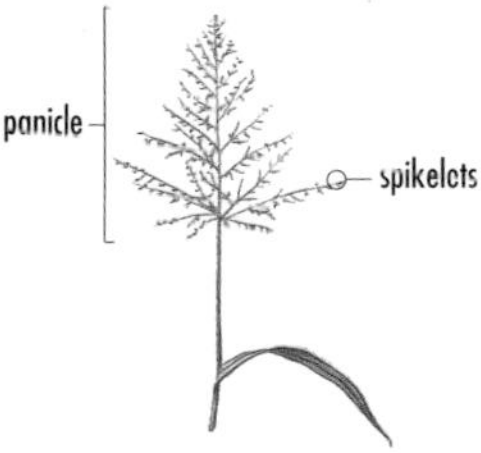

grass

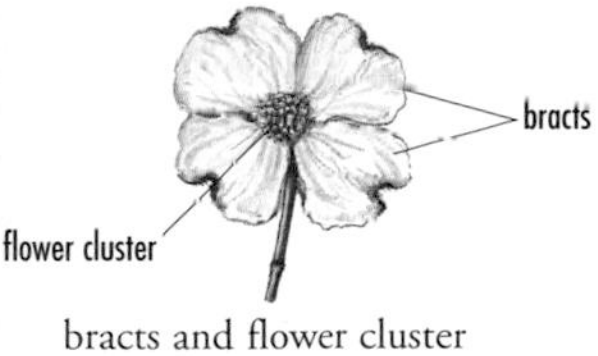

bracts and flower cluster

catkin

Flower Cluster Types

elongated

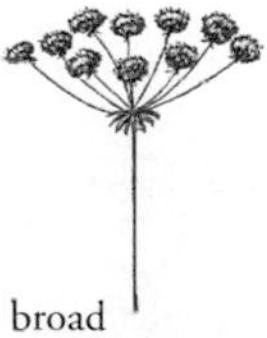

broad

branching

Wildflowers

Southwest flora is composed of several thousand species of flowering plants in approximately 160 families. This section covers a broad selection of common and interesting wildflowers. The term "wildflower" has many connotations: one person's wildflower is another person's weed—a plant growing where it's not wanted. For the purposes of this field guide, wildflowers are defined as relatively small, noncultivated flowering plants that die back after each growing season.

The wildflowers included here are mainly herbaceous (nonwoody); some are woody but too small to be placed with the shrubs; a few have a woody base with herbaceous stems. These plants come in numerous forms. Many have a single, delicate, unbranched, erect stem terminated by a single flower or a flower cluster. Some have very robust stems, others are many-branched and shrubby. In some, the stems trail along the ground, sometimes spreading by runners. Those known as "vines" have a long, slender, often flexible stem that either trails on the ground or climbs, sometimes with tendrils to hold it in place. Plants of the grass family have erect, jointed stems and blade-like leaves; some other plants, such as rushes and sedges, are described as grass-like because they have narrow leaves and slender stems.

Wildflowers, like all plants, are identified by features of their flowers. The flowers or flower clusters may be borne in the leaf axils along the main stem or on branches off the stem. Modified leaves called *bracts* are often situated at the base of the flower or flower cluster. Flowers are typically composed of four sets, or whorls, of modified leaves. The outermost set in a "complete" flower is the typically green, leaf-like *sepals* (known collectively as the *calyx*) that protect the often colorful second set—the *petals.* (The inner whorl of separate or fused petals is known as the *corolla.*) The next set is the *stamens,* the "male" part of the flower, each consisting of pollen sacs *(anthers)* typically on a stalk *(filament).* The innermost set is the "female" part of the flower, with one or more *pistils,* each of which typically has a swollen base, the *ovary* (containing the ovules that after fertilization become the seeds), and a stalk *(style)* topped by the pollen-collecting *stigma.* The fruit develops from the ovary, forming a covering for the seed or seeds. The form of the fruit varies from species to species. Members of the aster family (often called the sunflower family) have a *pappus,* an appendage or tuft of appendages that crowns the ovary or fruit and functions in the dispersal of the fruit; this pappus is a modified calyx.

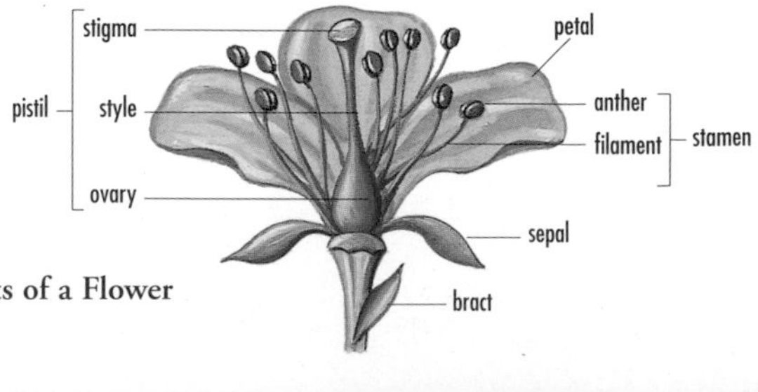

Parts of a Flower

Although many plants have flowers with both stamens and pistils, some species have unisexual flowers that may occur on the same or separate plants. Many wind-pollinated species, such as grasses, sedges, and cattails, have reduced flowers that lack petals and/or sepals. These wind-pollinated flowers tend to be inconspicuous, unlike flowers that need to attract insects for pollination. Seed dispersal is often aided by animals: migrating birds and other animals eat fruit or seeds whole and disperse seeds in their droppings; fruits that are bur-like or covered with various kinds of sticky hairs attach to animals on contact and later fall off or are shed along with fur. Plants such as dandelions bear tiny fruits that have parachute-like tops and are carried by the wind far from the parent plant.

Flowers of a few representative types are illustrated on page 145. Members of the buttercup and lily families are *regular* flowers; their parts radiate in a wheel-like (radially symmetrical) fashion. Pea and orchid flowers are considered *irregular* (bilaterally symmetrical); the irregular pea-flowers have one broad upper petal, two lateral petals, and two joined bottom petals. Many plants in the mint and snapdragon families have tubular, *two-lipped* flowers. The *composite* "flower" of the daisy or aster is actually a head of many flowers; tiny tubular *disk florets* form a disk in the center, encircled by petal-like *ray florets.* (Dandelions have flower heads made up of all ray florets; true thistles have flower heads of all disk florets.) Grasses have tiny, reduced florets. Each floret is composed of an outer *lemma* and an inner *palea* that envelope the stamens and pistil. The florets are organized in overlapping arrangements called *spikelets.* Each spikelet has a pair of bract-like *glumes* at the base. Spikelets typically form a larger, often plume-like arrangement called a *panicle* or *spike.*

The "flower" of the four-o'clock family consists of a dense head of tiny flowers encircled by several large, petal-like bracts. What resembles a single flower is actually a cluster of many tiny flowers. The tiny unisexual flowers of oaks, willows, and numerous other species of trees and shrubs are clustered into slender pendulous spikes called *catkins.* Many plants bear flowers in clusters along or atop the stems or branches. Flower clusters take many forms, such as small round bunches, elongated spikes, feathery plumes, and broad, flat-topped, or branching arrangements.

Unless otherwise noted, in the accounts that follow, sizes given are typical heights of mature specimens.

Southwest Bloom Times

In the deserts of the Southwest region, unlike most of the United States and Canada, wildflowers can be found year-round. However, the peak of the wildflower season varies greatly with latitude and elevation and from year to year.

At low elevations, peak bloom time is generally April and May, ending with the approach of summer and the long dry season. In more southern areas, peak bloom time is earlier: mid-March to early April at higher elevations. These peak times vary depending on average daily temperatures and the amount and timing of rainfall. In years when the first rains fall in October and are followed by a mild winter, flowers may bloom up to a month earlier, whereas in years of little rainfall, desert wildflower bloom may be spotty or nonexistent. In years with numerous late-summer desert thunderstorms, such as in southern New Mexico, there may be a second bloom season that extends through October. During this rather unique and sometimes spectacular fall bloom, shrubs flower once again and summer wildflowers abound; at such times the desert becomes even more colorful as the late rains also trigger a second butterfly breeding season.

In the lower montane zone and higher, there is snow in winter and the seasons resemble those of the northeastern United States. Flowers therefore do not bloom in earnest until summer. July and August is the mountain bloom time for the many red tubular flowers—such as Red Columbine, Scarlet Monkeyflower, and Scarlet Gilia—favored by hummingbirds migrating south through the area at that time of year.

FRINGED AMARANTH
Amaranthus fimbriatus
AMARANTH FAMILY

24″. Flowers in axillary clusters, with 12″ terminal spike-like cluster; sepals of female flowers fan-shaped, fringe-tipped. Stems red, erect. Leaves linear or narrowly lanceolate. Abundant after plentiful summer rains. **BLOOMS** Aug.–Oct. **HABITAT** Sandy or fine gravels, washes, benches, plains.

YARROW
Achillea millefolium
ASTER FAMILY

30″. Flowers ½″; ray florets white or pink; disk florets creamy-white; in dense flat clusters. Stem single, fibrous. Leaves narrow, fern-like, soft, finely pinnately divided into numerous segments; fragrant when crushed. Widely distributed. **BLOOMS** May–Sept. **HABITAT** Sagebrush to coniferous woods, high-mtn. meadows, alpine communities.

ACOURTIA
"Fluffroot"
Acourtia wrightii
ASTER FAMILY

4′ Glandular-stalked; basal buds hairy. Flowers ½″, numerous; disk florets rose-purple, ray florets lacking, 2-lipped; pappus of bristles. Leaves 5″, alternate, ovate to lanceolate, broad at base, clasping, margins minutely spiny-toothed. **BLOOMS** Jan.–Nov. **HABITAT** Foothills, rocky slopes, canyons in Creosote Bush, pinyon-juniper communities.

RUSSIAN KNAPWEED
Acroptilon (Centaurea) repens
ASTER FAMILY

3′. From underground stems; cobwebby-hairy. Flowers ½″; ray florets white to blue; pappus of somewhat feathery bristles. Leaves 3″, oblong to linear, entire to pinnately lobed, smooth to tooth margined. Introduced from Eurasia; noxious weed. **BLOOMS** May–Oct. **HABITAT** Fields, lots, roadside ditches.

ORANGE MOUNTAIN DANDELION
Agoseris aurantiaca
ASTER FAMILY

20″. Dandelion-like. Flowers 1″, coppery-orange, 1 per stem. Stems unbranched; sap milky. Leaves 12″, lanceolate, very slender, unlobed or with few pairs of slight lobes, in basal cluster. **BLOOMS** June–Sept. **HABITAT** Grassy slopes, meadows, mixed shrub, aspen, coniferous mtn. woods.

PALE MOUNTAIN DANDELION
Agoseris glauca
ASTER FAMILY

17″; less than 6″ in alpine zone. Flowers ¾″; ray florets pale yellow, dry pinkish, waxy; 1 per stem. Stems unbranched, milky-juiced. Leaves lanceolate, sometimes wavy-edged. Seed heads dandelion-like. **BLOOMS** May–Oct. **HABITAT** Arid, open slopes, streamsides, moist meadows, sagebrush, coniferous woods, alpine communities in foothills and mtns.

ROSY PUSSYTOES
Antennaria microphylla (rosea)
ASTER FAMILY

10″. Slender stalk above leafy mat. Flowers tiny tufts of minute white bristles, surrounded by pink- or white-tipped, greenish-based papery bracts; in rounded, 1″ clusters. Leaves oblanceolate, whitish-wooly, mostly basal. **BLOOMS** May–Aug. **HABITAT** Dry, open areas, meadows, open woods.

ROCKY MOUNTAIN PUSSYTOES
Antennaria parvifolia (aprica)
ASTER FAMILY

6″. Short, stout stalk above leafy mat. Flowers tiny tufts of minute white bristles, surrounded by white-tipped papery bracts; in rounded, 1″ clusters. Leaves oblanceolate, whitish-wooly, mostly basal. **BLOOMS** May–Aug. **HABITAT** Dry, open rocky to gravelly areas, meadows, hillsides, mtn. slopes, sagebrush, mixed shrub, coniferous woods.

HEARTLEAF ARNICA
Arnica cordifolia
ASTER FAMILY

12"; 6" in alpine zone. Flowers 2½"; ray florets yellow, 8–15. Leaves heart-shaped, toothed; 2–4 opposite pairs per stem, lowest pair long-stalked; often ovate and untoothed on alpine variety. **BLOOMS** May–Aug. **HABITAT** Streamsides, moist, shaded areas in coniferous woods, dry, open areas in sagebrush, high-mtn. meadows, alpine communities.

BIGELOW'S ASTER
Aster bigelovii
ASTER FAMILY

3′. Glandular. Flowers ¼", ray florets purple, disk florets yellow; pappus of bristles. Leaves 4", lanceolate to oblong, entire or margins spiny-toothed. **BLOOMS** Mar.–Nov. **HABITAT** Mtn. areas, mixed shrub communities, woodland openings, alpine meadows. **RANGE** UT, AZ, NM.

RAGLEAF BAHIA
"Yellow Ragweed" "Cutleaf"
Bahia dissecta
ASTER FAMILY

3′. Finely hairy; upper portion glandular-stalked. Flowers ½"; ray florets yellow; pappus lacking; numerous. Leaves 4", alternate, 2–3 times pinnately compound. **BLOOMS** Aug.–Oct. **HABITAT** Dry, sandy, gravelly, rocky slopes of sagebrush, mixed shrub communities, coniferous woods, open meadows.

DESERT MARIGOLD
Baileya multiradiata
ASTER FAMILY

24". Erect. Flowers ½", yellow-orange; oblong ray florets persist and become papery. Stems slender, branching in lower half. Upper leaves linear; lower leaves deeply pinnately lobed. **BLOOMS** Mar.–Nov. **HABITAT** Sandy, gravelly, open areas, plains, slopes, washes, roadsides with Creosote Bush, Blackbrush, pinyon-juniper communities.

WOOLY MARIGOLD
Baileya pleniradiata
ASTER FAMILY

15". Leafy above and below; covered with wooly hairs. Flowers yellow-orange; ½", oblong ray florets persist and become papery; on 4" stalks. Stems slender; branching in lower half. Upper leaves linear; lower leaves deeply pinnately lobed. **BLOOMS** Feb.–Nov. **HABITAT** Plains, slopes, washes, sandy roadsides, dunes, Creosote Bush, Blackbrush, sagebrush, pinyon-juniper communities. **RANGE** UT, NV, AZ.

DUSTY MAIDEN

Chaenactis douglasii

ASTER FAMILY

20″; 5″ at high elevs. Flowers ¾″; ray florets white to pinkish; disk florets 5-lobed, 50–70; in flat clusters. Leaves fern-like, white wooly, thick. Suggestive of yarrow but lacks fragrance. **BLOOMS** May–Oct. **HABITAT** Dry, gravelly, sandy, open areas on slopes, flats, washes, canyons, pinyon-juniper woods to alpine communities.

NEW MEXICAN THISTLE

Cirsium neomexicanum

ASTER FAMILY

7′. Flowers 2½″; ray florets white, lavender, or pink. Leaves 10″, pinnately cleft, spiny-toothed or cobwebby-hairy, in basal rosettes; lower stem leaves 14″, reduced upward in size, spiny wing-margined at clasping base. **BLOOMS** Mar.–Sept. **HABITAT** Arid canyons, washes, slopes, Creosote Bush to pinyon-juniper communities.

ORANGE SNEEZEWEED

Dugaldia hoopesii

ASTER FAMILY

3′. Sometimes hairy. Flowers 1″, yellow to orange; pappus of scales. Leaves 12″, ovate to lanceolate, thick, simple, alternate, entire, clasping, basal. **BLOOMS** June–Sept. **HABITAT** Open areas in moist meadows, streamsides, sagebrush, mixed shrub, coniferous woods.

GREAT BASIN RAYLESS FLEABANE

Erigeron aphanactis

ASTER FAMILY

10″. Stiff-hairy, spreading. Flowers ½″, disk florets yellow, ray florets lacking; pappus of bristles, with short, narrow scales. Basal leaves 3″, stalked, spatula-shaped; smaller or lacking on stem. **BLOOMS** May–July. **HABITAT** Arid, sandy, rocky slopes, plains, washes, sagebrush, pinyon-juniper, Ponderosa Pine communities.

SPREADING FLEABANE

Erigeron divergens

ASTER FAMILY

18″. Stiff-hairy, glandular, spreading. Flowers ½″; ray florets blue, pink, or white, numerous; disk florets yellow; pappus of bristles, with outer narrow, short scales. Basal leaves spatula-shaped; blade 1″, smaller on stem; on 2″ stalk. **BLOOMS** Feb.–Oct. **HABITAT** Arid, open slopes, plains, washes, mixed desert shrub, sagebrush, pinyon-juniper, Ponderosa Pine communities.

HAIRY FLEABANE
"Vernal Daisy"
Erigeron pumilus
ASTER FAMILY

18″. Hairy, glandular. Flowers ½″; ray florets pink, white, or purple, numerous; double pappus: inner bristles longer, outer bristles shorter or narrow scales. Basal leaves 3″, linear to lanceolate; stem leaves reduced in size. **BLOOMS** Apr.–Oct. **HABITAT** Arid, rocky, sandy slopes, plains, washes, Blackbrush, sagebrush, pinyon-juniper communities.

SHOWY FLEABANE
Erigeron speciosus
ASTER FAMILY

3′. From woody base or underground stem; clump- or thick patch-forming. Flowers 1″; ray florets blue or white, numerous; disk florets yellow; pappus of bristles, with shorter outer bristles. Basal leaves 4″, stalked, sometimes hairy; stem leaves stalkless, reduced in size. **BLOOMS** June–Oct. **HABITAT** Wooded areas in mtn. regions, subalpine meadows.

WOOLY DAISY
Eriophyllum wallacei
ASTER FAMILY

3″. Hairy-wooly. Flowers ½″; ray and disk florets yellow; pappus of scales, or none. Leaves spatula-shaped, alternate, entire or 3-lobed at tip. Sometimes so abundant as to carpet the ground yellow. **BLOOMS** Mar.–June. **HABITAT** Sandy to fine gravels, washes, plains, Creosote Bush, Blackbrush, Joshua Tree communities. **RANGE** NV, UT, AZ.

SLENDER BLANKETFLOWER
Gaillardia pinnatifida
ASTER FAMILY

18″. Hairy. Flowers 1″; ray florets yellow, reddish at bases; disk florets brownish- to reddish-purple; pappus of bristle-tipped scales; solitary on long, slender stalks. Leaves 6″, spatula-shaped, mostly at stem bases, pinnatified on stalks below, entire and smaller above. **BLOOMS** Apr.–Oct. **HABITAT** Arid, sandy, gravelly, open areas, washes, plains, slopes, roadsides in mixed shrub, pinyon-juniper communities.

FIREWHEEL BLANKETFLOWER
Gaillardia pulchella
ASTER FAMILY

18″. Hairy. Flowers 1½″; ray florets reddish purple with yellow tip; disk florets brownish- to reddish-purple, with bristle-tipped lobes; pappus of bristle-tipped scales; solitary on stalks. Leaves 4″, linear to oblong, entire to toothed. Commonly cultivated, sometimes escaping. **BLOOMS** Apr.–Sept. **HABITAT** Arid, sandy, gravelly slopes, flats, disturbed areas.

DESERT SUNFLOWER
Geraea canescens
ASTER FAMILY

23". Hairy, glandular-stalked. Flowers 2"; ray florets yellow, 10–20; disk florets yellow; pappus of 2 bristles; showy. Leaves 4", ovate, alternate, mostly entire or toothed, stalked below. Sometimes so abundant as to color hillsides yellow. **BLOOMS** Jan.–June. **HABITAT** Arid, open, sandy, gravelly flats, slopes, Creosote Bush communities. **RANGE** NV, UT, AZ.

CURLYCUP GUMWEED
Grindelia squarrosa
ASTER FAMILY

24". Flowers 1½", yellow; ray florets approx. 30; gummy, bulbous base with long down-curved bract tips. Leaves dark green, linear to oblong to elliptical, fine-toothed to smooth; clasping or basal. **CAUTION** Mildly toxic; used medicinally. **BLOOMS** June–Oct. **HABITAT** Arid, open, disturbed areas, overgrazed rangeland, fields, roadsides.

COMMON SUNFLOWER
Helianthus annuus
ASTER FAMILY

4′. Bristly-hairy. Flowers 5"; ray florets yellow, disk brown. Stems branched. Lower leaves heart-shaped, upper leaves elliptical. **BLOOMS** Mar.–Oct. Escapes cultivation. **HABITAT** Fields, roadsides, disturbed areas.

MANY-FLOWERED GOLDENEYE
Heliomeris (Viguiera) multiflora
ASTER FAMILY

3′. Many-stemmed. Flowers 1¼", yellow; ray florets 10–16; disk domed. Leaves linear to elliptical, finely hairy, rough; lower leaves opposite. **BLOOMS** May–Oct. **HABITAT** Dry, rocky slopes, flats, washes, sagebrush, pinyon-juniper, Ponderosa Pine communities.

HAIRY GOLDEN ASTER
Heterotheca (Chrysopsis) villosa
ASTER FAMILY

4′. Many-stemmed; erect to spreading. Flowers 1", golden yellow; ray florets approx. 16; numerous. Stems and leaves usu. coarsely hairy. Leaves oblanceolate, mainly on stem. **BLOOMS** May–Oct. **HABITAT** Dry, rocky, gravelly slopes, flats, washes, fissures and crevices in bedrock, low elevs. to pinyon-juniper woods.

HYALINEHERB
Hymenopappus filifolius
ASTER FAMILY

3′. Hairy-wooly. Flowers ¾″; disk florets yellow or white, ray florets lacking; pappus of 10–20 scales. Basal leaves 6″, twice pinnately cleft, ultimate segments linear; stem leaves alternate, reduced upward or lacking. **BLOOMS** May–Oct. **HABITAT** Arid areas, sandy, gravelly slopes, flats, rocky outcrops, Blackbrush, sagebrush communities to pinyon-juniper, oak, Ponderosa Pine woods.

STEMLESS HYMENOXYS
Hymenoxys acaulis
ASTER FAMILY

18″. Stemless. Flowers yellow; ray florets ¾″, 5–15; pappus of scales; solitary on leafless, 12″ stalks. Leaves linear or spatula-shaped, often soft-hairy, glandular, basal, entire. **BLOOMS** Apr.–Oct. **HABITAT** Arid, rocky slopes, ridges, plains in mixed desert shrub communities, pinyon-juniper, Ponderosa Pine woods, to above tree line.

COLORADO RUBBER-PLANT
Hymenoxys richardsonii
ASTER FAMILY

8″. From woody stem base; finely hairy, smooth or hairy-wooly at base or in leaf axils. Flowers ¾″; ray florets yellow, 5–15 or lacking; pappus of narrow, pointed scales. Leaves 6″, basal and on stem, divided into 3–7 linear segments. **BLOOMS** May–Sept. **HABITAT** Arid, sandy, rocky slopes, mixed desert shrub communities to pinyon-juniper, coniferous woods. **RANGE** UT, AZ, NM.

TIDYTIPS
Layia glandulosa
ASTER FAMILY

18″. Glandular-stalked. Flowers 1″; ray florets white, 3-lobed; disk florets yellow; pappus of feathery, bristle-like scales. Leaves alternate, linear to lanceolate, toothed below to entire above. **BLOOMS** Mar.–July. **HABITAT** Arid, mostly sandy slopes, washes, benches, flats, mixed desert shrub communities to pinyon-juniper woods.

HOARY ASTER
Machaeranthera canescens
ASTER FAMILY

24″. Branched; finely hairy, glandular. Flowers with 10–25 purple, ½″ ray florets; disk florets yellow; pappus of numerous bristles. Leaves 4″, spiny-toothed to entire, basal; stem leaves reduced in size. **BLOOMS** Apr.–Oct. **HABITAT** Arid mtn. areas, slopes, washes, roadsides, disturbed areas, Creosote Bush to pinyon-juniper, Ponderosa Pine woods.

DESERT DANDELION

Malacothrix glabrata

ASTER FAMILY

16". Carpet-forming. Flowers 2"; ray florets pale yellow, overlapping; young flowers have central red spot. Stems erect, smooth, hollow. Leaves pinnately divided into long, narrow lobes. Often so abundant as to paint low-elev. deserts yellow. **BLOOMS** Mar.–July. **HABITAT** Arid, sandy, fine gravelly plains, washes, Creosote Bush, sagebrush, Joshua Tree, pinyon-juniper communities. **RANGE** NV, UT, AZ.

DESERT STAR

Monoptilon bellidiforme

ASTER FAMILY

2". Low-growing, prostrate; with stiff, spreading hairs. Flowers ½"; ray florets white, fading light purple, approx. 20; disk florets yellow; pappus of minute scales and 1 feathery bristle. Leaves spatula-shaped, alternate, entire. **BLOOMS** Mar.–June. **HABITAT** Sandy, fine gravelly washes, benches, plains in Creosote Bush communities. **RANGE** NV, UT, AZ.

ROCK DAISY

Perityle emoryi

ASTER FAMILY

24". Usu. many-branched; finely hairy, glandular. Flowers ½"; ray florets white, approx. 10; disk florets yellow; pappus of scales and 1 longer bristle. Leaves heart-shaped, alternate, cleft-margined, stalked. **BLOOMS** Feb.–Oct. **HABITAT** Rocky slopes, cliffs, washes in Creosote Bush communities. **RANGE** NV, UT, AZ.

ROCK GOLDENROD

Petradoria pumila

ASTER FAMILY

12". Slightly woody at base; smooth, resinous. Flowers in flattened clusters; ray florets ¼", 1–3; disk florets approx. 5; pappus of fine bristles. Leaves 5", alternate, entire, somewhat leathery; linear to elliptical near base; reduced in size up stem. **BLOOMS** June–Sept. **HABITAT** Rock outcrops, limestone, rocky ridges, slopes, pinyon-juniper, Mountain Mahogany, Ponderosa Pine communities.

DESERT CHICORY

Rafinesquia neomexicana

ASTER FAMILY

24". Smooth, hollow-stemmed, milky-juiced. Flowers 1¾"; ray florets white, rose on outer surface, strap-shaped, 5-toothed; pappus of long, feathery bristles. Leaves 4", oblong, pinnately cleft, in basal rosettes; stem leaves reduced in size, clasping. **BLOOMS** Feb.–July. **HABITAT** Sandy, gravelly flats, slopes in Creosote Bush, Blackbrush, Joshua Tree communities.

MEXICAN HAT CONEFLOWER

Ratibida columnifera

ASTER FAMILY

3′. Leggy, in clumps. Flowers 2″; ray florets yellow, drooping, 3–7; disk 1½″, red-brown, columnar. Leaves pinnately narrow-lobed; all on stem. Introduced in UT from plains and prairies of central U.S. **BLOOMS** June–Nov. **HABITAT** Disturbed areas, roadsides, slopes, plains, open areas, sagebrush, Ponderosa Pine communities. **RANGE** UT, AZ, NM.

CUTLEAF CONEFLOWER

Rudbeckia laciniata

ASTER FAMILY

6′. Leggy, single-stemmed. Flowers 4″; ray florets yellow, somewhat droopy, 6–16; disk yellowish, domed. Leaves 8″, palmately narrow-lobed or compound. **BLOOMS** July–Sept. **HABITAT** Moist meadows, streamsides in aspen and coniferous woods. **RANGE** UT, AZ, NM. **Western Coneflower** *(R. occidentalis)* has 1½″, blackish, conical disk florets and lacks ray florets.

THREAD-LEAF GROUNDSEL

Senecio flaccidus (douglasii)

ASTER FAMILY

6′. Woody at base; felty-hairy. Flowers yellow; ray florets ½″, 10–15 yellow; pappus of soft, white bristles. Leaves 5″, pinnately cleft into linear segments. **BLOOMS** Year-round. **HABITAT** Wash gravels, rocky slopes, canyons, Creosote Bush, sagebrush, pinyon-juniper communities.

CANADA GOLDENROD

Solidago canadensis

ASTER FAMILY

6′. Thicket-forming. Flowers tiny, golden, numerous; pyramidal clusters form dense, branching, 5″ plume atop each minutely hairy stem. Leaves lanceolate, 3-veined, crowded. **BLOOMS** July–Oct. **HABITAT** Dry to moist areas, open to wooded slopes, plains, seeps, bottomlands, streamsides, moist meadows.

COMMON DANDELION

Taraxacum officinale

ASTER FAMILY

12″. Flowers 1½″; ray florets tiny, yellow, numerous; mature into fluffy, white, globular seed balls. Stems hollow; sap milky. Leaves lanceolate, toothed, lobed, in basal rosettes. **BLOOMS** Apr.–Dec. **HABITAT** Disturbed areas, lawns, meadows, fields.

NAVAJO TEA

"Hopi Tea"

Thelesperma megapotamicum

ASTER FAMILY

30". Flowers ½"; disk florets yellow to brownish; ray florets lacking; pappus of 2 bristles. Leaves opposite, 1–2 times pinnately divided into few, linear segments. **BLOOMS** May–Oct. **HABITAT** Open slopes, plains, mixed desert shrub, woodland communities. **RANGE** UT, AZ, NM.

STEMLESS DAISY

Townsendia exscapa

ASTER FAMILY

2". Stemless. Flowers 1¼"; ray florets white or pink, disk florets yellow; pappus of capillary bristles. Leaves linear or spatula-shaped, basal. **BLOOMS** Apr.–Aug. **HABITAT** Dry, open slopes, plains in sagebrush, pinyon-juniper, Ponderosa Pine communities.

YELLOW SALSIFY

Tragopogon dubius

ASTER FAMILY

30". Dandelion-like. Flowers 2", yellow; with narrow, long-pointed bracts; fold up in midday heat; seed heads huge. Stems branched, milky-juiced. Leaves grass-like, clasping. Introduced from Europe. **BLOOMS** May–Sept. **HABITAT** Disturbed areas, fields, meadows, roadsides.

GOLDEN CROWNBEARD

Verbesina encelioides

ASTER FAMILY

3′. Grayish, covered by fine, stiff hairs. Flowers 1¼"; ray florets golden-yellow, 3-cleft; pappus of 2 slender bristles. Leaves 4", triangular, toothed, stalked; opposite below, alternate above. **BLOOMS** Apr.–Nov. **HABITAT** Disturbed areas, roadsides, fields, sagebrush, pinyon-juniper, Ponderosa Pine woods.

COCKLEBUR

Xanthium strumarium

ASTER FAMILY

3′. Flowers tiny, greenish. Stems coarse, red- or black-spotted. Leaves triangular to heart-shaped, usu. 3-lobed and toothed. Egg-shaped seedpods ("porcupine eggs") have numerous tiny, hooked barbs. **BLOOMS** Apr.–Oct. **HABITAT** Moist, disturbed areas, cultivated areas, ditches, streambeds.

PRAIRIE ZINNIA
Zinnia grandiflora
ASTER FAMILY

8″. Branched; finely rough-hairy. Flowers with ¾″ yellow ray florets, often red at bases, drooping; disk florets red. Leaves entire, linear, opposite. **BLOOMS** May–Oct. **HABITAT** Arid hills, slopes, plains, sagebrush, grasslands, roadsides. **RANGE** AZ, NM.

PARRY'S BELLFLOWER
Campanula parryi
BELLFLOWER FAMILY

15″. From slender roots; erect-stemmed. Flowers 1″; corollas blue to purple; bell-shaped; usu. borne singly (but up to 3). Leaves linear to narrowly lanceolate, entire or small-toothed; stiff hairs on margins of leaf stalk, basal portion of blade. Fruit many-seeded capsules. **BLOOMS** July–Sept. **HABITAT** High-elev. moist areas, meadows, streamsides, coniferous woods. **RANGE** UT, AZ, NM.

HAREBELL
"Bluebells-of-Scotland"
Campanula rotundifolia
BELLFLOWER FAMILY

16″; 4″ alpine zone. Flowers 1″, pale blue, bell-shaped; nodding; stalks thread-like. Stem leaves linear; basal leaves stalked, oblanceolate to heart-shaped, often withers before flowers open. Seed pods nodding. Alpine form 1-flowered. **BLOOMS** June–Oct. **HABITAT** Subalpine meadows, slopes, high-elev. coniferous woods. **RANGE** UT, AZ, NM.

CARDINAL FLOWER
Lobelia cardinalis
BELLFLOWER FAMILY

4′. Flowers 1½″, scarlet, tubular, 2-lipped; upper lip 2-lobed, lower lip 3-lobed; stamens united into projecting tube; showy; in slender spikes. Stems leafy, erect. Leaves lanceolate, toothed. Name refers to bright red robes worn by Roman Catholic cardinals. **BLOOMS** June–Oct. **HABITAT** Moist areas, seeps, springs, streamsides.

CLUSTERED BROOMRAPE
Orobanche fasciculata
BROOMRAPE FAMILY

10″. Flowers 4–10; corollas 1″, yellow, pink, or purple, tubular, slightly curved, irreg. Stems 8″, yellow or purplish, fleshy, glandular-hairy. Leaves reduced to small scales. Fruit many-seeded capsules. Parasitic on roots of other plants; lacks chlorophyll. **BLOOMS** May–Aug. **HABITAT** On sagebrush, buckwheat, other woody perennials in mixed shrub communities, coniferous woods.

SULPHUR BUCKWHEAT
Eriogonum umbellatum
BUCKWHEAT FAMILY

7″. Mat-forming subshrub. Flowers tiny, cream to sulphur-yellow to reddish, bell-shaped, 6-lobed, in ball-like clusters that form looser, branched clusters. Stems wooly. Leaves ovate, gray-wooly below, clustered at ends of short, woody branches. Widely distributed. **BLOOMS** May–Oct. **HABITAT** Sandy, gravelly, rocky, open, dry areas, sagebrush, mixed desert shrub, pinyon-juniper, coniferous, alpine woods.

AMERICAN BISTORT
"Western Bistort"
Polygonum bistortoides
BUCKWHEAT FAMILY

20″. Flowers tiny, white to pinkish, in fuzzy 1″ ball-like clusters atop slender, unbranched, reddish stems. Leaves lanceolate, mostly at stem base. Abundant at high elev. **BLOOMS** June–Oct. **HABITAT** Moist meadows, bogs, streamsides, coniferous to alpine woods.

CANAIGRE DOCK
Rumex hymenosepalus
BUCKWHEAT FAMILY

3′. Smooth, stout-stemmed. Flowers pinkish; in dense, 18″ clusters. Basal leaves on long, slender stems supporting 10″, elliptical to lanceolate blades; stem leaves reduced in size. Utilized as substitute for rhubarb. **BLOOMS** Feb.–June. **HABITAT** Low-elev. sandy areas, washes, Creosote Bush, Blackbrush communities.

WESTERN MONKSHOOD
Aconitum columbianum
BUTTERCUP FAMILY

5′. Flowers 1″, blue-purple; with 5 petal-like sepals, uppermost sepal forming large, helmet-shaped hood; several in showy, 20″ spikes. Leaves deeply palmately 5-lobed, long-toothed. **CAUTION** Poisonous, esp. roots. **BLOOMS** June–Sept. **HABITAT** Moist, rich mtn. meadows, open wooded areas, bogs, springs, streamsides, aspen and coniferous woods.

GOLDEN COLUMBINE
Aquilegia chrysantha
BUTTERCUP FAMILY

4′. Flowers 3″, yellow; with petal-like sepals; petals have slender, 2½″ bulb-tipped spurs. Leaves 18″, including slender stalk; 2–3 times compound, in groups of 3; finely hairy on lower surfaces. **BLOOMS** Apr.–Sept. **HABITAT** Moist canyons, streamsides, springs, seeps.

COLORADO BLUE COLUMBINE

Aquilegia coerulea

BUTTERCUP FAMILY

20″. Bushy. Flowers 2½″; 5 white to blue, spreading, petal-like sepals; 5 white, tubular petals with rearward spurs; numerous yellow stamens. Leaves repeatedly divided into round-lobed leaflets. **BLOOMS** June–Aug. **HABITAT** Mtn. meadows, rocky slopes, cliffs, streamsides, aspen and coniferous woodland openings.

RED COLUMBINE

Aquilegia formosa

BUTTERCUP FAMILY

3′6″. Flowers 2″; with 5 red or orange, spreading, petal-like sepals; 5 tubular yellow petals with rearward spurs; numerous yellow stamens. Stems many-branched. Leaves repeatedly divided into round-lobed leaflets. Nectar-bearing spurs attract sphinx moth pollinators. **BLOOMS** June–Aug. **HABITAT** Moist, wooded areas, canyons, streamsides, springs, seeps. **RANGE** UT, NV.

WHITE MARSH MARIGOLD

Caltha leptosepala

BUTTERCUP FAMILY

12″. Succulent, patch-forming. Flowers 1″, white or rarely bluish; with 6–11 petal-like sepals; stamens yellow, numerous; bowl-shaped; usu. 1 per stem. Stems smooth. Leaves oblong, notched at base. **CAUTION** Poisonous. **BLOOMS** May–Sept., as snow melts. **HABITAT** High-elev. moist mtn. meadows, marshes, pondsides, streamsides, seeps.

NUTTALL'S LARKSPUR

Delphinium nuttallianum

BUTTERCUP FAMILY

3′. Flowers 1¼″; with 5 indigo sepals (upper 1 spurred) around 4 white to brownish-purple, smaller petals; lower 2 petals deeply notched; in 1 loose spike per delicate stem. Leaves deeply divided into narrow lobes; mostly basal. **CAUTION** Poisonous. **BLOOMS** Apr.–July. **HABITAT** Slopes, valleys, meadows, sagebrush, mixed desert shrub, pinyon-juniper, coniferous woods.

ALPINE BUTTERCUP

Ranunculus eschscholtzii

BUTTERCUP FAMILY

12″. Flowers 1″; with 5 glossy, yellow petals; 5 sepals; numerous stamens; saucer-shaped. Leaves vary from deeply 3-lobed to compound with 3 several-lobed leaflets. **BLOOMS** July–Aug., as snow melts. **HABITAT** Moist areas, coniferous woodland openings, subalpine to alpine meadows, rocky talus slopes.

SAGEBRUSH BUTTERCUP
Ranunculus glaberrimus
BUTTERCUP FAMILY

10″. Flowers 1″; with 5 or more glossy, yellow petals; 5 sepals; numerous stamens; saucer-shaped. Leaves elliptical, round, or shallowly 3-lobed. Plant withers in midsummer. **BLOOMS** Jan.–July. **HABITAT** Moist meadows, sagebrush, coniferous woods.

FENDLER'S MEADOWRUE
Thalictrum fendleri
BUTTERCUP FAMILY

3′. Flowers lacking petals; sepals ¼″, whitish or greenish; stamens ½″, 15–25; male and female on separate plants. Stems purplish. Leaves 24″; 2–4 times compound, in groups of 3; blades very slender, ultimate segments 3-lobed. Fruit ¼″, hard, dry, elliptical, nerved, 1-seeded; 10 per plant; styles tiny, persistent. **BLOOMS** May–Aug. **HABITAT** Moist, open, coniferous woods, aspen stands.

ARIZONA CALTROP
"Arizona Poppy"
Kallstroemia grandiflora
CALTROP FAMILY

24″. Mat-forming with prostrate stems; silky to bristly-hairy. Flowers orange to yellow; petals 1″. Leaves pinnately compound; leaflets in 5–9 pairs. Fruit tiny, 10-lobed, splitting into 1-seeded segments. **BLOOMS** Feb.–Sept. **HABITAT** Arid hills, slopes, sandy areas, roadsides, Creosote Bush communities. **RANGE** AZ, NM.

PUNCTURE VINE
Tribulus terrestris
CALTROP FAMILY

L 3′. Mat-forming, prostrate; silky-hairy to hairless. Flowers yellow; petals ½″; solitary on stalks. Leaves hairy, even-pinnately compound; leaflets oblong, in 3–8 pairs. Fruit ½″, splitting into 5 segments with stout, ¼″ spines. Noxious weed; introduced from Mediterranean. **CAUTION** Spines sharp, capable of puncturing bicycle tires. **BLOOMS** Mar.–Oct. **HABITAT** Roadsides, fields, vacant lots, disturbed areas.

YELLOW BEE PLANT
Cleome lutea
CAPER FAMILY

4′. Flowers ½″, yellow, 4-petaled; stamens very long; in fuzzy, rounded clusters atop bluish-waxy, tall stems. Leaves palmately compound; leaflets lanceolate. Fruit slender seedpods. Rich nectar source. **BLOOMS** May–Oct. **HABITAT** Arid hills, plains, sandy, alkaline areas, bottomlands, streamsides, roadsides, disturbed areas, Creosote Bush and pinyon-juniper communities.

ROCKY MOUNTAIN BEE PLANT
Cleome serrulata
CAPER FAMILY

3′. Flowers ½″, pink to purple (occ. white), 4-petaled; stamens usu. long; in fuzzy, rounded clusters atop tall stems. Leaves compound, with 3 linear leaflets; sharply fetid. Fruit slender seedpods. Rich nectar source. **BLOOMS** June–Oct. **HABITAT** Arid hills, plains, disturbed areas, roadsides, waste areas, Creosote Bush and pinyon-juniper communities.

SOUTHERN CATTAIL
Typha domingensis
CATTAIL FAMILY

12′. Flowers minute, greenish to brownish, dense, in club-like spike; upper male flowers separated by naked stem from lower female flowers; atop erect stem. Leaves 3′, flat, stiff, sheathing. **BLOOMS** July–Aug. **HABITAT** Shallow water of ponds, lakes, marshes, moist meadows, springs, seeps, ditches, streamsides, canyon bottoms.

BROAD-LEAVED CATTAIL
Typha latifolia
CATTAIL FAMILY

9′. Flowers minute, in yellowish 4″ tail of male flowers above brown 6″ cylinder of flowers; in brown, furry spike atop slender stem. Leaves 5′, sparse, narrow, blade-like, flat at ends, sheathing. **BLOOMS** July–Aug. **HABITAT** Shallow water of ponds, lakes, marshes, springs, ditches.

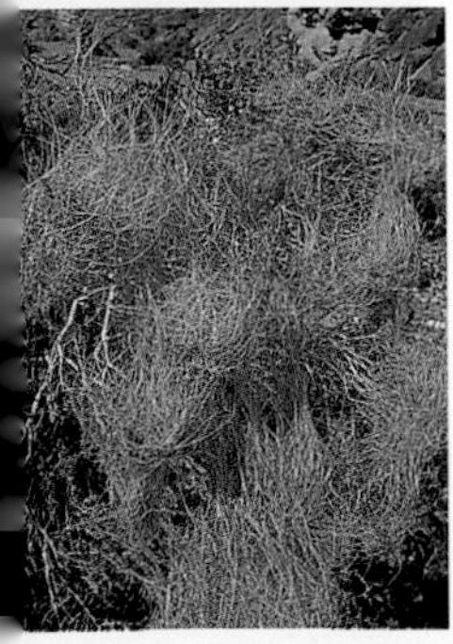

DODDERS
Cuscuta species
DODDER FAMILY

L variable. Twining, parasitic vine. Flowers tiny, usu. whitish. Stems usu. orange to yellow, hairless, attached to host by sucker-like structures that penetrate tissues of host. Leaves alternate, reduced to scales or lacking. Initial root system degenerates, leaving mature plant without connection to ground; some species seriously damage alfalfa crops. **BLOOMS** May–Oct. **HABITAT** On wide variety of hosts, mostly at low elev.

LAVENDER-LEAF SUNDROPS
Calylophus lavandulifolius
EVENING-PRIMROSE FAMILY

12″. Low-growing; slightly woody at base, hairy. Flowers yellow, aging red or orange; 4-sepaled; 4 1″ petals; in 4″ floral tube above ovary; stigma distinctly disk-like; open in early evening, wither in morning. Leaves alternate, entire, linear or somewhat broader. **BLOOMS** May–Aug. **HABITAT** Mtn. slopes, ridges, Blackbrush, pinyon-juniper, coniferous woods.

YELLOW-CUPS EVENING-PRIMROSE
"Desert Evening-primrose"
Camissonia brevipes
EVENING-PRIMROSE FAMILY

24″. Erect, hairy. Flowers with 4 yellow, ¾″ petals, occ. red-spotted; showy. Leaves pinnately cleft; leaflets of variable size and shape, terminal segment 3″. Fruit 4″, capsules. Can form spectacular carpets. **BLOOMS** Feb.–July. **HABITAT** Sandy, gravelly, rocky alluvium, arid washes, flats, slopes, Creosote Bush, Joshua Tree communities. **RANGE** NV, UT, AZ.

FIREWEED
Epilobium (Chamerion) angustifolium
EVENING-PRIMROSE FAMILY

6′. Flowers 2″, pink to purple, 4-petaled; in conical spikes. Leaves long, slender, with veins joined at edges. Fruit 3″, slender seedpods, splitting into 4 strips; release white fluffy seeds. **BLOOMS** June–Sept. **HABITAT** Open areas, meadows, gravel streambeds, burned areas, sagebrush to coniferous woods.

CALIFORNIA FUCHSIA
Epilobium canum
EVENING-PRIMROSE FAMILY

24″. Flowers ½″, scarlet, trumpet-shaped, with slightly bulging base; stamens and pistil protrude. Stems woody, sometimes wooly; densely spreading. Leaves gray-green, ovate to linear, wooly. **BLOOMS** June–Dec. **HABITAT** Clefts, fissures in bedrock, talus slopes, high-elev. pinyon-juniper, aspen, coniferous woods.

SCARLET GAURA
Gaura coccinea
EVENING-PRIMROSE FAMILY

3′6″. Slender, in clumps. Flowers ½″, 4 petals turn from white in evening to pink, red, or maroon by mid-morning; with 8 protruding stamens; bloom in sequence upward in spike; fragrant. Stems sprawl, bend upward. Leaves lanceolate. **BLOOMS** Mar.–Nov. **HABITAT** Open, arid areas, mtn. slopes, flats, washes, Creosote Bush, Blackbrush, sagebrush, pinyon-juniper communities.

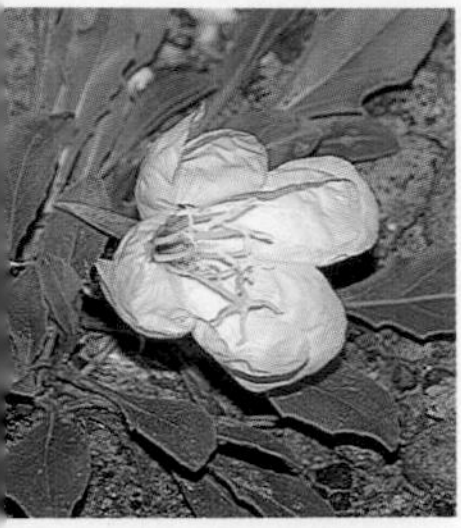

TUFTED EVENING-PRIMROSE
"Sand-lily" "Morning-lily"
Oenothera caespitosa
EVENING-PRIMROSE FAMILY

6″. Stemless clumps. Flowers 3″; 4 broad petals, white then pink or purple; stamens yellow; bloom in evening, wither next morning; fragrant. Leaves 7″, oblanceolate, jagged-toothed, basal. **BLOOMS** Apr.–Aug. **HABITAT** Dry, rocky, sandy, gravelly clay slopes, flats, rock outcrops, mixed shrub, sagebrush, pinyon-juniper, coniferous communities.

BIRDCAGE PRIMROSE
"Dune Primrose"
Oenothera deltoides
EVENING-PRIMROSE FAMILY

H 12″; W 3′6″. Flowers 3″, white to pink, 4-petaled; open in early evening. Leaves gray-green, lanceolate, pinnately lobed. Branches extend along ground; dry to form "birdcage." **BLOOMS** Feb.–June. **HABITAT** Low-elev. sandy areas, dunes. **RANGE** NV, UT, AZ.

HOOKER'S EVENING-PRIMROSE
Oenothera elata (hookeri)
EVENING-PRIMROSE FAMILY

8′. Flowers 3″, yellow to red-orange; 4 slightly notched petals; in spike on single erect stem; bloom in evening, wither in morning. Leaves lanceolate, abundant on stem. **BLOOMS** June–Oct. **HABITAT** Moist areas, meadows, springs, drainages, streamsides, sagebrush, pinyon-juniper, coniferous woods.

SPRING EVENING-PRIMROSE
Oenothera primiveris
EVENING-PRIMROSE FAMILY

10″. Usu. stemless. Flowers with 1½″ yellow petals, age orange-red; open in evening. Leaves 10″, finely hairy, entire to 1–2 times pinnately lobed; in basal rosettes. **BLOOMS** Feb.–May. **HABITAT** Sandy areas, dunes, low-elev. Creosote Bush, Blackbrush, pinyon-juniper communities.

WILD BLUE FLAX
Linum lewisii
FLAX FAMILY

18″. Flowers 1½″, sky-blue with yellow center, 5-petaled; nearly flat. Leaves linear. **BLOOMS** Mar.–Sept. **HABITAT** Well-drained slopes, washes, foothills in sagebrush, pinyon-juniper communities to coniferous, alpine woods.

FIDDLE-NECK

"Devil's Lettuce"

Amsinckia tessellata

FORGET-ME-NOT FAMILY

24". Bristly. Flowers orange; corollas ½", tubular; in 1-sided clusters, coiled at tips. Leaves lanceolate, alternate, entire. Fruit 4 nutlets. **BLOOMS** Feb.–June. **HABITAT** Arid, sandy, gravelly areas, plains, slopes, Creosote Bush communities.

WING-NUT CRYPTANTHA

Cryptantha pterocarya

FORGET-ME-NOT FAMILY

12". Bristly-hairy. Flowers white; corollas tiny, tubular. Leaves linear or slightly broader. Fruit 4 nutlets; 3 or 4 have broad wing. **BLOOMS** Mar.–June. **HABITAT** Sandy, gravelly washes, plains, slopes, Creosote Bush, Blackbrush, sagebrush, pinyon-juniper communities.

SWEET-SCENTED HELIOTROPE

"Showy Heliotrope"

Heliotropium convolvulaceum

FORGET-ME-NOT FAMILY

12". Hairy. Flowers ¾", corollas ½", white with yellow throat; scattered along stems; open in late afternoon. Leaves ovate or narrower, alternate, entire. Fruit 4 silky-hairy nutlets. **BLOOMS** Mar.–Oct. **HABITAT** Dry, sandy areas, dunes, Creosote Bush, sagebrush, mixed shrub communities.

FRINGED GROMWELL

Lithospermum incisum

FORGET-ME-NOT FAMILY

14". Clump-forming; hairy. Flowers 1¼", bright yellow, trumpet-shaped, 5 fine-toothed lobes; crowded together with leaves at stem ends; fragrant. Leaves linear, stalkless. Fruit stony nutlets, borne mainly in lower leaf axils. **BLOOMS** Mar.–July. **HABITAT** Arid, open, sandy, gravelly, rocky slopes, flats, washes, sagebrush, mixed shrub, pinyon-juniper, Ponderosa Pine communities.

FRANCISCAN BLUEBELLS

Mertensia franciscana

FORGET-ME-NOT FAMILY

4'. Robust, somewhat hairy. Flowers blue; corollas ½", tubular; bell-shaped, nodding. Leaves 8", lanceolate, short-stalked or stalkless. **BLOOMS** June–Sept. **HABITAT** Moist meadows, streamsides, canyons, high-elev. wooded slopes.

WISHBONE BUSH
Mirabilis bigelovii
FOUR-O'CLOCK FAMILY

3′. Smooth- to rough-hairy. Flowers white; sepals ½″, petal-like, fused in whorl of sepal-like bracts; open in late afternoon, close in morning. Stems forked-branched; old stems often persistent. Leaves oval, opposite, entire. **BLOOMS** Mar.–Oct. **HABITAT** Arid, rocky areas, fissures in bedrock, canyon walls, Creosote Bush, Blackbrush, sagebrush, pinyon-juniper communities. **RANGE** NV, UT, AZ.

SNOWBALL SAND VERBENA
Abronia fragrans (elliptica)
FOUR-O'CLOCK FAMILY

16″. Clump-forming. Flowers ¾″, white to pink, long-necked, trumpet-shaped, 5-lobed; in pom-poms; fragrant. Stems whitish, occ. red; sticky-wooly. Leaves obovate to oblong. Fruit 1-seeded pods; 2–5 pliable, papery wings. **BLOOMS** Apr.–Sept. **HABITAT** Arid, sandy areas, canyons, slopes, washes, Creosote Bush, Blackbrush, sagebrush, pinyon-juniper, Ponderosa Pine communities.

DESERT SAND VERBENA
Abronia villosa
FOUR-O'CLOCK FAMILY

30″. Prostrate; glandular-hairy. Flowers lacking petals; sepals pink, fused to form 1¼″ tube; in ball-like clusters. Leaves opposite; blades roundish, entire, stalked. **BLOOMS** Feb.–June. **HABITAT** Arid, sandy areas, canyons, slopes, washes, Creosote Bush, Blackbrush, sagebrush, pinyon-juniper, Ponderosa Pine woods. **RANGE** NV, UT, AZ.

TRAILING FOUR-O'CLOCK
Allionia incarnata
FOUR-O'CLOCK FAMILY

L 3′. Prostrate, with trailing stems; glandular-hairy. Flowers ½″, reddish purple, 3-lobed; in whorled groups of 3, each group resembling single flower. Leaves stalked, oval, opposite, unequal in size. **BLOOMS** Apr.–Oct. **HABITAT** Arid, sandy, gravelly, rocky flats, slopes, washes, Creosote Bush, Blackbrush communities.

DESERT FOUR-O'CLOCK
Mirabilis multiflora
FOUR-O'CLOCK FAMILY

24″. Sprawling, dense mass. Flowers 1¼″, magenta, funnel-shaped; in groups of 6 from cup of fused bracts; showy; open in late afternoon. Leaves 4″, heart-shaped, ovate. **BLOOMS** Apr.–Oct. **HABITAT** Coarse sandy to rocky washes, arid flats, slopes, Creosote Bush, Blackbrush, pinyon-juniper communities.

PARRY'S GENTIAN
Gentiana parryi
GENTIAN FAMILY

18". Erect, unbranched. Flowers violet to blue, streaked with green; corollas 1½", bell-shaped; in sparse clusters. Leaves opposite, oval to lanceolate, finely hairy on margins, in lines on stems; basal leaves reduced in size. **BLOOMS** July–Sept. **HABITAT** Alpine and subalpine meadows, mixed shrub, coniferous woods. **RANGE** UT, AZ, NM.

WESTERN FRINGED GENTIAN
Gentianopsis detonsa (thermalis)
GENTIAN FAMILY

24". Hairless; single- or few-stemmed. Flowers deep blue to violet; corollas 2", funnel-shaped, lobes fringed; borne singly on 12" stalks. Leaves linear to spatula-shaped, opposite, entire, stalkless; basal leaves 2½", elliptical to spatula-shaped, in stalkless rosettes. **BLOOMS** July–Oct. **HABITAT** Moist meadows, seeps, springs, sagebrush communities, coniferous woods.

DESERT SWERTIA
Swertia (Frasera) albomarginata
GENTIAN FAMILY

24". Single- or few-stemmed; hairless or finely hairy. Flowers greenish white, dark green–spotted; petals ½"; with 4-part symmetry. Leaves 10", white-margined, linear to spatula-shaped, whorled on stems; in basal rosettes. Dies after flowering. **BLOOMS** May–Sept. **HABITAT** Dry openings on slopes, flats in wooded areas. **RANGE** UT, NV, AZ.

MONUMENT PLANT
Swertia radiata
GENTIAN FAMILY

4'. Robust. Flowers 1¼", pale green, purple-spotted; 4-petaled, with 4 linear sepals; saucer-shaped; clustered in upper leaf axils. Leaves lanceolate, in whorls; basal leaves longest, 20". **BLOOMS** May–Aug. **HABITAT** Rich mtn. slopes, meadows, open woods in pinyon-juniper, sagebrush, Mountain Mahogany communities, coniferous woods.

RED-STEM FILAREE
"Heron's Bill"
Erodium cicutarium
GERANIUM FAMILY

14". Flowers ½", magenta, 5-petaled. Stems slender, hairy, reclining. Leaves pinnately compound; leaflets 9–13, deeply lobed. Fruit pointed, resembles bird bill; splits into 5 seeds with corkscrew tails that drive seeds into ground. Introduced from Eurasia; well-integrated into native flora. **BLOOMS** Feb.–July. **HABITAT** Dry, disturbed areas.

RICHARDSON'S GERANIUM

Geranium richardsonii

GERANIUM FAMILY

3′. Glandular-hairy. Flowers white to lavender with reddish-purple veins; petals 1″; sepals tiny, ovate, bristle-tipped. Lowest leaves on 9″ stalks; leaf blades 3″, palmately divided into coarsely toothed lobes. **BLOOMS** June–Oct. **HABITAT** Moist wooded areas, aspen and coniferous woods, streamsides, seeps, moist meadows.

HALOGETON

Halogeton glomeratus

GOOSEFOOT FAMILY

16″. Basally branched, clump-forming; pale blue-green in spring, turn red (esp. stems) or yellow by late summer. Flowers minute, green, along stems. Leaves tubular, bristle-tipped, fleshy. Seriously invasive, esp. in overgrazed areas. **CAUTION** Poisonous to livestock. **BLOOMS** June–Sept. **HABITAT** Disturbed, waste areas, alkaline flats in saltbush, Creosote Bush, sagebrush, pinyon-juniper communities.

GLASSWORTS

Salicornia species

GOOSEFOOT FAMILY

12″. Smooth. Flowers minute, greenish; have both male and female parts. Stems highly branched, jointed, fleshy. Leaves opposite, stalkless, scale-like, basally fused. **BLOOMS** July–Nov. **HABITAT** Salt marshes, alkaline flats. **RANGE** UT, NV, NM.

RUSSIAN THISTLE

Salsola tragus

GOOSEFOOT FAMILY

3′. Bushy, ferociously spiny. Flowers tiny, magenta or green. Stems purple-striped. Early leaves linear, soft; later leaves thorn-like. Dies, turns rigid in fall, tumbles over open areas, scattering seeds; seriously invasive, esp. in overgrazed areas. **BLOOMS** May–Oct. **HABITAT** Disturbed areas, roadsides, vacant lots.

BUFFALO GOURD

Cucurbita foetidissima

GOURD FAMILY

L variable. Coarse, sprawling vine. Flowers 2½″, yellow-orange, funnel-shaped, 5-lobed. Stems succulent; fetid. Leaves 8″, narrowly heart-shaped; hide flowers. Fruit 3″, green-striped ripening yellow, hard, spherical gourds. **CAUTION** Poisonous. **BLOOMS** May–Oct. **HABITAT** Sandy, fine gravelly, disturbed or cultivated areas, canyon bottoms, Creosote Bush, Joshua Tree, Blackbrush, pinyon-juniper woods.

INDIAN RICEGRASS
Achnatherum hymenoides
GRASS FAMILY

24″. Flowers in delicate, open, branching, 4½″ panicles of tiny, white florets on fine branchlets. Leaves 12″, tightly rolled, in upright bundle. Utilized for food by Native Americans. **BLOOMS** Apr.–Aug. **HABITAT** Dry, rocky slopes, well-drained areas, dunes, Creosote Bush, sagebrush, Blackbrush, mixed shrub, pinyon-juniper communities.

PURPLE THREE-AWN
Aristida purpurea
GRASS FAMILY

3′. Tufted, erect-stemmed. Flowers in narrow, 12″ clusters; spikelets purplish; first glume ½″, second 1″; lemmas 3 bristled, 2½″ each, fused at base, forming column. Leaf blades 5″, narrow, mostly inrolled. **BLOOMS** Mar.–Sept. **HABITAT** Dry slopes, plains, canyons, roadsides, gravelly to rocky areas, outcrops, Creosote Bush, Blackbrush, pinyon juniper communities.

SIDEOATS GRAMA
Bouteloua curtipendula
GRASS FAMILY

28″. Forms open patches, scarcely clumping. Flowers in 1-sided, open, 7″ panicles atop stems; spikelets purplish. Often a major component of grasslands; a valuable forage plant. **BLOOMS** Apr.–Oct. **HABITAT** Arid, open, rocky or fine-textured areas, slopes, flats, mixed shrub, pinyon-juniper, Ponderosa Pine woods.

BLUE GRAMA
Bouteloua gracilis
GRASS FAMILY

12″. Sod-forming. Flowers in 1–3 distinctive flag- or sickle-like, 1-sided, tight 1½″ spikes; spikelets usu. purplish, bristly. Leaves mostly basal, from underground stem. Dominant plant in short-grass prairies; valuable forage plant and soil-building species. **BLOOMS** May–Oct. **HABITAT** Open, arid areas, fine gravelly to rocky plains, slopes, sagebrush, pinyon-juniper, Ponderosa Pine communities.

FOXTAIL CHESS
"Red Brome"
Bromus madritensis (rubens)
GRASS FAMILY

24″. Finely hairy. Flowers in erect, dense, elliptical, 4″ clusters; usu. turning purple; spikelets cylindrical to somewhat flattened, with 3–9 florets; lemmas with 1″ bristle between 2 teeth. Leaves flat. Introduced from Eurasia; widely distributed. **BLOOMS** Mar.–July. **HABITAT** Open, disturbed areas.

CHEATGRASS
"Downy Brome"
Bromus tectorum
GRASS FAMILY

14″. Forms small tufts. Flowers in loose, arching, reddish panicles; spikelets ¾″, stiff-hairy. Leaves flat, finely hairy. Introduced from Eurasia; stubbornly invasive; depletes soil moisture, preventing germination of native species; dies in midsummer, becoming fire hazard. **BLOOMS** May–Sept. **HABITAT** Open, disturbed areas.

HAIRY CRABGRASS
Digitaria sanguinalis
GRASS FAMILY

30″. Hairy, ascending, often prostrate, mat-forming, node-rooting. Flowers in fan-like clusters of several dense 6″ spikes; spikelets have 2 bristleless florets, lower sterile; glumes have distinctive raised veins. Leaf blades 6″, flat, narrow. Introduced from Europe; invasive. **BLOOMS** June–Oct. **HABITAT** Gardens, lawns, fields, disturbed areas.

SALTGRASS
Distichlis spicata
GRASS FAMILY

18″. Smooth, with hairy nodes; ascending to erect; from creeping runners and underground stems; occ. forms dense patches. Flowers in sparse, 4″ clusters; spikelets 1″, flattened, closely spaced, with 5–15 bristleless florets; male and female flowers on separate plants. Leaves overlapping; blades 4″, very narrow, stiff. **BLOOMS** May–Oct. **HABITAT** Salty alkaline flats, playa margins, seeps, springs, ditches.

SQUIRRELTAIL
Elymus elymoides
GRASS FAMILY

24″. Tufted; smooth to finely hairy. Flowers in pointed, bristly 6″ spike, readily shattering at maturity; spikelets in pairs at each spike joint, with 2–4 florets; glumes and lemmas have 3½″ bristles. Leaf blades flat, narrow, firm, folded or inrolled. **CAUTION** Spikes can seriously injure livestock. **BLOOMS** Mar.–Sept. **HABITAT** Dry sandy or gravelly plains, rocky slopes, meadows, wooded areas above tree line.

FLUFFGRASS
Erioneuron (Tridens) pulchellum
GRASS FAMILY

6″. Low-growing; stems tufted, some forming runners, rooting. Flowers in 2″ clusters; spikelets ½″, hairy, nestled among leaves, with 5–8 florets; lemmas hairy, cleft into two lobes, short-bristled between segments. Leaves ½″, very narrow, inrolled; in clusters. **BLOOMS** Feb.–Oct. **HABITAT** Dry sandy to gravelly plains, rocky slopes, Creosote Bush to pinyon-juniper communities.

NEEDLE-AND-THREAD GRASS

Heterostipa (Stipa) comata

GRASS FAMILY

4′. Erect, tufted; smooth or short-hairy at nodes. Flowers in 10½″ clusters; spikelets 1-flowered; glumes 1″; lemmas ½″, with single 6½″ bristle, bent once or twice, twisted. Leaves 12″, flat and very flat or inrolled. **BLOOMS** May–Aug. **HABITAT** Dry hills, sandy, gravelly, rocky areas, dunes, sagebrush, pinyon-juniper woods, open coniferous woods.

WALL BARLEY

Hordeum murinum

GRASS FAMILY

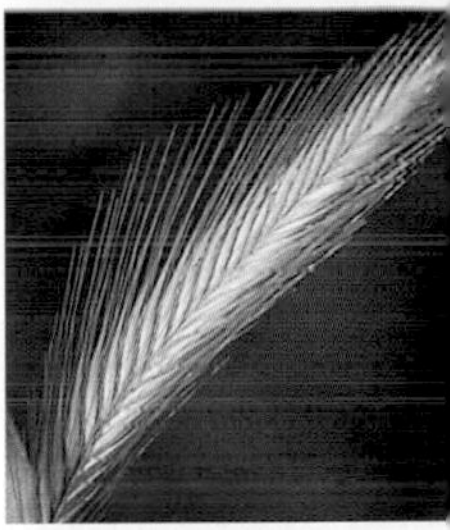

3′. Erect, smooth-stemmed. Flowers in 5″ spikes, readily shattering at maturity; spikelets in groups of 3, central bisexual, lateral sterile or male; glumes with ½″ bristle; lemmas with 2″ bristle. Leaves hairy; blades flat and narrow or folded, distinctly lobed at base. Introduced from Europe. **BLOOMS** May–July. **HABITAT** Moist to dry disturbed areas, pastures, fields, ditches, roadsides.

GREAT BASIN WILDRYE

Leymus cinereus

GRASS FAMILY

H 6′; W 3′. Erect; forming robust clumps. Flowers in dense, 9″ spikes; spikelets ¾″, 2–6 per node, with 2–5 florets; lemmas bristle-tipped or acute. Leaf blades narrow. **BLOOMS** June–Sept. **HABITAT** Moist or dry canyons, valley floors, streamsides, sagebrush, mixed shrub, pinyon-juniper, Ponderosa Pine communities. **RANGE** UT, NV, AZ.

COMMON REED

Phragmites australis

GRASS FAMILY

12′. Tufted. Flowers in reddish (turning silver), 12″ panicles. Leaves bluish, linear, sharp. Often forms pure stands; invasive, replaces other marsh grasses and cattails; perhaps most widely distributed of all seed-producing plants. **BLOOMS** July–Nov. **HABITAT** Moist areas, streamsides, in ponds, springs, ditches, marshes.

KENTUCKY BLUEGRASS

Poa pratensis

GRASS FAMILY

24″. Sod-forming. Flowers in open, delicate, conical or arching, purple panicles; 2–4 per flattened spikelet. Leaves sometimes bluish, slender, soft, numerous. Introduced from Europe; an important cultivated species for lawns, pastures. **BLOOMS** Apr.–Sept. **HABITAT** Roadsides, fields, meadows, streamsides, springs.

RABBITFOOT GRASS

Polypogon monspeliensis

GRASS FAMILY

3′. Flowers in cylindrical, 6″ spikes; spikelets numerous, 1-flowered, appearing soft-hairy due to glume and lemma bristles. Leaf blades 10″, narrow, flat. Introduced from Europe. **BLOOMS** Apr.–Nov. **HABITAT** Moist areas, streamsides, springs, seeps, ditches.

ALKALI SACATON

Sporobolus airoides

GRASS FAMILY

5′. Robust, tufted clumps. Flowers in open, loosely flowered, 16″ clusters; spikelets tiny, 1-flowered, mostly at tips of branches; glumes and lemmas bristleless. Leaf blades 18″, very narrow, flat or inrolled. **BLOOMS** Apr.–Oct. **HABITAT** Dry plains, slopes, Saltgrass communities in alkaline meadows.

SIX-WEEKS FESCUE

Vulpia octoflora

GRASS FAMILY

12″. Erect; smooth to finely hairy. Flowers in 4″ clusters, branches ascend or lay flat; 5–15 per flattened spikelet; lemmas with single ¼″ bristle. Leaf blades inrolled, very narrow. **BLOOMS** Apr.–June. **HABITAT** Dry, rocky, gravelly, sandy plains, slopes, Creosote Bush, mixed shrub, sagebrush, pinyon-juniper communities.

WESTERN BLUE FLAG

Iris missouriensis

IRIS FAMILY

18″. Forms dense clumps. Flowers 3″, pale blue or blue-violet, with petal-like parts in 3s: down-curved sepals, erect petals, style branches; 1–4 per stalk. Leaves folded flat, sword-like. **BLOOMS** May–Sept. **HABITAT** Moist meadows, pastures, springs, marshes.

HOOKER'S ONION

Allium acuminatum

LILY FAMILY

9″. Flowers ½″, rose-purple to white, vase-shaped; in rounded, branched clusters; atop bare, slender, single stem. Leaves linear, rolled, basal. **BLOOMS** May–July. **HABITAT** Dry, open, rocky slopes, plains, sagebrush, mixed shrub, pinyon-juniper, Ponderosa Pine communities. **RANGE** NV, UT, AZ.

NEVADA ONION

Allium nevadense

LILY FAMILY

6″. Flowers ½″, white or pink, in clusters of 5–25, on ¾″ stalks; 2–3 bracts below. Leaves usu. solitary; cylindrical, tapering at ends; tip coiled, withered, sometimes missing. **BLOOMS** Apr.–July. **HABITAT** Gravelly, rocky slopes, clay flats in sagebrush, Blackbrush, mixed shrub, pinyon-juniper communities. **RANGE** NV, UT, AZ.

STRAGGLING MARIPOSA LILY

Calochortus flexuosus

LILY FAMILY

18″. Erect-stemmed to sprawling; not parasitic but often twisting around branches of other plants for support. Flowers pink, lavender, or white; petals 1¾″; 1–2 per plant. Basal leaves 12″, withering; stem leaves 8″, linear. Fruit 1½″, angled capsules. **BLOOMS** Apr.–June. **HABITAT** Arid, gravelly, rocky slopes, flats, mixed shrub, Joshua Tree, pinyon-juniper communities. **RANGE** NV, UT, AZ.

DESERT MARIPOSA LILY

Calochortus kennedyi

LILY FAMILY

8″. Flowers 1½″, vermilion to orange, usu. purple-spotted inside, bell-shaped, 3-petaled; 1–6 on short, sometimes twisted stems. Leaves gray-green, linear, basal, with long grooves. **BLOOMS** Mar.–May. **HABITAT** Arid, gravelly, rocky slopes, flats, Creosote Bush, Blackbrush, mixed shrub, Joshua Tree, pinyon-juniper communities. **RANGE** NV, UT, AZ.

SEGO LILY

Calochortus nuttallii

LILY FAMILY

14″. Flowers 2″, lilac-tinged white; 3 very broad, small-pointed petals with maroon crescent and yellow blush at base; 3 shorter, lanceolate, white sepals; 1–4 per stem; showy. Leaves grass-like, sparse. UT state flower. **BLOOMS** May–July. **HABITAT** Arid clay, gravelly, rocky, open slopes, ridges, flats, Blackbrush, mixed shrub, pinyon-juniper, Ponderosa Pine communities.

COMMON BLUE CAMAS

Camassia quamash

LILY FAMILY

20″. Grass-like. Flowers 1½″, blue-violet; 6 nearly flat, spreading petals, lowest one somewhat isolated; numerous; in tall conical clusters. Leaves linear, sheathing lowest part of stem. **BLOOMS** Apr.–July. **HABITAT** Moist meadows, spring moist sagebrush communities. **RANGE** UT, NV.

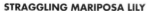

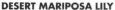

BLUE DICKS
Dichelostemma pulchellum (capitatum)
LILY FAMILY

24″. Flowers ¾″, violet, blue to white; in 6-segmented fan-shaped clusters, united at base to form tube; 2–15 per stem. Leaves 16″, narrow, linear, basal, 2–5. **BLOOMS** Feb.–May. **HABITAT** Creosote Bush, Blackbrush, Joshua Tree, sagebrush, mixed shrub communities.

LEOPARD LILY
Fritillaria atropurpurea
LILY FAMILY

24″. Flowers 1″, yellowish-, greenish- to purplish-brown mottled with yellow or white; 6-segmented, bell-shaped, hanging down; 1–4 per plant. Leaves 4″, narrow, linear, alternate or whorled; on upper stem. Fruit 1″, 6-angled, many-seeded capsules. The bulbs were consumed by Native Americans. **BLOOMS** Apr.–July. **HABITAT** Rich wooded or grassy mtn. slopes. **RANGE** UT, NV, AZ.

STARRY FALSE SOLOMON'S-SEAL
Smilacina stellata
LILY FAMILY

16″. Flowers ½″, white; in open clusters of 3–15; fragrant. Stems arch out from rootstock. Leaves 6″, elliptical, parallel-veined. Fruit green berries, ripen dark red. **BLOOMS** Apr.–Sept. **HABITAT** Moist, rich, wooded areas on mtn. slopes, streamsides, seeps.

FALSE HELLEBORE
"California Corn Lily"
Veratrum californicum
LILY FAMILY

5′. Flowers ½″; 6-petaled, each white with green V at base; in dense, branched, 12″ clusters. Stems stout. Leaves 12″, ovate, parallel-veined. Exceptional abundance of this plant can indicate overgrazing. **CAUTION** Poisonous. **BLOOMS** June–Aug. **HABITAT** Moist meadows, boggy areas, streamsides, montane coniferous woodland openings.

ELEGANT DEATH CAMAS
Zigadenus elegans
LILY FAMILY

20″. Flowers ¾″, saucer-shaped; 6-petaled, each greenish white with heart-shaped, green spot near base; in open 8″ spikes. Leaves 10″, grass-like. **CAUTION** Possibly poisonous. **BLOOMS** June–Aug. **HABITAT** Rich meadows, streamsides, montane woodland openings.

YERBA MANSA
Anemopsis californica
LIZARD'S-TAIL FAMILY

14″. Flowers tiny, greenish, in conical 1″ spike; surrounded by 5–8 larger, white, petal-like bracts; solitary atop long stems. Leaves lanceolate, long-stalked, basal. **BLOOMS** May–Oct. **HABITAT** Moist, saline, alkaline areas, springs, streamsides.

DESERT FIVESPOT
Eremalche (Malvastrum) rotundifolia
MALLOW FAMILY

24″. Bristly-hairy, slightly stellate-hairy. Flowers lavender; petals 1¼″, with red spot near base. Leaves stalked, alternate, kidney-shaped, tooth-margined. **BLOOMS** Year-round; mainly Mar.–June. **HABITAT** Arid, rocky slopes, gravels, sandy washes, open plains in Creosote Bush communities. **RANGE** NV, AZ.

DESERT ROSEMALLOW
Hibiscus coulteri
MALLOW FAMILY

8″. Woody at stem base; cloaked with white, forked hairs. Flowers yellow; petals 1″, with red spot near base; stalked. Leaves ovate or lanceolate, with toothed or 3-lobed margins. Fruit bears numerous hair-covered seeds in capsules. **BLOOMS** Year-round; mainly Apr.–Sept. **HABITAT** Rocky slopes, canyons. **RANGE** AZ, NM.

ROCK HIBISCUS
Hibiscus denudatus
MALLOW FAMILY

3′. Woody at stem base; stellate-hairy. Flowers white to lavender; petals 1″, red-purple at base; short-stalked. Leaf blades ovate, heart-shaped at base, finely toothed margins. Fruit bears numerous hair-covered seeds in capsules. **BLOOMS** Jan.–Oct. **HABITAT** Rocky slopes, canyons, sandy washes. **RANGE** NV, AZ, NM.

CHECKER MALLOW
Sidalcea neomexicana
MALLOW FAMILY

3′. Thick, clustered roots; occ. stellate-hairy on stems, calyx. Flowers purple or rose; petals 1″. Stems with simple or branched hairs. Leaves 3″, circular, irreg. toothed, lobed, or parted. **BLOOMS** June–Sept. **HABITAT** Moist meadows, streamsides, springs, seeps.

DESERT GLOBE MALLOW

Sphaeralcea ambigua

MALLOW FAMILY

2′. Flowers 1″, apricot to orange-red, cup-shaped, 5-petaled. Stems erect, rather woody. Leaves yellow-hairy or gray-hairy, shallow-palmately 3-lobed, toothed. **BLOOMS** Year-round; mainly Mar.–June. **HABITAT** Arid, rocky, sandy, gravelly washes, open plains, slopes, roadsides, Creosote Bush, Joshua Tree communities. **RANGE** NV, UT, AZ.

SCARLET GLOBE MALLOW

Sphaeralcea coccinea

MALLOW FAMILY

8″. Velvety; patch-forming. Flowers 1″, brick-red to red-orange, 5-petaled, with several stamens; in numerous, small, elongated clusters. Stems often weak, leaning; in clumps. Leaves grayish, compound with 3 narrow-lobed leaflets. **BLOOMS** May–Oct. **HABITAT** Arid, gravelly slopes, plains, sagebrush, pinyon-juniper, Ponderosa Pine, mixed shrub communities.

SHOWY MILKWEED

Asclepias speciosa

MILKWEED FAMILY

3′6″. Coarse, gray-wooly. Flowers ¾″, pink to maroon; 5-petaled, each sharply bent back; 5 incurved, horn-like stamens; in broad clusters. Stems milky-juiced. Leaves 6″, opposite, lanceolate. Seedpods velvety, spiny; release silky, white fluff. **CAUTION** Mildly poisonous. **BLOOMS** Apr.–Sept. **HABITAT** Coniferous woods, streamsides, disturbed areas, cultivated fields, roadsides, ditches.

ORANGE MILKWEED

"Butterfly Weed"

Asclepias tuberosa

MILKWEED FAMILY

2′3″. Hairy. Flowers tiny, orange, star-like; in 2″ clusters at branch ends. Leaves oblong, watery-juiced. Seedpods narrow, hairy, erect. **BLOOMS** May–Sept. **HABITAT** Sandy, gravelly areas, canyons, sagebrush, pinyon-juniper, Ponderosa Pine communities. **RANGE** UT, AZ, NM.

FIELD MINT

Mentha arvensis

MINT FAMILY

2′4″. Flowers tiny, white, pale pink, or lavender; tubular; 4-lobed; 4 protruding stamens; in tight clusters in leaf axils along stem. Stems square, hairy, weak. Leaves elliptical, sharp-toothed; fragrant. Leaves used for tea. **BLOOMS** June–Oct. **HABITAT** Moist meadows, streamsides, springs, ditches.

CHIA
Salvia columbariae
MINT FAMILY

24″. Skunky-smelling. Flowers light to dark blue; corollas ½″, bilaterally symmetrical; in spherical, terminal clusters (clusters occ. in pagoda-like arrangements). Basal leaves 5″, pinnate; in rosettes, stem leaves reduced or lacking. Fruit 4 tiny nutlets. **BLOOMS** Mar.–July. **HABITAT** Arid, well-drained, sandy, gravelly areas, Creosote Bush, Blackbrush, Joshua Tree, pinyon-juniper communities.

SCARLET HEDGE-NETTLE
"Scarlet Sage"
Stachys coccinea
MINT FAMILY

30″. Sparsely to densely fine-hairy. Flowers 1″, bright red, with irreg. symmetry, tubular; densely fine-hairy on outer surface. Stems 4-angled. Leaves opposite, on 2½″ stalks, bearing 3″ elliptical blades with serrated margins. A very showy plant. **BLOOMS** Mar.–Oct. **HABITAT** Dry, rocky slopes, canyons. **RANGE** AZ, NM.

DESERT MISTLETOE
Phoradendron californicum
MISTLETOE FAMILY

24″. Flowers minute, lacking petals; male and female flowers on separate plants. Stems often reddish, slender, jointed; finely hairy when young, hairy when mature. Leaves reduced to scales, opposite. Fruit ¼″ red, white, or pink berries. A parasitic plant. **BLOOMS** July–Aug. **HABITAT** On Catclaw Acacia, mesquite, paloverde, ironwood, occ. Creosote Bush.

JUNIPER MISTLETOE
Phoradendron juniperinum
MISTLETOE FAMILY

12″. Flowers minute, lacking petals; male and female flowers on separate plants. Stems yellow-green to yellow-brown, smooth, stout, jointed. Leaves reduced to scales, opposite. Fruit tiny, white or pink berries. A parasitic plant. **BLOOMS** May–Sept. **HABITAT** On junipers.

BINDWEED
"Field Bindweed"
Convolvulus arvensis
MORNING GLORY FAMILY

L 3′6″. Aggressive twining vine. Flowers 1″, white to purplish, funnel-shaped, shallowly 5-lobed. Leaves triangular to arrowhead-shaped. Introduced from Europe; widely distributed noxious weed. **BLOOMS** May–Sept. **HABITAT** Fields, gardens, orchards, roadsides.

HEART-LEAF BITTERCRESS

Cardamine cordifolia

MUSTARD FAMILY

24″. Flowers white; petals ½″. Stems smooth to hairy. Leaves ovate to heart-shaped, stalked, simple, smooth, alternate. Fruit 1½″, linear, flattened, with numerous seeds. **BLOOMS** June–Sept. **HABITAT** Moist areas, streamsides, seeps, springs, alpine meadows, high-elev. coniferous woods.

HOARY CRESS

"Whitetop"

Cardaria draba

MUSTARD FAMILY

24″. Flowers white, petals tiny. Stems hairy. Leaves 3½″, simple, ovate or elliptical, toothed, hairy, alternate; basal leaves stalked; stem leaves clasping. Fruit tiny, heart-shaped to globose, inflated. Introduced from Europe; a noxious weed. **BLOOMS** Mar.–Aug. **HABITAT** Cultivated fields, pastures, ditches, roadsides, waste areas.

SPINDLESTEM

"Thick-stem Wild Cabbage"

Caulanthus crassicaulis

MUSTARD FAMILY

3′. Flowers with brown to purple petals; sepals ½″, often densely hairy, with pouch at base. Stems stout, somewhat inflated. Basal leaf blades 4″, pinnately cleft to entire; stem leaves reduced in size, linear, entire. Fruit 5″, linear. **BLOOMS** May–July. **HABITAT** Arid slopes, Blackbrush, pinyon-juniper, Joshua Tree, sagebrush communities. **RANGE** NV, UT, AZ.

TANSY MUSTARD

Descurainia pinnata

MUSTARD FAMILY

3′. Finely stellate-hairy. Flowers yellow; petals tiny. Basal and stem leaves 4″, pinnately compound. Fruits ½″, linear. **BLOOMS** Mar.–Aug. **HABITAT** Arid slopes, flats in many soil and vegetation types.

WESTERN WALLFLOWER

Erysimum capitatum (asperum)

MUSTARD FAMILY

24″. Erect. Flowers 1″, orange-yellow, 4-petaled, short-stalked; in loose, terminal clusters. Leaves linear to spoon-shaped; upper leaves reduced in size. **BLOOMS** Mar.–Sept. **HABITAT** Arid, rocky, gravelly slopes, flats, Creosote Bush, Blackbrush, sagebrush, coniferous woods, alpine communities.

TRUE WATERCRESS

Rorippa nasturtium aquaticum

MUSTARD FAMILY

10″. Flowers tiny, white; in rounded clusters. Stems float or creep. Leaves with several oval leaflets, terminal leaflet largest; often submerged. Leaves utilized in salads. **BLOOMS** Apr.–Aug. **HABITAT** Streamsides, springs, lakesides, pondsides, ditches.

LONDON ROCKET

Sisymbrium irio

MUSTARD FAMILY

30″. Nearly smooth. Flowers yellow; petals ¼″. Leaves pinnately cleft; lower leaves 6″. Fruit 2½″, linear. Introduced from Europe; widely established. **BLOOMS** Feb.–May. **HABITAT** Disturbed areas, roadsides, fields, gardens.

DESERT PRINCE'S PLUME

Stanleya pinnata

MUSTARD FAMILY

4′. Woody, erect-stemmed. Flowers ½″, yellow; 4-petaled, with 4 shorter, petal-like sepals; in elongated, plume-like, 18″ clusters. Basal and lower leaves lanceolate, deeply pinnately lobed; upper leaves lanceolate to ovate. **CAUTION** Poisonous to livestock. **BLOOMS** Apr.–Sept. **HABITAT** Selenium-rich soils on slopes, flats, in Creosote Bush, Blackbrush, sagebrush, pinyon-juniper communities.

WILD CANDYTUFT

Thlaspi montanum

MUSTARD FAMILY

12″. Flowers ¼″, white, narrow, 4-petaled, erect bells; in dense clusters atop slender stems. Leaves stalked, ovate, in basal rosettes; smaller stem leaves clasping. **BLOOMS** Feb.–Aug. **HABITAT** Mtn. areas, coniferous woods, meadows, talus slopes.

SACRED DATURA
"Angel Trumpet"
Datura wrightii (meteloides)
NIGHTSHADE FAMILY

4′. Densely fine-hairy. Flowers white or purplish-tinged; corollas 8″, tubular. Leaves 8″, ovate, entire to lobed. Fruit 5″, spherical, prickly capsules. **CAUTION** Entire plant is toxic. **BLOOMS** May–Oct. **HABITAT** Sandy, gravelly plains, roadsides, washes, Creosote Bush, Blackbrush, sagebrush, Joshua Tree, pinyon-juniper communities.

DESERT TOBACCO
Nicotiana obtusifolia (trigonophylla)
NIGHTSHADE FAMILY

18″. Erect, glandular-hairy. Flowers creamy white to greenish-tinged; petals united to form 1″ tube. Leaves ovate, alternate, entire; basal leaves stalked; stem leaves stalkless with clasping base. Contains nicotine; was smoked by Native Americans. **BLOOMS** Year-round. **HABITAT** Gravelly, sandy washes, among boulders, canyon walls, cliffs, Creosote Bush, mixed shrub communities.

Poisonous Plants

Poisonous plants are those that contain potentially harmful substances in high enough concentrations to cause injury if touched or swallowed. Determining whether a plant species is "poison" or "food" requires expertise. The information in this guide is not to be used to identify plants for edible or medicinal purposes.

Sensitivity to a toxin varies with a person's age, weight, physical condition, and individual susceptibility. Children are most vulnerable because of their curiosity and small size. Toxicity can vary in a plant according to season, the plant's different parts, and its stage of growth; plants can also absorb toxic substances, such as herbicides, pesticides, and pollutants from the water, air, and soil. Potentially deadly plants in the Southwest region, including Sacred Datura, are noted as such this guide.

Physical contact with plants that contain irritating resinous compounds causes rashes in many individuals. The Southwest's Desert Rock-nettle is covered with hypodermic-like stinging hairs that actually inject pain-inducing substances into the skin when touched. Scorpionweed produces a contact dermatitis in sensitive people, indistinguishable from that of poison oak or poison ivy; other glandular species of *Phacelia* also produce the same effect.

Puncture wounds involving spines, thorns, or prickles of a number of Southwest plants—trees, shrubs, and wildflowers—may result in tissue damage and serious infection. Plants that can inflict mechanical damage include Catclaw Acacia, Honey Mesquite, Screwbean Mesquite, New Mexico Locust—all members of the pea family—Puncture Vine, Woods's Rose, and various cacti and agaves.

IVY-LEAF GROUND-CHERRY
Physalis hederifolia
NIGHTSHADE FAMILY

24″. Erect, finely hairy. Flowers yellow; petals ½″, united; calyx ¼″, enlarging to 1″, encloses berry fruit. Leaves ovate to lanceolate, alternate, entire or toothed. **BLOOMS** Apr.–Oct. **HABITAT** Rocky slopes, canyons, Blackbrush, pinyon-juniper communities.

BUFFALO BUR
Solanum rostratum
NIGHTSHADE FAMILY

24″. Prickly. Flowers 1″, yellow, trumpet-shaped, with 5 flat-spreading, shallow lobes. Stems very spiny. Leaves 5″, deeply pinnately lobed. Burs covered with long straight spines. **BLOOMS** Mar.–Sept. **HABITAT** Disturbed areas, cultivated fields, roadsides.

GIANT HELLEBORINE
"Stream Orchid"
Epipactus gigantea
ORCHID FAMILY

3′. Flowers ¾″, 2–15; in 1-sided clusters, sepals green with purple veins; petals green to yellow, lined with purple or red veins. Stems erect, nearly smooth. Leaves 8″, ovate to lanceolate, alternate, clasping stem, reduced in size upward. Fruit 1″ capsules. **BLOOMS** Apr.–Aug. **HABITAT** Seeps, springs, streamsides, moist meadows.

FRECKLED MILKVETCH
Astragalus lentiginosus
PEA FAMILY

18″. Pea-flowers pink-purple; 5-petaled, each 1″. Stems prostrate to ascending, finely hairy. Leaves 6″, pinnately compound. Fruit 1″, ovoid, often inflated, hairless pods; often red- or purple-tinged. Highly variable species. **CAUTION** Potentially deadly to livestock. **BLOOMS** Feb.–July, Sept.–Oct. **HABITAT** Roadsides, sandy, gravelly, clay, rocky slopes, flats, mixed brush, Joshua Tree, pinyon-juniper communities.

WRIGHT'S DEERVETCH

"Wright's Trefoil"

Lotus wrightii

PEA FAMILY

24″. Wiry, minutely hairy. Pea-flowers ¾″, borne singly or in pairs in stem leaf axils; petals yellow, tinged with red. Stems erect or ascending, incurved. Leaves palmately compound; leaflets 3–5. Fruit 1½″, narrow, straight pods. **BLOOMS** May–Sept. **HABITAT** Dry, open pine, oak woods. **RANGE** UT, AZ, NM.

SILVERY LUPINE

Lupinus argenteus

PEA FAMILY

18″; smaller in alpine zone. Silvery-hairy, ex. upper petal. Pea-flowers ¾″, blue, occ. bicolored with pink or white; whorled in conical clusters. Stems often purple. Leaves palmately compound. A common plant, with many named varieties. **CAUTION** Poisonous to livestock. **BLOOMS** Apr.–Oct. **HABITAT** Dry slopes, meadows, flats, sagebrush, mixed shrub communities, coniferous woods.

SHORTSTEM LUPINE

"Sand Lupine"

Lupinus brevicaulis

PEA FAMILY

5″. Low-growing; hairy. Pea-flowers ¼″, blue; in clusters of 4–16. Stemless or short-stemmed. Leaves stalked, palmately compound; leaflets 3–9; persistent seed leaves form disk at root-shoot junction. Fruit ½″ pods; 1–3 seeds. **BLOOMS** Apr.–July. **HABITAT** Arid, sandy, gravelly hills, washes, Blackbrush, sagebrush, Joshua Tree, pinyon-juniper communities.

MOJAVE LUPINE

"Coulter's Lupine"

Lupinus sparsiflorus

PEA FAMILY

18″. Hairy. Pea-flowers ½″, bluish purple with yellow or white "eye"; in 10″ clusters of 10–50. Leaves long-stalked, palmately compound; leaflets 5–9. Fruit 1″ pods; 4–6 seeds. **BLOOMS** Jan.–May. **HABITAT** Sandy, gravelly areas, esp. washes, Creosote Bush, mixed shrub, Joshua Tree communities.

ALFALFA

Medicago sativa

PEA FAMILY

3′. Pea-flowers ½″, blue-violet; in short spikes on low or prostrate stems. Leaves clover-like, divided in 3s. Fruit coiled, spiral seedpods. Introduced from Eurasia; cultivated for forage and widely established. **BLOOMS** Apr.–Oct. **HABITAT** Disturbed areas, cultivated fields, roadsides, ditches.

YELLOW SWEET CLOVER
Melilotus officinalis
PEA FAMILY

6′. Pea-flowers ¼″, pale yellow; in 3½″ spikes on most branches. Leaves divided into 3 obovate, fine-toothed leaflets. Introduced from Eurasia; sweet scent attracts bees. **BLOOMS** June–Aug. **HABITAT** Cultivated fields, disturbed areas, roadsides, ditches, streamsides, springs, seeps, washes. **White Sweet Clover** *(M. alba)* has white flowers. **Sourclover** *(M. indicus)* has smaller yellow flowers.

PURPLE LOCOWEED
Oxytropis lambertii
PEA FAMILY

12″. Pea-flowers 1″, pink-purple; in clusters of 10–40. Stemless. Leaves 9″, silvery-hairy, pinnately compound; leaflets 2″, linear to oblong, 7–17. Fruit 1″ pods. **CAUTION** Potentially deadly to livestock. **BLOOMS** Apr.–Oct. **HABITAT** Open, sandy plains, mtn. slopes, pinyon-juniper, oak, pinewoods. **RANGE** UT, AZ, NM.

RED CLOVER
Trifolium pratense
PEA FAMILY

24″. Pea-flowers ¾″, red, curving; in rounded, 1″ clusters. Stems sparsely hairy. Leaves compound, with 3 ovate to elliptical leaflets, each usu. marked with a pale V. Introduced from Eurasia; cultivated for forage, soil enrichment, and honey production; escapes and naturalizes. **BLOOMS** May–Sept. **HABITAT** Ditches, disturbed areas, lawns, roadsides.

WHITE CLOVER
Trifolium repens
PEA FAMILY

5″. Pea-flowers tiny, white or pinkish; in rounded, ¾″ clusters. Leaves divided into 3 round, fine-toothed leaflets with slightly notched tips. Introduced from Eurasia; provides forage, soil enrichment, honey; roots freely from runners; escapes and naturalizes. **BLOOMS** May–Oct. **HABITAT** Ditches, disturbed areas, fields, pastures, lawns, gardens, roadsides.

WESTERN PEONY
Paeonia brownii
PEONY FAMILY

16″. Flowers 2″, maroon to brown, globular, drooping; petals often yellow-edged, 5–10; sepals reddish green, 5–6. Stems fleshy; become floppy. Leaves bluish green, thick, twice divided in 3s, lobed. **BLOOMS** May–Aug. **HABITAT** Arid slopes, sagebrush, mixed shrub, coniferous woods. **RANGE** UT, NV.

SAND GILIA
Gilia leptomeria
PHLOX FAMILY

8″. Branching; glandular-stalked, hairy. Flowers white, pink, or rose; corollas ¼″; with 3-toothed or single-pointed lobes. Basal leaves 3½″, toothed or lobed, form rosettes; stem leaves greatly reduced, toothed to entire. **BLOOMS** Apr.–June. **HABITAT** Arid, rocky hillsides, Creosote Bush, Blackbrush, sagebrush, mixed shrub, pinyon-juniper, pine communities; one variety common in sand.

SCARLET GILIA
"Skyrocket"
Ipomopsis (Gilia) aggregata
PHLOX FAMILY

24″. Patch-forming. Flowers 1″, scarlet with white speckles, trumpet-shaped, with 5 pointed lobes; very showy. Leaves finely pinnately lobed; skunky-smelling. Hummingbird-pollinated; a highly variable species. **BLOOMS** May–Sept. **HABITAT** Arid, rocky slopes, flats, dry meadows, open sagebrush, mixed shrub, pinyon-juniper, pinewoods.

LONG-LEAVED PHLOX
Phlox longifolia
PHLOX FAMILY

12″. Densely branched, semiwoody. Flowers 1″, pink with white center, lilac, or white; with 5 lobes spreading flat from tubular base; in loose clusters. Leaves linear. **BLOOMS** Apr.–June. **HABITAT** Mtn. areas, open, arid, rocky slopes, canyons, plains, sagebrush, mixed shrub, coniferous woods.

SKY PILOT
Polemonium viscosum
PHLOX FAMILY

10″. Sticky; skunky-smelling. Flowers ¾″, purple (rarely white) with orange stamens, narrowly funnel-shaped, 5-lobed; in dense clusters. Leaves compound; leaflets tiny, numerous, whorled around stalk. **BLOOMS** June–Sept. **HABITAT** High mtns., open, rocky areas, meadows, talus slopes, coniferous woods, alpine communities.

MEXICAN SILENE
Silene laciniata
PINK FAMILY

24″. Glandular-hairy above. Flowers cardinal red; calyx ¾″; petals deeply irregularly lobed into 4–6 segments. Leaves 4″, oblong to lanceolate; upper linear; blades thrust out ½″ beyond calyx. **BLOOMS** July–Oct. **HABITAT** Wooded slopes, chaparral, pine, oak woods. **RANGE** AZ, NM.

PLANTAIN

Plantago ovata (insularis)
PLANTAIN FAMILY

7″. Slender, soft silky-hairy. Flowers minute; in spike-like 1″, cylindrical, terminal clusters atop leafless stalks. Leaves 6″, entire, broadly linear. Sometimes abundant, carpet-forming. **BLOOMS** Jan.–May. **HABITAT** Arid slopes, alluvial plains, gravels, clays, Creosote Bush, Blackbrush, Joshua Tree communities. **RANGE** NV, UT, AZ.

GOLDEN BEARCLAW-POPPY

Arctomecon californica
POPPY FAMILY

24″. Soft-hairy. Flowers bright yellow; 6-petaled, each 1½″; 3–20 per long stalk. Leaves 8″, wedge-shaped; in basal rosettes, 3–7 lobed at tips. Fruit 1″, oblong capsules, open at top. A rare, showy plant. **BLOOMS** Apr.–May. **HABITAT** Gypsum-rich areas, barren flats, slopes. **RANGE** s NV, nw AZ.

PRICKLY POPPY

Argemone munita
POPPY FAMILY

3′. Stout, branching. Flowers 4″, white; 6-petaled, flat, crinkled; stamens bright yellow, numerous. Stems spiny, yellow-sapped. Leaves deeply pinnately lobed, spiny, clasping. **BLOOMS** May–Sept. **HABITAT** Open slopes, foothills, washes, roadsides, disturbed areas, sandy, gravelly, clay areas, Creosote Bush, Blackbrush, sagebrush, pinyon-juniper communities. **RANGE** NV, UT, AZ.

GOLDEN CORYDALIS

"Golden Smoke"
Corydalis aurea
POPPY FAMILY

12″. Sprawling; soft, watery-juiced. Flowers ½″, yellow, irreg., tube-like, attached at midlength; in elongated clusters. Leaves bluish, fern-like. Fruit 1″, curved beanpods. **BLOOMS** Feb.–Sept. **HABITAT** Dry or moist, open areas, loose gravels, rocky hillsides, talus slopes, mixed shrub, sagebrush, pinyon-juniper, coniferous woods.

STEER'S HEAD

Dicentra uniflora
POPPY FAMILY

3″. Flowers ½″, pinkish, resembling upside-down water buffalo head: 2 back-curved petals, 2 fused petals; 1 per stalk. Leaves much divided, rather lacy, round-tipped, long-stalked; basal. Leaf and flower stalks joined below ground. **BLOOMS** Feb.–June. **HABITAT** Well-drained gravels, rocky areas on mtn. slopes, mixed shrub, sagebrush, aspen communities. **RANGE** UT, NV.

MEXICAN GOLD POPPY

Eschscholzia californica var. *mexicana*

POPPY FAMILY

12″. Smooth. Flowers orange to yellow; 4-petaled, each 2″; 2 united sepals, fall off after flowering. Basal leaves alternate; stem leaves 2″, finely dissected. Fruit 4″, elongated, many-seeded capsules. A showy plant, it can carpet hillsides and flats; often planted as an ornamental. **BLOOMS** Feb.–May. **HABITAT** Roadsides, Creosote Bush, Joshua Tree communities.

WESTERN SHOOTING STAR

Dodecatheon pulchellum

PRIMROSE FAMILY

9″. Flowers 1″, deep pink, dart-like; 5 petals upswept from dark purple stamens; yellow "neck," white "collar"; atop single stem. Leaves lanceolate, basal, somewhat succulent. **BLOOMS** Apr.–Aug. **HABITAT** Springs, seeps, moist meadows, streamsides, to near tree line.

PARRY'S PRIMROSE

Primula parryi

PRIMROSE FAMILY

12″. Flowers ¾″, deep pink with yellow throat, tubular base, 5 slightly notched lobes; several atop single stem; fetid. Leaves 10″, oblanceolate, somewhat fleshy, with heavy midvein, basal. **BLOOMS** June–Aug. **HABITAT** Meadows, ledges, among rocks, talus slopes, streamsides, subalpine to alpine areas.

WESTERN SPRING BEAUTY

Claytonia lanceolata

PURSLANE FAMILY

4″. Slightly succulent. Flowers ¾″, white (rarely yellow, orange, or pink) with red veins, 5-petaled, loosely clustered. Leaves lanceolate, single pair at midstem; basal leaves wither early. **BLOOMS** Feb.–July. **HABITAT** Mtn. meadows, slopes (esp. north-facing), rich moist areas, sagebrush, coniferous woods, subalpine communities.

PYGMY BITTERROOT
Lewisia pygmaea
PURSLANE FAMILY

2″. Alpine dwarf. Flowers ½″, rose-pink (occ. white); 6–9 petals; 2 green to red sepals; atop several short stems. Leaves fleshy, basal, linear, taller than stems; 1 pair of tiny, papery leaflets midway up stem. **BLOOMS** May–Aug. **HABITAT** Open mtn. ridges, rocky slopes, moist meadows, streamsides, gravelly, coarse sandy areas, sagebrush, coniferous woods, alpine communities.

MONTANA BITTERROOT
Lewisia rediviva
PURSLANE FAMILY

2″. Flowers 2″, pink to white or apricot; 10–18 petals; atop unbranched stems. Leaves linear, thick, fleshy, basal; usu. wither before flowering. **BLOOMS** May–July. **HABITAT** Ridges, coarse sandy, gravelly, rocky areas, sagebrush, mixed shrub, coniferous woodland communities. **RANGE** NV, UT, AZ.

OLD MAN'S WHISKERS
Geum triflorum
ROSE FAMILY

18″. Silky-hairy; patch-forming; from underground stems. Flowers yellow to cream, pink- or red tinged; petals ½″; sepals greenish, suffused with pink, red, or purple; 1–3 per stalk. Basal leaves 8″, pinnately cleft, segments wedge-shaped, in rosettes; 1–2 pairs tiny stem leaves. Styles feathery. **BLOOMS** May–Aug. **HABITAT** Open slopes, streamsides, sagebrush, high-elev. pine, coniferous woods, moist alpine meadows.

ROCKMAT
"Rock-spiraea"
Petrophyton caespitosum
ROSE FAMILY

3″. Sprawling, shrubby mat. Flowers minute, creamy-white; stamens long, numerous; in dense, rounded, 1½″ spikes. Stems unbranched, somewhat woody. Basal leaves oblanceolate, crowded, grayish-silky; stem leaves tiny, few. Roots in crevices and cracks of bare rock; mat-like stems conform to contours of substrate. **BLOOMS** June–Oct. **HABITAT** Rock (esp. limestone), Blackbrush, pinyon-juniper, coniferous woods.

SOFT RUSH
Juncus effusus
RUSH FAMILY

3′. Grass-like clumps. Flowers tiny, green to brown, numerous; in 4″, spray-like, dense clusters; atop tubular, pointed stems. Leaves brown sheaths around stem bases. **BLOOMS** June–Sept. **HABITAT** Moist mtn. meadows, marshy areas near ponds, streamsides, lakesides. **RANGE** NV, AZ, NM.

BASTARD TOADFLAX
Comandra umbellata
SANDALWOOD FAMILY

9″. Pale gray-green; patch-forming. Flowers tiny, white, 5-lobed, cobwebby on inside; in rounded clusters atop stems. Leaves linear, thick, gray-coated. Roots blue where cut. A root parasite. **BLOOMS** Apr.–Aug. **HABITAT** Dry, rocky, gravelly, sandy areas, canyons, slopes, plains, Blackbrush, sagebrush, pinewoods.

RED ALUM-ROOT
Heuchera rubescens
SAXIFRAGE FAMILY

12″. Smooth to glandular-hairy. Flowers ¼″; sepals tiny, white or pinkish, green-tipped; petals ¼″, white to pink, very narrow. Leaves basal, on 2″ stalks; blades round, lobed, toothed. **BLOOMS** Apr.–Sept. **HABITAT** Cliffs, rock outcrops, ledges, Blackbrush, sagebrush, pinewoods.

HARD-STEM BULRUSH
"Tule"
Scirpus acutus
SEDGE FAMILY

12′. Densely colony-forming. Flowers tiny; in loose sprays of numerous, brownish, ½″ spikelets. Stems thick, cylindrical, grass-like. Leaves long sheaths around stem bases. **BLOOMS** May–Aug. **HABITAT** Marshes, pondsides, lakesides, streamsides, springs, ditches.

SOFT-STEM BULRUSH
"Great Bulrush"
Scirpus tabernaemontani (validus)
SEDGE FAMILY

10′. Densely colony-forming; from underground stems. Flowers tiny; in orangish- or reddish-brown, ½″ spikelets. Aerial stems erect, cylindrical, tapering at ends; clustered. Leaves basal; blades 4″ or lacking. **BLOOMS** May–Aug. **HABITAT** Marshes, pondsides, lakesides, streamsides, springs, ditches. **RANGE** UT, AZ, NM.

DESERT PAINTBRUSH
Castilleja angustifolia (chromosa)
SNAPDRAGON FAMILY

18″. Flowers and floral bracts form red to orange (occ. yellow) ragged "paintbrush" spikes; size varies, depending on weather conditions. Outer bracts, upper leaves have several long, narrow lobes, lower leaves linear. Partly parasitic; roots connect with those of other plants. **BLOOMS** Mar.–Aug. **HABITAT** Arid, open areas, Creosote Bush, Joshua Tree, sagebrush, Blackbrush, pinyon-juniper communities.

BUTTER-AND-EGGS
Linaria vulgaris
SNAPDRAGON FAMILY

3′. Flowers 1″, pale yellow, with deep yellow center, long rearward spur; in dense spikes. Stems unbranched. Leaves linear. Introduced from Eurasia; widely established. **BLOOMS** June–Sept. **HABITAT** Disturbed areas, fields, ditches, pastures, roadsides.

TWINING SNAPDRAGON
Maurandya antirrhiniflora
SNAPDRAGON FAMILY

30″. Smooth vine; climbs by twining, slender stems. Flowers 1″; corollas bilaterally symmetrical, with pink to purple lobes, yellow to white throat, light-colored tube; stalked, solitary. Leaves alternate, triangular, lobed, stalked. **BLOOMS** Apr.–Oct. **HABITAT** Coarse sandy, rocky slopes, cliff crevices, among boulders, in shelter of shrubs.

SCARLET MONKEYFLOWER
Mimulus cardinalis
SNAPDRAGON FAMILY

24″. From underground stems. Flowers 2″, scarlet to orangish red; corollas bilaterally symmetrical; 2-lipped; atop 3″ stalks. Leaves 4″, oblong, opposite, stalkless, with toothed margins, 3–5 palmately veined. **BLOOMS** Mar.–Oct. **HABITAT** Seeps, springs, streamsides.

COMMON MONKEYFLOWER
Mimulus guttatus
SNAPDRAGON FAMILY

3′. Flowers 2″, brilliant yellow, with hairy, red-spotted throat; 2-lipped. Stems unbranched to many-branched. Leaves ovate, toothed. Individual plants vary in size, hairiness. **BLOOMS** Mar.–Oct. **HABITAT** Marshy areas around seeps, springs, streamsides.

YELLOW OWL'S-CLOVER
Orthocarpus luteus
SNAPDRAGON FAMILY

15″. Flowers ½″, tubular; tips divided into upper and lower lips of equal length, extend past 3-lobed, yellow-tipped bracts; in ragged, pale yellow "paintbrush" spikes; atop sticky-hairy, usu. unbranched stems. Leaves linear. **BLOOMS** July–Sept. **HABITAT** Moist meadows, fields, slopes, sagebrush, pine, oak, aspen woods.

PURPLE OWL'S-CLOVER
Orthocarpus purpureo-albus
SNAPDRAGON FAMILY

18″. Erect, glandular-hairy; purplish. Flowers ¾″; calyx pink and green; corollas purple and white, bilaterally symmetrical; 3–5 lobed bracts, broad, leaf-like, green with rose tips; in dense 4″ clusters. Leaves alternate, linear, entire to 3-cleft. **BLOOMS** July–Sept. **HABITAT** Hillsides, plains, openings in sagebrush, pinyon-juniper, Ponderosa Pine communities. **RANGE** UT, AZ, NM.

DWARF LOUSEWORT
Pedicularis centranthera
SNAPDRAGON FAMILY

8″. Smooth. Flowers 1½″, light purple or yellowish; corollas hooded, bilaterally symmetrical; in dense, 4″ clusters. Leaves 6″, stalked, alternate, lanceolate, pinnately cleft; extend beyond flower clusters. **BLOOMS** Apr.–July. **HABITAT** Sagebrush slopes, mixed shrub, pinyon-juniper, Ponderosa Pine communities.

ELEPHANT'S HEAD
Pedicularis groenlandica
SNAPDRAGON FAMILY

24″. Flowers ¾″, pink, numerous; in dense spikes, each unmistakably shaped like an elephant's head with up-curved trunk. Leaves fern-like, pinnately lobed, toothed. **BLOOMS** June–Aug. **HABITAT** High-elev. coniferous woods, moist meadows, bogs, streamsides, alpine tundra.

TOADFLAX PENSTEMON
Penstemon linarioides
SNAPDRAGON FAMILY

12″. Erect; finely hairy, slightly woody at base. Flowers ¾″, blue; corollas bilaterally symmetrical. Leaves linear, entire, opposite. **BLOOMS** May–Aug. **HABITAT** Rocky slopes, sandy, clay areas, mixed shrub, sagebrush, pinyon-juniper, Ponderosa Pine communities.

PALMER'S PENSTEMON

Penstemon palmeri

SNAPDRAGON FAMILY

6′. Erect; smooth, occ. glandular-hairy. Flowers 1″, pink or white, red-streaked, throat inflated; sterile, hairy-tipped stamen protrudes from corolla; fragrant. Leaves 5″, ovate to lanceolate, toothed; basal leaves stalked; upper leaves stalkless. **BLOOMS** Mar.–Sept. **HABITAT** Gravelly, rocky areas, washes, roadsides, Creosote Bush, Blackbrush, mixed shrub, sagebrush, pinyon-juniper, Ponderosa Pine woods.

COMMON MULLEIN

Verbascum thapsus

SNAPDRAGON FAMILY

6′. Flowers 1″, yellow, with 5 flat-spreading lobes; in dense spike atop stout, erect stalk. Leaves gray-wooly, thick, lanceolate; basal leaves 16″, upper leaves shorter. Produces clump of leaves one year; adds flowering stalk next year. Introduced from Eurasia; widely distributed. **BLOOMS** June–Sept. **HABITAT** Roadsides, pastures, disturbed areas around human habitation.

WATER SPEEDWELL

Veronica anagallis-aquatica

SNAPDRAGON FAMILY

30″. Smooth. Flowers ¼″, blue; corolla bilaterally symmetrical. Leaves opposite, elliptical, toothed, stalkless. Introduced from Europe; widely established. **BLOOMS** Mar.–Sept. **HABITAT** Aquatic areas such as marshes, bogs, muddy streamsides, springs, pools, ditches.

RATTLESNAKE-WEED

Chamaesyce albomarginata

SPURGE FAMILY

12″. Smooth; prostrate, mat-forming. Male flowers: tiny, numerous, within cup-like structure bearing 4 glands, each with 1 white, petal-like appendage; female flowers: 1 pistil, maturing into 3-lobed capsule fruit. Leaves entire, ovate; bases asymmetrical. **BLOOMS** Feb.–Oct. **HABITAT** Arid, open areas, clay, gravelly, sandy slopes, flats, Creosote Bush, Joshua Tree, Blackbrush, pinyon-juniper communities.

DESERT ROCK-NETTLE
Eucnide urens
STICKLEAF FAMILY

30″. Slightly woody at base; clump-forming. Flowers 2″, cream or pale yellow, 5-petaled; stamens numerous. Leaves 4″, short-stalked or stalkless, ovate, toothed. Fruit seeded capsules. **CAUTION** Covered with sharp, stinging hairs that inject pain-inducing substances. **BLOOMS** Mar.–Sept. **HABITAT** Rocky outcrops, washes, canyons, Creosote Bush, Blackbrush, Joshua Tree communities. **RANGE** NV, UT, AZ.

WHITE-STEMMED BLAZING STAR
Mentzelia albicaulis
STICKLEAF FAMILY

18″. Minutely barbed, stiff-hairy. Flowers yellow; 5-petaled, each ¼″. Stems white, shiny, smooth. Leaves 4″, stalkless, linear to lanceolate, entire or lobed. Fruit narrow, tapered, cylindrical capsules, from inferior ovaries. **BLOOMS** Feb.–Aug. **HABITAT** Sandy, gravelly, alluvial areas, plains, washes, Creosote Bush, Blackbrush, Joshua Tree, pinyon-juniper communities.

DESERT BLAZING STAR
Mentzelia pumila
STICKLEAF FAMILY

3′. Minutely barbed, stiff-hairy. Flowers ½″, yellow, 5-petaled; stamens numerous, outermost petal-like. Stems white. Leaves 4″, oblong, pinnately cleft to toothed, on stems; basal leaves stalked, clasping, in rosettes. Fruit oblong or club-shaped capsules, from inferior ovaries. **BLOOMS** Feb.–Oct. **HABITAT** Sandy, gravelly, alluvial areas, plains, washes, sagebrush, mixed shrub, pinyon-juniper communities.

DEVIL'S CLAW
Proboscidea parviflora
UNICORN PLANT FAMILY

H 30″; W 6′. Sticky-hairy; clump-forming, spreading. Flowers 1½″, yellow to pink or purplish, 5-lobed; corollas bilaterally symmetrical. Leaves 10″, heart-shaped, stalked, entire to lobed. Fruit 10″ tapering capsules, split lengthwise; linear beak incurved, forms pair of hook-like "claws." **BLOOMS** Apr.–Oct. **HABITAT** Dry slopes, plains, open fields, washes, roadsides, Creosote Bush communities.

BRACT VERVAIN
Verbena bracteata
VERBENA FAMILY

24″. Coarse, sparsely hairy; prostrate, mat-forming. Flowers ¼″, blue to purple; corollas tubular; bracts ½″, leaf-like, linear; in dense clusters. Stems ascending. Leaves oblong, opposite, 3-parted; lobes toothed; stalked; blades 2″. **BLOOMS** May–Sept. **HABITAT** Disturbed areas, roadsides, fields, pastures, streamsides, ponds, lakes, Creosote Bush, pinyon-juniper communities.

GOODDING'S VERBENA

Verbena gooddingii

VERBENA FAMILY

24″. Glandular-hairy. Flower ½″, blue, pink-purple, or white; corollas tubular; in clusters. Stems ascending. Leaves pinnately divided; lobes toothed. **BLOOMS** Year-round. **HABITAT** Dry, rocky, gravelly canyons, mtn. slopes, Creosote Bush, Blackbrush, pinyon-juniper, Ponderosa Pine communities.

MACDOUGAL'S VERBENA

Verbena macdougalii

VERBENA FAMILY

3′. Slender; hairy. Flowers ¼″, blue-violet, 5-lobed, slightly irreg.; stamens and pistils hidden; in several dense spikes, bloom upward 1 ring at a time. Stems 4-sided. Leaves opposite, lanceolate, coarse-toothed, on stem. **BLOOMS** June–Sept. **HABITAT** Mtn. meadows, valleys, Ponderosa Pine woods. **RANGE** UT, AZ, NM.

YELLOW PRAIRIE VIOLET

Viola nuttallii

VIOLET FAMILY

10″. Flowers ½″; 5 yellow petals with veins, occ. brownish purple on outside; solitary on stem. Leaves ovate to linear, smooth-edged, long-stalked, basal. Tolerates dry sites by going dormant in summer heat. **BLOOMS** Apr.–July. **HABITAT** Dry plains, slopes, hills, sagebrush, mixed shrub, coniferous woods.

SCORPIONWEED

Phacelia crenulata

WATERLEAF FAMILY

3′. Simple to branched; covered with hairs. Flowers ¼″, purple; petals united; in 1-sided clusters, coiled like scorpion's tail. Leaves elliptical, lobed to nearly entire; lower leaves stalked. Fruit 4-seeded, globose capsules. **CAUTION** Gland-tipped hairs can cause severe rash. **BLOOMS** Feb.–July. **HABITAT** Dry, sandy, rocky hills, canyons, washes, Creosote Bush, sagebrush, mixed shrub, pinyon-juniper communities.

Invertebrates

Biologists divide the animal kingdom into two broad groupings—vertebrates, animals with a backbone, and invertebrates, those without. Invertebrates constitute the vast majority of animal life-forms that inhabit water, air, and land. They have thrived on earth for more than a billion years, with species evolving and disappearing through the eons, and they include a fascinating spectrum of phyla with extraordinarily diverse lifestyles and evolutionary developments. This guide describes selected species from two phyla found in freshwater and terrestrial environments.

Phylum Annelida	Earthworms
Phylum Arthropoda	Crustaceans, millipedes, centipedes, arachnids, and insects

There are two basic invertebrate body structures. *Radially symmetrical* invertebrates, such as many marine invertebrates, have a circular body plan with a central mouth cavity and a nervous system that encircles the mouth. *Bilateral* invertebrates have virtually identical left and right sides like vertebrates, with paired nerve cords that run along the belly, not the back, and a brain (in species with a head). All invertebrates are cold-blooded, and either become dormant or die when temperatures become too high or low.

Tens of thousands of invertebrate species thrive in the Southwest's freshwater and terrestrial environments. Ponds and meadows may contain billions of invertebrates per acre. The phylum Annelida includes the earthworms, which can occur at an average of 1,000 pounds per acre; they help fertilize and oxygenate soil by pulling vegetation underground. The phylum Arthropoda comprises the largest number of terrestrial invertebrates, with five classes covered here: crustaceans, millipedes, centipedes, arachnids, and insects. Crustaceans include pillbugs, commonly found under rocks and logs, and freshwater shrimp, which survive many years of drought as eggs. Arachnids—spiders, daddy-long-legs (harvestmen), ticks, and mites—are discussed on page 196. Insects, introduced on page 200, comprise many well-known orders, including dragonflies, grasshoppers, beetles, flies, butterflies and moths, and ants, wasps, and bees (see their separate introductions within the section).

EARTHWORMS
Lumbricus species
EARTHWORM CLASS

L to 8″. Body soft, cylindrical, legless, with about 150 segments; purplish orange. Aerates moist soil; common on surface after heavy rains. Feeds on decaying plant matter. **HABITAT** Moist soils.

COMMON PILLBUG
Armadillidium vulgare
CRUSTACEAN CLASS

3/8". Body convex, with gray, shrimp-like plates, 7 pairs short legs; can roll into ball. Head has 2 short antennae. Feeds on decaying plant matter. Burrows into soil in dry season. **HABITAT** Moist places, under rocks, logs.

FAIRY SHRIMPS
Brachinecta species
CRUSTACEAN CLASS

1". Body elongated, lacks carapace; transparent, colorfully tinted. 11 pairs flattened "feet." Eggs survive drought and cold in mud. **HABITAT** Abundant in temporary ponds and salt lakes after heavy rains.

TADPOLE SHRIMP
Triops longicaudatus
CRUSTACEAN CLASS

1½". Body elongated, segmented, with oval carapace; pale-colored. Dozens of pairs of broad "feet." 2 long appendages at rear. Swims on back, creeps on pool bottoms. Eggs lie dormant in soil, hatch when pond fills. **HABITAT** Deserts, in temporary ponds.

DESERT MILLIPEDE
Orthoporus ornatus
MILLIPEDE CLASS

4". Body cylindrical, black or brown. About 80 segments, each with 2 pairs short legs. 2 short antennae at front. Slow-moving; rolls into ball, spraying foul odor if threatened. Common after summer rains. Vegetarian. **HABITAT** Desert scrub; most common in Sonoran Desert.

GIANT DESERT CENTIPEDE
Scolopendra heros
CENTIPEDE CLASS

7". Body elongated; brownish yellow, with blue-black head and rear. About 20 segments, each with 1 pair legs. 2 antennae at front. 2 rear legs raised when threatened; resemble antennae to confuse predator. Fast runner. Nocturnal; feeds on arthropods. **CAUTION** Bites; mildly poisonous. **HABITAT** Low-elev. deserts.

Spiders and Kin

The class Arachnida includes spiders, ticks, mites, daddy-long-legs (harvestmen), scorpions, and pseudoscorpions. Spiders have two body parts and eight legs. Most also have eight simple eyes, the arrangement of which differs from family to family. On jumping spiders, which hunt without benefit of a web, two of the eyes are tremendously enlarged, a trait that enables them to accurately judge distances to their prey. All spiders extrude up to three or four types of silk from spinnerets on the tips of their abdomens: one to make cocoons for their eggs; another, much finer, for lowering themselves; sturdy strands to construct radial web lines; and finally, the sticky silk they use to entrap prey.

Head of a spider

Spiders hunt by stalking, ambushing, or ensnaring their victims, then subduing or killing them with a poisonous bite. Their venom acts as a powerful digestive fluid, which liquifies their prey so they can suck it up. Almost all spiders are venomous, but most are entirely harmless to humans. Spiders are not parasitic on humans or domesticated animals, nor do they transmit any diseases to humans. They can be incredibly abundant, especially in meadows and grasslands, where hundreds of thousands can inhabit a single acre. Their hearty appetites help to control the insect population.

In addition to spiders, there are many other arachnids among us. Daddy-long-legs, also called harvestmen, are nonvenomous and have one body part and very long, fragile legs. They are normally solitary, but in winter they may huddle together in masses. Scorpions look like tiny lobsters with stingers on the tips of their up-turned tails. Great care should be taken while examining scorpions: their sting can be quite painful, and in the case of one southwestern species, potentially fatal. Ticks are parasites with little foreclaws that grasp onto passing animals. To feed, they bury their heads under the skin and draw blood.

Arachnids in buildings and at lower elevations may be active all year; those at higher elevations are active chiefly from spring through fall. The accounts below give typical lengths of females, not including legs; the infrequently seen males are often much smaller.

Bark Scorpion with young on back

DESERT TARANTULA
Aphonopelma chalcodes
ARACHNID CLASS

3″. Body, legs very large, hairy. Female yellowish to brown; male blackish with red hairs on abdomen. Nocturnal; hides by day in deep, silk-lined burrow. **CAUTION** Bites; releases irritating abdominal hairs if roughly handled. **HABITAT** Deserts. **SEASON** Late Aug.–Oct. **RANGE** s AZ, NM.

FIDDLE-BACK SPIDERS
Loxosceles species
ARACHNID CLASS

⅜″. Cephalothorax yellow-brown to light brown, with distinct violin-shaped marking. Legs long, slender. Several Southwest species. **CAUTION** Not aggressive, but bite may be serious and heal slowly. **HABITAT** Ground litter, woodpiles, clothing piles; below 5,000′. **SEASON** Year-round.

FUNNEL WEB SPIDER
Calilena restricta
ARACHNID CLASS

1″. Body and legs gray with lighter markings. Young hatches in spring; builds funnel that reaches about 3′ diameter by late summer; retreats to bottom of funnel, in debris, old rodent burrow. **HABITAT** Deserts at low to mid-elev. **SEASON** Mar.–Oct. **RANGE** s AZ.

NET WEB SPIDER
Kukulcania arizonensis
ARACHNID CLASS

1″. Body and legs black, velvety. Constructs lacy web in retreat under rocks, debris, human constructs; web radiates out from retreat. **HABITAT** Varied, at mid-elev. **SEASON** Year-round.

WESTERN BLACK WIDOW SPIDER
Latrodectus hesperus
ARACHNID CLASS

½″. Female black, glossy; abdomen bulbous, with red hourglass pattern below. Male and imm. much smaller (¼″); appear paler due to fine white, yellow, or red lines on sides and back; usu. have red hourglass below. Web irreg., with funnel-like exit. **CAUTION** Poisonous (mainly female). **HABITAT** Debris, buildings. **SEASON** Year-round.

GREEN LYNX SPIDER
Peucetia viridans
ARACHNID CLASS

⅜″. Body green to tan. Legs long, skinny; armed with prominent narrow spines. Eyes arranged in hexagonal pattern on top of head. Spins irreg. web only for egg sac; hunts by jumping and running. **HABITAT** Shrubs, grasses. **SEASON** Summer.

GIANT CRAB SPIDER
Olios giganteus
ARACHNID CLASS

¾″. Body gray with dark markings. Legs gray. Female spins golfball-size cocoon around herself to lay eggs. Runs fast on smooth vertical surfaces, ceilings. **HABITAT** Deserts, woodlands at low elev. **SEASON** Apr.–Oct. **RANGE** s AZ, NM.

GIANT HAIRY SCORPION
Hadrurus arizonensis
ARACHNID CLASS

4″. Body darker than sand-colored legs and abdominal "tail." Nocturnal; hides by day in burrow; occ. under rocks, human debris. Genus contains largest scorpions in N. Amer. **CAUTION** Stings if molested. **HABITAT** Desert valleys. **SEASON** Chiefly summer. **RANGE** w AZ, extreme s UT and NV.

BARK SCORPION
Centruroides exilicauda
ARACHNID CLASS

1½″. Body tan or beige; "tail" and pincers slender. Nocturnal. Hibernates in groups. **CAUTION** Most dangerous Southwest scorpion; sting is life-threatening to young children. **HABITAT** Under rocks, debris, dead tree bark, at low to mid-elev. **SEASON** Summer. **RANGE** s and w AZ, s UT, s NV.

DADDY-LONG-LEGS
Leiobunum species
ARACHNID CLASS

¼″. Body oval. Legs extremely long, thin; second pair longest, used as antennae. Most often seen singly, but sometimes mass together with legs intertwined. Nonvenomous. **HABITAT** Varied, from deserts to woodlands. **SEASON** Year-round.

VELVET MITES
Dinothrombium species
ARACHNID CLASS

¼". Body rounded, velvety, red. Lives in soil below surface; emerges during summer rains to feed on winged termites (its sole food), mate, and lay eggs. Sometimes stays underground for several years. **HABITAT** Deserts, at low elev. **SEASON** Summer.

ROCKY MOUNTAIN WOOD TICK
Dermacentor andersoni
ARACHNID CLASS

⅛". Female reddish brown with white shield on back; male mottled gray. Waits on grasses for passing mammals. **CAUTION** Can transmit serious diseases: Rocky Mountain spotted fever, Colorado tick fever, tularemia, tick paralysis. **HABITAT** Open, rocky areas. **SEASON** Year-round; chiefly spring–fall.

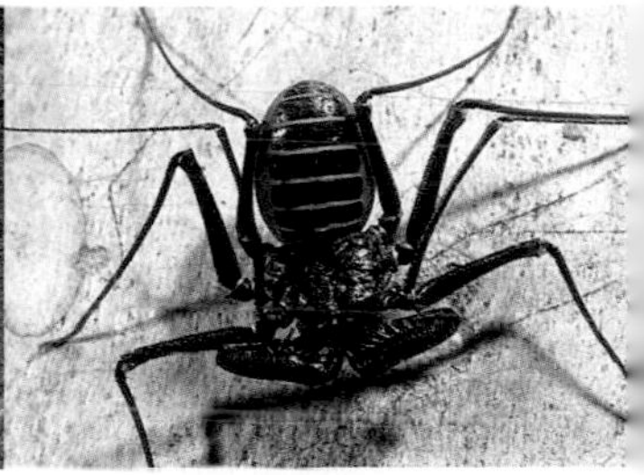

GIANT VINEGARONE
Mastigoproctus giganteus
ARACHNID CLASS

3". Body elongated; brown or black. Large pincers held forward; long "tail" at abdomen tip. Releases vinegar (85% acetic acid) secretion when disturbed. Nocturnal. **HABITAT** Under logs, wood, debris; in houses. **SEASON** Summer rainy season. **RANGE** se AZ and east.

TAIL-LESS WHIPSCORPION
Paraphrynus mexicanus
ARACHNID CLASS

1". Body disk-like, dark brown to black. Front legs antenna-like. Can move quickly in any direction. Nocturnal; feeds on insects. **HABITAT** Low-elev. deserts, in rodent burrows and under rocks, wood. **SEASON** Summer. **RANGE** s AZ.

WINDSCORPIONS
Eremobates species
ARACHNID CLASS

1¼". Body yellow-brown. Head pointed; abdomen large, segmented, oval. Large mouthparts on head used to masticate prey. Very fast runner and voracious predator on insects, arachnids. Nonvenomous. **HABITAT** Arid, nonurban areas at low elev. **SEASON** Chiefly summer.

Insects

Insects, of the class Insecta, include over a million different species worldwide and are found almost everywhere. Their importance to the ecological health of the planet cannot be overstated. In the Southwest and other temperate regions, insects pollinate approximately 80 percent of the flowering plants. They are a vital link in every ecosystem.

All insects have three main body parts—head, thorax, and abdomen—to which various other structures are attached. The head has a pair of antennae, which may be narrow, feathery, pointed, short, or long (sometimes much longer than the body). The eyes are compound and the mouthparts are adapted to chewing, biting, piercing, sucking, and/or licking. Insect wings (usually four) and legs (six) attach at the thorax. The abdomen, usually the largest section, houses the reproductive and other internal organs.

A remarkable aspect of insect life is the transformation from egg to adult, known as metamorphosis. In complete metamorphosis, which includes a pupal stage and is unique to insects, the adults lay eggs from which the larvae are hatched. The larva feeds and grows, molting its skin several times, until it prepares for its immobile pupal state by hiding or camouflaging itself. Within the pupa, larval organs dissolve and adult organs develop. Moths, butterflies, beetles, and flies undergo complete metamorphosis. In incomplete metamorphosis, there is no pupal stage, and insects such as mayflies, dragonflies, grasshoppers, and bugs gradually develop from hatched nymphs into adults. The metamorphic timetable varies widely; some insects complete the transformation in a matter of days while others, like cicadas, take up to 17 years. More primitive insects such as Firebrats undergo no metamorphosis, and young and adults are similar except in size.

Horse Lubber Grasshoppers

This book introduces representative species or genera of insects from many orders. They are sequenced from primitive to more advanced. We have placed the large butterfly and moth section last, although traditionally these insects precede the ants, bees, and wasps. For many insects there is no commonly accepted English name at the species level. Descriptions and seasonal information refer to typical adult forms unless otherwise noted. Measurements indicate typical adult body lengths except in the butterfly accounts, in which wingspan measurements are given.

FIREBRAT
Thermobia domestica
SILVERFISH ORDER

½". Body brown and white, flattened; antennae long. Three long bristles at end of abdomen. Often found near stoves, boilers. **HABITAT** Warm, humid areas, houses. **SEASON** Year-round.

Dragonflies

Dragonflies (order Odonata) are large predatory insects, many of which specialize in killing mosquitoes. The order is 300 million years old and comprises two major groups—dragonflies and damselflies. Both have movable heads and large compound eyes that in dragonflies nearly cover the head and in damselflies bulge out from the sides. Their legs are attached to the thorax just behind their heads, a feature that makes walking all but impossible but greatly facilitates their ability to grasp and hold prey while tearing into it with sharp mouthparts. They have four powerful wings that move independently, allowing for both forward and backward flight. At rest, the wings are held horizontally by dragonflies, and together over the top of the abdomen by damselflies. Nymphs, called naiads, live among the vegetation and muck in ponds and streams and feed on mosquito larvae, other insects, tadpoles, and small fish. Many of the Southwest's colorful species have captured the interest of bird and butterfly enthusiasts. A few species are migratory, gathering in the fall for southbound flights. In the accounts that follow, all species not noted as damselflies are dragonflies. The size given for dragonflies is the typical adult body length (not the wingspread).

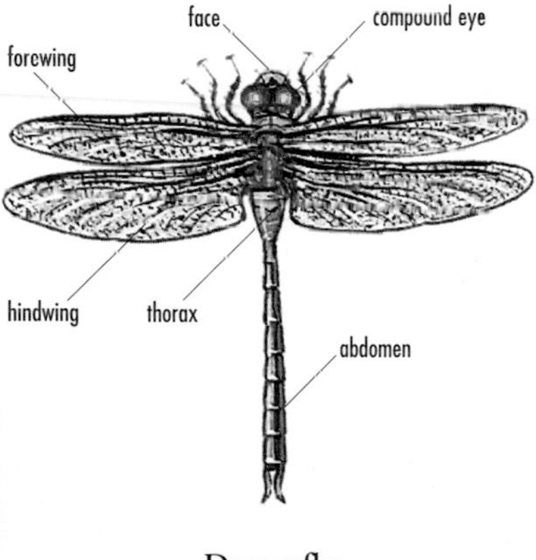

Dragonfly

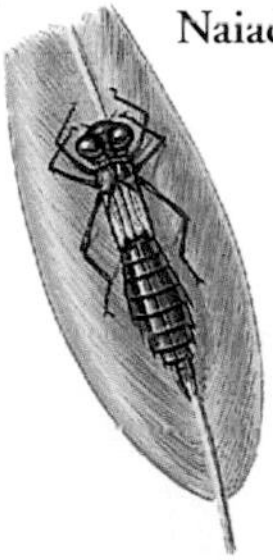

Naiad

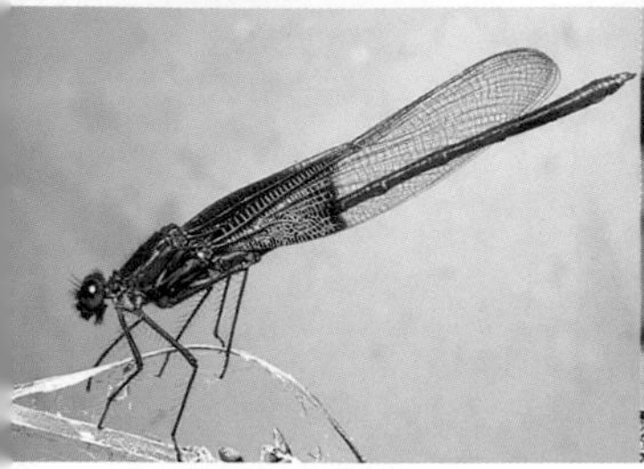

AMERICAN RUBYSPOT
Hetaerina americana
DRAGONFLY ORDER

1¾″. Damselfly. Male abdomen iridescent bronze-green; female greener. Wings clear, male's bright red at base, female's brown at base. **HABITAT** Rapid streams. **SEASON** Apr.–Nov.

GREAT SPREADWING
Archilestes grandis
DRAGONFLY ORDER

2¼″. Damselfly. Body dark with bright yellowish-white stripe on each side of thorax, whitish tip to abdomen. Wings clear. Very large damselfly. **HABITAT** Ponds, slow streams. **SEASON** June–Nov.

FAMILIAR BLUET
Enallagma civile
DRAGONFLY ORDER

1⅜″. Damselfly. Body blue with black markings along top of thorax and abdomen. Wings clear. Frequents newly disturbed areas. Most widespread N. Amer. damselfly. **HABITAT** Permanent and temporary ponds, slow streams. **SEASON** Apr.–Nov.

DESERT FIRETAIL
Telebasis salva
DRAGONFLY ORDER

1″. Damselfly. Thorax dark; abdomen bright red (male) or brownish-yellow (female). Wings clear. **HABITAT** Sunny ponds and slow streams with emergent vegetation. **SEASON** May–Oct.

BLUE-EYED DARNER
Aeshna multicolor
DRAGONFLY ORDER

2¾″. Thorax bright blue with black stripes; abdomen has black and blue checkered pattern. Eyes blue. Wings clear. Strong flier; rarely perches. **HABITAT** Open lowlands, occ. far from water. Breeds in slow or still waters. **SEASON** May–Oct.

BLUE DASHER
Pachydiplax longipennis
DRAGONFLY ORDER

1½″. Male thorax striped black and yellow; abdomen blue with black tip. Female and imm. duller. Wings mostly clear. Common near quiet waters. **HABITAT** Ponds, marshes, slow streams. **SEASON** July–Sept.

MEXICAN AMBERWING
Perithemis intensa
DRAGONFLY ORDER

1″. Thorax and abdomen golden and greenish. Thorax with dark streaks on sides. Wings bright orange-yellow, female's with golden to brown crossbands. **HABITAT** Low-elev. deserts. **SEASON** Aug.–Oct. **RANGE** AZ.

VARIEGATED MEADOWHAWK
Sympetrum corruptum
DRAGONFLY ORDER

1⅝″. Body light brownish orange. Thorax with 2 yellowish-white stripes or spots on sides; abdomen with light blue-gray patches along sides. Wings have several orange veins at front edge. **HABITAT** Still water, slow streams. **SEASON** Year-round.

BLACK SADDLEBAGS
Tramea lacerata
DRAGONFLY ORDER

2″. Body purplish blue; abdomen with yellow spots above. Wings clear, with black "saddlebag" bands covering basal fourth of each hindwing. **HABITAT** Near slow-moving or still fresh water. **SEASON** Mar.–Nov. **RANGE** NV, UT, AZ.

ARID LAND SUBTERRANEAN TERMITE
Reticulitermes tibialis
TERMITE ORDER

¼″. Worker yellowish white with darker abdomen; soldier has large yellow head, blackish mandibles. Builds underground nest of dirt and saliva. Common, destructive, eats wood from inside out. **HABITAT** Low- to mid-elev. deserts. **SEASON** Below 4,000′: Jan.–Mar.; above 4,000′: June–July.

DESERT ROACHES
Arenivega species
COCKROACH ORDER

1¼″. Body tan to light brown (male) or brown (female). Winged male attracted to lights; female flightless, rarely seen. A scavenger, feeding on rodent feces, food scraps. Not a household pest. **HABITAT** Desert areas. **SEASON** Chiefly summer.

AMERICAN COCKROACH
Periplaneta americana
COCKROACH ORDER

1¾″. Body shiny reddish brown; large, pale yellow head shield with 2 brown blotches; antennae longer than body. **HABITAT** Buildings, sewers. **SEASON** Year-round.

EUROPEAN EARWIG
Forficula auricularia
EARWIG ORDER

⅝″. Body slender, brownish to black. Legs yellowish. Antennae bead-like. Pincers at abdomen tip curved (male) or straight (female). Female guards eggs, feeds young nymphs. **HABITAT** Decaying logs, leaf litter, yards, at low to mid-elev. **SEASON** Year-round.

GROUND MANTIS
Litaneutria minor
MANTID ORDER

1½″. Body long, gray. Female wings short; male's long, with large black spot in center of hindwings. Preys on insects, other arthropods. **HABITAT** Deserts, chaparral scrub. **SEASON** Apr.–Nov.

WESTERN SHORT-HORNED WALKINGSTICK
Parabacillus hesperus
WALKINGSTICK ORDER

3″. Body very slender and stick-like; brown. Antennae slender, short. Is parthenogenetic (produces young without mating); overwinters as eggs. **HABITAT** Trees, shrubs, other vegetation. **SEASON** Apr.–Sept.

Grasshoppers and Kin

Members of the order Orthoptera are beloved for their musical abilities and despised for their voracious appetites. All species have mouthparts designed to bite and chew, and straight membranous wings. Grasshoppers and crickets have greatly developed hindlegs for jumping. Females have long ovipositors, straight in most species but sickle-shaped in katydids; they lay eggs in soil or tree vegetation. While no insects have true voices, orthopterans manage to make themselves heard in a variety of distinctive ways; most melodies are produced by males trying to attract mates. Crickets and katydids raise their wings and rub together specialized parts to produce their well-known calls. Most crickets are "right-winged," rubbing their right wings over their left, while katydids are "left-winged." Grasshoppers rub their hindlegs and wings together, and also make rattling, in-flight sounds by vibrating their forewings against their hindwings.

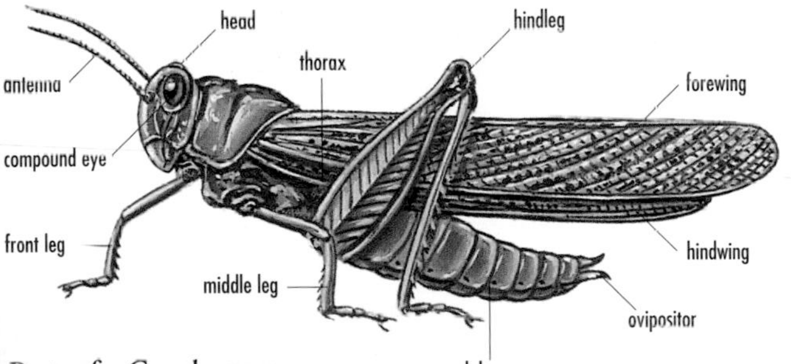

Parts of a Grasshopper

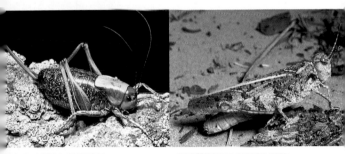

MORMON CRICKET
Anabrus simplex
GRASSHOPPER ORDER

1¾". A katydid. Body brown to blackish, with large head shield, sword-like ovipositor. Antennae as long as body. Wings small, obscured by shield. Serious pest to crops. California Gull monument in Utah commemorates cricket-hungry gulls who saved Mormons' crops in 1848. **HABITAT** Fields. **SEASON** Chiefly June–Oct.

SPECKLED RANGELAND GRASSHOPPER
Arphia conspersa
GRASSHOPPER ORDER

1¼". Forewings brownish gray. Body and most of hindwings brightly and variably colored; hindwings visible in flight. **HABITAT** Prairies, fields, croplands. **SEASON** May–July.

PALLID-WINGED GRASSHOPPER
Trimerotropis pallidipennis
GRASSHOPPER ORDER

1½″. Body tan to brown, with dark camouflaging bands. Hindwings translucent pale yellow with dark edge; visible in flight. Several related "band-winged" grasshoppers have blue, red, yellow, or orange hindwings. **HABITAT** Grasslands, desert scrub. **SEASON** June–Oct.

HORSE LUBBER GRASSHOPPER
Taeniopoda eques
GRASSHOPPER ORDER

2″. Body shiny black with yellow or orange stripes. Forewings green-veined, hindwings pink with black edges. **HABITAT** Rolling grasslands at 3,000–4,000′. **SEASON** June–Aug. **RANGE** s AZ.

BROAD-WINGED KATYDID
Microcentrum rhombifolium
GRASSHOPPER ORDER

2″. Body bright green; humped appearance. Wings have vein-like markings. Resembles a leaf. Feeds on cottonwoods, willows, occ. citrus. Overwinters as large, flat eggs glued in rows to twigs or leaf edges. **HABITAT** Desert riparian areas, oak woodlands. **SEASON** June–Dec.

JERUSALEM CRICKET
Stenopelmatus fuscus
GRASSHOPPER ORDER

1¾″. Body humpbacked, shiny, brown; abdomen large, with darker brown bands. Head large, round, light-colored; resembles bald human head. Wingless. Burrows in soft, damp ground; eats insects, roots, decaying plants. **CAUTION** Bites. **HABITAT** Moist soils. **SEASON** Year-round.

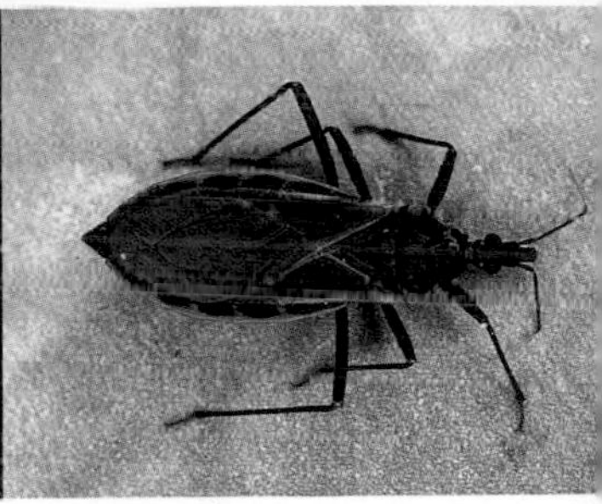

COMMON WATER STRIDERS
Gerris species
TRUE BUG ORDER

⅝". Body brown, long, slender. Middle and hindlegs very long, spiderlike. Winged or wingless. Skates over water using surface tension. Eats mosquito larvae, small insects. **HABITAT** Slow-moving streams, ponds. **SEASON** Year-round.

KISSING BUG
"Bloodsucking Conenose"
Triatoma rubida
TRUE BUG ORDER

¾". Body reddish brown, with red along margins. Head elongated. Nocturnal; attracted to lights. **CAUTION** Bites. **HABITAT** Nests of Wood Rats and other small animals. **SEASON** May–June.

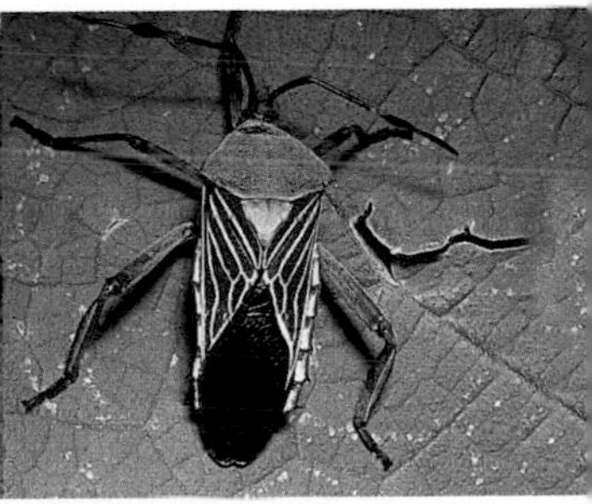

SMALL MILKWEED BUG
Lygaeus kalmii
TRUE BUG ORDER

½". Body oval, dark gray; red band behind head; bright red X on forewings. Eats milkweeds, asters; distasteful to predators. Lays eggs on milkweeds. **HABITAT** Fields, meadows. **SEASON** Feb.–Oct.

GIANT MESQUITE BUG
Thasus gigas
TRUE BUG ORDER

1½". Body oval. Forewings brown with yellowish markings. Legs banded black and red. Sucks sap from mesquite trees. **HABITAT** Areas with mesquite. **SEASON** May–July. **RANGE** s AZ.

LEAF-FOOTED BUG
Leptoglossus occidentalis
TRUE BUG ORDER

¾″. Body hourglass-shaped, brown. Hindlegs have flattened, leaf-like expansions on sides. Wings have white markings. **HABITAT** Crop fields, grasslands. **SEASON** Apr.–Sept.

STINK BUG
Brochymena sulcata
TRUE BUG ORDER

⅝″. Body rounded at rear, pointed at front; mottled gray and brown. Rear edge of thorax angled outward. Upper surfaces pebbly, superbly camouflaged for resting on bark. **HABITAT** Orchards, woodlands, deserts. **SEASON** Apr.–Oct.

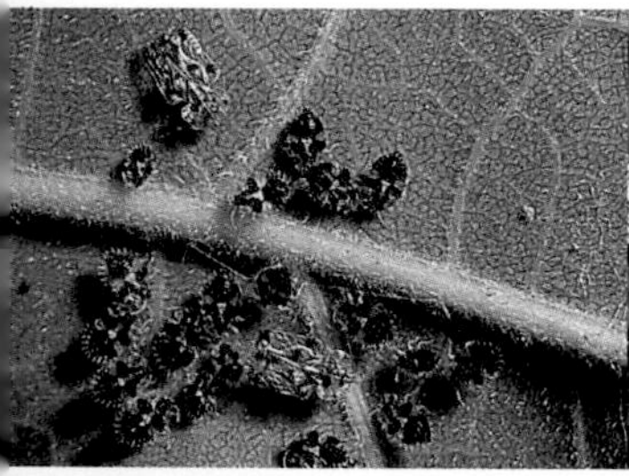

LACE BUGS
Corythucha and other genera
TRUE BUG ORDER

¼″. Body white, lace-like. Feeds chiefly on leaves of trees and shrubs; causes leaves to yellow and fall. Lays eggs on undersides of leaves. Nymph black, spiny. **HABITAT** Mid- to high elev. **SEASON** Apr.–Sept.

COCHINEAL BUG
Dactylopius confusus
SCALE INSECT ORDER

1⁄16″. Body reddish; hidden under white, thread-like, waxy plates. Female wingless, remains stationary on plant surface. Male half-size, winged. Occurs in clustered colonies. Insects are gathered and dried to produce red "cochineal" dye. **HABITAT** Cactuses, principally prickly-pears. **SEASON** Summer. **RANGE** s half of SW.

DESERT LAC INSECTS
Tachardiella species
SCALE INSECT ORDER

1⁄16″. Body oval, covered with resin secreted from body for protection. Male winged; female wingless. **HABITAT** Arid areas with Wolfberry. **SEASON** Chiefly summer.

DESERT CICADA
Diceroprocta apache
CICADA ORDER

1″. Body robust; blackish brown with yellow "collar," flattened head, tapered abdomen. Wing veins lighter on outer half. Call very noisy, high-pitched. Nymph dark brown, with downcurved abdomen. **HABITAT** Desert areas. **SEASON** May–July. **RANGE** s AZ.

SNOW SCORPIONFLIES
Boreus species
SCORPIONFLY ORDER

⅛″. Body spindle-shaped, with greatly elongated face; dark. Female's ovipositor long. Wings tiny. Hops about on snow on warm winter days. A dozen western species. **HABITAT** On mosses in woods. **SEASON** Year-round.

COMMON SNAKEFLIES
Raphidia species
NERVEWING ORDER

⅝″. Body elongated, dark brown. Head and prothorax long, narrow, snake-like. Wings transparent; folded tent-like over back. Female ovipositor long, slender. **HABITAT** Stumps and vegetation in woodlands. **SEASON** Apr.–Sept.

OWLFLIES
Ascaloptynx and other genera
NERVEWING ORDER

1¼″. Adult resembles dragonfly. Antennae long, clubbed. Predatory larva (¾″) similar to Antlion, with long mandibles, but does not dig pit. **HABITAT** Deserts, woodlands, at mid-elev. **SEASON** Adult: June–Sept.; larva: year-round.

ANTLIONS
Bracynemerus species
NERVEWING ORDER

1¾″. Resembles a damselfly, but softer. Wings heavily veined; held roof-like over body at rest; weak flier. Mainly nocturnal. Larva (Doodlebug or Antlion) oval with large jaws. Larva and most adults carnivorous. **HABITAT** Grasslands, open sandy areas, yards. **SEASON** Summer.

GREEN LACEWINGS
Chrysoperla species
NERVEWING ORDER

⅝″. Body elongated, pale green; head narrow; eyes large, coppery; antennae long. Wings clear, veined; at least ¼″ longer than body; fold together over back. Adult and larva eat destructive aphids. **HABITAT** Gardens, woodland edges. **SEASON** Mar.–Sept.

Beetles

There are more species of beetles (order Coleoptera) than any other animals on earth. Beetles' forewings are hardened dense sheaths known as *elytra,* which meet in a straight line down the back. Their hindwings underneath function as the organs of flight. Beetle legs and antennae vary from long and straight to stout and angled. Both adults and larvae, known as grubs, have mouthparts adapted for biting and chewing. They are vegetarians, predators, scavengers, and in a few instances parasites. Some, like lady beetles, are highly prized by gardeners because they eat aphids and other garden pests, while others are nuisances at best. They range in size from microscopic organisms to some of the largest insects in the world.

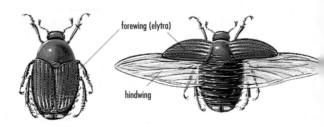

OREGON TIGER BEETLE
Cicindela oregona
BEETLE ORDER

½″. Head and thorax narrow, abdomen wide; dark brown. Forewings have white spots. Adult quick, ferocious, runs down prey; in flight resembles a fly. Larva ambushes from burrows. **HABITAT** Moist areas. **SEASON** Summer.

GROUND BEETLES
Harpalus species
BEETLE ORDER

½″. Body an elongated oval, black. Attracted to lights at night. Many similar species. **HABITAT** Underground debris, incl. logs. **SEASON** July.

SUNBURST DIVING BEETLE
Thermonectus marmoratus
BEETLE ORDER

⅝″. Body oval, smooth, black with yellow spots. Hindlegs oar-like, for swimming. Surfaces to renew air supply captured under wings. Eats insects, tadpoles, small fishes. Aquatic larva (Water Tiger) also predatory, breathes with gills. **HABITAT** Streams in oak woodlands. **SEASON** Apr.–Oct.

LARGE WHIRLIGIG BEETLES
Dineutus species
BEETLE ORDER

½″. Body oval, flat; black with bronzy sheen. Forewings have shallow grooves. Hindlegs short, paddle-like. Gathers in groups that swim in circles. **HABITAT** Surface of ponds, streams. **SEASON** Summer.

ROVE BEETLE
Creophilus maxillosus
BEETLE ORDER

¾″. Body elongated, shiny black. Hindwings and several abdominal segments have yellow bands. Feeds on dead animals; appears at first sign of decay. **HABITAT** On dead animals. **SEASON** Year-round.

MAY BEETLES
"June Bugs"
Phyllophaga species
BEETLE ORDER

1⅜″. Body bulky. Thorax shield chestnut. Forewings lighter brown, ungrooved. Antennae end in right angles. Attracted by lights; slow, noisy, buzzing flight. Larva one of most common white grubs. **HABITAT** Broadleaf woods, fields. **SEASON** May–Aug.

TEN-LINED JUNE BEETLE
Polyphylla decemlineata
BEETLE ORDER

1″. Body oval; brown, with white stripes on head, thorax, and forewings: each wing has 1 short and 4 long stripes. Eats conifer needles. Larva white; eats shrub and tree roots. **HABITAT** Forests, woodlands. **SEASON** Mar.–July.

RHINOCEROS BEETLE
"Southwestern Hercules Beetle"
Dynastes granti
BEETLE ORDER

2″. Largest U.S. beetle. Body búlky, gray-green. Male has 2 horns: 1 projects from head, 1 from prothorax; female lacks horns. Attracted to lights at night. **HABITAT** Riparian areas with sycamores. **SEASON** July–Sept.

COMMON CLICK BEETLES
Melanotus species
BEETLE ORDER

⅝″. Body elongated, somewhat flattened; dark brown to blackish. If overturned, arches back and quickly flips upright with audible "click." **HABITAT** Under tree bark, vegetation. **SEASON** Apr.–Sept.

CONVERGENT LADY BEETLE
Hippodamia convergens
BEETLE ORDER

¼″. Body oval. Thorax has converging white stripes. Forewings reddish orange, often with many black spots. Adult and larva eat aphids, soft-bodied insects. From May through winter, adults migrate to mtn. canyons. **HABITAT** Gardens, meadows, woodlands. **SEASON** Feb.–Apr.: valleys; May–Jan.: mtns.

ARMORED STINK BEETLE
Eleodes armata
BEETLE ORDER

¾″. Body oval, black. When disturbed, raises abdomen at 45-degree angle, releases foul-smelling black liquid. A very common desert insect. **HABITAT** Desert scrub. **SEASON** Year-round.

CACTUS LONGHORN BEETLES
Moneilema species
BEETLE ORDER

1½". Body oval, black. Long antennae look short due to white markings halfway up. Flightless. Color and shape closely resemble unpalatable Stink Beetle, but does not possess stink glands. **HABITAT** Desert areas where cholla and prickly-pear cactuses occur. **SEASON** June–Sept.

SPOTTED BLISTER BEETLES
Epicauta species
BEETLE ORDER

½". Body elongated, oval, with wide head. Forewings gray with black spots. Abundant at a given site for 1 or 2 days, then disappears. **CAUTION** When disturbed, secretes "blood" that causes blisters. **HABITAT** Agricultural fields, gardens, deserts. **SEASON** June–Sept.

SPOTTED CUCUMBER BEETLE
Diabrotica undecimpunctata
BEETLE ORDER

¼". Thorax narrow, dark; head, legs, antennae black. Forewings oval, pale green with large black spots. Adult eats leaf epidermis, esp. of gourd family; larva eats host plant roots. **HABITAT** Meadows, weedy fields, farms. **SEASON** Spring–fall. **RANGE** AZ, NM.

LONG-JAWED LONGHORN BEETLE
Dendrobis mandibularis
BEETLE ORDER

1". Body an elongated oval, black with orange patches. Antennae long (male's longer than body), banded black and orange. Feeds on fruits of Saguaro, prickly-pear cactuses. **HABITAT** Deserts. **SEASON** July–Aug. **RANGE** s AZ, s NM.

RAGWEED LEAF BEETLE
Physonata arizone
BEETLE ORDER

½". Body oval, mottled with gray and white. Antennae short. When threatened, larva raises abdomen, smears feces on predator's face. **HABITAT** Deserts, canyons. **SEASON** June–Aug. **RANGE** s AZ.

ACORN WEEVILS
Curculio species
BEETLE ORDER

½". Weevils have more species than any other family in the animal kingdom. Body light brown; snout slender, nearly as long as body. Adult bores into acorns and other nuts to eat; lays eggs in the holes. Numerous species throughout region. **HABITAT** Woodlands. **SEASON** May–Sept.

SILVER TWIG WEEVIL
Ophryastes argentata
BEETLE ORDER

¾". Body elongated, with long snout; silver-gray. Larva a legless grub; feeds inside seeds, stems, roots. This species harmless, but many weevils cause serious damage to crops and stored foods. **HABITAT** Desert areas with Creosote. **SEASON** May–July.

Flies and Mosquitoes

All flies and mosquitoes have two wings and mouthparts formed for sucking, or for piercing and sucking combined. The legless and wingless larvåe undergo complete metamorphosis, and can be either terrestrial (maggots) or aquatic (called by various names). Adults fly with a wingbeat frequency often of hundreds of beats per second. This incredible speed produces the familiar in-flight buzzing sounds. Flies feed on decomposing matter, nectar, and sometimes blood. Mosquitoes' lower lips form a proboscis with six knife-sharp organs, some smooth and some saw-toothed, that cut into skin.

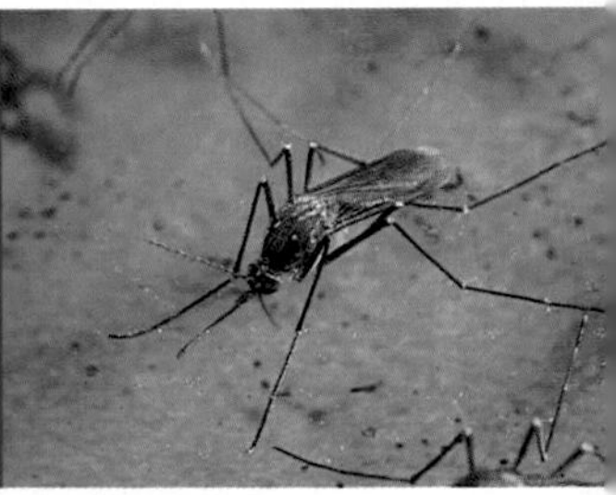

CRANE FLIES
Tipula species
FLY ORDER

2½". Body long, delicate, gray to gold; legs very long, slender. Wings clear, veined. Feeds on plants; mistaken for gigantic mosquito, but does not bite humans. **HABITAT** Watersides; may enter houses. **SEASON** Feb.–Apr.

HOUSE MOSQUITOES
Aedes and *Culex* species
FLY ORDER

⅜". Body narrow, with long proboscis; dark. Male antennae feathery, female's hairy. Both sexes feed on sap and nectar; female also feeds on blood. Larva, pupa aquatic; very active pupa (called wriggler) does not feed. **HABITAT** Near still water. **SEASON** Year-round; most active spring–fall.

DEER FLIES
Chrysops species
FLY ORDER

½″. Head small. Body dull gray-brown to black. Wings have brownish-black patches. **CAUTION** Bites; often lands on head. **HABITAT** Woodlands, roadsides near water. **SEASON** May–Sept.

BIG BLACK HORSE FLY
Tabanus punctifer
FLY ORDER

⅞″. Body large, black; male thorax has white hairy edges above, female back end white. Wings black, nearly opaque. Male eyes large. Male drinks nectar; female sucks blood, esp. of livestock. Gives painful bite. **HABITAT** Marshy ponds, streamsides. **SEASON** Spring–fall.

GIANT ROBBER FLY
Proctacanthus rodecki
FLY ORDER

1″. Thorax bulging; abdomen long, tapering. Brownish gray, with many bristly spines on body and legs. Effective predator; snatches insects from ground and vegetation. **HABITAT** Meadows, fields. **SEASON** June–Sept.

BRINE FLIES
Ephydra species
FLY ORDER

⅛″. Body gnat-like, brown, with long bristly hairs; face yellow. Adult eats small insects, larva eats decaying plants. Larva aquatic; can survive very salty habitats. May be so abundant at Great Salt Lake that water appears black from pupae and adults. **HABITAT** Salt marshes, desert salt lakes. **SEASON** Summer.

HOUSE FLY
Musca domestica
FLY ORDER

¼″. Body gray with dark stripes. Wings clear. Eyes large, red-brown; legs hairy. Egg hatches in 10–24 hours; matures to adult in 10 days; lives 15 (male) to 26 (female) days. Sucks liquid sugars from garbage; spreads disease. **HABITAT** Human habitation. **SEASON** Year-round.

Ants, Wasps, and Bees

Insects of the order Hymenoptera include narrow-waisted bees, wasps, and ants. Hymenopterans have two pairs of membranous transparent wings, mouthparts modified to chew and lick, and, in adult females, an ovipositor. All species undergo complete metamorphosis.

The narrow-waists are divided into two broad groupings. The first, parasitic wasps, include the large and varied assemblage of nonstinging ichneumon wasps, which live as parasites during their larval stage. Some ichneumons are feared by humans for their astonishingly long ovipositors, which are used not for stinging but to probe about in woody vegetation for suitable insects on which to lay eggs. The second group of narrow-waists are the stinging insects, with ovipositors that have been modified into stinging organs. These include the vespid wasps (such as yellow jackets), bees, and many ants.

paper wasp nest

Ants and some wasps and bees are highly social creatures, but some species in this order live solitary lives. Their nests vary in complexity from a single-celled hole in the ground to the Honey Bee's elaborate comb structure. Many ant species excavate in soil or wood, building multi-chambered homes mostly hidden from sight. Bumble bees and yellow jackets build similar homes. Unlike ants, they build a separate six-sided chamber for each of their young. Paper wasps often construct their nests in open situations, while Honey Bees utilize man-made hives or hollow trees or logs. The Honey Bee's two-sided, vertically hanging beeswax combs can contain more than 50,000 cells.

CARPENTER ANTS
Camponotus species
ANT, WASP, AND BEE ORDER

3/8″. Body amber to dark. Preys on insects; does not sting. Lives in large colonies. **HABITAT** In tree holes, under rocks; also found indoors, in drapery folds, kitchen cabinets, etc. **SEASON** Chiefly summer.

RED MOUND ANTS
Formica species
ANT, WASP, AND BEE ORDER

1/4″. Head, thorax rusty red; abdomen, legs blackish brown. Builds dome-like nest mound. One species of mound ant, *F. sanguinea,* raids nests of other *Formica* species and carries off pupae as slaves. **HABITAT** Woodlands. **SEASON** Most active June–Sept.

DESERT LEAFCUTTER ANT

Acromyrmex versicolor

ANT, WASP, AND BEE ORDER

½". Body reddish brown; 3 pairs of prominent spines on thorax. Cuts leaves, carries to nest, uses as mulch to culture a symbiotic fungus that larvae and adults eat. Known as farmers of the insect world. **HABITAT** Desert areas. **SEASON** Summer. **RANGE** s AZ, NM.

LONG-LEGGED ANTS

Aphaenogaster species

ANT, WASP, AND BEE ORDER

⅝". Body reddish black, with long legs. One of the largest, most conspicuous ants in region. Nest entrance covered with ⅛" layer of pebbles. Preys on insects. **HABITAT** Deserts, grasslands. **RANGE** s AZ, s NM.

HARVESTER ANTS

Pogonomyrmex species

ANT, WASP, AND BEE ORDER

½". Body reddish brown to black, depending on species. Harvester ants clear all vegetation in a conspicuous circle around their nests, sometimes causing crop damage. Feeds on seeds. **CAUTION** Stings painfully if molested at nest. **HABITAT** Deserts, other dry areas. **SEASON** Warm months.

THISTLEDOWN VELVET ANT

Dasymutilla gloriosa

ANT, WASP, AND BEE ORDER

⅝". Body robust; black with long white hairs. Male has wings. Wingless female armed with powerful stinger; frequently seen searching ground for other wasps to prey upon. **CAUTION** Female stings. **HABITAT** Areas with Creosote. **SEASON** Apr.–Sept.

TARANTULA HAWKS

Pepsis and *Hemipepsis* species

ANT, WASP, AND BEE ORDER

1½". Body shiny blue-black; wings blue-black, bright red, or orange. Searches out, stings, and paralyzes tarantulas to lay eggs on. Rarely stings. **HABITAT** Open areas, flower blossoms. **SEASON** Apr.–Oct.

GOLDEN PAPER WASPS
Polistes species
ANT, WASP, AND BEE ORDER
¾″. Body slender, with very narrow waist; yellow and black markings. Builds small, open-faced, stalked nest, often in conspicuous place. **CAUTION** Stings painfully if nest is disturbed. **HABITAT** Man-made structures. **SEASON** Warm months.

WESTERN YELLOW JACKET
Vespula pensylvanica
ANT, WASP, AND BEE ORDER
⅝″. Body stout, wider than head; yellow with heavy black bands and spots. Aggressively defends nests in burrows, logs. Raids picnic food, trash cans. **CAUTION** Stings. **HABITAT** Towns, foothills, mtns. **SEASON** Spring–fall.

BALD-FACED HORNET
Dolichovespula maculata
ANT, WASP, AND BEE ORDER
¾″. Body rotund, black. Yellowish-white spots on short head, base of wings, waist, and abdomen tip. Builds football-size paper nest under overhang or in bush. **CAUTION** Stings. **HABITAT** Woodland edges. **SEASON** May–Sept.

BLACK-AND-YELLOW MUD DAUBER
Sceliphron caementarium
ANT, WASP, AND BEE ORDER
1⅛″. Body slender; waist long, narrow; black with yellow markings. Wings brown to black. Legs mostly yellow. Mud nests under rocks, cliff overhangs, eaves stocked with paralyzed spiders. **HABITAT** Meadows, cliffs, buildings. **SEASON** Apr.–Oct.

CARPENTER BEES
Xylocopa species
ANT, WASP, AND BEE ORDER
1″. Body rotund, usu. blue-black. Head, thorax hairy; abdomen shiny. Female hindlegs have dense pollen brush hairs. Bores into wood to build nest. Loud buzzing flight; rarely stings. **HABITAT** Meadows, woods, buildings, desert mtns. **SEASON** Apr.–Sept.

LEAFCUTTER BEES
Megachile, Osmia, other species
ANT, WASP, AND BEE ORDER
½". Body black, with dark or light hairs. Wings clear, veined. Nests in beetle burrows in wood; cuts rose, ash, bougainvillea leaves into circular pieces to line nests with. One species is important pollinator of Alfalfa. **HABITAT** Deserts, grasslands, woods. **SEASON** Spring–summer.

HONEY BEE
Apis mellifera
ANT, WASP, AND BEE ORDER
⅝". Thorax hairy, brown; abdomen banded black and orange. Wings short, dusky. Makes honey; pollinates crops; nests in tree holes, rocks, crevices. **CAUTION** Stings but is not aggressive; if stung, remove stinger immediately. **HABITAT** Open areas. **SEASON** Year-round in all but coldest areas.

SONORAN BUMBLE BEE
Bombus sonorus
ANT, WASP, AND BEE ORDER
1". Body stout, fuzzy; largely yellow, with black head, black stripe on thorax, black tip on abdomen. Rarely stings. **HABITAT** In soil. **SEASON** Warm months. **RANGE** s AZ.

Butterflies and Moths

The order Lepidoptera comprises the familiar groups of moths and butterflies. *Lepidoptera* means "scale-winged," and refers to the minute scales that cover the four wings of all butterfly and moth species. All lepidopterans share the same general life cycle—egg to larva to pupa to adult. Eggs are laid singly, or in rows, stacks, or masses, depending on the species. The emergent larva, usually referred to as a caterpillar, feeds on plant life, and grows through several stages, or instars, shedding its skin each time. When fully grown, the caterpillar prepares to pupate by spinning a silken cocoon (moth) or finding a secure hiding place (butterfly). Then the caterpillar sheds its last larval skin, revealing the pupa, an outer shell with no head or feet, within which the wings and other adult features fully develop. Finally, the pupal skin breaks open and the winged moth or butterfly emerges. The time required for this process is different for each species. Many have only one emergence of adults per year; others have two or three. Most Southwest lepidopterans live out their entire lives within the region, although a few species, like the famous Monarch, are strongly migratory. In some springs, large incursions of Painted Ladies head northward into the Southwest from the deserts of Mexico. Most species overwinter as eggs, larvae, or pupae, but because of the mild winters in the southern parts of the region, a number of species survive the winter in their adult state, including Mourning Cloaks, Common Buckeyes, and Queens.

Several key differences distinguish moths and butterflies. Moths' antennae are either feathery or wiry, and lack the clubbed tip of butterflies' antennae. Moths rest with their wings outstretched, folded, or at an angle above the body; butterflies rest with their wings outstretched or held together vertically, like a sail. Moths can fly day and night, while butterflies fly only by day. Color and size are poor general distinguishing features between the two groups. When trying to identify a species, pay special attention to the wing colors, shape, and pattern. Most of the characteristic wing markings on moths are found on the uppersides. In butterflies, look for distinguishing markings on the uppersides of those species that rest with outstretched wings and on the undersides of those that rest with their wings folded up.

Butterflies drink nectar from many species of wildflowers and shrubs. Among the best wild nectar plants in the Southwest are milkweeds, asters, clovers and vetches, buckwheats, and *Ceanothus* species. Excellent garden flowers that attract butterflies and moths include lantanas, butterfly bushes, verbenas, heliotropes, and coreopsis. Nocturnal moths are also drawn to lights.

newly metamorphosed Monarch

Each larva, or caterpillar, species has its own select food plants, and the accounts that follow list several of these. Measurements indicate typical wingspans for adult forms, from tip to tip. The season given is the normal time these butterflies and moths are found flying in the region. However, in the north or high up in the mountains, the season generally begins later and ends earlier.

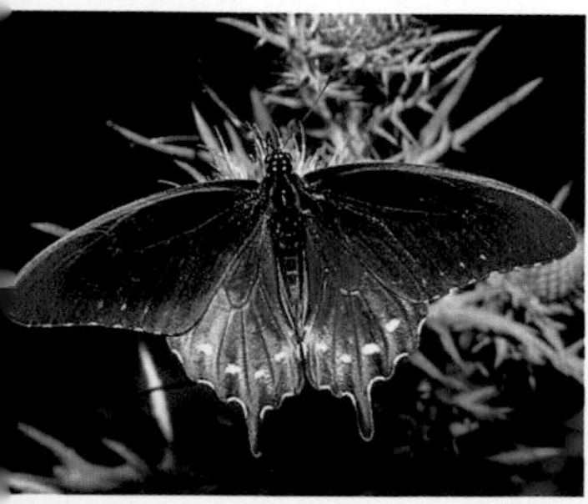

PIPEVINE SWALLOWTAIL

Battus philenor

SWALLOWTAIL FAMILY

3⅛". Forewings black above; hindwings iridescent blue-black with row of cream spots around rim, stubby tail. Below, hindwings have curved row of large orange dots. Caterpillar black to dark red with red tubercules. **HABITAT** Open woodlands, fields, streamsides, roadsides. **FOOD PLANTS** Dutchman's Pipe. **SEASON** Feb.–Oct. **RANGE** AZ, NM, s UT, s NV.

GIANT SWALLOWTAIL
Papilio cresphontes
SWALLOWTAIL FAMILY

4½″. Brownish black above, with broad yellow diagonal band across forewings and yellow band along margins. Spatulate tail has yellow spot at end. Below, mostly yellow with black veins. Caterpillar brown with large white patches, red horns. **HABITAT** Citrus groves, open woods. **FOOD PLANTS** Citruses, Torchwood. **SEASON** Mar.–Nov. **RANGE** Much of AZ and NM, extreme s NV.

WESTERN TIGER SWALLOWTAIL
Papilio rutulus
SWALLOWTAIL FAMILY

3¼″. Yellow with black "tiger" stripes; hindwings have several blue and 2 orange spots near long black tail. Caterpillar bright green with 2 large yellow eyespots. **HABITAT** Parks, gardens, riparian areas. **FOOD PLANTS** Cottonwoods, willows, sycamores, alders. **SEASON** June–July.

TWO-TAILED SWALLOWTAIL
Papilio multicaudatus
SWALLOWTAIL FAMILY

4¼″. Very large. Yellow above, with black borders; forewings have 4 narrow black stripes; hindwings have 1 narrow black stripe, blue spots near rear edge; 2 distinct tails. Below, bright yellow with narrow black stripes. **HABITAT** Canyons, gardens. **FOOD PLANTS** Cherries, plums, ashes. **SEASON** Northward: May–July, Aug.; southward: Mar.–Oct.

CABBAGE WHITE
Pieris rapae
WHITE AND SULPHUR FAMILY

1⅝″. White above; forewings have slaty tip, 1 black spot (male) or 2 (female); hindwings have 1 black spot. Yellow-white below. Caterpillar green with yellow stripes; eats crops. **HABITAT** Fields, gardens, parks. **FOOD PLANTS** Mustard family, incl. cabbages, radishes. **SEASON** Year-round.

SARA ORANGETIP
Anthocharis sara
WHITE AND SULPHUR FAMILY

1½″. White above (female occ. yellow); forewings have bright orange tip. Below, hindwings have dark gray marbling; forewing tips paler orange. Unmistakable as it bounces along trails. Caterpillar dull green. **HABITAT** Sunny canyons, slopes, streamsides, meadows. **FOOD PLANTS** Mustards. **SEASON** Northward: Mar.–June; southward: Jan.–Apr. **RANGE** Entire region, ex. extreme e NM.

ORANGE SULPHUR
Colias eurytheme
WHITE AND SULPHUR FAMILY

2″. Yellow-orange above (female occ. white), with black spot on mid-forewings, orange spot on hindwings; outer wings solid black (male) or black with yellow spots (female). Below, olive green or yellow, with silver spots: 1 ringed black, 1 or 2 ringed red. Caterpillar green with red or pale stripes. **HABITAT** Fields. **FOOD PLANTS** Pea family, incl. White Clover, Alfalfa. **SEASON** Northward: Mar.–Nov.; southward: year-round.

SOUTHERN DOGFACE
Colias cesonia
WHITE AND SULPHUR FAMILY

2¼″. Yellow above; forewings with pointed tips, black markings in poodle-head shape, complete with black "eye"; hindwings have scalloped black edges. Below, mostly yellow. **HABITAT** Open woods, fields, roadsides. **FOOD PLANTS** Pea family, incl. False Indigo, Alfalfa, clovers. **SEASON** Northward: spring–fall; southward: year-round. **RANGE** Entire region, ex. n UT, n NV.

CLOUDLESS SULPHUR
Phoebis sennae
WHITE AND SULPHUR FAMILY

2½″. Male clear yellow above; below, yellow with tiny brown dots. Female yellow or white above and below, with dark spot on forewings, brownish dots along outer margins. Migrant. **HABITAT** Deserts, open areas, fields. **FOOD PLANTS** Pea family, incl. Partridge Pea, sennas. **SEASON** Northward: June–Sept.; southward: Mar.–Dec. **RANGE** AZ, NM, s UT.

SLEEPY ORANGE
Eurema nicippe
WHITE AND SULPHUR FAMILY

1⅝″. Deep orange above, with heavy dark wing margins; forewings have thin dark line near front. Duller below, with brown spotting. **HABITAT** Fields, desert scrub, meadows. **FOOD PLANTS** Pea family, incl. sennas, clovers. **SEASON** Northward: June–Aug.; southward: year-round.

DAINTY SULPHUR
Nathalis iole
WHITE AND SULPHUR FAMILY

1″. Yellow above; forewings broadly tipped black, black bar along rear of forewings, front of hindwings. Below, yellowish or olive, with orange on forewing margins. Smallest N. Amer. sulphur. Migrant. **HABITAT** Fields, roadsides, grasslands. **FOOD PLANTS** Many, incl. aster and pink families. **SEASON** Northward: Apr.–Oct.; southward: year-round.

TAILED COPPER
Lycaena arola
GOSSAMER-WING FAMILY

1″. Above, male dull copper with purple sheen; female brown with extensive orange patches; short tail. Below, light brown with heavy dark markings, orange bar near tail. Male makes many quick forays from eye-level vegetation when defending territory. **HABITAT** Streamsides, clearings, mtn. meadows. **FOOD PLANTS** Currants, gooseberries. **SEASON** July–Aug. **RANGE** Patchily distributed throughout region.

COLORADO HAIRSTREAK
Hypaurotis crysalus
GOSSAMER-WING FAMILY

1½″. Unmistakable hairstreak. Purple above; wide black margins with few orange spots; 2 prominent tails. Below, light gray-brown, with white-edged dark band; hindwings have blue shading along outer edge, black-centered orange spot. **HABITAT** Oak canyons in mtns., foothills. **FOOD PLANTS** Gambel's Oak. **SEASON** June–Sept. **RANGE** Patchily distributed in UT, AZ, NM.

GREAT PURPLE HAIRSTREAK
Atlides halesus
GOSSAMER-WING FAMILY

1¾″. Iridescent blue (not purple) above, with black borders, 2 black tails. Below, grayish or brownish, with 3 reddish spots at base and patch of blue. Body red-orange below. **HABITAT** Junipers with Mistletoe. **FOOD PLANTS** Mistletoe. **SEASON** Northward: Apr.–Aug.; southward: Mar.–Nov. **RANGE** Patchily distributed throughout region.

JUNIPER HAIRSTREAK
Callophrys gryneus
GOSSAMER-WING FAMILY

1″. Brown above, with rusty wash near hindwing tails and scattered over forewings; 2 tails. Below, green crossed by prominent white line; forewings have rusty patch; hindwings have black-spotted gray-violet patch. Some populations purplish below. **HABITAT** Mtn. foothills, canyons, plains. **FOOD PLANTS** Junipers. **SEASON** Northward: Mar.–May, July–Aug.; southward: Mar.–Nov.

GRAY HAIRSTREAK
Strymon melinus
GOSSAMER-WING FAMILY

1⅛″. Dark gray above; hindwings have 2 orange spots, 1 long black tail at trailing edge. Below, pale to medium gray, with thin orange, black, and white line across both wings, 2 orange dots near tail. **HABITAT** Many, incl. gardens, meadows, woodland edges. **FOOD PLANTS** Varied, incl. mallow family, buckwheats, lupines, beans, hops, cotton. **SEASON** Northward: Apr.–Sept.; southward: year-round.

WESTERN PYGMY-BLUE
Brephidium exilis
GOSSAMER-WING FAMILY

½″. Above, male purple-blue at base blending to brown at edges; female less blue. Below, gray at base; outer wings orange-brown with small, white, wavy lines; hindwings have 4 iridescent spots on margin. World's smallest butterfly; low-flying. Migrant northward. **HABITAT** Weedy fields, roadsides, desert alkali flats. **FOOD PLANTS** Goosefoot family, incl. saltbushes, Lamb's Quarters. **SEASON** Northward: Mar.–Oct.; southward: year-round.

MARINE BLUE
Leptotes marina
GOSSAMER-WING FAMILY

⅞″. Male light purplish blue above; female broadly washed with brown. Below, both sexes with light brown and off-white banding; hindwings with 2 dark, orange-ringed eyespots on outer margin. Migratory northward. **HABITAT** Weedy fields, roadsides, yards, riparian areas. **FOOD PLANTS** Pea family, incl. clovers, Alfalfa, Crazyweed. **SEASON** Northward: June–Oct.; southward: year-round.

REAKIRT'S BLUE
Hemiargus isola
GOSSAMER-WING FAMILY

1″. Above, male blue with narrow black and white outer edges, female brownish, blue at base; hindwings with 2 black spots on lower edge. Below, light gray-brown; forewings have band of white-ringed black spots, hindwings have spots and short bands. Migratory northward. **HABITAT** Weedy fields, gardens, roadsides. **FOOD PLANTS** Pea family. **SEASON** Northward: May–Sept.; southward: year-round.

WESTERN TAILED-BLUE
Everes amyntula
GOSSAMER-WING FAMILY

1″. Pale blue above (female darker), with narrow dark margins. Whitish below, lightly marked with thin dark lines and spots; hindwings have orange spot over small thin tail. Low-flying. **HABITAT** Roadsides, canyons, woodland edges, meadows. **FOOD PLANTS** Pea family, incl. locoweeds, vetches, wild peas. **SEASON** Apr.–Aug.

SPRING AZURE
Celastrina ladon
GOSSAMER-WING FAMILY

1″. Male entirely pale blue above; female with black border. Below, grayish white with numerous black markings on hindwings (most common in spring) or with small dark spots (most common in summer). **HABITAT** Woodland openings, shrubby areas. **FOOD PLANTS** Many, incl. Snowbush, Cliffbush, viburnums. **SEASON** Northward: Mar.–Sept.; southward: year-round.

BOISDUVAL'S BLUE
Plebejus icarioides
GOSSAMER-WING FAMILY

1¼″. The largest N. Amer. blue. Male blue above, with narrow black borders; female brownish, sometimes with blue at base. Below, light gray with white-ringed black spots, larger on forewings. **HABITAT** Woodland openings, meadows, sagelands. **FOOD PLANTS** Lupines. **SEASON** May–July. **RANGE** Entire region, ex. extreme s AZ and NM.

ACMON BLUE
Plebejus acmon
GOSSAMER-WING FAMILY

⅞″. Male lilac-blue above, with thin black margins; hindwings have iridescent pinkish-orange trailing edge with black spots; female duller blue or brown with orange trailing edge. Below, white with many small black spots; hindwings have row of red-orange spots. **HABITAT** Everywhere, ex. dense forests, driest deserts. **FOOD PLANTS** Buckwheats; pea family, incl. locoweeds, clovers. **SEASON** Northward: Apr.–Sept.; southward: year-round.

MORMON METALMARK
Apodemia mormo
METALMARK FAMILY

1″. Boldly and variably patterned. Above, frequently blackish with reddish-brown inner areas and numerous large white spots; southernmost populations mostly reddish brown. Below, forewings reddish brown; hindwings and forewing margins variably colored; numerous white spots. **HABITAT** Rocky, dry hillsides. **FOOD PLANTS** Buckwheats. **SEASON** Northward: May–June, Aug.–Oct.; southward: Feb.–Nov.

AMERICAN SNOUT
Libytheana carinenta
BRUSHFOOT FAMILY

1¾″. Brown above, with orange patches; white spots on squared forewing tips. Below, hindwings grayish. Extremely long palpi (facial appendages) form unmistakable "snout." Migrant in summer and fall, sometimes in remarkable numbers. **HABITAT** River valleys, riparian canyons, desert scrub, towns. **FOOD PLANTS** Hackberries, Wolfberry. **SEASON** Year-round. **RANGE** Entire region, ex. n UT, n NV.

GULF FRITILLARY
Agraulis vanillae
BRUSHFOOT FAMILY

2¾″. Forewings long, fairly narrow. Glowing red-orange above, with black spots and lines. Below, pale brownish orange, with many large silvery spots. Caterpillar black, with black, branching spines and 4 red-orange stripes. **HABITAT** Parks, gardens, fields. **FOOD PLANTS** Passionflower. **SEASON** Year-round. **RANGE** AZ, NM, se UT.

VARIEGATED FRITILLARY
Euptoieta claudia
BRUSHFOOT FAMILY

2″. Tawny above with numerous black lines on basal half of wings, followed by row of black spots and 2 black lines along edges. Below, orange at base of forewings, otherwise mottled light brown and white. **HABITAT** Grasslands, lower open mtn. slopes. **FOOD PLANTS** Very varied, incl. stonecrops, violets. **SEASON** Northward: Mar.–Nov.; southward: year-round.

FIELD CRESCENT
Phyciodes campestris
BRUSHFOOT FAMILY

1¼″. Blackish brown above, with rows of orange and yellow spots. Below, forewings orange with small dark patches near margin; hindwings dull yellow and orange, with small whitish crescents in brownish trailing edge. **HABITAT** Fields, meadows, grasslands, streamsides. **FOOD PLANTS** Aster family. **SEASON** May–Sept. **RANGE** Entire region, ex. s AZ.

MYLITTA CRESCENT
Phyciodes mylitta
BRUSHFOOT FAMILY

1¼″. Mostly orange above, with evenly spaced wavy dark lines, blackish borders. Below, yellowish brown with complex darker brown markings. **HABITAT** Meadows, canyons, agricultural fields, roadsides. **FOOD PLANTS** Thistles. **SEASON** Mar.–Oct. **Pearl Crescent** *(P. tharos)* similar, has wider black borders above; widespread.

VARIABLE CHECKERSPOT
Euphydryas chalcedona
BRUSHFOOT FAMILY

1¾″. Variable amounts of black and orange above, with creamy patches, red-orange spots along margins. Below, forewings mostly orange, with white spots near outer margin; hindwings have red and cream bands. **HABITAT** Mtn. meadows, sagelands, desert hills, woodland clearings. **FOOD PLANTS** Snapdragons, monkeyflowers, paintbrushes. **SEASON** Mar.–Aug.

MOURNING CLOAK
Nymphalis antiopa
BRUSHFOOT FAMILY

3″. Mainly dark brown above, with blue-spotted black band and creamy edges. Below, blackish brown with pale borders. Adult overwinters; flies year-round. Caterpillar dark purple with reddish spots on back. **HABITAT** Riparian areas, parks, gardens. **FOOD PLANTS** Many broadleaf trees, incl. cottonwoods, willows, elms. **SEASON** Year-round.

PAINTED LADY
Vanessa cardui
BRUSHFOOT FAMILY

2⅛″. Orange above, with black markings; forewings have black tip with white spots, bar; hindwings have row of small, blue, black-rimmed spots. Below, forewings rose with black, white, and olive markings; hindwings have olive-brown network with small blue eyespots. Most widespread butterfly in world. Irreg. mass migrations from Mexico. **HABITAT** Deserts, mtns., grasslands, gardens. **FOOD PLANTS** Very varied, incl. mallow family, aster family, incl. thistles. **SEASON** Northward: Mar.–Nov.; southward: year-round.

WEST COAST LADY
Vanessa annabella
BRUSHFOOT FAMILY

2″. Above, very similar to Painted Lady, but with orange bar on forewing tip (white on Painted Lady). Below, marbled olive, beige, and whitish. Caterpillar tan or black with yellow lines. Population fluctuates. **HABITAT** Riparian canyons, open areas. **FOOD PLANTS** Mallows. **SEASON** Northward: May–Oct.; southward: year-round.

RED ADMIRAL
Vanessa atalanta
BRUSHFOOT FAMILY

2″. Brownish black above, with wide orange-red semicircle; forewings have white spots near tip. Below, heavily mottled brown, black, and blue; forewings have pale reddish-orange band. Prefers rotting fruit, sap, or scat to nectar. Migrant. Caterpillar black with yellow spots. **HABITAT** Streamsides, riparian canyons, parks, gardens. **FOOD PLANTS** Nettles. **SEASON** Northward: Mar.–Sept.; southward: year-round.

COMMON BUCKEYE
Junonia coenia
BRUSHFOOT FAMILY

2¼″. Brown above, with large eyespots; forewings crossed with pale bar. Below, lighter brown; forewings have large eyespot, paler bar; hindwings have 2 smaller dark spots. Flies with a few flaps and a short glide. Territorial. Caterpillar dark with pale yellow stripes, short spines. **HABITAT** Many, incl. roadsides, grasslands, weedy fields. **FOOD PLANTS** Plantains, snapdragons, monkeyflowers. **SEASON** Northward: June–Sept.; southward: year-round.

WEIDEMEYER'S ADMIRAL
Limenitis weidemeyerii
BRUSHFOOT FAMILY

3″. Blackish above, with broad white band across wings; small white spots near forewing edges. Below, whitish with black veins; black-bordered orange band near margins. Caterpillar gray and white, humpbacked. **HABITAT** Willow- and aspen-lined watercourses. **FOOD PLANTS** Willows, aspens, cottonwoods. **SEASON** June–July.

CALIFORNIA SISTER
Adelpha bredowii
BRUSHFOOT FAMILY

3¼″. Black above, with wide white median band across all wings; forewings have large orange spot near tip. Paler below, with pattern of auburn, pale blue, and orange; white bands, spots. Slow, gliding flight. **HABITAT** Oak woodlands, riparian canyons. **FOOD PLANTS** Oaks. **SEASON** Mar.–Nov.

HACKBERRY EMPEROR
Asterocampa celtis
BRUSHFOOT FAMILY

2″. Tawny above; forewings pointed, outer half blackish with numerous white spots, one tawny-ringed black eyespot; hindwings lighter with row of black eyespots along orange-brown margin. Below, marbled brownish gray with black eyespots. Often lands on humans. Caterpillar green with 2 projections at each end. **HABITAT** Woodland paths, clearings. **FOOD PLANTS** Hackberries. **SEASON** May–Oct. **RANGE** Patchily distributed throughout region.

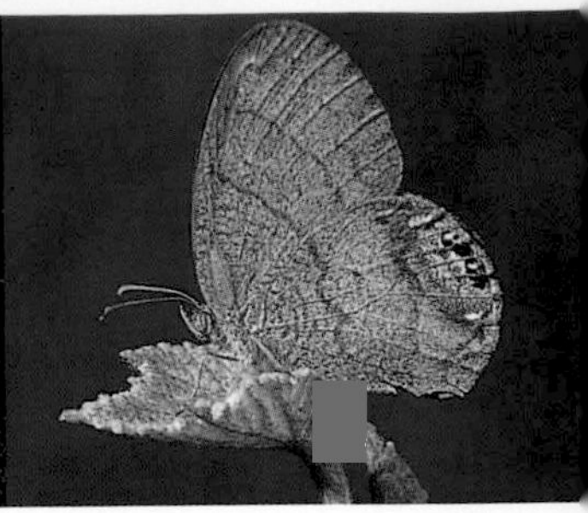

CANYONLAND SATYR
Cyllopsis pertepida
BRUSHFOOT FAMILY

1½″. Reddish brown above. Below, reddish brown (female hindwings purplish brown), with several brown lines; hindwings with silvery edges and small blue-black central spots. **HABITAT** Arid foothill canyons. **FOOD PLANTS** Unknown; presumably grasses. **SEASON** May–June, Aug.–Nov. **RANGE** AZ, NM, extreme s NV and UT. **Nabokov's Satyr** *(C. pyracmon)* very similar.

RIDINGS' SATYR
Neominois ridingsii
BRUSHFOOT FAMILY

1¾″. Dark brown above, with unique light gray-brown oval patches on outer half; 2 eyespots on forewings, small black spot occ. on hindwings. Below, grayish, darker at base; cryptically patterned. **HABITAT** Grasslands, prairies. **FOOD PLANTS** Grasses. **SEASON** June–Aug. **RANGE** n NV, UT, northern half of AZ and NM.

QUEEN
Danaus gilippus
BRUSHFOOT FAMILY

3¼″. Rich brownish orange above; black border dotted with fine white spots; other white spots on forewings. Below, hindwings have prominent black veins. Caterpillar brownish white with yellow and brown bands and yellow-green lateral stripes. Adult and caterpillar toxic to predators. Migrant. **HABITAT** Deserts, riparian canyons. **FOOD PLANTS** Milkweed family. **SEASON** Northward: May–Sept.; southward: year-round.

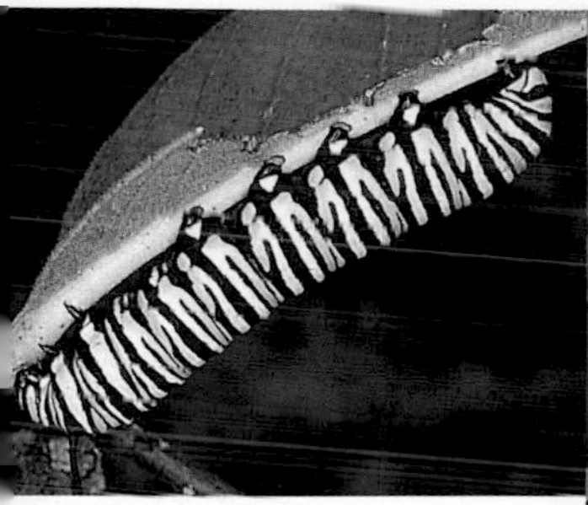

MONARCH

Danaus plexippus

BRUSHFOOT FAMILY

3¾″. Orange above, with black veins, orange- and white-spotted blackish margins; male has black spot on vein of hindwing. Below, yellow-orange. Glides slowly with wings held at an angle. Caterpillar banded black, white, and yellow. Adult and caterpillar poisonous to predators. Migrates south in fall to overwinter in Mexican mountains. **HABITAT** Weedy fields, meadows. **FOOD PLANTS** Milkweeds. **SEASON** Apr.–Nov.

caterpillar (upper left), butterfly (top right), chrysalis (bottom)

SILVER-SPOTTED SKIPPER

Epargyreus clarus

SKIPPER FAMILY

2″. Chocolate brown above, with golden patches on forewings. Below, hindwings have large silver patch. Fast flier. Territorial; aggressively chases other butterflies. **HABITAT** Fields, gardens. **FOOD PLANTS** Pea family, incl. locust trees. **SEASON** May–Sept. **RANGE** Patchily distributed in region; absent from most of NV.

FUNEREAL DUSKYWING

Erynnis funeralis

SKIPPER FAMILY

1½″. Dark gray-brown above; forewings have dark mottling, small clear spots; hindwings have white trailing edge. Defends territory from perch along open area. Migrant northward. **HABITAT** Varied, from deserts to spruce-fir forests. **FOOD PLANTS** Pea family, incl. Deerweed, vetches, Alfalfa. **SEASON** Northward: Mar.–Oct.; southward: year-round. **RANGE** s NV, s UT, AZ, NM.

COMMON CHECKERED-SKIPPER

Pyrgus communis

SKIPPER FAMILY

1″. Dark brown with white checkered pattern above; bluish body and base of wings; below, white with pale rusty-brown pattern. Male aggressively defends territory. Caterpillar yellowish white with gray-green stripes, dark head. **HABITAT** Foothills, weedy fields, roadsides, parks. **FOOD PLANTS** Mallow family. **SEASON** Apr.–Oct.

FIERY SKIPPER

Hylephila phyleus

SKIPPER FAMILY

1⅛″. Above, male orange with few dark marginal markings, narrow black stigma (streak of scent-producing scales) across forewings; female brown with complex orange markings. Below, yellow-orange with small dark spots. Can be extremely common in towns. **HABITAT** Lawns, gardens, agricultural fields. **FOOD PLANTS** Grasses. **SEASON** Northward: Mar.–Oct.; southward: year-round. **RANGE** Entire region, ex. ne NV, n UT.

COMMON BRANDED SKIPPER

Hesperia comma

SKIPPER FAMILY

1″. Very variably patterned. Above, tawny with dark borders; male has dark stigma across forewings. Below, greenish to ocher; hindwings with white markings that are separate or form a crooked band. **HABITAT** Open areas, streamsides in mtns.; sagebrush grasslands. **FOOD PLANTS** Grasses. **SEASON** July–Aug. **RANGE** Entire region, ex. w AZ, se NM.

BUMBLEBEE MOTH

Hemaris diffinis

SPHINX MOTH FAMILY

1¾″. Wings clear, mostly scaleless, with reddish black base, veins, outer edges. Thorax fuzzy, golden brown; abdomen black with yellow band; resembles large bee. Caterpillar pale green with small white raised spots, long hair. **HABITAT** Forest edges, meadows, gardens. **FOOD PLANTS** Honeysuckle family, esp. Snowberry. **SEASON** May–Sept.

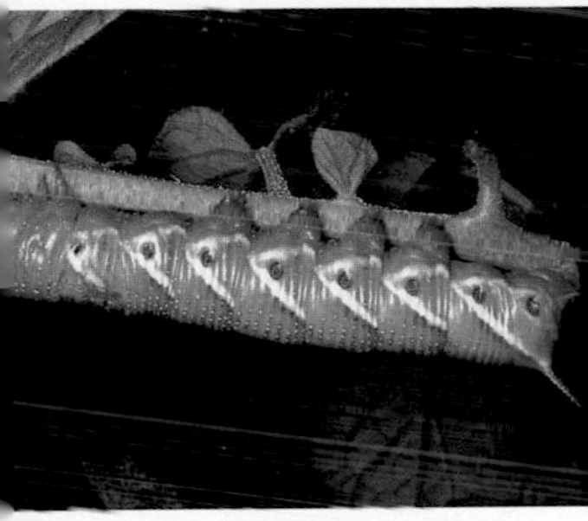

TOMATO HORNWORM MOTH

Manduca quinquemaculata

SPHINX MOTH FAMILY

4″. Wings narrow, pointed, gray-brown. Body very large, tapered, with 5–6 pairs of yellow spots on abdomen. Caterpillar bright green with white, V-shaped lines; green and black horn at rear. **HABITAT** Gardens, crop fields. **FOOD PLANTS** Tomato, tobacco, potato plants. **SEASON** June–Sept.

EYED SPHINX

Smerinthus cerisyi

SPHINX MOTH FAMILY

3″. Forewings and body mostly gray to gray-brown, with contrasting light and dark patches; hindwings rose pink with large black and blue eyespot. Nocturnal. Caterpillar green with yellow lines, horn at rear; if disturbed, arches back, tucks head, assuming sphinx-like stance. **HABITAT** Low-elev. rivers, streams. **FOOD PLANTS** Willows, poplars. **SEASON** May–July.

PAMINA MOTH

Automeris cecrops pamina

GIANT SILKWORM MOTH FAMILY

2½″. Forewings beige with white diagonal stripe; hindwings orangish with prominent black, white-centered eyespot. Body reddish, robust. Nocturnal. Caterpillar light gray, with black and white on sides; branching gray spines; stings. **HABITAT** Open woods. **FOOD PLANTS** Oaks, mountain-mahoganies, ceanothus. **SEASON** May–mid-Aug. **RANGE** se AZ, sw NM.

MESQUITE MOTH

Sphingicampa hubbardi

GIANT SILKWORM MOTH FAMILY

1½″. Body and forewings gray. Hindwings pink with black dot. Nocturnal; attracted to lights. Caterpillar green; covered with shiny, reflective spines. **HABITAT** Low- to mid-elev. **FOOD PLANTS** Mesquite, Acacia. **SEASON** July–Sept. (some appear as early as Apr.). **RANGE** s NM, s and w AZ, extreme s NV.

PICTURED TIGER MOTH

Arachnis picta

TIGER MOTH FAMILY

2″. Forewings whitish with wavy gray bars; hindwings reddish pink with patches and wavy bands of gray. Abdomen red with black-outlined blue spots on sides. Nocturnal. Caterpillar blackish brown, very hairy. **HABITAT** Grasslands. **FOOD PLANTS** Acanthus, Wild Radish, other weedy plants. **SEASON** Summer. **RANGE** s AZ.

ACREA MOTH

Estigmene acraea

TIGER MOTH FAMILY

2¼″. Forewings white with scattered black dots; male hindwings yellow-orange, female's white. Abdomen orange and white with black bars. Nocturnal. Caterpillar dark, hairy; large numbers on roads in fall. **HABITAT** Open areas, fields, deserts. **FOOD PLANTS** Nonwoody plants, incl. corn, cabbage, other crops. **SEASON** May–Aug.

WOOLLY BEAR CATERPILLAR MOTH

Pyrrharctia isabella

TIGER MOTH FAMILY

1¾″. Forewings rusty orange, with rows of small black spots; hindwings lighter. Body rusty orange. Nocturnal. Caterpillar very hairy, reddish brown and black, often wanders onto roadways. **HABITAT** Shrubby fields, roadsides. **FOOD PLANTS** Dandelions, plantains, low-growing weeds. **SEASON** Summer.

TENT CATERPILLAR MOTHS

Malacosoma species

TENT CATERPILLAR MOTH FAMILY

1″. Male body, wings dull red-brown; forewings have 2 yellow stripes. Female body, wings tan; forewings have pale red-brown stripes. Caterpillar brown or black with yellow stripes; bristly; groups build large silken tents in tree branches for protection; can denude trees, but rarely kill them. **HABITAT** Woodlands at mid-elev. **FOOD PLANTS** Willows, cottonwoods, fruit trees, oaks, ceanothus. **SEASON** Mar.–May.

CHOCOLATE LOOPER
Autographa californica
OWLET MOTH FAMILY

1¼". Forewings gray-black with purple highlights. Hindwings buffy on inner two-thirds, medium to dark brown on outer third. Body dull gray to brownish. Nocturnal. Caterpillar dark olive-green with pale head. **HABITAT** Open areas. **FOOD PLANTS** Varied. **SEASON** Summer.

UNDERWING MOTHS
Catocala species
OWLET MOTH FAMILY

2½". Forewings mottled gray; hindwings red to orange, with black band, edge. Body mottled gray-brown. Nocturnal. Caterpillar mottled brown. **HABITAT** River- and streamsides, woodland edges. **FOOD PLANTS** Willows, poplars, alders. **SEASON** May–Sept.

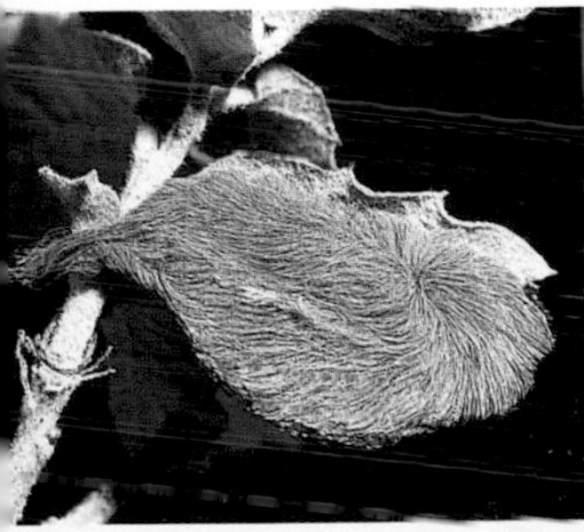

PUSS CATERPILLAR MOTH
Megalopyge bissesa
FLANNEL MOTH FAMILY

1". Wings yellowish white. Body yellowish white; "feet" black. Caterpillar bristly, gray, with hidden venomous spines. Nocturnal. **HABITAT** Oak woodlands. **FOOD PLANTS** Oaks. **SEASON** July–Aug. **RANGE** s AZ.

BAGWORM MOTHS
Thyridopteryx and other genera
BAGWORM MOTH FAMILY

1". Male brown, inconspicuous. Female legless, wingless; stays in cocoon after maturing. Caterpillar ½–1½"; spins protective silken cocoon (bag), incorporating leaves and twigs; cocoon is carried around as caterpillar feeds, anchored prior to pupating. Female dies after laying overwintering eggs in cocoon. **HABITAT** Mid-elev. **FOOD PLANTS** Various trees and shrubs. **SEASON** May–Sept.

Mountain Lion

Vertebrates

There are approximately 43,000 vertebrate species on earth. The evolution of a variety of anatomical structures has made them extraordinarily successful for half a billion years. Today vertebrates are one of the most widespread groups of animals, inhabiting every corner of the globe, from ocean depths to mountaintops, deserts, and polar regions.

The evolution of the vertebrates stemmed from an invertebrate sea squirt–like animal, passed through a "missing link" invertebrate-to-vertebrate stage with the lancelets, and reached the beginnings of the vertebrate stage some 500 million years ago (mya) with the appearance of the first jawless fishes. During the following 350 million years, the various classes of vertebrates evolved. The ancestors of modern fishes developed from their jawless ancestors about 400 mya; 100 million years further into vertebrate development, amphibians evolved from fishes crawling about in search of water during the droughts of the Devonian period. Reptiles first appeared about 250 mya and flourished because of their ability to reproduce on land. Mammals and birds, warm-blooded and able to live successfully in places too cold for fishes, amphibians, and reptiles, spread across the world's environments, mammals beginning about 170 mya and birds about 150 mya.

Roadrunner with lizard

Today's vertebrates share a number of characteristics that separate them from the estimated 50 million or so invertebrate species with which they share the earth. Virtually all vertebrates are bilaterally symmetrical; that is, their left and right sides are essentially mirror images of one another. A strong but flexible backbone, composed of vertebrae, protects the spinal cord and serves as the main structural component of the internal skeletal frame and the segmented muscles that attach to it. Vertebrates are well-coordinated runners, jumpers, swimmers, and/or fliers because of this unique combination of skeletal and muscular development. Other shared characteristics of nearly all vertebrates include one pair of bony jaws (with or without teeth), one or two pairs of appendages, a ventrally located heart (protected by a rib cage), and blood contained in vessels.

The subphylum Vertebrata of the phylum Chordata includes several classes: three classes of living fishes, the amphibians, the reptiles, the birds, and the mammals.

Fishes

Living fishes fall into three major groups: the primitive hagfishes and lampreys, the cartilaginous fishes (sharks, skates, and rays), and the bony fishes. Aquatic, mostly cold-blooded vertebrates with fins and internal gills, fish are typically streamlined and have a muscular tail. Most move through the water by weaving movements of their bodies and tail fins, using their other fins to control their direction. The skin of a fish is coated with a slimy secretion that decreases friction with the water; this secretion, along with the scales that cover most fish, provides their bodies with a nearly waterproof covering. The gills are located in passages that usually lead from the throat to a pair of openings on the side, just behind the head. With rare exceptions, fish breathe by taking water in through the mouth and forcing it past the gills and out through the gill openings; the thin-walled gills capture oxygen from the water and emit carbon dioxide.

The body shapes of fishes vary from cylindrical and elongated trout to vertically compressed (flattened) sunfishes. Body colors can vary within a species due to season, sex, age, individual variation, relative ambient light in the aquatic environment, and water temperature. Brighter colors normally fade after breeding or with capture. Most fishes have one or more dorsal (back) fins that may be spiny or soft (a few fishes, such as trout and salmon, have an additional fleshy fin behind the dorsal fins, called an adipose fin); a tail (caudal) fin, usually with an upper and a lower lobe; and an anal fin, just in front of the tail along the edge of the ventral (belly) side. Most also have a pair of pectoral fins, usually on the sides behind the head, and a pair of pelvic fins, generally under the middle of the body. Some fishes lack one or more of these fins.

The mouths of fishes are usually wide and lipped; a few are disk-shaped or tubular. Depending on the species, the upper jaw (the snout) projects beyond the lower, the two parts of the jaw are of equal length, or the lower jaw projects beyond the upper. Some species have whisker-like sensory barbels around the jaw that detect objects in muddy or murky water. Most fish are covered with scales, but some species lack scales altogether, and others lack scales on the head or other areas; sometimes the scales have been modified into bony plates. The lateral line is a sensory organ beneath the skin that responds to vibrations and/or electrical fields in the water. It may be invisible or appear as a thin stripe along the side (branching in some fish). Some fish species are solitary, some live in small groups, and others are found mainly in enormous schools, in which members respond as a unit to stimuli while feeding, fleeing danger, or migrating.

Bony Fishes

Bony fishes normally have harder, less flexible bony skeletons than cartilaginous fishes (such as sharks, skates, and rays, which are chiefly marine), as well as a gas- or fat-filled swim bladder that keeps them buoyant. Most bony fishes have overlapping scales embedded in flexible connective tissue, although some lack scales entirely. There is a

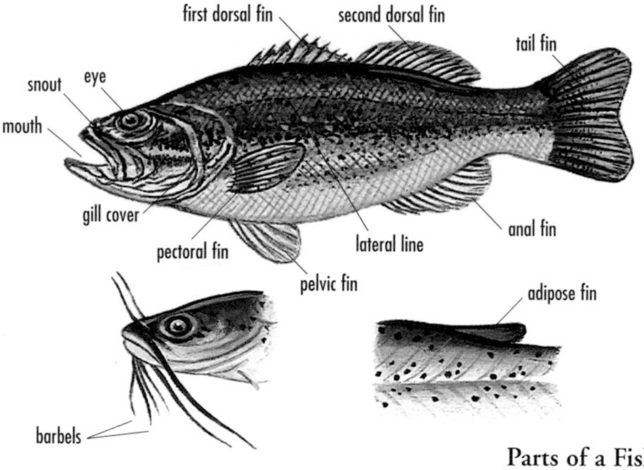

Parts of a Fish

single gill opening on each side protected by a hard gill cover. The fins of ray-finned bony fishes consist of a web of skin supported by bony rays (either segmented soft rays or stiffer spines), each moved by a set of muscles; this makes the fins very flexible. The tail fin is typically symmetrical. Most bony fishes reproduce by spawning; males directly fertilize eggs after the females release them from their bodies into the water. The eggs may float at mid-levels, rise to the surface, or sink to the bottom. A few fish species, usually the males, guard nests or incubate eggs in a pouch or the mouth. Newborn fish are called larvae; within a few weeks or months, a larva develops to resemble a miniature adult and is called a juvenile or fry.

Lengths given (from the tip of the snout to the tip of the tail) are for typical adults, although fish grow throughout their lives, and both smaller and larger individuals will be encountered.

THREADFIN SHAD
Dorosoma petenense
HERRING FAMILY

4½–5½". Deep, compressed. Back blue; sides and belly silvery; single black spot above, behind gills; belly has sharp, saw-like keel along its length. Single high dorsal fin, last ray elongated, thread-like; tail fin deeply forked. Native to sc U.S. and FL. **HABITAT** Reservoirs, rivers. **RANGE** Introduced widely into AZ, se NV.

RED SHINER
Cyprinella (Notropis) lutrensis
CARP AND MINNOW FAMILY

3". Body deep. Back brownish, sides silvery; blue wash behind gills. Breeding male has blue back, bright red-orange below and on fins. Single dorsal fin rounded; tail fin forked. **HABITAT** Rivers, ponds; tolerates silt. **RANGE** Native of Rio Grande and e NM; introduced to AZ, se NV, s UT.

COMMON CARP
Cyprinus carpio
CARP AND MINNOW FAMILY

18–22". Oval; back high, rounded. Dark olive above, shading to yellowish gray below. Dorsal fin long, begins at high point of back, with thickened forward spine; tail fin forked, lobes rounded. 2 pairs of barbels on upper lip. Male thrashes about surface waters in spring spawning frenzy. Introduced from Eurasia. Destroys bottom plants needed as cover for eggs and fry of native fish. **HABITAT** Clear or turbid rivers, lakes, reservoirs. **RANGE** se NV, UT, AZ, s NM.

UTAH CHUB
Gila atraria
CARP AND MINNOW FAMILY

12–18". Body compressed. Olive-brown to dark blue above, sides brassy yellowish. Snout short, blunt; eyes large. Dorsal fin triangular; tail fin deeply forked, lobes rounded. **HABITAT** Lakes, small rivers. **RANGE** Native to w and n UT; introduced to e UT. Five similar chubs live in the SW: **Tui Chub** *(G. bicolor)* of NV; **Rio Grande Chub** *(G. pandora)* of NM; and 3 Colorado R. species, the most common of which is the **Roundtail Chub** *(G. robusta)*.

GOLDEN SHINER
Notemigonus crysoleucas
CARP AND MINNOW FAMILY

4–8″. Body deeper, more vertically compressed than most minnows; greenish or pale silver (shining gold when breeding); scales large. Mouth tiny. Single dorsal fin; tail fin forked. Usu. in schools near surface. Common bait fish. Native to e and c U.S. **HABITAT** Near surface of shallow, weedy lakes, ponds, streams. **RANGE** se NV, AZ, s NM.

COLORADO SQUAWFISH
Ptychocheilus lucius
CARP AND MINNOW FAMILY

3′. Elongated; back olive, sides silvery. Head flattened, eyes small, mouth large. Single dorsal fin; tail fin forked. Now extinct in Gila Basin and Colorado R. below Glen Canyon. Once to 6′ and an important food fish; now endangered. **HABITAT** Larger rivers. **RANGE** Colorado R. basin of UT.

SPECKLED DACE
Rhinichthys osculus
CARP AND MINNOW FAMILY

3½″. Elongated; back rounded, belly flattened. Back dark green; sides gray, green, or yellowish mottled with dark brown spots. Mouth small, ventral; eyes small. Fins pale, unspotted; single dorsal fin; tail fin forked, lobes equal; fins have red bases in breeding male. **HABITAT** Over gravel in springs, creeks, rivers, lakes. **RANGE** NV, UT, AZ, w NM.

RED-SIDED SHINER
Richardsonius balteatus
CARP AND MINNOW FAMILY

5–7″. Compressed. Back dark olive-brown, golden and blackish line on sides; breeding males pinkish below. Single dorsal fin; tail fin forked; both yellowish. **HABITAT** Ponds, slow streams. **RANGE** Native of ne NV, w UT; introduced to Colorado R. basin of e UT, n AZ.

DESERT SUCKER

Catostomus (Pantosteus) clarki

SUCKER FAMILY

8–12". Elongated. Back and sides brown, belly white; breeding male has orange over black side stripe. Single dorsal fin; tail fin forked. Mouth round, sucker-like, below and behind eye. **HABITAT** Small and medium rivers; usu. in mtns. **RANGE** ec NV, sw UT, c and se AZ, wc NM. Similar **Utah Sucker** *(C. ardens)* is found in lakes and creeks of c and n UT.

BLACK BULLHEAD

Ameiurus (Ictalurus) melas

BULLHEAD CATFISH FAMILY

6–12". Robust; front heavy, compressed toward tail. Back blackish brown; sides shade to yellow brown; belly yellowish. Head wide, rounded; upper lip and chin have long black barbels. Tall, thin dorsal fin and adipose fin above. **HABITAT** Muddy bottoms of lakes, ponds, rivers. **RANGE** s NV, se UT, much of AZ, NM.

CHANNEL CATFISH

Ictalurus punctatus

BULLHEAD CATFISH FAMILY

22–24". Elongated, slender. Back blue-gray; sides tan or silvery blue with few scattered blackish spots; belly white. Single dorsal fin short, high, rounded; adipose fin; anal fin long, with rounded outer edge; tail fin forked. Head long; upper jaw overhangs lower; 4 pairs of barbels, upper 2 black, lower ones white. **HABITAT** Flowing rivers with clear bottoms; lakes and ponds. **RANGE** Native to NM; introduced to all SW.

FLATHEAD CATFISH

Pylodictis olivaris

BULLHEAD CATFISH FAMILY

15–35". Back and sides black or yellow, sometimes spotted; below white. Head long, flat; mouth very wide; whiskers black and white. Dorsal fin rounded; adipose fin large; tail fin fan-shaped. **HABITAT** Deep river pools. **RANGE** Native to Rio Grande and Pecos rivers of NM; introduced to AZ, sw NV, and drainages of other areas.

Lost Fish of the Colorado River

Before the Colorado River was dammed, it contained large populations of fish adapted to its turbulent waters, temperatures, and sources of food. The Colorado Squawfish (page 240), grew to 6 feet long and weighed as much as 80 pounds. Other fish common in much of the river were the Bonytail Chub *(Gila elegans)*, the Humpback Chub *(Gila cypha)*, and the Razorback Sucker *(Xyrauchen texanus)*. For millenia, native Amerindians of the Colorado River valley harvested, dried, and ate these fish; many later settlers lived on squawfish until the 1900s.

Today, all of these once plentiful native Colorado River fish are rare or endangered. The massive Glen Canyon, Hoover, Davis, Parker, and Imperial dams created large, still reservoirs with calm, silty bottoms—impossible foraging grounds for these river fish. The dams blocked migratory routes and water released from the bottoms of the dams was too cold for the fry of these fish. Dozens of alien species of bait and game fish were introduced, to the detriment of local species. Below the diversion canals, what little water remains is frequently too warm for the river fish. Now small in number and in size, these native species hang on chiefly in hatcheries and upstream branches of the river in eastern Utah, western Colorado, and southwestern Wyoming. The Colorado River Fish Recovery Team and other groups are working to bring native species back to stretches of river between the dams.

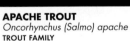

APACHE TROUT
Oncorhynchus (Salmo) apache
TROUT FAMILY

6″ (streams)–18″ (lakes). Stout, compressed. Body bright golden yellow with many large black spots. Dorsal fin white-tipped; adipose and tail fins also black-spotted. Black line through eye. Threatened due to hybridization and competition with introduced trout. **HABITAT** Headwater streams, mtn. lakes. **RANGE** Upper Salt and Little Colorado river systems, ec AZ. **Gila Trout** *(O. gilae)*, 10–14″, often pink along lateral line; rare in streams of ec AZ.

CUTTHROAT TROUT
Oncorhynchus (Salmo) clarki
TROUT FAMILY

12–20″. Elongated. Olive above; sides orange with faint red stripe, black spotting; bright red slash mark on throat. 1 triangular dorsal fin; small adipose fin; crescent-shaped tail fin greenish with black spotting. Head and mouth large; jaw extends behind eye. **HABITAT** Gravel-bottomed rivers and streams; lakes. **RANGE** n and c NV, UT; introduced to n AZ, n and c NM.

RAINBOW TROUT
Oncorhynchus mykiss
(Salmo gairdneri)
TROUT FAMILY

10–30″. Elongated. Colors, patterns variable. Olive above, with large spots; sides have long, rosy-red stripe; many races and hybrids where introduced. Dorsal fin triangular; adipose fin small; tail fin slightly forked. Mouth white. **HABITAT** Rivers, headwater streams, lakes. **RANGE** Native to n and w NV; introduced to all SW, ex. sw AZ.

BROWN TROUT
Salmo trutta
TROUT FAMILY

8–25″. Elongated; head large. Brown above; sides olive with dark brown and red spots haloed by white; belly silvery; head spotted. Dorsal fin rounded; tail fin squarish. Tolerates higher water temperatures than other trout. Native to Europe; danger to native species. **HABITAT** Lakes, fast-flowing streams. **RANGE** e NV, ec AZ, NM.

BROOK TROUT
Salvelinus fontinalis
TROUT FAMILY

8–16″. Elongated. Olive-green above, with dark, wavy lines; sides olive, with many large yellowish spots and a few small red spots with blue halos; belly white (reddish in adult male). Dorsal fin spotted, triangular; tail fin squared or slightly forked; ventral fins reddish, with white and black leading edges. Large jaws extend well behind eyes. Native to e U.S., e Canada. **HABITAT** Cold, clear streams, cold lakes. **RANGE** Introduced widely throughout SW, esp. n NV and mtns. of c AZ, NM; in some cases, threatens native trout.

LAKE TROUT
Salvelinus namaycush
TROUT FAMILY

14–20″. Elongated, slightly compressed. Dark green above, paler green on sides; large, irreg., whitish spots. Triangular dorsal fin and deeply forked tail fin both spotted with yellow; ventral fins olive or reddish, with white leading edges. Head and mouth large. Native to n U.S., Canada. **HABITAT** Deep, cold lakes. **RANGE** Introduced to Lake Tahoe, NV, and c UT lakes.

WESTERN MOSQUITOFISH

Gambusia affinis

LIVEBEARER FAMILY

¾–2″. Male pencil-shaped, shorter than robust female. Pale olive-brown above, sides silvery, pale yellow below. Scales dark-edged in net-like pattern. Rows of black spots on clear dorsal and rounded tail fin. Snout high on flat forehead; mouth slanted up; dark smudge below eye. 3–4 broods of 200+ live young a year. **HABITAT** Ponds, slow streams. **RANGE** Native to NM; introduced to w and s NV, nc UT, AZ.

STRIPED BASS

Morone saxatilis

TEMPERATE BASS FAMILY

22–28″. Elongated, moderately compressed, streamlined, with small fins. Pale olive or slaty blue above; sides silvery, with 6–9 blackish side stripes; belly white. 2 dorsal fins triangular; tail fin notched. Lower jaw projects slightly. Native to e U.S. **HABITAT** Large rivers. **RANGE** Introduced to Colorado R. of w AZ, se NV, s UT.

SACRAMENTO PERCH

Archoplites interruptus

SUNFISH FAMILY

9–11″. Compressed, moderately elongated. Back dark olive or black; sides grayish olive with 6–8 irreg. bands of dark brown spots; belly whitish. Dorsal fins joined, 1st low, spiny, 2nd high, rounded; tail fin has 2 rounded lobes. Head pointed; lower lip longer than upper; eyes red. Native to the Central Valley of CA; tolerates alkaline and saline waters. **HABITAT** Sluggish streams, sloughs, lakes. **RANGE** Introduced to NV, UT.

GREEN SUNFISH

Lepomis cyanellus

SUNFISH FAMILY

4–8″. Oval, deep. Olive-brown above; sides paler olive-green; some have 6 brown bands on sides; belly pale orange. Head and mouth large; head pale green with fine blue lines. Wide gill cover ends with reddish-edged black spot. Fins darker at base; dorsal fins continuous; tail fin notched, lobes rounded; pectoral fin rounded. **HABITAT** Streams, swamps, ponds; often near brush, dense vegetation. **RANGE** Native to NM; introduced to w and s NV, UT, AZ.

BLUEGILL
Lepomis macrochirus
SUNFISH FAMILY

6–8″. Oval, extremely compressed. Olive above, with 5–9 vertical dusky green bands; breeding male orange below, with blue gill covers; female whitish below. Dark spot on rear of single dorsal fin; tail fin slightly forked. Region's most common sunfish. **HABITAT** Shallow, vegetated lakes, stream pools. **RANGE** Native to se NM; introduced to all SW.

SMALLMOUTH BASS
Micropterus dolomieu
SUNFISH FAMILY

13–17″. Elongated. Dark brown above; sides greenish yellow with diffuse, vertical, brownish bands; belly whitish. 1st dorsal fin spiny, 2nd rounded; tail fin notched, lobes rounded. Mouth extends to below front of eye. Native to e U.S. **HABITAT** Low- to mid-elev. deep lakes; cool, clear streams over rocks. **RANGE** Introduced to all SW.

LARGEMOUTH BASS
Micropterus salmoides
SUNFISH FAMILY

14–18″. Elongated. Dark green above; sides olive-green with brownish mottling; belly whitish. Dark lateral stripe disappears with age. 1st dorsal fin spiny, 2nd rounded; tail fin slightly forked. Head large; mouth extends to below rear of eye. Native to e U.S. **HABITAT** Warm, shallow, low-elev. waters with vegetation. **RANGE** Introduced to all SW.

BLACK CRAPPIE
Pomoxis nigromaculatus
SUNFISH FAMILY

12–14″. Oval, extremely compressed; forehead concave; lower jaw protrudes. Pale brown or sooty green, heavily mottled with dark brown spots. Single dorsal fin and anal fin large, rounded, begin with 6–8 spines; tail fin forked; most fins distinctly spotted. Native of e U.S. **HABITAT** Ponds, warm streams, some in brackish waters. Favors brushy areas and regions with considerable bottom structure. **RANGE** Introduced to w and s NV, nc UT, AZ, and NM.

WALLEYE
Stizostedion vitreum
PERCH FAMILY

13–20″. Elongated. Head long; mouth large; teeth strong. Olive-brown to brassy greenish yellow; sides speckled with black dots. Separate dorsal fins; 1st spiny, with last 3 membranes black; tail fin forked, tip of lower lobe white. Native to nc U.S., Canada. **HABITAT** Lakes, deep rivers. **RANGE** Introduced to n and se NV, UT, n and c AZ, n NM. **Yellow Perch** *(Perca flavescens),* 4–10″, is yellowish with dark brown bands on sides; introduced to ne NV, n UT.

MOZAMBIQUE TILAPIA
Tilapia mossambica
CICHLID FAMILY

10–15″. Deep, compressed. Forehead concave, sloping; mouth small. Back and sides dark olive fading to yellowish on belly. Continuous dorsal fin and anal fin long, pointed toward rear, speckled green and black; tail fin ends in straight line. Breeding male blacker; mouth swollen, blue; lower jaw white; tail fin edged in red. Accidentally introduced from se Africa; now competes with native fish for prey. **HABITAT** Slow, vegetated streams, canals, ponds. **RANGE** s AZ.

Amphibians

Members of the class Amphibia typically start life in fresh water and later live primarily on land. Most undergo metamorphosis (a series of developmental stages) from aquatic, gilled larvae to terrestrial, air-breathing adults. The most primitive of terrestrial vertebrates, amphibians lack claws and external ear openings. They have thin, moist, scaleless skin and are cold-blooded; their body temperature varies with that of their surroundings. In winter, they burrow deep into leaf litter, soft soils, and the mud in ponds, and maintain an inactive state. Due to the great variety of elevations and erratic swings in rainfall and temperatures, the actual months of activity are difficult to pinpoint exactly. Unlike reptiles, amphibians can become dehydrated in dry environments and must live near water at least part of the year and for breeding. Their eggs lack shells, and most are laid in water.

Salamanders

Salamanders (order Caudata) have blunt, rounded heads, long slender bodies, short legs, and long tails. The eggs, which are usually laid in fresh water, hatch into four-legged larvae with tufted external gills; after several months or years, the larvae typically lose their gills and go ashore. Some salamanders lay eggs on land and skip the gilled larval stage. Mole salamanders, which breathe through lungs, burrow into soft soil. During all life stages, salamanders eat small animal life. They are generally voiceless and hard to see as they feed under wet leaves and logs; they are easiest to spot at night, when they congregate to mate and lay eggs in temporary pools of fresh water created by heavy rains. When inactive, they reside in decaying logs, between roots of trees, and in soil. Salamanders differ from lizards, which are reptiles, in having thin moist skin (not scales), four toes on the front feet (not five), and in their lack of claws and external ear openings. Like frogs, salamanders are fast declining in number worldwide, due to habitat destruction and perhaps also acid rain, pesticides, and increasing ultraviolet light. The Southwest has very few salamanders compared to the Pacific coast and the eastern U.S.

The size given for salamanders is the typical length from the tip of the nose to the end of the tail.

TIGER SALAMANDER Arizona race (left), barred race (right)
Ambystoma tigrinum
MOLE SALAMANDER FAMILY

8″. Stout; head broad; snout rounded. AZ race of plateaus s of Grand Canyon brownish olive with black and yellow spots above, yellow below. UT race of UT, n AZ, and nw NM gray or brown with black spots. Barred race of e NM black with yellow blotches and bands. Lives in mammal burrows, under lakeside debris. **HABITAT** Sagebrush deserts, dry coniferous forests, watersides; to 8,000′. **ACTIVITY** Feb.–Aug.: mainly nocturnal. **RANGE** UT, n and e AZ, NM.

Frogs

Adult frogs and toads (order Anura) have large heads and eyes and wide, usually toothless, mouths; most lack tails. Many can rapidly extend a long tongue for capturing insects. They have two long, muscular hindlegs and two smaller front legs. All must keep their skin moist. Some frogs spend cold or dry periods in a state of torpor, burying themselves in mud at the edge of a pond or crawling between the bark and trunk of a large tree. When breeding, the male vocalizes to attract the larger female and clings to her while fertilizing eggs as she lays them, usually in water. The eggs hatch into round-bodied, long-tailed aquatic larvae called tadpoles or pollywogs, which begin life with external gills that are soon covered with skin. The tadpole later transforms into a tail-less ground, tree, or marsh dweller with air-breathing lungs. Toads are a family (Bufonidae) of frogs that have shorter legs for hopping and warty skin that secretes poisons that cause irritations. In the treefrog family (Hylidae), tadpoles live in water and adults live in trees; treefrogs have disks on their toes for clinging. The true frogs (Ranidae) are

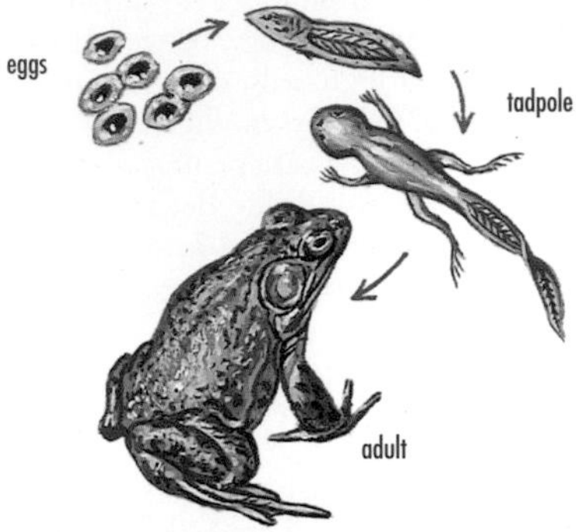

Life Cycle of a Frog

large, with slim waists, long legs, pointed toes, and webs on their hindfeet; most live in or near water and are good jumpers. Like salamanders, frogs are declining in number worldwide.

Frogs and toads have excellent hearing and vocal capabilities. Their ears are well developed (the external eardrum is a conspicuous round disk behind the eye). In spring or summer, most male frogs announce their presence with vocalizations that vary from species to species. When calling, the animals rapidly inflate and deflate balloon-like vocal sacs on the throat that amplify the sound. Calls are primarily used during the breeding season to attract mates, some by day, some at night; other species give calls to defend feeding territories. Most Southwestern frogs have rather soft voices, but the calls of the Bullfrog and some other species are conspicuous waterside sounds from spring into summer, mainly at night.

The size given for frogs is the typical length from the tip of the nose to the end of the body (not including the extended legs).

GREAT PLAINS TOAD
Bufo cognatus
TOAD FAMILY

3″. Skin has many small warts. Gray, olive, or brown above, with large, dark brown oval blotches; white or buff mid-back line. Long, swollen glands behind eye meet V-shaped crown patch. **VOICE** Shrill riveting trill of 20+ seconds. **HABITAT** Grasslands, sagebrush deserts. Breeds in ditches, streams, temporary pools. **ACTIVITY** Apr.–Oct.: forages at night and on rainy days. **RANGE** se NV, sc UT, w and s AZ, s, c, and e NM.

RED-SPOTTED TOAD
Bufo punctatus
TOAD FAMILY

2½″. Olive to grayish above, with many raised red spots; lacks pale stripe down back. Round, swollen glands behind eyes; appears fairly flat, thin. **VOICE** High musical trill. **HABITAT** Rocky areas, open grasslands near seepages, cattle tanks for range livestock; to 6,000′. **ACTIVITY** Breeds Mar.–Sept. **RANGE** s NV, s UT, AZ, NM. **Colorado River Toad** *(B. alvarius),* 3″, is dark brown with white wart at mouth corner; s AZ.

CANYON TREEFROG
Hyla arenicola
TREEFROG FAMILY

2″. Toad-like; skin warty. Gray-brown, changeable; plain or with greenish-brown spots (small or large). Dark bar under eye. Orange under legs. Distinguished from toads by its round toe pads. **VOICE** A hoarse trill. **HABITAT** Bouldery canyons with some permanent water. **ACTIVITY** Nocturnal; breeds May–July. **RANGE** s UT, AZ (ex. sw), w NM.

BULLFROG
Rana catesbeiana
TRUE FROG FAMILY

6″. Above yellowish green or brown, with dark mottling; below pale yellow. Ridge from eye to eardrum. Legs long, dark-banded; feet mainly webbed. Introduced from c U.S.; wiping out native frogs. Feeds on insects, minnows, other frogs. **VOICE** Deep *jug-o-rum.* **HABITAT** Ponds, lakes, streams. **ACTIVITY** Seen by day; feeds mainly at night. **RANGE** Most of SW, ex. ne AZ, s UT.

NORTHERN LEOPARD FROG
Rana pipiens
TRUE FROG FAMILY

3″. Slender; snout pointed. Body and legs have large oval spots with thin yellow edges. Light green with dark green spots, or light brown with dark brown spots. Raised yellow ridges flank back and run along upper jaw. Ear drum usu. plain brown. Declining in numbers. **VOICE** Low 3-second snore, mixed with grunts and moans. **HABITAT** Marshes, rivers, meadows. **ACTIVITY** Day and night; Mar.–Nov.: in lowlands, shorter season in mtns. **RANGE** NV, UT, mtns. of n and c AZ, n NM.

Reptiles

Members of the class Reptilia are cold-blooded, like amphibians. Their body temperature varies with that of their surroundings; reptilian activities come to a halt in cold weather, when they hibernate alone or in communal dens. Actual months of activity vary by elevation and year, due to erratic rainfall and temperatures. Of the four orders of living reptiles, the Southwest has two: turtles and scaled reptiles; the latter order includes both snakes and lizards. The reptilian body is low-slung and has a long tail and, except for the snakes and some lizards, four short legs. Unlike the thin-skinned amphibians, reptiles are covered with protective scales (some are modified into plates in turtles) that waterproof their bodies and help keep them from becoming dehydrated. They breathe via lungs. All breed on land and mate via internal fertilization; their eggs have brittle or leathery shells. Some give birth to live young. Newborns and young are shaped like adults, but often differ in color. Reptiles grow throughout their lives, though growth rates are much slower after maturity.

Turtles

Members of the order Testudines, turtles are the oldest living group of reptiles, dating back to the time of the earliest dinosaurs. The upper part of their characteristic bony shell is the carapace, the lower part the plastron; both parts are covered with hard plates called scutes. Some species have ridges, called keels, on the carapace and tail. Most can withdraw the head and legs inside the shell for protection. Aquatic species have flipper-like legs. Turtles are the only toothless reptiles, but their horny beaks have sharp biting edges. The exposed skin of turtles is scaly and dry. Most turtles spend hours basking in the sun. Southwestern turtles hibernate during the winter. All turtles lay eggs; most dig a hollow, lay the eggs, cover them up, and leave them alone. When the eggs hatch, the young claw their way to the surface and must fend for themselves.

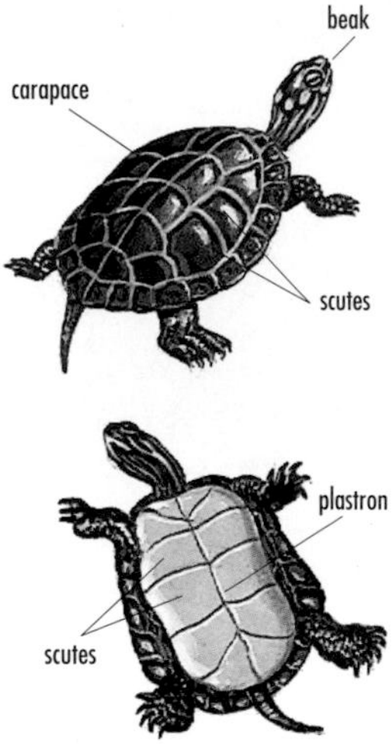

Parts of a Turtle

Lengths given below are for the carapace of a typical adult, not from the extended nose to the tip of the tail.

DESERT TORTOISE
Gopherus agassizii
TORTOISE FAMILY

12″. Carapace domed, brown; sides rounded due to joining of carapace and plastron. Each scute has grooved concentric rings; raised center of scute yellowish or orange. Plastron yellowish with brown on margins; extends forward of carapace in adults, even further in males. Head rounded, buffy, with black scales. Front limbs flattened for digging, rear limbs round, covered with heavy blackish scales; claws heavy. Tail short. Leaves lines of rounded dents in sand. Digs nearly horizontal tunnels in firm sand on sides of desert washes for egg-laying and rest. Takes 15–20 years to reach maturity. In breeding season, males fight by bobbing heads, clashing, and attempting to flip over rivals. Populations reduced due to easy capture and off-road vehicle activities. **HABITAT** Deserts with creosote, cactus, grass. **ACTIVITY** Morning and late afternoon, Mar.–Oct. Escapes midday heat and overwinters in burrows. **RANGE** Mojave and Colorado Deserts of s NV, w and s AZ.

YELLOW MUD TURTLE

Kinosternon flavescens

MUD TURTLE FAMILY

5". Carapace smooth, high; scutes brown or olive with black seams. Plastron pale yellow or brown with black seams; concave in male. Head slaty above; jaws and throat yellow. **HABITAT** Streams and ponds with muddy bottoms. **ACTIVITY** Aquatic; basks some days; Apr.–Oct.: forages on land at night. **RANGE** e and s NM, se AZ. **Sonora Mud Turtle** *(K. sonoriense)* has spotted head; is found in wooded canyons of c and s AZ, w NM.

PAINTED TURTLE

Chrysemys picta

POND AND BOX TURTLE FAMILY

6". Carapace oval, fairly flat, smooth; has 3 rows of olive-brown to black scutes with pale yellow edges; fringing scutes of carapace edged red. Plastron red with black and yellow pattern in middle. Head, neck, and legs lined with yellow and red. **HABITAT** Ponds, swamps, rivers. **ACTIVITY** Chiefly by day. **RANGE** Pecos, Rio Grande, and San Juan rivers of NM. Red-eared race of **Common Slider** *(Trachemys scripta elegans)*, 10", has large red ear patch; found along rivers of e NM.

ORNATE BOX TURTLE

"Western Box Turtle"

Terrapene ornata

POND AND BOX TURTLE FAMILY

5". Carapace thick, high, flat on top; black or dark brown with yellow lines radiating from 3 spots on each side; thin yellow stripe at midline of dome. Plastron black with maze of yellow lines (older ones plain brown); forward hinge lets it protect head. Eyes and foreleg scales reddish in male, yellow in female. Mainly eats large insects. **HABITAT** Grasslands, sandhills, open woodlands. **ACTIVITY** Mar.–Nov.: by day in spring and fall; nocturnal on hot summer days. **RANGE** e and s NM, se AZ.

SPINY SOFTSHELL TURTLE

Apalone spinifera

SOFTSHELL TURTLE FAMILY

Female 13"; male 6½". Carapace flattish, rounded, covered in leathery skin; olive or tan with black spots; near edge, pale yellow-orange with black line. Plastron smooth, flat, gray. Head brown; yellow stripe through eye; snout tubular. Feet paddle-like, fully webbed. **HABITAT** Rivers, irrigation ditches. **ACTIVITY** By day; floats in still waters; basks on sandbars. **RANGE** Colorado and Gila rivers of AZ, Rio Grande and Pecos rivers of NM.

Lizards

Lizards (suborder Sauria of the scaled reptile order, Squamata) generally have long tails (sometimes lost to predators); most species have legs and are capable of running, climbing, and clinging, although in a few the legs are tiny or even lacking. Typical lizards resemble salamanders but can be distinguished from them by their dry scaly skin, clawed feet, and external ear openings. Lizard species vary greatly in size, shape, and color; in many, colors and patterns differ among adult males, adult females, and young. The horned lizards, erroneously called horned toads, are quite spiny; they squirt blood from the corners of their eyes at an attacker. Most lizards are active by day, and many are particularly active in the midday heat. Most do not swim. Fertilization is internal; most lay eggs rather than give birth to live young.

The size given in the following species accounts is the length from the tip of the snout to the end of the tail.

male (left), female (right)

COLLARED LIZARD
Crotaphytus collaris
IGUANA FAMILY

12″. Many races; highly variable in color and pattern. Head large; neck narrow with 2 white- or yellow-edged black collars; tail longer than body, thin, not flattened. Male: head swollen, plain gray or yellow; brown or blue-green above, with many yellow spots; blue-gray or greenish below; throat blue-green or orange; tail gray with brown spots. Female: gray or brown with creamy spots; may show rusty barring. Runs from danger on hind legs. **HABITAT** Rocky canyons, ledges, open woods, scrub. **ACTIVITY** Apr.–Oct.: by day. **RANGE** e UT, c and e AZ, NM.

MOJAVE BLACK-COLLARED LIZARD
Crotaphytus bicinctores
IGUANA FAMILY

11″. Head large; neck narrow; tail long, thin. Head brown with network of white lines; 2 black collars separated by white collar; brown above, with many white spots (male) or crossbands of orange dots (female); feet yellowish; tail buffy. Male has blue and black throat. **HABITAT** Rocky desert canyons and hills. **ACTIVITY** By day; often basks on large boulders. **RANGE** NV, w UT, w AZ.

ZEBRATAIL LIZARD
Callisaurus draconoides
IGUANA FAMILY

8″. Brown with yellow dots, 2 rows of brown spots; 2 black bands on sides; belly pale. Nose blunt. Legs long, slender. Heavy black bands on pale gray tail. Swift; curls tail over body when running. **HABITAT** Hard-packed bare desert soils. **ACTIVITY** By day. **RANGE** w and s NV, sw UT, w and s AZ.

DESERT IGUANA
Dipsosaurus dorsalis
IGUANA FAMILY

14″. Brown above, with bands of white spots; whitish below, pink when breeding. Head small, pale gray; snout short. Row of raised scales down middle of back and tail. Legs gray; claws long. Tail long, gray with many brown bands. Eats leaves high up in bushes. **HABITAT** Sandy creosote bush deserts with rocks, streambeds. **ACTIVITY** By day. **RANGE** s NV, sw UT, w AZ.

LONGNOSE LEOPARD LIZARD
Gambelia wislizenii
IGUANA FAMILY

12″. Tan or pale gray with dark spots (when hot) to brown (when cool); thin yellowish bands. Snout long. Can run upright on hindlegs. Scans for prey from shade of bush. **CAUTION** Hisses when cornered; will bite if picked up. **HABITAT** Deserts with scattered bushes. **ACTIVITY** By day. **RANGE** NV, w and s UT, AZ, sw NM.

CHUCKWALLA
Sauromalus obesus
IGUANA FAMILY

14″. Neck and body have loose folds of sandpapery skin; tail long, buffy, with blunt tip. Adult male back reddish or gray; head, neck, legs blackish. Female and young banded gray and yellow. Avoids capture by inflating itself in rock crevice. **HABITAT** Near large boulders in creosote bush deserts. **ACTIVITY** By day. **RANGE** s NV, s UT, w AZ.

SHORT-HORNED LIZARD

Phrynosoma douglassi
IGUANA FAMILY

3″. Head small, plain; fan of short spines behind eyes. Body squat, flat. Brown or bluish gray above (color matches local soil); 2 dark blotches at back of neck; smaller dark spots with pale rear edges along either side of back; sides and short tail edged with whitish spines. **HABITAT** Rocky to sandy open areas, open juniper and pine woodlands. **ACTIVITY** By day, Apr.–Oct. **RANGE** n NV, UT, c and e AZ, w, c, and n NM.

DESERT HORNED LIZARD

Phrynosoma platyrhinos
IGUANA FAMILY

4½″. Body flat; brown, gray, black, or sandy, with dark wavy bands; nose blunt; crown of thin spines on nape; rows of short spines on back and sides; tail short. Less spiny than other horned lizards. Eats ants. Relies on camouflage, not speed, to elude capture. **HABITAT** Desert scrub. **ACTIVITY** By day; basks on rocks. **RANGE** se AZ, s and c NM.

REGAL HORNED LIZARD

Phrynosoma solare
IGUANA FAMILY

4″. Body flattened. Head fringed, with thick spines. Above gray, buff, or reddish brown with paler center stripe on back. Fringes with single row of spines; tail short. **HABITAT** Rock and gravel deserts in canyons and plains. **ACTIVITY** Chiefly early morning, late afternoon. **RANGE** s AZ.

TEXAS HORNED LIZARD

Phrynosoma cornutum
IGUANA FAMILY

4″. Body flat. Brown or gray with dark brown spots edged white at rear; white line down back. Head has crown of spines (2 long ones in center); edges of body and short tail also spiny. Face blunt; dark lines below eye. Fairly fast runner. **HABITAT** Sandy or rocky areas with little vegetation. **ACTIVITY** Above ground on hot days. **RANGE** se AZ, s and e NM.

SAGEBRUSH LIZARD
Sceloporus graciosus
IGUANA FAMILY

6". Male striped brown and grayish white above; throat and belly blue with irreg. white line down middle; reddish-orange spot on sides. Female has faint or no blue below. Skin has small, spiny scales. **HABITAT** Sagebrush deserts, chaparral, open dry conifer forests. **ACTIVITY** Mar.–Oct.: by day. **RANGE** NV, UT, n AZ, nw NM.

YARROW'S SPINY LIZARD
Sceloporus jarrovii
IGUANA FAMILY

7". Body scaly, with iridescent pink and blue green scales on body and tail. Head blackish with few pale stripes and broad black neck collar edged in white. Adult male has blue sides and throat. Not watchful when sunning on boulder. Bears live young. **HABITAT** Rocky canyons in pine-oak zone of mtns. **ACTIVITY** Daytime. **RANGE** Mtns. of se AZ, sw NM.

DESERT SPINY LIZARD
Sceloporus magister
IGUANA FAMILY

10". Rough spiny scales. Adult male buffy brown, dark spots above; black patches on neck; throat, sides, tail blue-green. Female and imm. banded dark and light; lacks blue. Tail long. Wary and alert. **CAUTION** Bites if held. **HABITAT** Desert scrub. **ACTIVITY** By day; often in trees or burrows. **RANGE** s NV, s UT, n, w, and s AZ, nw and sw NM.

LONG-TAILED BRUSH LIZARD
Urosaurus graciosus
IGUANA FAMILY

6½". Slender. Yellowish with gray crossbars; male has bluish belly patches. Throat, yellow or orange, has folds on sides. Tail up to twice length of body. Sits on branches with head hanging down; timid on ground. **HABITAT** Mesquite, catclaw, paloverde trees of desert washes. **RANGE** s NV, w and sc AZ.

WESTERN FENCE LIZARD
Sceloporus occidentalis
IGUANA FAMILY

8″. Skin has coarse, spiny scales. Male gray-brown above with triangular pattern of blue-edged brown chevrons on back; throat and patches on belly dark blue; limbs orange below. Female has faint or no blue on belly. Feeds on ground. **HABITAT** Woodlands, desert canyons, boulders, buildings. **ACTIVITY** By day; basks in morning sun; all year in warm areas; Apr.–Sept. in high country. **RANGE** NV, w UT.

EASTERN FENCE LIZARD
Sceloporus undulatus
IGUANA FAMILY

6″. Slender; head blunt; scales rough. Gray to tan, with dark brown markings and pale gray side stripe. Male has bright blue patches on sides of belly and sides of throat. Female has dark, wavy crossbars on back, bluish wash below. Plateau races have less prominent side stripes than Prairie races of NM. Feeds in trees and on ground. **HABITAT** Fences, stumps, trees, open pinewoods, fields. **ACTIVITY** By day. **RANGE** se UT, ne AZ, NM.

TREE LIZARD
Urosaurus ornatus
IGUANA FAMILY

5½″. Slender; tail 1½ times body length. Pale gray-brown above with irreg. small dark blotches; scales vary in size. Fold of skin at base of throat. Male has blue or orange throat, bright blue belly patches. Feeds mainly in trees; perches upright with head bobbing on trunks, boulders; wary. **HABITAT** Valleys with trees; buildings; rocks in arid areas. **ACTIVITY** Apr.–Oct.: by day. **RANGE** se NV, e and s UT, AZ, NM (ex. ne).

SIDE-BLOTCHED LIZARD
Uta stansburiana
IGUANA FAMILY

5½″. Scales small; fold of skin on neck. Coloration variable. Head and body gray to brown; large black blotch behind foreleg, on side. Male back, sides, and tail buff speckled with blue, or pale brown with white-edged dark brown arrow-shaped spots. Female pale brown, pale stripe behind eye. Often bobs head. **HABITAT** Cliffs, sagebrush deserts, juniper scrub, valleys. **ACTIVITY** By day, Apr.–Oct. **RANGE** Widespread at low and mid-elev. in all states.

WESTERN BANDED GECKO
Coleonyx variegatus
GECKO FAMILY

5″. Light tan with broad yellow and brown bands, spots; belly plain whitish. Protruding movable eyelids and vertical pupils. Legs pinkish; toes slender. Tail thick. **HABITAT** Rocky areas, canyons, creosote bush deserts, pinyon-juniper belt. **ACTIVITY** Mainly nocturnal. **RANGE** s NV, sw UT, w and s AZ, sw NM.

DESERT NIGHT LIZARD
Xantusia vigilis
NIGHT LIZARD FAMILY

4½″. Head narrow; skin velvety; belly scales large, square. Top of head, back, and tail olive, gray, or brown speckled with black; snout has buffy stripe from eye to shoulder. Arizona race of e AZ mtns. and plateau edge large, 6″, yellow or gray above, heavy black spots. **HABITAT** Rocky outcrops; leaf litter below Joshua Trees, cacti, pines. **ACTIVITY** Nocturnal in summer; by day spring–fall. **RANGE** s NV, s UT, w AZ.

CANYON SPOTTED WHIPTAIL
"Giant Spotted Whiptail"
Cnemidophorus burti
WHIPTAIL FAMILY

15″. All whiptails slim and long-tailed. They walk fast, erratically, often testing the air with their forked tongues. This species dark brown with large buffy yellow spots and/or stripes on body; tail pale buff. Desert race of sw AZ thinner, spots small, back reddish. **HABITAT** Dense shrubbery of canyons, nearby grassy areas. **ACTIVITY** By day. **RANGE** s AZ mtns.

CHIHUAHUAN SPOTTED WHIPTAIL
Cnemidophorus exsanguis
WHIPTAIL FAMILY

11″. Dark reddish brown with 6 yellow stripes and numerous buffy spots. Below pale bluish white, unmarked. Tail dark brown with greenish cast in adult, orange in juv. **HABITAT** Desert grasslands; rocky and sandy areas in pine and oak woodlands. **ACTIVITY** By day. **RANGE** se AZ, c and s NM.

CHECKERED WHIPTAIL

Cnemidophorus tesselatus

WHIPTAIL FAMILY

14″. Slender. Back, sides brown with buffy stripes and coarse black spots arranged in rows or bars. Below whitish with small spots. Tail long, yellowish, lightly spotted with black. **HABITAT** Rocky areas in grasslands, canyons, floodplains. **ACTIVITY** By day. **RANGE** ne, c, and s NM.

DESERT GRASSLAND WHIPTAIL

Cnemidophorus uniparens

WHIPTAIL FAMILY

8½″. Small, slender. Back and sides blackish with 4 buffy brown stripes above, whiter stripes on sides; lacks spots. Below white, chin blue. Tail plain olive in adult; bluish in juv. **HABITAT** Desert plains and foothills with mesquite and yucca. **ACTIVITY** By day. **RANGE** c and s AZ, sw NM.

WESTERN WHIPTAIL

Cnemidophorus tigris

WHIPTAIL FAMILY

10″. Striped above; chest spotted; tail very long, thin, gray-brown in adult, blue in young. Great Basin race (NV, w UT, and w AZ) has 4 light stripes above, dark bars on sides, white throat. Northern race (e UT and n AZ) has 6 yellow stripes, black spots on throat. Southern race (se AZ) has brown stripes with pale spots and dark bands; throat and chest black. Marbled race (s NM) has faded stripes with black barring; below rusty. Active runner; digs burrows. **HABITAT** Open woodlands without tall grass; desert scrub. **ACTIVITY** By day. **RANGE** All SW, ex. c AZ, n NM.

MANY-LINED SKINK

Eumeces multivirgatus

SKINK FAMILY

7″. Slim, long-bodied, long-tailed. Mid-back pale gray stripe bordered by narrow dark and pale brown stripes or rows of spots; creamy below. Tail looks swollen; buffy brown with rows of dark spots; blue in juv. Some individuals unstriped plain brown above, buffy below in lower, drier areas. **HABITAT** Loose, sandy soils in plains; pinyon-juniper woods and rocky, scrubby areas in mtns. **ACTIVITY** By day. **RANGE** se UT, c and ne AZ, NM (ex. sw). **Western Skink** *(E. skiltonianus)* bolder brown back, whitish side stripe, black sides; UT, w NV.

GREAT PLAINS SKINK

Eumeces obsoletus

SKINK FAMILY

12″. Uniformly colored, no stripes; scales on sides obliquely angled forward. Adult speckled due to brown scales with black edges; belly buffy. Juv. black with blue-black tail; lips speckled white. Seldom seen in open; usu. stays under rocks, logs, boards on ground. **HABITAT** Sandhills, canyons, floodplain valleys; near water. **ACTIVITY** By day. **RANGE** c and se AZ, all NM (ex. nw).

ARIZONA ALLIGATOR LIZARD

Elgaria kingii

ANGUID FAMILY

11″. Robust. Back, sides, and tail have wide reddish-brown and buffy-yellow crossbands. Head buffy with fine black spots. Juv. has black dots lining crossbands, black and white spots on lips. Forages on ground and climbs trees for insects, scorpions, and other lizards. **HABITAT** Rocky areas near water in mtn. scrub; cottonwood, pine, oak, and fir woodlands. **ACTIVITY** By day. **RANGE** c and se AZ, sw NM.

banded race (left), juvenile (right)

GILA MONSTER

Heloderma suspectum

VENOMOUS LIZARD FAMILY

22″. Body heavy; legs short, claws strong. Tail quite short, thick, sausage-shaped. Head massive, face black; jaws wide with sharp teeth. Reticulate race adult covered with shiny bead-like black scales, intermingled with spots and larger blotches of either red, pink, orange, or yellow. Banded race of s AZ, sw NM has 4 broad double crossbands. Juvenile of both races has distinct black bands. Stores fat in tail; swollen tail indicates it is well fed. Stays in burrows when very hot or very cold. Carnivorous; uses taste and smell to track prey. Frequently flicks forked tongue to taste ground. Generally slow-moving, but can lunge quickly. Poison glands by teeth of lower jaw; venom flows as jaws grip and chew on larger prey. Rarely uses venom on eggs in nests, insects, scorpions, smaller birds, rodents, and lizards. World's only other poisonous lizard is Mexico's **Beaded Lizard** *(H. horridum).* **CAUTION** Venomous; powerful grip; hard to dislodge. Venom causes pain but rarely death. **HABITAT** Shrubby desert and foothill grasslands; usu. close to moisture, shrubs, small trees. **ACTIVITY** Warm winter and spring days; chiefly nocturnal and crepuscular in summer and fall. **RANGE** se NV, w, c, and se AZ, sw NM.

Snakes

Snakes (suborder Serpentes of the scaled reptile order, Squamata) have elongated, scaly bodies with no limbs, eyelids, or external ear openings. They grow throughout their lives, shedding their skin from snout to tail several times a year. Snakes are carnivorous, swallowing prey whole. The flicking, forked tongue serves as an olfactory organ. Snakes mate via internal fertilization, most species in fall, before their winter hibernation, which usually begins in November and ends in March or April. Most species lay eggs from March through June that hatch July through September; a few give birth to live young in late summer. While most snakes in the Southwest are harmless, the rattlesnakes and coral snakes are poisonous (see the essay on snakebites, page 266). The size given is the length of a typical adult.

RUBBER BOA
Lichanura bottae
BOA FAMILY

24″. Thick; looks rubbery. Tail short, shaped like head. Snout short, broad. Head scales large; body scales small, smooth, shiny. Plain brown or olive above, yellowish below. Climbs trees; good burrower and swimmer. **HABITAT** Woodlands, grasslands, mtns., sandy watersides. **ACTIVITY** Feeds mainly at night and on warm overcast days. **RANGE** n and w NV, n and c UT.

ROSY BOA
Lichanura trivirgata
BOA FAMILY

3′. Head blunt; lacks large scales; neck slightly thinner. Tail short, blunt. Eyes tiny. Skin smooth, shiny. Wide stripes of gray and rosy reddish brown from head to tail; sometimes blotched. Good climber. Coils around birds, mammals; coils into ball when cornered. **HABITAT** Desert scrub, usu. near springs, permanent water, canyons. **ACTIVITY** Nocturnal. **RANGE** sw AZ.

RACER
Coluber constrictor
COLUBRID SNAKE FAMILY

4′2″. Body scales small, smooth. Adults of yellow-bellied races unpatterned olive-green to grayish above, pale yellow below. Young yellowish with many brown spots on back, smaller brown spots on sides. Alert; moves fast, often with head off ground. Climbs trees. Not a constrictor. **CAUTION** Not poisonous, but bites hard, thrashes violently if handled. **HABITAT** Woodland edges, grasslands, sagebrush deserts. **ACTIVITY** By day. **RANGE** w, n, and se NV, most of UT, n NM.

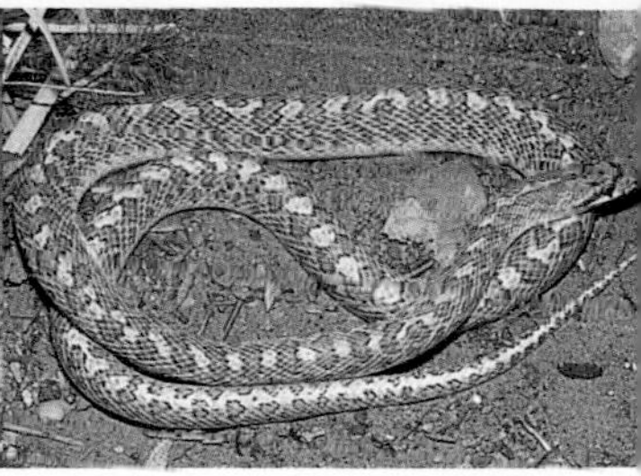

GLOSSY SNAKE Arizona race (left), Painted Desert race (right)
Arizona elegans
COLUBRID SNAKE FAMILY

5′. Scales glossy, unkeeled. Arizona race has numerous black-edged brown spots over yellow or gray mid-back stripe. Painted Desert race has paler, "bleached out" coloration. Snout pointed, overhangs jaw; dark line connects rear of jaw and eye. **HABITAT** Barren deserts, sagebrush, brushy grasslands near woods; usu. on sand, loam, or rocks. **ACTIVITY** Evenings and nights. Excavates its own burrow; spends day inside. **RANGE** s NV, far sw UT, w and s AZ, most of NM; absent in higher mtns.

RINGNECK SNAKE regal race (left), prairie race (right)
Diadophis punctatus
COLUBRID SNAKE FAMILY

18″. Head small. Regal race plain gray, olive, or brown; underside yellow, spotted with black grading to bright reddish orange under tail; lacks neck ring. Prairie race of e NM red below, red neck ring. Secretive; lives under logs, rocks, leaves. Constricts smaller reptiles, invertebrates. **HABITAT** Moist areas in forests, brushlands, grasslands, farms. **ACTIVITY** Mainly night. **RANGE** e NV, w and c UT, c, c, and se AZ, most of NM.

WESTERN HOGNOSE SNAKE
Heterodon nasicus
COLUBRID SNAKE FAMILY

28″. Heavy-bodied; neck broad; snout spade-like, upturned. Base color pale brown, buffy, or gray; large dark brown spots on back, smaller spots on sides; washed blackish below. If cornered, flattens head like a cobra and hisses; may then "play possum" and lie on its back with tongue hanging out. Good burrower. **HABITAT** Sand and gravel prairie, scrub, floodplains. **ACTIVITY** Apr.–Oct.: by day; stays in burrow when cold or very hot. **RANGE** se AZ, all NM (ex. nw).

COMMON KINGSNAKE

California race (left), desert race (right)

Lampropeltis getulus

COLUBRID SNAKE FAMILY

3′6″. Head small, rounded. California race black with white bands (wider on sides); face white; crown black with white spot. Striped form black or dark brown above with single mid-back row of broken white stripes; white below. Desert race of se AZ and NM has chain-like pattern; mid-back dark brown with thin yellow bands; sides speckled with yellow; belly blackish. Bites snakes, lizards behind head, then coils around them. **HABITAT** Near rocks, streams in woodlands; grasslands, deserts, mtns. to 7,000′. **ACTIVITY** Mainly by day. **RANGE** w and s NM, sw UT, w and s AZ, s, c, and e NM.

SONORAN MOUNTAIN KINGSNAKE

Lampropeltis pyromelana

COLUBRID SNAKE FAMILY

35″. Beautifully banded red, black, and white. Black bands between all red and white (sometimes yellowish) bands, meet over much of snake; not poisonous, like similar-looking coral snakes. A protected species in AZ. **HABITAT** Mtns. from juniper, pine, and oak zones up to fir zone. **ACTIVITY** Mainly by day. **RANGE** c and sw UT, nc to se AZ, sw NM.

STRIPED WHIPSNAKE

Masticophis taeniatus

COLUBRID SNAKE FAMILY

5′. Slender; tail long, thin; scales smooth. Back slaty; sides finely striped in black and white; white on throat, buffy below at midbody, pinkish below tail; small head has large, slaty, white-edged scales on top. Alert; moves fast, with head held off ground; often rests and hunts in bushes. **HABITAT** High grasslands, sagebrush flats, dry canyons; juniper, pine, and oak woods. **ACTIVITY** By day. **RANGE** NV, UT (ex. mtns.), AZ (ex. Sonoran Desert), NM (ex. Rockies).

COACHWHIP

red race (left), western race (right)

Masticophis flagellum

COLUBRID SNAKE FAMILY

5′. Tail whip-like. Red race of NV, UT, and AZ has 2 phases. Most are reddish pink with black bands on neck. In s AZ some are black, with red undertail. Western race plain light brown, pink, or orangy; some trace of dark crossbands. **CAUTION** Strikes repeatedly if cornered. **HABITAT** Grasslands, brush, deserts; mtns. to 7,000′. **ACTIVITY** By day. **RANGE** w and s NV, sw UT, AZ (ex. ne), NM (ex. nw). **Sonoran Whipsnake** *(M. bilineatus)*, 4′, grayish-brown body with 3 dark-edged light stripes on each side. Hunts lizards and bird nestlings.

MILK SNAKE

Utah race (left), New Mexico race (right)

"Milk Kingsnake"

Lampropeltis triangulum

COLUBRID SNAKE FAMILY

25″. Conspicuously banded in red, black, and white (or yellow). In UT race black bands fuse and join red rings; snout black or light with black blotches. NM race has red bands encircling entire body. Head equal to or slightly smaller than body. Scales smooth. Constricts rodents and other snakes. Common name is based on absurd notion that this snake milks cows. It feeds on small rodents, birds, lizards, and other snakes. **HABITAT** Woodlands of juniper, pine, or oak. **ACTIVITY** Often by night; esp. in hot weather; warm days in spring and fall. **RANGE** Chiefly UT, n and e NM.

GOPHER SNAKE

Pituophis catenifer

COLUBRID SNAKE FAMILY

4′. Stocky to medium; head yellowish brown with dark line across top. Great Basin race buffy with round, dark brown blotches; dark line on sides of neck. Sonora race of most of AZ, NM has reddish-brown blotches above, darker to rear. Bullsnake race of e NM yellowish with brown blotches, darker on both head and tail. If threatened puffs up, hisses, strikes; mimics rattlers by rustling dead leaves with tail. **HABITAT** Woodlands, grasslands, farms, sagebrush deserts. **ACTIVITY** By day, warm nights.

WESTERN PATCH-NOSED SNAKE

Salvadora hexalepis

COLUBRID SNAKE FAMILY

3′. Blunt snout has triangular front flap; useful in sand. Scales smooth. Yellowish midback stripe and sides separated by broad blackish band. Below gray; washed orange under tail. **CAUTION** Fast-moving; may bite if cornered. **HABITAT** Creosote flats, sagebrush deserts; to 7,000′. **ACTIVITY** All day, even when hot. **RANGE** w and s NV, sw UT, nw, c, and s AZ, s NM.

WESTERN TERRESTRIAL GARTER SNAKE

Thamnophis elegans

COLUBRID SNAKE FAMILY

30″. Back gray-brown; markings variable. Wandering race: mid-back stripe narrow, yellow; rest of back brown, some heavily spotted with black; sides and belly pale gray. Feeds in water and on land. **HABITAT** Watersides, nearby wooded areas, grassland, mtns. to 10,500′. **ACTIVITY** By day; basks. **RANGE** n and c NV, UT, ne AZ, nw and sc NM.

CHECKERED GARTER SNAKE

Thamnophis marcianus

COLUBRID SNAKE FAMILY

3′. Brown, olive, or tan above; white or yellow stripe on mid-back, another on side; covered with large, bold, black spots. Top of head plain brown; black and white lines below eye; white crescent above black patch on neck. **HABITAT** Arid grasslands near water. **ACTIVITY** By day or night. **RANGE** s AZ, s and e NM. **Black-necked Garter Snake** *(T. cyrtopsis)* is darker brown above, spots less distinct; canyons from desert to 8,750′, e AZ, se UT, most of NM.

COMMON GARTER SNAKE

valley race (left), New Mexico race (right)

Thamnophis sirtalis

COLUBRID SNAKE FAMILY

35". Extremely variable in color and pattern. Valley race of NV, UT brown or gray above; back has wide yellowish stripe; red dots on sides; top of head blackish. NM race brown above with black and red spots on sides, yellow midback stripe. **HABITAT** Marshy areas, ditches, open woods, grasslands, brush, incl. urban areas. **ACTIVITY** By day. **RANGE** w NV, n UT, Rio Grande Valley of NM. **Plains Garter Snake** *(T. radix)* has orangy mid-back stripe, checkerboard of black spots above; ne NM.

LYRE SNAKE

Trimorphodon biscutatus

COLUBRID SNAKE FAMILY

3'. Slim. Light brown or gray above, with light-centered dark brown diamonds. Head has oversized cat-like eyes with vertical pupils; lyre-shaped mark on top of head. Climbs boulders and trees. Feeds on lizards, birds, and small mammals. **HABITAT** Rocky hillsides from desert up to pine-oak forests. **ACTIVITY** Nocturnal. **RANGE** s NV, sw UT, w, c, and s AZ, sw NM.

WESTERN CORAL SNAKE

"Arizona Coral Snake"

Micruroides euryxanthus

ELAPID SNAKE FAMILY

20". Striking and colorful. Head small, snout blunt; face and jaws black; rear half of head yellow. Rest of body has encircling wide red and black bands that never touch, as narrower yellow bands separate each: thus, red next to yellow is a coral; similar snake (with red next to black) a harmless mimic. Rarely seen; spends most of its time in crevices, burrows; usu. not aggressive when approached. **CAUTION** Poisonous; venom attacks nerves; bites are rare but can be fatal. **HABITAT** Rocky areas of plains, valleys, and foothills, esp. near water. **ACTIVITY** Nocturnal, but also active on overcast and rainy days. **RANGE** c and se AZ.

Poisonous Snakes and Snakebites

The Southwest has 12 poisonous snake species, 11 of which are rattlesnakes. All except for 2 small, rare mountain species found near Mexico are covered in this guide. Rattlesnakes are pit vipers with wide triangular heads, narrow necks, and rattles on their tails. Long, hollow fangs fold back against the roof of the mouth when not in use. Rattlers locate prey by using their heat-sensing organs at night. Pit viper venom attacks blood vessels, red blood cells, and nerves. The only non–pit viper poisonous snake in the region is the Western Coral Snake (page 265); its poison acts on the nervous system rather than the blood.

Most snakes will flee from footsteps. If you encounter a snake, freeze to let it withdraw, then step away. Although bites sting and can be extremely painful, they are rarely fatal. However, for any poisonous snakebite the best course of action is to get medical care as soon as possible, with the dead snake as positive identification, so the proper antivenin can be administered. Meanwhile, the victim should avoid moving, as movement helps the venom spread through the system, and keep the injured body part motionless and just below heart level. The victim should be kept warm, calm, and at rest while on the way to medical care. If you are alone and on foot, start walking slowly toward help, exerting the injured area as little as possible.

WESTERN DIAMONDBACK RATTLESNAKE
Crotalus atrox
PIT VIPER FAMILY

6′. Heavy body with triangular head much thicker than neck. Gray or brown above; 4- or 6-sided dark-edged pale diamonds on back separated by short white lines. Pattern sometimes weak; often with erratic dark spots. Diagonal pale stripes on either side of eye to jaw. Tail banded black and white above rattles. Coils, lifts head, and rattles to warn intruders to back away. **CAUTION** Poisonous; bites can be fatal. **HABITAT** Desert plains, brush, rocky foothills to 7,000′. **ACTIVITY** Day or night. **RANGE** c and s AZ, c and s NM.

SIDEWINDER
Crotalus cerastes
PIT VIPER FAMILY

25″. Base color matches local soil: buffy, pinkish, or gray; back has inconspicuous pattern of cream and light brown blotches. Head has prominent pointed projection over each eye, blackish tear-line behind. Like all rattlers, has large triangular head, long hollow fangs, rattles on tail. Moves with peculiar sideways motion, leaving J-shaped tracks in sand; hook of J shows direction of travel. Feeds mainly on kangaroo rats. **CAUTION** Poisonous. **HABITAT** Sand dunes, rocky hillsides, to 6,000′. **ACTIVITY** Chiefly nocturnal. **RANGE** s NV, sw UT, w and s AZ.

ROCK RATTLESNAKE

Crotalus lepidus

PIT VIPER FAMILY

20". Banded race (pictured): plain or lightly spotted bluish gray; solid dark brown bands encircle body, wider at mid-back. Head wide; lacks stripes behind eyes. Mottled race of Guadalupe Mtns., se NM: gray with blackish bands and many dark spots between. **CAUTION** Poisonous and aggressive. **HABITAT** Rocky slopes, wooded canyons in mtns. **ACTIVITY** Day and night. **RANGE** Mtns. of se AZ (Santa Ritas eastward) and s NM.

SPECKLED RATTLESNAKE

Crotalus mitchellii

PIT VIPER FAMILY

3'4". Color matches local soil: buffy, brown, pinkish, or gray, with muted pattern of dark bands or diamond-like blotches with blackish speckles. Pattern often muted; looks like granite. Head speckled. **CAUTION** Alert, nervous; holds ground rather than flees from danger. **HABITAT** Rocky areas in canyons, deserts. **ACTIVITY** By day spring and fall; nocturnal in summer. **RANGE** s NV, w AZ (west of Phoenix).

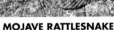

BLACK-TAILED RATTLESNAKE

Crotalus molossus

PIT VIPER FAMILY

3½'. Gray, olive, or yellowish above; dark brown crossbands that expand into dark diamonds with small, pale centers. Head has dark line over snout, diagonal to behind eye. Tail abruptly black (without white bands) above rattle. Less aggressive than other rattlers. **CAUTION** Poisonous. **HABITAT** Rock piles, canyons, and cliffs from desert washes up to pine-oak woodlands in mtns. **ACTIVITY** Day and night. **RANGE** AZ northward to Grand Canyon, but not along Colorado R.; c and s NM.

MOJAVE RATTLESNAKE

Crotalus scutulatus

PIT VIPER FAMILY

3'4". Greenish gray, occ. yellowish or brown; lined with dark brown ovals with paler brown centers; sides gray or buff. Tail light with thin black bands above rattle. Green or brown patch, flanked by pale lines below eye. **CAUTION** Most venomous and possibly most aggressive species in SW; venom highly toxic. **HABITAT** Desert scrub, arid plains; mesquite, creosote, and cactus areas; mtns. to 6,000'. **ACTIVITY** Nocturnal; also cooler hours of day. **RANGE** s NV, sw UT, AZ (ex. ne), sw NM.

TIGER RATTLESNAKE
Crotalus tigris
PIT VIPER FAMILY

30″. Tiger-like bands, rather than diamonds; color appears washed out. Above gray, pink, or buff with brown bands; below creamy. Head fairly small; rattle quite large. No black or white on tail above rattle. **CAUTION** Poisonous. **HABITAT** Desert foothills and canyons, incl. ocotillo and saguaro cactus areas. **ACTIVITY** Day and night. **RANGE** c and sc AZ.

MASSASAUGA
Sistrurus catenatus
PIT VIPER FAMILY

26″. Nine enlarged scales on top of head, unlike most rattlers. Light gray or tan; numerous large, dark brown blotches above, smaller blotches on sides; below gray. Horizontal dark and light lines on head and neck. **CAUTION** Poisonous, but usu. not aggressive. **HABITAT** Grasslands, esp. if boulders present. **ACTIVITY** Nocturnal in summer; suns and hunts on cooler days. **RANGE** All NM (ex. nw), se AZ.

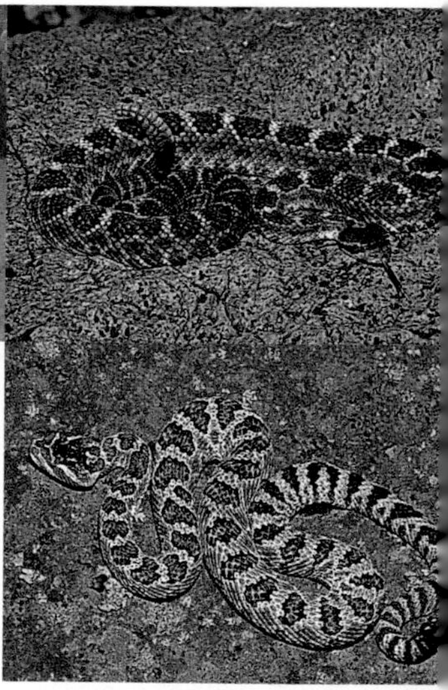

prairie race (upper left), Arizona black race (top right), Great Basin race (bottom right)

WESTERN RATTLESNAKE
Crotalus viridis
PIT VIPER FAMILY

4′. Varies widely by race and individual; most have diagonal dark stripe below eye, flanked by white. Great Basin race buffy brown with dark brown bands. Grand Canyon race pinkish, pale brown hourglass blotches on back. AZ black race blackish, yellow bands on back. Prairie race of NM buffy with lengthwise ovals in forehalf, becoming bands towards tail. Large, dark brown blotches on back edged with narrow whitish or yellow lines; pattern faded in older individuals. Head wide, top solid brown; diagonal dark patch below eye. **CAUTION** Aggressive; gives warning by rattling tail; holds its ground. **HABITAT** Forests, grasslands, rocky areas, mtns. to 11,000′. **ACTIVITY** Day and night. **RANGE** All SW, ex. s NV, sw AZ.

Birds

Members of the class Aves, birds are the only animals that have feathers, and all U.S. species are capable of flight. Like their reptile ancestors, they lay eggs; like mammals, they are warm-blooded. They generally have excellent sight and hearing, but few have a good sense of smell. The bird skeleton is adapted for flight: the bones are lightweight, with a sponge-like interior. The forelimbs have become wings, with strong pectoral muscles attached to a keeled breastbone, and the hindlimbs are modified for running, grasping, or perching. Wing shapes vary among types of birds, ranging, for example, from the long, broad wings of the soaring raptors to the narrow, fast-moving wings of hummingbirds.

Although all Black Phoebes in one area look the same regardless of their age or gender or the time of year, this is not the case for most birds. Plumages may vary from immature to adult, from male to female, and from breeding to nonbreeding seasons—summer and winter, respectively. (If both sexes have a summer plumage distinct from nonbreeding plumage, we note this as "summer adult." If only the male has such a summer plumage, we note "summer male.") In some species, groups living in different geographic areas (subspecies, or races) have slightly or distinctly different plumages. Some birds within a given species have different colorations (called morphs or phases) that have nothing to do with where they live. Some birds have ornamental plumes, often developed in the breeding season. This guide describes one or more of the plumages most often seen in the Southwest. The photograph shows the adult male or either adult (if adults look alike) unless otherwise noted.

Flight allows birds to migrate great distances, though a number are resident year-round in some or all of the region. Many birds that spend the winter in warmer, southern climes migrate north to breed, taking advantage of the abundant animal life in the summertime Southwest. Other birds breed to the north—in Alaska, Canada, and elsewhere in the western United States—and spend only the winter in the Southwest or pass through only in migration. Cold and snow rarely kill birds directly but may reduce the amount of food (insects, animals, berries) they can obtain to maintain their ideal body temperature. Because of this, a number of mountain birds descend to lower elevations for the winter, or migrate to Mexico or Central America. Many individuals return to the same breeding and wintering grounds several years in a row.

Northbound migration occurs from late February to early June, southbound from July into December. Migrants often wait until the wind is at their backs before continuing their journey. Western migration tends to be steady and gradual, building to a peak and tapering off, unlike the migration of eastern birds, which has periodic waves influenced by weather fronts. For more about bird migration, see the essay on bird-watching on page 271.

In bird species that do not nest in colonies, a male that is ready to breed stakes out and defends a nesting territory from other males.

The female chooses a male in part on the quality and size of his territory, the presence of a secure nest site, and the quality of his plumage and song. The avian life cycle typically starts with the female laying one or more eggs in a nest, which, depending on the species, may be a scrape in the sand, a cup of rootlets and fibers, a woven basket, a stick platform, or another type of structure. After an incubation period of roughly two to four weeks, the young are hatched and fed by their parents for a period varying from a few days (shorebirds) to a few weeks (most species) to many months (raptors). Smaller birds tend to breed the year following their birth, while many larger birds remain immature for several years before breeding. During the breeding season, many male birds exhibit more colorful and elaborate plumages and courtship displays and rituals in order to attract a mate. Most species mate in solitary pairs, the males competing for breeding territories; other species nest colonially. In this section of the guide, assume a bird is a solitary nester unless the description notes that it nests in colonies. Space limitations rarely allow us to give descriptions of nests in this guide.

Birds use their voices in different ways. In many species, contact and alarm call notes are given year-round by both sexes. The more musical songs, usually given only in spring and summer by the male, attract mates and define territory. Once the young are born, many birds stop singing.

This section's descriptions give the length of the bird from the tip of the beak to the end of the tail. For some large species, wingspan is also given.

> For suggestions on attracting birds to your yard, see page 318. In this section, the icon denotes species that will come into a yard to a feeder. The icon indicates species that might use a suitable nest box in a yard within its range and habitat.

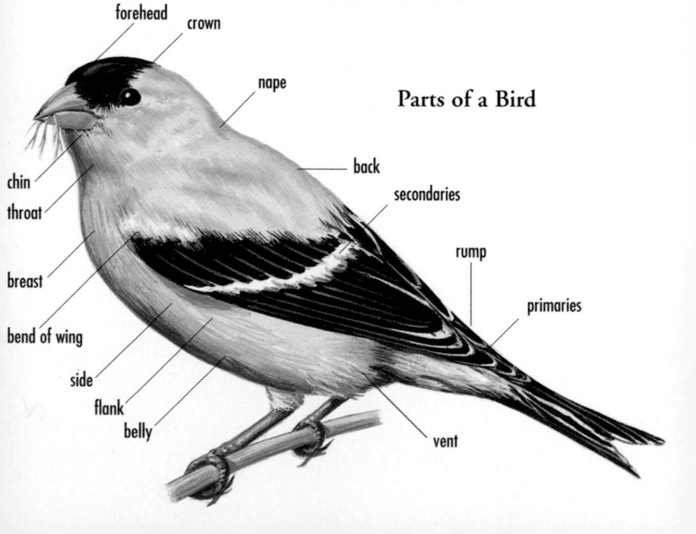

Parts of a Bird

Bird-Watching

Bird-watching, or birding, as it is often termed, can be a casual activity, develop into a hobby, or become a passion. Some observers enjoy generally keeping track of birds they come across in their daily activities or while hiking, driving, or boating, while others become intent on seeing as many different types of birds as possible. It's possible to see 200 to 300 species or more in a year in the Southwest.

In breeding season, many birds live in only one habitat and are active at certain times of day. Freshwater marsh birds (rails, bitterns, and marsh songbirds) are most often calling and active at dawn and dusk. Until mid-morning on hot days, songbirds search woodlands, fields, and thickets for food; from mid-morning to late afternoon, they tend to be quiet; they forage again late in the day. Birds that live near lakes and other aquatic habitats (herons, cormorants, ducks, sandpipers) may be active all day. Make an after-dark visit to a canyon or pine-oak woodland to listen for owls, which may respond to taped or imitated calls and can be viewed with spotlights.

Waterfowl, cranes, and shorebirds fly north–south along inland valleys on a route known as a flyway. The greatest variety of birds can be seen during migration seasons. In early spring (March and April), hawks and waterfowl that have wintered in South America return to the Southwest, while many birds that have wintered in the Southwest move northward. Most songbirds migrate to the Southwest from April to May; males arrive a week or so before females in order to stake out territories. When the land bird migration tapers off in late May, sandpipers and plovers are still flying through. Larger birds migrate by day, but most species, especially smaller, insect-eating ones (except swallows), fly at night, resting and feeding during the day, usually in quiet places with ample food. In a light woodland along a stream, where there are newly opened leaves and plenty of small insects, it is possible to see many birds, including warblers, on a spring morning. Migrating songbirds also concentrate in orchards, tree farms, and parks.

Fall migration is underway by July, when the first southbound sandpipers and plovers reappear; adults in these groups migrate a week to a month before their offspring. From August to November, most of the songbirds pass through. Ducks, geese, and raptors migrate from September into November. During severe weather, many birds may shift southward.

For the serious birder, at least one good field guide is essential; many excellent ones are available, including the *National Audubon Society Field Guide to North American Birds (Western Region).* Binoculars (7-, 8-, 9-, or 10-power) are a must; a close-focusing pair is especially helpful. A 15-, 20-, or 30-power telescope with a wide field of view, mounted on a sturdy, collapsible tripod, is invaluable for viewing waterfowl, shorebirds, and raptors.

Many birds are shy or secretive. Learn to move slowly and quietly, and avoid wearing brightly colored or patterned clothing and making loud noises. Please respect local laws, do not unduly frighten birds, and take great care not to disrupt nesting or resting birds.

COMMON LOON

Gavia immer

LOON FAMILY

32″. Body stout, duck-like. Summer: back black, with large white spots; head, neck, and bill black; white bands on neck; eyes red. Winter (pictured): slate gray above, white below; bill slaty. Bill heavy, pointed. In flight, legs extend beyond tail. **VOICE** Quavering laughter, yodeling; heard mainly on summer nights. **HABITAT** Lakes, reservoirs, large rivers. **RANGE** Oct.–Mar.: Colorado R. of s NV, w AZ; local elsewhere.

CLARK'S GREBE

Aechmorphorus clarkii

GREBE FAMILY

25″. Swan-like with its long, curving neck. Crown, rear of neck, and upperparts black. Area above eye, throat, foreneck, and below white. Bill long, thin, yellow. Courtship display is dance on water with body raised and head held forward. **VOICE** Rising *creeek.* **HABITAT** Marsh-fringed lakes, reservoirs. **RANGE** Apr.–Sept.: NV, UT. Oct.–Mar.: s NV, w AZ. **Western Grebe** *(A. occidentalis)* has similar range; black of crown surrounds red eye; bill olive-yellow.

summer (left), winter (right)

EARED GREBE

Podiceps nigricollis

GREBE FAMILY

13″. Slate gray above, whitish below; undertail coverts white, often fluffed up. Forehead high; bill short, slender, black, slightly up-turned; eyes red. Summer: sides rusty; head and neck black; sides of face streaked yellow. Winter: neck gray; crown and cheeks black; throat and nape white. Called Black-necked Grebe in Europe. **VOICE** Soft *poo-eep* when breeding. **HABITAT** Lakes, marshes. **RANGE** Apr.–Oct.: n NV, UT, ne AZ, nw NM. Mar.–Apr., Sept.–Nov.: all SW. Dec.–Apr.: s NV, s AZ, s NM.

PIED-BILLED GREBE
Podilymbus podiceps
GREBE FAMILY

13″. Summer: body brown; chin black; bill white with black ring. Winter: body brown; chin white; bill yellow or gray, lacks ring. Dives frequently for small fish. **VOICE** Series of 8 *cow* notes. **HABITAT** Marsh-edged ponds, reservoirs. **RANGE** All SW, local.

AMERICAN WHITE PELICAN
adult (left), in flight (right)
Pelecanus erythrorhynchos
PELICAN FAMILY

L 5′2″; WS 8′. Adult all white at rest. Bill long, flat, with orange-yellow pouch; knob on top in summer. Neck long; tail short. Legs short; feet wide, webbed; both orange-yellow. Flight reveals black primaries. Imm. grayish white; bill and pouch gray. Feeds in groups in water; dips bill and pouch into water for small schooling fish. Often flies in V-formation or wheels high in sky on thermals; does not dive from air. Nests in colonies on islands. **VOICE** Usu. silent; grunts at nest. **HABITAT** Large lakes. **RANGE** Apr.–Oct.: n NV, n UT. Mar.–Apr., Aug.–Oct.: all SW, local. Oct.–Apr.: w AZ.

DOUBLE-CRESTED CORMORANT
immature (left), adult (right)
Phalacrocorax auritus
CORMORANT FAMILY

33″. Adult: dark green (appears black); back and wings brownish; breeding crest (2 small tufts) hard to see. Bill narrow, hooked; throat skin orange. Imm grayish brown; chest and foreneck white. Swims with bill angled upwar spreads wings to dry while resting. Flocks often fly in V-formation with ne kinked. Nests in colonies, in nest of sticks and weeds in trees and on r of islands. **VOICE** Usu. silent; croaks at nest. **HABITAT** Lakes, rivers. **RANGE** ident in s NV, w and s AZ, s NM. Mar.–Nov.: nw NV, n UT.

Herons

Members of the heron family (Ardeidae)—herons, egrets, and bitterns—are large, long-legged, long-necked birds up to 4 feet long. They wade in shallows and marshes, where they use their longish, dagger-like bills to seize slippery fish and aquatic frogs, snakes, and invertebrates. Although storks, ibises, spoonbills, and cranes fly with outstretched necks, herons normally fold theirs into an S shape when airborne. During courtship (two to four weeks a year), adults of many of these species have ornamental plumes and bright facial colors. Their nests are usually large platforms of sticks, often in large colonies that may include several species of herons and other large waders. Predominantly white heron species are called egrets. Bitterns are shy denizens of marshes with distinct voices.

AMERICAN BITTERN
Botaurus lentiginosus
HERON FAMILY

28″. Adult light buffy brown, with thin white eyebrow and dark streaks on neck; black stripe partway down neck (unlike imm. night-herons). Neck thick; legs greenish. Imm. lacks black neck stripe. Shy; points bill skyward if disturbed. **VOICE** Loud, pumping *uunk-KA-lunk*. **HABITAT** Marshes. **RANGE** Apr.–Nov.: n NV, n UT, n NM. Sept.–Apr.: s NV, w and s AZ, s NM.

GREAT BLUE HERON
Ardea herodias
HERON FAMILY

breeding adult (left), in flight (right)

4′; WS 6′. Adult back and wings blue-gray; belly blackish; sides of breast d belly have black patches; crown black with white center; black plumes m back of head; face white; most of neck gray; foreneck striped black white. Legs very long, dark. Bill yellow. Imm. crown all black, lacks es. Nest of sticks in treetop colonies. **VOICE** Deep squawk. **HABITAT** es, lakesides, riversides. **RANGE** Resident in SW; most withdraw from JT in winter.

GREAT EGRET breeding (left), in flight (right)
Ardea alba
HERON FAMILY

L 3′3″; WS 4′3″. All white. Bill yellow; legs and feet black. Neck long, thin. During breeding, back has long, lacy, white plumes; facial skin green. Nests in treetop colonies with other species. **VOICE** Deep croak, but usu. silent. **HABITAT** Marshes, riversides, lakeshores. **RANGE** Resident in s NV, w and s AZ, s NM.

CATTLE EGRET breeding (left), nonbreeding (right)
Bubulcus ibis
HERON FAMILY

20″. Adult all white. Bill, legs, and feet yellow; legs short for a heron. During breeding, back, chest, and crown have buffy plumes; bill, legs, feet orange. Imm. all white; bill yellow; legs olive or blackish. Social; small flocks feed together, nest in colonies. Range expanding; self-introduced from Africa. Chases large insects disturbed by feeding cattle and horses. **VOICE** Occ. hoarse croaks; usu. silent. **HABITAT** Meadows, watersides, farms. **RANGE** Resident in s AZ. Apr.–Sept.: erratic in w NV, n UT, c NM.

SNOWY EGRET

immature (left), breeding (right)

Egretta thula

HERON FAMILY

L 24″; WS 3′2″. All white. Bill slender, black; lores yellow. Neck long. Legs black; feet yellow. During breeding, back, chest, and crown have long, lacy, white plumes. Imm. back of legs yellow-green. Nests in colonies. **VOICE** Harsh *aah.* **HABITAT** Marshes, ponds. **RANGE** Resident in w AZ. Apr.–Sept.: local in NV, UT, n and e AZ, NM.

BLACK-CROWNED NIGHT-HERON

breeding adult (left), immature (right)

Nycticorax nycticorax

HERON FAMILY

26″. Adult crown, back black; wings gray; lores and underparts white; eyes red. Neck thick; legs shortish, yellow. Imm. back and wings brown with large whitish spots; brown and white streaked below. Nests in colonies. **VOICE** Low *kwock.* **HABITAT** Ponds, riversides, marshes. **RANGE** Resident in s NV, w and s AZ, s NM. Mar.–Oct.: rest of SW; few winter in UT.

WHITE-FACED IBIS

Plegadis chihi

IBIS FAMILY

24″. Summer: glossy chestnut with glossy green wings. Eye encircled by white line; bare red skin at base of long, drooping, silvery bill. Neck and legs long. Flies with neck out. Nests in colonies in reeds. **VOICE** Low grunts. **HABITAT** Marshes, flooded fields. **RANGE** Apr.–May, Aug.–Oct.: all SW. May–Sept.: n NV, n UT. Nov.–Mar.: s AZ.

breeding adult (left), immature (right)

GREEN HERON
Butorides virescens
HERON FAMILY

19″. Adult body slaty green; cap black; neck chestnut. Legs greenish yellow (breeding male has orange legs), short for a heron; bill dark. Imm. brownish; neck pale with heavy dark brown streaks. Often feeds by leaning over water from logs, rocks; also wades. **VOICE** Harsh *keyow.* **HABITAT** Ponds, streams, marshes. **RANGE** Resident in s NV, w and s AZ, s NM.

Waterfowl

The waterfowl family (Anatidae) includes the huge white swans, the medium-size geese, and a wide variety of ducks. All have webbed feet and thick bills designed for filtering small organisms in the water or for grasping underwater vegetation and invertebrates, including mollusks. Most waterfowl undergo lengthy migrations between northern or inland breeding areas and southern and/or coastal wintering waters. Their nests, made of grasses and lined with feathers, are usually on the ground, hidden in tall grass or reeds, and contain many eggs. Ducks may be split into two main groups. Dabbling ducks upend on the surface of waters and can jump up and take flight straight out of the water. Diving ducks dive well under the surface of waters; in taking flight, they run and flap horizontally over the water's surface before gaining altitude. Mergansers are diving ducks with saw-edged bills for grasping fish. Swans and geese upend like dabbling ducks, rather than dive for food; most patter across the water to get airborne. Waterfowl males are in breeding plumage all winter and spring, and in late summer develop a drab nonbreeding plumage similar to that of females.

Mallard taking off, straight up, from surface of water

Mallard dabbling

Canada Goose taking off by running across water

TUNDRA SWAN
Cygnus columbianus
WATERFOWL FAMILY

L 4′5″; WS 7′. Adult mostly white; head and neck often stained buffy; bill thick, black, tapers to eye; yellow spot before eye. Neck extremely long. Feet black; tail short. Imm. light brown; bill mostly pink. Flies with neck outstretched. **VOICE** Mellow, high-pitched *hoo-oo-hoo.* **HABITAT** Lakes, marshes. **RANGE** Oct.–Apr.: w NV, n UT, sw AZ, s NM.

GREATER WHITE-FRONTED GOOSE
Anser albifrons
WATERFOWL FAMILY

29″. Adult body brown; wings gray-brown. Head, neck dark brown. Bill pink; white ring at base. Legs, feet orange; vent white. Gregarious; often flocks with other geese. **VOICE** Barking *kla-hah.* **HABITAT** Wetlands, fallow grain fields. **RANGE** Feb.–Mar., Oct.–Nov.: all SW, local. Nov.–Mar.: sw AZ, c and se NM.

CANADA GOOSE
Branta canadensis
WATERFOWL FAMILY

adults feeding (left), in flight (right)

L 3′4″; WS 6′. Adult back and wings dark brown; head and long neck black, with large, white chinstrap; breast pale brown; vent and rump white. Tail short, black. Often flies in V-formation. **VOICE** Honking *car-uunk.* **HABITAT** Marshes, mudflats, ponds, lawns, fallow fields. **RANGE** Resident in n NV, UT, n NM. Oct.–Mar.: s NV, AZ, s and e NM.

SNOW GOOSE
Chen caerulescens
WATERFOWL FAMILY

28″. Adult pure white with black primaries; bill pink with black "lips"; legs pink. Imm. pale gray; bill and legs black. Flies in V-formation high overhead. **VOICE** High, nasal honks. **HABITAT** Muddy fields, esp. corn stubble. **RANGE** Mar.–Apr., Oct.–Dec.: all SW. Nov.–Mar.: w NV, sw AZ, s and e NM. **Ross's Goose** *(C. rossii),* 23″, often with Snow Goose.

GREEN-WINGED TEAL
Anas crecca
WATERFOWL FAMILY

14″. Dabbler. Male body gray, with vertical white stripe behind chest; head chestnut; green eye patch extends to fluffy nape; vent patch yellow. Female brown. Bill small, black. Flight reveals green wing patch. SW's smallest duck. **VOICE** Male: whistled *crick-et.* **HABITAT** Marshes, ponds. **RANGE** Resident in n NV, n UT, n NM. Aug.–Apr.: all SW.

BLUE-WINGED TEAL
Anas discors
WATERFOWL FAMILY

15″. Dabbler. Male brown, with black dots; head dull blue-gray; white crescent in front of eye; crown black. Female mottled brown. In flight, pale blue shoulders. Bill heavier, longer than Green-wing. **VOICE** Male: peeps. Female: high quack. **HABITAT** Marshes, weedy ponds. **RANGE** Apr.–Oct.: n NV, n UT, NM. Migrant in all SW. Sept.–May: s AZ, s NM.

MALLARD male (left), female (right)
Anas platyrhynchos
WATERFOWL FAMILY

24″. Dabbler. Male body and wings gray; head and neck green; purplish chest has white ring above; bill yellow; rump black; tail white. Female buffy, heavily mottled with brown; bill pale orange with dark saddle. Legs orange. Flight reveals blue secondaries, bordered with white. **VOICE** Male: quiet; gives *reeb* call when fighting. Female: quack. **HABITAT** Ponds, rivers, marshes, towns. **RANGE** Resident in n NV, UT, n AZ, NM. Sept.–Mar.: s NV, s AZ.

NORTHERN PINTAIL
Anas acuta
WATERFOWL FAMILY

26″. Dabbler. Male back, wings, and sides gray; head and hindneck brown; foreneck and belly white; white line tapers onto rear of head; tail pointed, long. Female pale brown. Neck thin; bill gray. **VOICE** Male: wheezy *prip prip.* Female: quack. **HABITAT** Ponds, marshes. **RANGE** Resident in n NV, n and c UT, mtns. of n AZ, c and ne NM. Sept.–Apr.: all SW.

CINNAMON TEAL
Anas cyanoptera
WATERFOWL FAMILY

15″. Dabbler. Male back scalloped brown; head, neck, sides, and belly reddish chestnut; crown black. Female mottled brown. In flight, both sexes have pale blue forewing patch. **VOICE** Male: soft *chuck*. Female: soft quack. **HABITAT** Shallow lakes, marshes. **RANGE** Apr.–Nov.: all SW. Nov.–Apr.: s AZ, s NM.

NORTHERN SHOVELER
Anas clypeata
WATERFOWL FAMILY

18″. Dabbler. Male head green; chest white; sides rusty; bill black. Female brown, speckled; bill black or orange. Eyes yellow; neck short. Bill long, wide, held close to water. In flight, both sexes have pale blue forewing patch. **VOICE** Male: low *took*. Female: quack. **HABITAT** Marshes, ponds. **RANGE** Apr.–Nov.: n NV, UT, n NM. Migrant in all SW. Aug.–Apr.: s NV, s AZ, NM; local in UT.

GADWALL
Anas strepera
WATERFOWL FAMILY

20″. Dabbler. Male body and head gray; rump and bill black. Female brown; bill black with orange edge. Flight reveals square white wing patch and pale belly on both sexes. **VOICE** Male: croaks, whistles. Female: subdued quack. **HABITAT** Lakes, marshes. **RANGE** Apr.–Oct.: n NV, UT, n AZ, n and c NM. Oct.–Apr.: all SW.

AMERICAN WIGEON
Anas americana
WATERFOWL FAMILY

21″. Dabbler. Both sexes brownish with dull rusty orange sides, speckled head. Male forehead white; green patch behind eye; vent black and white. Flight reveals white forewing patch on both sexes. **VOICE** Whistled *whee whee whew*. **HABITAT** Shallow lakes. **RANGE** Resident in n NV, n UT, n NM. Mar.–May, Sept.–Nov.: all SW. Oct.–Mar.: w and s AZ, NM.

REDHEAD
Aythya americana
WATERFOWL FAMILY

20″. Diver. Male body gray; head rufous; chest and rear end black; eyes yellow. Female all plain brown; whitish eye ring. Forehead steep, rounded; bill blue-gray, with black tip. Flight reveals dark gray wings. **VOICE** Male: cat-like *meeow* in courtship. Female: soft quack. **HABITAT** Ponds, lakes. **RANGE** May–Sept.: n NV, n UT, c AZ. Sept.–Apr.: all SW, local.

RING-NECKED DUCK
Aythya collaris
WATERFOWL FAMILY

17″. Diver. Male chest, back, and tail black; sides gray; shoulder stripe white; head dark purple; crown peaked; brown neck ring hard to see. Female brown; pale buffy wash on face; pale eye ring. Flight reveals black shoulder, gray flight feathers. Bill patterned. **VOICE** Usu. silent. **HABITAT** Lakes, rivers. **RANGE** Oct.–Apr.: all SW. A few breed in mtns.

CANVASBACK
Aythya valisineria
WATERFOWL FAMILY

21″. Diver. Male back, wings, and sides white; chest and tail black; head reddish brown; eyes red. Female back, wings, sides gray; chest dark brown; head light brown, with white eye ring, dark eyes; tail blackish. Sloping forehead forms straight line with long, black bill. Flight reveals plain gray wings. **VOICE** Male: coos in courtship. Female: soft *ker-ker.* **HABITAT** Lakes, reservoirs. **RANGE** May–Sept.: n NV, n UT. Mar.–May, Oct.–Nov.: all SW (local). Nov.–Mar.: s NV, s AZ, c and e NM.

LESSER SCAUP
Aythya affinis
WATERFOWL FAMILY

17″. Diver. Male back gray; head black (dark purple gloss); sides pale gray; chest and tail black. Female dark brown, with distinct white face. Bill blue-gray; eyes yellow. Flight reveals white stripe on base of gray wings. Often flocks in "rafts" of 100s. Dives for seeds, snails, crustaceans. **VOICE** Usu. silent. **HABITAT** Lakes, rivers. **RANGE** Mar.–May, Oct.–Nov.: all SW. Nov.–Mar.: n UT, w and s AZ, s NM.

COMMON GOLDENEYE

Bucephala clangula

WATERFOWL FAMILY

18″. Diver. Male black above; thin black lines over wings; white below; head black (dark green gloss), fluffed out at rear; large white spot near bill. Female head all dark brown, white neck ring; body paler brown. Eyes golden. **VOICE** Quiet; wings whistle in flight. **HABITAT** Estuaries, harbors, lakes, rivers. **RANGE** Oct.–Apr.: all SW. **Barrow's Goldeneye** *(B. islandica),* 19″; male has purple head, white crescent on face; winters in NV, n UT, w AZ (rarer).

BUFFLEHEAD

Bucephala albeola

WATERFOWL FAMILY

14″. Diver. Male back black; chest and underparts white; rear half of head, with greenish-purple gloss, has white wedge. Female brown, with large white spot behind eye. Bill short. Flight reveals extensive white secondaries. **VOICE** Usu. silent in SW. **HABITAT** Lakes, rivers. **RANGE** Oct.–Apr.: all SW. **Hooded Merganser** *(Lophodytes cucullatus),* 18″; male has fan-shaped white crest with black fringe; bill thin, black; sides rusty; uncommon winterer in SW.

COMMON MERGANSER

Mergus merganser

WATERFOWL FAMILY

25″. Diver. Male back black; chest and underparts white; head dark green, rounded. Female body gray; head and neck rusty; chin distinctly white. Bill red, slender but with thick base. **VOICE** Usu. silent. **HABITAT** Lakes, rivers. **RANGE** Apr.–Oct.: mtns. of w NV, c UT, c AZ, n and w NM. Nov.–Mar.: all SW. **Red-breasted Merganser** *(M. serrator),* 23″, winters on Colorado R. lakes of s NV, w AZ; male has green crest, buffy chest, gray sides.

RUDDY DUCK

Oxyura jamaicensis

WATERFOWL FAMILY

16″. Diver. Breeding male: body ruddy brown; top of head black, bottom white; bill thick, bright blue. Winter male: head same as breeding; body slaty brown; bill gray. Female body and cap brown; pale buff cheeks have dark line. Tail black, stiff, fan-shaped, often raised. Usu. in flocks or rafts of several dozen when not breeding. **VOICE** Usu. silent. **HABITAT** Reedy lakes, ponds. **RANGE** Mar.–Nov.: n NV, UT, n AZ, n NM. Migrant in all SW. Oct.–Apr.: chiefly w and s AZ, s NM.

Raptors

The word "raptor" is usually used to refer to birds of prey that are active in the daytime (some experts also use the term for the nocturnal owls, described on page 300). Families found in the Southwest include the American vultures (Carthartidae, recently aligned with storks), the hawks and eagles (Accipitridae), and the falcons (Falconidae). The bills of raptors are strong for tearing flesh, while the feet (usually yellow) are generally powerful (except vultures), with curved talons for grasping prey. Some of our breeding raptors migrate to South America in winter; others come to the Southwest from the north and east for the winter. The carrion-feeding vultures are black, with broad wings and bare heads. Members of the hawk and eagle family are the very large eagles, with feathered legs; the Osprey, an eagle-size "fish hawk"; harriers, which fly low over open areas and use their superb hearing as an aid in hunting; and the hawks. There are two main types of hawks: the accipiters, whose shorter wings allow them to achieve rapid, twisting flight, and the broad-winged, soaring buteos. Buteos and eagles ride rising thermals of air on sunny days. Acute vision allows them to spot unsuspecting prey from great heights. The pointed-winged falcons are fast fliers. Immature raptors, often striped below, take a year or more to reach adulthood. Females are 10 to 20 percent larger than males in most species. Raptors migrate during the day.

Flight silhouettes of raptors *(illustrations not to relative scale)*

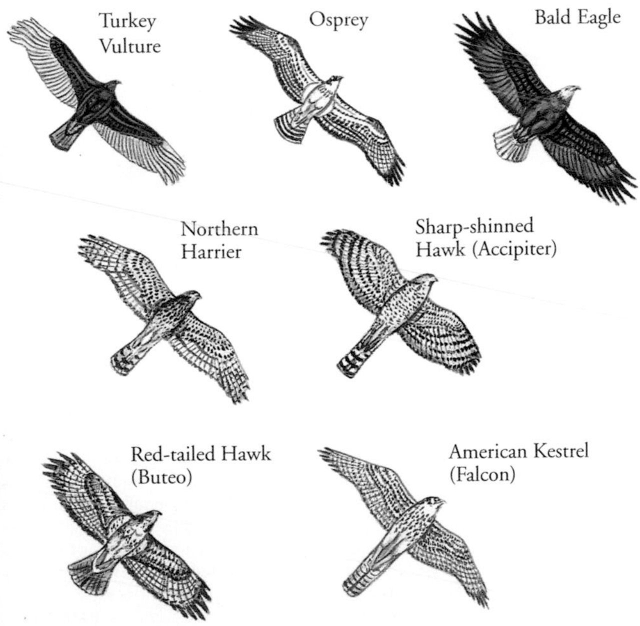

TURKEY VULTURE
Cathartes aura
AMERICAN VULTURE FAMILY

L 28"; WS 6'. Adult mostly black, brown-tinged above; head small, naked, red; bill yellow. Imm. head naked, gray. Soars with wings held at 25 degrees above horizontal; seldom flaps wings. Tail long, rounded; pale silver flight feathers can be seen from below. Finds carcasses by sight and smell. Gathers at nightly communal roosts. **VOICE** Occ. grunts and hisses; usu. silent. **HABITAT** Soars over all habitats. **RANGE** Mar.–Oct.: all SW. Some winter in s AZ.

CALIFORNIA CONDOR
Gymnogyps californianus
AMERICAN VULTURE FAMILY

L 4'; WS 9'. Adult black, with small white patch on closed wing; neck has black ruff; head naked, orange; tail fan-shaped. Flight reveals white wing linings, "fingered" primaries. In flight, wings held out flat; bird doesn't rock or tilt. Imm. has gray head; lacks white underwing. Largest raptor in N. Amer. Endangered. **VOICE** Usu. quiet. **HABITAT** Over grasslands, canyons, forests. **RANGE** Some captive-bred birds released into the wild on north rim of Grand Canyon in AZ.

OSPREY
Pandion haliaetus
HAWK AND EAGLE FAMILY

L 24"; WS 5'6". Adult brown above with white crown, white below. Imm. similar, but crown buffy. Flies with wings bent at "wrist," like flattened M; flight feathers and tail finely banded. Hovers frequently; often flies grasping fish in talons. Nest is mass of sticks topping dead tree or platform on Osprey pole. **VOICE** Emphatic *kee-uk* and repeated *cheep*. **HABITAT** Rivers, lakes. **RANGE** Mar.–May, Sept.–Nov.: all SW. Local nester in UT, c AZ. Winters in sw AZ.

BALD EAGLE
Haliaeetus leucocephalus
HAWK AND EAGLE FAMILY

L 32"; WS 7'. Adult body, thighs, wings dark brown; head white; bill yellow, hooked; eyes, feet, legs yellow; tail white. Imm. dark brown perched; flight reveals whitish wing linings, base of tail. Flies with slow wingbeats, wings held flat, primaries spread. Perches on tall trees. Eats fish and carrion. Once endangered but making a comeback. Captive-bred birds released in many areas; many nesting. **VOICE** Loud cackle. **HABITAT** Rivers, lakes, grasslands. **RANGE** Resident in c AZ. Nov.–Mar.: all SW.

GOLDEN EAGLE
Aquila chrysaetos
HAWK AND EAGLE FAMILY

L 3′; WS 6′6″. Adult dark brown, golden nape; legs heavily feathered; feet yellow; tail base banded gray. Imm. dark brown; tail base has wide white band. Flight reveals white at base of primaries, esp. in imm. (pictured). An upland hunter, it preys primarily on mammals. Flies with wings slightly angled up, few wingbeats. **VOICE** High *kee-kee-kee;* screams. **HABITAT** Mtns., forests, grasslands. **RANGE** Resident in all SW.

NORTHERN HARRIER
Circus cyaneus
HAWK AND EAGLE FAMILY

L 22″; WS 4′. Wings and tail long, narrow; rump white; head, bill small; owl-like facial disks. Adult male pearl gray, whiter below. Adult female brown above, off-white with brown stripes below. Imm. brown above, rusty orange below. Flies low over open areas, wings raised at an angle; often hovers and drops. **VOICE** Weak *pee.* **HABITAT** Marshes, fields. **RANGE** Resident in NV, UT, n AZ, n NM. Sept.–Apr.: c and s AZ, c and s NM.

SHARP-SHINNED HAWK
Accipiter striatus
HAWK AND EAGLE FAMILY

L 12″; WS 21″. All accipiters have shortish, rounded wings and long, narrow tails. Adult upperparts slate gray; underparts barred, rusty; crown gray; feet small, yellow. Tail square with notch in middle. Imm. brown above, striped below. Flies with fast wingbeats followed by glides. Expert at capturing small birds. Soars during migration. **VOICE** High *kek* notes. **HABITAT** Wooded mtns. in summer; woodlands, parks, scrub in other seasons. **RANGE** Resident in mtns. of SW. Sept.–Apr.: all SW.

COOPER'S HAWK
Accipiter cooperii
HAWK AND EAGLE FAMILY

L 17″; WS 28″. Plumages nearly identical to Sharp-shinned Hawk, but head larger and tail longer, distinctly rounded; adult has black cap. Imm. belly whiter, with fewer streaks than Sharp-shinned. Flies like Sharp-shinned but perches in open more often. **VOICE** High *kek* notes. **HABITAT** Woodlands, brush, canyons, mtns. **RANGE** Resident in most of SW. Oct.–Mar.: s NV, w AZ.

NORTHERN GOSHAWK
Accipiter gentilis
HAWK AND EAGLE FAMILY

L 23"; WS 3′7". Adult dark gray above, fine gray barring below; black crown and stripe behind eye; wide white eyebrow. Imm. has heavy stripes below; wide white eyebrow. Flight reveals long, rounded tail; fluffy white undertail feathers in adult. A fierce and aggressive deep woods hunter. **VOICE** Harsh *kek* notes. **HABITAT** Chiefly mtn. forests. **RANGE** Resident in mtns.; spreads onto plains in winter.

COMMON BLACK-HAWK
Buteogallus anthracinus
HAWK AND EAGLE FAMILY

22". Adult all black; base of bill and legs yellowish. Flight reveals broad, rounded wings. Tail black, short, fan-shaped, with broad white band and tip. **VOICE** Harsh whistles. **HABITAT** Wooded streamsides, wet canyons. **RANGE** Mid-Mar.–Sept.: c and se AZ. **Gray Hawk** *(Buteo nitidus),* 17"; adult all pearly gray, with white bands on black tail; Mar.–Oct., se AZ streamsides.

HARRIS'S HAWK
"Bay-winged Hawk"
Parabuteo unicinctus
HAWK AND EAGLE FAMILY

25". Adult slender, mainly black; shoulders and fluffy thighs reddish chestnut; vent white; base of bill and legs yellow. Flight reveals long, narrow wings with chestnut wing linings; long tail narrow, rounded, white with broad black band. Very social, with 3–6 adults hunting and helping at nest together. **VOICE** Long *keeeerrr.* **HABITAT** Cactus deserts; mesquite woods, canyons. **RANGE** Resident in s and c AZ (chiefly n and w of Tucson), se NM.

SWAINSON'S HAWK
Buteo swainsoni
HAWK AND EAGLE FAMILY

L 20"; WS 4′. Adult plain brown above; throat white; upper chest rufous; rest of underparts whitish. Flight reveals white underwing linings and blackish flight feathers; wingtips pointy for a buteo; tail gray with fine black bands. Dark-morph adult solid brown, with rufous underwing linings. Formerly more common; suffering from pesticides in Argentine wintering grounds. **VOICE** Whistled *kreee.* **HABITAT** Grasslands, farms. **RANGE** Mid-Mar.–Oct.: all SW; migrant only in sw AZ.

RED-TAILED HAWK adult perched (left), in flight (right)
Buteo jamaicensis
HAWK AND EAGLE FAMILY

L 22"; WS 4'2". Head, back, and wings dark brown; underparts light rufous and white; lower chest may have band of heavy brown streaks; tail pale orange below, rufous above. Adults vary from whitish to dark rufous or blackish below. Imm. striped below; tail pale brown with many indistinct bands. Seen from below, underwing mainly white, with dark leading edge, black crescent beyond wrist. Harlan's race winters from nw N. Amer.; all black, with whitish tail base. In deserts, face pale, washed-out; tail pale rusty in adults. Red-tailed Hawk most frequently seen large hawk in SW year-round; perches conspicuously in trees along highways. Often mobbed by crows, redwings, kingbirds. **VOICE** Down-slurred squeal: *keee-rrr.* **HABITAT** Woodland edges, scrub, grasslands, farms. **RANGE** Resident in all SW; more common Apr.–Sept. in n NV, n UT.

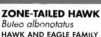

ZONE-TAILED HAWK
Buteo albonotatus
HAWK AND EAGLE FAMILY

20". Adult all black, ex. yellow base of bill and legs. Flight reveals long, narrow wings; wing lining black, but undersides of flight feathers silvery; tail black with 1–2 white bands and white tip. Mimics a Turkey Vulture in flight, as it often flies with wings angled up. **VOICE** Long whistle. **HABITAT** Wooded mtns., desert canyons, valley farms. **RANGE** Mar.–Sept.: c, e, and se AZ; c and s NM.

FERRUGINOUS HAWK
Buteo regalis
HAWK AND EAGLE FAMILY

L 24"; WS 4'8". Adult rufous above, white below; thighs rufous; head streaked brown. Flight reveals white breast, flight feathers, and tail; rusty wing linings; dark thighs that form a V. Dark-morph adult body and wing linings brown; tail and flight feathers white. Imm. brownish above, all white below. **VOICE** Descending *kree-ahh.* **HABITAT** Arid grasslands, farms, canyons. **RANGE** Apr.–Oct.: most of NV, UT, n AZ, n NM. Oct.–Mar.: all SW, ex. e UT.

ROUGH-LEGGED HAWK

Buteo lagopus

HAWK AND EAGLE FAMILY

L 22″; WS 4′8″. Adult head and upper chest striped black and white; back and wings dark brown; black patch across lower belly; tail white, with broad black terminal band. Adult dark morph black, with paler flight feathers. Flight reveals, from above, white patch at base of primaries; from below, black wrist patch at bend of wing. Often hovers. **VOICE** Usu. silent. **HABITAT** Open areas. **RANGE** Nov.–Mar.: all SW; uncommon in s AZ, s NM.

AMERICAN KESTREL

Falco sparverius

FALCON FAMILY

L 11″; WS 23″. Male back rufous; chest pale buffy; wings blue-gray; tail rufous with black terminal band. Female rufous above, with fine black bars. Both have 2 thin black sideburns on white face. In flight, pointed wings obvious; often hovers. **VOICE** Shrill *killy killy.* **HABITAT** Open grasslands, sagebrush, woodland edges, farms, towns, deserts. **RANGE** Resident in all SW; withdraws from mtns. in winter.

MERLIN

Falco columbarius

FALCON FAMILY

L 12″; WS 25″. Adult male medium to dark gray above; pale buffy below, with heavy brown streaks; tail has wide black band near tip. Female and imm. dark brown above, heavily striped below; tail finely banded. Both have 1 thin black sideburn. Flies fast and low when chasing small birds. **VOICE** High *ki ki ki ki.* **HABITAT** Watersides, grasslands with clumps of trees, farms. **RANGE** Oct.–Apr.: all SW.

PRAIRIE FALCON

Falco mexicanus

FALCON FAMILY

L 18″; WS 3′6″. Adult pale brown above; whitish below, speckled brown; crown brown; eyebrow pale; throat white; 1 narrow "mustache" below eye; bill base orange. Imm. streaked below; bill base blue or yellow. Flight reveals pointed wings, longish tail, black patch at base of wing linings. **VOICE** Loud *ki-ki-ki-ki.* **HABITAT** Grasslands, sagebrush, canyons, farms. **RANGE** Resident in most of SW; widespread in winter.

PEREGRINE FALCON
Falco peregrinus
FALCON FAMILY

adult perched (left), in flight (right)

L 18″; WS 3′4″. Adult dark slate gray above; underparts and underwing finely gray-barred. Head and thick sideburns black; throat and chest white or buffy. Feet powerful. Imm. brown above, streaked below. Flight reveals pointed wings, broad at base (lacks black patch); tail tapers to square end. Flies both high and low; targets injured birds in flight. Almost died out, due to DDT poisoning; numbers now increasing with DDT ban and captive breeding/releases. **VOICE** Harsh *kak kak* at nest. **HABITAT** Nests on cliffs, canyons, cities; feeds anywhere, incl. wetlands. **RANGE** Resident and migrant in all SW.

CHUKAR
Alectoris chukar
PARTRIDGE FAMILY

14″. Plain gray above and on chest; sides barred chestnut and black; wings brown. Thick black line through eye and down foreneck frames white throat. Bill and legs red. Tail short, outer tail feathers rufous. Introduced from Mideast. **VOICE** Loud *chuk-chuk-chukar.* **HABITAT** Arid rocky hills, canyons. **RANGE** NV, UT.

BLUE GROUSE
Dendragapus obscurus
PARTRIDGE FAMILY

18″. Male mainly blue-gray; wings brown; tail fairly long, black, with pale gray band at end in w NV; in courtship display, has rosy fried-egg-like patch on neck. Female brown, finely barred with black. **VOICE** Male: 5–7 deep *whoop* notes. **HABITAT** Coniferous and mixed forests, brush. **RANGE** Resident in forested mtns. of w and ne NV, UT; nw and ec AZ; w and n NM.

RUFFED GROUSE
Bonasa umbellus
PARTRIDGE FAMILY

18″. Adult reddish brown or gray, speckled white and black; head small, slightly crested; neck patch and terminal tail band black. Tail longish. Male "drums" on low perch in spring by thumping wings against chest. **VOICE** Alarm call: *quit quit.* **HABITAT** Broadleaf and mixed woods. Favors heavy cover. **RANGE** Resident in n and c UT. **White-tailed Ptarmigan** *(Lagopus leucurus),* 13″, of alpine tundra of ne UT, is speckled gray in summer, white in winter.

SAGE GROUSE
Centrocercus urophasianus
PARTRIDGE FAMILY

Male 28″; female 22″. Mottled gray-brown above, belly black. Male chest white; yellow wattle over eye; throat black; black V on white foreneck; tail long, with pointed feathers. Female head and chest scaled brown. In early spring male fans tail, inflates 2 naked, yellowish-orange air sacs on chest. **VOICE** When flushed, *kuk-kuk-kuk.* Courting male: weak *wom-poo;* popping sound of air sacs. **HABITAT** Sagebrush. **RANGE** Resident in c and n NV, UT.

WILD TURKEY
Meleagris gallopavo
PARTRIDGE FAMILY

Male 4′; female 3′. Male body dark brown; looks iridescent coppery green at close range; flight feathers black, banded white; tail rufous, with black bands. Head bare, warty, red and/or blue; black "beard" hangs from chest (most noticeable on Toms). Legs red. Female similar, with smaller, duller head. Feeds on ground; roosts in trees at night. **VOICE** Male: repeated gobble. **HABITAT** Mtn. forests, clearings. **RANGE** Native to c and se AZ, NM mtns.; introduced to s UT.

RING-NECKED PHEASANT
Phasianus colchicus
PARTRIDGE FAMILY

Male 34″; female 22″. Male head and neck iridescent dark green, often with white necklace, bare red skin around eye; rest of body rufous and bronze, with 19 black and white chevrons above. Female and imm. warm buffy, with black spots above. Tail feathers long, pointed. Flies with rapid wingbeats followed by glides. Introduced from Asia. **VOICE** Male: loud *kaw kawk.* **HABITAT** Farms, meadows. **RANGE** Resident in w and n NV, UT, c and e NM.

SCALED QUAIL
Callipepla squamata
NEW WORLD QUAIL FAMILY

11″. Back, wings, tail, and sides pale gray; sides have white stripes; entire neck and chest gray with black scales; head gray with white crest ("cottontop"). **VOICE** Call: *pay-cos.* **HABITAT** Arid scrub and grasslands. **RANGE** Resident in much of se AZ, most of NM, ex. nw. Masked race of **Northern Bobwhite** *(Colinus virginianus),* male 10″, has black throat, rusty below; reintroduced sw of Tucson, AZ.

CALIFORNIA QUAIL female, male
Callipepla californica
NEW WORLD QUAIL FAMILY

10″. Male pale brown above, chest gray; crown chestnut; forehead has rounded black plume; eyebrow and necklace white; throat black. Female paler; plume smaller; rusty sides have white stripes; white belly has black scaling. **VOICE** *Chi-CAH-go.* **HABITAT** Woodland edges, scrub, towns. **RANGE** Resident in w and n NV, n UT; introduced from California.

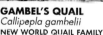

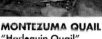

GAMBEL'S QUAIL
Callipepla gambelii
NEW WORLD QUAIL FAMILY

11″. Male crown, chestnut, has comma-shaped, forward-leaning topknot; face and throat patch black, bordered in white. Upperparts and chest gray; belly yellow with large black spot; sides chestnut, striped white. Female drabber; head plain gray; topknot thinner. **VOICE** Musical *chi-ca-go-go.* **HABITAT** Desert washes, canyons, towns, farms. **RANGE** Resident in s NV, s UT, all AZ (ex. ne), sw, c, and se NM.

MONTEZUMA QUAIL
"Harlequin Quail"
Cyrtonyx montezumae
NEW WORLD QUAIL FAMILY

9″. Rotund; tail very short. Male face black-and-white pied, like clown's; nape crest rusty; above brown with thin white stripes; sides blue with many large white spots; wide mid-belly stripe chestnut. Female drab brown, washed rufous below. Freezes on approach; sometimes acts tame. **VOICE** Soft, quavering cry; hard to pinpoint. **HABITAT** Canyons and mtns. with oaks, pines, tall bunch grasses. **RANGE** Resident in nc and se AZ, wc and s NM.

VIRGINIA RAIL
Rallus limicola
RAIL FAMILY

10″. Adult brown above, chest and wings rufous; sides barred black and white. Cheeks gray, eyes red; bill long, thin, drooping, red with black tip. Legs dull red. Usu. secretive. **VOICE** Repeated *kid-ick;* grunting *oink* notes. **HABITAT** Freshwater marshes. **RANGE** Local in all SW; some in winter.

SORA
Porzana carolina
RAIL FAMILY

9″. Adult brown above, sides of chest slate gray; belly barred blackish; face and foreneck black. Bill short, thick, yellow. Legs olive-green. Imm. throat white. **VOICE** Whistled *ker-wee;* descending whinny. **HABITAT** Marshes. **RANGE** Apr.–Sept.: NV, UT, n AZ, n NM. Sept.–Apr.: s NV, s AZ, s NM.

COMMON MOORHEN
"Common Gallinule"
Gallinula chloropus
RAIL FAMILY

14″. Adult back brown; slaty below; white stripe along sides and vent; head black; frontal shield red; bill bright red, yellow-tipped. **VOICE** Variety of clucks, grating notes. **HABITAT** Cattail marshes. **RANGE** Resident in s NV, sw UT, w and s AZ, s NM.

AMERICAN COOT
Fulica americana
RAIL FAMILY

15″. Adult sooty gray. Head and neck black; bill thick, white, black near tip; sides of undertail white. Dives; skitters over water surface to become airborne. Often in flocks. **VOICE** Grating *kuk* notes. **HABITAT** Marshes, lakes, parks. **RANGE** Resident in SW; summer only in ne UT.

SANDHILL CRANE
Grus canadensis
CRANE FAMILY

L 3′4″; WS 6′. Adult mostly gray, often stained rusty; forecrown red; cheeks white. Neck long, thin; bill shortish, thin, straight, black; legs long, black. Imm. gray-brown. Flies with neck outstretched. **VOICE** Loud, rattling *kar-r-r-r-o-o-o,* often given in flight. **HABITAT** Summer: shallow marshes. Winter: also fallow fields, salt flats. **RANGE** Apr.–Nov.: n NV, n UT. Oct.–Mar.: sw and se AZ, s and c NM (local, esp. Bosque del Apache NWR).

Shorebirds

The term "shorebird" is used for certain members of the order Charadriiformes: plovers, avocets, stilts, and sandpipers, including godwits, dowitchers, yellowlegs, curlews, and small sandpipers informally known as "peeps." Most shorebirds frequent open muddy, sandy, or rocky shores around wetlands; a few live in open areas far from water. Most American shorebirds have a distinct breeding plumage in late spring and early summer. Most seen in the Southwest travel thousands of miles yearly between their breeding and wintering grounds. In the Southwest, shorebirds are most numerous from March to May and again from July through October. Small numbers of nonbreeding individuals oversummer without going to the Arctic. Southbound migrating adults often return from Alaskan, Canadian, and northern plains breeding grounds by July. In identifying shorebirds, proportion and shape, as well as behavior and voice, are often more important than plumage color.

KILLDEER
Charadrius vociferus
PLOVER FAMILY

10″. Adult brown above, white below; 2 black chest bands; face pied, with red eye ring; legs usu. pinkish gray. Flight reveals wing stripe, unique orange rump. Imm. has 1 black breast band. Common inland plover in open habitats, often far from water. **VOICE** Strident *kill-dee.* **HABITAT** Farms, fields, parks. **RANGE** Resident in SW; withdraws from mtns. in winter.

SNOWY PLOVER
Charadrius alexandrinus
PLOVER FAMILY

6″. Pale brown above, white below; bill short, thin, black; legs dark gray. Breeding male forecrown, patch behind eye, and partial neck ring black. Female and imm. eye patch and partial neck ring dark brown. **VOICE** Musical *chu wee.* **HABITAT** Edges of shallow alkaline lakes. **RANGE** Apr.–Sept.: n and c NV, n UT, se NM; local elsewhere.

BLACK-NECKED STILT
Himantopus mexicanus
STILT FAMILY

14″. Black above, white below; rump and tail white. Head dark, with large white spot over eye; bill long, thin, black. Legs very long, red. Feeds in flocks; wades up to its belly, eating aquatic insects. **VOICE** Sharp *yip yip yip.* **HABITAT** Shallow lakeshores, wastewater ponds. **RANGE** Apr.–Sept.: NV, n UT, w AZ, NM. Apr.–May, Aug.–Sept.: migrant in all SW.

AMERICAN AVOCET
Recurvirostra americana
STILT FAMILY

18″. Back and wings pied black and white; below white; rump, tail white. Neck long; bill long, slender, upturned, black. Legs long, light blue. Nonbreeding: head and neck gray. Breeding: head and neck pale rusty orange. Feeds in flocks; sweeps bill from side to side in water when feeding. Nests in colonies; often seen near stilts. **VOICE** Loud *wheep.* **HABITAT** Shallow lakeshores, mudflats. **RANGE** Mar.–Oct.: n and c NV, n UT, c and se AZ, c and e NM.

LONG-BILLED CURLEW
Numenius americanus
SANDPIPER FAMILY

23″. Head, neck, and upperparts brown with buffy spots; buffy below. Neck long; legs long, gray. Bill very long, downcurved, lower mandible red at base. In flight, appears uniformly buffy, with rufous wing linings. **VOICE** Loud *cur-leee;* rapid *kli-li-li-li.* **HABITAT** Summer: open grasslands near marshes. Other seasons: mudflats and nearby grasslands. **RANGE** Mar.–Apr., Aug.–Oct.: all SW (local). Apr.–Aug.: n and c NV, n UT.

GREATER YELLOWLEGS
Tringa melanoleuca
SANDPIPER FAMILY

14″. Breeding: back dark brown with white dots; head, neck, sides speckled dark brown. Nonbreeding: paler gray-brown; belly and rump white. Neck long; legs long, bright yellow. Bill 1½ times longer than head; has relatively thick gray base and thin, black, slightly up-curved tip. Often nods head. **VOICE** Excited *tew tew tew.* **HABITAT** Marshes, mudflats, flooded fields. **RANGE** Mar.–May, July–Oct.: all SW. Oct.–Mar.: w AZ.

LESSER YELLOWLEGS
Tringa flavipes
SANDPIPER FAMILY

11″. Smaller version of Greater Yellowlegs. Plumages similar; legs also bright yellow; bill shorter (equal to length of head), straight, all black. Nonbreeding Wilson's Phalarope has duller yellow legs, gray (not white) lower back. **VOICE** 1–2 mellow *tew* notes. **HABITAT** Mudflats, marsh pools. **RANGE** Apr.–May, July–Oct.: all SW.

MARBLED GODWIT
Limosa fedoa
SANDPIPER FAMILY

18″. Breeding: head, neck, and upperparts brown with buffy spots; buffy below, with streaks on neck, bars on breast. Nonbreeding: clear, unbarred buff below. Neck long; legs long, blackish. Bill very long, slightly up-curved, red with black tip. In flight, appears uniformly buffy, with rufous wing linings. **VOICE** Loud *god-WIT.* **HABITAT** Lakesides, mudflats. **RANGE** Apr.–May, July–Oct.: all SW (local).

WILLET
Catoptrophorus semipalmatus
SANDPIPER FAMILY

15″. Breeding: speckled brownish gray. Nonbreeding: plain gray. Bill fairly long, straight; base of bill thick, gray; legs blue-gray; tail gray. Flight reveals startling black wings with broad white central stripe. **VOICE** Song: *pill-will-willet.* Call: *kip, kip, kip.* **HABITAT** Marshes, mudflats. **RANGE** Apr.–May, July–Aug.: all SW (local). Apr.–Sept.: n and c NV, n UT.

LONG-BILLED DOWITCHER
Limnodromus scolopaceus
SANDPIPER FAMILY

12″. Breeding: speckled brown above, orange below; sides black-barred. Nonbreeding: gray-brown above, whitish below. Juv. brown above; breast buffy orange. Bill very long, straight; legs greenish. In flight, white V on lower back, narrow white bars on tail. Feeds with rapid, sewing-machine motion. **VOICE** High, sharp *keek.* **HABITAT** Mudflats, pond shores. **RANGE** Mar.–May: all SW. Winters in s AZ, s NM. **Short-billed Dowitcher** *(L. griseus)* has wider white bars on tail; migrant only, uncommon.

COMMON SNIPE
Gallinago gallinago
SANDPIPER FAMILY

11″. Adult and imm. dark brown above, with few white stripes; sides barred; mid-belly white; head has bold blackish stripes; tail rusty. Legs short; bill very long, straight. Flies in erratic zigzag. **VOICE** Hoarse *skaip.* **HABITAT** Damp meadows, marshes. **RANGE** Apr.–Oct.: n NV, n UT. Sept.–Apr.: all SW.

SPOTTED SANDPIPER
Actitis macularia
SANDPIPER FAMILY

8″. Breeding: brown above; white below, with large black spots. Nonbreeding: unspotted; smudges on sides of chest. Often teeters rump. **VOICE** *Pee-weet-weet.* **HABITAT** Riversides, ponds. **RANGE** Apr.–May, Aug.–Oct.: all SW. May–Sept.: NV, UT, n AZ, n NM. Oct.–Apr.: AZ, s NM.

WESTERN SANDPIPER
Calidris mauri
SANDPIPER FAMILY

6½″. Breeding: rusty above; foreparts have fine black dots. Nonbreeding: gray above, white below. Bill fairly long, black, droops at tip; legs black. Fall imm. rusty on sides of back. **VOICE** High *cheep.* **HABITAT** Lakesides, mudflats. **RANGE** Mar.–May, July–Oct.: all SW (local).

LEAST SANDPIPER
Calidris minutilla
SANDPIPER FAMILY

6″. Breeding: reddish brown above; chest buffy brown, lightly spotted. Nonbreeding: browner than other small sandpipers. Bill short, thin, slightly drooping; legs yellow or green. **VOICE** High *kreet.* **HABITAT** Lakeside mudflats, reedy pools. **RANGE** Mar.–May, July–Oct.: all SW. Oct.– Mar.: s and w AZ, se NM.

WILSON'S PHALAROPE
Phalaropus tricolor
SANDPIPER FAMILY

9″. Breeding female: back gray with reddish stripes; white below; crown and hindneck silvery; line through eye and on sides of neck black, becoming reddish; foreneck buffy orange; legs black. Male is duller. Bill needle-like. Swims in circles. **VOICE** Soft *chek-chek-chek;* nasal *wurk.* **HABITAT** Mudflats, shallow ponds, lakes. **RANGE** Apr.–May, Aug.–Sept.: all SW. May–Aug.: n and c NV, n UT.

Gulls and Terns

Gulls and terns have webbed feet and breed in the open, in colonies, mainly on islands free of land predators; their nests are usually mere depressions in the ground. Although gulls are common near the sea, many breed far inland near lakes. Superb fliers, most gulls have wings with white trailing edges and fairly long, strong bills that are slightly hooked at the tip. These generalist feeders and scavengers eat living and dead animal life, and many have adapted to feed on human refuse. Gulls go through a confusing array of plumages and molts until they reach adulthood in two years (small species), three years (medium), or four years (large). For many gull species, this guide describes selected life-stage categories, such as juvenile (the bird's birth summer), first winter, first summer (bird is one year old), second winter, summer adult, or winter adult. The small to medium-size terns, sleek and slender-billed, fly in a buoyant or hovering manner, diving headfirst for small fish or snatching insects in air; most have black caps (in summer) and forked tails.

RING-BILLED GULL
Larus delawarensis
GULL AND TERN FAMILY

summer adult (left), 1st winter (right)

L 19"; WS 4'. Summer adult: head, underparts white; wings silvery; wingtips black with white spots; bill yellow with black ring near tip; legs greenish yellow. Winter adult: head flecked brown. 1st winter: back gray; wing coverts speckled brown; tail whitish with black terminal band; bill pink with black tip; legs pink. Juv.: pale brown, speckled; bill black; legs pink. Nests in colonies on lakes. **VOICE** High-pitched *high-er.* **HABITAT** Rivers, lakes, parks. **RANGE** Sept.–May: all SW.

CALIFORNIA GULL
Larus californicus
GULL AND TERN FAMILY

L 21"; WS 4'6". Adult: dark gray above; head, tail, and underparts white; eyes dark; legs pale yellow-green; bill yellow, with red and black spot near tip (in summer). 1st winter: bill base pink. **VOICE** High *kee-yah;* low *cow-cow-cow.* **HABITAT** Lakes, fallow fields, dumps. **RANGE** Apr.–May, Aug.–Nov.: all SW (local). Apr.–Sept.: n UT, w NV. Nov.–Apr.: w AZ.

FRANKLIN'S GULL
Larus pipixcan
GULL AND TERN FAMILY

14". Summer adult: back, wings gray; white band above black primary patch; feather tips white. Underparts white, washed rosy in spring. Head black; bill red. Feeds on insects in summer. Usu. in flocks. **VOICE** Variety of *yuk* notes, cries. **HABITAT** Ponds, lakes, wet fields. **RANGE** Apr.–May, Sept.–Oct.: migrant (local). Apr.–Sept.: n UT, c NV.

BLACK TERN
Chlidonias niger
GULL AND TERN FAMILY

10″. Summer: back, wings, and tail uniformly gray; head and underparts black; bill and legs black; vent white. Winter: dark gray above; face and underparts white; nape and earspot black. Tail short, notched. Nests in small colonies. **VOICE** Sharp *kreek.* **HABITAT** Reedy lakes. **RANGE** May–June, Aug.–Sept.: all SW (local). May–Sept.: n NV, n UT.

FORSTER'S TERN
Sterna forsteri
GULL AND TERN FAMILY

15″. Pale silvery above, white below; primaries white; tail forked, long. Summer adult: cap black; bill red-orange with black tip; legs red. Winter adult: crown white; eye mask long, black; bill black. Feeds on aerial insects; dives for fish. Nests in colonies. **VOICE** Grating *kay-r-r-r;* repeated *kip.* **HABITAT** Marshes, lakes, beaches. **RANGE** Apr.–May, Aug.–Oct.: all SW (local). May–Sept.: w and n NV, n UT.

ROCK DOVE
"Rock Pigeon"
Columba livia
PIGEON AND DOVE FAMILY

13″. Typical head dark gray, with coppery iridescence on neck; body pale gray; 2 black bars on secondaries. Bill short, black; legs short, red. Variations range from black to pale brown and white. Powerful flier; flight reveals pointed wings, white mid-back. This is the common pigeon of cities and farms. **VOICE** Gurgling *coo-cuk-cooo.* **HABITAT** Cities, towns, farms, to 8,000′. **RANGE** All settled areas of SW.

BAND-TAILED PIGEON
Columba fasciata
PIGEON AND DOVE FAMILY

15″. Back, wings, and tail slaty; white crescent on nape; head, underparts soft purplish gray; eyes red. Bill and feet yellow. Imm. (to 1st winter) all gray; bill and feet gray to yellow. Flight reveals pale gray rump, blackish base of tail, tip pale gray. In courtship, flying male circles with stiff wings and fanned tail. **VOICE** Low, owl-like *hoo-hooo.* **HABITAT** Mtn. forests, urban parks. **RANGE** May–Oct.: UT; n, c, and se AZ; w and c NM. A few winter in se AZ.

WHITE-WINGED DOVE
Zenaida asiatica
PIGEON AND DOVE FAMILY

11″. Adult gray-brown above; head and underparts pale buffy brown; eye ring blue; black dash below eye; wing has white band at edge of closed wing (conspicuous); feet reddish. Tail fan-shaped, corners white. **VOICE** Drawn out *Who-cooks-for-you?* **HABITAT** Desert scrub, towns. **RANGE** Mar.–Oct.: s NV; far sw UT; w, c, and s AZ; s NM. Some winter in s AZ.

MOURNING DOVE
Zenaida macroura
PIGEON AND DOVE FAMILY

12″. Head small. Back, wings, and tail dull brown; head and underparts pale buffy; bill short, black; black spot below eye; legs short, red. Tail long, pointed, wedge-shaped, with black and white edges. Wings whistle when taking flight. **VOICE** Mournful coo: *WHO-o coo, coo, coo.* **HABITAT** Open woodlands, fields, farms, suburbs. **RANGE** Resident in all SW; leaves from high mtns. in winter.

INCA DOVE
Columbina (Scardafella) inca
PIGEON AND DOVE FAMILY

8″. Small dove with long, squared tail. Head and entire body pale gray brown; feathers black-tipped, giving scaly look. Flight reveals reddish-chestnut primaries; outer tail feathers white. Roosts in flocks. Raises and fans tail in courtship. **VOICE** Monotonous *no hope* given in long series. **HABITAT** Cities, towns, parks, farms. **RANGE** Resident in c and s AZ, sw NM.

COMMON GROUND-DOVE
Columbina passerina
PIGEON AND DOVE FAMILY

7″. Body pale brown; black spots on wing coverts; primaries bright rufous. Head and chest pinkish gray, scaled black; legs pinkish; white sides extend to short black tail. Pairs walk sandy paths together; fairly approachable. Smallest dove in N. Amer. **VOICE** Soft, rising, repeated *coo-ah.* **HABITAT** Waterside thickets, brush, orchards. **RANGE** Resident in s AZ, far s NM.

YELLOW-BILLED CUCKOO
Coccyzus americanus
CUCKOO FAMILY

12″. Upperparts gray-brown; primaries rufous, white below. Tail long, rounded, gray above, black below, with 3 wide white bars. Bill slender, downcurved; black above, yellow below. Eye ring yellow. Often secretive; mainly seen on wing or heard. **VOICE** Song: long, hollow, descending *kuk* notes, ending with drawn-out *kowlp* notes. **HABITAT** Chiefly riverside thickets. **RANGE** Mid-May–mid-Sept.: s NV, n and sw UT, much of AZ and NM (not in higher mtns.).

GREATER ROADRUNNER
Geococcyx californianus
CUCKOO FAMILY

22″. Adult buffy white with dark brown stripes, dark brown fluffy crown; blue and red skin behind yellow eye. Legs fairly long; tail long, brown, wedge-shaped, outer tail feathers tipped white. Runs after lizards and snakes (incl. rattlers); also eats scorpions, beetles, small birds, mammals. **VOICE** Clucks; 6–8 dove-like, descending *coo* notes. **HABITAT** Desert brush, open woodland, ranches. **RANGE** Resident in s NV, sw UT, most of AZ and NM (ex. high plateaus).

Owls

Owls are nocturnal birds of prey that range in size in the Southwest from about 6 to 23 inches long. They have large heads, with large, forward-facing yellow or brown eyes. Their eyesight and hearing are both acute. Distinct facial disks conceal large ear openings that provide them with keen hearing, which can pinpoint a squeak or rustle in the grass in total darkness. The ears are asymmetrically placed on either side of the head, providing greater range of sound and better triangulation for pinpointing sources of sounds. Some owls have tufts of feathers at the corners of the head that look like ears or horns and are called ear tufts. The fluffy-looking bodies of owls are cryptically colored and patterned to blend with the background of their daytime nest or roost. Their bills are short but strongly hooked. The legs are also typically short, and the feet have sharp, curved talons. Owls fly silently; their pinions are delicately fringed and very soft. Imitations and tapes of their distinctive voices, given or played at night, often bring a response from an owl, which may call or fly in close to the source of the call, or both; in daytime, the same sound may bring crows, jays, and songbirds, which usually mob any roosting owls they discover.

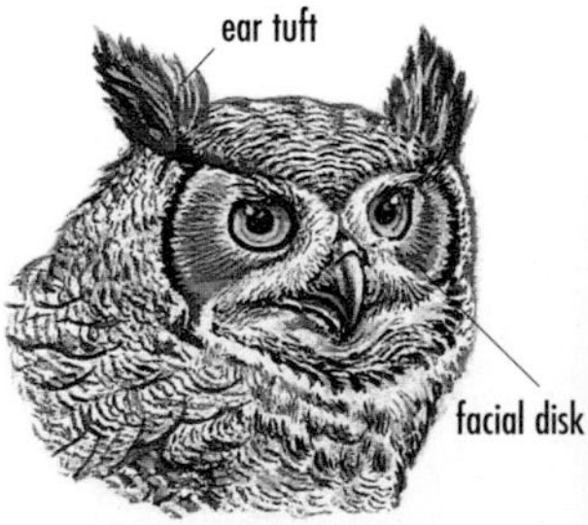

Parts of an Owl

NORTHERN PYGMY-OWL

Glaucidium gnoma

OWL FAMILY

7". Crown, upperparts, and chest brown or gray with fine whitish dots; breast white, striped brown or gray. Eyes yellow; back of head has false black eyes with white eyebrows; lacks ear tufts; tail long, banded dark and light brown. Feeds by day on small birds; often mobbed by them. **VOICE** Long series of even *toot* notes. **HABITAT** Oak and pine forests. **RANGE** Resident in all mtn. forests of SW.

ELF OWL

Micrathene whitneyi

OWL FAMILY

6". Smallest owl. Above brown, rows of white spots on wing; below dingy gray. Lacks ear tufts. Eyes yellow, eyebrows white; no false eyes on back; tail very short. Strictly nocturnal; spends day in tree cavity, saguaro cactus, or telephone pole. **VOICE** Series of high *chewk* notes. Calls into July. **HABITAT** Wooded canyons in oak zone, saguaro deserts. **RANGE** Mid-Mar.–Sept.: w and s AZ, far sw NM.

GREAT HORNED OWL

Great Horned Owl (left), desert race (right)

Bubo virginianus

OWL FAMILY

L 23"; WS 4'7". Dark brown with black spots above; underparts pale brown with heavy, dark brown bars; upper chest has dark streaks. Facial disks rich reddish brown, ringed in black. Desert race very pallid, washed out. Head large; eyes yellow; ear tufts fluffy. **VOICE** 5–8 deep hoots, 2nd and 3rd rapid and doubled. **HABITAT** Mtn. and riverine forests, parks, deserts. **RANGE** Resident in all SW.

BARN OWL

Tyto alba

BARN OWL FAMILY

18". Pale buffy washed with gray above; white or buff flecked with black dots below. Head large, without ear tufts; white, heart-shaped facial disk; eyes dark. Superb mouser. Strictly nocturnal; perches on poles. **VOICE** Screams, hisses, clicks. **HABITAT** Old farm buildings, riversides, deserts, towns, mtns. to 7,000'. **RANGE** Resident in most of SW.

BURROWING OWL
Athene cunicularia
OWL FAMILY

9″. Brown above, spotted with white; white below, barred brown. Head rounded, lacks ear tufts; facial disks light brown; eyes yellow. Legs long, grayish; tail short. Digs burrow nest in open field; sentinels stand guard on earthen mound by burrows in daytime. Often appropriates old burrows of ground squirrels, prairie dogs, and badgers. **VOICE** Mellow *coo-coo* at night; quick notes if alarmed. **HABITAT** Dry grasslands, sagebrush deserts, farms. **RANGE** Resident in s AZ, s NM. Mar.–Oct.: all SW.

SPOTTED OWL
Strix occidentalis
OWL FAMILY

18″. Dark brown with white spots above; underparts barred brown on white; facial disks edged in black; crown brown with white dots. Eyes brown; lacks ear tufts. Restricted to larger old-growth forest tracts. **VOICE** Dog-like, barking *hoo-hoo-hoo-hoooah.* **HABITAT** Mature oak woodlands, canyons with water. **RANGE** Resident in forested mtns. of s UT; nw, c, and se AZ; w and c NM.

FLAMMULATED OWL
Otus flammeolus
OWL FAMILY

7″. Looks like a screech-owl, but with dark eyes. Gray with black streaks and bars; face gray with black fringe; ear tufts short. Strictly nocturnal; remains well hidden by day. **VOICE** Long, slow series of single or double hoots. **HABITAT** Oak and ponderosa pine woodlands in mtns. **RANGE** Apr.–Sept.: all forested mtns. in SW.

WESTERN SCREECH-OWL
Otus kennicottii
OWL FAMILY

9″. Mainly gray. Facial disks ringed in black; back has row of white spots on either side; finely barred breast has blackish streaks. Fluffy ear tufts can lie flat. Eyes yellow; bill black; tail short. **VOICE** Low, short whistles that speed up; series of evenly spaced, quick hoots. **HABITAT** Low- to mid-elev. broadleaf and riparian woodlands, towns. **RANGE** Resident in most of SW.

LONG-EARED OWL
Asio otus
OWL FAMILY

15″. Slimmer than Great Horned Owl. Speckled dark brown above; striped blackish below over finer brown banding. Ear tufts long, placed close together on smallish head; eye disks rufous-orange, edged in black. Dozens may roost in same tree in winter. **VOICE** Varied: 1 or 2 long *hoooos;* wails and screams. **HABITAT** Riverine woodlands near fields and marshes; in winter, also conifers in parks. **RANGE** Uncommon resident or winterer in much of SW. **Short-eared Owl** *(A. flammeus),* 16″, breeds in n NV, n UT; winters in all SW; elongated; buffy brown; lacks ear tufts; has black eye shadow; often hunts in daylight.

COMMON POORWILL
Phalaenoptilus nuttallii
NIGHTJAR FAMILY

8″. Adult mottled gray-brown; throat black above white half-collar. Wings rounded (no white band); tail short, corners white. Often sits on dirt roads at night; some hibernate in rocky crevices for winter in s AZ. **VOICE** Loud *pour-wheeel,* given at night. **HABITAT** Desert washes, sagebrush flats, arid hills and canyons, pinyon-juniper woodlands; to 10,000′ in dry mtns. **RANGE** Mar.–Oct.: all SW. **Whip-poor-will** *(Caprimulgus vociferus),* 10″, is darker, tail longer; Apr.–Oct.: forested mtns. of s NV, AZ, s NM.

LESSER NIGHTHAWK
Chordeiles acutipennis
NIGHTJAR FAMILY

9″. Adult warm brown with darker spots above and bars below; throat white. Bill and legs very short; wings and tail long. Flight reveals white band (buffy white in female) near end of primaries. Flies low to ground; on wing evening to midmorning. **VOICE** Soft, toad-like trill. **HABITAT** Desert floors, scrub, towns, near water. **RANGE** May–Oct.: s NV; far sw UT; w, c, and s AZ; s NM.

COMMON NIGHTHAWK
Chordeiles minor
NIGHTJAR FAMILY

10″. Dark brown, heavily gray-spotted; throat white; legs very short. Flight reveals long, pointed, black primaries with prominent white bar in middle of primaries; long, notched tail. Flies high, erratically. Hunts at night for insects. **VOICE** Nasal *peeent.* **HABITAT** Fields, towns. **RANGE** May–Sept.: n NV, UT, n and se AZ, NM.

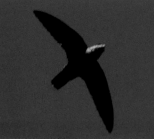

WHITE-THROATED SWIFT
Aeronautes saxatalis
SWIFT FAMILY

6½″. Mainly black; white throat narrows down to mid-belly; flanks and trailing edge of secondaries white; bill tiny; tail deeply notched. Flight reveals long, pointed wings. Very fast flier. Does not perch; clings upright. Nests in small colonies. **VOICE** Shrill, descending *ji-ji-ji-ji-ji.* **HABITAT** Over cliffs, canyons, deserts, lakes. **RANGE** Resident in w and s AZ, sw NM.

VAUX'S SWIFT
Chaetura vauxi
SWIFT FAMILY

4½″. Sooty gray with diffuse whitish throat; bill and feet tiny; wings extend beyond short, spiny tail. Flight reveals long, pointed wings, bowed in crescent when gliding. Does not perch; clings upright, though rarely seen at rest. In migration, roosts communally in hollow trees and chimneys. **VOICE** High *chitter* and *chip* notes. **HABITAT** Over forests, lakes, towns. **RANGE** Apr.–May, Sept.–mid-Oct.: all SW.

Hummingbirds

North America's 14 species of hummingbirds live mainly in the western half of the continent, especially in the Southwest. "Hummers" are among the most colorful of birds, with glittering, iridescent plumage, especially on the throats of the males; the throat appears black until the angle of viewing is just right and a bright flash of red or purple is seen. Hummingbirds are the only birds known to fly backward. They hover in front of flowers, using a long, slender bill to probe deep within and sip the nectar, pollinating the flowers in return. They also pick off insects while on the wing. These birds are attracted to specially designed red hummingbird feeders filled with a sugar-water solution (one part sugar to three parts water) that should be boiled first and changed regularly. Most have rapid *chit* notes and twitters as calls and lack a true song; therefore, voices are often omitted here.

COSTA'S HUMMINGBIRD
Calypte costae
HUMMINGBIRD FAMILY

3″. Male back green; belly white; crown and throat patch purple; tail black, notched. Female has red spots on middle of throat; tail corners white. Often soars to next clump of flowers. **VOICE** Call: short *sik.* **HABITAT** Deserts with ocotillo, yucca, cactus; chaparral; exotic gardens to 6,000′. **RANGE** Jan.–Sept.: s NV; w, c, and s AZ (most common Feb.–May). A few winter in s AZ.

MAGNIFICENT HUMMINGBIRD
"Rivoli's Hummingbird"
Eugenes fulgens
HUMMINGBIRD FAMILY

5″. Large hummer with long, black bill. Male green above and below, chest blackish; crown purple, throat emerald green; bright white spot behind eye; tail large, forked, black. Female all gray below; retains white spot behind eye; small white corners on tail. **HABITAT** Mtn. canyons in pine-oak woodlands. **RANGE** Mar.–Oct.: se AZ, far sw NM; a few in winter.

BLUE-THROATED HUMMINGBIRD
Lampornis clemenciae
HUMMINGBIRD FAMILY

5″. Large hummer with long, black bill. Male green above, gray below; thin white stripe behind eye and another at top of blue throat; tail large, square-ended, black with large white corners. Female lacks blue throat. **HABITAT** Wooded mtn. canyons with streams. **RANGE** Apr.–Oct.: se AZ mtns., far sw NM; a few in winter.

CALLIOPE HUMMINGBIRD
Stellula calliope
HUMMINGBIRD FAMILY

3″. Male crown and upperparts green, white below; throat patch striped red and white; tail very short, black. Female green above, white below; washed buffy on sides; tail corners white. Bill short for hummer. Smallest bird in N. Amer. **VOICE** High *tsik*. **HABITAT** Coniferous forests, wooded canyons. **RANGE** May–Sept.: mtns. of NV, UT. Apr.–May, July–Sept.: all SW, ex. deserts.

BLACK-CHINNED HUMMINGBIRD
Archilochus alexandri
HUMMINGBIRD FAMILY

3½″. Male green above and on sides; chest crescent and mid-belly stripe white; throat patch black above, violet below; tail black, notched. Female green above; throat and underparts white; tail green with white corners. **VOICE** Low *te euw*. **HABITAT** Riverine woodlands, mtns., canyons, towns. **RANGE** Mar.–Sept.: all SW.

ANNA'S HUMMINGBIRD
Calypte anna
HUMMINGBIRD FAMILY

4″. Male back, nape, and sides green; belly gray; crown and flared throat patch red; tail black, notched. Female has red spots on middle of throat; tail corners white. **VOICE** Call: sharp *chik*. Song: squeaks from perch; "popping" sound in aerial display. **HABITAT** Open oak woodlands, towns, gardens. **RANGE** Resident in w and s AZ; range expanding to s NV, s NM.

BROAD-BILLED HUMMINGBIRD
Cynanthus latirostris
HUMMINGBIRD FAMILY

4″. Bill broad, bright red with black tip. Male glittering green above and below; throat dark blue; vent white. Tail bluish black, forked. Female has white stripe behind eye; mainly gray below. **HABITAT** Wooded canyons with streams; desert washes. **RANGE** Apr.–Sept.: se AZ.; a few in winter. **White-eared Hummingbird** *(Hylocharis leucotis)* male has purple face, bold white patch behind eye, bill mostly red; summer in pine-oak woodlands of se AZ mtns. (rare).

RUFOUS HUMMINGBIRD
Selasphorus rufus
HUMMINGBIRD FAMILY

3½″. Male crown, upperparts, and sides rufous; chest crescent and mid-belly stripe white; throat patch red; tail rufous, feathers pointed; in display flight, wings make loud whistles. Female green above, white below; sides buffy; outer tail feathers rufous, black, and white. **HABITAT** Coniferous, broadleaf, and riparian woodlands; parks. **RANGE** Mar.–Apr.: AZ lowlands, w NV. July–Sept. (fall migration): mainly mtns. to 12,600′.

BROAD-TAILED HUMMINGBIRD
Selasphorus platycercus
HUMMINGBIRD FAMILY

4″. Male green above and on sides; chest and mid-belly white; throat red; tail black, wide, notched. Female sides buffy; tail square with white corners. Male's wings produce loud, shrill *whir* in flight. **HABITAT** Mtn. meadows near open pine-oak woodlands. **RANGE** Mid-Mar.–Sept.: mtns. of NV; UT; n, c, and se AZ; w and c NM.

ELEGANT TROGON
Trogon elegans
TROGON FAMILY

12″. Long, squared tail; stubby yellow bill. Male head, back, and rump dark green; chest band white; belly vent red. Top of tail coppery, below barred. Female mainly brown; rosy wash on belly; white spot behind eye. **VOICE** *Kum* notes. **HABITAT** Sycamore canyons in mtn. pine-oak woodlands. **RANGE** Apr.–Oct.: Santa Rita, Huachuca, Chiricahua Mtns., se AZ.

BELTED KINGFISHER
Ceryle alcyon
KINGFISHER FAMILY

13″. Male blue above; throat, neck, and belly white; blue belt on chest. Female (pictured) has 2nd (rufous) belt extending onto sides. Head large, with ragged crests; bill long, thick, black; white spot before eye. Dives headfirst to seize small fish. **VOICE** Loud, woody rattle. **HABITAT** Rivers, lakes, ponds. **RANGE** Resident in n NV, UT, NM. Aug.–May: s NV, AZ, c and s NM.

Woodpeckers

Woodpeckers, which range in size from small to midsize birds, cling to the trunks and large branches of trees and large cactus with their sharp claws (on short legs) and stiff, spine-tipped tails that help support them in the vertical position. Their long, pointed bills are like chisels, able to bore into wood. Curled inside the woodpecker's head is a narrow tongue twice the length of the bill, tipped with spear-like barbs that impale wood-boring insects. Members of this family laboriously dig out nest holes in tall cactus and living or dead tree trunks and limbs. The sexes are very much alike, but the red (or yellow) patches on the heads of the males are reduced or lacking in the females of many species. In spring, males rapidly bang their bills against resonant wood on trees and buildings in a territorial drumming that is louder and more rapid than the tapping made while feeding. Most Southwest woodpeckers are year round residents, but some sapsuckers migrate southward for the winter.

LEWIS'S WOODPECKER
Melanerpes lewis
WOODPECKER FAMILY

11″. Crown, back, and wings black (glossed dark green); face and cheeks dark red; chest and complete collar silvery; belly pink. In flight, all dark above. Flight is crow-like, with steady wingbeats. Takes large insects in trees, in air, on ground. **VOICE** Harsh *churr;* drums softly. **HABITAT** Open areas with pine, oak, cottonwood trees; farms; orchards. **RANGE** Resident in n NV, much of UT, n and ec AZ, n and c NM. A few wander to s AZ in winter.

ACORN WOODPECKER
Melanerpes formicivorus
WOODPECKER FAMILY

9″. Male black above; white forehead joined to white throat in front of eye; belly white; sides streaked black; crown red. Female crown black over eye; hindcrown red. Eyes white. Rump and base of primaries white. Caches acorns in trees and poles. **VOICE** Loud, repeated *wake-up.* **HABITAT** Open oak and pine-oak woodlands; mtns., towns. **RANGE** Resident in mtns. of AZ from Grand Canyon to se AZ; c and s NM.

GILA WOODPECKER
Melanerpes uropygialis
WOODPECKER FAMILY

9″. Male back, wings, and middle of tail zebra-barred; cap red; rest of head and below plain gray-brown. Flight reveals white patch on black primaries, white rump. Female lacks red cap. Common, noisy, and conspicuous. **VOICE** A descending *churrr;* rapid series of *kip* notes. **HABITAT** Cities, towns, wooded desert washes, saguaro cactus. **RANGE** Resident in c and s AZ, far sw NM.

RED-NAPED SAPSUCKER
Sphyrapicus nuchalis
WOODPECKER FAMILY

8″. Male black above, weakly barred white; long white patch on wing; pale yellow below, with dark speckles; head boldly pied; forecrown and nape red, split by black line; throat red. Female upper throat white. Drills holes in bark, returns for sap, insects. **VOICE** Slurred mewing note. **HABITAT** Pine, aspen, alder, and riverine woodlands. **RANGE** May–Oct.: NV mtns., UT, n AZ, n NM. Sept.–Apr.: s NV, sw UT, s AZ, s NM.

WILLIAMSON'S SAPSUCKER
Sphyrapicus thyroideus
WOODPECKER FAMILY

9″. Sexes very different. Adult male mainly black; shoulder and rump white; 2 thin white head stripes; throat red; mid-belly yellowish. Adult female mainly barred black and buff; head plain dull brown; belly pale yellow; rump white. **VOICE** Slurred, nasal *cheer;* drum irreg. **HABITAT** Coniferous forests. **RANGE** Apr.–Oct.: mtns. of NV, UT, n and c AZ, nw NM. Sept.–May: c and se AZ, sw NM.

LADDER-BACKED WOODPECKER

Picoides scalaris

WOODPECKER FAMILY

7″. Male back has even bars of black and white; creamy below, with black dots on sides; crown and upper nape red; face white with black ring behind eye. Female crown and nape black. **VOICE** Sharp *peeck;* descending whinny. **HABITAT** Wooded desert washes, woods in foothills (up to 4,500′). **RANGE** Resident in s NV, far sw UT, all AZ (ex. ne), all NM (ex. nw).

DOWNY WOODPECKER

Picoides pubescens

WOODPECKER FAMILY

6½″. Like Hairy, head boldly pied; mid-back white; wings black, with very few white dots; underparts white; male has red nape patch. Downy is smaller than Hairy, with shorter bill and black spots on white outer tail feathers. **VOICE** Rapid, descending whinny; flat *pick;* long drum. **HABITAT** Broadleaf and riparian woodlands; thickets. **RANGE** Resident in n NV, UT, c AZ, w and n NM.

HAIRY WOODPECKER

Picoides villosus

WOODPECKER FAMILY

9″. Like Downy, head boldly pied; mid-back white; wings black, with few white dots; underparts white; male has red nape patch. Hairy is larger than Downy, with longer bill and unspotted white outer tail feathers. **VOICE** Loud, woody rattle; sharp *peek;* long drum. **HABITAT** Coniferous and mixed forests. **RANGE** Resident in all wooded mtns. of SW.

STRICKLAND'S WOODPECKER

"Arizona Woodpecker"

Picoides stricklandi

WOODPECKER FAMILY

8″. Back, rump, and tail solid brown in both sexes; below white with dark brown spots. Crown, ear patch, and mustache slaty brown; ear patch ringed with white. Male has red nape patch. Inconspicuous compared to Acorn and Gila woodpeckers. **VOICE** Sharp *peek;* 2-second drum. **HABITAT** Pine-oak woodlands at 4,000–7,000′. **RANGE** Resident in se AZ, far sw NM.

NORTHERN FLICKER
"Red-shafted Flicker"
Colaptes auratus
WOODPECKER FAMILY

13". Red-shafted race of west: male back brown with blackish bars; belly buff with black spots; crown brown; cheeks and throat gray, with thick red mustache; chest has black crescent. Female lacks red mustache. Bill long. In flight, white rump, reddish pink underwing and tail. **VOICE** Rapid *wic* and *woika* notes; loud *klee-err.* **HABITAT** Woodlands; mtns. to 10,000′; farms, towns. **RANGE** Resident in most of NV, UT, AZ mtns., NM.

GILDED FLICKER
Colaptes chrysoides
WOODPECKER FAMILY

12". Both sexes brown above with black banding; chest has black crescent; belly white with black spots; crown cinnamon; face and throat pale gray. Male has red mustache. Flight reveals yellow underwings and undertail; rump white. Recently split from Northern Flicker. **VOICE** Loud *woika;* loud series of *kee* notes. **HABITAT** Saguaro deserts, cottonwood-lined streams, towns. **RANGE** Resident in AZ lowlands.

Songbirds

The birds described from here to the end of the birds section belong to a single order called Passeriformes. Known as passerines or, more commonly, perching birds or songbirds, they are the most recently evolved of the 25 bird orders. Members of this order make up about half of the world's nearly 10,000 bird species. Their sizes range from 3½-inch kinglets to 24-inch ravens, but they are generally small land birds with pleasing songs; among the finest songsters are the wrens, thrushes, and orioles. Songbirds use call notes year-round, while most give their songs only during the breeding season (spring and early summer). In some species, the male has a particularly colorful summer breeding plumage that changes in winter to a drabber, female-like coloration. In the spring, migrant males generally arrive in the Southwest seven to ten days before the females and stake out breeding territories, which they defend against neighboring males. After a male shows a female around his territory, she may be satisfied (especially if the vegetation and insect life are plentiful) and stay with him, or search for another singing male whose territory is more to her liking. Most songbirds build open-topped, rounded nests of grasses, sticks, vegetable fibers, and rootlets in a tree fork, in a shrub, or tucked under tall grass. Some eat insects year-round, while others focus on seeds, grains, or fruit; all feed insects to their hatchlings. In the fall, the sexes may migrate south together, the adults often several weeks or more before the young born that year.

OLIVE-SIDED FLYCATCHER

Contopus cooperi

TYRANT FLYCATCHER FAMILY

7½". Upperparts and crown dark olive-brown; sides olive-brown, form a vest; throat and mid-belly stripe white. Bill fairly thick; tail medium length. Perches on highest twigs of trees, esp. dead ones. **VOICE** Song: whistled *hic . . . three-beers.* Call: rapid *pip-pip-pip.* **HABITAT** Summer: coniferous forests, in mtns. Migration: also broadleaf woodlands, parks. **RANGE** May, Aug.–Sept.: all SW. May–Aug.: mtns. of NV, UT, n and c AZ, n and w NM.

GREATER PEWEE

"Coues' Flycatcher"

Contopus pertinax

TYRANT FLYCATCHER FAMILY

7¼". Plain slaty brown above, no wing bars (as seen in smaller wood-pewees); chest and sides uniformly dusky; vent whitish; usu. small, pointed crest on top of head; bill black above, orange below; tail fairly long. Sits on exposed branches. **VOICE** Song: whistled *Jo-say-Ma-ri-a.* Call: *pip-pip.* **HABITAT** Pine-oak mtn. woodlands. **RANGE** Apr.–Sept.: c and se AZ, sw NM.

WESTERN WOOD-PEWEE

Contopus sordidulus

TYRANT FLYCATCHER FAMILY

6½". Adult pale grayish brown above; 1 or 2 pale whitish wing bars; dingy whitish below; sides grayish. Bill thin, often orangy at base. Head peaked at rear; tail fairly long. Imm. wing bars buffy, bill black. **VOICE** Song: harsh, nasal *peee-err.* **HABITAT** Broadleaf, pine, and riverine woodlands. **RANGE** Apr., Sept.–Oct.: all SW. May–Sept.: mtns. of NV; UT; n, c, and se AZ; w and c NM.

WILLOW FLYCATCHER

Empidonax traillii

TYRANT FLYCATCHER FAMILY

5¾". The Southwest has 8 species of confusing *Empidonax* flycatchers, most told by song and breeding habitat. This species: olive-brown above; white throat and dusky chest drab; faint yellowish wash on belly; eye ring very thin. Flicks tail up. **VOICE** Song: sneeze-like *fitz-beuw.* Call: soft *whit.* **HABITAT** Riverside and lakeside thickets; dry washes. **RANGE** Mid-May–mid-June, mid-Aug.–Sept.: all SW. June–Aug.: n NV; UT, w, n, and e AZ; w and c NM.

GRAY FLYCATCHER
Empidonax wrightii
TYRANT FLYCATCHER FAMILY

5½". Above pale gray, 2 whitish wing bars; below whitish. Bill long, pink below. Slowly dips tail down. **VOICE** Song: rising *che whe.* Call: unmusical *whit.* **HABITAT** Sagebrush, pinyon, juniper, thickets. **RANGE** Apr.–May, Aug.–Sept.: all SW. May–Aug.: NV, UT, ne AZ, nw NM. Winter: s AZ.

CORDILLERAN FLYCATCHER
"Western Flycatcher"
Empidonax occidentalis
TYRANT FLYCATCHER FAMILY

5½". Olive-brown above; sides washed olive; throat and belly yellow; 2 wing bars; eye ring white. **VOICE** Song: loud *pit-SEET.* **HABITAT** Aspen, conifer forests; sagebrush in migration. **RANGE** May–Sept.: NV mtns., UT, c and e AZ, w and c NM.

male (left), female (right)

VERMILION FLYCATCHER
Pyrocephalus rubinus
TYRANT FLYCATCHER FAMILY

6". Adult male has bright red crown and underparts; line through eye, back, and wings blackish brown; trace of wing bars; tail blackish. Adult female dull brown above; chest whitish with brown streaks; belly washed pink (yellow on imm. female). Wonderful flight songs in spring with male circling about with fluffed-up chest. Perches high to low in trees, on wires. **VOICE** Song: clear *pit-pit-pit-a see.* Call: sharp *pit* notes. **HABITAT** Riverine woods; tree rows of farms, desert washes. **RANGE** Resident in s NV; w, c, and se AZ; s NM.

BLACK PHOEBE
Sayornis nigricans
TYRANT FLYCATCHER FAMILY

7". Adult head, back, chest, sides, and tail black; belly white; wings and outer tail feathers have white edging. Sits upright; wags tail frequently. Fly-catches over fresh water and meadows near woodlands or brush. **VOICE** Song: rising *pee-yee-yit-see.* Call: down-slurred *chuurp.* **HABITAT** Wooded streams, ponds, ranches. **RANGE** Resident in s NV, w and se AZ, s NM. Apr.–Oct.: also sw UT, nw and c AZ, c NM.

SAY'S PHOEBE
Sayornis saya
TYRANT FLYCATCHER FAMILY

7½″. Dull brown above; throat gray; belly and vent cinnamon; 2 faint wing bars; tail long, black, often wagged. Bill thin. **VOICE** Song: *pit-cedar.* Call: falling *peeurr.* **HABITAT** Shrubby grasslands, farms, deserts. **RANGE** Apr.–Sept.: all SW. Oct.–Mar.: s NV; w, c, and se AZ; s NM.

DUSKY-CAPPED FLYCATCHER
"Olivaceous Flycatcher"
Myiarchus tuberculifer
TYRANT FLYCATCHER FAMILY

7″. Upperparts and tail dusky brown (no rufous); wing bars faint rufous; throat grayish; belly lemon yellow. **VOICE** Song: *wheat peeyer.* Call: *queeer.* **HABITAT** Mtn. pine, oak, and juniper woodlands; canyons. **RANGE** Apr.–Sept.: mtns., se AZ, far sw NM.

ASH-THROATED FLYCATCHER
Myiarchus cinerascens
TYRANT FLYCATCHER FAMILY

8″. Dull brown above; throat, chest pale gray; belly yellow; 1 whitish wing bar; wings and tail rusty. Head fluffy at rear; bill black. **VOICE** Soft *pur-weer* and *pwit;* harsher *ka-brick.* **HABITAT** Open woodlands, brush, mtns. to 7,500′. **RANGE** Apr.–Sept.: all SW; some winter in s AZ.

SULPHUR-BELLIED FLYCATCHER
Myiodynastes luteiventris
TYRANT FLYCATCHER FAMILY

8″. Above brown, striped black; below pale yellow, striped brown. Head striped; bill very large, black. Rump and tail bright rufous. **VOICE** Song: high, emphatic *kee-zeee-ick.* **HABITAT** Mtn. canyons with sycamores, walnuts. **RANGE** May–mid-Sept.: se AZ mtns.

BROWN-CRESTED FLYCATCHER
"Wied's Crested Flycatcher"
Myiarchus tyrannulus
TYRANT FLYCATCHER FAMILY

9″. Brown above; throat pale gray; belly yellow; trace of pale wing bars; wings and tail edged rufous; bill large, black. Nests in holes in trees, saguaros. **VOICE** Song: *wheer-pur-bert.* Call: loud *whit.* **HABITAT** Desert washes, saguaro forests, riverine and canyon woods. **RANGE** Apr.–Aug.: c and s AZ.

CASSIN'S KINGBIRD
Tyrannus vociferans
TYRANT FLYCATCHER FAMILY

8½". Adult back olive; crown dark gray; throat white; chest slaty gray; belly yellow; tail blackish with pale tip. **VOICE** Husky *chi-beeer* and *chi-be-be-be-be.* **HABITAT** Hillsides with scrub; usu. higher elev. than Western. **RANGE** Apr.–Oct.: s NV, s and e UT, all AZ (ex. sw), NM (ex. se). **Thick-billed Kingbird** *(T. crassirostris),* 9½", plain slaty above, white below; bill thick, black, no white in tail; se AZ riverine woods, May–Aug.

WESTERN KINGBIRD
Tyrannus verticalis
TYRANT FLYCATCHER FAMILY

8½". Crown and back gray; thin blackish line through eye; throat and chest pale gray; belly yellow; tail black with white outer feathers. Bill short. Aggressive toward larger birds near nest. Prefers exposed perches (e.g., wires and fences). **VOICE** Shrill *kit* and *kit-kit-kiddledit.* **HABITAT** Grasslands, riparian woodlands, farms. **RANGE** Apr.–Oct.: all SW. **Scissor-tailed Flycatcher** *(T. forficatus),* 14", breeds in se NM; silvery; sides pink; very long, forked tail.

EASTERN KINGBIRD
Tyrannus tyrannus
TYRANT FLYCATCHER FAMILY

8". Back and wings slaty; throat and underparts white; head black; tail black, with white terminal band. Often flies slowly, with quivering wings. Flies fast when attacking crows and hawks that come near its territory. Perches on tips of trees and on wires. **VOICE** Rapid, agitated *kit-kit-kittery;* nasal *tzeer.* **HABITAT** Trees near fields, waterways, roads. **RANGE** May–Sept.: n NV, n UT, ne NM; some migrants elsewhere in SW.

HORNED LARK
Eremophila alpestris
LARK FAMILY

7½". Brown above, with few black streaks; belly white; crown stripe black. Male has 2 tiny "horns." Black chest crescent and stripe below eye. Bill slender, pointed. Tail black; outer tail feathers white. Flight reveals white underwing. Has extended range due to commercial livestock grazing. **VOICE** Song: high tinkling. Call: *tsee-titi.* **HABITAT** Open grasslands. **RANGE** Resident in all SW, ex. forested areas.

PURPLE MARTIN
Progne subis
SWALLOW FAMILY

8″. Male mainly dark iridescent blue-purple. Female dull purplish above; throat and chest dusky gray, with darker scales; belly and vent white. Tail forked. Glides more than other swallows; often circles with short flaps, then a glide. **VOICE** Song: low, gurgling series. Call: throaty *chew chew.* **HABITAT** Saguaro stands, woodland edges, fields, marshes, towns. **RANGE** May–mid-Oct.: n UT, much of AZ (ex. sw), w NM.

TREE SWALLOW
Tachycineta bicolor
SWALLOW FAMILY

6″. Adult dark iridescent green-blue above; 1st year female and imm. brown above. Tail notched; entirely snowy white below. Slow flier; short, flapping circles and a climb. Flocks in migration. **VOICE** Song: *weet-trit-weet.* Call: *cheat cheat.* **HABITAT** Fields; over lakes, ponds, and rivers. **RANGE** Mid-Feb.–Apr., Aug.–Oct.: all SW. Apr.–mid-Sept.: n NV, UT, ne AZ, nw NM.

VIOLET-GREEN SWALLOW
Tachycineta thalassina
SWALLOW FAMILY

5″. Crown, back, and forewing green; back of neck, flight feathers, mid-rump stripe, and tail dark violet; white underparts continue up behind eye; sides of rump white. Tail short, notched; bill tiny. Flight very fluttery. Usu. in small flocks. **VOICE** Thin *chip;* rapid *chit-chit-chit-weet-weet.* **HABITAT** Woodland edges, chiefly in mtns. **RANGE** Mar.–Oct.: all SW, ex. sw AZ.

NORTHERN ROUGH-WINGED SWALLOW
Stelgidopteryx serripennis
SWALLOW FAMILY

5½″. Dull brown above; throat and chest pale brown; breast and vent dull white. Tail notched. Flies with slow, deep wingbeats. Often in solitary pairs. **VOICE** Raspy *brit.* **HABITAT** Ponds, rivers, fields. **RANGE** Feb.–Oct.: all SW; few winter in sw AZ. **Bank Swallow** *(Riparia riparia),* 5″, is brown above, white below, with brown necklace; breeds in colonies in n NV and UT; migrant in all SW.

CLIFF SWALLOW
Petrochelidon pyrrhonota
SWALLOW FAMILY

6″. Adult crown, back, and wings blue; rump buffy; underparts grayish white; forehead cream; foreneck chestnut; hindneck gray. Tail black, short, square. Flies in circles high in air. Nests in colonies under bridges, on buildings. **VOICE** Song: harsh creaking. Call: grating *syrup*. **HABITAT** Low- to mid-elev. farms, fields, waterways. **RANGE** Mar.–Sept.: all SW.

BARN SWALLOW
Hirundo rustica
SWALLOW FAMILY

7″. Adult glossy blue above, mainly pale orange below; forehead chestnut; throat deep orange. Tail forked, outer tail streamers very long. Imm. has dark necklace; lacks tail streamers. Nest is open cup of mud pellets and grass, inside or under overhang of barn or bridge. Fast flier. **VOICE** Song: long twittering. Calls: soft *vit vit* and *zee-zay.* **HABITAT** Fields, farms, waterways. **RANGE** Apr.–Sept.: n NV, UT, c and e AZ, NM. Mar.–May, Aug.–Oct.: all SW.

GRAY JAY
Perisoreus canadensis
CROW AND JAY FAMILY

11½″. Adult back, wings, and tail dull, dark gray; crown, cheeks, and underparts white; nape black. Bill black; tail long, rounded. Imm. all slaty; white mustache. Bold food robber at human campsites. Northern Mockingbird similar, but has white wing patch, white outer tail feathers. **VOICE** Low *chuck.* **HABITAT** Spruce, fir woods. **RANGE** Resident in ne UT, ec AZ, ne NM.

STELLER'S JAY
Cyanocitta stelleri
CROW AND JAY FAMILY

12″. All dark; bill heavy. Crest long, shaggy, black with thin white stripes; head, back, and upper breast blackish; belly and rump plain blue; wings and tail blue with fine black barring. Brash and nearly omnivorous; visits campsites for scraps. **VOICE** Loud *shaq-shaq-shaq.* **HABITAT** Coniferous forests. **RANGE** Resident in NV (local), UT, higher mtns. of AZ, NM.

WESTERN SCRUB JAY

Aphelocoma californica

CROW AND JAY FAMILY

13″. Back gray-brown; belly gray; crown, hindneck, partial necklace, wings, rump, and tail blue; throat white with faint blue streaks; no crest. Tail long, rounded. Shy at nest, but bold rest of year at picnic sites and parks. Caches acorns in ground for winter. **VOICE** Loud series of *kwesh* or *check* notes. **HABITAT** Low- to mid-elev. oak woodlands, scrubby grasslands. **RANGE** Resident in most of SW, ex. sw AZ, se NM.

MEXICAN JAY

Aphelocoma ultramarina

CROW AND JAY FAMILY

13″. Large, crestless jay of Mexican border. Back and cheeks gray-brown; crown, wings, and long tail bright blue; underparts gray, darker on chest. Lacks streaked throat and blue necklace of Western Scrub Jay. Brash and noisy. **VOICE** Loud *shrink shrink.* **HABITAT** Foothill scrub, mtn. pine-oak woodlands. **RANGE** c and se AZ, sw NM.

PINYON JAY

Gymnorhinus cyanocephalus

CROW AND JAY FAMILY

10″. Adult all dull blue; faint white streaks on throat. Bill black, chisel-like; tail shorter than other jays; no crest. Imm. paler with grayish underparts. Even, crow-like flight. Very social; usu. seen in large flocks. Stores pine nuts for winter and spring. **VOICE** High, descending *kra-a-a-a;* series of *kway* notes. **HABITAT** Stunted forests of pinyon pine, juniper; mtns. **RANGE** Resident of NV, UT, n AZ, n NM. Some winters, disperses to s AZ, s NM.

CLARK'S NUTCRACKER

Nucifraga columbiana

CROW AND JAY FAMILY

13″. Head, back, and underparts plain silvery gray; vent white; wings black; trailing edge of secondaries white. Tail fairly short, black in center, with white outer tail feathers. Bill long, pointed, black. Walks like crow on ground (jays hop); begs scraps at picnic sites. Caches nuts, seeds on south-facing slopes. **VOICE** Guttural *kraaah.* **HABITAT** Subalpine forests, esp. Whitebark Pine, mainly above 8,000′. **RANGE** Resident in mtns. of NV, UT, n and c AZ, n and c NM.

BLACK-BILLED MAGPIE
Pica pica
CROW AND JAY FAMILY

20″. Head, chest, back, rump, and vent black; belly and long shoulder patch white; wings and tail iridescent purple and green. Bill stout, black; tail very long, with wedge-shaped tip. Flight reveals mainly white primaries. Feeds on insects, fruit, baby birds, roadkill. Mobs hawks, larger birds. Uses communal roosts. **VOICE** Rapid series of *jack* notes; rising *maayg?* **HABITAT** Riverine woodlands, sagebrush deserts, farms. **RANGE** Resident in n and c NV, UT, ne AZ, n NM.

AMERICAN CROW
Corvus brachyrhynchos
CROW AND JAY FAMILY

18″. All glossy black; bill heavy, black. Flight reveals rounded wings, "fingered" wingtips, squarish tail with rounded corners. Bold, noisy. Huge night roosts in winter. **VOICE** Loud, descending *caw.* **HABITAT** Shores, cities, farms, woodlands, fields. **RANGE** Resident in w and n NV, n and e UT, ne AZ, n and c NM.

Attracting Birds to Your Yard

Many people enjoy attracting birds to their yards, and supplemental feeding helps birds in winter, when naturally occurring seeds may be covered by snow in higher country. Once started, winter feeding should be continued into spring. Throughout the birds section, most species that will come into a yard to feed are indicated by the icon .

Birdfeeders come in many designs. Hanging, clear seed feeders with short perch sticks are popular with goldfinches and siskins. Window boxes and platforms on a pole are good for medium-size birds such as chickadees, titmice, nuthatches, and many finches. Quail, doves, blackbirds, juncos, and sparrows prefer to feed on the ground.

Grains and seeds are the best all-purpose fare for feeders. Many species like sunflower seeds. Thistle seed is popular with goldfinches; white millet seed is good for small species, and cracked corn is appreciated by large, ground-feeding birds.

Many seed mixes are available at supermarkets plus garden and wild bird supply stores. Birds also like fruit. In summer, you can lay out orange slices for orioles and tanagers; diced apples and grapes can also be put out on a platform. The fat and protein in nuts make these foods very desirable. Suet, in a mesh holder suspended from a branch or mounted on a tree trunk, attracts birds

CHIHUAHUAN RAVEN

Corvus cryptoleucus

CROW AND JAY FAMILY

20". All glossy black; bill black, heavy; throat has shaggy feathers. White on base of neck feathers rarely seen. Flight reveals pointed wings; "fingered" wingtips; long, wedge-shaped tail. Often flies fairly high; will soar. More gregarious than Common Raven; call a bit higher. **VOICE** Flat *kraack.* **HABITAT** Arid, grassy plains and deserts with yucca, cactus, mesquite; nearby foothills; roadsides; flocks at dumps watchful. **RANGE** sc and se AZ, s and e NM.

COMMON RAVEN

"Northern Raven"

Corvus corax

CROW AND JAY FAMILY

24". All glossy black; bill black, very heavy; throat has long, shaggy feathers. Flight reveals pointed wings; "fingered" wingtips; long, wedge-shaped tail. Soars frequently. Shy but conspicuous. **VOICE** Very low *croonk;* metallic *tok.* **HABITAT** Chiefly mtns. and forests. **RANGE** Resident in all SW; valleys to tops of mtns.

such as nuthatches, woodpeckers, starlings, and a few wrens; it should be discontinued in hot months, when it spoils quickly and mats feathers. Hummingbirds and orioles will come to specially designed red plastic dispensers of sugar water. (See page 304 for more on hummingbirds.)

Water is important, especially during periods when natural water sources dry up or freeze over. Many species are attracted to a bird bath and a drip or spray fountain, which should be regularly scrubbed with a brush to rid it of algae and prevent diseases from spreading.

You might want to make or purchase a nest box to attract breeding birds. The most inviting to chickadees, nuthatches, wrens, bluebirds, and even small owls, is an enclosed box with a square floor area 4 to 7 inches wide and deep, and about twice as high as it is wide (8 to 12 inches). Specifications for such a box vary depending on the species and include floor area, the size of the entrance hole, height from the base of the box to the hole, and proper siting of the box. Other birds will nest in open-fronted shelves or in martin houses. Information on building and siting nest boxes and feeders is available at your local Audubon Society or nature center. In the birds section, the icon denotes species that have used nest boxes in the right habitat.

BLACK-CAPPED CHICKADEE
Poecile (Parus) atricapillus
CHICKADEE FAMILY

5½″. Gray above; white below; sides buffy; wings edged white; cap and throat black; face white. Friendly, inquisitive; often in family groups. **VOICE** Song: clear *fee-bee.* Call: *chick-a-dee-dee-dee-dee.* **HABITAT** Broadleaf and riverine woods, thickets, towns. **RANGE** Resident in UT and n NM.

MOUNTAIN CHICKADEE
Poecile (Parus) gambeli
CHICKADEE FAMILY

5½″. Mostly gray; crown, throat black; cheek, eye line white. **VOICE** Song: high, whistled *fee-bee-bee.* Call: raspy *chick-a dee-dee-dee.* **HABITAT** Coniferous forests, thickets, towns, mtns. **RANGE** Resident in mtns. of NV; UT; n and c AZ (south to Santa Catalinas); mtns. of NM.

BRIDLED TITMOUSE
Baeolophus (Parus) wollweberi
CHICKADEE FAMILY

5″. Above gray; below pale gray. Head pied; crest at rear. Common within its range; often found in small groups. **VOICE** Fairly high *peter peter peter.* **HABITAT** Canyons with sycamore; pine-oak woodlands on mtn. slopes. **RANGE** Mtns. of c and se AZ, sw NM.

JUNIPER TITMOUSE
"Plain Titmouse"
Baeolophus (Parus) ridgwayi
CHICKADEE FAMILY

5½″. Adult plain gray above, paler gray below; crest gray; head plain. **VOICE** Harsh *see-dee-dee.* **HABITAT** Broadleaf woodlands, esp. oaks, pinyon-juniper. **RANGE** Resident in NV; UT; n, c, and se AZ; n, w, and c NM.

VERDIN
Auriparus flaviceps
VERDIN FAMILY

4″. Adult gray above; pale gray below; shoulder patch chestnut; head and throat yellow. Imm. gray-brown above; lacks yellow head. Feeds low in desert shrubs. Nest is large grass ball with side entrance. **VOICE** Song: high *see-tsee-see.* Call: loud *zee-lip.* **HABITAT** Desert scrub, washes to 4,500′. **RANGE** Resident in s NV; w, c, and s AZ; s NM.

BUSHTIT
Psaltriparus minimus
BUSHTIT FAMILY

4″. Gray above with brown or black cheeks; paler gray below. Bill tiny; tail long. Eyes dark in male, yellow in female. In flocks of up to 30 birds. **VOICE** Song: high trill. Call: weak *teet.* **HABITAT** Oak, pinyon, juniper woodlands, thickets. **RANGE** Resident in NV, UT; mtns. of AZ, NM.

RED-BREASTED NUTHATCH
Sitta canadensis
NUTHATCH FAMILY

4½″. Male blue above; orange below; cap black; white line over eye. Female duller. Tail short. Feeds on trunks and outer branches. **VOICE** High, nasal *enk* series. **HABITAT** Conifer forests, broadleaf woodlands. **RANGE** Resident of all SW mtns. Sept.–Apr.: some in lowlands.

WHITE-BREASTED NUTHATCH
Sitta carolinensis
NUTHATCH FAMILY

6″. Back gray-blue; face and underparts white; crown narrow, black; vent and sides washed rusty. Creeps headfirst down tree trunks. **VOICE** Song: rapid *wer* notes. Call: loud *yank.* **HABITAT** Broadleaf and mixed woodlands. **RANGE** Resident in mtns. of all SW.

PYGMY NUTHATCH
Sitta pygmaea
NUTHATCH FAMILY

4″. Blue-gray above, pale buffy below; crown brown; throat white. Tail short. Climbs over trunks and branches, often upside-down. Often in small flocks. **VOICE** High series of *peep* notes. **HABITAT** Dry coniferous forests, esp. Ponderosa Pine. **RANGE** Resident in mtns. of SW.

BROWN CREEPER
Certhia americana
CREEPER FAMILY

5½″. Brown with buff stripes above; white below; wing stripe buffy; eye line white; rump rufous; tail tips spiny. Climbs trees, probing bark with slender bill. **VOICE** Song: high *see see see tu wee.* Call: 1–2 high *tsee* notes. **HABITAT** Forests. **RANGE** Resident in mtns. of SW. Sept.–Apr.: some visit lowlands.

CACTUS WREN
Campylorhynchus brunneicapillus
WREN FAMILY

8″. Huge speckled and striped wren with brown crown; white eye line; black chest; long white-spotted tail. Builds bulky stick nest. **VOICE** Song: long series of *chug* notes. **HABITAT** Desert scrub, cactus, yucca, foothill woods. **RANGE** Resident in s NV, far sw UT, w, c, and s AZ, s NM.

ROCK WREN
Salpinctes obsoletus
WREN FAMILY

6″. Gray-brown above, speckled white; whitish below; sides washed buffy; eyebrow thin, buffy. Often bobs head. **VOICE** Song: loud repeated *cha-wee.* Call: sharp *tee-keer.* **HABITAT** Canyons, rocky areas in deserts, foothills. **RANGE** Resident in s NV, s UT, AZ, NM. Apr.–Sept.: n NV, n UT.

CANYON WREN
Catherpes mexicanus
WREN FAMILY

5½″. Rufous with white speckling, ex. brown crown, white throat. Bill long, down-curved. Creeps over rocks. **VOICE** Song: descending *tee-tee-tee-tew-tew-tew-tew.* Call: harsh *jeet.* **HABITAT** Cliff faces, canyons with streams. **RANGE** Resident in all SW, ex. desert flats.

BEWICK'S WREN
Thryomanes bewickii
WREN FAMILY

5½″. Crown and upperparts gray-brown; pale gray below; white eyebrow; faintly striped cheeks. Tail fairly long, rounded, outer tail feathers white. **VOICE** Song: melodious, complex. **HABITAT** Broadleaf and riparian woodlands, thickets, towns. **RANGE** Resident in most of SW.

HOUSE WREN
Troglodytes aedon
WREN FAMILY

5″. Head and back plain dull brown; light brown below; sides finely barred; wings and tail barred black. Tail often cocked. **VOICE** Song: long, pleasing, descending gurgle. Call: *chuurr.* **HABITAT** Shrubs, vines, suburbs. **RANGE** Apr.–Sept.: n and c NV, UT, n, c, and se AZ, NM. Sept.–Apr.: w and s AZ, s NM.

WINTER WREN
Troglodytes troglodytes
WREN FAMILY

4″. Dark brown; fine black bars on sides, wings, and extremely short tail; indistinct eyebrow; throat buffy. **VOICE** Song: long series of warbles and trills. Call: *kip kip*. **HABITAT** Conifer forest ravines, brush piles. **RANGE** Oct.–Mar.: all SW.

MARSH WREN
Cistothorus palustris
WREN FAMILY

5″. Back black with white stripes; wings, rump, and tail rufous; white below; sides buffy; white eyebrow under dark brown crown. Tail often cocked. **VOICE** Song: gurgling rattle. Call: loud *check*. **HABITAT** Large cattail marshes. **RANGE** Resident in NV, UT, w AZ. Oct.–Mar.: rest of AZ, NM.

AMERICAN DIPPER
Cinclus mexicanus
DIPPER FAMILY

8″. Adult gray; white eye ring; eyelids transparent; legs pale pink. Tail short. Walks underwater to feed on insect larvae. **VOICE** Song: musical, varied; repeats phrases. Call: piercing *zeet*. **HABITAT** Mtn. streams. **RANGE** Resident in NV mtns., UT, nw, c, and e AZ, n and w NM.

GOLDEN-CROWNED KINGLET
Regulus satrapa
KINGLET FAMILY

3½″. Back olive; paler below; crown black, with orange (male) or yellow (female) center; eyebrow white. Tail short, notched. Often flicks wings. **VOICE** Song: high *see-see-see* then chatter. Call: 3 high notes. **HABITAT** Spruce and mixed forests. **RANGE** Resident in higher mtns.; lowlands in winter.

RUBY-CROWNED KINGLET
Regulus calendula
KINGLET FAMILY

4″. Drab olive all over, but paler below; 2 white wing bars; eye ring large, white. Males red mid-crown patch usu. not visible. Often flicks wings. **VOICE** Song: high warbles ending with 3 *look-at-me*'s. Call: scolding *je-dit*. **HABITAT** Mtn. forests, scrub. **RANGE** Apr.–Oct.: mtns. of NV, UT, n and c AZ, n and c NM. Oct.–Apr.: all SW.

BLUE-GRAY GNATCATCHER
Polioptila caerulea
OLD WORLD WARBLER FAMILY

4½". Blue-gray above, white below. Eye ring white; male has black line over eye in summer; tail black with white outer feathers. Often wags tail sideways. **VOICE** Song: thin, wheezy warble. Call: single *pweee?* **HABITAT** Open broadleaf woodlands, thickets. **RANGE** Apr.–Sept.: all SW, ex. s NV, sw AZ. Sept.–Apr.: w and s AZ.

BLACK-TAILED GNATCATCHER
Polioptila melanura
OLD WORLD WARBLER FAMILY

4½". Breeding male gray above with black cap down to eye; no eye ring; below whitish; thin white edge on black tail feathers. Winter male and female have gray crown. **VOICE** Call: double or triple raspy *cheese.* **HABITAT** Desert, foothill thorn scrub, washes. **RANGE** w, c, and s AZ, sc NM.

TOWNSEND'S SOLITAIRE
Myadestes townsendi
THRUSH FAMILY

9". Brownish gray; eye ring white; buffy patches on wings; white outer tail feathers. Bill short. **VOICE** Song: rising and falling fluty whistles. Call: high *eeek.* **HABITAT** Forests, parks. **RANGE** Resident n and c NV, UT, n and ec AZ, n and w NM. Sept.–May: rest of SW.

WESTERN BLUEBIRD
Sialia mexicana
THRUSH FAMILY

7". Male blue above; chest, sides, part of back rusty orange. Female head gray; wings and tail pale blue; orange wash on chest. **VOICE** Song: musical *cheer cheer-lee churr.* Call: soft *pheew.* **HABITAT** Open woodlands, mtns., farms. **RANGE** Mar.–Oct.: n NV, UT, mtns. of AZ and NM. Oct.–Mar.: s NV, AZ, s NM.

MOUNTAIN BLUEBIRD
Sialia currucoides
THRUSH FAMILY

7". Male all blue, paler below. Female head, back, and chest gray; wings and tail blue. Often in large flocks. **VOICE** Song: short, weak warbling. Call: low *churr.* **HABITAT** Open pines, sagebrush deserts, grasslands, farms. **RANGE** Feb.–Oct.: n and c NV, UT, n AZ, n and c NM. Nov.–Mar.: s NV, s UT, AZ, NM.

SWAINSON'S THRUSH
Catharus ustulatus
THRUSH FAMILY

7″. Olive brown above; dark brown spots on buffy throat and chest; eye ring buffy. **VOICE** Song: beautiful, upslurred whistles. Calls: *whit* and *heep*. **HABITAT** Streamside thickets, forest understories, gardens, ranches. **RANGE** Apr.–Aug.: mtns. of NV, n UT. May, Sept.–Oct.: all SW.

HERMIT THRUSH
Catharus guttatus
THRUSH FAMILY

7″. Grayish brown above; upper chest spotted dark brown; belly whitish; tail rufous brown. **VOICE** Song: clear, flute-like phrases repeated at different pitches. Call: low *chuck*. **HABITAT** Forests, thickets. **RANGE** Resident c and se AZ, s NM. Apr.–Oct.: mtns. of NV, UT, n AZ, n NM.

AMERICAN ROBIN
Turdus migratorius
THRUSH FAMILY

10″. Breast orange; gray-brown above; head blackish; white eye ring; yellow bill. Juv. has blackish spots below. **VOICE** Song: *cheery-up cheery-me*. Calls: *tut tut tut; tseep*. **HABITAT** Woodlands, fields, gardens, towns. **RANGE** Resident in SW; to high elev. in summer, low in winter.

NORTHERN MOCKINGBIRD
Mimus polyglottos
MOCKINGBIRD FAMILY

10″. Mainly gray; paler below; 2 thin wing bars and wing patch white; tail blackish with white outer tail feathers. Bill short, thin. Sings conspicuously day and night. **VOICE** Song: mimics other birds, repeats songs 3–6 times. Calls: loud *chack*, softer *chair*. **HABITAT** Shrubs, gardens, fields, cities. **RANGE** Resident in all SW.

SAGE THRASHER
Oreoscoptes montanus
MOCKINGBIRD FAMILY

8″. Dull brown above, whitish below, with dark brownish stripes; pale white corners on tail. Bill slightly curved; eyes yellow. **VOICE** Song: clear, sweet warbling. Call: harsh *chuck*. **HABITAT** Sagebrush deserts. **RANGE** Mar.–Aug.: n and c NV, UT, ne AZ, nw NM. Mid-Sept.–Mar.: s NV, s, c, and s AZ, s and e NM.

BENDIRE'S THRASHER
Toxostoma bendirei
MOCKINGBIRD FAMILY

10″. Dull gray-brown above; fine dots on pale rusty chest; bill a bit shorter than Curve-billed. Eyes usu. yellow. **VOICE** Song: continuous, double-noted warbles. Call: soft *tear-up.* **HABITAT** Thorn scrub in deserts, foothills; cholla cactus. **RANGE** Resident in s AZ. Mar.–Oct.: also s NV, far s UT, rest of AZ, w NM.

CURVE-BILLED THRASHER
Toxostoma curvirostre
MOCKINGBIRD FAMILY

11″. Adult gray above; diffuse gray spots below. Tail tipped white. Eyes orange; bill slender. Young similar to Bendire's. **VOICE** Song: varied musical phrases. Call: loud *whit-wheat.* **HABITAT** Cactus scrub, desert washes, towns. **RANGE** Resident in s AZ, s and e NM.

CRISSAL THRASHER
Toxostoma crissale (dorsale)
MOCKINGBIRD FAMILY

12″. Mostly gray-brown; strong mustache; bill deeply downcurved; vent dark rufous; tail blackish. **VOICE** Song: sweeter than other thrashers. Call: whistled *cheet-er-ee.* **HABITAT** Thickets and woodlands near riverbeds and washes. **RANGE** s NV; far sw UT; w, c, and s AZ; s and c NM.

AMERICAN PIPIT
Anthus rubescens
PIPIT FAMILY

6″. Gray-brown above; buffy below; weak brown streaks on chest. Bill thin; outer tail feathers white. **VOICE** Flight song: series of *chwee* notes. Call: *pi-pit.* **HABITAT** Summer: alpine meadows. Winter: plains, fields. **RANGE** Apr.–Sept.: high peaks of NV, UT, n AZ, n NM. Oct.–Apr.: w and s NV, n UT, c AZ, n NM.

BOHEMIAN WAXWING
Bombycilla garrulus
WAXWING FAMILY

7″. Adult mostly gray; head and crest brown; throat and line through eye black; white lines on black primaries; red-tipped secondaries. Tail slaty with yellow tip; vent rusty. **VOICE** High, buzzy *zeeee.* **HABITAT** Summer: coniferous forests. Winter: fruiting trees in all habitats. **RANGE** Nov.–Mar.: NV, UT, n AZ, n NM.

CEDAR WAXWING
Bombycilla cedrorum
WAXWING FAMILY

7″. Soft brown (incl. crest); belly yellow; eye mask black, edged in white; tail gray with yellow band at tip; secondaries red-tipped. Flies in tight flocks, esp. in winter. **VOICE** Call: high, thin *seee.* **HABITAT** Woodland edges, shrubs, gardens. **RANGE** May–Sept.: mtns. of n NV, n UT. Oct.–May: all SW.

NORTHERN SHRIKE
Lanius excubitor
SHRIKE FAMILY

10″. Adult back and crown gray; white below; wings black with large white spot; narrow black eye mask; long black tail. Bill heavy, hooked. Preys on small birds and rodents. **VOICE** Call: loud *chek-chek.* **HABITAT** Trees in open country. **RANGE** Sept.–Mar.: n NV, UT, n AZ, n NM.

LOGGERHEAD SHRIKE
Lanius ludovicianus
SHRIKE FAMILY

9″. Gray above; white below; wide black eye mask; wings and tail mainly black. Bill heavy, hooked; feet short. Preys on large insects, lizards, small birds. **VOICE** Song: repeated phrases. Call: harsh *shack.* **HABITAT** Shrubby grassland, farms, deserts. **RANGE** Resident in SW.

EUROPEAN STARLING
Sturnus vulgaris
STARLING FAMILY

summer adult (left), winter adult (right)

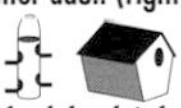

8″. Summer adult glossy green-purple; bill yellow. Winter adult blackish, heavily speckled with white; bill dark. Wings short, pointed, rusty-edged; legs dull red; tail square. Imm. gray-brown. Usu. in flocks. Introduced from Europe; detrimental to native birds; boldly takes over most nest holes and birdhouses, occupied or not; depletes wild fruit stock, feeder suet. **VOICE** Song: mix of whistles, squeals, chuckles; will mimic other birds. Calls: rising, then falling *hoooeee,* harsh *jeer.* **HABITAT** Cities, towns, farms, fields. **RANGE** Resident in all SW since 1950s.

PHAINOPEPLA
Phainopepla nitens
SILKY-FLYCATCHER FAMILY

7½″. Male glossy, dark purple; white on primaries in flight. Female dark gray, white wing bars. Crest pointed; eyes red; bill thin. Spreads mistletoe seeds. **VOICE** Song: short warbling. Call: low *wurp.* **HABITAT** Trees of desert washes; scrubland. **RANGE** Resident in s AZ. Apr.–Sept.: also s NV, sw UT, n AZ, c NM.

BELL'S VIREO
Vireo bellii
VIREO FAMILY

5″. Nondescript; gray above, dingy white below; 1 medium and (usu.) 1 short, thin white wing bar. **VOICE** Song: 3-part, raspy *needle needle me, needle needle you.* **HABITAT** Riverine woods, mesquite-lined desert washes. **RANGE** Apr.–Sept.: s NV, far sw UT, w, c, and s AZ, s NM.

GRAY VIREO
Vireo vicinior
VIREO FAMILY

5½″. Fairly dark gray above; 1 thin, whitish wing bar; paler gray below; crown and cheeks gray; very thin white eye ring. **VOICE** Song: fast *chawee chawee.* **HABITAT** Oak scrub, juniper, open woods. **RANGE** Apr.–Sept.: s NV, s UT, n, c and se AZ, w and s NM.

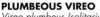

PLUMBEOUS VIREO
Vireo plumbeus (solitarius)
VIREO FAMILY

5½″. Head and upperparts slaty gray; 2 white wing bars; sides pale gray; spectacles and throat white. **VOICE** Song: low, burry phrases with long pauses. Call: husky *churr.* **HABITAT** Forests, woodlands. **RANGE** Apr.–Sept.: mtns. of NV, UT, nw, c, and se AZ, w and c NM. A few winter in s AZ.

HUTTON'S VIREO
Vireo huttoni
VIREO FAMILY

4½″. Crown and upperparts dark olive-gray; pale dingy olive-gray below; 2 white wing bars; eye ring white, incomplete at top. **VOICE** Song: oft-repeated *zu-weep.* Call: hoarse *day-dee-dee.* **HABITAT** Evergreen oak woodlands, mixed forests in mtns. **RANGE** Resident in c, se AZ, sw NM.

WARBLING VIREO
Vireo gilvus
VIREO FAMILY

5". Drab-looking. Pale gray above, with slight olive cast; dusky white below; no wing bars; eyebrow white. **VOICE** Song: melodious warbling. Call: wheezy *twee*. **HABITAT** Broadleaf woodlands. **RANGE** mid-Mar.–May, Aug.–Sept.: all SW. Breeds n and c NV, UT, n, c, and se AZ, NM.

Wood Warblers

Warblers native to the New World, often called wood warblers, were once dubbed subfamily Parulinae, part of the warbler, grosbeak, and sparrow family (Emberizidae). They are are now considered their own family, Parulidae. Many adult males have the same plumage year-round, but some have breeding (summer) and nonbreeding (winter) plumages. Females, fall males, and immature birds often have a trace of the summer male pattern. They are confusing at first; consult specialized field guides. Each species has a distinct song, but the call tends to be a simple *chip*. During the summer, these birds breed in a variety of woodland and scrub habitats. Most nests are cups on small forks of branches or hidden under bushes. Warblers glean insects from leaves with their thin, unhooked bills. In early autumn, most return to Mexico or Central and South America. Many are in serious decline because of habitat destruction. A number of "eastern" warblers occur in both spring and fall migrations at moist wooded sites.

ORANGE-CROWNED WARBLER
Vermivora celata
WOOD WARBLER FAMILY

5". Very plain. Adult gray; back and wings olive-green; olive-yellow below. Imm. head and back grayish; pale olive below; vent yellow. **VOICE** Song: high trill, tapers at end. **HABITAT** Woodlands, thickets. **RANGE** Apr.–Sept.: mtns. of NV, UT, ec AZ, and NM; Mar.–May, Aug.–Nov.: all SW. Dec.–Feb.: AZ.

NASHVILLE WARBLER
Vermivora ruficapilla
WOOD WARBLER FAMILY

4¼". Back, wings, and tail olive-green; no wing bars; throat and underparts clear, unstriped yellow; most of head gray with white eye ring. **VOICE** Song: 2-part *see-it see-it see-it titititititi*. **HABITAT** Young broadleaf forests, woodland edges. **RANGE** May–Sept.: w NV. mid-Mar.–May, Aug.–Sept.: all SW.

VIRGINIA'S WARBLER

Vermivora virginiae

WOOD WARBLER FAMILY

4½". Plain gray above; throat, upper chest, and rump yellow; belly whitish; thin white eye ring. **VOICE** Song: colorless *chip-chip-chip-chip-wik-wik*. Call: *chink*. **HABITAT** Brushy areas, pinyon-juniper woodlands in mtn. canyons. **RANGE** Apr.–Sept.: s and e NV, UT, n, c, and se AZ; NM.

LUCY'S WARBLER

Vermivora luciae

WOOD WARBLER FAMILY

4¼". Adult plain gray above, with thin white eye ring; rump rufous; whitish below. Male has rufous crown patch. **VOICE** Song: high *wheeta wheeta chi chi chi*. **HABITAT** Shrubby areas in deserts, foothills. **RANGE** Mar.–Sept.: s NV; sw UT; w, c, and s AZ, s NM.

Audubon's race summer male (left), female (right)

YELLOW-RUMPED WARBLER

"Audubon's Warbler"

Dendroica coronata (auduboni)

WOOD WARBLER FAMILY

5½". Audubon's race summer male: gray above, with black streaks; chest black; belly white; yellow rump, throat, crown, sides; large white wing patch; broken white eye ring. Summer female: gray-brown above; whitish below, streaked brown. Winter adults and imm.: brown, heavily striped. **VOICE** Song: warbling *seet-seet-seet-seet-turrrr*. Call: soft *check*. **HABITAT** Summer: coniferous forests. Winter: Woodlands, thickets. **RANGE** Apr.–Oct.: NV, UT, n, c, and se AZ, NM. Sept.–May: lowlands s NV, w and s AZ, s NM.

BLACK-THROATED GRAY WARBLER

Dendroica nigrescens

WOOD WARBLER FAMILY

5". Adult male gray above; white below, with black streaks; 2 white wing bars; head pied; lore spot yellow. Adult female and imm. have white chin. **VOICE** Song: buzzy *weze-weze-weze-weze-weet*. **HABITAT** Oak, pinyon, juniper. **RANGE** Apr.–Sept.: NV, UT, n, c, and se AZ, w and c NM. Oct.–Mar.: few winter in s AZ.

YELLOW WARBLER male, female
Dendroica petechia
WOOD WARBLER FAMILY
5″. Male olive-yellow above; head, underparts bright yellow; chest has rusty stripes. Female lacks stripes. **VOICE** Song: rapid *sweet sweet sweet, I'm so sweet.* **HABITAT** Shrubby areas, esp. watersides, to 9,000′. **RANGE** May–Sept.: all SW, ex. sw AZ deserts. Apr.–May, Sept.: all SW.

TOWNSEND'S WARBLER
Dendroica townsendi
WOOD WARBLER FAMILY
5″. Male greenish above; breast yellow with black streaks; 2 white wing bars; head black and yellow. Female throat yellow. **VOICE** Song: buzzy *zir zir-zir-zir-see-see.* Call: soft *chip.* **HABITAT** Lowland woods, mtn. pine-oak forests. **RANGE** Apr.–May, Aug.–Oct. (esp. mtns.): all SW.

HERMIT WARBLER
Dendroica occidentalis
WOOD WARBLER FAMILY
5″. Male gray above, clear white below; 2 white wing bars; forehead and face yellow; rear of crown and throat black. Female has little or no black on throat. **VOICE** Song: *sweety-sweety-sweety-chup-chup* **HABITAT** Conifer forests. **RANGE** Apr.–May, Aug.–Oct.: forested mtns. of SW.

GRACE'S WARBLER
Dendroica graciae
WOOD WARBLER FAMILY
5″. Gray above, 2 white wing bars; eyebrow, throat, and upper chest yellow; belly white with black streaks on sides. Female paler above. **VOICE** Song: pleasing *chedle chedle che-che-che-che.* **HABITAT** Pine forests. **RANGE** Apr.–Sept.: s NV mtns., s UT, n, c, and se AZ, w and c NM.

MACGILLIVRAY'S WARBLER
Oporornis tolmiei
WOOD WARBLER FAMILY
5″. Male olive above, yellow below; head slaty gray, throat scaled black. Female has white throat. Eye ring white, incomplete; legs pink. **VOICE** Song: loud *chitle-chitle-chitle-cheer-cheer.* Call: loud *check.* **HABITAT** Woodland undergrowth. **RANGE** Apr.–Sept.: n and c NV, UT, n AZ mtns., NM. Apr.–May, Aug.–Oct: all SW.

COMMON YELLOWTHROAT
Geothlypis trichas
WOOD WARBLER FAMILY

5″. Male olive above; throat and chest yellow; broad white line above black mask. Female head olive. **VOICE** Song: rollicking *witchity-witchity-witchity-witch.* Call: flat *chep.* **HABITAT** Marshes, riverine thickets, lake edges. **RANGE** Apr.–Sept.: all SW. Oct.–Mar.: s and w AZ.

WILSON'S WARBLER
Wilsonia pusilla
WOOD WARBLER FAMILY

4¾″. Male olive above; face and underparts yellow; cap round, black. Female has trace of black cap. **VOICE** Song: rapid, thin *chi chi chi chi jet jet.* **HABITAT** Woodland edges, waterside thickets. **RANGE** Apr.–Sept.: n and c NV, UT. Mar.–May, Aug.–Oct.: all SW. Some winter in s AZ.

RED-FACED WARBLER
Cardellina rubrifrons
WOOD WARBLER FAMILY

5¼″. Sexes alike: gray above; 1 white wing bar; below whitish; head bright red, ex. for black "headphone" patch and white nape. **VOICE** Song: a pleasing *tink tink tink tsee tsee suu sweet.* **HABITAT** Pine-oak forests above 6,000′. **RANGE** Apr.–mid-Sept.: c and se AZ, sw NM.

PAINTED REDSTART
"Painted Whitestart"
Myioborus pictus
WOOD WARBLER FAMILY

5½″. Mainly black; wing patch and outer tail feathers white; belly bright rose. **VOICE** Song: ringing *weetah weetah weetah weee.* Call: 2-note *klee-it.* **HABITAT** Pine-oak woodlands. **RANGE** mid-Mar.–Sept: c and se AZ, sw NM. Winter: few in se AZ.

YELLOW-BREASTED CHAT
Icteria virens
WOOD WARBLER FAMILY

7″. The largest warbler. Olive above; throat and breast yellow; "spectacles" white; lores black in male, gray in female. Low, fluttering, courtship flight. Tail fairly long. **VOICE** Song: long series of scolds, whistles, and soft, crow-like *caw* notes. Call: loud *chack.* **HABITAT** Dense thickets, riverine scrub. **RANGE** Apr.–Sept.: all SW.

OLIVE WARBLER
Peucedramus taeniatus
OLIVE WARBLER FAMILY

5″. Male gray above, 2 white wing bars. Head and chest burnt orange; face mask black; belly whitish. Female head and chest yellow. **VOICE** Song: loud *peeta peeta peeta.* Call: short whistle. **HABITAT** Open pine forests in mtns. **RANGE** Mar.–Sept.: c and se AZ, sw NM.

HEPATIC TANAGER
Piranga flava
TANAGER FAMILY

7½″. Thick bill pale gray. Male back, wings, cheek patch grayish; crown, underparts red. Female olive-gray above; crown, chest yellow. **VOICE** Song: pleasing jumble. Call: flat *tup.* **HABITAT** Pine-oak woods of mtn. canyons. **RANGE** Apr.–Sept.: c and se AZ, w and c NM; few in s NV, sw UT.

SUMMER TANAGER male, female
Piranga rubra
TANAGER FAMILY

7½″. Adult male entirely rosy red. Female yellowish olive. Bill thick, whitish, conical. **VOICE** Song: melodious; oft-repeated *chur wee sue weet.* Call: fast *trick-ee dick-ee.* **HABITAT** Riverine woods, foothill canyons. **RANGE** mid-Apr.–Sept.: s NV, far sw UT, w, c, and se AZ, s NM.

WESTERN TANAGER
Piranga ludoviciana
TANAGER FAMILY

7″. In all plumages yellow underparts, blackish wings with 1 yellow, 1 white wing bar. Summer male has red head, black back. Bill conical. **VOICE** Song: 3 slurred, hoarse phrases. Call: *per-dick.* **HABITAT** Mtn. forests, woods. **RANGE** Apr.–May, Aug.–Sept.: all SW. June–Aug.: mtns. of all SW.

PYRRHULOXIA
"Silver Cardinal"
Cardinalis sinuatus
GROSBEAK FAMILY

8″. Adults silvery; crest wings and tail reddish; bill yellow, parrot-like. Adult male has red face and midchest. **VOICE** Song: series of *queenk* notes; repeated *whit cheer.* Call: flat *chip.* **HABITAT** Desert scrub, bushy grasslands, wooded canyons. **RANGE** s AZ, s NM.

BLACK-HEADED GROSBEAK
Pheucticus melanocephalus
GROSBEAK FAMILY

7½″. Adult male head black; chest, sides, and rump rusty orange; wing has white patches. Female head striped brown; buffy orange below. **VOICE** Song: sweet, fast warble. Call: low *eek.* **HABITAT** Mtn. forests, thickets. **RANGE** Apr.–Sept.: all SW, ex. sw AZ deserts.

NORTHERN CARDINAL
Cardinalis cardinalis
GROSBEAK FAMILY

male (left), female (right)

9″. Male grayish red above; underparts, crest, and cheeks bright red; black face encircles thick, red bill. Female buffy brown; top of crest red; face black; bill red; wings and tail dusky red. Imm. like female, but bill black. Sought-after feeder bird that likes sunflower and safflower seeds, cracked corn. **VOICE** Song: pleasing clear whistles; variations on *wait wait wait cheer cheer cheer.* Call: short *chip.* **HABITAT** Desert scrub, wooded foothill canyons, towns. **RANGE** Resident in c and se AZ, s NM.

BLUE GROSBEAK
Guiraca caerulea
GROSBEAK FAMILY

7″. Adult male dark blue; shoulder and wing bar chestnut; face black. Female and imm. brown; 2 buffy wing bars. Bill thick, silvery. Feeds on ground. **VOICE** Song: sweet, warbled phrases. Call: loud *chink.* **HABITAT** Brushy pastures, thickets, mesquite grassland. **RANGE** May–Oct.: s NV, s and e UT, AZ (ex. w deserts), NM.

LAZULI BUNTING
Passerina amoena
GROSBEAK FAMILY

5½″. Male pale azure blue above; 2 white wing bars; chest rusty orange; belly white. Female brown; 2 buffy wing bars. **VOICE** Song: series of rising and falling warbles. Call: short *pit.* **HABITAT** Riverine woodlands, thickets. **RANGE** Apr.–Sept.: NV, UT, n AZ, n NM. Apr.–May, Aug.–Sept.: all SW. A few winter in s AZ.

GREEN-TAILED TOWHEE

Pipilo chlorurus

AMERICAN SPARROW FAMILY

7". Adult olive above; face, neck, and sides gray; crown rufous; black mustache on white; throat white. **VOICE** Song: slurred *weet-weet-churrr.* Call: cat-like *meeow.* **HABITAT** Thickets, desert scrub. **RANGE** Apr.–Oct.: n and c NV, UT, n and c AZ, n NM. Sept.–Apr.: s AZ, s NM.

SPOTTED TOWHEE

male (left), female (right)

"Rufous-sided Towhee"

Pipilo maculatus

AMERICAN SPARROW FAMILY

8". Male head, chest, rump, and tail black; back and wings black, with many white spots; sides rufous; mid-belly white. Female: brown replaces black of male. Eyes red; tail corners and outer feathers white. Juv. streaked below. Scratches on ground under brush. **VOICE** Song: long, buzzy *cheweeeee.* Call: cat-like *meee.* **HABITAT** Understories of forests, thickets. **RANGE** Resident in mtns. of NV, UT, n, c, and se AZ, NM. Some descend to lowland valleys in winter.

CANYON TOWHEE

Pipilo fuscus

AMERICAN SPARROW FAMILY

8½". Plain brown above, pale gray below. Crown rufous; throat buffy; necklace of brown dots; large brown chest spot; eye yellow. Tail long, rounded, no white; Feeds on ground. **VOICE** Song: chipping trill. Call: rising *chee-up.* **HABITAT** Brushy foothill canyons, arid desert scrub. **RANGE** Resident in c and s AZ, most of NM.

ABERT'S TOWHEE

Pipilo aberti

AMERICAN SPARROW FAMILY

8½". Above dark grayish brown; below pale buffy-grayish without dotted necklace. Black mask encircles bill. Eye yellow; crown brown, not rufous. **VOICE** Song: rapid *chink chink chink chink.* Call: sharp *peek.* **HABITAT** Heavy brush along desert washes. **RANGE** Resident in s NV, far sw UT, w, c, and se AZ, sw NM.

CASSIN'S SPARROW
Aimophila cassinii
AMERICAN SPARROW FAMILY

5½". Back, rump, and crown pale gray with brown stripes; head fairly flat; long, rounded tail with white corners. Best identified by its "skylarking" flight song. **VOICE** Song: *tea tea tsseeeeee tay tay;* long, high note in middle. **HABITAT** Open arid grasslands with scattered bushes. **RANGE** Apr.–Sept.: c and se AZ, s, c, and e NM.

RUFOUS-CROWNED SPARROW
Aimophila ruficeps
AMERICAN SPARROW FAMILY

5½". Striped rufous above; clear grayish below; rufous crown; black mustache. Tail rounded. **VOICE** Song: a few *mew* notes, then a wrenlike warble. Call: thin *mew*, nasal, repeated *dear*. **HABITAT** Rocky areas with brush. **RANGE** Resident in nw, c, and s AZ, s, c, and ne NM.

CHIPPING SPARROW
Spizella passerina
AMERICAN SPARROW FAMILY

5½". Summer: brown above, gray below; cap rufous; eyebrow white; eye line black. Winter: crown striped brown. **VOICE** Song: series of 20 dry *chip* notes. **HABITAT** Woodland edges, fields, farms. **RANGE** Apr.–Oct.: n and c NV, UT, n, c, and se AZ, NM. Oct.–Apr.: w and s AZ, s NM.

BREWER'S SPARROW
Spizella breweri
AMERICAN SPARROW FAMILY

5½". Back and crown buffy brown, finely streaked; clear grayish below. **VOICE** Song: series of long musical trills. Call: soft *seep,* given in flight. **HABITAT** Sagebrush deserts, weedy fields. **RANGE** Apr.–Oct.: NV, UT, n AZ, nw NM. Sept.–Apr.: w, c, and s AZ, s NM.

VESPER SPARROW
Pooecetes gramineus
AMERICAN SPARROW FAMILY

6". Pale brown with darker stripes above and below; small rusty shoulder patch; 2 buffy wing bars; white outer tail feathers. **VOICE** Song: melodious *slurr-slurr-slee-slee-teuw-teuw-teuw.* **HABITAT** Grasslands, sagebrush deserts. **RANGE** Mar.–Nov.: n and c NV, UT, n AZ, n NM. Oct.–Apr.: w, c, and s AZ, s NM.

LARK SPARROW
Chondestes grammacus
AMERICAN SPARROW FAMILY

6″. Striped brown above; white below; black spot on chest. Harlequin head pattern. Tail edged white. **VOICE** Song: complicated, broken trills, buzzes, clear notes. Call: sharp *tsip*. **HABITAT** Grasslands, deserts, farms. **RANGE** Apr.–Sept.: NV, UT; n, c, and se AZ, NM. Sept.–Apr.: s AZ, s NM.

BLACK-THROATED SPARROW
Amphispiza bilineata
AMERICAN SPARROW FAMILY

5″. Adult dark brown above, white below; crown and cheeks gray; eyebrow and mustache white; black throat becomes V on chest. **VOICE** Song: sweet *chit chit cheeeeeeee*. **HABITAT** Desert scrub, sagebrush. **RANGE** Apr.–Sept.: all SW, ex. forested mtns. Sept–Apr.: w and s AZ, s NM.

SAGE SPARROW
Amphispiza belli
AMERICAN SPARROW FAMILY

6″. Gray above; white below with black breast spot, fine side stripes; weak white eyebrow, black mustache. **VOICE** Song: soft *sit-sit-soo-see-say-soo-see*. **HABITAT** Sagebrush, desert scrub. **RANGE** Mar.–Nov.: n and c NV, UT, nc AZ, nw NM. Oct.–Mar.: s NV, AZ, w and s NM.

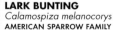

LARK BUNTING
Calamospiza melanocorys
AMERICAN SPARROW FAMILY

summer male (left), female (right)

7″. Summer male all black, ex. for large white wing patch; bill thick, gray. Female and winter male look like heavy sparrow: brown above with darker streaks; white eye line over brown cheek; creamy wing patch; white with brown stripes below. Dense flocks in migration and winter. **VOICE** Song: whistles, trills, and slurs, each repeated up to 10 times. **HABITAT** Prairie grasslands, weedy fields, feedlots, roadsides. **RANGE** May–Sept.: n UT, e NM, Aug.–Apr.: w and s AZ, s NM.

SAVANNAH SPARROW
Passerculus sandwichensis
AMERICAN SPARROW FAMILY

5½″. Blackish stripes on brown back and whitish breast; eyebrow all or partly yellow. Small bill and legs pink. Tail short, notched. **VOICE** Song: high, buzzy *zit zit zit zeee zaaay.* Call: light *tzip.* **HABITAT** Open grasslands, farm fields. **RANGE** Apr.–Oct.: NV, UT, n NM. Sept.–Apr.: s NV, w and s AZ, s NM.

FOX SPARROW
Passerella iliaca
AMERICAN SPARROW FAMILY

7″. Grayish brown above; wings and long tail tinged rufous; heavily spotted below. **VOICE** Song: musical series of clear whistles. Call: sharp *chink.* **HABITAT** Forest understories, thickets. **RANGE** Apr.–Oct.: mtns. of NV, n and c UT. Apr.–Oct.: all SW. Nov.–Mar.: s AZ, s and e NM.

SONG SPARROW
Melospiza melodia
AMERICAN SPARROW FAMILY

6¼″. Brown stripes on back (pale brown in desert) and on white underparts; eyebrow grayish; chest has central dark spot. **VOICE** Song: sweet *zeet zeet zeee diddle diddle dee.* **HABITAT** Shrubs, marshes, fields. **RANGE** Resident in NV, UT, much of AZ, n NM.

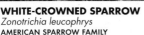

WHITE-CROWNED SPARROW
adult (left), immature (right)

Zonotrichia leucophrys
AMERICAN SPARROW FAMILY

7″. Adult back brown, with heavy black streaks; unstriped gray below; 2 thin white wing bars; crown striped black and white; bill pink or yellow. Imm. crown striped brown and buff. **VOICE** Song: 1–3 clear notes, then a trill. Call: sharp *pink.* **HABITAT** Forests, thickets, towns. **RANGE** Apr.–Sept.: mtns. of NV, UT. Sept.–Apr.: widespread all SW. **White-throated Sparrow** *(Z. albicollis)* has a distinct white throat, yellow lores; winters NM, s AZ.

LINCOLN'S SPARROW
Melospiza lincolnii
AMERICAN SPARROW FAMILY

5½". Striped brown above; chest buffy, with fine black streaks; head striped gray. **VOICE** Song: musical gurgling. Call: flat *chup*, buzzy *zeee*. **HABITAT** Summer: bogs. Winter: thickets. **RANGE** Apr.–Sept.: mtns. of w NV and UT (local). Mar.–May, Sept.–Oct.: all SW. Oct.–Apr.: s NV, s AZ, s NM.

DARK-EYED JUNCO
Junco hyemalis
AMERICAN SPARROW FAMILY

6". Gray-headed race: gray above, ex. rusty back; whitish below; eyes dark; white outer tail feather. Often in flocks. **VOICE** Song: loose musical trill. Call: light *smack*. **HABITAT** Woodlands, brush. **RANGE** Apr.–Oct.: mtns. of NV, UT; n and c AZ; NM mtns. Oct.–Mar.: all SW.

YELLOW-EYED JUNCO
Junco phaeonotus
AMERICAN SPARROW FAMILY

5½". Basically gray with rusty back; lores black, eye yellow, outer tail feathers white; bill dark above, pink below. **VOICE** Song: musical *chit chit chit weedle weedle che che che che che*. Call: *seet*. **HABITAT** Floor of mtn. pine-oak and fir forests. **RANGE** Resident in se AZ and sw NM mtns.

RED-WINGED BLACKBIRD

breeding male (left), female (right)

Agelaius phoeniceus
BLACKBIRD FAMILY

9". Male all glossy black, with red shoulder bordered by yellow; yellow and much of red less visible during nonbreeding months. Female heavily streaked brown; crown and eye line dark brown; eyebrow buffy. Bill fairly long, pointed; eyes black; tail medium length, rounded. In winter, feeds and roosts in huge groups with other blackbirds, starlings, and cowbirds. **VOICE** Song: gurgling *conk-a-ree*. Calls: harsh *check*; high *tee-eek*. Calls from trees, shrubs, tall reeds. **HABITAT** Marshes, fields, feedlots; withdraws from higher mtns. in winter. **RANGE** Resident in all SW.

WESTERN MEADOWLARK
Sturnella neglecta
BLACKBIRD FAMILY

10″. Speckled brown above; throat and breast yellow; chest has black V; crown striped brown and white; outer tail feathers white. **VOICE** Song: low, flute-like *too tee too tiddleyou.* Call: *chupp.* **HABITAT** Grasslands. **RANGE** Resident in NV, UT, n and c AZ, n and c NM. Sept.–Mar.: also s AZ, s NM.

YELLOW-HEADED BLACKBIRD
Xanthocephalus xanthocephalus
BLACKBIRD FAMILY

10″. Male black; head and chest yellow; white patch on wing. Female dark brown; eyebrow, throat, chest yellow. Nests in colonies. **VOICE** Song: gurgling *choke-a-weee.* Call: *kruck.* **HABITAT** Marshes, feedlots. **RANGE** Apr.–Oct.: NV, UT, w and ec AZ, n NM. Sept.–Apr.: w and s AZ, s NM.

BREWER'S BLACKBIRD
Euphagus cyanocephalus
BLACKBIRD FAMILY

9″. Male black with iridescent purple sheen; eyes yellow. Female all grayish brown; eyes dark. Bill thin. In enormous roosts at night. **VOICE** Song: creaky squeak. Call: *chek.* **HABITAT** Farms, parks, grasslands. **RANGE** Resident in NV, UT, n AZ, n NM. Sept.–Apr.: also c and s AZ, c and s NM.

GREAT-TAILED GRACKLE
Quiscalus mexicanus
BLACKBIRD FAMILY

Male 15″; female 11″. Male purplish black; tail long, wedged-shaped. Female dark brown above; underparts buffy; tail flat. Eyes yellow. Often in flocks. **VOICE** Series of harsh creaks and whistles. **HABITAT** Farms, marshes, towns. **RANGE** Apr.–Oct.: s NV, s UT, AZ, NM. Resident in s AZ, s NM.

BRONZED COWBIRD
Molothrus aeneus
BLACKBIRD FAMILY

8″. Male glossy black with bluish shine above. Female solid grayish brown. Both sexes have red eye. Displaying male raises ruff on back of neck. Female lays single egg in nest of other birds, esp. orioles. **VOICE** Song: mechanical squeaks. Call: low *chuk.* **HABITAT** Short grass of lawns, fields; feedlots. **RANGE** Apr.–Aug.: c and se AZ. Some winter in s AZ.

BROWN-HEADED COWBIRD male (left), female (right)
Molothrus ater
BLACKBIRD FAMILY

7″. Adult male dark, shiny, greenish black, with brown head. Adult female uniformly dull brown. Juv. brownish, paler below, faintly streaked. Bill conical. Travels in tight flocks outside nesting season. Female lays single eggs in several nests of native songbirds; baby cowbird pushes out other eggs and babies and is raised by foster parents. Implicated in the decline of many songbirds. **VOICE** Song: bubbly, creaking *bubble-lee come seee*. Flight call: high *weee teetee*. **HABITAT** Open fields, farms, lawns. **RANGE** May–Sept.: all SW, ex. w AZ. Sept.–May: s NV, w and s AZ, s NM.

HOODED ORIOLE
Icterus cucullatus
BLACKBIRD FAMILY

7½″. Adult male back, wings, and tail black; wing bars white; head, underparts orange; black patch from eye to chest. Female olive above, yellow below; 2 faint wing bars. **VOICE** Song: *chut-chut-chut whew-whew*. **HABITAT** Shade trees, esp. palms. **RANGE** Mar.–Aug.: s NV, w, c, and s AZ; sw NM.

BULLOCK'S ORIOLE
Icterus bullockii
BLACKBIRD FAMILY

8″. Adult male black above, ex. white wing patch; orange below with black bib. Female olive above; 2 white wing bars; throat yellow; belly whitish. **VOICE** Song: 4–8 musical whistles. Call: rapid chatter. **HABITAT** Broadleaf woodlands, towns. **RANGE** Apr.–Sept.: all SW, ex. sw AZ. Few winter in AZ.

SCOTT'S ORIOLE
Icterus parisorum
BLACKBIRD FAMILY

8″. Adult male back, wings, head, chest, and part of tail black; wing bar white; shoulder, belly, and base of tail lemon yellow. Female olive above, yellow below; 2 white wing bars. **VOICE** Song: clear, whistled phrases. Call: loud *chak*. **HABITAT** Desert scrub, dry wooded hillsides, yucca. **RANGE** Mar.–Sept.: s NV, s UT, AZ, most of NM.

CASSIN'S FINCH
Carpodacus cassinii
FINCH FAMILY

6″. Male striped brown above; chest rosy; sides lightly streaked; crown red; cheeks striped brown. Female heavily striped brown. **VOICE** Song: lively, fluty warbling. Call: high *pwee-de-lip.* **HABITAT** Woodlands, parks. **RANGE** May–Oct.: mtns. of NV, UT, n AZ, nw NM. Oct.–Apr.: lowlands of all SW (erratic).

HOUSE FINCH
male (left), female (right)

Carpodacus mexicanus
FINCH FAMILY

5½″. Male back, mid-crown, wings, and tail brown; sides and belly whitish, streaked brown; 2 pale wing bars; wide eyebrow, throat, chest, and rump rosy red. Female upperparts and head plain dull brown; dusky below, with brown streaks. Abundant; often nests in hanging planters. **VOICE** Song: musical warbling ending with a down-slurred *jeer.* **HABITAT** Cities, residential areas, backyards; farms, desert, woods. **RANGE** Resident in all SW.

RED CROSSBILL
Loxia curvirostra
FINCH FAMILY

6″. Adult male brick red; wings and tail blackish. Adult female head and body yellow-olive. Tips of bill cross; bill used for prying seeds from conifer cones. **VOICE** Song: *chipa-chipa-chipa-che-chee-chee.* Call: sharp, repeated *kip.* **HABITAT** Coniferous forests. **RANGE** Resident in mtns. of all SW.

PINE SISKIN
Carduelis pinus
FINCH FAMILY

5″. Very heavily striped brown above and below; wing has yellow stripe. Bill thin, pointed. **VOICE** Song: wheezy trills and warbles mixed with calls. Calls: loud *clee-up* and rising *shreee.* **HABITAT** Coniferous and mixed woodlands, yards. **RANGE** Resident in mtns. of SW. Oct.–Apr.: some disperse into lowlands.

LESSER GOLDFINCH
Carduelis psaltria
FINCH FAMILY

4½". Adult male back, cheeks, and rump olive; crown, wings, and tail black; wing has white patches; yellow below. In NM, male black above. Female greenish above, yellow below; 2 white wing bars. **VOICE** Song: repeated phrases. Call: rising *tee-yee,* falling *tee-yer.* **HABITAT** Woodland edges, brushy fields. **RANGE** Resident in SW.

AMERICAN GOLDFINCH
Carduelis tristis
FINCH FAMILY

5". Summer male yellow; cap, wings, tail black. Summer female olive above; yellow below. In winter brownish; yellow throat. **VOICE** Song: canary-like. Call: *per chicory;* rising *sweee-eat.* **HABITAT** Fields, forest edges, yards. **RANGE** Resident: n and c NV, UT. Nov.–Apr.: also s NV, AZ, NM.

EVENING GROSBEAK
Coccothraustes vespertinus
FINCH FAMILY

8". Male brown; yellow below; head dark brown; wings black, white secondaries. Female gray-brown; wings black, white spots. Bill thick, ivory. **VOICE** Song: short warble. Call: ringing *cleeer.* **HABITAT** Mixed woodlands. **RANGE** Resident: mtns. of NV, AZ, and NM. Nov.–Apr.: erratic in all SW.

HOUSE SPARROW
male (left), female (right)
Passer domesticus
OLD WORLD SPARROW FAMILY

6". Male rufous streaked with black above; underparts, crown, cheeks, rump gray; 1 white wing bar; throat and upper chest black (only chin black in winter); chestnut stripe behind eye. Female brown with blackish back streaks, buffy streak above eye; paler below. Abundant European import. Like Starlings and Brown-headed Cowbirds, exerts profound, negative effect on many songbird species. Hogs seed at feeders; kills nestlings and eggs of other birds when taking over nest cavities. **VOICE** Song: frequent *chireep* and *chereep* notes. Call: *chir-rup.* **HABITAT** Cities, parks, farms, mtns. **RANGE** Resident in all SW.

Mammals

All members of the vertebrate class Mammalia are warm-blooded and able to maintain a near-constant body temperature. Males generally have an external penis for direct internal fertilization of the female's eggs. Almost all mammals are born live rather than hatching from eggs (exceptions are the Platypus and the echidnas of Australasia). Mammary glands, unique to mammals, produce milk that is high in nutrients and fat and promotes rapid growth in the young. Mammals have abundant skin glands, used for temperature regulation (sweating), coat maintenance, territory-marking, sex and species recognition, breeding cycle signals, and even defense, as in skunks and others that can repel predators with powerful secretions.

Eight mammalian orders are represented in the Southwest, including humans (members of the primate order). Opossums (order Didelphimorphia) give birth to young in an embryonic state; they then develop in a separate fur-lined pouch on the mother's belly. The tiny energetic shrews and moles (Insectivora), which eat insects and other invertebrates, have long snouts, short dense fur, and five toes on each foot. Bats (Chiroptera), with their enlarged, membrane-covered forelimbs, are the only mammals that truly fly. Lagomorphs (hares, rabbits, and pikas) resemble large rodents but have four upper incisor teeth—a large front pair and a small pair directly behind them—that grow continuously, and five toes on their front feet and five in back; digits on all feet are very small. Rodents (Rodentia—including chipmunks, marmots, squirrels, mice, rats, muskrats, voles, porcupines, and beavers) have two upper incisor teeth that grow continuously, and most have four toes on their front feet and five in back. Carnivores (Carnivora)—bears, the Coyote, foxes, weasels, raccoons, and cats—have long canine teeth and sharp cheek teeth for killing and eating prey. The even-toed hoofed mammals (Artiodactyla), represented in the Southwest by peccaries, deer, the Pronghorn, goats, and sheep, have two or four toes that form a cloven hoof.

Most mammals have an insulating layer of fur that allows them to maintain a fairly constant body temperature independent of their surroundings, thus making them successful in cold climates. Many molt twice a year and have a noticeably thicker coat in winter. Some, such as certain weasels and hares, change colors, developing a concealing white coat in winter. The ability to maintain a high body temperature allows many mammals to prosper in below-freezing temperatures.

The body parts and appendages of mammals exhibit a wide and adaptive variety of sizes, shapes, and functions. Most mammals have well-developed eyes, ears, and noses that provide good night vision, hearing, and sense of smell. Mammalian teeth range from fine points for capturing insects (bats and insectivores) to chisel-like gnawing teeth (rabbits, rodents, and hoofed mammals), wide plant-crushers (rodents and hoofed mammals), and heavy, pointed instruments for flesh-ripping (carnivores). Mammals generally have four limbs. In many rodents, in some carnivores, and in primates, the ends of the forelimbs are modified into complex, manipulative hands. Solid hooves support the heavy weight of sheep, deer, and the Pronghorn.

In the species accounts that follow, the typical adult length given is from the tip of the nose to the end of the tail, followed by the tail length alone; for larger mammals, shoulder height is also given. Wingspan is given for bats, when known.

Mammal Signs and Tracks

The evidence that a particular animal is or has been in a certain area is called its "sign." The sign can be scat (fecal matter), burrow openings, nutshells, tracks, or other evidence. Tracks are a useful aid in confirming the presence of mammal species. Impressions vary depending on the substrate and whether the animal was walking or running. Animals can leave clear tracks in mud, dirt, snow, and sand, usually larger ones in wet mud and snow. Because animals come to ponds or streams to drink or feed, tracks are likely to be found on their shores; damp mud often records tracks in fine detail, sometimes showing claws or webbing. Prints in snow may leave a less clear impression but can often be followed for a long distance and may show the pattern of the animal's stride. The track drawings below, of selected mammals that live in the Southwest, are not to relative scale.

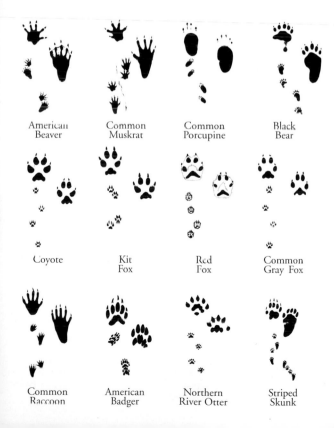

American Beaver

Common Muskrat

Common Porcupine

Black Bear

Coyote

Kit Fox

Red Fox

Common Gray Fox

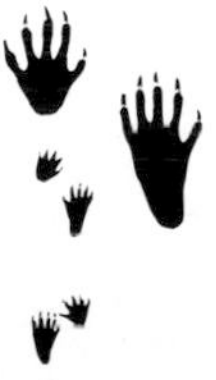

Common Raccoon

American Badger

Northern River Otter

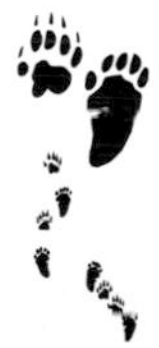

Striped Skunk

Mountain Lion

Bobcat

Collared Peccary

Elk

White-tailed Deer

Mule Deer

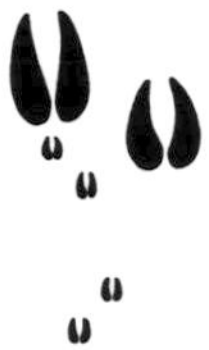

Pronghorn

Bighorn Sheep

VIRGINIA OPOSSUM

Didelphis virginiana

OPOSSUM FAMILY

L 30″; T 12″. Grizzled gray, with mix of black underfur and longer white guard hairs. Head pointed; nose long; face white, with long whiskers; ears small, round, black with white tip. Legs short, black; feet have 5 digits; hindfeet have opposable, grasping inner thumbs. Tail long, tapered, naked, pink with black base. Eats fruit, nuts, bird eggs, large insects, carrion. Hangs from branches using wrap-around, prehensile tail. If surprised at close range, may "play possum" (play dead). **BREEDING** 1–14 (avg. 8) pea-size young attach themselves to nipples in mother's pouch for 2 months; 2–3 litters per year. **SIGN** Tracks: 2″ hindprint, 3 middle toes close, outer toes well spread; foreprint slightly smaller, star-like. **HABITAT** Broadleaf woods, watersides, farms, coverts, residential areas. **ACTIVITY** Nocturnal; much less active in winter. **RANGE** se AZ, c, s, and e NM.

VAGRANT SHREW

Sorex vagrans

SHREW FAMILY

L 4″; T 2″. Reddish brown in summer, black in winter. Tail gray. Nose long, conical; eyes tiny; ears hidden on sides of head. Legs and feet short. Feeds on invertebrates and fungi in vole runways. **BREEDING** 2 litters of 2–9 young born in Feb.–May, Oct.–Nov. **HABITAT** Mixed forests, meadows, bogs. **ACTIVITY** Very active day and night, year-round. **RANGE** Mtns. of all SW.

Bats

Bats are the only mammals that truly fly (flying squirrels glide). The bones and muscles in the forelimbs of bats are elongated; thin, usually black, wing membranes are attached to four extremely long fingers. When bats are at rest, the wings are folded along the forearm; the short, claw-like thumbs are used for crawling about. Small insectivorous bats beat their wings six to eight times a second.

Bats are mainly nocturnal, though some species are occasionally active in the early morning and late afternoon. Their slender bodies are well-furred, and their eyesight, although not excellent, is quite adequate to detect predators and general landscape features. Most use echolocation (sonar) to locate flying insects and avoid obstacles. In flight, they emit dozens of high-frequency calls per second that rebound off objects. Their large ears receive these reflected sounds and the bats interpret them as they close in on prey or evade an obstacle. Echolocation sounds are mainly inaudible to humans, but bats also give shrill squeaks most humans can hear. By day, most bats hang upside-down from the ceilings of caves, tree hollows, or attics, using one or both feet. Members of solitary species may roost alone under a branch or in the foliage of a tall tree. In other species, large colonies gather in caves and under natural and manmade overhangs.

Parts of a Bat

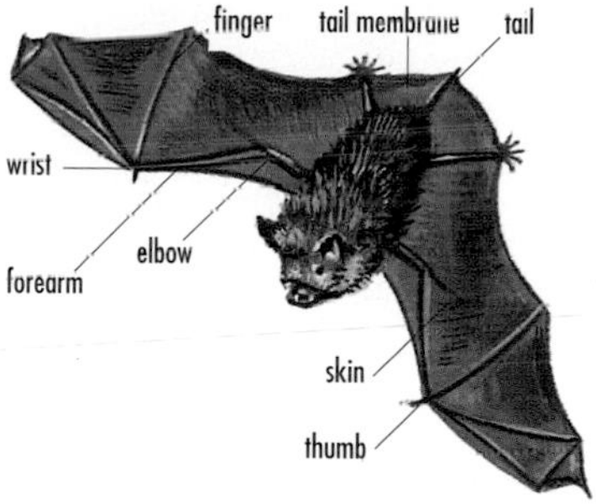

Echolocation

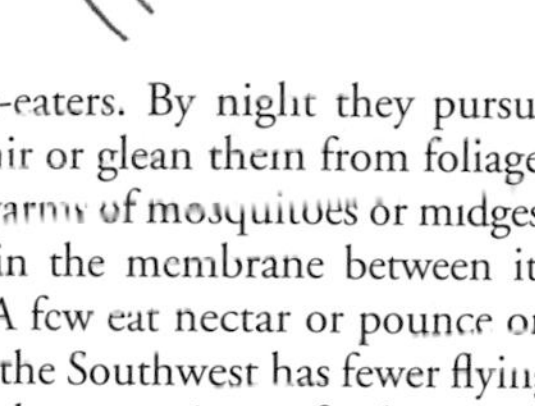

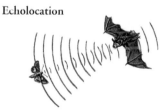

Most southwestern bats are insect-eaters. By night they pursue larger individual insects through the air or glean them from foliage. Some skim open-mouthed through swarms of mosquitoes or midges. A bat can trap a large flying insect in the membrane between its hindlegs, then seize it with its teeth. A few eat nectar or pounce on small animals on the ground. Because the Southwest has fewer flying insects in winter, bats either hibernate here or migrate further south to hibernate or feed in winter. Sheltered hibernation roosts provide protection from extreme cold. Many species are in decline due to habitat destruction, pesticides, and obliteration of colonies by vandals.

Watch for bats overhead on warm evenings, especially around water, where insects are abundant and where bats may skim the water surface to drink.

SOUTHERN LONG-NOSED BAT

Leptonycteris curasoae (sanborni)

LEAF-NOSED BAT FAMILY

L 3″. Above reddish brown, underparts buffy; nose long, with erect, leaf-like projection; medium-size ears; tail absent. Hovers or perches to lap nectar at night flowers. Also eats fruit, insects. Becoming rare; pollination of some cacti and agaves threatened. **BREEDING** 1–2 young born in Apr.–June. **HABITAT** Desert scrub, cactus forests. **ACTIVITY** Hangs in caves, mines, and buildings by day. Feeds late in evening. **RANGE** Spring–fall: sc and se AZ.

PALLID BAT

Antrozous pallidus

VESPERTILIONID BAT FAMILY

5″. Above creamy pale brown, below whitish; pink ears large, separated at base. Wing membranes pale, naked. Wingbeats fairly slow. Often feeds on ground; catches beetles, scorpions, crickets, grasshoppers, lizards. Gives variety of audible high-pitched calls. Has foul skunk-like odor. **BREEDING** 1–2 young born in May–June. **HABITAT** All SW; desert to mtn. forest. **ACTIVITY** Roosts of up to 100 in buildings, crevices. **RANGE** w and s NV, c and s UT, AZ, NM.

LITTLE BROWN MYOTIS

"Little Brown Bat"

Myotis lucifugus

VESPERTILIONID BAT FAMILY

L 3½″; WS 9″. Rich glossy brown above, buffy below. Face broad, blunt, furry; ears short, rounded, black. Often flies before dusk; flight erratic. Squeaks audible. Maternal colonies sometimes in thousands. **BREEDING** 1 young born in June. **HABITAT** Woodlands, fields, water; roosts and breeds in trees, caves, mines, attics. **ACTIVITY** Summer: active. Winter: hibernates in caves; emerges every 2 weeks without feeding. **RANGE** n and c NV, UT, ne NM.

HOARY BAT

Lasiurus cinereus

VESPERTILIONID BAT FAMILY

L 5″; WS 15″. Mahogany brown above, heavily frosted with white hairs; throat buffy yellow. Ears short, rounded, with naked black rims. Nose blunt. Tail membrane heavily furred, brown. Usu. solitary. Most migratory bat in SW; many winter in Chile or Argentina. **BREEDING** 2 young born in June. **HABITAT** Wooded areas; roosts in foliage of trees. **ACTIVITY** Emerges late in evening to feed on moths. **RANGE** Summer: all SW.

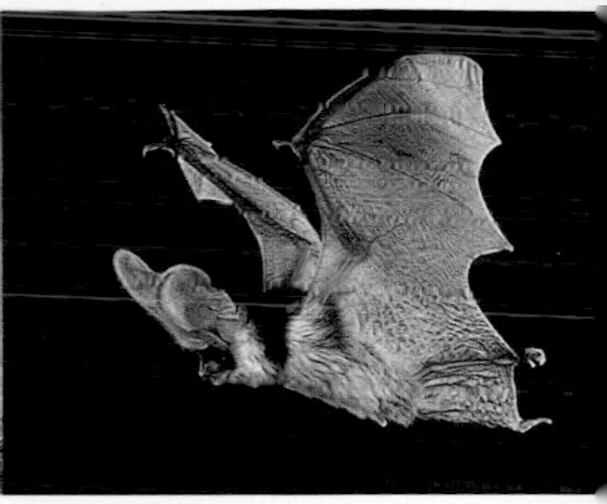

BIG BROWN BAT

Eptesicus fuscus

VESPERTILIONID BAT FAMILY

L 4½"; WS 12". Dark brown above, pale brown below. Wings and tail membranes furless. Face and ears broad, black. Flight straight, fast. Usu. in small groups. Flies later in autumn, earlier in spring than others. **BREEDING** 2 young born in June. **HABITAT** Roosts and breeds in attics, barns, tree hollows, behind shutters, under bridges; often in cities. **ACTIVITY** Spring–fall: active. Winter: hibernates. **RANGE** All SW, low to high elev.

SPOTTED BAT

Euderma maculatum

VESPERTILIONID BAT FAMILY

4½". Above dark sepia brown with large, round, white patches on rump and both shoulders; below white. Ears huge, long, pink, folded back at roost, bent forward in flight. Loud, high-pitched call. Feeds mainly on moths. Rare but spectacular-looking. **BREEDING** 1 young born in June. **HABITAT** Ponderosa pine belt in mtns., pinyon-juniper zone of plateau and mesa country. **ACTIVITY** Roosts in caves, cliffs by day; flies late in evening. **RANGE** s NV, s UT, AZ, w NM.

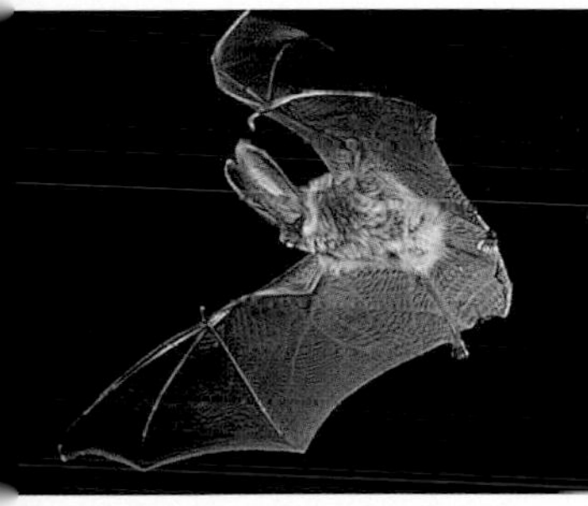

TOWNSEND'S BIG EARED BAT

Plecotus townsendii

VESPERTILIONID BAT FAMILY

L 4"; WS 13". Pale gray or brown above, buffy below. Enormous ears (to 1½") with rounded tip; joined in middle of crown; extend to middle of body when laid back. 2 large lumps on nose. **BREEDING** Females form nursery colonies in caves and buildings; 1 young born in May–June. **HABITAT** Open or forested areas with crevices for roosting, caves for hibernation. **ACTIVITY** Emerges in late evening to feed on moths. **RANGE** All SW; more common in mtns., plateaus.

BRAZILIAN FREE-TAILED BAT

"Mexican Free-tailed Bat"

Tadarida brasiliensis

VESPERTILIONID BAT FAMILY

4". Dark brown above; ears separated at base; outer half of tail, beyond membrane, free. Enormous colonies in some caves, incl., Carlsbad Caverns, NM. They exit caves by the 1000s; feed up to 150 miles away. **BREEDING** 1 young born in June. **HABITAT** Deserts, canyons, farms; low to mid-elev. **ACTIVITY** Roosts in mines, caves, buildings; flies from dusk on. **RANGE** Mar.–Oct.: w and c NV, c and s UT, AZ, NM. A few winter in caves.

Lagomorphs

Black-tailed Jackrabbit

Lagomorph families of the Southwest include, along with the more familiar hares and rabbits, the distinctive pikas. Pikas have four upper incisor teeth; rodents have only two. Pikas have short ears and hind limbs, no tail, and are restricted to rocky, mountainous habitats. The hares and rabbits, with their long ears and hindlegs, cotton-ball tails, and large eyes, are found everywhere else. Hares, including the misnamed jackrabbits (jackhares would be more correct), are larger and have longer ears than rabbits. Their powerful hind limbs allow them to obtain speeds of up to 35 mph for long distances and leaps of 20 feet. They do not build nests. Young hares are born with hair and can see and hop around within hours of birth, and follow their parents by the second day. True rabbits are smaller and dash off to nearby cover when startled. They line their nests, which are hidden, with fur, grasses, and leaves. Their young are born naked and blind; they need two weeks before they can face the world.

AMERICAN PIKA
"Cony"
Ochotona princeps
PIKA FAMILY

8½". Gray-brown. Ears round, black with white edges. Legs short; no visible tail. Sits on rock piles; gives bleats, jerks body. Feeds on stored hay under snow in winter. **BREEDING** 2–6 young born in May–June; occ. 2nd litter in Aug. **SIGN** Fresh hay amid rocks or out to dry in sun. Scat: round, black pellets; white urine stains on rocks. **HABITAT** Rocky slopes; usu. near timberline. **ACTIVITY** Mainly by day. **RANGE** Higher mtns. of w, c, and ne NV, UT, nc NM.

PYGMY RABBIT
Brachylagus idahoensis
HARE AND RABBIT FAMILY

L 11"; T 1". Slate gray with pinkish tinge. Ears fairly short (1½"), pale. White spot at side of nostril. Tail short, gray below. Digs own burrow system, unlike other rabbits. Scampers rather than leaps. Feeds on sagebrush leaves and grasses. **BREEDING** 4–8 young born in June–July. **SIGN** Burrows have 2–5 entrances, each entrance 3". **HABITAT** Clumps of tall sagebrush in deserts. **ACTIVITY** Appears by day, but mainly nocturnal. **RANGE** n and c NV, w UT (scarce and local).

DESERT COTTONTAIL
"Audubon's Cottontail"
Sylvilagus audubonii
HARE AND RABBIT FAMILY

L 15"; T 2". Buffy brown or pale gray washed yellow above, white below; nape rusty; ears slightly larger than Mountain. Runs up to 15 mph. Climbs up-ended logs to check for predators. **BREEDING** Several litters of 2–6 young born year-round. **SIGN** Piles of pellets on logs, stumps. **HABITAT** Grasslands, farms, Creosote Bush, deserts. **ACTIVITY** Day and night, year-round. **RANGE** c and s NV, w and e UT, most of AZ and NM.

EASTERN COTTONTAIL
Sylvilagus floridanus
HARE AND RABBIT FAMILY

L 17"; T 1½". Grayish brown; belly white. White eye ring. Ears to 2½" long, with thin black stripe on upper edges. Rusty wash on nape. Legs buffy. **BREEDING** 4–5 young; several litters each year. **SIGN** Tracks: 3" hindprints in front of small, round foreprints. Scat: piles of dark brown, pea-size pellets. **HABITAT** Woodland edges in mtns., thickets, gardens. **ACTIVITY** By day (usu. early or late) or night. **RANGE** Mtns. of nw, c, and se AZ; sw and ec NM.

MOUNTAIN COTTONTAIL
"Nuttall's Cottontail"
Sylvilagus nuttallii
HARE AND RABBIT FAMILY

L 15"; T 2". Pale grayish brown above, white below. Ears medium-length (2½"), black-tipped. Legs medium-length. Tail short, white below. Spends most of day resting in tall grass or rocky crevice. **BREEDING** 3–8 young Mar.–July; several litters each year. **SIGN** Tracks: foreprint round, 1"; hindprint oblong, 3½". **HABITAT** Shrubby canyons in plateau country, sagebrush. **ACTIVITY** Mainly nocturnal. **RANGE** NV (ex. se), UT, n and ec AZ, nw and n NM.

ANTELOPE JACKRABBIT
Lepus alleni
HARE AND RABBIT FAMILY

L 24"; T 2½". Hare. Above grayish brown, lower sides white; head buffy; ears extremely long (7"), buffy with white tip; tail black above. Flashes white sides during tremendous leaps when fleeing. Stands on hindfeet when browsing shrubs; does not need to drink water. **BREEDING** 1–5 young in 3–4 litters a year. **HABITAT** Brush, desert, and foothill grasslands. **ACTIVITY** Rests in shade of bush during midday heat, active dawn, dusk, and night. **RANGE** sc AZ eastward to Santa Rita Mtns.

BLACK-TAILED JACKRABBIT
Lepus californicus
HARE AND RABBIT FAMILY

L 24"; T 4". Hare. Buffy brown above, peppered with black; white below. Neck longer than rabbits'. Ears very long (5"), tipped brownish black. Legs long, thin, with large hindfeet (5"). Tail black above (black extends onto rump), white below. Usu. hops rather than walks; can run up to 35 mph; every 5th leap higher to check for predators. Gives squeals, thumps feet when distressed. **BREEDING** 2–4 litters of 2–4 young born in Mar.–Oct. **SIGN** Tracks: foreprint round, 1½" hindprint oval, 2½"; 5–20' apart, depending on speed. **HABITAT** Prairies, scrubby deserts, farms. **ACTIVITY** Day and night; avoids midday summer heat. **RANGE** All SW, ex. higher mtns.

WHITE-TAILED JACKRABBIT
Lepus townsendii
HARE AND RABBIT FAMILY

L 26"; T 3½". Hare. Summer: gray-brown above, peppered with black; paler below; ears tipped black. Winter: all white. Ears to 4½" long. Legs long, thin, with large hindfeet (almost 7"). Tail all white. Usu. solitary. Can run up to 45 mph. **BREEDING** Males kick and bite each other over females. 1–3 litters of 1–6 young born in Apr.–Sept. **SIGN** Tunnels in snow. Tracks: foreprint round, 1½"; hindprint oval, 2½"; tracks 5–20' apart. **HABITAT** Open grassy and sagebrush plains. **ACTIVITY** Mainly nocturnal. **RANGE** n and c NV, all UT (ex. se). **Snowshoe Hare** *(L. americanus)* smaller (20"); brown in summer, white in winter; in coniferous forests of far w NV, UT, n NM.

Rodents

Rodentia is the world's largest mammalian order; more than half of all mammal species and many more than half of all mammal individuals on earth are rodents. In addition to the mice and rats (a family that also includes the mouse-like but chubbier voles and the muskrats), other rodent families in the Southwest are the squirrels (including chipmunks and marmots), pocket mice and kangaroo rats, pocket gophers, porcupines, and beavers. Southwestern species range from mice weighing roughly an ounce to the American Beaver, which may weigh up to 65 pounds, but most rodents are relatively small. They are the only mammals that have just two pairs of incisors—one upper and one lower—and no canines, leaving a wide gap between incisors and molars. Rodent incisors are enameled on the front only; the working of the upper teeth against the lower ones wears away the softer inner surfaces, producing a short, chisel-like, beveled edge ideal for gnawing. The incisors grow throughout an animal's life (if they did not, they shortly would be worn away), and rodents must gnaw enough to keep the incisors from growing too long. The eyes are bulbous and placed high on the sides of the head, enabling the animals to detect danger over a wide arc.

GRAY-COLLARED CHIPMUNK
Tamias cinereicollis
SQUIRREL FAMILY

L 9"; T 4". Above dark gray with 5 dark brown and 4 white stripes; sides have rusty patches. Head has 2 white stripes; cheeks, upper back, and neck pale gray. Often feeds in shrubs and trees. **BREEDING** 1 litter of 4–6 young born in June–July. **HABITAT** Ponderosa Pine and spruce forests with fallen logs. **ACTIVITY** By day. **RANGE** Mtns. of c and ec AZ, s NM. **Colorado Chipmunk** *(T. quadrivittatus)* is mainly orange; feeds high in trees; e UT, ne AZ, n NM.

CLIFF CHIPMUNK
Tamias dorsalis
SQUIRREL FAMILY

L 10"; T 4". Above gray with single, bold black mid-back stripe and fainter, thinner black and pale gray stripe; sides have trace of rusty. Head has 2 bold white stripes; tail gray above, rusty below. Very vocal, with variety of barks and chirps. **BREEDING** 4–8 young born in summer. **HABITAT** Cliff faces and rocky areas in pinyon-juniper and Ponderosa Pine zones. **ACTIVITY** By day. **RANGE** c and e NV, UT mtns., AZ mtns. southward to Chiricahuas, w NM.

LEAST CHIPMUNK
Tamias minimus
SQUIRREL FAMILY

L 8"; T 4". 5 brown and 4 whitish stripes on back (reaching tail); sides yellow-gray; belly pale. 3 brown, 2 whitish stripes each side of face. Tail light brown. Calls incl. high-pitched *chip*. **BREEDING** 4–7 young born in May, in tunnel or tree hole. **HABITAT** Juniper and pine woodlands; sagebrush deserts; cliffs. **ACTIVITY** By day; hibernates in winter. **RANGE** n and c NV, UT, nc and ec AZ, n and sc NM.

UINTA CHIPMUNK
Tamias umbrinus
SQUIRREL FAMILY

L 8½", T 4". Back has 4 gray stripes, 2 brown stripes, and median blackish stripe reaching base of tail; sides washed tawny. Head strongly striped; forehead brown; ears blackish in front, whitish behind; white patch behind ears. Tail black-tipped, white-bordered. Feeds mainly in trees. **BREEDING** 5 young born in early summer. **HABITAT** Pine, juniper, and scrub oaks. **ACTIVITY** By day; hibernates in winter. **RANGE** Mtns. of c and e NV, UT, n AZ.

YELLOW-BELLIED MARMOT
Marmota flaviventris
SQUIRREL FAMILY

L 24"; T 7". Coat reddish brown. Head dark brown; muzzle has pale brown patches; sides of neck, belly, and bushy tail rufous. Feet brown, short, strongly clawed. Often sits on boulder above burrow. **VOICE** High, soft chirps and shrill whistles. **BREEDING** 5 young born in Apr. **SIGN** Den near large boulder. **HABITAT** Rocky areas in foothills, mtns. **ACTIVITY** Mainly by day; hibernates Aug.–Apr. **RANGE** n and c NV, UT, nc NM.

HARRIS'S ANTELOPE SQUIRREL
"Yuma Antelope Squirrel"
Ammospermophilus harrisii
SQUIRREL FAMILY

L 9"; T 3½". Above buffy, washed rosy in summer, gray in winter; single white stripe on each side; below white. Tail gray above, mixed black and white below. Runs fast, with tail arched over back. Will climb bushes and cactus to feed. **BREEDING** 4–9 young born Jan.–Mar. **HABITAT** Open deserts and grasslands with few shrubs, cactus. **ACTIVITY** By day, even in midday heat. **RANGE** w, c, and s AZ, sw NM.

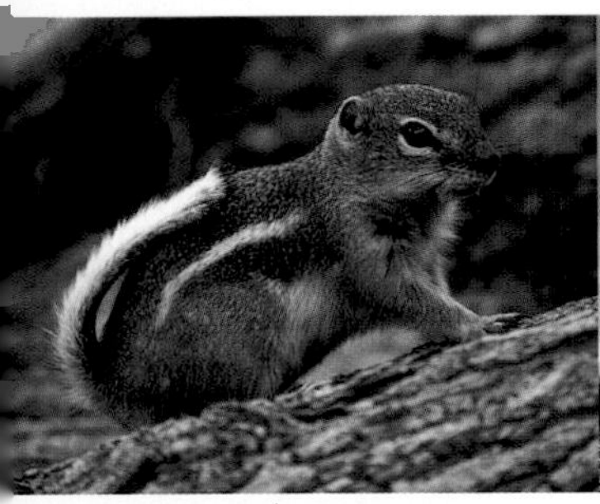

WHITE-TAILED ANTELOPE SQUIRREL
Ammospermophilus leucurus
SQUIRREL FAMILY

L 9"; T 2¾". Back pale grayish buff; sides and thighs pale orange; 1 white stripe on each side; white below. Head pale sandy; whitish eye ring; ears small. Tail flattened, gray above, white below. Runs fast, with tail arched over back. **BREEDING** 5–14 young born in Apr. **SIGN** Burrows with pathways radiating out, but no mound. **HABITAT** Rocky or gravelly desert scrub. **ACTIVITY** By day; hibernates in winter. **RANGE** Deserts of NV, UT, ne AZ, nw, c, and se NM.

UINTA GROUND SQUIRREL
Spermophilus armatus
SQUIRREL FAMILY

L 11½"; T 3". Mid-back brown; rest of back, neck, and sides gray; muzzle and ears cinnamon; top of head has grayish spots; legs washed buffy; belly whitish; tail mixed black and buff. **BREEDING** 4–7 young born in May. **HABITAT** Sagebrush, high grasslands, towns. **ACTIVITY** By day; adults active Apr.–July, juvs. into Sept. **RANGE** Mtns. of n UT. **Belding's Ground Squirrel** *(S. beldingi)* is gray with brown stripe on back; black-tipped tail is reddish below; found in n and c NV, nw UT.

GOLDEN-MANTLED GROUND SQUIRREL

Spermophilus lateralis

SQUIRREL FAMILY

L 11"; T 4". Back gray-brown or buff; 1 white stripe on each side bordered by heavy black stripe. Head and shoulders plain golden orange. Tail grizzled grayish on black. **VOICE** Variety of *chip* notes and squeals. **BREEDING** 4–6 young born in June. **HABITAT** Moist mtn. coniferous and mixed woods; sagebrush. **ACTIVITY** By day; hibernates Oct.–Apr. **RANGE** NV, UT (ex. se), n and ec AZ, n and wc NM.

SPOTTED GROUND SQUIRREL

Spermophilus spilosoma

SQUIRREL FAMILY

L 9"; T 2½". Back and sides pale gray or pale brown with many large buffy or white spots; ears small; belly whitish. Tail flat, thin, top has blackish spot near tip, buffy below. **BREEDING** 2 litters of 5–7 young, born Apr., July–Aug. **SIGN** 2" wide burrow under rocks or shrubs. **HABITAT** Dry, sandy soils of semiarid grasslands. **ACTIVITY** By day, Apr.–Sept.; born in burrow during midday heat. **RANGE** se UT, n and se AZ, most of NM.

ROUND-TAILED GROUND SQUIRREL

Spermophilus tereticaudus

SQUIRREL FAMILY

L 10", T 4". Rusty brown above, silvery gray below; no stripes or mottling. Cheeks silvery; ears small. Tail long, slender, cinnamon. Usu. shy, secretive. **BREEDING** 6–12 young born in Apr.–June. **SIGN** Burrow entrance without mound. **HABITAT** Creosote Bush, mesquite, cactus scrub in flat, sandy deserts. **ACTIVITY** By day; active year-round or hibernates Oct.–Jan. Rests during midday heat in bush or burrow. **RANGE** s NV; w and sc AZ eastward to Tucson.

TOWNSEND'S GROUND SQUIRREL

Spermophilus townsendii

SQUIRREL FAMILY

L 9"; T 2". Smoky gray above, washed with pinkish buff; belly paler gray or pale buff. Head plain gray-brown; eye ring white. Tail tawny with white edge. **BREEDING** 4–10 young in Mar. **SIGN** Burrow openings rimmed with dirt piles. **HABITAT** Sagebrush and Greasewood deserts. **ACTIVITY** By day; hibernates July–Feb. **RANGE** All NV (ex. far s), w UT.

THIRTEEN-LINED GROUND SQUIRREL

Spermophilus tridecemlineatus
SQUIRREL FAMILY

L 10″; T 4″. Basic color buffy or dull brown; nape and back have thick, dark brown stripes with alternating buffy lines and rows of spots; belly whitish; tail flat, brown, fringed buffy. **BREEDING** 8–10 young born in May. **SIGN** Radiating runways from burrow without mound. **HABITAT** Prairie grasslands, roadsides, lawns, towns. **ACTIVITY** By day, Mar.–Oct. **RANGE** ne UT, n and c NM.

ROCK SQUIRREL

Spermophilus variegatus
SQUIRREL FAMILY

L 19″; T 8″. Region's largest ground squirrel. Above gray or grayish brown, finely mottled with black and buff; eye ring whitish; belly pale buff. Tail somewhat bushy, black near tip. Climbs bushes, trees, rock piles. **BREEDING** 2 litters of 3–9 young born Apr.–June, Aug.–Sept. **HABITAT** Cliffs, boulder piles, road-cuts; juniper and oaks in canyons. **ACTIVITY** By day, mostly Mar.–Oct.; warm spells in winter. **RANGE** c and se NV, UT (ex. nw), AZ, NM.

GUNNISON'S PRAIRIE DOG

Cynomys gunnisoni
SQUIRREL FAMILY

L 14″; T 2″. Rotund. Back, sides, and legs yellowish buff, paler buff below. Tail short, white-tipped, grayish in center. Lives in colonies of a few dozen. **BREEDING** 1–8 young born in May. **HABITAT** Shortgrass prairies on plateau and intermontane valleys. **ACTIVITY** By day, chiefly early and late; active Apr.–Oct. aboveground. **RANGE** se UT, ne AZ plateaus, c AZ mtns., nw NM. **Utah Prairie Dog** *(C. parvidens),* of sc and sw UT, reddish above; tail white-tipped with white center.

BLACK-TAILED PRAIRIE DOG

Cynomys ludovicianus
SQUIRREL FAMILY

L 16″; T 4″. Rotund. Back, sides, and legs warm buffy brown; paler below; small rusty tail black. Often sits on haunches atop mound. Sociable; often seen "kissing"; colonies of 100s. **VOICE** Highly vocal; many calls, incl. bark. **BREEDING** 4–5 young born in Mar.–Apr. **SIGN** Bare mounds of earth 1–2′ high. **HABITAT** Short-grass prairie. **ACTIVITY** By day; avoids midday heat and winter storms. **RANGE** s, c, and e NM (now local); exterminated in se AZ.

ABERT'S SQUIRREL
"Tassel-eared Squirrel"
Sciurus aberti
SQUIRREL FAMILY

L 21″; T 9″. Typical races: above dark gray with chestnut patch on back, below white; tail gray above, white below. Ears have long tassles (to 1¾″) from fall to spring. Kaibab race (n rim of Grand Canyon) has black belly; tail all white. **BREEDING** 4 young born Apr.–May. **HABITAT** Pine woodlands of mtns. and plateaus. **ACTIVITY** By day year-round. **RANGE** nw to cc AZ (introduced to Santa Catalina Mtns.), w and n NM.

ARIZONA GRAY SQUIRREL
Sciurus arizonensis
SQUIRREL FAMILY

L 21″; T 11″. Plain gray above with faint bands of buff; tail long, gray, fringed in white; ears lack tassles; feet pale. **BREEDING** 1 litter born in early summer. **HABITAT** Sycamore, cotton wood, and walnut woodlands in pine-oak belt of mtns. **ACTIVITY** By day. **RANGE** c AZ plateaus, se AZ mtns. (Santa Catalinas, Santa Ritas, and Huachucas).

RED SQUIRREL
Tamiasciurus hudsonicus
SQUIRREL FAMILY

L 13″; T 5″. Underparts white; tail long, bushy, reddish. Summer: dark reddish gray above, with black side stripe; ears rounded. Winter: paler above, no side stripe; ears tufted. Mainly arboreal. Noisy; chattering *chick-r-r-r-r.* **BREEDING** 4–5 young Apr.–May and/or Aug.–Sept. in tree cavity or leaf-and-stick nest in treetop. **SIGN** Tracks: hindprint 1½″; 5-toe print. **HABITAT** Coniferous and mixed woods. **ACTIVITY** Mainly by day, year-round. **RANGE** Mtns. of UT, AZ (southward to Mt. Graham), NM.

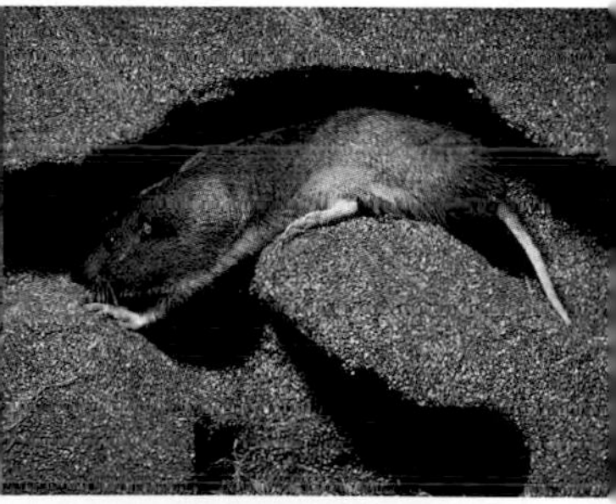

BOTTA'S POCKET GOPHER
"Valley Pocket Gopher"
Thomomys bottae (umbrinus)
POCKET GOPHER FAMILY

L 9″; T 3″. Dull dark brown, buffy gray, or whitish, matching local soil color. 2 orange, chisel-like upper and lower incisors. Forefeet have long digging claws. Tail round, naked, rat-like. Solitary. Pest in farm country. **BREEDING** Several litters of 2–12 young born year-round. **SIGN** Mounds and raised underground tunnels. **HABITAT** Farms, lawns, fields. **ACTIVITY** Mainly nocturnal; occ. seen aboveground. **RANGE** c and s NV, UT, AZ, w and c NM.

GREAT BASIN POCKET MOUSE
Perognathus parvus
POCKET MOUSE AND KANGAROO RAT FAMILY

L 7″; T 3½″. Above gray-brown, below white. Ears small; fur-lined cheek pouch. Tail long, bicolored. Makes extensive burrows with chambers for sleeping, nesting, food storage. Eats seeds. Other species in southern deserts. **BREEDING** 2 litters of 2–8 young born in May–Aug. **SIGN** Mounds of soil at burrow entrance. **HABITAT** Sagebrush, juniper woodlands. **ACTIVITY** Nocturnal; hibernates in winter. **RANGE** NV, w and c UT, nw AZ.

DESERT KANGAROO RAT
Dipodomys deserti
POCKET MOUSE AND KANGAROO RAT FAMILY

L 14″; T 8″. Above pale yellow-buff, below white. Head large; white area behind eye. White stripe on thighs. Hindfeet large, white. Tail longer than body; mostly white with tufted tip preceded by dusky band. Hops. Stomps its feet and kicks sand at unfamiliar objects. **BREEDING** 1–2 litters of 1–6 young Jan.–July. **SIGN** Well-worn trails radiating from burrows. **HABITAT** Soft sand, dunes, desert scrub. **ACTIVITY** Mainly nocturnal; avoids moonlit nights. **RANGE** c and s NV, w and sw AZ.

ORD'S KANGAROO RAT
Dipodomys ordii
POCKET MOUSE AND KANGAROO RAT FAMILY

L 10″; T 5″. Tan above, white below. White spot above eye, below ear. Hindfeet 2″ long. Tail striped brown and white with dark tip. Jumps to 8′. **BREEDING** 3–5 young. **SIGN** 3″ burrow openings on slopes; scooped-out dusting areas nearby. Narrow, 1½″ hindprints. **HABITAT** Open deserts with hard or sandy soils. **ACTIVITY** Nocturnal; winters in burrows. **RANGE** n and c NV, UT, n, c, and se AZ, NM.

BANNER-TAILED KANGAROO RAT
Dipodomys spectabilis
POCKET MOUSE AND KANGAROO RAT FAMILY

L 14″; T 8″. Back and sides brown, belly white; white spots above eyes and ears. Tail black above, sides white, black band near all-white fluffy tip. **BREEDING** 1–2 litters a year; born in Apr. in high country, Dec. and June in low. **HABITAT** Arid grassland with scattered mesquite or junipers. **ACTIVITY** Nocturnal. **RANGE** sc and se AZ, w, c, and se NM.

beaver gnawing tree (left), lodge (right)

AMERICAN BEAVER
Castor canadensis
BEAVER FAMILY

L 3′4″; T 16″. Rich dark brown on mtns. (pale buffy in desert waterways). Eyes and ears small. Legs short; feet webbed; claws small. Tail paddle-shaped, black, scaly, flattened. Eats bark and twigs of broadleaf trees; stashes branches underwater for winter use. Swims with only head above water. Slaps tail loudly on water to warn family of danger. Fells trees by gnawing trunk down to a "waist" that finally cannot support tree. Dams small streams with sticks, reeds, and saplings caulked with mud. Builds dome-like lodge up to 6′ high and 20′ wide; underwater tunnels reach up to dry chambers above water level. Ponds formed by dams promote growth of trees favored by beavers and help form marshes for other wildlife. Some will den in waterside burrows and not build a dam or lodge. N. Amer.'s largest rodent. **BREEDING** Usu. 3–5 young born in May–July inside lodge. **SIGN** Dams; lodges; cone-shaped tree stumps. Tracks: 5″ 5-toed hindprint covers smaller foreprint. **HABITAT** Ponds, rivers, adjacent woodlands. **ACTIVITY** Mainly at dusk and night, year-round. **RANGE** All SW, incl. Colorado R., but local. Increasing.

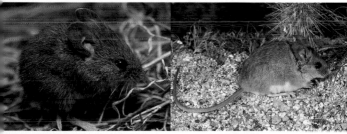

WESTERN HARVEST MOUSE
Reithrodontomys megalotis
MOUSE AND RAT FAMILY

L 6″; T 3″. Brown above; sides buffy; white or gray below. Ears medium-size, round. Tail dusky above, pale below. Travels in vole runways. Nimble climber. Eats new growth in summer, seeds in fall and winter. **BREEDING** Several litters of 2–6 young. **SIGN** Builds round, woven nest, entrance at bottom. **HABITAT** Cultivated and weedy fields, grasslands. **ACTIVITY** Nocturnal, year-round.

CACTUS MOUSE
Peromyscus eremicus
MOUSE AND RAT FAMILY

L 7″; T 4″. Back gray brown, sides yellowish brown; below pale gray. Ears fairly large. Tail long, faintly bicolored, few hairs. Body darker in lava areas. Climbs shrubs for seeds, fruit. **BREEDING** Several litters of 2–3 young born year-round; nests in rocks, cactus. **HABITAT** Lowland deserts with sandy soil; rocky areas up to pinyon pine zone. **ACTIVITY** Chiefly nocturnal. **RANGE** s NV, far sw UT, AZ (ex. ne and mtns.), s NM.

DEER MOUSE
Peromyscus maniculatus
MOUSE AND RAT FAMILY

L 7″; T 3″. Above brown (adult) or gray (juv.), below white. Ears round, medium-size. Feet white. Tail dark above, white below. In some habitats, outnumbers all other rodents combined. Agile climber. Feeds on seeds, insects, fungi. **BREEDING** 2–4 litters of 3–5 young born in Mar.–Oct. **HABITAT** Forests, grasslands; all elevations. **ACTIVITY** Nocturnal, year-round. **RANGE** All SW, ex. se NM.

SOUTHERN GRASSHOPPER MOUSE
Onychomys torridus
MOUSE AND RAT FAMILY

L 6″; T 2″. Grayish cinnamon above, white below. Feet white. Tail short, tip and underside white. Eats scorpions, insects, other mice. Male has high-pitched whistle. **BREEDING** 1–2 litters of 2–6 young born in June–Aug. **HABITAT** Low deserts. **ACTIVITY** Mainly nocturnal, year-round. **RANGE** s NV, far sw UT, w and s AZ, s NM. **Northern Grasshopper Mouse** *(O. leucogaster)*, 7″, is similar; n NV, UT, n and e AZ, all NM.

WHITE-THROATED WOODRAT
Neotoma albigula
MOUSE AND RAT FAMILY

L 14″; T 7″. Back and forehead gray, sides washed tawny. Belly, throat, and feet white. Tail brown above, white below. Communicates by hindfoot drumming. **BREEDING** Several litters of 2–3 young. **SIGN** Builds bulky nest of sticks, stems, and cactus parts at base of thorny plant or in rock pile. **HABITAT** Arid areas: cactus deserts, yucca grasslands, pinyon pine zone in mtns. **ACTIVITY** Chiefly nocturnal. **RANGE** se UT, AZ south of Colorado R., NM.

BUSHY-TAILED WOODRAT
Neotoma cinerea
MOUSE AND RAT FAMILY

L 17″; T 8″. Tan above, peppered with black; white below. Ears large. Feet white. Tail bushy, brown. Brings shiny, metal objects to nest. Makes tapping sound with hindfeet. Eats foliage, seeds, fruit. **BREEDING** 1–2 litters of 2–6 young born in May–Sept. **SIGN** Large nest of sticks under log or in crevice; piles of leaves in autumn. **HABITAT** Rocky areas in all habitats, up to alpine zone. **ACTIVITY** Nocturnal, year-round. **RANGE** Most of NV, all UT, n AZ, n NM.

DESERT WOODRAT

Neotoma lepida

MOUSE AND RAT FAMILY

L 12"; T 5". Pale buffy gray above, whitish below; hairs slaty near skin. Feet white. Tail gray above, with fine hair. **BREEDING** 2–4 young born in Mar.–May. **SIGN** Sticks, cactus spines piled on ground. **HABITAT** Cactus deserts, stunted pinyon-juniper woodlands. **ACTIVITY** Mainly nocturnal, year-round. **RANGE** NV, w and se UT, nw and sw AZ.

BROWN RAT

"Norway Rat"

Rattus norvegicus

MOUSE AND RAT FAMILY

L 15"; T 7". Naturalized from Europe. Grayish brown above, belly gray; ears partly hidden in fur; tail long, scaly. Digs network of tunnels 2–3" wide in ground. Eats insects, stored grain, garbage. **BREEDING** 6 litters of 6–8 young a year. **SIGN** Holes in walls, paths to food supplies. **HABITAT** Towns, farms. **ACTIVITY** Mostly nocturnal, year-round. **RANGE** Populated areas of SW.

SAGEBRUSH VOLE

Lemmiscus curtatus

MOUSE AND RAT FAMILY

L 5"; T 1". Ashy gray above, silvery below. Nose and small ears buff. Feet silvery. Tail very short. Feeds on grasses in summer; bark, twigs, and roots in winter. **BREEDING** Several litters of 2–11 young born in Apr.–Nov. **SIGN** Colonial burrow entrances under bush clumps. **HABITAT** Sagebrush and bunchgrass flats. **ACTIVITY** Day and night, year-round. **RANGE** NV, w and c UT.

COMMON MUSKRAT

Ondatra zibethicus

MOUSE AND RAT FAMILY

L 23"; T 10". Fur rich brown in mtns., paler in desert; belly silver. Tail long, scaly, blackish; tapers to point. Hindfeet partially webbed. Swims with head, back, and sculling tail visible. **BREEDING** 2–3 litters of usu. 6–7 young born in Mar.–June. **SIGN** Lodge of cattails, roots, and mud floats up to 3′ above surface of water. Tracks: often incl. tail drag mark. **HABITAT** Freshwater marshes, ponds, rivers, canals. **ACTIVITY** Day and night. **RANGE** Colorado Valley and n NV, n and e UT, ec AZ, most of NM.

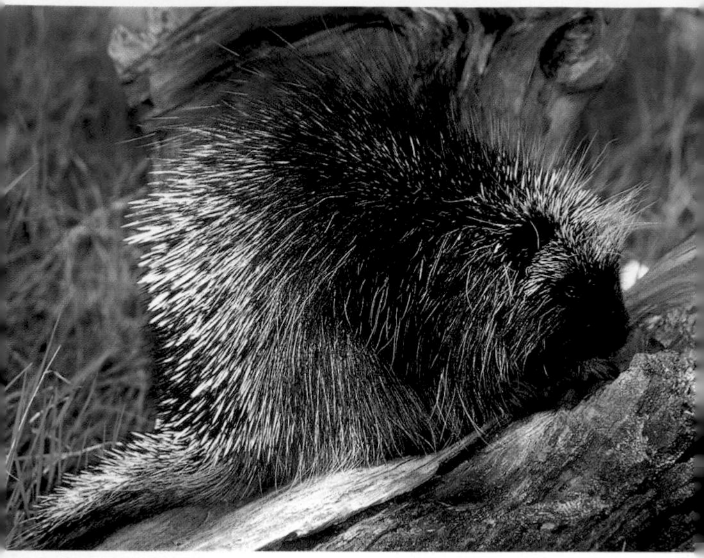

COMMON PORCUPINE
Erethizon dorsatum
NEW WORLD PORCUPINE FAMILY

L 33″; T 8″. Blackish. Long, wiry guard hairs on front half of body; thousands of shorter, heavier quills (hairs modified into sharp, mostly hollow spines) mainly on rump and longish, rounded tail, but also some on front of body; underfur long, soft, wooly. Back high-arching. Legs short; soles of feet knobbed; claws long, curved. Walks pigeon-toed on ground. Eats green plants and twigs, buds, and bark of trees; sometimes damages wooden buildings and poles. **VOICE** Squeals, grunts. **BREEDING** 1 young born in Apr.–June. **SIGN** Tooth marks on bark; irreg. patches of bark stripped from tree trunks and limbs. Tracks: inward-facing, up to 3″; claw tips well forward. Scat: piles of variably shaped pellets near crevice or base of feeding tree. **HABITAT** Forests (esp. coniferous), meadows, mtns. **ACTIVITY** Mainly nocturnal, year-round. **RANGE** NV, UT, AZ (ex. sw), NM (ex. se).

Carnivores

Short-tailed Weasel, winter coat

Members of the order Carnivora eat meat, although many also eat fruit, berries, and vegetation. They have long canine teeth for stabbing prey, and most have sharp cheek teeth for slicing meat. None truly hibernate, but several retire to logs or burrows and sleep soundly during a cold winter. Most live on land, although otters spend most of their time in water. Most carnivores have a single yearly litter of offspring, which are born blind and receive many months to a year or more of parental care. Southwestern carnivore families include the bears, canids (coyotes and foxes), weasels (martens, skunks, badgers, otters, fishers, and minks), raccoons, and cats.

BLACK BEAR
Ursus americanus
BEAR FAMILY

mother and cub

H 3′4″; L 5′; T 4″; female smaller. Long hair varies from black through brown to dark yellow; often has white patch on chest. Some individuals cinnamon-brown. Head round; muzzle long, brownish; ears short, rounded. Legs short. More vegetarian than most carnivores; eats inner layer of tree bark, berries, fruit, plants, honeycombs, insects in rotten logs, and vertebrates, incl. fish and small mammals. Powerful swimmer and climber; can run up to 30 mph. **CAUTION** Do not feed, approach, or get between one and its food or cubs; will usu. flee, but can cause serious injury. Campers must firmly seal up food. Will break into unattended vehicles if it smells food. **BREEDING** Usu. 2 cubs, about ½ lb at birth, born in den Jan.–Feb. **SIGN** Torn apart stumps; turned-over boulders; torn-up burrows; hair on shaggy-barked trees. Tracks: foreprint 5″ wide; hindprint up to 9″ long. Scat: dog-like. **HABITAT** Forests, dumps. **ACTIVITY** Mainly nocturnal, but often out in daytime; does not hibernate. **RANGE** Lake Tahoe area of NV; mtns. of UT, AZ, and NM.

cinnamon-brown coat

COYOTE

"Song Dog"

Canis latrans

DOG FAMILY

H 25"; L 4'; T 13". Coat long, coarse; grizzled gray, buffy, and black. Muzzle long, narrow, brownish; ears rufous. Tail bushy, black-tipped. Runs up to 40 mph. Eats small mammals, birds, frogs, snakes, berries. **VOICE** Bark, flat howl; series of *yip* notes followed by wavering howl at night. **BREEDING** 4–8 pups born in spring. **SIGN** 24" den mouths on slopes. Tracks: dog-like, but in nearly straight lines; foreprint larger, 2⅜". Scat: dog-like, but usu. full of hair or fruit stains. **HABITAT** Open plains, scrub deserts, farms, towns, forests. **ACTIVITY** Day and night, year-round.

KIT FOX

Vulpes velox

DOG FAMILY

L 28"; T 10½". Desert Kit races: back, sides, and top of tail silvery; belly, thin legs, and underside of tail buffy red. Forehead and narrow muzzle gray; throat white; ears large, pointed, rusty. Tip of long bushy tail black. Swift race of e NM has shorter ears. **VOICE** Shrill yap, whines. **BREEDING** 3–7 young born in Feb.–May; mates for life. **SIGN** Den with several 8" entrances, mound of dirt and bones at side. Tracks: about 1½"; shows 4 toes and claws. **HABITAT** Deserts, dry grasslands. **ACTIVITY** Mainly nocturnal, year-round. **RANGE** NV, w UT, w, s, and ne AZ, NM.

RED FOX
Vulpes vulpes
DOG FAMILY

L 3′2″; T 14″. Rusty orange; underparts whitish; narrow legs, reddish above, black below. Some are gray-brown with black markings above. Muzzle narrow; ears pointed, black. Tail bushy, white-tipped. Eats rodents, rabbits, birds, insects, berries, fruit. Has strong scent. **VOICE** Short yap and long howls. **BREEDING** 1–10 young Mar.–Apr. **SIGN** Den entrance, up to 3′ wide, on slope. Tracks: foreprint slightly larger, 2½″; shows 4 toe pads. **HABITAT** Brushy and open areas in forested regions, mtns.; wetlands and other open areas. **ACTIVITY** Mainly nocturnal, year-round. **RANGE** c NV, UT, n and c NM (all Rio Grande Valley).

COMMON GRAY FOX
Urocyon cinereoargenteus
DOG FAMILY

H 15″; L 3′2″; T 13″. Grizzled silvery gray above, throat and mid-belly white; collar, lower sides, legs, and sides of tail rusty; top and tip of tail black. Eats rabbits, rodents, birds, grasshoppers, fruit, berries. Often climbs trees, unlike Red Fox and Coyote. **BREEDING** 2–7 young Apr.–May. **SIGN** Den hidden in natural crevice in woods; often has snagged hair, bone scraps near entrance. Tracks: foreprint 1½″; hindprint slightly narrower. **HABITAT** Wooded and brushy areas. **ACTIVITY** Mainly nocturnal, year-round. **RANGE** c and s NV, s and e UT, AZ, NM.

RINGTAIL
"Ring-tailed Cat"
Bassariscus astutus
RACCOON FAMILY

L 28"; T 14". Above yellowish brown or gray, below whitish buff. Face short; eyes large, ringed with whitish fur; ears pointed. Legs short. Tail long; black with 7–8 white rings (bands). **BREEDING** 3–4 young born in May–June; den hidden under boulders. **SIGN** Tracks: up to 2¾", round; shows 5 toes but no claws. **HABITAT** Rocky areas, canyons, large trees with hollows, old buildings. **ACTIVITY** Strictly nocturnal. **RANGE** s NV, s and e UT, AZ, NM.

COMMON RACCOON
Procyon lotor
RACCOON FAMILY

L 32"; T 9". Coat long, grizzled grayish brown. Black mask on white muzzle. Legs short; paws buffy. Tail banded yellow-brown and black. Omnivorous; raids trash bins. **BREEDING** Usu. 4 young born in Apr.–May. **SIGN** Den in hollow tree or crevice. Tracks: flat-footed; hindprint much longer than wide, 4"; foreprint rounded, 3"; claws show on all 5 toes. **HABITAT** Forests, scrub near water; towns, cities. **ACTIVITY** Mainly nocturnal. **RANGE** n, w, and se NV, sw and se UT, most of AZ and NM.

WHITE-NOSED COATI
"Coatimundi"
Nasua narica
RACCOON FAMILY

L 4'; T 20". Back and sides dark brown, grayish below. Snout long, pointed; eye ring and muzzle white; ears small. Tail long, fluffy, brown, 6–7 faint bands. Walks with tail held high; often climbs trees. **BREEDING** 4–6 young born in spring. **SIGN** Fore- and hindprints 3" long, 2" wide; claws print only on forefeet. **HABITAT** Mtn. forests near water; rocky wooded canyons. **ACTIVITY** Chiefly by day. **RANGE** c and se AZ, sw NM.

AMERICAN BADGER
Taxidea taxus
WEASEL FAMILY

L 28"; T 5". Coat shaggy, gray-brown above, white below. White stripe from nose over crown to mid-back. Snout pointed. Legs short, black; feet heavily clawed. Tail short, bushy, yellowish. Waddles in clumsy trot. Digs out burrowing rodents, snakes. **BREEDING** 1–5 young born in Apr. **SIGN** Burrow entrances to 12" wide, elliptical; nearby mound of dirt with bones, fur, dung. Tracks: toes point inward; prints round, 2". **HABITAT** Grasslands, sagebrush, open juniper and pine woodlands; farms. **ACTIVITY** Day and night, year-round.

SHORT-TAILED WEASEL

"Ermine"

Mustela erminea

WEASEL FAMILY

L 11"; T 2"; female smaller. Brown above; underparts, inside of legs, and feet white. Tail thin, furred, with black tip. White with black tail tip in winter. Expert mouser; also takes rabbits, birds, frogs, insects. Tireless, active hunter. **BREEDING** 4–9 young born in Apr. **SIGN** Spiral scat along trails. **HABITAT** Brush, fields, wetlands. **ACTIVITY** Day and night, year-round. **RANGE** n and c NV, n and c UT, nc NM.

LONG-TAILED WEASEL

Mustela frenata

WEASEL FAMILY

L 15"; T 5"; female smaller. Brown above, white below; feet brown. Tail thin, furred, black tip. Some in lowlands have blackish muzzle with large white patches between eye and ear. In high country only: white with black tail tip in winter. **BREEDING** 6–8 young born in Apr.–May. **SIGN** Cache of dead rodents under log. Tracks: hindprint ¾" wide, 1" long; foreprint a bit wider, ½" long. **HABITAT** Woodlands, brush, fields. **ACTIVITY** Day and night, year-round. **RANGE** n and c NV, UT, mtns. of AZ, NM.

MINK

Mustela vison

WEASEL FAMILY

L 24"; T 7"; female much smaller. Lustrous blackish brown above and below; chin white. Muzzle pointed; ears tiny. Tail bushy. Swims often. Eats fish, birds, rodents, frogs. **BREEDING** 3–4 young born in Apr.–May. **SIGN** Holes in snow (where mink has pounced on vole); 4" burrow entrance in stream bank. Tracks: round, 2", in snow. **HABITAT** Freshwater shores. **ACTIVITY** Late afternoon to early morning, year-round; dens up in coldest, stormiest periods. **RANGE** w and ne NV, n and c UT, n NM.

NORTHERN RIVER OTTER

Lutra canadensis

WEASEL FAMILY

L 3'7"; T 16". Fur dense, dark brown, often silvery on chin and chest. Ears and eyes small. Legs short; feet webbed. Tail long, thick based, tapering to a point. Swims and runs rapidly. Eats fish, frogs, turtles, muskrats. **BREEDING** 2–3 young born in Apr. **SIGN** 12"-wide slides on sloping riverbanks. Tracks: 3¼", toes fanned. **HABITAT** Clean rivers, wood-edged ponds, lakes. **ACTIVITY** Day and night, year-round. **RANGE** n and w NV, n and c UT, n, c, and w AZ, w and n NM.

WESTERN SPOTTED SKUNK
Spilogale gracilis
WEASEL FAMILY

L 16″; T 6″. Body black with several long, wavy, white stripes. Head small, black with small white spots; ears tiny, at sides of head. Feet short, black. Tail short for a skunk, bushy, black with white tip. **CAUTION** If threatened, stands on forepaws; can spray foul-smelling liquid to 13′. **BREEDING** 4–7 young born in June. **SIGN** Lingering stench. Tracks: like Striped Skunk's, but smaller. **HABITAT** Woodlands, scrub, farms. **ACTIVITY** Nocturnal; dens up in winter.

HOODED SKUNK
Mephitis macroura
WEASEL FAMILY

28″; T 14″. Usu. all black, ex. for 1–2 thin white stripes on sides. Some have white backs mixed with black hairs. Tail usu. all black, as long as body. Hair on neck forms a ruff. Top of snout furred, not naked as in Hog-nosed. **BREEDING** 3–5 young born May–June. **HABITAT** Brushy streambeds, rocky areas. **ACTIVITY** Nocturnal. **RANGE** sc and se AZ, sw NM.

STRIPED SKUNK
Mephitis mephitis
WEASEL FAMILY

L 24″; T 9″. Coat mainly black, large white nape patch, continues as 2 stripes along sides of back, usu. reaching tail; forehead has narrow white stripe. Tail long, bushy. In some individuals, most of upper back and tail white. **CAUTION** Can emit sulphurous spray that travels to 15′, stings eyes of predators, pets, humans. **BREEDING** 6–7 young born in May–June. **SIGN** Foul odor. Tracks: round foreprint 1″; hindprint broader at front, flat-footed, 1½″. **HABITAT** Woodlands, fields, towns. **ACTIVITY** Dusk to dawn; dens up and sleeps much of winter.

COMMON HOG-NOSED SKUNK
Conepatus mesoleucus
WEASEL FAMILY

L 30″; T 14″. Nape, and top half of body fluffy white; bushy tail all white; underparts and face black. Snout naked on top. No white stripe on forehead. Tears up ground searching for insects, reptiles, small rodents, tubers, bulbs, and roots; often called "Rooter." **BREEDING** 2–4 young born in May. **SIGN** Rootings. Tracks: longer front foot toe prints than other skunks. **HABITAT** Oak and semi-desert scrub, pinyon-juniper woodlands. **ACTIVITY** Nocturnal in summer; forages on some winter days. **RANGE** c and se AZ, s, c, and ne NM.

MOUNTAIN LION

"Puma" "Cougar"

Felis concolor

CAT FAMILY

H 30″; L 8′; T 30″; female smaller. Tawny reddish or grayish above, whitish below. Head fairly small; dark spot at base of whiskers; ears erect, blackish on back. Legs long, paws wide; claws long, sharp, retractile. Tail long, blackish at end. Young dark-spotted for 6 months. Feeds on deer, rabbits, large rodents, birds. Solitary territorial hunter, ex. for mother with older cubs; good climber. **CAUTION** Usu. shy of humans, but fatal attacks have occurred. **VOICE** Screams, hisses, growls. **BREEDING** 2–4 young born in July, every other year. **SIGN** Scratch marks left 6–10′ up tree. Tracks: round; 4 toe prints show no claws. **HABITAT** Semiarid canyons, mtns., forests. **ACTIVITY** Mainly nocturnal, year-round. **RANGE** All SW; absent from most populated areas.

BOBCAT

Lynx rufus

CAT FAMILY

H 20″; L 33″; T 4″. Orange-brown in summer, pale grayish in winter; black spots and bars on long legs and rear; underparts and inside of legs white. Face wide, flat; black lines radiate onto facial ruff. Ears slightly tufted, back side black. Stalks and ambushes mammals, birds. **VOICE** Occ. yowls and screams, though mostly silent. **BREEDING** 2–3 young born in May. **SIGN** Tracks in snow at scent posts and scratching trees. Tracks: like domestic cat, but 2″ vs. 1″. **HABITAT** All terrestrial habitats. **ACTIVITY** Mainly nocturnal, year-round. **Ocelot** *(Felis pardalis)* 4′, T 14″; buffy with black-bordered brown spots; rare in se AZ.

Hoofed Mammals

Most hoofed mammals worldwide are in the order Artiodactyla, the even-toed ungulates. Ungulates are mammals that have hooves, an adaptation for running. The order Perissodactyla—the odd-toed ungulates: horses, zebras, rhinos, and tapirs—has no extant native species in North America, but escaped horses (called mustangs) roam as herds in many remote areas, especially in Nevada, Utah, and northern Arizona. Even-toed ungulates have a split, two-part hoof (actually two modified toes) and two small dewclaws (vestigial toes) above the hoof on the rear of the leg. Their lower incisors are adapted for nipping or tearing vegetation, their molars for grinding it. Most hastily swallow their food, which is stored temporarily in the first compartment of their four-chambered stomachs; the food then passes to the second stomach, where it is shaped into small pellets of partly digested plant fiber (the cud). While the animal is at rest, the cud is returned to the mouth, slowly chewed to pulp, and swallowed; it then passes through all four chambers of the stomach. This process allows an animal to feed quickly, reducing its exposure to predators, and afterward chew its cud slowly in a concealed spot.

Members of the deer family (Cervidae) have paired bony antlers that grow, usually only on males, in summer, at which time they are soft and tender and covered with a fine-haired skin ("velvet") containing a network of blood vessels that nourishes the growing bone beneath. By late summer, the antlers reach full size, and the velvety skin dries up and peels off. The bare antlers then serve as sexual ornaments; rival males may use them as weapons in courtship battles in fall. As winter nears, the antlers fall off. As long as an individual has an adequate diet, its antlers become larger and have more points each year. The Pronghorn, the sole species in its family (Antilocapridae), has permanent short horns, each with one broad, short prong jutting forward; the horns develop keratin sheaths that are shed each year. Cows, goats, and sheep (family Bovidae) have permanent horns that grow continuously. Note that the well-known American Bison *(Bos bison)* has been introduced to some large ranches.

COLLARED PECCARY
"Javelina"
Tayassu tajacu
PECCARY FAMILY

L 38"; T 2"; H 22". Pig-like; massive head and shoulders; legs and rear small. Body grizzled gray with black and white hairs; collar faint, whitish. Tips of 1½" tusks protrude from jaws. All feet have split hooves. Often roams in large packs. **CAUTION** Families with young may charge aggressive humans. **BREEDING** 2 or more reddish young born in summer. **HABITAT** Desert washes, canyons, oak woodlands. **ACTIVITY** Day or night. **RANGE** c and se AZ, sw NM.

buck (left), female and young (right)

ELK
"Wapiti"
Cervus elaphus
DEER FAMILY

H 5′; L 9′; T 6″; female smaller. Pale gray, brown or tan. Neck thick, chestnut brown; shaggy on buck. Head and muzzle, brown. Buck develops large antlers: 2 rear-projecting beams up to 5′ long, with 6 upward-projecting points along each beam; sheds antlers in early winter. Legs long, brown; hooves black. Rump and very short tail white. Very social; bull herds on fringes of cow/calf herds. **VOICE** Bull in fall gives low bellow followed by far-carrying whistle; cow whistles in spring. **BREEDING** Mates Sept.–Nov.; 1–2 young born in June–July. **SIGN** Buck polishes antlers on small tree trunks during rut. Tracks: 4½″ "split hearts," larger than those of deer. **HABITAT** Summer: high mtn. pastures. Rest of year: forests at lower elevations. **ACTIVITY** Day and night, year-round. **RANGE** Mtns. and adjacent valleys of ne NV, UT, n and e AZ, NM.

White-tailed buck (left), Coue's race (right)

WHITE-TAILED DEER
Odocoileus virginianus
DEER FAMILY

H 3′3″; L 6′; T 12″. Rich reddish brown in summer, gray-brown in winter. Neck, legs, tail long; ears large. Nose and hooves black. Ring around nose, eye ring, throat, midbelly, and underside of tail white. Summer male develops antlers with main beam curving out and up, points issuing from it. Fawn reddish orange, with many white spots. Flees with tail erect, white underfur exposed. Coue's race of AZ, w NM smaller, paler; ears larger. **BREEDING** Mates Oct.–Nov.; 1–2 fawns born in late spring. **SIGN** Buck rubs bark off trees with antlers; flattened beds in grass or snow. Tracks: 2–3″ "split hearts," with narrow, pointed end forward, dots of dewclaws behind. **HABITAT** Broadleaf and mixed woodlands and edges, shrubs, fields, watersides. **ACTIVITY** Day and night, year-round. **RANGE** w NV, n UT, c and s AZ, all NM (ex. nw).

MULE DEER
Odocoileus hemionus
DEER FAMILY

H 3′4″; L 7′; T 8″; female smaller. Reddish brown in summer, light gray-brown in winter. White muzzle and eye ring contrast with black nose and eyes. Ears large, mule-like. Legs slender, buffy. In summer, buck develops antlers: 2 upward-angled beams fork twice into total of 4 points per beam. White rump extending above white, black-tipped tail. Juv. spotted. Runs with stiff-legged, bounding gait. In winter, forms small herds. Declining in many areas; esp. in areas with increasing Elk (Wapiti). **BREEDING** Mates Oct.–Jan.; 1–2 young born in June–Aug. **SIGN** Browse marks; buck rubs. Tracks: narrow "split hearts"; male's prints 3¼″, female's 2¾″. **HABITAT** Forests, sagebrush, meadows. **ACTIVITY** Day and night, year-round; mostly nocturnal where hunted.

bucks (left), female with young (right)

PRONGHORN
"Antelope"
Antilocapra americana
PRONGHORN FAMILY

H 3′4″; L 4′6″; T 4″; female smaller. Head and body pale reddish tan, white below. Neck tan with 2 partial white collars; buck has short, black mane. Horns black, straight; doe's 3″, buck's 6″. Each summer and fall, adult male grows a hard sheath another 9″ high that tapers to a point and has a separate forward prong that is shed in winter. Legs long, tan on outside. Rump white; tail short. Inexhaustible runner; can cruise at 30 mph for 15 miles, with spurts to 70 mph. Unable to leap over higher fences, as slower deer can. **BREEDING** Mates Sept.–Oct.; 1–2 young born in May–June. **SIGN** Tracks: "split hearts," about 3″. **HABITAT** Dry open grasslands with sagebrush and bunchgrass. **ACTIVITY** Day and night, year-round. **RANGE** All SW, but local or absent in many areas.

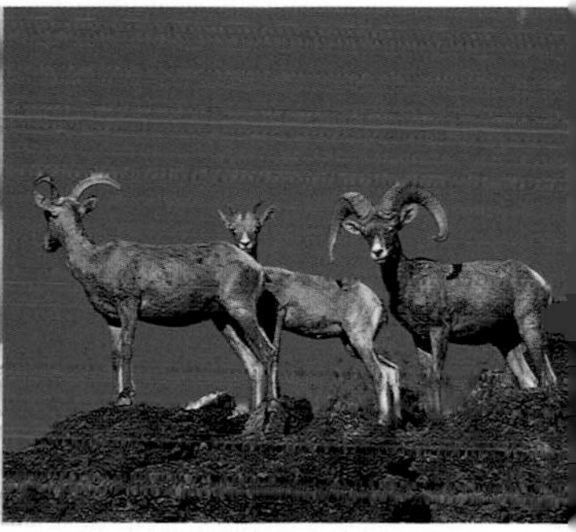

Bighorn rams (left), desert race family (right)

BIGHORN SHEEP
Ovis canadensis
CATTLE, GOAT, AND SHEEP FAMILY

H 3′4″; L 5′6″; T 5″; female smaller. Numerous subspecies and races; those of desert areas smaller, horns thinner. Coat brown; belly and muzzle whitish. Horns brown; male's extremely thick, ridged, curved backward, encircle ears; female's shorter, more slender, form half circles. Leading edges of legs black; hooves with rubbery soles for traction on rocks. Rump white; tail short, dark brown. Summer: small, segregated herds (3–5 rams, 5–15 ewes). Winter: sexes join in larger herds. Rams have autumn head-butting contests that last up to 20 hours, audible for miles. **BREEDING** Mates Oct.–Dec.; 1 young born in May–June. **SIGN** Snagged hair along steep trails. Tracks: splayed hoofprints 3–3½″, less pointed than deer's. **HABITAT** Lightly wooded canyons. **ACTIVITY** By day, year-round. **RANGE** NV, UT, AZ, n, w, and sc NM.

Parks and Preserves

Introduction

The hallmark of the Southwest is diversity. Each state includes wide lowlands of desert or grassland that rise upward into isolated mountain ranges or wide forested plateaus. As a result, the region can be visited at any season. In summer the high mountains are cool and pleasant, while winter brings mild temperatures to the low, sunny deserts that reach from southern New Mexico and Arizona into Nevada and the southwestern corner of Utah.

The Southwest also is a traveler's paradise because of its extensive tracts of public land, much of it protected in national parks and monuments and wilderness areas, as well as a smattering of private preserves. It would take many visits to plumb the wonders of the region's dozens of national parks and monuments alone, to say nothing of the hundreds of thousands of square miles of public land that are not specially designated. The extensive grasslands and deserts managed by the Bureau of Land Management (BLM), for example, offer unending camping, hiking, and wildlife-viewing opportunities.

This section, which includes descriptions of 50 of the most significant nature-viewing sites in the Southwest, is only a selective, bare-bones introduction. It is organized according to state. There is a small map of each state showing the locations of the sites, but a detailed road map is essential in making good use of the location information. Mailing addresses and telephone numbers are included. Most sites will send brochures upon request, sometimes for a small fee; many also publish comprehensive flora and fauna lists. An additional 57 locations are more briefly described.

Operating hours for preserves and visitor centers, as well as entrance fees, have not been included, as they may change rapidly. Most parks and refuges in the Southwest are open year-round, with a few exceptions. Parts of some refuges may be closed to nonhunters during hunting season, and to all visitors during nesting periods. High-elevation sites across the entire region, especially on national forest land, are often closed by snow accumulation during winter and well into spring. Road closures may also occur after summer rainstorms, some of which are violent enough to cause dangerous flash floods in canyons and washes; hikers and drivers should exercise caution at such times.

Important Bird Areas (IBAs) are sites where a significant population or exceptional diversity of birds occurs. IBAs are the focus of conservation strategies of National Audubon Society, working with other conservation groups, including American Bird Conservancy, and as a member of Partners in Flight. In the descriptions that follow, IBAs are noted.

Arizona

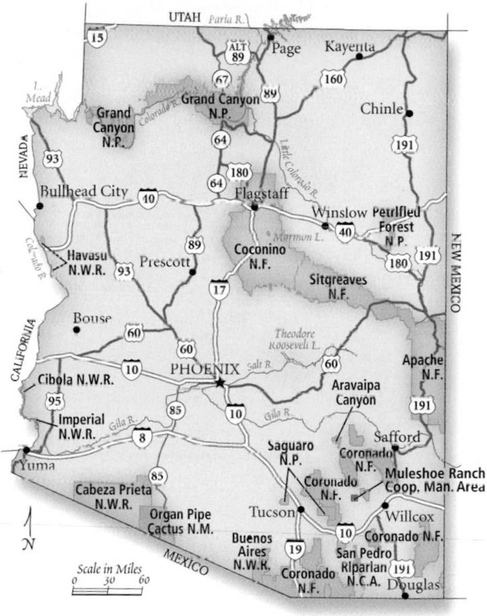

The Grand Canyon State offers residents and visitors far more than a large hole in the ground. Arizona includes elements of all four North American deserts, along with grasslands, forests, high mountains, and lush canyons and riparian areas, within its 114,000 square miles. Indeed, from most parts of the state a two-hour drive will take you into a dramatically different climate or ecosystem.

Generally speaking, the state is split into northern and southern halves by the Mogollon Rim, an escarpment hundreds of miles long that marks the southern edge of the Colorado Plateau. To the south and west lie the hot lowlands of the Chihuahuan, Sonoran, and Mojave Deserts; to the north are the extensive grasslands and forests of the Colorado Plateau. Some high mountains rise out of southern Arizona's lowlands, though, and a good deal of northern Arizona is desert. Ecosystems are further complicated by rugged topography, different soil types, and human intervention. The varied terrain, as well as a fortuitous location between the southern end of the Rocky Mountains and the northern edge of Mexico's Sierra Madre, contributes to the state's remarkable diversity of plants and animals.

A visit to Arizona can be as rugged or as comfortable as desired. Many parks and preserves are accessible via paved roads. Others, especially the wilderness areas managed by the U.S. Forest Service or the Bureau of Land Management (BLM), offer ample opportunity for backcountry hiking and camping. Arizona boasts seven national forests, two national parks, two national recreation areas, eight national wildlife refuges, and 26 state parks.

GRAND CANYON

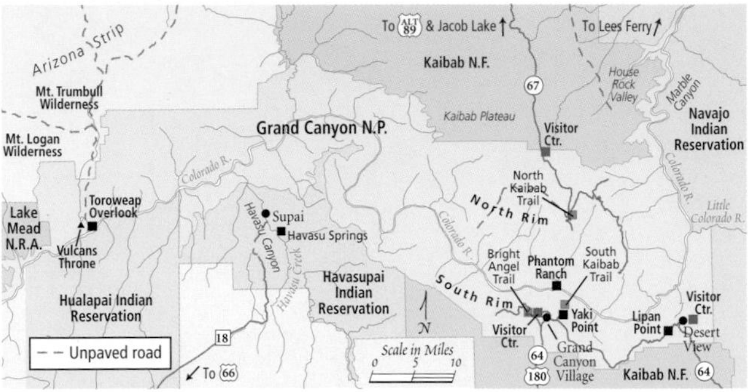

A place of superlatives, the Grand Canyon retains the power to astonish and humble both first-time visitors and those who have seen it many times. Officially 277 miles long, the gaping chasm carved by the erosive force of the Colorado River extends from 4 to 18 miles in width and, in places, to a mile in depth. Geologists believe it has been gouged out recently, in geologic terms—within the last 6 million years or so. The river, according to the current theory, carved the canyon as the Colorado Plateau rose straight up in response to the collision of continental plates.

What the river cut through is a stunning layer cake of geologic history, with rocks from one epoch stacked in orderly fashion above older materials. The oldest and deepest, the Vishnu schist, is estimated to be between 1.7 and 2 billion years old. The youngest and topmost layer of Kaibab limestone is a mere 245 million years old. Many of the layers were deposited as riverine or marine sediments whose fossils have told paleontologists a great deal about the area's prehistoric environment.

But the awesome power of these rocks to evoke the depth of time is only part of the Grand Canyon's appeal. Though much of the terrain here appears stark, almost lifeless, animals and plants thrive. They do so in an impressive variety, thanks to a diversity of habitats. Engelmann Spruce and Blue Grouse live on the cool, moist North Rim at 9,000 feet, while Brittlebush shrubs and Chuckwalla lizards live in the hot depths 6,000 feet below. Seeps and springs, returning high-country runoff to the surface, nourish gardens of hanging plants; the largest water sources, such as Havasu and Roaring Springs, support extensive riparian areas. The Colorado River itself is a ribbon of life, much altered by dam-building and the introduction of nonnative species, in which imperiled native species from American Beaver to Bonytail Chub have managed to persist.

Most of the canyon lies within the 1.2-million-acre Grand Canyon National Park; other reaches abut the Navajo, Havasupai, and Hualapai Indian Reservations, while extensive lands to the north are managed by the U.S. Forest Service and the Bureau of Land Management.

COLORADO RIVER A boat trip through the Grand Canyon is one of America's great wilderness adventures. Traversing quiet pools and turbulent rapids, the journey affords looks at Desert Bighorn Sheep, Peregrine Falcons, and other wildlife. The National Park Service allows both commercial and private trips (it can take years to acquire a permit for the latter). Trips begin at Lees Ferry and usually proceed to the head of Lake Mead, though some end at Diamond Creek on the Hualapai Indian Reservation, and sometimes passengers can disembark at Phantom Ranch.

NORTH RIM The North Rim of the Grand Canyon rears to 9,000 feet on the Kaibab Plateau, whose subalpine meadows and forests of Quaking Aspen and Engelmann Spruce remain locked in deep snow for much of the winter. Open only from about mid-April to mid-October, the North Rim offers a more primitive viewing experience than the heavily visited South Rim. Hikers can descend 6,000 feet on the well-maintained North Kaibab Trail, or on other more rugged routes most suited for those with extensive backcountry experience. Day trips along the rim reward viewers with astonishing vistas, while camping in the neighboring Kaibab National Forest provides the opportunity to see abundant wildlife, including Mule Deer, endemic Kaibab Squirrels, and Northern Goshawks.

View from South Rim to North Rim

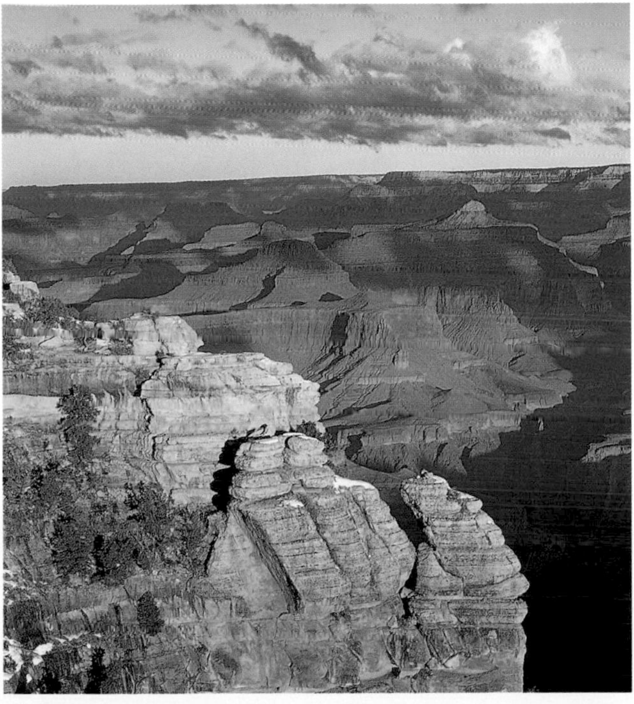

SOUTH RIM Busy at all times of year, but especially during the summer, the South Rim still affords opportunities for solitude to those willing to walk. Many hikers and mule riders make their way down the Bright Angel and South Kaibab Trails to Phantom Ranch, where a lodge and campground allow overnight stays along the Colorado River. The rim itself, much of it paralleled by a paved road, provides endless views, while the headquarters complex at Grand Canyon Village offers services including hotel rooms, campsites, restaurants, and shops. Some autumn days bring large flights of migrating hawks past Yaki Point and Lipan Point, where monitoring stations are maintained by HawkWatch International.

AROUND LEES FERRY The Grand Canyon is said to begin, and Glen Canyon (see page 426) to end, at Lees Ferry, where access to the river is possible from both sides. From there the river begins to incise itself deeply between cliffs of sandstone and limestone. Lees Ferry is the starting point for canyon river trips, but backcountry and wildlife-watching opportunities abound here too. Running through a narrow slot canyon that begins in southern Utah, the Paria River meets the Colorado at Lees Ferry and offers superb hiking, though it is dangerous during summer rains (see page 430 for contact information for the Paria River). To the west, the 3,000-foot Vermilion Cliffs are the new home of California Condors, reintroduced to the wild in 1996 after a 70-year absence from the area. The best place to spot these wide-ranging scavengers is the northwestern end of House Rock Valley, below the eastern rim of the Kaibab Plateau.

Inner gorge of the Grand Canyon

HAVASU CANYON Home of the Havasupai Indians, Havasu Canyon is an oasis in the desert. Fed by a large spring, Havasu Creek thunders through a deep canyon system and over a series of waterfalls. The calcium carbonate carried by its blue-green water slowly precipitates out, forming graceful travertine terraces and hanging rock curtains. The water nourishes both the farming efforts of the Havasupai—who live in the village of Supai, accessible only by foot, horseback, or helicopter—and a lush riparian area of Fremont Cottonwood and Velvet Ash trees. Visitors stay at either a lodge in Supai or a campground 2 miles downstream; from the campground, a strenuous 7-mile trail takes hikers to the point where the creek joins the Colorado River.

Colorado River from Toroweap Overlook

ARIZONA STRIP Separated from the rest of Arizona by the canyon, and managed primarily by the Bureau of Land Management, the Arizona Strip is a land apart. Its sagebrush plains, pinyon-juniper woodlands, and Joshua Tree stands have few visitors and fewer permanent human residents. One of the most visited sites here is Toroweap Overlook, from which it is possible to look almost straight down at the Colorado River more than 3,000 feet below. Nearby are the Mount Logan and Mount Trumbull Wildernesses, high volcanic outcrops that stand over jagged lava flows and are crowned with fine stands of old-growth Ponderosa Pine. Other parts of the Strip are likely to provide a large dose of solitude, as well as the possibility of seeing wild animals, among them Pronghorns and Ferruginous Hawks on the high grasslands and Desert Tortoises and Gila Monsters at low elevations to the west.

LOCATION Northwestern Arizona; nearest major urban areas are Flagstaff, AZ, Kanab, UT, and Las Vegas, NV. **CONTACTS** Grand Canyon N.P., P.O. Box 129, Grand Canyon, AZ 86023; 520-638-7888. Havasupai Tourist Enterprise, P.O. Box 160, Supai, AZ 86435; 520-448-2141; 520-448-2121. Kaibab N.F., North Kaibab Ranger District, P.O. Box 248, Fredonia, AZ 86022; 520-643-7395. Bureau of Land Management, Arizona Strip District, 345 E. Riverside Dr., St. George, UT 84790; 435-688-3246. **VISITOR CENTERS** Grand Canyon N.P.: on North Rim at end of Rte. 67; on South Rim at Desert View, on Rte. 64 at eastern entrance; and 6 miles north of southern park entrance in Grand Canyon village. Kaibab N.F.: Jacob Lake V.C. at junction of Rtes. 89A and 67, open mid-Apr. to mid-Oct. Havasu Canyon: in Supai village. Arizona Strip: at BLM office in St. George, UT (see address above).

COCONINO NATIONAL FOREST **Flagstaff**

Ranging in elevation from less than 4,000 to 12,633 feet and covering nearly 2 million acres, Coconino National Forest showcases climatic and floral diversity. Vegetation includes low-elevation grassland and pinyon-juniper woodland and extensive forests of Ponderosa Pine; higher elevations support mixed-conifer and spruce-fir forests, while the uppermost parts of the San Francisco Peaks (also called San Francisco Mountain) comprise Arizona's only true alpine tundra. Wildlife-watching opportunities abound: Numerous canyon riparian areas, ephemeral lakes, and man-made reservoirs offer the greatest diversity. Lava flows and cinder cones around Flagstaff reveal the area's volcanic heritage. Opportunities for downhill and cross-country skiing, hiking, biking, fishing, and hunting make the forest a recreational mecca. Many forest roads are closed by winter snows.

SAN FRANCISCO PEAKS Arizona's tallest mountain (the highest point is Humphreys Peak) is only a remnant of a much higher volcano that blew its top about a million years ago. The east-facing Inner Basin, where Quaking Aspen groves put on a popular foliage display each autumn, records the direction of the blast. Scientist C. Hart Merriam developed the idea of altitudinal "life zones" here a century ago, and the observant naturalist can still note how Ponderosa Pine forests give way to higher stands of Engelmann Spruce and Rocky Mountain Bristlecone Pine, which in turn yield to the krummholz Subalpine Firs of the timberline.

Quaking Aspens, San Francisco Peaks

MORMON LAKE Growing and shrinking in response to precipitation and evaporation, this shallow marshland (an IBA) is at times Arizona's largest natural lake. Its fish attract abundant Bald Eagles in winter, while summer brings nesting Ospreys, Western Grebes, Savannah Sparrows, and several species of ducks.

SUNSET CRATER AND WUPATKI NATIONAL MONUMENTS Surrounded by national forest land, Sunset Crater National Monument includes both jagged lava flows and shapely cinder cones that stand as evidence of Arizona's most recent volcanic activity. A thousand feet high, Sunset Crater's symmetrical cone reached its current extent less than 800 years ago. Nearby Wupatki National Monument, created to protect ancient stone dwellings built during the era of the eruptions, is a good place to see Pronghorns and other grassland animals, and to admire the colorful badlands of the Painted Desert on the far side of the Little Colorado River valley.

Lava flow and San Francisco Peaks, Sunset Crater National Monument

OAK CREEK CANYON One of Arizona's most scenic drives, Highway 89A winds along rushing Oak Creek in close proximity to riverside woodlands of Douglas Fir, Box Elder, Velvet Ash, and Arizona Walnut. The canyon's cliffs, many of them bright orange, expose some of the same geologic history visible at the Grand Canyon, but from a relatively short time period: mainly 240 to 330 million years ago. Some 15 species of bats have been found in these insect-rich surroundings, along with water-loving birds such as American Dippers. Numerous trails and campgrounds allow access to the creek and the surrounding forest, and Slide Rock State Park is a popular place for swimmers.

Oak Creek Canyon

SYCAMORE CANYON WILDERNESS Resembling Oak Creek Canyon, but with less water and far fewer people, Sycamore Canyon offers rugged backpacking and day-hiking possibilities. Thickets of Canyon Grape and Poison Ivy add to the challenge of negotiating cliffs and talus slopes. Black Bears, Mountain Lions, Golden Eagles, and Ringtails occupy this terrain; summer brings the sweet calls of Hermit Thrushes, Canyon Wrens, and numerous other songbirds.

LOCATION Surrounding Flagstaff and Sedona in north-central Arizona. **CONTACTS** Coconino N.F., 2323 E. Greenlaw La., Flagstaff, AZ 86004; 520-527-3600. Sunset Crater and Wupatki N.M.s, Rte. 3, Box 149, Flagstaff, AZ 86004; 520-526-0502. Slide Rock S.P., P.O. Box 10358, Sedona, AZ 86339; 520-282-3034. **VISITOR CENTERS** At Sunset Crater and Wupatki N.M.s, on Forest Rd. 545.

APACHE-SITGREAVES NATIONAL FOREST

Springerville

Biologically, the Apache and Sitgreaves National Forests, more than 2 million acres managed as a single unit, mark the meeting place of the Rocky Mountains and the Sierra Madre, the biologically rich Mexican massif where subtropical and montane ecosystems mingle. Northern species such as Common Mergansers and Pine Grosbeaks nest here, while subtropical animals such as White-nosed Coatis reach their northern range limits. Cleaved by the steep east–west escarpment of the Mogollon Rim, the forest includes boreal woods on its high northeastern mountains, a huge expanse of Ponderosa Pine forest, and pine-oak woodlands in the rugged canyon country to the south. It is pierced by rivers that carry off heavy snowmelt and the runoff from frequent summer storms. Eagle Creek, the Blue, Little Colorado, and Black Rivers, and other waterways are flanked by campgrounds popular with anglers and naturalists.

Mogollon Rim

The heart of the forest is the 173,762-acre Blue Range Primitive Area, which has remained largely unchanged since its designation in 1933. This rugged patch of mountains, forests, and canyons is accessible only by trail. One of the last strongholds for the large carnivores facing an onslaught of government-sponsored predator control earlier in this century, the Blue's heritage was partly restored in 1998 when captive-bred Mexican Wolves were reintroduced nearby.

Backpackers and cross-country skiers also head to the smaller Mount Baldy and Escudilla Wildernesses near the forest's northern edge, where Engelmann Spruces, Subalpine Firs, and Quaking Aspens cloak mountainsides that rise to 11,400 feet. Elk are common here. Coyotes, Pronghorns, Black Bears, and Long-tailed Weasels are among the other mammals that may be observed in forest openings and on extensive subalpine grasslands. The forest's unpaved roads are closed most winters.

LOCATION East-central Arizona. **CONTACT** Apache-Sitgreaves N.F., P.O. Box 640, Springerville, AZ 85938; 520-333-4301. **VISITOR CENTERS** Mogollon Rim V.C., on Hwy. 260 about 30 miles west of Heber; and at Ranger District office at junction of Rtes. 180 and 191 in Alpine.

PETRIFIED FOREST NATIONAL PARK **Holbrook**

These 93,000 acres of protected federal land preserve both a dense assemblage of 225-million-year-old fossilized logs and a scenic expanse of the starkly beautiful Painted Desert. Relics of an ancient floodplain forest, the logs were buried under mud and turned to colorful rock by the slow deposition of silica. Fossil remains of enormous amphibians and modest-sized dinosaurs, on display at the visitor centers, give a glimpse into the animal life of the Triassic Period (195–230 million years ago). Scenic drives and backcountry hiking allow visitors to peek into today's Painted Desert, a land of soft, easily erodable badlands stained by a palette of bright-colored minerals.

LOCATION About 25 miles east of Holbrook via I-40 or Rte. 180. **CONTACT** Petrified Forest N.P., P.O. Box 2217, Petrified Forest, AZ 86028; 520-524-6228. **VISITOR CENTERS** Rainbow Forest Museum, just north of Rte. 180 entrance; and Painted Desert V.C. and Painted Desert Inn Museum, adjacent to I-40 entrance.

MULESHOE RANCH COOPERATIVE MANAGEMENT AREA **Willcox**

The Nature Conservancy bought this parcel of rugged grassland in the 1980s, and is now managing it and adjacent leased lands (making a total of 48,120 acres) for the benefit of several endangered fish species that live in the ranch's perennial creeks. Periodic burning and the cessation of cattle grazing, which had contributed to the conversion of grassy slopes into scrubby thickets, are helping to restore grasslands and ensure high-quality runoff for the creeks. Mountain Lions, Lowland Leopard Frogs, and many other species also benefit from this progressive management. Visitors can camp and hike, and stay in comfortable accommodations at the preserve headquarters.

LOCATION 29 miles northwest of Willcox via Airport and Muleshoe Rds. **CONTACT** Muleshoe Ranch Cooperative Management Area, R.R. 1, Box 1542, Willcox, AZ 85643; 520-586-7072. **VISITOR CENTER** At preserve hdqtrs., off end of Muleshoe Rd.

ARAVAIPA CANYON — Klondyke

Arizonans say that their rivers are dry and their creeks wet. That's certainly true along perennial Aravaipa Creek, which provides habitat for seven native fish species: Longfin and Speckled Dace, Loach Minnow, Spikedace, Roundtail Chub, and two suckers. The water also supports dense stands of ash, cottonwood, willow, and other trees that furnish nest sites for the state's largest population of Common Black-Hawks. Desert Bighorn Sheep are often seen on neighboring cliffs, while White-nosed Coatis, Ringtails, and several species of rattlesnakes are generally more secretive. Hikers often spend several days here, traversing a 10-mile Bureau of Land Management wilderness area straddled by Nature Conservancy lands. Permits, required for hiking the wilderness, are often claimed up to three months in advance for peak weekends.

Aravaipa Creek

LOCATION Western end, 12 miles east of Rte. 77 on Aravaipa Rd.; eastern end, 45 miles northwest of Rte. 70 on Klondyke Rd. **CONTACTS** Bureau of Land Management, 711 14th Ave., Safford, AZ 85546; 520-348-4400. The Nature Conservancy, Box 4, Klondyke, AZ 85643; 520-828-3443. **VISITOR CENTER** At BLM office in Safford (see address above).

SAN PEDRO RIPARIAN NATIONAL CONSERVATION AREA — Sierra Vista

A southwestern rarity, an undammed river, the San Pedro has long lured people with its shade, water, and abundant food sources. Stone tools and animal bones reveal that hunters killed Woolly Mammoths and other ice-age mammals here 11,000 years ago. Today hiking and backcountry camping are popular at this 40-mile-long site, especially with birders. Since the Bureau of Land Management discontinued cattle grazing in the late 1980s, vegetation has made a quick comeback. Now such rare birds as Gray Hawks, Western Yellow-billed Cuckoos, and Southwestern Willow Flycatchers nest here, and hundreds of migrant and wintering species pass through. The river corridor also supports 86 mammal species, the greatest number in any area of comparable size north of Mexico.

San Pedro River

LOCATION South of I-10 between Benson and Sierra Vista. **CONTACT** San Pedro Riparian N.C.A., 1763 Paseo San Luis, Sierra Vista, AZ 85635; 520-458-3559. **VISITOR CENTER** San Pedro House, on Rte. 90, 7 miles east of Sierra Vista.

BUENOS AIRES NATIONAL WILDLIFE REFUGE

Arivaca

The grasslands of the Southwest have been heavily altered by more than a century of livestock grazing; at Buenos Aires, managers are trying to recreate what the landscape once looked like. The 114,000-acre refuge provides a reintroduction site for the endangered Masked Bobwhite, but its diverse habitats support many species. Extensive grasslands are home to Pronghorns and many sparrows, including Botteri's, Cassin's, and Rufous-winged. Arivaca Creek and Arivaca Cienega (a group of seven springs) are rare wetlands. Brown Canyon, a rugged Arizona Sycamore–lined cleft in the eastern side of the Baboquivari Mountains that provides access to pine-oak woodlands, offers splendid opportunities for wildflower, butterfly, and bird watching.

LOCATION About 60 miles southwest of Tucson via Rte. 286 or Arivaca Rd. **CONTACT** Buenos Aires N.W.R., P.O. Box 109, Sasabe, AZ 85633; 520-823-4251. **VISITOR CENTER** At hdqtrs. 38 miles south of Three Points off Hwy. 286, and on Arivaca Rd. in Arivaca.

SAGUARO NATIONAL PARK

Tucson

Giant Saguaros

Bracketing Tucson like bookends, the two halves of Saguaro National Park (an IBA) comprise 91,327 acres of urban recreation areas and prime expanses of desert and montane wilderness. Their washes and foothills preserve some of the finest examples of dense Giant Saguaro cactus forest. Trails in the arid Saguaro West district rise to over 4,600 feet, while those in the larger Saguaro East district penetrate the high, cool forests of the Rincon Mountains and provide a true wilderness experience. Loop drives in both sections provide splendid scenery and short trails for briefer visits. Gila Monsters, Elf Owls, Harris's Hawks, Collared Peccaries, and an array of other desert dwellers are often seen or heard. Couch's Spadefoot toads emerge in huge, cacophonous numbers following the first heavy summer rains.

LOCATION Saguaro East: main entrance off Old Spanish Trail east of Freeman Rd. Saguaro West: about 10 miles west of Tucson via Kinney Rd. **CONTACT** Saguaro N.P., 3693 Old Spanish Trail, Tucson, AZ 85730; 520-733-5153 (Saguaro East), 520-733-5158 (Saguaro West). **VISITOR CENTERS** Saguaro East: at park entrance. Saguaro West: just northwest of Kinney Rd. entrance.

CORONADO NATIONAL FOREST **Tucson**

Home to one of the greatest assemblages of biodiversity in the United States, the 1.7-million-acre Coronado National Forest and adjoining preserves shelter great numbers of plants, arthropods, and vertebrates, including many uncommon north of Mexico. Reports continue of such rarities as Jaguars and Eared Trogons. Because these montane forests are separated by desert or grassland, they offer puzzles in biogeography—Mexican Chickadees, for example, are found in the United States only in the Chiricahuas, and not in other areas of similar habitat. These "sky islands" also pose a conservation problem, as development threatens the suitability of lowlands used as wildlife corridors. Roads and campgrounds here are often closed by winter snow.

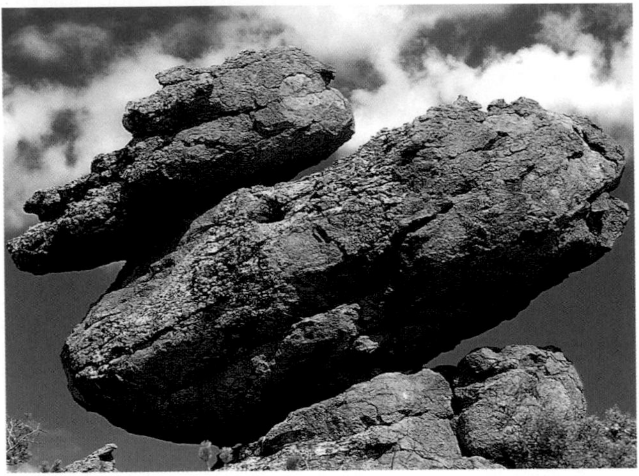

Duck on a Rock, Chiricahua National Monument

CHIRICAHUA NATIONAL MONUMENT Weirdly rounded towers of volcanic rhyolite are the hallmark of this national monument, which is a good place to see many of this range's unique plants and animals, including Chihuahua Pines, Arizona Cypresses, Apache Fox Squirrels, and White-nosed Coatis. Higher slopes atop this large north–south range support Mexican Chickadees, Evening Grosbeaks, and Twin-spotted Rattlesnakes. The cliffs and riparian trees of Cave Creek Canyon attract species from Peregrine Falcons to Strickland's Woodpeckers and Painted Redstarts.

THE PINALEÑOS The Pinaleños are the highest of the sky islands. The summit, Mount Graham, rearing up to 10,713 feet, is crowned with a relict forest of Engelmann Spruce and Corkbark Fir. The cones of these conifers constitute a major food source for the endangered Mount Graham Red Squirrel. A winding road leads visitors to over 9,000 feet; its top portion is closed to protect squirrel habitat and to facilitate construction of a controversial astronomical observatory.

RAMSEY CANYON This Nature Conservancy preserve forms a gateway into the Huachuca Mountains, next to the Mexican border. Its perennial creek is a lifeline for the Ramsey Canyon Leopard Frog, a rare and local species that differs from related species by calling underwater. Rare Lemon Lilies, Tepic Flame-flowers, and Ridge-nose Rattlesnakes thrive here, while feeders attract about a dozen hummingbird species. Reservations are often needed in spring and summer.

Canelo Hills below Huachuca Mountains

THE SANTA CATALINAS Tucson's backyard mountains rise to over 9,000 feet, providing a cool escape from desert heat. A highway winds up Mount Lemmon, allowing easy access to desert, grassland, oak woodland, and Ponderosa Pine forest before ending among Quaking Aspen and fir trees. Orange-crowned Warblers are among the birds typically found in moister climates that nest locally here; wildflowers and butterflies are abundant following summer rains. Trails beginning at Tucson's edge provide access to rugged canyons.

MADERA CANYON This birding hotspot in the Santa Rita Mountains is best known as one of the most reliable places to see Buff-collared Nightjars, Whiskered Screech-Owls, Elegant Trogons, Sulphur-bellied Flycatchers, and other subtropical species, including numerous hummingbirds. A lodge and campground provide accommodations, while foot trails allow access to the mountains' higher terrain.

PATAGONIA–SONOITA CREEK PRESERVE A rare perennial, lowland waterway sliding between the Santa Rita and Patagonia Mountains, Sonoita Creek (an IBA) is lined with Fremont Cottonwoods that attract a plethora of birds, including such primarily Mexican species as Gray and Zone-tailed Hawks, Green Kingfishers, Thick-billed Kingbirds, and Northern Beardless-Tyrannulets.

LOCATION Southeastern Arizona. **CONTACTS** Coronado N.F., 300 W. Congress, Tucson, AZ 85701; 520-670-4552. Chiricahua N.M., HCR 2 Box 6500, Willcox, AZ 85643; 520-824-3560. Ramsey Canyon Pres., 27 Ramsey Canyon Rd., Hereford, AZ 85615; 520-378-2785. Patagonia–Sonoita Creek Pres., P.O. Box 815, Patagonia, AZ 85624; 520-394-2400. **VISITOR CENTERS** Coronado N.F.: in town of Portal; on Rte. 366 in the Pinaleños; at Sabino Canyon in Tucson; and at milepost 19 on Mt. Lemmon Hwy. Chiricahua N.M.: 2 miles into park on main road. Ramsey Canyon Pres.: at hdqtrs. (see above). Patagonia–Sonoita Creek Pres.: at hdqtrs., west of Patagonia on Pennsylvania Ave.

ORGAN PIPE CACTUS NATIONAL MONUMENT

Ajo

Organ Pipe Cacti

This 330,690-acre preserve is both hot and—by desert standards—fairly moist, allowing huge columnar Giant Saguaro, Organ Pipe, and Senita cacti to thrive. The latter two, along with numerous other Mexican species, are at or near the northern edge of their range here. When the timing of fall and winter rains is right, this park's diverse plant communities offer prime opportunities to see spectacular spring wildflower displays. A great diversity of animal life relies on this wide variety of vegetation. Desert wildlife abounds, while a spring-fed pond at Quitobaquito supports the only wild population of an endangered Desert Pupfish subspecies. Scenic driving, hiking, and camping opportunities are ample.

LOCATION Entrance 35 miles south of Ajo on Rte. 85. **CONTACT** Organ Pipe Cactus N.M., Rte. 1, Box 100, Ajo, AZ 85321; 520-387-6849. **VISITOR CENTER** At monument hdqtrs., south of Why off Rte. 85.

CABEZA PRIETA NATIONAL WILDLIFE REFUGE

Ajo

The grandeur of this spare wilderness is commensurate with the difficulty of getting there. All visitors must have a permit, available free at the headquarters. Only four-wheel-drive vehicles are allowed, and then only on a handful of roads. Backcountry hiking is permitted, but opportunities are severely restricted by a lack of water and extreme summer heat. The few visitors to this 860,000-acre refuge, however, are treated to a wilderness experience that has become rare in the desert. Steep granite mountains rise like ships from wide fans of alluvial sediments, providing homes for nimble Desert Bighorn Sheep, while endangered Sonoran Pronghorns patrol the creosote flats below. Birds and reptiles, including six species of rattlesnakes, are common. Yet light, color, and silence are typically the greatest rewards of visits here.

Sand verbenas and evening-primroses

LOCATION West of Ajo and Organ Pipe Cactus N.M. **CONTACT** Cabeza Prieta N.W.R., 1611 N. Second Ave., Ajo, AZ 85321; 520-387-6483. **VISITOR CENTER** At hdqtrs. on Second Ave. (Rte. 85), at the northern end of Ajo.

IMPERIAL NATIONAL WILDLIFE REFUGE — Yuma

A study in contrasts, this 28,000-acre refuge (an IBA) includes both marshy sloughs of the Colorado River and stark, almost barren uplands watered by an average of only 3 inches of rain a year. Washes are rich with Desert Ironwood, Blue Paloverde, and Honey Mesquite trees. The Painted Desert Trail is a scenic, 1-mile footpath through lava flows and colorful eroded badlands. Lookout points north of the refuge headquarters provide views of the Colorado River, backwaters, and birds. The best way to see the refuge's 30 miles of river, though, is by boat. Wintering birds include Sandhill Cranes and numerous species of waterfowl.

Desert Ironwood

LOCATION About 27 miles north of Yuma via Rte. 95 and Martinez Lake Rd. **CONTACT** Imperial N.W.R., P.O. Box 72217, Martinez Lake, AZ 85365; 520-783-3371. **VISITOR CENTER** At hdqtrs., off Martinez Lake Rd.

ANTELOPE CANYON NAVAJO TRIBAL PARK — Page

A deep and sinuous slot, often little wider than an adult's shoulders, cuts through multi-hued sandstone in Glen Canyon drainage. This park offers superb hiking and photography. **CONTACT** Antelope Canyon Navajo Tribal Park., P.O. Box 4803, Page, AZ 86040; 520-698-3347.

Anasazi Indian ruins, Canyon de Chelly National Monument

CANYON DE CHELLY NATIONAL MONUMENT — Chinle

At this 83,000-acre site, steep-walled canyons carved into the sandstone of the Defiance Plateau shelter ancient cliff dwellings, contemporary Navajo farms, Peregrine Falcons, and White-throated Swifts. **CONTACT** Canyon de Chelly N.M., P.O. Box 588, Chinle, AZ 86503; 520-674-5500.

CIBOLA NATIONAL WILDLIFE REFUGE — Blythe, CA

In winter, tens of thousands of Canada Geese descend on this 16,267-acre Colorado River refuge, along with many other types of waterfowl. Summer residents include endangered Southwestern Willow Flycatchers and Yuma Clapper Rails, as well as Burrowing Owls, Kit Foxes, and numerous reptiles. **CONTACT** Cibola N.W.R., P.O. Box AP, Blythe, CA 92226; 520-857-3253.

EAST CACTUS PLAIN WILDERNESS — Bouse
CACTUS PLAIN WILDERNESS STUDY AREA — Parker

Neighboring tracts of stabilized sand dunes surrounded by distant mountains provide visitors with ever-shifting tableaux of desert light and color. Wildflower displays can be impressive after wet winters. **CONTACT**

Bureau of Land Management, 2610 Sweetwater Ave., Lake Havasu City, AZ 86406; 520-505-1200.

GILA BOX RIPARIAN NATIONAL CONSERVATION AREA Safford

Variable flows in the Gila River provide rafting, kayaking, and canoeing through riparian woodlands, while Zone-tailed Hawks and Common Black-Hawks circle overhead at this 22,000-acre site. CONTACT Gila Box Riparian N.C.A., 711 14th Ave., Safford, AZ 85546; 520-348-4400.

HAVASU NATIONAL WILDLIFE REFUGE Needles, CA

This 44,371-acre refuge (an IBA) encompasses a wildlife-rich Colorado River marsh, scenic Topock Gorge, and the rugged desert of the Needles Wilderness. CONTACT Havasu N.W.R., P.O. Box 3009, Needles, CA 92363; 760-326-3853.

KOFA NATIONAL WILDLIFE REFUGE Yuma

More than 665,400 acres of pristine Sonoran Desert allow visitors to experience solitude, along with looks at Desert Bighorn Sheep and a rare native California Fan Palm oasis. CONTACT Kofa N.W.R., 356 W. 1st St., Yuma, AZ 85364; 520-783-7861.

METEOR CRATER
Winslow

This 570-foot-deep and 3/4-mile-wide crater was formed 49,000 years ago by the impact of a meteor estimated to be 150 feet in diameter. A privately run facility offers impressive vantage points and meteorite displays. CONTACT Meteor Crater Enterprises, P.O. Box 70, Flagstaff, AZ 86002; 520-289-2362.

Meteor Crater

NAVAJO NATIONAL MONUMENT Kayenta

Established to protect ancient cliff dwellings, this scenic monument also offers visitors a look at steep canyons that shelter relict Quaking Aspen and Douglas Fir groves. CONTACT Navajo N.M., HC-71 Box 3, Tonalea, AZ 86044; 520-672-2366.

PRESCOTT NATIONAL FOREST Prescott

Two large swaths of desert and forest in central Arizona provide abundant outdoor recreation. Boating the Verde Wild and Scenic River and hiking the Granite Mountain Wilderness near Prescott are among the most popular attractions. CONTACT Prescott N.F., 344 S. Cortez St., Prescott, AZ 86303; 520-771-4700.

SAN BERNARDINO NATIONAL WILDLIFE REFUGE Douglas

Springs in the headwaters of the south-flowing Rio Yaqui provide habitat for threatened native fishes and frogs. Birding is excellent at this 2,300-acre refuge. CONTACT San Bernardino N.W.R., P.O. Box 3509, Douglas, AZ 85608; 520-364-2104.

TONTO NATIONAL FOREST Phoenix

Consisting largely of Sonoran Desert terrain, these almost 3 million acres also encompass seven rugged wilderness areas that rise to nearly 8,000 feet. Scenic and rugged stretches of the Salt and Verde Rivers provide nesting sites for rare desert-dwelling Bald Eagle. Many day-hiking and camping sites near Phoenix grow crowded, but large portions of the farther reaches are rarely visited. CONTACT Tonto N.F., 2324 E. McDowell Rd., Phoenix, AZ 85006; 602-225-5200.

WILLCOX PLAYA WILDLIFE AREA Willcox

Water levels vary in this huge ancient lake bed, depending upon precipitation in the surrounding mountains. Winter brings flocks of thousands of Sandhill Cranes as well as abundant raptors to this 555-acre preserve. CONTACT Arizona Game and Fish Dept., 555 N. Greasewood Rd., Tucson, AZ 85745; 520-628-5376.

Nevada

From the air Nevada looks as split and crinkled as the dried mud flakes that curl from its numerous playas in summer's heat. Fracturing of the earth's crust has resulted in the creation of mountain range after mountain range, each steep-sided parallel ridge separated from its neighbors by wide valleys full of sagebrush or, in some cases, lakes or alkali flats.

Nevada's wide-open, arid country appears monotonous at first glance. But it richly rewards exploration, and not just because of the ample solitude that can be gained on virtually any outing. Plants and animals have conformed themselves to the state's topography and climate. The higher mountains capture moisture and convey it to the basins through creeks and springs that form oases for wildlife—and for people. Boundary Peak, near the California border, is the highest point in the state at 13,140 feet.

The isolation of many ranges has resulted in endless applications of the rules of island biogeography. Biologists will no doubt busy themselves for a long time examining why certain ranges support certain plants and animals while neighboring mountains do not. In this sparsely populated region naturalists will no doubt continue to significantly contribute to an understanding of the state's ecology.

About 87 percent of Nevada is federal land, which means that the opportunities for exploration are virtually endless. This guide can only hint at a few highlights. In particular, the vast acreage managed by the Bureau of Land Management (BLM) will reward those who are willing to pore over topographic maps and set out for the backcountry with stout hiking boots, a hat, and plenty of water. Nevada's 110,561 square miles feature two national forests, one national park, six national wildlife refuges, one national recreation area, and 24 state parks.

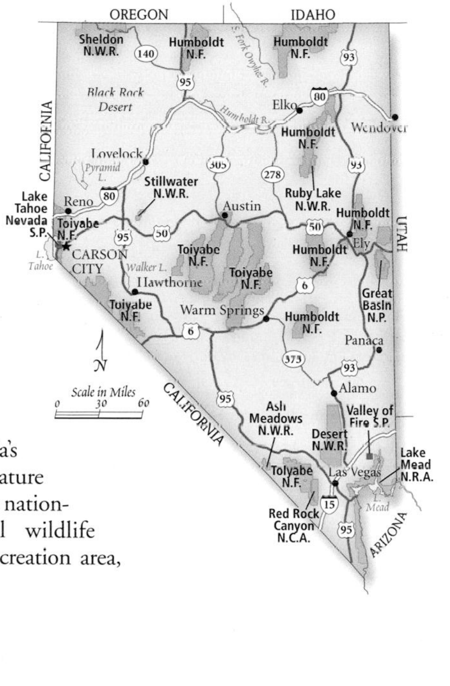

SHELDON NATIONAL WILDLIFE REFUGE — Denio

This 575,000-acre refuge was established in the 1930s to conserve Pronghorns, which thrive on the area's open sagebrush plains. Mule Deer and California Bighorn Sheep are also often seen here. Sage Grouse, too, are common, while raptors including Golden Eagles, Ferruginous Hawks, and Prairie Falcons nest on rimrock cliffs. Creeks and reservoirs support at least 10 nesting species of waterfowl and three native fish species—Alvord Chub, Tui Chub, and the threatened Lahontan Cutthroat Trout. Numerous dirt roads allow visitors to access dispersed, primitive campsites, wildlife-watching areas, and rockhounding sites.

Mule Deer

LOCATION Refuge hdqtrs. is on Rte. 140, 30 miles west of Denio, NV, and 95 miles east of Lakeview, OR. **CONTACT** Sheldon N.W.R., P.O. Box 111, Lakeview, OR 97630; 541-947-3315. **VISITOR CENTER** At refuge hdqtrs.

BLACK ROCK DESERT — Gerlach

The veritable definition of a desert, the Black Rock is a huge playa so flat that it has an elevation change of only 5 feet over its 25-mile length. Covered during the last ice age by 500-foot-deep Lake Lahontan, the lake bed is now generally dry in summer and muddy the rest of the year. Except at its edges, the playa is almost entirely lifeless. Exploring it is a stunning way to experience open space—even the curvature of the earth is visible—though care must be taken to ensure that hikers and vehicles do not get stuck in the glue-like alkali mud. Neighboring wild areas, including High Rock Canyon and the Black Rock Range, offer more conventional exploration and camping opportunities, as well as the chance to see Desert Bighorn Sheep, Feral Horses, and numerous raptors.

LOCATION Just northeast of Gerlach; inquire locally about road conditions. **CONTACT** Bureau of Land Management, Winnemucca District, 5100 E. Winnemucca Blvd., Winnemucca, NV 89445; 702-623-3672.

PYRAMID LAKE — Nixon

Fremont Pyramid and Pyramid Lake

Pyramid Lake—a relict lake that has not yet evaporated into the desert air—offers a glimpse into the Great Basin's ice-age past. Its surface has dropped about 100 feet in the last century, but this change resulted from human diversions of the Truckee River, the lake's main inflow. As a result, the native Cui-ui (a large sucker) and Lahontan Cutthroat Trout have become imperiled. American White Pelicans, which once nested in great numbers on Anaho Island, have become scarcer, too. Management of the 110,000-acre lake's water supply remains a contentious issue, but in the meantime visitors enjoy sensational fishing, birding, and the ever-changing play of light on the water and its surrounding pyramid-shaped tufa formations.

LOCATION Just north of Nixon, 14 miles north of I-80. **CONTACT** Paiute Tribe, P.O. Box 256, Nixon, NV 89424; 702-574-1000. **VISITOR CENTERS** Along the Truckee River in Nixon; also at marina in Sutcliffe, along Hwy. 445.

STILLWATER NATIONAL WILDLIFE REFUGE — Fallon

The wetlands in the Carson Sink—a huge, flat valley basin—can vary in extent from about 100 acres to more than 200,000, depending on the quantity of Sierra Nevada snowmelt that feeds the marshes and shallow lakes here. During drought years, migrating and nesting shorebirds mass on shrinking mudflats; in wet years, American White Pelicans, Double-crested Cormorants, and other fish-eating species spread out across miles of shallow water. Cattails, Alkali Bulrush, Brine Flies, and Fairy Shrimp form the basis for the area's simple but productive ecosystem. The neighboring Stillwater Wildlife Management Area and Fallon National Wildlife Refuge offer additional possibilities for wildlife-watching and primitive camping.

LOCATION 10 miles east of Fallon on Stillwater Rd. **CONTACT** Stillwater N.W.R., P.O. Box 1236, Fallon, NV 89407; 702-423-5128.

HUMBOLDT-TOIYABE NATIONAL FOREST

Encompassing nearly 6 million acres in Nevada and another 700,000 in eastern California, Humboldt-Toiyabe National Forest is a far-flung catch-all for many of the state's highest and most heavily forested mountain ranges. Its many units border California, Oregon, and Idaho, and almost reach Utah. While each of the forest's units provides abundant opportunities for hiking, camping, and encountering myriad species of plants and animals, a few stand out as particularly rich areas for naturalists to explore. Note that snowfall can be heavy in these mountains, whose high elevations are frequently inaccessible in winter.

Sagebrush prairie, Santa Rosa Mountains

SANTA ROSA MOUNTAINS Running south from the Oregon line, the Santa Rosas present intriguing lessons in geology and island biogeography. Comprised of both steep granite escarpments and gentler basalt mesas, they lack most of the conifers present on other Nevada ranges. Only Quaking Aspens and Limber Pines break the monotony of the sagebrush, though a diversity of perennial grasses has led to large populations of herbivores. Among the animals that like this open terrain are numerous species of gamebirds, including California Quail, Sage Grouse, and introduced Chukars and Hungarian Partridges.

JARBIDGE MOUNTAINS Hard by the Idaho border the classic Basin and Range topography of Nevada changes. Here the mountains are more jumbled as they descend to the north into the Snake River Basin, and Rocky Mountain influences become more pronounced. This is one of the few Nevada ranges with Whitebark Pines. The fossilized bones of American Martens—a species no longer found in the Great Basin—suggest that the range's forests once connected with the Rockies during cooler, wetter times. The 113,000-acre Jarbidge Wilderness offers high-elevation remoteness.

Ruby Mountains

RUBY MOUNTAINS The higher elevations of these mountains receive upward of 400 inches of snow each winter, making this the wettest range in Nevada and the one with the largest and most diverse alpine tundra habitat. Many of the alpine lakes and glacial cirques of the 90,000-acre Ruby Mountains Wilderness are accessible via the lengthy Ruby Crest Trail. Rocky Mountain Bighorn Sheep and introduced Mountain Goats are often spotted on the slopes. The continent's only self-sustaining population of introduced Himalayan Snowcocks lives here. The steep sides of scenic Lamoille Canyon are bright with wildflowers or, in autumn, the dappled golden yellow of Quaking Aspens.

TOIYABE RANGE One of the many parallel mountain chains that crinkle central Nevada, the long and narrow Toiyabe Range reaches northward from the 115,000-acre Arc Dome Wilderness, Nevada's largest. A 68-mile-long recreation trail follows much of the crest, and connects with other routes that rise to the high country from the east and west. Hikers on virtually any of these trails are assured large doses of solitude. Native trout can still be found in the range's numerous creeks.

Arc Dome Wilderness

SPRING MOUNTAINS Separated from the rest of the forest by more than a hundred miles of desert, the Spring Mountains form a cool backdrop for the sprawl of Las Vegas. At 11,918 feet, the summit of Mount Charleston is so high and exposed that even the hardy Bristlecone Pines of lower elevations—some of which are believed to be close to 5,000 years old—cannot grow on its crest. It is a measure of the range's isolation that at least 35 plants grow only here. Palmer's Chipmunk and a number of butterflies are found exclusively in the Spring Mountains. More widespread wildlife species include the Elk, Desert Bighorn Sheep, Northern Goshawk, and Flammulated Owl.

LOCATION Units scattered widely across the state. **CONTACT** Humboldt-Toiyabe N.F., 1200 Franklin Way, Sparks, NV 89431; 702-331-6444. **VISITOR CENTER** Spring Mountain Unit: in Kyle Canyon near end of Rte. 157.

LAKE TAHOE NEVADA STATE PARK — Incline Village

Along its western rim, Nevada rises into the heights of the Sierra Nevada, nowhere more scenically than along the shores of Lake Tahoe. The park here incorporates both an undeveloped stretch of shoreline and forested backcountry rich with such Sierra Nevada species as the Jeffrey Pine and the White-headed Woodpecker. Several smaller lakes are popular with day hikers. There is no camping in the 13,000-acre state park, but opportunities are ample in surrounding Humboldt-Toiyabe National Forest (page 396).

LOCATION Hdqtrs. is at Sand Harbor, on Rte. 28 about 3 miles south of Incline Village. **CONTACT** Lake Tahoe Nevada S.P., P.O. Box 8867, Incline Village, NV 89452; 702-831-0494.

RUBY LAKE NATIONAL WILDLIFE REFUGE — Ruby Valley

Sandhill Cranes

Throughout the Great Basin, mountain runoff drains into wide basins that lack an outlet. In the Ruby Valley, runoff collects in a long string of marshes and ponds that now are managed to provide optimal habitat for migrating and nesting waterfowl. Thousands of Canvasbacks and Redheads nest here each summer, as do smaller numbers of Trumpeter Swans, Sandhill Cranes, White-faced Ibises, Snowy Egrets, and many other wetland-dependent species. Eight fish species also reside at the 37,632-acre refuge (an IBA); the only known native—the Relict Dace—is restricted to a few basins in northeastern Nevada. Depending on water level, various parts of the marshes are best explored by boat or via a network of roads.

LOCATION Refuge hdqtrs. off Rte. 767, 65 miles south of Elko. **CONTACT** Ruby Lake N.W.R., H.C. 60 Box 860, Ruby Valley, NV 89833; 702-779-2237. **VISITOR CENTER** At refuge hdqtrs.

GREAT BASIN NATIONAL PARK

Baker

View from summit of Wheeler Peak

Located in the South Snake Range, Great Basin National Park includes a sampling of the habitats that make up its namesake region. From sagebrush plains, the mountains rise high into clear sky, clad in turn by pinyon-juniper woodlands, grassy meadows, Quaking Aspen groves, mountain scrub, ancient stands of Bristlecone and Limber Pine, and finally steep and rocky peaks above the tree line. Cradled just below the 13,063-foot summit of Wheeler Peak is the only remnant glacier in the Great Basin. Alpine lakes and perennial creeks provide further relief from the dominating aridity of the vertical succession of habitats.

The 77,100-acre park was created in 1986 by greatly expanding the existing Lehman Caves National Monument. Eroded by water out of limestone bedrock, the cavern was decorated over eons by the deposition of tiny amounts of calcite carried by remnant trickles of groundwater. The result is an array of exquisite stalactites, stalagmites, draperies, columns, shields, and other formations.

Bristlecone Pine

Visitors can also enjoy Wheeler Peak Scenic Drive, which ascends to over 10,000 feet on its way past several developed campgrounds. But much of the most rewarding exploration is done off-road, on a series of trails that penetrate the rugged backcountry (snow can close high-elevation roads and trails in winter). Commonly observed animals include Golden Eagles, Clark's Nutcrackers, Yellow-bellied Marmots, and Mule Deer.

LOCATION 5 miles west of Baker on Rte. 488. **CONTACT** Great Basin N.P., Baker, NV 89311; 702-234-7331. **VISITOR CENTER** At end of Rte. 488 near park entrance.

VALLEY OF FIRE STATE PARK

Overton

Elephant Rock

Erosion has turned the brightly colored sandstones, shales, and other rocks of this 36,000-acre park into a natural playground for children and adults alike. Sand dunes 150 million years old, frozen into place and now exposed to the elements, have been sculpted into weird gorges, domes, and pinnacles, such as Elephant Rock. Hiking is always entertaining here; short trails lead to numerous geological oddities, including a collection of ancient petrified logs. Visitors can also observe resident animals of the Mojave Desert, including Greater Roadrunners, Loggerhead Shrikes, Desert Tortoises, and an array of lizards.

LOCATION 50 miles east of Las Vegas via I-15 and Rte. 169. **CONTACT** Valley of Fire S.P., P.O. Box 515, Overton, NV 89040; 702-397-2088. **VISITOR CENTER** On main park road halfway between eastern and western entrances.

ASH MEADOWS NATIONAL WILDLIFE REFUGE

Pahrump

Ash Meadows is a desert surprise, a network of spring-fed wetlands that is a hotbed for rare and endangered species. Some 24 plant and animal species live only at this 22,117-acre refuge. Its four endangered native fishes include the Devils Hole Pupfish, whose range is restricted to a single natural pool. Like other pools in the area, it is fed by springs fueled by groundwater that fell as rain or snow thousands of years ago. After long years of agricultural use that heavily impacted the area and threatened the survival of the endemic species, the U.S. Fish and Wildlife Service is now attempting to return the area to its natural state as much as possible; visitors can witness restoration activities in process.

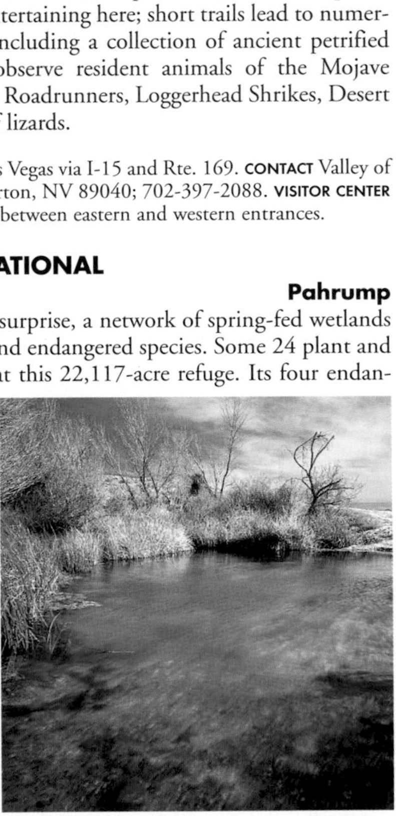

LOCATION 90 miles northwest of Las Vegas via Rte. 160. **CONTACT** Ash Meadows N.W.R., P.O. Box 115, Amargosa Valley, NV 89020; 702-372-5435. **VISITOR CENTER** At refuge hdqtrs., 22 miles west of Pahrump on Bell Vista Rd.

DESERT NATIONAL WILDLIFE RANGE — Las Vegas

This enormous 1.5-million-acre preserve, the most extensive in the lower 48 states, caters to the needs of Desert Bighorn Sheep rather than of people—indeed, the western half of the refuge overlaps an Air Force range and is entirely off-limits to recreational visitors. The refuge encompasses a representative array of plant communities, from lowland Mojave Desert to high-elevation stands of Ponderosa and Bristlecone Pine. There are scant facilities for visitors here, but a drive on the main refuge roads offers prime opportunities for solitude and wildlife-watching. Along with the native sheep, Golden Eagles, Pinyon Jays, Loggerhead Shrikes, and Mule Deer are among the commonly observed species.

Desert Bighorn Sheep

LOCATION Field hdqtrs. and main entrance about 23 miles northwest of Las Vegas on Rte. 93. **CONTACT** Desert National Wildlife Range, 1500 N. Decatur Blvd., Las Vegas, NV 89108; 702-646-3401.

RED ROCK CANYON NATIONAL CONSERVATION AREA — Las Vegas

Steep canyons carved into multi-colored sandstone characterize the terrain of this preserve, a popular outing destination. A stunning 3,000-foot escarpment separates Mojave Desert vegetation, including Joshua Trees, from montane plants such as Ponderosa Pines. Numerous springs emerge among the cliffs and canyons. Pine Creek, a perennial watercourse, flows through an area of lush riparian growth. Hiking opportunities are ample on the site's 195,610 acres; there is also a paved, 13-mile scenic loop road.

LOCATION About 10 miles west of Las Vegas via Rte. 159 or 160. **CONTACT** Bureau of Land Management, Las Vegas District Office, P.O. Box 26569, Las Vegas, NV 89126; 702-647-5000. **VISITOR CENTER** On Rte. 159 at beginning of scenic loop.

LAKE MEAD NATIONAL RECREATION AREA

Boulder City

Completed in 1935, Boulder Dam—later renamed Hoover Dam—set the stage for human control of the unpredictable Colorado River. It tamed floods, generated electricity, and allowed a steady supply of water for irrigation and development, meanwhile destroying riparian habitat and rugged canyon scenery. The dam created the largest reservoir in the United States. The 110-mile-long lake and its surroundings now comprise a recreation area of more than 2,500 square miles that is extremely popular for swimming, boating, and other water sports. Downstream, smaller and narrower Lake Mojave backs up behind Davis Dam.

More than 85 percent of the recreation area consists of rugged desert land, much of it little visited. The Sonoran, Mojave, and Great Basin deserts meet here, fostering an exceptional diversity of plant and animal life. The park's northeastern fringe, in Arizona, rises to high Ponderosa Pine forests. River's edge constitutes one of the best places to watch Desert Bighorn Sheep, especially in dry seasons when they descend to the water to drink. Introduced Burros are also common and often noisy. Endangered Desert Tortoises roam, while Lake Mojave supports relict populations of endangered Razorback Suckers and Bonytail Chubs.

Tamarisk tree at water's edge

Rental boats provide an easy means of accessing the reservoir's 550-mile shoreline. There are few maintained trails, but hiking is permitted and possible almost anywhere in this open desert terrain.

LOCATION Hdqtrs. on Rte. 93, 4 miles east of Boulder City. **CONTACT** Lake Mead N.R.A., 601 Nevada Hwy., Boulder City, NV 89005; 702-293-8947. **VISITOR CENTER** Alan Bible V.C., at hdqtrs.

BEAVER DAM STATE PARK **Panaca**

Hiking, fishing, and camping are popular at this remote and beautiful park, rich with deep canyons and perennial water. American Beaver, Mule Deer, and native fishes are abundant. **CONTACT** Beaver Dam S.P., P.O. Box 176, Panaca, NV 89042; 702-728-4460.

BERLIN-ICHTHYOSAUR STATE PARK **Austin**

The fossils of 225-million-year-old marine reptiles, recovered in this mining region, are on display at the park's Fossil House. **CONTACT** Berlin-Ichthyosaur S.P., HC 61 Box 61200, Austin, NV 89310; 702-964-2440.

CATHEDRAL GORGE STATE PARK **Panaca**

Cathedral Gorge State Park

Erosion has carved steep gorges and gullies into the soft, buff-colored sediments of an ancient lake bed here. Trails wind through 14,000 acres of Greasewood, Shadscale, saltbush, and other desert vegetation. **CONTACT** Cathedral Gorge S.P., P.O. Box 176, Panaca, NV 89042; 702-728-4460.

ELY ELK VIEWING AREA **Ely**

Nevada's largest Elk herd can be watched here, especially during spring and fall. Viewing is best on the 9-mile auto tour. **CONTACT** Bureau of Land Management, HC 33 Box 33500, Ely, NV 89301; 702-289-4865.

GOSHUTE MOUNTAINS **Wendover, UT**

Rising to 9,611 feet, the steep ridgeline of this north–south range attracts numerous migrating raptors in autumn. A steep trail leads to an observation point. **CONTACT** Bureau of Land Management, 3900 E. Idaho St., Elko, NV 89803; 702-753-0200.

HUMBOLDT WILDLIFE MANAGEMENT AREA **Lovelock**

The Humboldt River ends in a salty sink here, as its waters spread into wide marshes of Saltgrass and Tamarisk. Migratory ducks rely on the 32,000-acre area (an IBA) as a feeding stopover. **CONTACT** Humboldt W.M.A., 380 West B Street, Fallon, NV 89406; 702-423-3171.

OWYHEE RIVER CANYON **Elko**

Flowing north from Nevada into Idaho, the Owyhee has cut a steep canyon through volcanic rocks. Challenging river-running is generally possible from late March through early June. **CONTACT** Bureau of Land Management, 3900 E. Idaho St., Elko, NV 89803; 702-753-0200.

PAHRANAGAT NATIONAL WILDLIFE REFUGE **Alamo**

Named after a Paiute word meaning "place of many waters," the linear chain of ponds and marshes at this 5,380-acre refuge (an IBA) attracts abundant birds, especially in spring and fall. **CONTACT** Pahranagat N.W.R., 1500 N. Decatur Blvd., Las Vegas, NV 89108; 702-646-3401.

WALKER LAKE **Hawthorne**

Second only to Pyramid Lake in size, this 38,000-acre lake (an IBA) provides habitat for endangered Lahontan Cutthroat Trout as well as excellent birding. **CONTACT** Bureau of Land Management, 1535 Hot Springs Rd., Suite 300, Carson City, NV 90706; 702-885-6000.

New Mexico

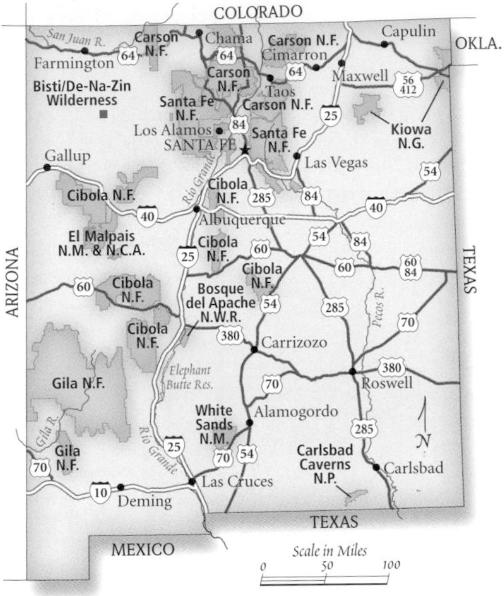

New Mexico was the first state in the Southwest to be settled by non-natives; Spanish explorers arrived here as early as 1538. Its development has proceeded slowly since then. Today the 121,593-square-mile state retains more small-scale agriculture and pastoralism than its later-blooming, faster-growing neighbors. It is also rich in Native American communities. The result is a state that is largely rural and diverse culturally as well as biologically, with small human settlements set amid stunning desert, mountain, and grassland scenery.

Geologists will find much of interest here, including lava flows, cinder cones, and hot springs that evince quite recent changes on the earth's surface. Wildlife is easily observed in some areas; the best places to watch wild animals are intensively managed, such as the refuges established for migratory birds. But much relatively pristine wilderness remains. The 3-million-acre, largely roadless Gila National Forest in the west-central part of the state is one of the Southwest's wild cores. Other national forests retain much of their original biodiversity and wild character, although grazing, logging, and predator control have altered ecological circumstances almost everywhere.

Northern mountains, especially the high Sangre de Cristos, are linked to the Rocky Mountains topographically and biologically. Often-neglected lowlands, including extensive Chihuahuan Desert basins in the south and the Great Plains grasslands that cover a large part of the eastern third of the state, also offer much to the naturalist who is willing to travel off the beaten path.

New Mexico has five national forests, one national grassland, six national wildlife refuges, one national park, and 40 state parks.

CARSON NATIONAL FOREST

Taos

Alpine lake, Latir Peak Wilderness

Rising to over 13,000 feet in the heights of the Sangre de Cristo Mountains, Carson National Forest includes New Mexico's highest point—13,160-foot Wheeler Peak—and its most substantial expanse of alpine tundra. The Sangre de Cristos are topographically a southern extension of the Rocky Mountains, and their high country shares an affinity with more northerly alpine areas, including traces of the effects of glaciation during the most recent ice age. Low willows and sedges create a dense tundra mat above the timberline here, studded with grasses and such cosmopolitan alpine wildflowers as Alpine Avens and Moss Campion. Hikers in the Wheeler Peak and Latir Peak Wilderness Areas often hear the sharp whistles of Yellow-bellied Marmots. White-tailed Ptarmigans, American Pikas, and Rocky Mountain Bighorn Sheep are other often-seen tundra residents.

Wheeler Peak Wilderness

The other units of the 1.4-million-acre forest are more lightly visited. West of Taos is a large expanse of rolling plateau where valley grasslands are interspersed with woods of Quaking Aspens, Subalpine Firs, and Blue and Engelmann Spruces. The Cruces Basin Wilderness, almost on the Colorado border, and the scenic Chama River Canyon—where the Carson meets the Santa Fe National Forest—are two of the more popular backcountry destinations here. As with most national forests in the Southwest, higher elevations are typically closed by snow in winter.

LOCATION Northern New Mexico, both east and west of Rio Grande valley.
CONTACT Carson N.F., 208 Cruz Alta Rd., Taos, NM 87571; 505-758-6200.
VISITOR CENTERS At forest hdqtrs. (see address above) in Taos; also at Ghost Ranch Living Museum, 14 miles northwest of Abiquiu on Hwy. 84.

SANTA FE NATIONAL FOREST **Santa Fe**

About a million years ago a massive volcanic eruption just west of the Rio Grande valley spewed out at least 100 cubic miles of dust and ash and left a caldera 14 miles across. This great circular depression—much of it privately owned—forms the center of the Pajarito Plateau, which with the Jemez Mountains forms the core of the western half of Santa Fe National Forest. Hot springs in the area show that geothermal activity just below the surface has not ceased.

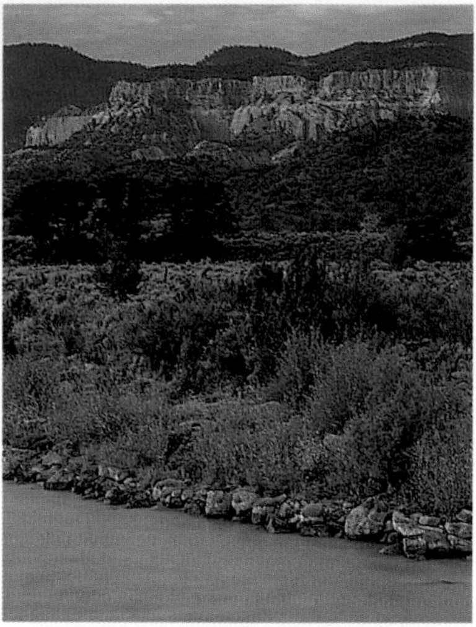

Chama River, Chama River Canyon Wilderness

Many recreationists opt for the cold-water thrills of the Chama River Canyon Wilderness (also in the forest's western half), which provides both scenic hiking and fine whitewater boating along a designated Wild and Scenic River.

The eastern half of the 1.5-million-acre forest sits astride the southern part of the Sangre de Cristo Range, which is perhaps best visited in the extensive Pecos Wilderness—a small adjacent part of which is administered by the Carson National Forest. The wilderness area's 15 high mountain lakes and dozens of perennial streams, along with a rich mix of alpine tundra and montane forests, have made it popular with campers and fishermen. Check with the forest headquarters or ranger station for information on camping restrictions in this popular and extremely scenic area.

Quaking Aspens

LOCATION Both east and west of Rio Grande near Santa Fe. **CONTACT** Santa Fe N.F., P.O. Box 1689, Santa Fe, NM 87504; 505-438-7542. **VISITOR CENTER** Public Land Information Ctr., 1474 Rodeo Rd., Santa Fe.

RIO GRANDE WILD AND SCENIC RIVER — Taos

Following the path of a major rift in the continent's surface, the Rio Grande lies at the bottom of a deep canyon in southern Colorado and northern New Mexico, in places running through ancient flows of basaltic lava more than 600 feet thick. From the Colorado border south, the designated Wild and Scenic portion runs for 48 miles. It is popular with whitewater rafters, but also accessible by foot on rim trails, and by car—the Wild Rivers Back Country Byway provides scenic overlooks west of the town of Questa. Patches of pinyon-juniper woodland occupy the canyon's cooler, protected niches, while the rims themselves support grassland and sagebrushes. Cottonwoods and other riparian vegetation attract numerous songbirds, raptors, Common Porcupines, and other animals.

LOCATION Along Rio Grande west and north of Taos to Colorado border. **CONTACT** Bureau of Land Management, 226 Cruz Alta Rd., Taos, NM 87571; 505-758-8851. **VISITOR CENTER** Rio Grande Gorge V.C., on Hwy. 68 in Pilar, about 15 miles southwest of Taos.

BISTI AND DE-NA-ZIN WILDERNESS AREAS — Farmington

Some 70 million years ago, lush coastal swamps covered what is now northwestern New Mexico. They were home to large dinosaurs and to small mammals that would soon undergo a great surge in diversity as the dinosaurs vanished. Today the landscape looks quite different: Steeply eroded and often brightly colored shales, mudstones, and sandstones make up a maze of badlands. Within them are preserved the fossil bones of those ancient swamp dwellers. No collecting is allowed, but the two linked wilderness areas offer a combined 45,000 acres of superb off-trail hiking and nature-observing opportunities. Facilities here are minimal: No water is available, and summer heat is often extreme.

Rock formation in Bisti Wilderness

LOCATION About 32 miles south of Farmington via Hwy. 371. **CONTACT** Bureau of Land Management, 1235 La Plata Hwy, Suite A, Farmington, NM 87401; 505-599-8900.

EL MALPAIS NATIONAL MONUMENT AND NATIONAL CONSERVATION AREA **Grants**

Within the last 3,000 years or so the earth has been restless in the area Spanish explorers would call "the badlands." Volcanic activity here pushed up dozens of cinder and spatter cones and coated much of the land surface around them with flows of black lava that dried into jagged rocks. The youngest of these rocks are only about a thousand years old.

Lava patterns, El Malpais National Monument

Though the sharp-edged, heat-absorbing rocks may seem inhospitable, life thrives here. Nooks and crannies create cooler, moister microclimates where stunted Alligator Junipers, Ponderosa Pines, Quaking Aspens, and Douglas Firs grow; some are at least 700 years old. Colorful lichens plaster some rocks. Perhaps the most unusual life-forms here are colonies of green algae that live on the ice accumulated in the cold caves of El Malpais. Cold air drains into the caves, which are the remains of collapsed tubes through which liquid lava ran. Runoff from rain and snow collects there and freezes, thanks to temperatures that never rise above the melting point.

The national monument and the national conservation area, managed by the National Park Service and the Bureau of Land Management, respectively, cover a total of 377,000 acres. Both sites include scenic drives, backcountry camping opportunities, and hikes that range from short and easy to long and strenuous. The neighboring Bandera Volcano and Ice Cave are on private land, open to visitors for a fee.

El Malpais National Conservation Area

LOCATION Just south of I-40 via Hwy. 53 or 117. **CONTACTS** National Park Service, P.O. Box 846, Grants, NM 87020; 505-287-7911. Ice Caves Trading Post, 12000 Ice Caves Rd., Grants, NM 87020; 505-783-4303. **VISITOR CENTERS** 9 miles south of I-40 on Hwy. 117, and 23 miles south of I-40 on Hwy. 53; also at Ice Caves Trading Post on Hwy. 53.

CIBOLA NATIONAL FOREST

Albuquerque

View from crest of Sandia Mountains

Scattered across the mid-elevation desert scrub, grassland, and pinyon-juniper woodland of central New Mexico are isolated patches of higher country that comprise the widely separated units of this 1.6-million-acre national forest. The steep Sandia and Manzano Mountains, just east of Albuquerque, are most popular with outdoor recreationists. The rapid change in elevation allows plants and animals of pinyon-juniper woodland, Ponderosa Pine forest, and mixed-conifer stands to be seen in close proximity. In autumn, updrafts enable migrating raptors to sail effortlessly near the mountains' ridgelines. HawkWatch International maintains watch sites where the birds are tallied and where novice birders can learn from experts. Most of the raptors known to breed in the western part of North America pass by here, some in impressive numbers.

The forest's other units are far less frequently visited. Mount Taylor, about 75 miles northwest of Albuquerque, is an ancient volcano whose 11,301-foot-high peak is crowned with a boreal forest of Engelmann Spruce. The forest's most remote parts center around the town of Magdalena, southwest of Albuquerque. The lowest elevations here show a strong Chihuahuan Desert influence, complete with such plants as Ocotillos. Higher up are isolated Ponderosa Pine and mixed-conifer forests that host Black Bears, Mountain Lions, Band-tailed Pigeons, and Wandering Garter Snakes, and other animals.

Maples in fall, Manzano Mountains

LOCATION Scattered units in central New Mexico. **CONTACT** Cibola N.F., 2113 Osuna Rd. NE, Suite A, Albuquerque, NM 87113; 505-761-4650. **VISITOR CENTER** Four Seasons V.C., at upper tram terminal in Sandia Mountains.

GILA NATIONAL FOREST — Silver City

A huge tract of rugged wooded terrain, these more than 3 million acres include three extensive wilderness areas and adjoin equally wild land on the Apache-Sitgreaves National Forest in Arizona. It is no exaggeration to say that hiking and backpacking opportunities are almost endless here, while the corridors of the Gila and San Francisco Rivers provide rafting and kayaking following wet winters.

Gila Wilderness

With habitats ranging from desert grassland and pinyon-juniper woodland to extensive Ponderosa Pine and mixed-conifer stands, along with riparian areas rich with cottonwoods, willows, Box Elders, and other trees, the forest is extraordinarily diverse. Southern species such as Elf Owls and Sonoran Mountain Kingsnakes here meet northerly species that include Long-eared Owls and Western Chorus Frogs.

It is fitting that one of the forest's three large wilderness areas—the more than 200,000- acre Aldo Leopold—should bear the name of one of the country's pioneer conservationists, who honed his ecological understanding during a stint here as a forest ranger. The nearby Gila Wilderness, designated in 1924, is the oldest and, at more than 550,000 acres, one of the largest wilderness areas in any national forest. The smaller Blue Range Wilderness abuts the Blue Range Primitive Area in Arizona and forms a new home for the Mexican Wolves reintroduced near the border beginning in 1998.

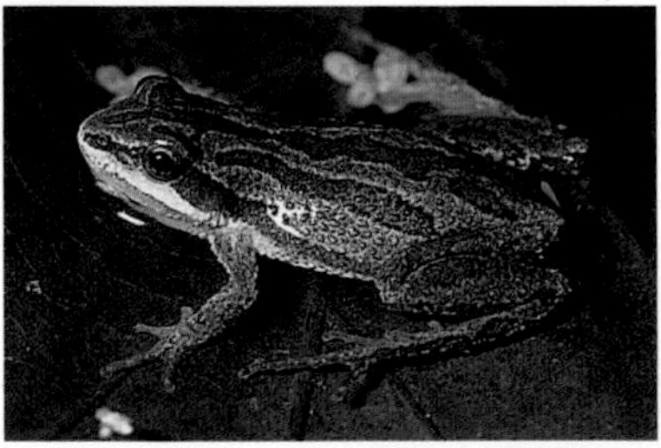
Western Chorus Frog

LOCATION West-central New Mexico. **CONTACT** Gila N.F., 3005 E. Camino del Bosque, Silver City, NM 88061; 505-388-8201. **VISITOR CENTER** At Gila Cliff Dwellings National Monument, 44 miles north of Silver City on Hwy. 15.

BOSQUE DEL APACHE NATIONAL WILDLIFE REFUGE

Socorro

Snow Geese

Part of the floodplain of the Rio Grande, the marshes, sloughs, cottonwood stands, and mesquite woods of the Bosque del Apache (*bosque* is Spanish for "woodland") have long hosted scores of animals and human communities. The area's hydrology has been extensively altered through flood control and diminution of the river's flow, but the Bosque still supports stunning numbers of animals, notably wintering waterbirds.

The network of marshes, fields, and woodlands at the 57,191-acre refuge (an IBA) is intensively managed to provide nesting, feeding, and roosting habitat for a wide variety of species. Much of the current management strategy involves an ongoing effort to replace dense thickets of nonnative Tamarisk—which has little value for wildlife—with native mesquites, willows, and cottonwoods, to the benefit of avian migrants such as the endangered Southwestern Willow Flycatcher.

The Bosque is most visited in winter, when huge flocks of Sandhill Cranes and Snow Geese feed in nearby fields, along with a few Whooping Cranes. Bald Eagles are easily seen from the tour loop road, as are numerous species of ducks. But every season allows naturalists the opportunity to see what a wide range of animals—migrants and permanent residents alike—benefits from an abundance of water in the desert.

LOCATION About 20 miles south of Socorro via I-25 or Hwy. 1. **CONTACT** Bosque del Apache N.W.R., P.O. Box 1246, Socorro, NM 87801; 505-835-1828. **VISITOR CENTER** At refuge hdqtrs., south of Socorro off Hwy 1.

WHITE SANDS NATIONAL MONUMENT

Alamogordo

Among the most striking of landscapes in the Southwest, White Sands comprises the largest gypsum dune field in the world. Normally gypsum, a form of calcium sulfate, dissolves in water and washes away. But geological forces here created a basin with no outlet. Gypsum, washed into the Tularosa Valley from the surrounding mountains, accumulates on the bed of Lake Lucero, a playa that fills with runoff after storms and heavy winters.

As the playa dries, the gypsum deposits turn into wind-borne sand and dune formations that now cover a total of 275 square miles. Changes in wind, plant life, and quantity of sand contribute to the formation of at least four different types of dunes; some move as much as 30 feet a year. A few species of perennials have evolved the ability to cope with these moving masses of sand. The Soaptree Yucca, for example, can grow as much as a foot per year in order to remain above the surface of a rising dune. Some animals, too, thrive here; reptiles such as the Bleached Earless Lizard have developed distinct races whose light coloration serves as camouflage.

Bleached Earless Lizard

Visitors to the monument can enjoy a scenic road, several nature trails, and ranger-led walks. There are no developed campgrounds, and only one hike-in backcountry campsite, for which registration is required. The park road and Highway 70 are occasionally closed for brief periods during tests at the adjacent White Sands Missile Range.

LOCATION 15 miles southwest of Alamogordo on Hwy. 70. **CONTACT** White Sands N.M., P.O. Box 1086, Holloman Air Force Base, NM 88330; 505-479-6124. **VISITOR CENTER** At park entrance on Hwy. 70.

CARLSBAD CAVERNS NATIONAL PARK Carlsbad

A wonderland of water-molded rock, Carlsbad Caverns is a vast underground expanse of limestone eroded away over millennia by seeping rainwater. What sets it apart from many other caves, though, is less its huge size than its spectacular ornamentation: The slow deposition of calcite has formed innumerable varieties of stalactites, stalagmites, columns, and an endless array of other structures both huge and delicately tiny. Trails, lights, and an elevator have made the main caverns' depths accessible to all.

More than 80 other caves pockmark the park's 46,000 desert acres; one, lovely Slaughter Canyon Cave, is open to visitors on a strenuous ranger-guided walk. Wild animals, too, have taken advantage of these underground shelters. Hundreds of thousands of Brazilian Free-tailed Bats roost in the main cave from April through October, hanging from the ceiling in densities as great as 300 per square foot. Their nightly emergence from the entrance is one of North America's great wildlife spectacles, coming as it does soon after the caverns' lesser but still considerable numbers of Cave Swallows have flown in for the evening. Other bats include the Fringed Myotis, which has been found as far as 1,000 feet below ground level. White-footed Mice, Ringtails, and Common Raccoons are among the animals that have colonized deep reaches of the cave.

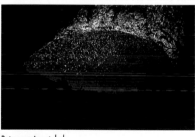

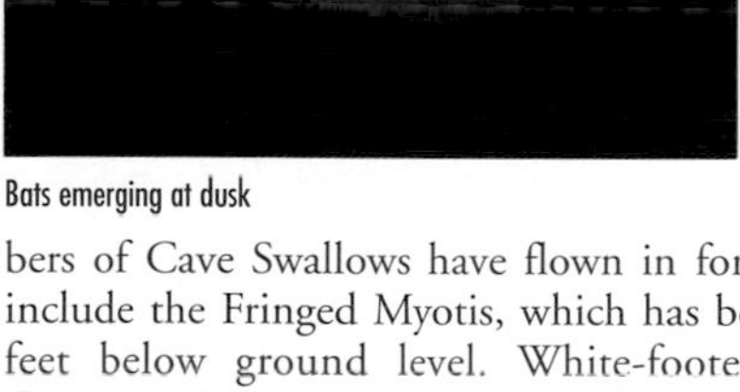

Bats emerging at dusk

LOCATION About 25 miles southwest of Carlsbad via Hwy. 62/180. **CONTACT** Carlsbad Caverns N.P., 3225 National Parks Hwy., Carlsbad, NM 88220; 505-785-2232. **VISITOR CENTER** At end of park entrance road, off Hwy. 62/180.

KIOWA NATIONAL GRASSLANDS — Clayton

These tracts of Great Plains shortgrass prairie were unwisely farmed early in this century. The Dust Bowl demonstrated how untenable

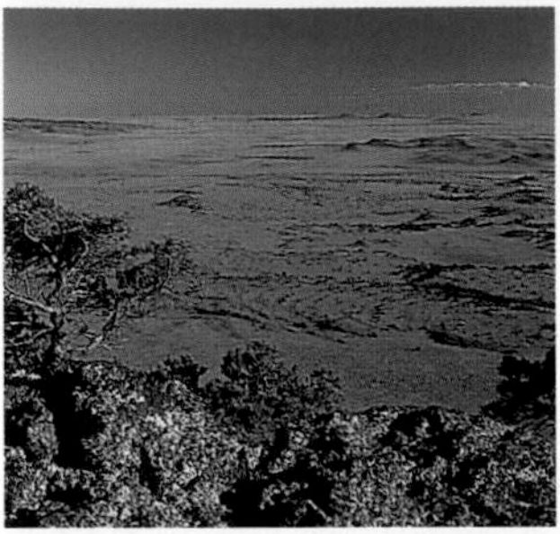

that practice was in a place with an average—and highly unpredictable—annual rainfall of only 15 inches. Now managed by the U.S. Forest Service, these 135,374 acres are still grazed by cattle but are slowly regaining their ecological health. Blue Grama and Buffalo Grass give way to taller bluestem grasses in moist swales. Grassland animals thrive. Pronghorns are common, while Scaled Quails, Burrowing Owls, and Long-billed Curlews are only a few of the open-country birds present seasonally or year-round. Where the Canadian River flows through a scenic 800-foot-deep canyon just west of the town of Mills, rimrock cliffs provide homes for Bald and Golden Eagles, Wild Turkeys, Mule Deer, and many other animals, including introduced Barbary Sheep.

LOCATION Units near Clayton and Mills, NM, as well as in adjacent Texas and Oklahoma. **CONTACT** Kiowa N.G., 714 Main St., Clayton, NM 88415; 505-374-9652.

Angel Peak Recreation Area

ANGEL PEAK RECREATION AREA — Farmington

Eroded shales and sandstones form the Nacimiento Badlands, colorfully sculpted and sparsely vegetated remnants of 40-million-year-old seas that can be enjoyed from trails and developed campsites at this 10,240-acre site. **CONTACT** Angel Peak R.A., 1235 La Plata Hwy., Suite A, Farmington, NM 87401; 505-599-8900.

BANDELIER NATIONAL MONUMENT — Los Alamos

Ancient Pueblo ruins dot an extensive 50-square-mile preserve that encompasses much pristine forest and canyon terrain, 70 percent of it designated wilderness. There are numerous day-hiking and backpacking possibilities here. Bird-watching is excellent in Frijoles Canyon. **CONTACT** Bandelier N.M., HCR 1 Box 1, Suite 15, Los Alamos, NM 87544; 505-672-3861.

BITTER LAKE NATIONAL WILDLIFE REFUGE — Roswell

Artificial impoundments along the Pecos River attract tens of thousands of migrant ducks, geese, and Sandhill Cranes. Late fall is the best time to visit the 24,500-acre refuge (an IBA). **CONTACT** Bitter Lake N.W.R., P.O. Box 7, Roswell, NM 88202; 505-622-6755.

CAPULIN VOLCANO NATIONAL MONUMENT — Capulin

This heavily vegetated, almost perfectly symmetrical cinder cone is a relic of volcanic activity some 62,000 years ago. Access is by car or by foot. Wildlife, including Common Porcupines and Mule Deer, is frequently seen. **CONTACT** Capulin Volcano N.M., P.O. Box 40, Capulin, NM 88414; 505-425-3581.

CIMARRON CANYON STATE PARK AND COLIN NEBLETT WILDLIFE AREA — **Cimarron**

Cimarron Canyon State Park

Developed campgrounds along the scenic Cimarron River constitute the state park, while the surrounding 33,000-acre wildlife area provides greater opportunities for solitary hiking. **CONTACTS** Cimarron Canyon S.P., P.O. Box 185, Eagle Nest, NM 87718; 505-377-6271. Colin Neblett W.A., New Mexico Dept. of Game and Fish, P.O. Box 1145, Raton, NM 87740; 505-445-2311.

CITY OF ROCKS STATE PARK — **Deming**

Wind and water have sculpted ancient volcanic rocks into fancifully rounded boulders, pillars, and blocks. There are maintained trails and a cactus garden at this 680-acre park. **CONTACT** City of Rocks S.P., P.O. Box 50, Faywood, NM 88034; 505-536-2800.

EDWARD SARGENT FISH AND WILDLIFE MANAGEMENT AREA — **Chama**

More than 20,000 acres of high Quaking Aspen meadows and small streams are home to numerous Elk and Black Bears. Trails penetrate the backcountry; camping is available in designated areas. **CONTACT** Edward Sargent F.W.M.A., P.O. Box 25112, Santa Fe, NM 87504; no telephone.

LAS VEGAS NATIONAL WILDLIFE REFUGE — **Las Vegas**

Rolling grasslands interspersed with wetlands and brushy areas attract a wide array of wildlife to this 8,750-acre refuge. Wintering birds include Snow Geese, Sandhill Cranes, and Bald Eagles. **CONTACT** Las Vegas N.W.R., Rte. 1 Box 399, Las Vegas, NM 87701; 505-425-3581.

LINCOLN NATIONAL FOREST — **Alamogordo**

Three separate units in southern New Mexico provide a variety of high-country recreation. The forest's 1 million acres include two wilderness areas, plus ample trails, fishing areas, and downhill and cross-country skiing. **CONTACT** Lincoln N.F., 1101 New York, Alamogordo, NM 88310; 505-434-7200.

Pronghorn, Living Desert State Park

LIVING DESERT STATE PARK — **Carlsbad**

Flora and fauna of the Chihuahuan Desert are featured in attractively landscaped exhibits. **CONTACT** Living Desert S.P., P.O. Box 100, Carlsbad, NM 88221; 505-887-5516.

MAXWELL NATIONAL WILDLIFE REFUGE — **Maxwell**

Three lakes set amid 3,600 acres of northeastern New Mexico's shortgrass prairie provide habitat for a variety of birds, especially wintering ducks and geese. **CONTACT** Maxwell N.W.R., P.O. Box 276, Maxwell, NM 87728; 505-375-2331.

VALLEY OF FIRES RECREATION AREA — **Carrizozo**

A nature trail, campground, and visitor center on this 125-square-mile lava flow created about 1,500 years ago provide opportunities to see how plants and animals have colonized new land. **CONTACT** Bureau of Land Management, P.O. Box 871, Carrizozo, NM 88301; 505-648-2241.

Utah

After Nevada, Utah is the second-driest state in the country, but thanks to its high mountains it includes many of the wettest places in the Southwest. The heights of the Wasatch Front capture abundant moisture from Pacific storms, feeding both lush montane forests and numerous wetlands, from bright mountain creeks to the vast saline expanse of Great Salt Lake. Much of that precipitation arrives in the winter in the form of fine, dry powder snow that makes for superb skiing.

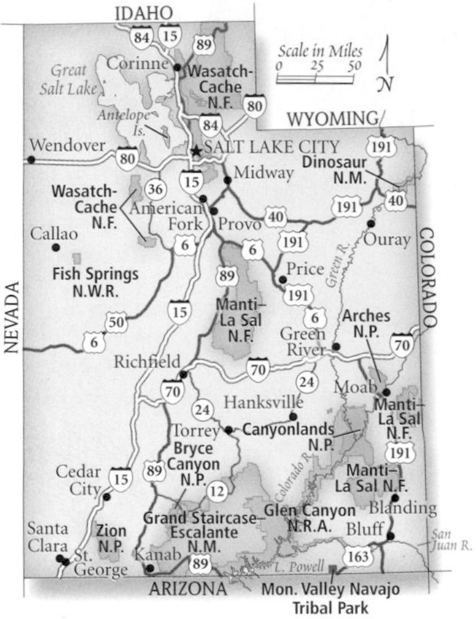

The erosive power of water has carved out the scenic wonders of southern Utah, where the arid sandstones of the Colorado Plateau have been dissected by deep, steep-walled canyons. From above, the landscape here appears open; at ground level, it is a land of mystery, where slot canyons reveal hidden alcoves and springs at every turn, where the ruins of ancient civilizations persist side-by-side with such reclusive animals as Desert Bighorn Sheep and Mexican Spotted-Owls.

West of the Wasatch Front is the sun-baked desert of the Great Basin. Here long north–south mountain ranges split low basins of sagebrush, Shadscale, or salt flats from one another, each replete with a unique mix of higher-elevation plants and animals.

Utah was settled in the 1840s by the Mormons, who took advantage of their tightly knit communal structure to organize large-scale irrigation agriculture. Though parts of the state are rapidly urbanizing, it still bears the same basic pattern: Towns and farms lie in the well-watered lowlands and canyon bottoms, while the uplands are left forested in order to preserve water quality and game populations. More than a century of grazing and logging have significantly altered natural balances, and today heavy recreational pressure threatens the diversity of some areas, especially fragile desert and tundra terrain. The visitor who is mindful of staying on trails and practicing low-impact techniques can enjoy Utah's vast open spaces and abundant wildlife without degrading what so many come to see.

Utah has six national forests, one national recreation area, five national parks, two national wildlife refuges, and 45 state parks.

THE GREEN RIVER

Vernal

Alternating stretches of flat, calm water with tumultuous rapids, the Green River knits together eastern Utah's highlands and lowlands as it runs from the mountains of Wyoming down to its junction with the Colorado in southern Utah. Endangered native fishes such as the Colorado Squawfish, Humpback Chub, and Bonytail Chub are still found in some areas.

Desolation Canyon, south of Ouray National Wildlife Refuge

FLAMING GORGE NATIONAL RECREATION AREA Flaming Gorge Dam backs the Green River up through 123,000 acres of multi-colored canyons on the Wyoming–Utah border. Boaters can camp at waterside, while hikers can view the scenic canyons from the Little Hole and Canyon Rim Trails. Sheep Creek Canyon Geological Area showcases twisted rocks that have been undergoing erosion since the uplift of the Uinta Mountains tens of millions of years ago.

Dinosaur National Monument

DINOSAUR NATIONAL MONUMENT The 210,000-acre monument's rich fossil beds memorialize the plants and animals that died on a river sandbar 145 million years ago. Exposed by modern-day erosion, the fossil deposit is now protected by a glass-sided building at the monument's western end. More remote are the Green River Canyon and surrounding lands, accessible by boat, dirt road, and foot.

OURAY NATIONAL WILDLIFE REFUGE Encompassing about 12,000 acres of riverside marshes, fields, and riparian thickets, the refuge is a magnet for migratory waterfowl; 14 species of ducks nest here. The preserve's diverse wetland and upland habitats can be viewed from a tour road or on foot.

LOCATION Eastern Utah. **CONTACTS** Flaming Gorge N.R.A., Ashley N.F., Box 279, Manila, UT 84046; 435-784-3445. Dinosaur N.M., 4545 Hwy. 40, Dinosaur, CO 81610; 970-374-3000. Ouray N.W.R., 266 West 100 North, Suite 2, Vernal, UT 84078; 435-545-2522. Bureau of Land Management, Price Field Office, 125 South 600 West, Price, UT 84501; 435-636-3600. **VISITOR CENTERS** At Flaming Gorge Dam and Red Canyon in Flaming Gorge N.R.A.; and 7 miles north of Jensen in Dinosaur N.M.

GREAT SALT LAKE

Salt Lake City

A mirror to the wide Great Basin sky, Great Salt Lake is a paradoxical place. The largest natural lake west of the Mississippi River, this shallow remnant of the much larger ice-age Lake Bonneville laps against bone-dry desert. It is at least three times as salty as the ocean, and scarcely any organisms can survive in it, but those that do are extraordinarily abundant.

The lake is fed by freshwater runoff from surrounding mountains, and variations in annual precipitation account for extreme changes in the lake's level—as much as 20 feet in the last century and a half. In recent decades its size has varied from about 610,000 acres to more than 1,470,000. Though high-water years such as those in the mid-1980s damage marshes and adjacent property, the fluctuations have stymied development of the shore, keeping much of it in a relatively natural state. Some of the area's extensive marshes, such as those at the Bear River Migratory Bird Refuge and the Ogden Bay Wildlife Management Area, support enormous concentrations of waterbirds.

The lake itself has a simple ecosystem. Green algae thrive in its warm, shallow waters, providing food for Brine Shrimp and Brine Flies, tiny winged insects that often scoot up harmlessly in swarms as a person walks the shoreline. Brine Shrimp are so common that their tiny floating eggs form miles-long red streaks on the lake's surface in winter. The lake's flies are estimated to be responsible for removing 120,000 tons of organic material from the lake each year.

Numerous birds thrive on this bounty. In summer a half million Wilson's Phalaropes stop here after breeding, nearly doubling their weight in preparation for long flights to southern wintering grounds. Tens of thousands of California Gulls nest on the lake's islands, while pale Snowy Plovers choose beaches and salt flats instead. American White Pelicans feed on fish in the freshwater inflows, but nest on remote lake islands.

GREAT SALT LAKE STATE PARK Encompassing 5 miles of shoreline about 17 miles west of Salt Lake City, the park offers opportunities for viewing the lake's common birds, including American Avocets, Black-necked Stilts, Wilson's Phalaropes, and various species of ducks, gulls, and terns.

Antelope Island and mudflats

ANTELOPE ISLAND STATE PARK The lake's largest island (an IBA), now connected to the mainland by a causeway, is home to American Bison, free-roaming descendants of animals brought to the island in the 1890s; to herds of Pronghorns, reintroduced in the 1990s after being extirpated; and to California

Bighorn Sheep, also introduced in the 1990s. Long-billed Curlews and Burrowing Owls nest on the island's grasslands. The rocky heights rise some 2,400 feet above lake level, providing excellent views from the 28,463-acre park's hiking trails. Camping is allowed at the island's northern end; backcountry trails are open only to day hiking, and only with a permit.

White-faced Ibises, Bear River Migratory Bird Refuge

BEAR RIVER MIGRATORY BIRD REFUGE Flooded during the 1980s, this 74,000-acre preserve (an IBA) is undergoing a slow process of healing as freshwater marshes reestablish themselves where salt water recently stood. Every season offers rewarding birding opportunities. Summer visitors can see fledgling Canada Geese, White-faced Ibises, Western Grebes, and ducks; American White Pelicans fish here, then return to lake islands to feed their nestlings. In fall up to a half million waterfowl congregate. Winter brings raptors such as Prairie Falcons, Rough-legged Hawks, Bald Eagles, and Northern Harriers. Biking or driving the refuge's 12-mile tour loop is the best way to see these and other species.

OGDEN BAY WATERFOWL MANAGEMENT AREA Some 20,000 acres of marshland, salt flats, and mudflats support thousands of breeding ducks each summer, but their numbers pale in comparison to the half-million waterfowl that appear in autumn. Visitors can walk or use canoes, bicycles, or cars to reach prime viewing sites.

BONNEVILLE SALT FLATS Reaching west of Great Salt Lake, this expanse of baked salt is the old lake bed of glacial Lake Bonneville. So flat that the earth's curvature can be seen—and that numerous land-speed world records have been set here—the white surface is lifeless but well worth a look, as it runs into the distance against a backdrop of stark, dark mountain ranges.

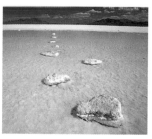

Bonneville Salt Flats

LOCATION North and west of Salt Lake City via I-15 and I-80. **CONTACTS** Great Salt Lake S.P., P.O. Box 323, Magna, UT 84044; 801-250-1898. Antelope Island S.P., 4528 West 1700 South, Syracuse, UT 84075; 801-773-2941. Bear River Migratory Bird Refuge, 58 South 950 West, Brigham City, UT 84302; 801-723-5887. Ogden Bay W.M.A., 4800 South 7500 West, Hooper, UT 84315; 801-773-1398. Bonneville Salt Flats, Bureau of Land Management, 2370 South 2300 West, Salt Lake City, UT 84119; 801-977-4300. **VISITOR CENTER** At northern end of Antelope Island.

WASATCH-CACHE NATIONAL FOREST

Salt Lake City

Wasatch Range

The Wasatch Front splits Utah in two, rising from the western desert as a sharp line of peaks and cliffs and tapering off as a series of high plateaus that slope down more gently to the east. The high elevations here trap moisture from Pacific storms; the result is large amounts of rain and snowfall that create numerous streams and small lakes, as well as lush forests and thickets of montane scrub. The northern reach of the escarpment, with associated ranges, forms much of Wasatch-Cache National Forest.

WELLSVILLE MOUNTAINS A steep-sided and isolated range, the Wellsvilles form a sharp north–south ridge whose updrafts attract numerous migrating raptors in late summer and autumn. A trailhead near the town of Mendon ascends more than 3,000 feet in 4 miles on its way to one of the best viewing points.

BEAR RIVER RANGE The Bear River Range is easily accessible but also has remote corners, especially in the extensive Mount Naomi Wilderness. The range's many wetlands provide places to see such water-loving species as Moose, American Beavers, and Lazuli Buntings. The highest terrain is dotted with gnarled Limber Pines. Motorists can experience some of the mountains' lovely scenery on winding Highway 89 through Logan Canyon; the road tops out at nearly 8,000 feet.

Summit of Mount Naomi

WASATCH RANGE Steep trails ascend the western face of the Wasatch Range, which forms the scenic backdrop for the booming cities and suburbs of the Ogden–Provo corridor. Some of these slopes are covered with dark stands of Douglas Fir and Subalpine Fir, while extensive shrubby thickets of oak, maple, and Quaking Aspen cloak other areas. Among the most popular access roads and trails are those that wind through canyons lush with Bigtooth Maples, Quaking Aspens, and spruces.

STANSBURY MOUNTAINS Though their cool heights provide an island home for many plants and animals that could not survive in the surrounding terrain, it is those surroundings that lend perhaps the greatest interest to the Stansbury Mountains, for they rise up out of the stark desert flats south of Great Salt Lake. Hikers who ascend the 6-mile trail up to the 11,031-foot summit of Deseret Peak are rewarded with astonishing vistas of the lake and desert at their feet and the forested wall of the Wasatch Range rising to the east.

UINTA MOUNTAINS The Uinta Mountains are an anomaly in the American West: a major range that trends east to west rather than north to south. They consist of a thick deposit of quartzite squeezed upward into a giant dome 150 miles long. Kings Peak, at 13,528 feet, is the highest point in the state. Perhaps most impressive is the extent of their high country—more than 300 square miles of alpine tundra, most of it in a continuous belt 60 miles long. Lakes and bogs fill glacial cirques, while streams run downward into thick coniferous forests of spruce and fir and, at lower elevations, dense stands of Lodgepole Pine more typical of the Rocky Mountains. The Uintas' cool, northerly aspect is apparent in its animal life, too. Moose and Elk browse its wetlands, and Rocky Mountain Bighorn Sheep are sometimes spotted in open areas. Pileated Woodpeckers, Saw-whet Owls, and American Martens are among the signature animals of the forests, while White-tailed Ptarmigans, White-crowned Sparrows, and Pikas inhabit the tundra.

Columbines, High Uintas Wilderness

Much of the range's high country is set aside as the High Uintas Wilderness—some 800 square miles split between the Wasatch-Cache and Ashley National Forests. Numerous trails penetrate the wilderness, which lies so high that it is generally closed off by snow from as early as October through June. Roads entering the adjacent forest lands from north and south lead to developed campgrounds.

LOCATION East of Logan and Salt Lake City. **CONTACTS** Wasatch-Cache N.F., 8230 Federal Bldg., 125 S. State St., Salt Lake City, UT 84138; 801-524-3900. Ashley N.F., 355 N. Vernal Ave., Vernal, UT 84078; 435-789-1181. **VISITOR CENTERS** Wasatch-Cache N.F.: on Hwy. 89 in Logan. Ashley N.F.: in Flaming Gorge N.R.A. (page 417), on forest's northeastern edge.

MANTI–LA SAL NATIONAL FOREST **Price**

Quaking Aspens below La Sal Mountains

Rising from the crenellated canyon country of southeastern Utah are several isolated, ice-etched ranges made up of laccoliths, huge domes of rock pushed upward by subsurface wellings of magma. The La Sal and Abajo Mountains provide a scenic, often snow-capped backdrop to the red rocks of Canyonlands and Arches National Parks, as well as cool relief from the desert's summer heat. Their lands are managed by the 1.3-million-acre Manti–La Sal National Forest, as is the forest's separate Manti Division, which covers a wide swath of the Wasatch Plateau in the state's center.

The plateau is easily accessed on the Skyline Drive Scenic Backway, an unpaved 87-mile route that transects much of the Manti Division's length. It passes through Quaking Aspen and spruce-fir woods, offering frequent looks at Elk, American Beavers, gliding raptors, and other animals. Views off the sides of the plateau are extensive. On the western side of the Abajos, meanwhile, hardy hikers gear up for a trip into the Dark Canyon Wilderness, where the high mountain terrain drops sharply into a steep and scenic system of red-rock canyons. This rugged area is studded with lush springs and "hanging gardens" high in rock alcoves; it abuts the lower Dark Canyon Primitive Area managed by the Bureau of Land Management.

Dark Canyon Wilderness

The forest's units feature numerous developed and primitive campsites and extensive hiking trails. High elevations are typically closed off by winter snows. Visitors to Dark Canyon and other steep-walled drainages should be mindful of the threat of flash flooding following summer storms.

LOCATION Southeastern and central Utah. **CONTACT** Manti–La Sal N.F., 599 W. Price River Dr., Price, UT 84501; 435-637-2817. **VISITOR CENTER** Moab Interagency V.C., on Hwy. 191 in Moab.

CANYONLANDS NATIONAL PARK **Moab**

Big Spring Canyon, Needles District

In 1869 the explorer John Wesley Powell took time during his trip down the Green River to describe the terrain where it joined the Colorado. "Wherever we look there is but a wilderness of rocks," he wrote, "deep gorges where the rivers are lost below the cliffs and towers and pinnacles, and ten thousand strangely carved forms in every direction."

Desert Prince's Plume, Island in the Sky District

Today many visitors view the same scene in what has become Canyonlands National Park. The two rivers still run through deep canyons separated from flat-topped plateaus above by sheer cliffs. Though the exposed rock layers showcase hundreds of millions of years of geological history, the canyons themselves are young, having been carved during the last 15 million years or so by uplifting of the land around the rivers. The ongoing work of erosion is everywhere visible here, in large part because the arid climate supports only sparse desert scrub, grassland, and pinyon-juniper woodland.

From Island in the Sky, a high peninsular mesa between the two rivers, steep-walled side canyons run into the main drainages. Two other park districts are more remote: the Needles, east of the Colorado, and the Maze, west of the Green River. Both include extensive arrays of fins, arches, spires, pinnacles, and other features.

Visits to the remoter parts of this 337,280-acre park can be challenging, as water is scarce, road access minimal, and route-finding difficult. Paved roads penetrate the Needles and the top of Island in the Sky; other areas can be reached by four-wheel-drive vehicle or on foot. River trips are popular too; Cataract Canyon, below the confluence, offers enthusiasts one of the supreme whitewater experiences in the West.

LOCATION Southwest of Moab via Hwy. 191. **CONTACT** Canyonlands N.P., 2282 South West Resource Blvd., Moab, UT 84532; 435-259-7164. **VISITOR CENTERS** At entrances to each of park's three districts.

ARCHES NATIONAL PARK **Moab**

Like a child's playground grown huge, Arches National Park is a landscape of smooth and rounded sandstone eroded into pillars, arches, hoodoos, and myriad other forms—a landscape that invites spontaneous exploration. Though its prominent arches and fins of pink and orange sandstone have been shaped by wind and water erosion, the reason for their existence actually lies far underground. Hundreds of millions of years ago deep layers of salt were deposited here by the evaporation of an ancient sea. Covered by thick layers of sand and sediment that were eventually compressed into rock, the salt buckled and shifted, causing the overlying rocks to heave into domes or settle into cavities. Erosion widened the resulting surface cracks into wide crevices separating free-standing fins, some of which have now been whittled into narrow arches by wind and water.

Turret Arch framed by North Window

Sparse pinyon-juniper woodland covers much of the park's 73,379 acres now, often growing amid carpets of black cryptobiotic crust, a melange of bacteria, algae, fungi, and lichens that conserves moisture and hinders soil erosion. Its presence and fragility is the prime reason for the park management's insistence that visitors remain on existing roads and trails. Trails allow visitors to approach many of the several thousand known arches. The starkness of the landscape is often enlivened by the sight of Common Ravens, Pinyon Jays, Mountain Bluebirds, and other birds, more rarely by a distant view of Desert Bighorn Sheep, Mule Deer, or Kit Foxes.

Camping is allowed year-round at a developed campground, though water is not available there in winter. Backcountry hiking and camping are allowed; a permit is required. Winter nights are quite cold at the park's more than 4,000-foot elevation, while summer temperatures can reach 110 degrees.

LOCATION 5 miles northwest of Moab on Hwy. 191. **CONTACT** Arches N.P., P.O. Box 907, Moab, UT 84532; 435-259-8161. **VISITOR CENTER** At park entrance.

GRAND STAIRCASE–ESCALANTE NATIONAL MONUMENT

Escalante

Waterfall near Escalante River

Established in 1996 to considerable fanfare as well as local opposition, this 1.7-million acre tract showcases three primary topographic features. The canyons of the Escalante River and its tributaries are carved out of easily eroded Navajo sandstone, and lined with lush stands of Fremont Cottonwood, Box Elder, Gambel's Oak, and other moisture-loving plants. Just to the west a long escarpment marks the eastern edge of the Kaiparowits Plateau, a rugged maze of mesas and canyons that occupies half of the monument; it rises as high as 8,300 feet and supports groves of Ponderosa Pine. Other parts of the plateau are topped with grayish shale impregnated with chemicals that are toxic to most plants; only a few types of shrubs, cactus, and other specialized species, such as the showy, yellow-flowered Desert Prince's Plume, survive here.

West of the plateau, the Grand Staircase is a series of brilliantly hued cliffs that document as much as 200 million years of geological history. They rise from the Vermilion Cliffs—exposed Moenkopi sandstone that extends south to the head of the Grand Canyon—to the Pink Cliffs, whose limey siltstone is also on display in neighboring Bryce Canyon National Park (see page 427).

The monument—the only one in the country managed by the Bureau of Land Management—is short on visitor facilities, long on scenery and solitude. Highways 12 and 89 traverse its northern and southern edges, respectively. A few dirt roads penetrate the interior, but they can be treacherous, especially after snowfall or summer thunderstorms. Information about road and travel conditions should be sought locally. Developed trails and campsites are few, but the opportunities for exploration with map and compass are ample.

LOCATION South-central Utah, along the Arizona state line. **CONTACT** Grand Staircase–Escalante N.M., 337 S. Main St., Suite 010, Cedar City, UT 84720; 435-865-5100.

MONUMENT VALLEY NAVAJO TRIBAL PARK

Goulding

One of the West's most-filmed landscapes, 29,817-acre Monument Valley is a great flat basin out of which rise strikingly tall spires, pillars, and buttes—the remnants of an uplifted plateau of sandstone that has been eroded away by wind and water. Wildlife-viewing opportunities are scarce in this stark, Great Basin terrain, but Black-throated Sparrows and lizards are often present on the ground, while Common Ravens, American Kestrels, Horned Larks, and an occasional Prairie Falcon dance on the winds above. The Navajo Nation runs a campground in the valley; it lies in Arizona, but the access road leaves Highway 163 in Utah. There is a 17-mile-long self-guided loop tour road, and other parts of the valley can be visited with a guide.

The Mitten buttes at sunset

LOCATION About 21 miles southwest of Mexican Hat on Hwy. 163. **CONTACT** Monument Valley Navajo Tribal Park, P.O. Box 360289, Monument Valley, UT 84536; 435-727-3353 or 435-727-3287. **VISITOR CENTER** At park entrance, off Hwy. 163 in Arizona.

GLEN CANYON NATIONAL RECREATION AREA

Page, Arizona

Created by the backing up of the Colorado River behind Glen Canyon Dam, Lake Powell contains up to two year's worth of the river's flow in its 186-mile length. Conservationists still mourn the reservoir's drowning of most of Glen Canyon, once a wonderland of sandstone cliffs dissected by tributary canyons and springs that supported lush groves. But the reservoir is only part of the 1.2-million-acre recreation area. It also includes large expanses of slickrock—smooth, sloping sandstone—along the Waterpocket Fold and the Escalante River, as well as corridors along the Colorado, San Juan, and Green Rivers. Roads and trails penetrate the backcountry, but hiking is possible almost anywhere in this terrain of open sandstone knolls and knobs. Rainbow Bridge, the world's largest known natural bridge, spans Rainbow Canyon on the reservoir's southern side.

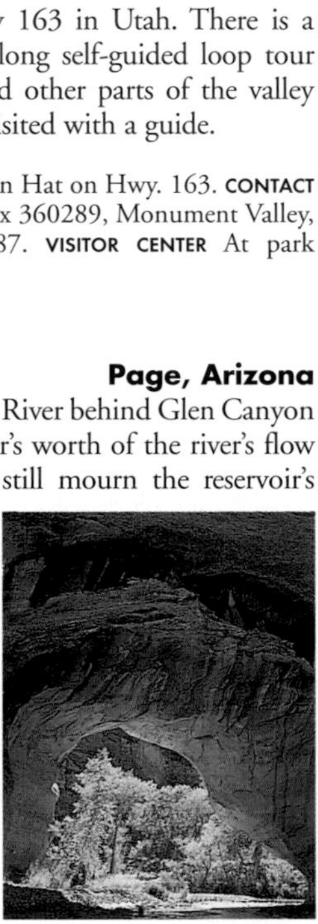
Coyote Natural Bridge, Escalante Canyon

LOCATION Along Colorado and San Juan Rivers in southern Utah and extreme northern Arizona. **CONTACT** Glen Canyon N.R.A., Box 1507, Page, AZ 86040; 520-608-6200. **VISITOR CENTERS** Carl Hayden V.C. on Hwy. 89 at Glen Canyon Dam; on Hwy. 276 at Bullfrog; and at Dangling Rope Marina, 40 miles uplake from Glen Canyon Dam and accessible only by boat.

ZION NATIONAL PARK — Springdale

Marking the western edge of the Colorado Plateau, Zion National Park is a lovely concatenation of colorful rock layers sliced into steep-walled canyons by some 15 million years of uplift and erosion by the Virgin River and its tributaries. The most striking layer is the reddish Navajo sandstone, whose smooth, sheer cliffs rise to over 2,000 feet at some points. Normally a small stream, the Virgin can flood following storms; some of its side drainages end in high "hanging valleys" that send spectacular waterfalls into the river gorge when runoff occurs. Drivers can view the Virgin River canyon from Zion Canyon Scenic Drive, while hikers take established trails or seek more difficult unmarked routes through washes and canyons. The Narrows, where visitors are dwarfed by 2,000- to 3,000-foot cliffs, and the parallel "finger canyons" of the Kolob Terrace in the northwestern corner of the 146,560-acre park are popular destinations.

LOCATION About 43 miles northeast of St. George via I-15 or Hwy. 9. **CONTACT** Zion N.P., Springdale, UT 84767; 435-772-3256. **VISITOR CENTERS** On Hwy. 9 just inside southern entrance, and at Kolob Canyons entrance off I-15.

BRYCE CANYON NATIONAL PARK — Tropic

A vast amphitheater of bizarrely eroded salmon- and orange-colored limestone, Bryce Canyon represents the top of the geological Grand Staircase of southern Utah. Here the forested Paunsaugunt Plateau suddenly gives way to a maze of spires, pinnacles, and fins. An 18-mile paved road parallels the amphitheater's rim; its overlooks provide access to hiking trails that meander both along and below the rim. The longer trails are studded with designated backcountry campsites. Scenery is the 35,000-acre park's selling point, but more than 400 plant species have been identified here. Animals, too, are abundant. Threatened Utah Prairie Dogs sound alarm calls in grassy meadows, where early morning and late afternoon may also bring a look at browsing Elk or Mule Deer. The cliff faces are enlivened by darting White-throated Swifts and Violet-green Swallows, and more rarely by soaring Golden Eagles.

LOCATION About 80 miles east of Cedar City via Hwys. 14, 89, and 12. **CONTACT** Bryce Canyon N.P., Bryce Canyon, UT 84717; 435-834-5322. **VISITOR CENTER** 1 mile past park entrance, off Hwy. 63.

FISH SPRINGS NATIONAL WILDLIFE REFUGE — Callao

An isolated oasis in the midst of Utah's stark western desert, Fish Springs encompasses 10,000 acres of marsh fed by numerous saline seeps and springs. The natural mosaic of marshy meadows and permanent water areas has been altered by the construction of dikes and canals intended to maximize habitat productivity for a wide array of native species. Several small native fishes live here, including the Utah Chub and the uncommon and recently reintroduced Least Chub. The refuge is also a stronghold for a local population of Northern Leopard Frogs. Most visitors, though, come to see the birds that overwinter or stop here during migration. During spring and fall the refuge hosts a wide variety of songbirds, raptors, shorebirds, and waterfowl; many remain to nest. Among the less common species are wintering Tundra Swans, Bald Eagles, and Merlins. Driving and hiking the refuge roads are the best ways to view the birds. Camping is not allowed on the refuge, but it is permitted on adjacent Bureau of Land Management lands.

Marsh below Fish Springs Range

LOCATION 104 miles southwest of Tooele via Hwy. 36 and the gravel Pony Express Route. **CONTACT** Fish Springs N.W.R., P.O. Box 568, Dugway, UT 84022; 435-831-5353.

DEEP CREEK RANGE — Callao

Rising above the southwestern edge of the Great Salt Lake Desert, hard by the Nevada line, the Deep Creek Range is a high "sky island" chain whose isolation raises fascinating questions in biogeography. Its slopes, rearing up to over 12,000 feet, support eight different conifer species, more than are found on most of the Great Basin ranges to the west. Native Bonneville Cutthroat Trout still live in some of its creeks, which wind down from glacial cirques carved out of gray granite. Getting to the base of the mountains is an expedition: Every approach demands lengthy stretches on unpaved roads. Foot trails are rough and steep; the route up Granite Creek to Mount Ibapah ascends about 5,300 feet in its 6-mile length. Visitors to the top are rewarded with expansive views and, in late summer and fall, flights of raptors migrating south.

Mount Ibapah

LOCATION South of Wendover, just east of the Nevada border. **CONTACT** Bureau of Land Management, Fillmore Field Office, 35 East 500 North, Fillmore, UT 84631; 435-743-6811.

CANYON RIMS RECREATION AREA **Moab**

Adjacent to the Needles District of Canyonlands National Park, this 85,000-acre area features scenic and rugged hiking and four-wheel driving opportunities. **CONTACT** Bureau of Land Management, Moab District, 82 E. Dogwood, Moab, UT 84532; 435-259-6111.

CAPITOL REEF NATIONAL PARK **Torrey**

High, buckled cliffs of the 100-mile-long Waterpocket Fold memorialize the ancient uplift of the Colorado Plateau, while riverside orchards at this 241,904-acre park commemorate the Mormons who settled the area. **CONTACT** Capitol Reef N.P., HC 70, Box 15, Torrey, UT 84775; 435-425-3791.

Capitol Reef National Park

CEDAR BREAKS NATIONAL MONUMENT **Cedar City**

The 6,000-acre monument provides scenic views of an awe-inspiring 2,000-foot-deep amphitheater of multi-colored eroded rocks. **CONTACT** Cedar Breaks N.M., 82 North 100 East, Cedar City, UT 84720; 435-586-9451.

CLEVELAND-LLOYD DINOSAUR QUARRY **Price**

More than 30 complete dinosaur skeletons have been found here; the 80-acre quarry showcases ongoing excavation. **CONTACT** Bureau of Land Management, 125 South 600 West, Price, UT 84501; 435-636-3600.

Dead Horse Point State Park

DEAD HORSE POINT STATE PARK **Moab**

Visit this 5,082-acre site for stunning views of the Colorado River far below. Trails and camping are available. **CONTACT** Dead Horse Point S.P., P.O. Box 609, Moab, UT 84532; 435-259-2614.

DIXIE NATIONAL FOREST **Cedar City**

The forested plateau of Boulder Mountain and the Pine Valley Mountain Wilderness are two of the popular destinations in this 1.9-million-acre forest of scattered southwestern Utah ranges. **CONTACT** Dixie N.F., 82 North 100 East, Cedar City, UT 84721; 435-865-3700.

FISHLAKE NATIONAL FOREST **Richfield**

These 1.4 million acres of high forestland in south-central Utah are split by sagebrush valleys. **CONTACT** Fishlake N.F., 115 East 900 North, Richfield, UT 84701; 435-896-9233.

GOLDEN SPIKE NATIONAL HISTORIC SITE **Corinne**

Sage and Sharp-tailed Grouse are among the species inhabiting sagebrush and grassland here. The best viewing is in spring. **CONTACT** Golden Spike National Historic Site, P.O. Box 897, Brigham City, UT 84302; 801-471-2209.

HENRY MOUNTAINS **Hanksville**

Free-ranging American Bison roam the highlands of a remote range of igneous rock. This is an area of prime hiking, backpacking, and solitude. **CONTACT** Bureau of Land Management, P.O. Box 99, Hanksville, UT 84734; 435-542-3461.

Gambel's Quail,
Joshua Tree Natural Area

JOSHUA TREE NATURAL AREA **St. George**

This northeasternmost extension of the Mojave Desert showcases Joshua Trees, Desert Tortoises, and ephemeral spring wildflowers. CONTACT Bureau of Land Management, Cedar City District, 176 East D.L. Sargent Drive, Cedar City, UT 84720; 435-586-2401.

NATURAL BRIDGES NATIONAL MONUMENT **Blanding**

Three large, dramatic spans show the life stages—young, middle-aged, and old—of bridges sculpted from stone. CONTACT Natural Bridges N.M., P.O. Box 1, Lake Powell, UT 84533; 435-692-1234.

PARIA RIVER **Kanab**

A twisting, narrow slot canyon lures hikers, who backpack down to the Colorado River. CONTACT Bureau of Land Management, Cedar City District, 176 East D.L. Sargent Drive, Cedar City, UT 84720; 435-586-2401.

PARIETTE WETLANDS **Ouray**

The marshes and wet meadows of this 11,600-acre refuge, are important to migrant and resident birds. CONTACT Bureau of Land Management, Vernal District, 170 South 500 East, Vernal, UT 84078; 435-789-1362.

SAN JUAN RIVER **Bluff**

A generally placid flow makes one- to six-day boat trips down the river a good opportunity for watching wildlife. CONTACT Bureau of Land Management, P.O. Box 7, Monticello, UT 84535; 435-587-1500.

SAN RAFAEL SWELL **Green River**

Canyon trails and an overlook provide views of colorful, bulging sandstone formations uplifted millions of years ago. There is extensive backcountry recreation here. CONTACT Bureau of Land Management, Moab District, 82 E. Dogwood, Moab, UT 84532; 435-259-6111.

SCOTT M. MATHESON WETLANDS PRESERVE **Moab**

Trails through 875 acres of rare remnant marshes and riparian thickets along the Colorado River attract birders. CONTACT The Nature Conservancy, P.O. Box 1329, Moab, UT 84532; 435-259-4629.

SNOW CANYON STATE PARK **Santa Clara**

Mojave Desert plants and animals inhabit a scenic canyon carved from red and white sandstone and dark lava at this 5,738-acre park. CONTACT Snow Canyon S.P., P.O. Box 140, Santa Clara, UT 84675; 435-628-2255.

Uinta National Forest

TIMPANOGOS CAVE NATIONAL MONUMENT **American Fork**

The 250-acre monument features a steep trail that leads to beautifully ornamented caves high on the limestone slopes of the Wasatch Range. CONTACT Timpanogos Cave N.M., R.R. 3, Box 200, American Fork, UT 84003; 435-756-5238.

UINTA NATIONAL FOREST **Provo**

Three wilderness areas dot the high peaks and plateaus of this nearly million-acre forest in central Utah. CONTACT Uinta N.F., 88 West 100 North, Provo, UT 84601; 801-342-5100.

WASATCH MOUNTAIN STATE PARK **Midway**

This large, popular state park provides 21,592 acres of extensive hiking and cross-country ski trails. CONTACT Wasatch Mountain S.P., P.O. Box 10, Wasatch, UT 84049; 435-654-1791.

The Authors

Peter Alden, principal author of this series, is a birder, naturalist, author, and lecturer. He has led nature tours to over 100 countries for the Massachusetts Audubon Society, Lindblad Travel, Friends of the Harvard Museum of Natural History, and cruises on all the world's oceans. Author of books on North American, Latin American, and African wildlife, Peter organized an event called Biodiversity Day, the first of which was held in his hometown of Concord, Massachusetts.

Brian Cassie, who co-wrote the invertebrates section of this guide, writes and teaches about natural history and is also the co-author of previous guides in the series. Brian lives with his family in Foxboro, Massachusetts.

Peter Friederici, author of the habitats, conservation and ecology, and parks and preserves sections of this guide, is a writer and field biologist who contributes articles and essays to many national and regional periodicals. Peter lives in Flagstaff, Arizona.

Jonathan D. W. Kahl, Ph.D., co-wrote the weather section of this book. He teaches and researches meteorology, air pollution, and climate at the University of Wisconsin–Milwaukee. Jon has published professional articles and children's books on atmospheric science and weather, including the *National Audubon Society First Field Guide: Weather.*

Patrick Leary, Ph.D., author of the flora section of this guide, is a professor of biology at the Community College of Southern Nevada. He lives with his family in Las Vegas, Nevada.

Amy Leventer, Ph.D., author of the topography and geology section of this guide, is a visiting assistant professor at Colgate University's Geology Department. She has published many articles on geology and co-authored the *National Audubon Society Pocket Guide to Earth from Space.* Amy has also written on geology for other guides in this series.

Wendy B. Zomlefer, Ph.D., co-authored the introductions in the flora section of this guide. She is a post-doctoral associate in the botany department at the University of Florida in Gainesville and courtesy assistant curator of the University of Florida Herbarium.

Acknowledgments

The authors collectively thank the many scientists, artists, photographers, and naturalists we have worked with over the years and whose books and papers provided a wealth of information for this book. The following organizations were especially helpful: National Audubon Society (and its local chapters), Massachusetts Audubon Society, Harvard Museum of Natural History, Arizona-Sonora Desert Museum, the Nature Conservancy, Sierra Club, Wildlife Conservation Society, American Birding Association, North American Butterfly Association, and University of Arizona. We also thank the staffs of the many federal and state land, game, and fish departments.

We thank the following experts for their help in writing and reviewing various sections of this guide: Kelly Allred (flora), Rudolf Arndt (fishes, reptiles, and amphibians), Bill Brace and Peggy Brace (grasses), Gary Mechler (weather and night sky), Larry Millman (mushrooms), Marc Minno (invertebrates), Steve Prchal (invertebrates), Stephen

Sharnoff and the late Sylvia Sharnoff (lichens), Louis Sorkin (invertebrates), and Jonathan Dey, Elizabeth Kneiper, and Bruce Ryan (lichens). Glen Martin reviewed most sections of the book. In addition, we continue to draw from material provided by authors of earlier guides in the series: Fred Heath, Richard Keen, Daniel Mathews, Eric A. Oches, and Dennis Paulson.

Special thanks go to David Alden, John Alden, James Baird, Abbie Berger, Clay Berger, Paul Boccardi, Rick Bowers, Richard Carey, Sidney Dunkle, Clare, John, and Joan Ellinwood and family, John Flicker, the late Richard Forster, Frank Gill, Karsten Hartel, Fred Heath, Steve Hilty, Steve Hoffman, John Kartesz, Kenn Kaufman, Boris Kondratieff, Vernon Laux, Katy Noble, Paul Opler, Simon Perkins, Wayne Petersen, the late Roger Tory Peterson, Virginia Peterson, Noble Proctor, Ruth Russell and Stephen Russell, John Schaefer, Judy Schwenk, Al Scott, Emily Scott, Guy Tudor, and Edward O. Wilson.

We are grateful to Andrew Stewart for his vision of a regional field guide encompassing the vast mosaic of the southwestern states' topography, habitats, and wildlife, and to the staff of Chanticleer Press for producing a book of such excellence. The success of the book is due largely to the skills and expertise of editor-in-chief Amy Hughes, series editor Pat Fogarty, managing editor George Scott, senior editor Miriam Harris, associate editor Michelle Bredeson, flora editor Lisa Lester, invertebrates editor Pamela Nelson, vertebrates editor Maury Solomon, assistant editor Elizabeth Wright, and editorial assistant Amy Oh, and editorial freelancers Carol Berglie, Eve Bowen, Jennifer Dixon, Ann ffolliott, Alyssa Okun, Mike Stanzilis, and Lara Stevens-McCormack.

Art director Drew Stevens and designers Kirsten Berger, Anthony Liptak, Vincent Mejia, and Bernadette Vibar took 1,500 images and tens of thousands of words of text and created a book that is both visually beautiful and eminently usable. Mark Abrams and Barbara Sturman assisted with layout. Howard S. Friedman created the beautiful and informative color illustrations. Wil Tirion produced the stunning night sky maps. Ortelius Design made the many detailed maps that appear throughout the book, and the mammal tracks illustrations were contributed by Dot Barlowe.

Photo director Zan Carter, photo editors Ruth Jeyaveeran and Jennifer McClanaghan, and assistant photo editor Meg Kuhta sifted through thousands of photographs in their search for the stunning images that contribute so much to the beauty and usefulness of this guide. Linda Patterson Eger and Lois Safrani of Artemis Picture Research Group, Inc., brought considerable skills and experience to the research and editing of many of the photographs. Permissions manager Alyssa Sachar and rights assistant Lauren Goldwert facilitated the acquisition of photographs and ensured that all photo credits were accurate. Photo editor Christine Heslin and photo assistants Leslie Fink, Karin Murphy, and Stephanie Wilson offered endless support.

Director of production Alicia Mills and production manager Philip Pfeifer saw the book through the complicated production and printing processes. They worked closely with Dai Nippon Printing to ensure the excellent quality of these books. Office manager Raquel Penzo and production intern Morgan Topman provided much support.

In addition, we thank all of the photographers who gathered and submitted the gorgeous pictures that make this book a delight to view.

—Peter Alden, Brian Cassie,
Peter Friederici, Jonathan D. W. Kahl,
Patrick Leary, Amy Leventer, Wendy B. Zomlefer

Picture Credits

The credits are listed alphabetically by photographer. Each photograph is listed by the number of the page on which it appears, followed by a letter indicating its position on the page (the letters follow a sequence from top left to bottom right).

Kevin Adams 148b
Walt Anderson 11b, 43a, 49b, 55a, 56c, 97b, 98f, 106d, 107b, 108d, 109b, 116e, 117d, 119e, 131d &e, 132c & f, 137d, 151e, 161c, 170d, 171a, 177c, 180b, 182d, 189e, 254a, 386b
Ron Austing 282b, 303a, 318b, 361b
Frank S. Balthis 150a
Robert E. Barber 41b, 186c, 190d, 198c, 256c
Roger W. Barbour/ Morehead State University 360b
R. D. Bartlett 247a, 251d, 252b, 255d, 256a, 261b
Tom & Susan Bean 428b
Bill Beatty 215c
Lance Beeny 97e, 166b, 168e, 199b, 430a
Steve Bentsen 290c
Niall Benvie/BBC Natural History Unit Picture Library 116a & b
Rick & Nora Bowers 355c
Rick & Nora Bowers/ The Wildlife Collection 328b
Tom Boyden 221b, 222a, 227c, 232d
Bruce Coleman, Inc.
Jen & Des Bartlett 192d
Erwin & Peggy Bauer 143b
Bob & Clara Calhoun 110b, 112d, 167b, 307c
Thase Daniel 110e
E. R. Degginger 240a
Jeff Foott 175b
John Shaw 98b, 109c
Steve Solum 112a
Wardene Weisser 126d, 161b
G. R. Zahm 150b
Joyce Burek 142e
Francis Caldwell 43b
Edgar Callaert 384, 425b
Scott Camazine 211c
John Cancalosi 352a
David Cavagnaro 98a, 106b, 109d, 110a, 115c, 122a, 123b, 125e, 126a, 133d, 169d, 177d, 181b
Rick Cech 220b, 223a, 224a, 225c & d, 228b, 229b & d, 231d & e, 232a & b
Patrice Ceisel/John G. Shedd Aquarium 241d
Kathy Adams Clark/KAC Productions 230a, 355b
Herbert Clarke 159d, 164b, 165e, 176a, 179c, 185c, 284b, 290b, 292a & e, 295b, 298a, 300a, 308d, 309b & c, 316c, 321d, 324d, 328a & e, 330d, 331d, 332a, 334a, 337c, 338b, c & d, 340d, 343e, 355d
Willard Clay 10b, 383a, 386a, 389, 390a & b, 407a, 422a, 424b, 426a, 427b
CNAAR
Suzanne L. Collins 248a, 249c, 261e
Suzanne L. & Joseph T. Collins 259a
Eliot Cohen 28b, 171d, 388
James C. Cokendolpher 198e, 217b
Colephoto
Mary Clay 66b
Phyllis Greenberg 333b
Michael Redmer 208a
Color-Pic, Inc.
E. R. Degginger 29a, 30a, 31b, 33a, c & d, 34b, 67a, 86a & e, 94c, 99e, f & g, 126b, 150d, 158d, 183d, 189a, 194, 204b, 207a & c, 214d, 218c, 219b, 227a, 229a, 231b, 243c, 257a, 260b, 262a, 297b
Phil Degginger 66a, 245c
Ed Cooper 15b, 39a, 64, 395a, 397a
Marty Cordano 217a, 304a
Gerald & Buff Corsi/Focus on Nature, Inc. 94b, 100c & d, 101b & c, 103c, 106c, 108c, 109e, 111b, 118a, 122b, 123d, 133a, 136b, 141a & c, 149e, 151a, 154a, 155b, c, & e, 159c, 161d, 164a, 166a & e, 172d, 173c, 174b & c, 176b, 181c, 185e, 187a & d, 190a, 193c, 253a, 254b, 291a, 319b, 399b, 417b
Daniel J. Cox/Natural Exposures, Inc. 65a, 363a & b, 365b, 373b
Sharon Cummings 339d, 357c, 369a
Richard Cummins 52b
Rob Curtis/The Early Birder 160c, 204c, 211d, 222b & c, 234c, 285d, 289b, 310b, 315d, 316d, 319a, 321b, 321e, 322b, 332d, 336e
Jaret C. Daniels 226d
Kent & Donna Dannen 28a, 167d, 182b, 383b, 414b
Mike Danzenbaker 295c, 304b, 330a & b, 333a
Larry Dech 91c, 93a, 138b
Dembinsky Photo Associates
Mike Barlow 54b
Stan Osolinski 372b
Jim Roetzel 364b
David M. Dennis 195e, 258a, 262b, 265b, c & d, 268c
Jack Dermid 284a
Alan & Linda Detrick 156e, 183a
Larry Ditto 299d, 324e
Christine M. Douglas 17c, 31a, 53b, 54a, 184e, 190e, 193a
Sidney W. Dunkle 202b, 203b & c
Michael Durham/ENP Images 373a
David Dvorak, Jr. 48a, 94a, 116d, 140b, 410a, 414a, 415a
Don Eastman 103d & e, 112c, 115a, 136d, 140d, 153a, 165a, 170a, 175e, 179b, 181d, 182c, 188d,

189c, 190c, 191c, 192b & e
Priscilla Alexander Eastman 168d, 173a, 178a, c & d, 184a, 188e
John Elk III 26b, 41a, 51b, 119c, 132e, 400a, 402b
Harry Ellis 86b, 87a & c, 91b
A. Murray Evans* 92b
Warren Faidley/ Weatherstock 63a
Dennis Flaherty 160b, 161e
Jeff Foott 24, 58b, 132b, 138c, 139b, 205a, 243a, 290a, 304c, 323c, 358b, 368c, 373d, 379, 380, 401a, 424a
Richard Forbes 240d, 254c, 356c, 357b
Michael H. Francis 212a, 278c, 284d, 327b & e, 357a, 364a, 366b, 367c, 372a, 373c
John P. George 156a
François Gohier 301c
Chuck Gordon 272c, 278b, 280a & c, 281a, 282a, 296d, 300b, 320e, 351c
Lois Theodora Grady 97c
Darrell Gulin 187b
Charles Gurche 387b
Thomas Hallstein/ Outsight 51a, 396
Calvin J. Hamilton 17b
Robert W. Hansen 253c
James H. Harding 264d
Harold Wilion Photography 203a
Jessie M. Harris 156c, 157a & d, 158a, 160e, 163a, 165c, 168c
Chip Hedgcock 195d, 198d
Ronald & Shirley Holle 67e
Diana Horton 92a, 164d
Stephen Ingram 111e, 114c & d, 121c, 129a, 130d & e, 135b, 137c, 163b, 164d, 166d, 171c, 191a, 192a
Dick James 52a, 174a
Judith Jango-Cohen 184d
John G. Shedd Aquarium 239c, 244d, 246a
Bill Johnson 163e, 174e, 216b
Emily Johnson 87b
Walter S. Judd 162b
Steve Junak 104a & b, 105c, 107d, 111d, 115b, 119a, 126e, 148a, 165b, 170e, 172c, 178b, 185a
Wolfgang Kaehler 57b, 184b
Dency Kane 176d
Kevin T. Karlson 275c & d, 288c, 292c, 322a, 334d, 336a
Richard A. Keen 69d
G. C. Kelley 124e, 267d, 279a, 282d, 291c, 294b, 301b, 306d, 313c, 334b, 340b, 352b, 353b, 354b, 355a, 370
Susan Cole Kelly 190b
Brian Kenney 199c, 214c, 215a & e, 218d, 221a & d, 222d, 230d, 244a, 255c, 263a, 264a, 266a & b, 267b, 273d
Breck P. Kent 34d, 236a, 249a
Larry Kimball 119b, 132d, 143a, 157b, 167a, 168a, 173b, 185d
Ed King 22b, 49a, 412a
Kirkendall-Spring Photographers 29b
Lee Kline 250, 350c
Eugene N. Kozloff 104d, 169e, 170b & c, 172a
Wayne Lankinen 327a
Patrick Leary 106e, 111c, 122d, 155d, 167c, 171b, 172b, 188c
William P. Leonard 248b, 251b, 252c, 253b, 262d, 265a
Jack N. Levy 227d
Michael H. Levy 65b
David Liebman 131a, 157e, 209a, 211c
Harold Lindstrom 277a, 281c, 295a, 322e, 336c, 343d
Kathy Lindstrom 281b
Bates Littlehales 272a, 289d, 314c
Barbara Magnuson 118e, 127e, 128b, 150c, 154e, 179d
Barbara Magnuson & Larry Kimball 42a
Stephen G. Maka 276c, 277b
Andrew J. Martinez 31c & d, 33b, 34a, 244b
Steve & Dave Maslowski 236b, 350a
Buddy Mays/Travel Stock 151b, 152d
Robert McCaw 154c
Joe McDonald 346a, 348c, 360a
Charles W. Melton 112e, 212d, 216a, 272b, 305a, 306b, 308b, 317b, 320c, 333e, 335d & e, 339c
Anthony Mercieca 361a
Anthony Mercieca/Root Resources 308a, 316a, 337a & b, 359d, 368a & b
C. Allan Morgan 108a & b, 109a, 131f, 135d, 201, 225a, 240b, 241a, 255b, 272d, 299c, 303b, 309a, 318a, 358d, 360c
Arthur Morris/BIRDS AS ART 273a, 275b, 276d, 278e, 279b, 284c, 286b, 288a, 292d, 294d, 297a, 298b & c, 299b, 314a, 324a, 336d, 338e
William Munoz 149a
NASA/JPL/Caltech 69b & c, 71c
National Audubon Society Collection, Photo Researchers, Inc.
Jeff Apoian 59b
Ron Austing 331a
Alan D. Carey 302c
Edna Bennett 67d
H. Berthoule/Jacana 243d
Biophoto Associates 30b
John Bova 68a, 202c, 233a
Tom Branch 86c
Joseph T. Collins 239b, 263c
Stephen Collins 179a
Stephen Dalton 413b
Donna Dannen 129c
Kent & Donna Dannen 178e, 182a, 299a
Betty Derig 130b
Alan & Linda Detrick 158c
Gregory G. Dimijian 133b
Joe DiStefano 206a
Phil A. Dotson 362b, 371a
John Eastcott & Yva Momatiuk 153c
R. J. Erwin 223d, 229c, 239d, 241b, 358a
Kenneth W. Fink 366c
John R. Foster 71a
S. C. Fried 320d, 339b
Michael P. Gadomski 249b
François Gohier 29c, 101a
Gilbert S. Grant 209e

David Hosking 354a
Kenneth M. Johns 310a
John Kaprielian 40b, 42b, 385b
G. C. Kelley 306a, 351d, 371d
Paolo Koch 30c
Stephen J. Krasemann 120c, 177b, 343c, 365a
Pat & Tom Leeson 100b, 286a, 359a, 367d
Jeff Lepore 278a, 286c, 349a, 369b
C. K. Lorenz 302b, 312c, 324b
Michael Lustbader 157c
David Macias 371b
Karl Maslowski 323e
Steve Maslowski 343b
Steve & Dave Maslowski 317a, 327c
Tom McHugh 31e, 239a, 246b, 357d, 361c
Anthony Mercieca 301e, 305c, 322d, 328d, 341e
Emil Muench 137a
Alan G. Nelson 287d
Charlie Ott 101e, 354c
Richard Parker 133c, 183b, 193b
Pekka Parviainen 68b
Rod Planck 83, 252a, 274b, 325c, 326e, 337d, 340a, 351a, 356d
Gary Retherford 234b
A. H. Rider 176e
David T. Roberts 211b
James H. Robinson 213c
Leonard Lee Rue III 302d, 315a, 371c
Jerry Schad 71b
M. H. Sharp 220a, 231a & c, 276a
James Simon 258d
Jim Steinberg 55b, 162a, 185b
Dan Sudia 333c
Karl H. Switak 137b
USGS/Science Photo Library 69a
R. Van Nostrand 287b, 367b
Virginia P. Weinland 132a
Jeanne White 366d

Nature's Images, Inc.
David T. Roberts 253d, 268b
David M. Schleser 125d, 139a, 142a & b, 208d, 213b

NEBRASKAland/ Nebraska Game and Parks Commisson 244c
Blair Nikula 202d, 203d
Dale O'Dell 22a
Frank Oberle 165d, 169c, 176c, 187c, 188b, 302a
Jack Olson 19b, 408b
Paul Opler 98c, 223b, 226b, 232c
Stan Osolinski 351b
Londie G. Padelsky 21b, 23b, 47a, 62, 138d, 160a
James F. Parnell 245a, 353a
Jerry Pavia 121f, 130a, 135a, 156b, 175a, 177a
Joanne Pavia 117b, 152b
B. Moose Peterson/WRP 242b, 359c
Chuck Place 12a & b, 46a, 134, 412b, 423a
Rod Planck 173d, 180a, 256b, 282c, 350b
Rick Poley 38b
Robert & Jean Pollock 353c
Steven J. Prchal 195c, 197b, c & d, 198b, 199a & d, 204a, 208c & e, 209d, 212b, 213a, d & e, 214b, 217d, 219a, 233c & d, 235c & d
Betty Randall 97a, 100e & f, 113c, 115d, 119d, 121b, 122e, 200, 305b, 311c, 341d, 360d, 367a
David Ransaw 183c, 189b
Jeffrey Rich 294a, 322c
James H. Robinson 17a, 44a, 206c, 208b, 218a, 356b
Jim Roetzel 287a, 293a, 339e, 341b
Eda Rogers 98e, 113e, 117c, 120d, 136a, 143c, 163d, 169b, 177d, 191b, 215d, 285b
Ernest H. Rogers/Sea Images 124c, 125c
Edward S. Ross 195a, 197e, 202a, 203e, 205b, 206b, 207d, 209c, 210a & b, 211a, 212e, 214a, 215b, 216c, 217c, 221c, 224b & c, 228a & c, 233b, 235a,
Phillip Roullard 138a, 162d, 218b, 219c, 228d
James P. Rowan 58a, 150e, 409a
Larry Sansone 105b, 113a & b, 126c, 151c, 152c, 158c, 166c, 202e, 223c, 224d, 226a & c, 291d, 311b, 312d, 325a, 336b, 364c
Kevin Schafer 366a
Perry Shankle, Jr. 368d
Stephen Sharnoff 88b, 89a, b, d & e, 90b & d, 91a
Sylvia Duran Sharnoff 88a, 89c, 90a & c
Wendy Shattil & Bob Rozinski 38a, 59a, 100a, 411, 419a
John Shaw 209b
Allen Blake Sheldon 235b, 251a, 259c, 261a & d, 263b, 264c, 410b
Rob & Ann Simpson 116c, 129b, 159e, 164c, 197a, 199e, 225b, 240c, 245d, 305d, 307b, 353d
Brian E. Small 273b, 274c, 280d, 288d, 293b, 297d, 307a, 309d, 311d, 312a, b, & e, 313b & d, 314b, 315c, 317d, 320b, 325b & e, 326a & c, 327d, 328c, 329a, b & c, 330e, 331b, c & e, 332b, c & e , 333d, 335c, 339a, 340e, 341c, 342e, 343a
Hugh P. Smith, Jr. 285c, 286d, 289c, 291b, 296b, 298d
Norm Smith 103b
Scott T. Smith 11a & c, 13b, 20, 36, 37a, 44b, 47b, 48b, 50a, 65b, 67b, c & f, 98d, 102a, 104c, 113d, 136c, 142d, 164e, 169a, 381, 394b, 395b, 397b, 398a & b, 399a, 400b, 401b, 402a, 403, 413a, 415b, 417a, 418, 419b, 420a & b, 422b, 426b, 427a, 428a, 429b, 430b
Ira & Bob Spring 97f
Joy Spurr 85, 86d, 87d, 93b, 94d, 99a & b, 101d & f, 102b, 107e, 111a, 114b, 117e, 118c, 120a, 122c, 124d, 127c, 128c & d, 131b & c, 149b & c, 151d, 152a, 154d, 159a & b, 160d, 161a, 162c, 163c, 167e, 172e, 174d, 183e, 184c, 186d, 188a, 189d
Doug Stamm/ProPhoto 241c, 243b
Steven M. Still 120c
George Stocking/Coyote Howls Photography 25, 39b, 56a, 142c, 387a

David Stone/Wildland Photography 19a
Nancy L. Strand 218e
Joseph G. Strauch, Jr. 103a, 153e, 156d
Rita Summers 362a
Dan Suzio 260a
Karl H. Switak 186a, 251c, 254d, 258c, 259b & d, 260c, 261c, 264b, 268a, d & e
Ian C. Tait 114a
Ronald J. Taylor 94e, 99d, 117a, 121d, 149d, 153b & d, 155a, 168b, 171e, 177e, 186b
Tom Till 15a, 16, 21a, 23a, 26a, 45a, 50b, 57a, 63b, 382, 385a, 391b, 392, 405a & b, 406a & b, 407b, 408a, 409b, 421, 423b, 425a, 429a
Thomas K. Todsen 107c, 175c
Hardie Truesdale 10a, 27
Mark Turner 87e, 97d, 99c, 123c, 173e, 234d
Merlin D. Tuttle/ Bat Conservation International 348a, b & d, 349b, c & d
Tom J. Ulrich 276e, 285a, 313a, 326b, 330c, 334c & e, 342a, 354d, 359b, 361d
R. W. Van Devender 247b, 256d, 257b, c & d, 258b, 267a
Jeff Vanuga 13a, 53a, 255a
Tom Vezo 273c, 274a, 275a, 276b, 278d, 279e, 280b, 281d, 288b, 293c, 294c, 296c, 303c & d, 320a, 321c, 323a, 325d, 335a, 338a, 342b

Visuals Unlimited
Walt Anderson 123a, 139c
Bill Beatty 212c
Gerald & Buff Corsi 110d, 118d, 121a, 123e, 127a & b, 129d, 130c, 141b, 175d, 191d, 204e
John D. Cunningham 128a
John Gerlach 107a, 273e, 337e
A. Kerstitch 121e
Ken Lucas 28c
Maslowski 245b
S. Maslowski 323b & d
Joe McDonald 37b, 267c, 289a
G. & C. Merker 263d
Gary Meszaros 154b, 262c
John C. Muegge 394a
Mark Newman 56b
Glen M. Oliver 242a
Science VU 129e
David Sieren 182e
Leroy Simon 152e, 227b, 230b, 234a
Doug Sokell 112b, 124a, 125b, 127d, 135c, 140a, 204d
Michael T. Stubben 105a, 118b, 125a, 148c, 158b, 181a, 192c, 193d
Gustav W. Verderber 195b

Richard A. Wagner 196, 207b
Harry M. Walker 140c, 341a
Mark F. Wallner 295d, 296a, 314d, 356a
B. Walsh, J. Beckett, M. Carruthers (Sample courtesy of American Museum of Natural History, NY) 34c
Steve Warble 45b
Joe Warfel 198a, 206d, 217e
Jan L. Wassink 346b
Neil Weidner 110c, 124b, 143d, 391a
Sally Weigand 106a, 128e
Brian K. Wheeler 287c
Gary C. Williams 18, 46b, 120b, 141d
Craig D. Wood 139d
George Wuerthner 301d
Dale & Marian Zimmerman 311a, 313e, 324c, 358c
H. Zirlin 230c
Tim Zurowski 279 c & d, 290d, 292b, 297c, 301a, 306c, 308c, 315b, 316b, 317c, 321a, 326d, 335b, 340c, 342c & d

*From *A Field Manual of Ferns and Fern Allies of the United States and Canada* by D. B. Lellinger. Smithsonian Institution Press, Washington, DC, 1985.

Front Cover: Rod Planck/ Photo Researchers, Inc. (a), Pat Caulfield/Photo Researchers, Inc. (b), John Gerlach/Earth Images (c), Craig K. Lorenz/Photo Researchers, Inc. (d)
Spine: Charles Gurche
Back Cover: Jerry Schad/ Photo Researchers, Inc. (a), Scott T. Smith (b), Frank Oberle (c), Willard Clay (d)
Title Page: Courthouse Towers, Arches National Park, Utah, by Willard Clay
Table of Contents: Chuck Place (6a), Scott T. Smith (6b), John Bova/Photo Researchers, Inc. (6c), Howard S. Friedman (7a, 7c), C. Allan Morgan (7b), Jeff Foott (7d)
Pages 8–9: Hickman Bridge, Capitol Reef National Park, Utah, by Charles Gurche
Pages 80–81: Sandhill Cranes by Jeff Vanuga
Pages 374–375: Colorado River, Canyonlands National Park, Utah, by Ed King

All original illustrations by Howard S. Friedman, except mammal tracks (pp. 345–346), by Dot Barlow

Maps by Ortelius Design

Night sky maps by Wil Tirion

Index

Converting to Metric

Limited space makes it impossible for us to give measurements expressed as metrics. Here is a simplified chart for converting standard measurements to their metric equivalents:

	MULTIPLY BY
inches to millimeters	25
inches to centimeters	2.5
feet to meters	0.3
yards to meters	0.9
miles to kilometers	1.6
square miles to square kilometers	2.6
acres to hectares	.40
ounces to grams	28.3
pounds to kilograms	.45
Fahrenheit to Celsius	subtract 32 and multiply by .55

OREGON
IDAHO
CALIFORNIA
Black Rock Desert
Santa Rosa Range
S. Fork Owyhee R.
Humboldt River
Great Salt Lake
Winnemucca Lake
Humboldt Range
Shoshone Range
Ruby Mountains
GREAT
Great Salt Lake Desert
Bonneville Salt Flats
Pyramid Lake
Lake Tahoe
CARSON CITY
Toiyabe Range
NEVADA
BASIN
Utah Lake
Walker Lake
Monitor Range
Snake Range
Sevier R.
Sevier Lake
White Mtns.
Boundary Peak
13,140'
Sevier River
Markagunt Plateau
Paunsaugunt Plateau
Grand Staircase
CALIFORNIA
MOJAVE
DESERT
Virgin R.
Lake Mead
Las Vegas
Hoover Dam
Kaibab Plateau
Colorado R.
Grand Canyon
San Francisco Peaks
Humphreys Peak
12,633'
Colorado R.
ARIZONA
PHOENIX
Salt River
SONORAN
Gila River
DESERT
Tucson
MEXICO